INTRODUCTION TO

Hospitality Management

INTRODUCTION TO

Hospitality Management

THIRD EDITION

John R. Walker

McKibbon Professor of Hotel and Restaurant Management
University of South Florida

Prentice Hall
Upper Saddle River, New Jersey
Columbus, Ohio

Library of Congress Cataloging-in-Publication Data

Walker, John R.
    Introduction to hospitality management / John R. Walker. — 3rd ed.
        p. cm.
    Includes bibliographical references and index.
    ISBN-13: 978-0-13-506138-1
    ISBN-10: 0-13-506138-5
    1. Hospitality industry—Management. I. Title.
    TX911.3.M27W3515 2010
    647.94'068—dc22   2008041068

Editor in Chief: Vernon Anthony
Acquisitions Editor: William Lawrensen
Development Editor: David Ploskonka
Editorial Assistant: Lara Dimmick
Production Coordination: Linda Zuk, Wordcraft LLC
Project Manager: Kris Roach
Managing Editor: Alexandrina Benedicto Wolf
Operations Specialist: Deidra Schwartz
Art Director, Interior: Diane Ernsberger
Interior Design: Wanda España
Art Director, Cover: Diane Ernsberger
Cover Designer: Bryan Huber
Cover Image: Getty One
Director, Image Resource Center: Melinda Patelli
Manager, Rights and Permissions: Zina Arabia
Manager, Cover Visual Research and Permissions: Karen Sanatar
Image Permission Coordinator: Joanna Dippel
Director of Marketing: David Gesell
Marketing Manager: Leigh Ann Sims
Senior Marketing Coordinator: Alicia Dysert
Marketing Assistant: Les Roberts
Copyeditor: Amy Schneider

This book was set in Sabon by S4Carlisle Publishers and was printed and bound by CJ Krehbiel. The cover was printed by Phoenix Color Corp.
Portions of this book were previously published under the title *Introduction to Hospitality*.

Pearson Education Ltd.   Pearson Education North Asia Ltd.
Pearson Education Singapore, Pte. Ltd.   Pearson Educación de Mexico, S.A. de C.V.
Pearson Education, Canada, Ltd.   Pearson Education Malaysia, Pte. Ltd.
Pearson Education–Japan   Pearson Education Australia Pty, Limited

Prentice Hall
is an imprint of

www.pearsonhighered.com

10 9 8 7 6 5 4 3
ISBN-13: 978-0-13-506138-1
ISBN-10:   0-13-506138-5

To Josielyn,
Christopher, and
Selina

BRIEF CONTENTS

CONTENTS

Thank you to the professors and students who have used the previous editions of this text. This new edition of *Introduction to Hospitality Management* focuses on the hospitality industry and has been written in response to professors and students who wanted a broader view of the world's largest industry. *Introduction to Hospitality Management* complements *Introduction to Hospitality* and *Exploring the Hospitality Industry,* also written by John R. Walker. Adopters may select the title best suited to their needs. Each text offers a comprehensive overview of the industry plus chapters on the managerial and operational areas of the hospitality industry.

This text is designed for the hospitality management professionals of tomorrow. By involving readers in each step of this exciting journey, *Introduction to Hospitality Management* invites students to share the unique enthusiasm surrounding the hospitality industry. Each chapter has been vetted by industry professionals and includes several hands-on examples that help students understand the how-to aspects of the hospitality industry.

The primary goals and objectives of this text are to:

- Prepare students to advance in their hospitality career by offering a foundation of knowledge about the hospitality industry presented in a lively, interesting manner with an extensive array of features to facilitate the learning process.
- Assist students in learning the details of the hospitality industry by offering chapters on the operational areas of the industry.
- Offer students information on the array of careers available in the various segments of the hospitality industry.
- Facilitate learning by offering a student-friendly text to students and an outstanding instructional package to professors.

Organization of the Text

In response to faculty suggestions, this third edition has been divided into six parts:

Part 1   The Hospitality Industry and Tourism
Part 2   Lodging
Part 3   Restaurants, Managed Services, and Beverages
Part 4   Recreation, Theme Parks, Clubs, and Gaming Entertainment
Part 5   Assemblies and Event Management
Part 6   Managerial Areas of the Hospitality Industry

New to this edition: broader coverage of globalization and the greening of the hospitality industry, a chapter on Event Management, and the Hospitality Careers Companion Website packaged with this text.

The Hospitality Careers DVD includes material to help students advance in their coursework and in their career:

- Job readiness and career advice
- Resume writing
- Additional resources
- Scholarship information

New and continuing features include:

1. Completely revised and updated text, new photos, and new page layouts
2. Focus boxes written by leading academicians that provide real-world applications of the information presented in each chapter
3. Corporate and Personal Profiles
4. Case Studies
5. Check Your Knowledge questions dispersed throughout the chapters that serve as reminders and reinforce learning
6. Key words and concepts set in boldface in text, listed at the ends of chapters, and defined in the Glossary
7. Review Questions
8. Internet Exercises
9. Apply Your Knowledge questions
10. Summaries at the ends of chapters that correspond to the learning objectives
11. New! Suggested Activities

Supplement Package

1. Companion Website with Web-based activities and resources for each chapter reinforce the material and offer self-tests and links to numerous hospitality Websites; available at *www.pearsonhighered.com/johnwalker*
2. Professional PowerPoint presentation is available online to qualified text adopters
3. Updated Online Test Bank of class-tested questions
4. Video DVD including corporate videos and PowerPoint presentations with videos, which bring industry professionals into the classroom
5. Online Instructors Manual
6. Blackboard Course

To access supplementary materials online, instructors need to request an instructor access code. Go to **www.pearsonhighered.com/irc,** where you can register for an instructor access code. Within 48 hours after registering, you will receive a confirming e-mail, including an instructor access code. Once you have received your code, go to the site and log on for full instructions on downloading the materials you wish to use.

Dear Future Hospitality Professional:

This textbook is written to empower you and help you on your way to becoming a future leader of this great industry. It will give you an in-depth overview of the world's largest and fastest growing business. Each chapter contains **profiles of industry practitioners and leaders, case studies,** and **corporate profiles.** Additionally, industry experts speak on their area of specialization in **focus boxes.**

Read the Book

Read and study the text, including the profiles, focus boxes, applications, and case studies. Answer the Check Your Knowledge questions and review questions. By using the many tools throughout this textbook—including boldface key words and concepts—you will be amazed at how much more you get out of class by preparing ahead of time.

Use the Resources Accompanying This Book

Make use of the excellent **Companion Website** (*www.prenhall.com/walker*) with its sample questions, a complete PowerPoint presentation (that you can download and bring to class), and links to hospitality websites. You will improve your chances of achieving success in this class and will find that you enjoy learning.

Success in the Classroom

Faculty constantly says that the best students are the ones who come to class prepared. I know that, as a hospitality student, you have many demands on your time: work, a heavy course load, family commitments, and, yes, fun—plus a lot of reading and studying for your other courses. With these thoughts in mind, I tried to make this book as visually appealing, easy and engaging to read, and enjoyable as possible.

Wishing you success in your studies and career.

Sincerely,
John Walker

Take some time to turn the page and review descriptions of all the features and tools in this book and find out how they will facilitate your reading and understanding of the concepts. **Discover** the exciting opportunities in the numerous and varied segments of the hospitality industry.

Boxed Features Connect You to the Real World

These boxed features introduce you to *real people* and *real jobs* with engaging *true-to-life scenarios*.

Introducing ...

INTRODUCING CONRAD HILTON AND HILTON HOTELS CORPORATION

"King of Innkeepers" and Master of Hotel Finance

Hilton's success was attributed to two main strategies: (1) hiring the best managers and letting them have total autonomy, and (2) being a careful bargainer who, in later years, was careful not to overextend his finances. Conrad Hilton had begun a successful career in the banking business before he embarked on what was to become one of the most successful hotel careers ever.

In 1919, while on bank business in Cisco, Texas, he bought the Mobley Hotel with an investment of $5,000. Hilton rented rooms to oil industry prospectors and construction workers. Because of high demand for accommodations and very little supply, Hilton rented rooms in eight-hour shifts, for 300 percent occupancy. On some occasions, he even rented out his own room and slept in a lobby chair.

Because Hilton knew the banking business well and had maintained contacts who would lend him money for down payments on properties, he quickly expanded to seven Texas hotels. Hilton's strategy was to borrow as much money as possible to expand as rapidly as possible. This worked well until the Great Depression of the early 1930s. Hilton was unable to meet the payments on his properties and lost several but did not declare bankruptcy.[1]

Hilton, like many great leaders, even during the Depression years had the determination to bounce back. To reduce costs, he borrowed money against his life insurance and even formed an alliance with the National Hotels Corporation.

Hilton's business and financial acumen is legendary. The *New York Times* described Conrad Hilton as "a master of finance and a cautious bargainer who was careful not to overfinance" and someone who had "a flawless sense of timing."[2]

Hilton was the first per~~~~ast lobbies with people s~~~~ in comfortable c~~~~~~

You're introduced to industry practitioners' careers, the issues and challenges they encounter, and their achievements and contributions. These features give a "from-the-heart" up-close and personal view of their work. From dreams to reality . . . follow the career path to success for industry leaders and learn from their experiences.

Corporate Profiles

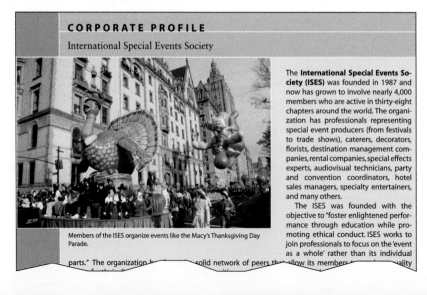

CORPORATE PROFILE

International Special Events Society

The **International Special Events Society (ISES)** was founded in 1987 and now has grown to involve nearly 4,000 members who are active in thirty-eight chapters around the world. The organization has professionals representing special event producers (from festivals to trade shows), caterers, decorators, florists, destination management companies, rental companies, special effects experts, audiovisual technicians, party and convention coordinators, hotel sales managers, specialty entertainers, and many others.

The ISES was founded with the objective to "foster enlightened performance through education while promoting ethical conduct. ISES works to join professionals to focus on the 'event as a whole' rather than its individual

Members of the ISES organize events like the Macy's Thanksgiving Day Parade.

parts." The organization h~~~~ ~~~~olid network of peers th~~~ ~~llow its members~~~~ ~~~~uality

Learn about the practices, growth, and scope of leading corporations and organizations. For example, Marriott International did not start out as a multibillion-dollar company; the company began as a nine-seat root beer stand in 1927.

Trends

Trends in Human Resources

There is increasing diversity among new employees in the hospita
More women and minorities are not only entering the industry, but
ing supervisory and managerial positions.

- Understanding the emotional aspects of motivation will change
  manage. Emotional intelligence refers to skills in intrapersonal
  interpersonal relations. In the future, managers will view empl
  deeper emotional standpoint rather than on the surface level.

- Increased globalization is making the hospitality workplace eve
  diverse. Individual differences go past traditional demographic
  deep-level attitudes and beliefs, particularly with nontraditiona

A list of trends appears in each chapter to give you an up-to-date and realistic picture of factors shaping the future of that segment of the industry.

Focus on . . .

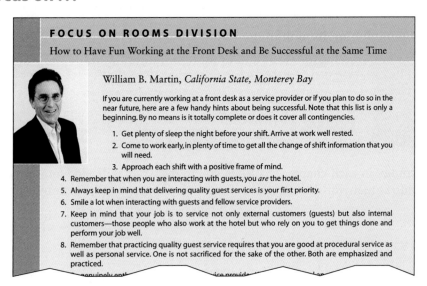

Written by contributing expert authors, these boxes offer unique personal perspectives on chapter topics.

Objectives

> **OBJECTIVES**
>
> After reading and studying this chapter, you should be able to:
>
> - Explain the importance of job descriptions.
> - Give an example of how productivity standards are determined.
> - Name and describe the employment-related laws.
> - Discuss how to select, recruit, and orient employees.
> - Identify methods of employee appraisal and compensation.
> - Describe motivation theories and industry practice.

At the start of each chapter, this list gives you a "heads up" to what will be discussed and how to organize your thoughts. The learning objectives summarize what you need to know after studying the chapter and doing the exercises, case questions, and Apply Your Knowledge.

Case Studies

> **CASE STUDY**
>
> Latasha's Challenge
>
> Latasha Hinkson recently graduated with a bachelor's degree in hospitality management and has been hired as the front-desk manager in a medium-sized hotel in New York City. The hotel's clientele is truly international, and so is its staff, which originates from more than 20 different nations. Many of the employees speak more than one language, often at work. Latasha is from the midwestern United States and has had little experience in managing and motivating a multicultural work group. Indeed, she knows little or nothing about many of the cultures that surround her.
>
> One challenge put to Latasha when she was hired was to give a "lift" to the staff and try to create more of a team atmosphere. Currently, the employees at the front desk operate as a bunch of individuals, with little sense of teamwork. It seems as though the differences in culture are preventing the group from getting closer. As a result, the atmosphere at the front desk is cool and functional, rather than warm and friendly.
>
> In addition, Latasha must contend with a number of employee problems if the department is going to function properly. For example, Maria, who originally comes from Spain, is excellent with customers but often comes to work late. Even when confronted by past supervisors about her tardiness, Maria failed to see this as a real problem. Bjorn is a Norwegian hospitality student working part time in the hotel. Although Bjorn is always on time and works very efficiently, his demeanor with the customers is lacking. Often, guests and coworkers perceive him as being aloof or standoffish. Bjorn rarely smiles at guests. Finally, Peng from Asia is very diligent about his work and gives 100 percent to any task he is given. Unfortunately Peng has some dif-

Case studies in each chapter challenge you to test your skills and knowledge as you address real-world situations and recommend appropriate actions.

Internet Exericses

> ## Internet Exercise
>
> Organization: Your choice of company
>   Web site: The company's URL
>   Summary: Pick a major corporation, such as one mentioned in the text, and go to its web site to look for answers to the following questions.
>   (a) What different types of product offerings does the company have?
>
> (b) In how many countries or regions is it represented?
> (c) What kind of divisions does it have?
> (d) Have different types of guest groups been identified?

Surf the Net to uncover answers to specific hospitality questions. The Internet Exercises challenge you to learn more and prepare you for a career in this fascinating industry.

Apply Your Knowledge

> ## Apply Your Knowledge
>
> 1. Develop the criteria for and role-play an employee appraisal.
> 2. Write a job description and the performance evaluation criteria for a position in the hospitality industry.
> 3. Plan and role-play an interview for a position in the hospitality industry.
> 4. Interview three hospitality associates—preferably one manager, one supervisor, and one associate—to find out what motives them.
> 5. Ask your librarian for help in finding interesting hospitality trade magazine articles in an area of human resources that interests you. Share your findings with your classmates.

Apply the knowledge and skills learned in each chapter to real-life industry topics.

Check Your Knowledge

> ## ► Check Your Knowledge
>
> 1. What is the difference between interpersonal and organizational communication?
> 2. What are three ways of communicating interpersonally?
> 3. Describe the interpersonal communication process.

Every few pages, the Check Your Knowledge section helps you review and reinforce the material that has just been covered.

Chapter Summary

The chapter summary highlights the most important points in the chapter. It provides a brief review of the chapter and reinforces the main terms, concepts, and topics.

Key Words and Concepts

Highlighted in bold with easy-to-understand definitions in the Glossary, the key words and concepts help you recall the importance of and meaning of these important terms. Master the key words and concepts of the text and improve your test scores.

Review Questions

By answering these review questions, you will reinforce your mastery of the materials presented in the text and most likely improve your test scores.

Visuals

WINE	SMELL AND TASTE ASSOCIATED WITH WINE	FOOD PAIRING
Gewürztraminer (Alsace in France)	grapefruit, apple, nectarine, peach, nutmeg, clove, cinnamon	Thai, Indian, Tex-Mex, Szechwan, ham, sausage, curry, garlic
Chardonnay Chablis (Burgundy in France)	citrus fruit, apple, pear, pineapple, other tropical fruit	pork, salmon, chicken, pheasant, rabbit
Sauvignon Blanc Sancerre (Loire in France)	citrus fruit, gooseberry, bell pepper, black pepper, green olives, herbs	goat cheese, oysters, fish, chicken, pork, garlic
Pinot Blanc	citrus fruit, apple, pear, melon	shrimp, shellfish, fish, chicken
Pinot Noir Cote d' Or (Burgundy in France)	strawberry, cherry, raspberry, clove, mint, vanilla, cinnamon	duck, chicken, turkey, mushrooms, grilled meats, fish and vegetables, pork
Merlot Gamay (Beaujolais in France)	cherry, raspberry, plum, pepper, herbs, mint	beef, lamb, duck, barbecued meats, pork ribs
Cabernet Sauvignon Medoc (Bordeaux in France)	cherry, plum, pepper, bell pepper, herbs, mint, tea, chocolate	beef, lamb, braised, barbecued and grilled meats, aged cheddar, chocolate
Late harvest white wines	citrus fruit, apple, pear, apricot, peach, mango, honey	custard, vanilla, ginger, carrot cake, cheesecake, cream puffs, apricot cobbler

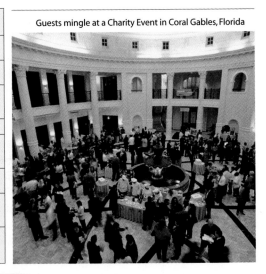
Guests mingle at a Charity Event in Coral Gables, Florida

Figure 9–3 • Matching Wine with Food.
(Courtesy of Jay R Schrock.)

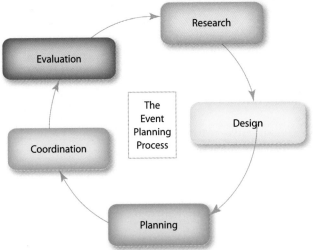

Figure 13–1 • Event Planning Process Diagram.

Color format with lively photographs, drawings, and tables maintains your interest and provides visual aids to learning.

Additional Student Resources

Companion Website www.prenhall.com/walker

This free online student study guide has been designed specifically to help you review, reinforce, and apply the concepts presented in the book. This interactive site features chapter-specific modules—practice exams with immediate answer assessment, help in the "hints" section, relevant Internet links, and PowerPoint slides.

Message from John Walker

To obtain great hospitality jobs—the ones that you really want when you graduate—you must take full advantage of all that college has to offer. Today's job market is highly competitive, with the best jobs going to the best prepared individuals. If a particular job sounds great, you can be sure many graduates also consider it great—meaning strong competition for those positions. There is a direct correlation between the quality of a position and the number of applicants. This competition is not only from your classmates, but from hospitality graduates from around the country and around the world.

For many students, it is difficult to see far ahead to graduation day, since it is years ahead. It appears that there will always be time to improve grades, get better work experience, or join more clubs for leadership experience. But the years go by quickly and graduation does happen.

Students can set themselves up for future success by being proactive throughout each year at college. Hospitality graduates already have the major, but also need the combination of activities, grades, work experience, communication ability, and attitude in order to do well when seeking a position upon graduation.

By setting their standards high as early in college as possible, students can establish a pattern of habits that will lead to taking full advantage of all that college has to offer while at the same time preparing to excel upon graduation.

Hospitality students who start building their resume early in their college career will be building toward the goal of obtaining their job of choice upon graduation.

ACKNOWLEDGMENTS

Thanks to the students and professors, especially those who have made valuable contributions to this edition, and to the industry professionals who contributed to this text.

I am particularly grateful to Beth Lukens, Katerina Annaraud, and Flora Guidry for their important contributions to Chapters 2 and 17. Ken Jarvis did an exceptional job of finalizing Chapter 17.

Thanks to all of my CHRIE colleagues, many of whom encouraged me to undertake this project and made valuable suggestions. I would like to thank the following contributing authors, who graciously allowed their materials and expertise to be included in this and previous editions: Charlie Adams, Bart Bartlett, Hank Christen, Lynne Christen, Fred DeMicco, Kathleen Doeller, William Fisher, Claudia Green, Kathryn Hashimoto, Christine Jaszay, John Self, Robert Kok, Peter La Macchia, Jim Makens, Paul Maniscalco, William B. Martin, Brian Miller, Catherine Rabb, James Reid, Jay Schrock, Stowe Shoemaker, Andrea Sigler, Karen Smith, Dave Tucker, Cliff Wener, and Mike Zema.

The following reviewers made valuable suggestions regarding the organization and content: Edward Addo, St. Cloud State University; Diana S. Barber, Georgia State University; Robert Bennett, Delaware County Community College; Jane Boyland, Johnson & Wales University, Providence, RI; John M. Courtney, Johnson County Community College; Ken Jarvis, Anne Arundel Community College; Tammie J. Kaufman, University of Central Florida; Chris Roberts, University of Massachusetts; Eva Smith, Spartanburg Technical College; Muzzo Uysal, Virginia Polytechnic Institute and State University; Gary Ward, Scottsdale Community College; William H. Weber, Johnson & Wales University, Charleston, SC; and Jim Whitlock, Brenau University.

Eva Smith, thank you for the great job you did on the PowerPoints and Study Guide. Gary Ward, your work on the Companion Website is greatly appreciated. Michael Petrillose, thank you for your work on the Instructor's Manual. And gratitude to James Bennett for your authorship of the Test Bank. It was a pleasure working with all of you.

This book would not have been possible without the extraordinary help of Yasmeen Hossain; Simone Trafford; Yolanda Rucker; Bart Bartlett, Ph.D., Pennsylvania State University; Karl Titz, Ph.D., Conrad N. Hilton College, University of Houston; Denny Bhatka; Alfred Lewis, D.B.A. Alliant International University; Jay Schrock, Ph.D., University of South Florida; Ken Crocker, Ph.D., Bowling Green State University; Ed Rothenberg; Esther Lee, Evans Hotels; Tim Mulligan; Roger Huldi; Jody Nicholas; Mark Testa, Ph.D., San Diego University; MICROS Systems, Inc.; and Sodexho.

Dr. John R. Walker, DBA, FMP, CHA, is the McKibbon Professor of Hotel and Restaurant Management at the University of South Florida. John's years of industry experience began with management training at the Savoy Hotel London. This was followed by terms as food and beverage manager, assistant rooms division manager, catering manager, and general manager with Grand Metropolitan Hotels, Selsdon Park Hotel, Rank Hotels, Inter-Continental Hotels, and the Coral Reef Resort, Barbados, West Indies.

John has taught at two- and four-year schools in Canada and the United States. In addition to being a hospitality management consultant and text author, he has been published in *The Cornell Hotel Restaurant Administration Quarterly* and *The Hospitality Educators Journal*. He is a ten-time recipient of the President's Award for teaching, scholarship, and service; and he has received the Patnubay Award for exemplary professional performance through teaching and authorship of tourism and hospitality publications.

Dr. Walker is an editorial advisory board member for Progress in Tourism and Hospitality Research. He is a past president of the Pacific Chapter of the Council on Hotel, Restaurant, and Institutional Education (CHRIE). He is a certified hotel administrator (CHA) and a certified Foodservice Management Professional (FMP).

John is married to Josielyn T. Walker and they have twins, Christopher and Selina. The Walkers live in Sarasota, Florida.

PART I

The Hospitality Industry and Tourism

CHAPTER 1

Hospitality Spirit

OBJECTIVES

After reading and studying this chapter, you should be able to:

- Describe the characteristics of the hospitality industry.

- Explain corporate philosophy.

- Discuss why service has become such an important facet of the hospitality industry.

- Suggest ways to improve service.

Welcome to You, the Future Hospitality Industry Leaders!

The hospitality industry is a fascinating, fun, and stimulating one in which to enjoy a career, plus you get compensated quite well and have excellent advancement opportunities. We often hear from industry professionals that it (the industry) gets in your blood—meaning we become one with the hospitality industry. On countless class industry visits, the persons speaking to the class said that they wouldn't change their job—even if they had a chance to. Only one speaker said, "You must be nuts if you want to work in this industry"—of course, he was joking! But there are some realities you need to be aware of, and they are discussed in the section titled "Characteristics of the Hospitality Industry" later in this chapter. Many examples exist of people graduating and being offered positions that enable them to gain a good foundation of knowledge and experience in the industry. Possible career paths are illustrated in Figure 1–1. In most cases, it does not take long for advancement opportunities to come along. Let's begin our journey with a look at *service spirit,* which plays a crucial role in the success of our industry, no matter what your position or title is.

Ever think about why Marriott International is so successful? Well, one of the reasons is given by Jim Collins writing in the foreword to Bill Marriott's book, *The Spirit to Serve: Marriott's Way.* Collins says Marriott has *timeless core values and enduring purpose,* including the belief that their people are number one: "Take care of Marriott people and they will take care of the guests." Also, Marriott's commitment to continuous improvement and good old-fashioned dedication to hard work and having fun while doing it provide a foundation of stability and enduring character. Collins adds that Marriott's core purpose—making people away from home feel that they are among friends and are really wanted—serves as a fixed point of guidance and inspiration.

So, where does *hospitality spirit* fit into all this? It's simple; it begins with each and every time we have a guest encounter. People with a *service spirit* are happy to do something extra to make a guest's experience memorable. The hospitality spirit means that it is our passion to give pleasure to others, or as one human resources director, Charlotte Jordan, calls it, "Creating memorable experiences for others and being an Ambassador of the world, adding warmth and caring."[1] Every day we encounter guests who rely on us for service, which can make or break their experience. We want to WOW guests and have them return often with their friends. Yes, we are in the people business, and it's "we the people" who succeed in the hospitality industry when we take pride in the words of the Ritz-Carlton hotel company: We are ladies and gentlemen taking care of ladies and gentlemen.

The **National Restaurant Association (NRA)** forecasts a need for thousands of supervisors and managers for the hospitality and tourism industries. Are you wondering if there's room in this dynamic industry for you? You bet! There's room for everyone. The best advice is to consider what you love to do most and get some experience in that area—to see if you really like it—because our industry has some distinct characteristics. For starters, we are in the business of giving service. When Kurt Wachtveilt, thirty-year veteran general manager of the

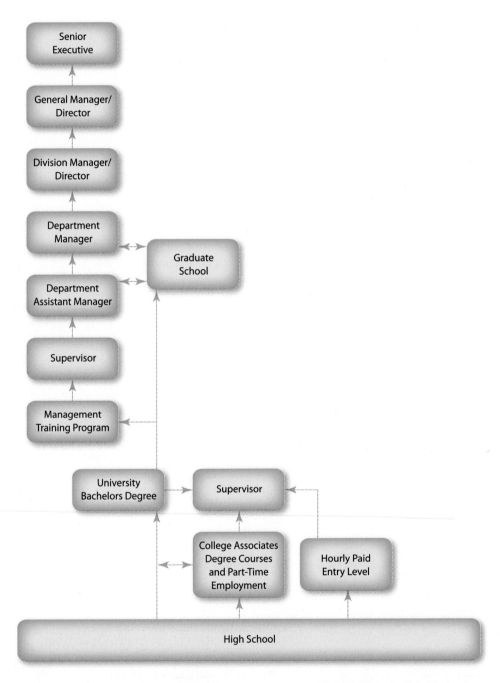

Figure 1–1 • A Likely Career Path in the Hospitality Industry. Is Education Worth it? You Bet! Just Think—the Difference in Salary Over a Career Between an Associate's and a Bachelor's Degree is $500,000. Yes, That's Half a Million Bucks!

(*Source:* U.S. Census Bureau Average Lifetime Earnings—Different Levels of Education.)

Oriental Hotel in Bangkok, Thailand, considered by many to be one of the best hotels in the world—was asked, "What is the secret of being the best?" he replied, "Service, service, service!" But what is service? Service is defined in *Webster's New World Dictionary* as "the act or means of serving." To serve is to "provide goods and services for" and "be of assistance to." With thousands of guest encounters each day, it is critical to give our guests exceptional service at each encounter. And that's the challenge!

The hospitality industry can also be a good choice for entrepreneurs who prefer to do their own thing, whether it be running a bar, catering company, restaurant, or night club; being involved in event management; or being a tour guide or wedding planner or whatever. The prospects are good for starting a successful endeavor. Think about it: You could begin with one restaurant concept, open a second, and then begin to franchise. Whatever your dreams and goals, the hospitality industry likely has an opportunity for you.

Consider that a company like Marriott International started out as a small root beer place, in Washington, D.C., with a counter and a few stools. And that an immigrant, who opened up a hot dog stand outside Dodger Stadium in Los Angeles later became a multi-millionaire chain restaurant owner (Karl Kartcher, owner of Carl's Jr.). And that a former dishwasher, Ralph Rubio, now owns a successful chain of Rubio's Fresh Mexican Grill quick-service restaurants that have sold more than 50 million fish tacos since opening the first restaurant in 1983. Then, there is Peter Morton, who in the early 1970s lived in London, England, and missed American food, so he borrowed $60,000 from family and friends and opened the Great American Disaster. It was an immediate success with a line of customers around the block. Morton quickly realized that London needed a restaurant that not only served American food but also embodied the energy and excitement of music past and present. He opened the Hard Rock Café and offered a hearty American meal at a reasonable price in an atmosphere charged with energy, fun, and the excitement of rock and roll.[2] More recently, Howard Schultz, who while in Italy in the early 1980s was impressed with the popularity of espresso bars in Milan. He saw the potential to develop the coffee bar culture in the United States and beyond—there are now well over 8,000 Starbucks.[3] Any ideas on what the next hot entrepreneurial idea will be?

A pineapple is the symbol of hospitality

The Pineapple Tradition

The pineapple has enjoyed a rich and romantic heritage as a symbol of welcome, friendship, and **hospitality**. Pineapples were brought back from the West Indies by early European explorers during the seventeenth century. From that time on, the pineapple was cultivated in Europe and became the favored fruit to serve to royalty and the elite. The pineapple was later introduced into North America and became a part of North American hospitality as well. No, pineapples were displayed at doors or on gateposts, announcing to friends and acquaintances: "The ship is in! Come join us. Food and drink for all!"

Since its introduction, the pineapple has been internationally recognized as a symbol of hospitality and a sign of friendliness, warmth, cheer, graciousness, and conviviality.

The Interrelated Nature of Hospitality and Tourism

The hospitality and **tourism** industries are the largest and fastest-growing industries in the world. One of the most exciting aspects of this industry is that it is made up of so many different professions. What picture comes to mind when you think about a career in hospitality and tourism? Do you picture a chef, a general manager, owners of their own businesses, a director of marketing, or an event manager? The possibilities are many and varied, ranging from positions in restaurants, resorts, air and cruise lines, theme parks, and casinos, to name a few of the several sectors of the hospitality and tourism industries (see Figures 1–2. and 1–3). The CD-ROM that accompanies this book has more information on the following topics: scholarships; sample test questions; advice from industry leaders; whether the hospitality industry is for you; careers, career preparation, career paths; your career in the hospitality

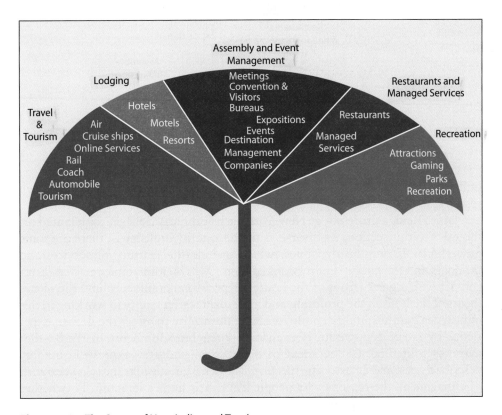

Figure 1–2 • The Scope of Hospitality and Tourism.

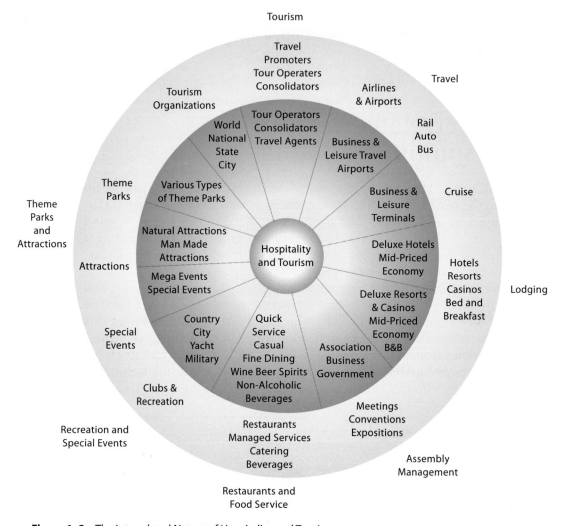

Figure 1–3 • The Interrelated Nature of Hospitality and Tourism.

industry; resume writing; interviewing skills, and related web sites, and web resources.

James Reid, a professor at New York City Technical College, contributed his thoughts to this section. As diverse as the hospitality industry is, there are some powerful and common dynamics, which include the delivery of services and products and the guests' impressions of them. Whether an employee is in direct contact with a guest (**front of the house**) or performing duties behind the scenes (**heart of the house**), the profound and most challenging reality of working in this industry is that hospitality employees have the ability to affect the human experience by creating powerful impressions—even brief moments of truth—that may last a lifetime. (A "moment of truth" is an industry expression used to describe a guest and an associate meeting, as when a guest walks into a restaurant.)

Imagine all the reasons why people leave their homes temporarily (whether alone or with others) to go to other places near and far.

People travel for many reasons. A trip away from home might be for vacation, work, to attend a conference, or maybe even to visit a college campus, just to name a few. Regardless of the reason, under the umbrella of travel and tourism, many professions are necessary to meet the needs and wants of people away from home. Think of the many people who provide services to travelers and have the responsibility of representing their communities and creating experiences that, when delivered successfully, are pleasurable and memorable for travelers. These people welcome, inform, comfort, and care for tourists and are collectively a part of a process that can positively affect human lives and well-being.

The Venezia Tower rises from the glowing grounds of the Venetian Resort Hotel Casino on the Las Vegas strip

The hotel business provides career opportunities for many associates who help make reservations and greet, assist, and serve guests in hospitality operations of varied sizes and in locations all over the world. Examples include a husband and wife who operate their own bed and breakfast (B&B) in upstate Vermont. This couple provides the ideal weekend retreat for avid skiers during a frosty February, making their guests want to return year after year. Another example is the hundreds of employees necessary to keep the 5,505-room MGM Grand in full swing 365 days a year! Room attendants, engineers, front-desk agents, food servers, and managers are just a few of the positions that are vital to creating experiences for visitors who come to Las Vegas from around the globe.

The restaurant business is also a vital component under the travel and tourism umbrella. People go to restaurants to fulfill diverse needs and wants. Eating is a biological need that restaurants accommodate, but restaurants and the people who work in them fulfill numerous other human desires, such as the need for socialization and to be entertained.

Gramercy Tavern restaurant in New York may be the perfect location for a certain group of friends to celebrate a twenty-first birthday. The individual guest who turned twenty-one may remember this fête for a lifetime because the service and food quality were excellent and added value to the experiences for all the celebrants. For this kind of collective and powerful impression to be made, many key players are needed to operate and support the service delivery system: several front-of-the-house staff members, such as the food servers, bartenders, greeters, managers, and bus attendants; plus the back-of-the-house employees, such as the chefs, dishwashers, food purchaser, and stewards (to name a few). All these people had to coordinate a diversity of activities and responsibilities to create this dynamic, successful, and, for the restaurant ownership, profitable event.

In managed services, foodservices are provided for airlines, military facilities, schools, colleges and universities, health care operations, and business and industry. These foodservice operations have the dual challenge of meeting the needs and wants of both the guests and the client (i.e., the institution that hired the foodservices). The employees who are part of foodservices enterprises have responsibilities very much like those of other restaurant operations. The quality of food products delivered in an airline, for example, may be the key to winning

Beverages add to the many celebrations of life

customers back in the future and creating positive word-of-mouth promotion that attracts new customers.

Since history has been recorded, beverages have provided a biological need that has expanded the beverage menu far beyond water alone! Whether it is the cool iced tea garnished with lemon and mint served poolside at a Riviera resort or the champagne toast offered at a fiftieth wedding anniversary party in Boston, beverages play a major role in satisfying people and adding to the many celebrations of life.

As with food products, the creation and delivery systems for beverage products are vital components of the hospitality industry. These operations involve many people who consumers rarely see: the farmer in Napa Valley who tends to the vineyard every day of the year, the coffee bean harvester in Colombia, the sake server in Tokyo, or the orchard owner who crates oranges in Florida. These individuals behind the scenes have diverse and crucial responsibilities so that guests, whether in a resort, office, hospital, college, or roadside snack bar, can have the quality of products they want.

Characteristics of the Hospitality Industry

Hospitality businesses are open 365 days a year and 24 hours a day. No, we don't have to work all of these days, but we do tend to work longer hours than people in other industries. Those on their way to senior positions in the hospitality industry, and many others for that matter, often work 10 hours per day. However, because of managerial burnout, there is a trend in the industry of reducing working hours of managers to 50 hours a week to attract and retain generation Xers. Evenings and weekends are included in the workweek—so we have to accept that we may be working when others are enjoying leisure time.

The hospitality industry depends heavily on shift work. Early in your career, depending on the department, you will likely work on a particular shift. Basically, there are four shifts, beginning with the morning shift, so you may be getting up as early as 5 A.M. to get to the shift that starts at 7 A.M. The midshift is usually from 10 A.M. to 7 P.M.; the evening shift starts at 3 P.M. and goes on until 11:30 P.M.;

and finally there is the night shift that begins at 11 P.M. and lasts until 7:30 A.M. Supervisors and managers often begin at 8 A.M. and work until 6 or 8 P.M. Success does not come easily.

In the hospitality industry, we constantly strive for outstanding **guest satisfaction,** which leads to guest loyalty and, yes, profit. Our services are mostly **intangible,** meaning the guest cannot "test drive" a night's stay or "taste the steak" before dining. Our product is for the guest's use only, not for possession. Even more unique, for us to produce our product—hospitality—we must get the guest's input. Imagine General Electric building a refrigerator with the customer in the factory, participating in the actual construction of the product! Seems preposterous, yet we do it every single day, numerous times per day, and in a uniquely different way each time. This is referred to as the **inseparability** of production and consumption of the service product, which presents a special challenge because each guest may have his or her own requests.

The other unique dimension of our industry is the **perishability** of our product. For example, we have 1,400 rooms in inventory—that is, available to sell—but we sell only 1,200 rooms. What do we do with the 200 unsold rooms? Nothing. We have permanently lost 200 room-nights and their revenue.

▶ Check Your Knowledge

1. List and describe the four shifts in the hospitality industry.
2. Identify and explain two differences between the hospitality business and the other business sectors.

Each year, the National Restaurant Association (NRA) invites the best and brightest students from universities and colleges to participate in the annual restaurant show in Chicago. The highlight of the show is the "Salute to Excellence" day when students and faculty attend forums, workshops, and a gala award banquet with industry leaders. Coca-Cola sponsors the event and several other corporations involved in the industry.

During the day students are invited to write their dreams on a large panel, which is later displayed for all to enjoy reading. Here are a few of a previous year's hopes and dreams:

- To help all people learn and grow. (Jason P.)
- To be the best I can. (NMC)
- To establish a chain of jazz cafés in six years and go public in ten years. (Richard)
- To successfully please my customers. (J. Calicendo)
- To be happy and to make others happy, too.
- To put smiles on all faces.

- To be one of the most creative chefs—I would like to be happy with everything I create.
- To make a difference in the lives of people through food! (Mitz Dardony)
- To be successful professionally, socially, and financially. (Marcy W.)
- To preserve our natural resources by operating a restaurant called Green. (Kimberley Mauren)
- Anything I do I like to do it in such a way that I can always be meaningful to people. (Christian Ellis-Schmidt)
- To reach the top because I know there is a lot of space up there. (P. W., Lexington College)
- To use the knowledge that I've gained throughout my career and pass it on to others in hopes of touching their lives in a positive way! To smile and to make smiles. (Armey P. DaCalo)
- I want to be prosperous in my desire to achieve more than $. Happiness and peace are the keys to life. (D. McKinney)
- To teach and be as good as those who have taught me. (Thomas)

So what are your dreams and goals? Take a moment to think about your personal dreams and goals. Keep them in mind and look back on them often. Be prepared to amend them as you develop your career.

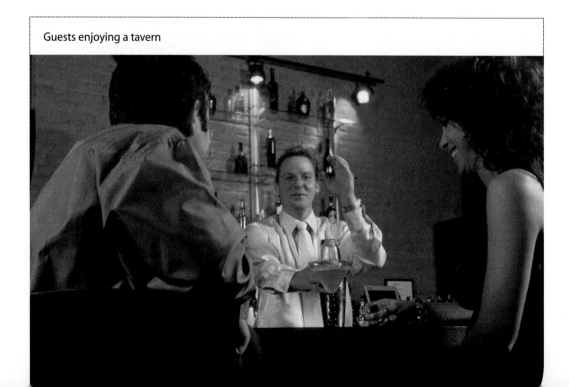

Guests enjoying a tavern

Hospitality Industry Philosophy

Current **hospitality industry philosophy** has changed from one of managers' planning, organizing, implementing, and measuring to that of managers' counseling associates, giving them resources, and helping them to think for themselves. The outcome is a more participative management style, which results in associate **empowerment,** increased productivity, and guest and employee satisfaction. For example, Ritz-Carlton associates are empowered to spend up to $2,000 to make a guest completely happy. Imagine a bride-to-be arriving at a hotel and sending her wedding dress to be pressed. Unfortunately, the iron burns the dress. Luckily, the concierge comes to the rescue by taking the bride to a wedding dress store where they select a gorgeous dress for around $1,800 and the bride is happy because it is a nicer dress than the original one was. Corporate philosophy has strong links to quality leadership and the **total quality management (TQM)** process. (TQM is discussed in a later section.)

Corporate philosophy embraces the values of the organization, including ethics, morals, fairness, and equality. The new paradigm in corporate American hospitality is the shift in emphasis from the production aspect of our business to the focus on guest-related services. The philosophy of "whatever it takes" is winning over "it's not my job." Innovation and creativity are winning over "that's the way we've always done it." Successful organizations are those that are able to impart corporate philosophies to employees and guests alike. Disney Corporation, as discussed later, is a good example of a corporation that has a permeating corporate philosophy.

Service Philosophy Is a Way of Life

J. W. (Bill) Marriott Jr. is chairman of the board of directors of Marriott International. Marriott's web site defines the "Marriott Way" as "about serving the associates, the customer, and the community." These ideals serve as the cornerstone for all Marriott associates who strive to fulfill the "Spirit to Serve."[4] The values originate from deep inside the people themselves—authentic, bone-deep, and passionately held. Marriott's core values include the belief that people are number one ("Take care of Marriott people and they'll take good care of Marriott guests"), a commitment to continuous improvement and overcoming adversity, and a good old-fashioned dedication to hard work and having fun while doing it.

Marriott's core values drive the culture. Similarly, regardless of which service organization we work for, our culture influences the way we treat associates, guests, and the community, and that affects the success of everyone. In the words of J. W. Marriott Jr., "Culture is the life-thread and glue that links our past, present, and future."[5]

▶ Check Your Knowledge

1. Describe Marriott's "Spirit to serve."

Bill Marriott showing his appreciation to some of his associates

Success in Service

What must happen to achieve success in service? Given that approximately 70 percent of the U.S. and Canadian economies and an increasing percentage of other countries' are engaged in service industries, it is critical to offer guests exceptional service. With thousands of guest encounters, or moments of truth, each day, it is critical to incorporate service excellence in each hospitality organization. Some corporations adopt the expression, "If you're not serving the guest, you had better be serving someone who is." This is the essence of teamwork: Someone in the back of the house is serving someone in the front of the house, who is serving the guest.

A guest is anyone who receives or benefits from the output of someone's work. The external guest is the guest most people think of in the traditional sense. The satisfaction of external guests ultimately measures a company's success, because they are the people who are willing to pay for its services. The internal guests are the people inside a company who receive or benefit from the output of work done by others in the company, for example, the server or busser preparing the restaurant to serve lunch has been "served" by the dishwasher, who has prepared clean plates, knives, forks, spoons, and glassware.

For success in service, we need to do the following:

1. Focus on the guest.
2. Understand the role of the guest-contact employee.
3. Weave a service culture into education and training systems.
4. Emphasize high-touch instead of just high-tech.
5. Thrive on change.

As hospitality professionals, we need to recognize a variety of guest-related situations and act to relieve them or avoid them. Imagine how an associate can win points by showing empathy—that is, putting herself in someone else's shoes—in the following situation: A party of eight people arrives at a restaurant: Mom, Dad, and the kids, who are running all over the place. Mom and Dad just had a huge fight in the minivan. Obviously, the associate would want to welcome the party to the restaurant, seat them as quickly as possible, and then give the

INTRODUCING HORST SCHULZE

West Paces Hotel Group

Horst Schulze is a legendary leader in the hospitality industry and one of the most influential hospitality industry leaders of our times. His vision helped reshape concepts of guest service throughout the hospitality and service industries.

Mr. Schulze grew up in a small village in Germany, and he was eleven years old when he told his parents that he wanted to work in a hotel. When he was fourteen, his parents took him to the finest hotel in the region where they had "an audience" with the general manager—it lasted ten minutes, and never spoke to him for the next two years! Everyone, including young Schulze's mother, the general manager, and the restaurant maître d' told him how important the guests were, so with knees shaking, young Schulze found himself in the restaurant working as a buser. The maître d' made a favorable impression on the young man because he was respected by both guests and staff alike. So, when Horst had to do an essay for his hotel school (he attended hotel school on Wednesdays), he chose the title "We Are Ladies and Gentlemen Serving Ladies and Gentlemen." He kept the essay because it was the only A he received, but that A also became the foundation of his philosophy to create service excellence.

Mr. Schulze now speaks on guest service to thousands every year, graciously sharing with others his knowledge and experiments. He says that there are three aspects of service:

1. Service should be defect free.
2. Service should be timely.
3. People should care.

It is the caring piece that is service. The guest relationship begins when a guest perceives that he or she has contacted you, and the human contact should begin with a warm welcome. Mr. Schulze adds that all hospitality businesses should be doing four things:

1. Keeping guests equals loyalty, meaning guests trust you and are happy to form a relationship with you.
2. Find new guests.
3. Get as much money as you can from the guest without losing him or her.
4. Create efficiencies.

Mr. Schulze spent nine years with Hyatt Hotels Corporation, where he was a hotel GM, regional VP, and corporate VP. Before his association with Hyatt, he worked for Hilton Hotels. After joining the Ritz-Carlton as a charter member and VP of operations in 1983, Mr. Schulze was instrumental in creating the operating and service standards that have become world famous. He was appointed Executive Vice President in 1987, and president and chief operating officer (COO) in 1988. When he left the Ritz-Carlton in 2002, Mr. Schulze was responsible for the $2 billion Ritz-Carlton operations worldwide.

Mr. Schulze served as vice chairman of the Ritz-Carlton Hotel Company from 2001 to 2002, after serving as president and COO of the Ritz-Carlton Group starting in 1988. Under his leadership, the group was awarded the Malcolm Baldrige National Quality Award in both 1992 and 1999; it was the first and only hotel company to win even one such award. In addition, Ritz-Carlton is continuously voted "best hotel company in

INTRODUCING HORST SCHULZE (continued)

the world" by convention and trade publications. Mr. Schulze has been recognized as "corporate hotelier of the world" by *HOTELS* magazine, and he was awarded the Ishikawa Medal for his personal contributions to the quality movement.

In 2002, Mr. Schulze along with several former Ritz-Carlton executives formed West Paces Hotel Group to create and operate branded hotels in several distinctive market segments. The canon of the company is as follows:

The West Paces Hotel Group is in business to create value and unparalleled results for our owners by creating products which fulfill individual customer expectations.

We deliver reliable, genuinely caring and timely service superior to our competition, with respected and empowered employees who work in an environment of belonging and purpose.

We are supportive and contributing members of society, operating with uncompromising values, honor and integrity.

West Paces has hotels and resorts under two brands: Solis and Capella. They can be viewed at **http://www.westpaceshotels.com.**

kids something to play with or munch on until the food comes. Also, it would be a good idea to offer everyone a beverage.

Another key objective in the service equation is to encourage guest loyalty. We not only need to keep guests happy during their stay, but also to keep them returning—with their friends, we hope! It costs several times more to attract new guests than it does to retain existing ones. Imagine how much more profitable a hospitality business would be if it could retain just 10 percent of its guests as loyal guests. Losing a guest equates to losing much more than one sale; it has the potential to be a loss of a lifetime guest. Consider a $20 restaurant lunch for two people. If the guests return twice a month over several years—say, ten—the amount they have contributed to the restaurant quickly becomes huge ($4,800). If they bring their friends, this amount is even higher.

We know that service is a complex yet critical component of the hospitality industry. In their book *Service America!*, Albrecht and Zemke suggest two basic kinds of service: "Help me!" and "Fix it."[6] "Help me" refers to guests' regular and special needs, such as, "Help me find the function room" or, "Help me to get a reservation at the best restaurant in town." "Fix it" refers to services such as, "Please fix my toilet; it won't flush" or, "Please fix the TV so that we can watch the World Series."

Moments of Truth

"Moments of truth" is a term coined by Jan Carlson. When Carlson became president of Scandinavian Airline System (SAS), it was ranked at the bottom of the European airline market. He quickly realized that he had to spend a lot of time on the front line coaching SAS associates in how to handle guest encounters, or as he called them, "moments of truth." As a result of his efforts, SAS was soon ranked at the top of the European airlines for service. Service

FOCUS ON SERVICE

Hospitality is Offering a Cup of Kindness

William B. Martin, *Cal Tech—Monterey Bay*

Customer service is a central focus of hospitality. It is what hospitality is all about—what we do. If you are interested in a hospitality career, it is important to understand and learn as much as possible about customer service and particularly how to be successful at it. Your success will come from a complete understanding of hospitality.

Let's begin by exploring why we provide hospitality. Why are hospitality businesses in business? What is the primary purpose of a foodservice operation? A lodging establishment? A travel- or tourism-related business? Is it just for the money? Many of you might answer an easy yes to this question. But, as you will see, hospitality is much more than just about money. Money is important, but it is important as a means and as a necessary ingredient to help us get to where we want to go. Money is not the primary reason for hospitality. Then, what is the primary purpose of hospitality?

Our job, first and foremost, is to enhance the lives of those people (guests, customers, passengers, etc.) to whom we are dedicated to serve. Yes, it is that simple (and complex at the same time). Our job is to make the lives of others better in a small way or big way; it makes no difference. Whatever it is, we are out to make people's lives on this planet a little bit better, or maybe even a lot better. This is our purpose. It is where we find meaning. We in the hospitality industry are about enhancing the lives of others—period. Ultimately, that is what makes it all worthwhile.

With that said, where does customer service fit in? Good question. If you are a sharp student, you've already got it. You can readily see that if the purpose of hospitality is to enhance the lives of others, the way we do that is through service. And what is service? It is how we go about treating our guests—how we make (or fail to make) their lives better by how we treat them. And we can go a long way toward treating them well by simply offering them a cup of kindness.

What does this mean? What does it take to be kind? What do we have to do? How do we enhance the lives of others through kindness? We begin by *understanding* what it is that they need. The problem is that all of our guests come to us with many needs. Some we can meet, some we can't. But of all the needs they come with, four of them are specifically hospitality related. If you can work toward helping them satisfy these needs, you can go a long way toward making their lives better through kindness. Quality customer service demands that service providers understand what it is that you want. Kindness, after all, comes through understanding. Kindness is demonstrated by making everyone feel *welcome*.

Quality customer service requires that we make all guests feel *comfortable*—that we provide the assurance, and follow through, that they will be taken care of. They don't need to worry; they are in good hands. In short, when we can do this we are filling their cups with more kindness. Whether they deserve it or not, be made to feel important. Why? Because, we all have a *need to feel important*. This is a part of our job. Moreover, it is another important way we can show kindness to our guests.

We need to stay focused on the primary purposes of hospitality. We need to understand the power of kindness and the importance of satisfying the four basic customer service needs of our guests. In the final analysis, hospitality and customer service success are found in our ability to enhance the lives of others through how we treat them—with a little cup of kindness.

commitment is a total organizational approach that makes the quality of service, as perceived by the customer, the number one driving force for the operation of the business.[7]

Every hospitality organization has thousands of moments of truth every day. This leads to tremendous challenges in maintaining the expected levels of service. Let's look at just some of the moments of truth in a restaurant dining experience:[8]

1. Guest calls the restaurant for a table reservation.
2. Guest tries to find the restaurant.
3. Guest parks.
4. Guest is welcomed.
5. Guest is informed that the table is not ready.
6. Guest either waits or goes to the lounge for a cocktail.
7. Guest tries to attract the bartender's attention for a cocktail because there are no seats available.
8. Guest is called over a loudspeaker or paged.
9. Guest is seated at the table.
10. Server takes order.
11. Server brings beverages or food.
12. Server clears food or beverages.
13. Server brings check.
14. Guest pays for meal.
15. Guest departs restaurant.

From your own experiences, you can imagine just how many moments of truth there are in a restaurant dining experience.

▶ Check Your Knowledge

1. What is the purpose of a mission statement?
2. Why is service so important?
3. What is a moment of truth?

The Focus on Service

Giving good service is a very difficult task; few businesses give enough priority to training associates in how to provide service. We suffer from an overreliance on technology so that service providers are often not motivated to give good service. For example, when checking a guest into the hotel, the front-desk associate may greet the guest but then look down at the computer for the remainder of the service encounter, even when asking for the guest's name.

Or consider the reservations associate who says nothing when asked for a specific type of guest room because he is waiting for the computer to indicate availability.

In his best-selling book *At America's Service,* Karl Albrecht lists the "Seven Deadly Sins of Service":

1. Apathy
2. Brush-off
3. Coldness
4. Condescension
5. Robotics
6. Rule book
7. Runaround

Money magazine published a list called "The Six Rudest Restaurants in America."[9] It detailed a number of characteristically negative experiences guests had with restaurants noted more for their high ideals than their hors d'oeuvres—and these included some of the swankiest of the swank. The author, Michael Williams, identifies the most common insults to guests as the following:

1. Grossly overbooked reservations
2. Holding better tables for favorite guests
3. Maître d's who could suddenly conjure up a table for a heavy tip
4. Treating guests with attitudes bordering on arrogance

Perfecting Service

To help improve service in the hospitality industry, the Educational Foundation of the National Restaurant Association, one of the hospitality industry's leading associations, developed a number of great programs that will enhance your professional development. Further information may be obtained from the NRA's web site (**www.restaurant.org**).

Among the various programs and courses is one titled Foodservice Leadership. Effective leaders are those who make things happen because they have developed the knowledge, skills, and attitude required to get the most out of the people in their operation. Leadership involves change; in fact, change is the one thing we can be sure of in the coming years. Our guests are constantly changing; so is technology, product availability, and, of course, our competition. To cope with this constant change, the NRA's group suggests that (1) all change is likely to meet with some resistance, and (2) when implementing change, do the following:

1. State the purpose of the change.
2. Involve all employees in the process.
3. Monitor, update, and take corrective action to get back on track.

One way in which leaders involve employees in the process is through total quality management (TQM) and empowerment.

Service and Total Quality Management

The increasingly open and fiercely competitive marketplace is exerting enormous pressure on service industries to deliver superior service. Inspired by rising guest expectations and competitive necessity, many hospitality companies have jumped on the service quality bandwagon.

The Malcolm Baldrige National Quality Award is the highest level of national recognition for quality that a U.S. company can receive. The award promotes an understanding of quality excellence, greater awareness of quality as a critical competitive element, and the sharing of quality information and strategies.

The Ritz-Carlton Hotel Company, the only hospitality company to win two Malcolm Baldrige National Quality Awards, was founded on principles of excellence in guest service. The essence of this philosophy was refined into a set of core values collectively called the Gold Standards. The credo is printed on a small laminated card that all employees must memorize or carry on their person at all times when on duty. The card lists the three steps of service:

1. A warm and sincere greeting; use the guest name, if and when possible.
2. Anticipation and compliance with guests' needs.
3. Fond farewell; give them a warm good-bye and use their names if and when possible.

The quality movement began at the turn of the century as a means of ensuring consistency among the parts produced in the different plants of a single company so that they could be used interchangeably. In the area of service, TQM is a participatory process that empowers all levels of employees to work in groups to establish guest service expectations and determine the best way to meet or exceed these expectations. Notice that the term *guest* is preferred over the term *customer*. The inference here is that if we treat customers like guests, we are more likely to exceed their expectations. One successful hotelier has insisted for a long time that all employees treat guests as they would like to be treated themselves.

TQM is a continuous process that works best when managers are also good leaders. A successful company will employ leader–managers who create a stimulating work environment in which guests and employees (sometimes called internal guests: one employee serves another employee, who in turn serves a guest) become integral parts of the mission by participating in **goal** and objective setting.

Implementing TQM is exciting because after everyone becomes involved, there is no stopping the creative ways employees will find to solve guest-related problems and improve service. Other benefits

The Employee Promise

At the Ritz-Carlton, our Ladies and Gentlemen are the most important resource in our service commitment to our guests.

By applying the principles of trust, honesty, respect, integrity, and commitment, we nurture and maximize talent to the benefit of each individual and the company.

The Ritz-Carlton fosters a work environment where diversity is valued, quality of life is enhanced, individual aspirations are fulfilled, and the Ritz-Carlton mystique is strengthened.

A DAY IN THE LIFE OF RYAN LASHWAY

Assistant Manager, Mar Vista Dockside Restaurant, Longboat Key, Florida

To describe a typical day of work for me at the Mar Vista, I must first tell you a little bit about the restaurant. Located on Sarasota Bay on the north end of Longboat Key in historic Long-beach Village, the Mar Vista has existed for over 60 years. Built in the early 1940s, "The Pub" was originally a bait and tackle shop until the 1950s when the owners started selling ham-burgers and beer to the local fishermen crowd. The Mar Vista operated like this until coming under the ownership of Ed Chiles of the Chiles Group Corporation in 1990. Chiles is the son of the former governor of Florida, Lawton Chiles, and also owns the Beachhouse and Sand-bar restaurants on Anna Maria Island. The Mar Vista is an authentic part of Old Florida, and our history and ambiance make it a fun and relaxing place. Our goal at the Mar Vista is to provide our guests with the finest in food and courteous, prompt service. For further information about the Chiles Group Corporation, visit our web site at **www.groupersandwich.com**.

A typical day for a manager at the Mar Vista goes like this:

8:30am – Arrive and check the premises for any unusual activity. Unlock the doors and turn on all lights and A/C units. Check to see that the overnight cleaning crew has done a thorough job, especially in the kitchen, restrooms, and behind the bars. Then, the manager must look at the schedules to see which employees are working on any given day and make ready for the kitchen staff's arrival at 9:00 A.M.

9:00am – Upon arrival, the kitchen staff is entered into our in-house computer system so that their hours for the day will be recorded. Towels and cleaning materials must also be supplied for the entire staff. The rest-rooms must be checked and stocked with hand towels, liquid soap, and toilet paper. The premises are then walked again and the grounds checked for trash. All windows and mirrors must be cleaned.

10:30am – The wait staff and bar staff arrive. The cash banks for the bar must be counted and paired up for daily use. The safe in the manager's office must then be opened and the money from the previous day is made ready for pickup by our financial officer. The manager then meets with the kitchen manager and discusses the daily specials. Upon agreement of the best use for food items, the specials must then be printed and inserted into the menus.

11:30am – Open for lunch business. Throughout the day, management focuses on customer relations and mak-ing sure the restaurant runs smoothly. Incoming paperwork from deliveries for the kitchen and bar must be fully documented, and all incoming orders must be checked in and signed for. Any problems with food orders or guest service must be handled in such a way that the customer is never scorned; return business is the primary focus. In general, the customers are always right, and in this business we must do whatever is necessary to keep them happy.

3:00pm – Toward the end of the lunch shift, servers are finishing their daily work and will require checkout forms to do their money drops. Managers must check each server out individually and make sure that all side-work is completed and the restaurant will be ready for the next shift crew arriving at 4:00. Managers must meet with the kitchen manager again and prepare the dinner specials. The P.M. bartender will also be arriving and will require a night bank, while the A.M. bartender will need to be checked out and his or her bank checked for correct money transactions.

5:00pm – Dinner begins and the night manager arrives. Discuss the events and highlights of the day with the P.M. manager and notify of any problems.

Then it's off to rest up and prepare to do it again tomorrow!

include cost reductions and increased guest and employee satisfaction, leading ultimately to increased profits.

Top executives and line managers are responsible for the success of the TQM process; when they commit to ownership of the process, it will be successful. Focused commitment is the foundation of a quality service initiative, and leadership is the critical component in promoting commitment. Achieving TQM is a top-down, bottom-up process that must have the active commitment and participation of all employees from the top executives down to those at the bottom of the corporate ladder. The expression, "If you are not serving the guest, then you had better be serving someone who is" still holds true today.

The difference between TQM and quality control (QC) is that QC focuses on error detection, whereas TQM focuses on error prevention. Quality control is generally based on industrial systems and, because of this, tends to be product oriented rather than service oriented. To the guest, services are experiential; they are felt, lived through, and sensed. The moment of truth is the actual guest contact.

Establishment of a continuous TQM program begins with the introduction of the concept and philosophy to all associates by the most senior member of management to underscore the importance of the continuous TQM process. One of the best examples of a TQM philosophy is the Ritz-Carlton Hotel Company, which has built a reputation on exceptional guest service. Horst Schulze, former president and CEO, who led the company to the Baldrige awards, began with the motto "We are ladies and gentlemen serving ladies and gentlemen,"…and with the mission of "providing the finest personal service and facilities, install[ing] well-being, and even fulfill[ing] the unexpressed wishes of our guests."[10]

The first step in the process is to assess the leadership capabilities of line managers and, if necessary, make changes to have excellent leaders at all levels of management.

The second step is to form departmental teams of volunteers who will work on TQM and train the teams in problem-solving.

The third step is to create an organizational and departmental mission, goals, and strategies on how the goals will be met.

The fourth step is for the teams to decide on and document the level of guest service expected and to determine the importance of each element.

The fifth step is to identify and record gaps in service (examples of service deficiencies).

The sixth step is to empower and coach teams to create strategies to overcome the challenges of service deficiencies and provide exceptional guest service.

The seventh step is to use team problem-solving techniques to solve all issues relating to guest service deficiencies.

The eighth step is to make improvements to the service.

The ninth step is to monitor and record results.

The tenth step is to celebrate the successes and continue the process.

These steps combine to make for a continuous quality improvement process that is used by hundreds of hospitality companies today. Ritz-Carlton recently

THE RITZ-CARLTON SERVICE VALUES*

I am proud to be Ritz-Carlton.

1. I build strong relationships and create Ritz-Carlton guests for life.
2. I am always responsive to the expressed and unexpressed wishes and needs of our guests
3. I am empowered to create unique, memorable, and personal experiences for our guests.
4. I understand my role in achieving the Key Success Factors, embracing Community Footprints, and creating The Ritz-Carlton Mystique.
5. I continuously seek opportunities to innovate and improve The Ritz-Carlton experience.
6. I own and immediately resolve guest problems.
7. I create a work environment of teamwork and lateral service so that the needs of our guests and each other are met.
8. I have the opportunity to continuously learn and grow.
9. I am involved in the planning of the work that affects me.
10. I am proud of my professional apppearance, language, and behavior.
11. I protect the privacy and security of our guests, my fellow employees, and the company's confidential information and assests .
12. I am responsible for uncompromising levels of cleanliness and creating a safe and accident-free environment.

© The Ritz-Carlton Hotel Company, L.L.C. All rights reserved. Reprinted with the permission of The Ritz-Carlton Hotel Company, L.L.C.

amended their service values, which are shown above. Notice how they underscore the philosophy of the company.

The nature of business has changed. Leaders empower employees who welcome change. Empowerment is a feeling of partnership in which employees feel responsible for their jobs and have a stake in the organization's success. Empowered employees tend to do the following:

- Speak out about their problems and concerns.
- Take responsibility for their actions.
- Consider themselves a network of professionals.
- Accept the authority to make their own decisions when serving guests.

To empower employees, managers must do the following:

1. Take risks.
2. Delegate.
3. Foster a learning environment.
4. Share information and encourage self-expression.
5. Involve employees in defining their own vision.
6. Be thorough and patient with employees.

CORPORATE PROFILE

Carlson

Based in Minneapolis, Carlson's brands and services employ about 170,000 people in nearly 150 countries and territories. Carlson's 2006 systemwide sales, including franchised operations, totaled $37.1 billion. Following the November 2007 launch of their new brand identity, the company is known simply as "Carlson".

Led by Chairperson and Chief Executive Officer Marilyn Carlson Nelson, Carlson Companies continues to build on a cornerstone set by her father, Curt Carlson nearly 65 years ago: developing long-lasting relationships with clients.

The history of Carlson Companies is one of the classic business success stories in the American free enterprise system. Starting in 1938 with merely an idea and $55 of borrowed capital, entrepreneur Curtis L. Carlson founded the Gold Bond Stamp Company in his home city of Minneapolis, Minnesota. His trading stamp concept, designed to stimulate sales and loyalty for food stores and other merchants, proved to be right for the times and swept the nation in a wave of dramatic growth.

Through the years, Carlson diversified into hotels, travel, and other related businesses. In the 1960s, Carlson and several other partners collectively bought an interest in the original Radisson Hotel in downtown Minneapolis. Eventually, Carlson became sole owner of the hotel brand and expanded it around the globe. Today, there are 435 Radissons in 61 countries.

Among the names in the Carlson family of brands and services are: Regent Hotels & Resorts® Radisson Hotels & Resorts® Park Plaza® Hotels & Resorts, Country Inn & Suites By Carlson℠, Park Inn® hotels, Regent Seven Seas Cruises®, T.G.I. Friday's® and Pick Up Stix® restaurants, Carlson Wagonlit Travel, Cruise Holidays, All Aboard Travel, Cruise Specialists, Fly4less.com, Dazzle Travel, Partners in Travel, Cruise Deals.com, Results Travel, Carlson Destination Marketing Services, Carlson Leisure Travel Services, SeaMaster Cruises®, SinglesCruise.com, Carlson Marketing®, Peppers & Rogers Group®, and Gold Points Reward Network®.

Carlson Hospitality Worldwide encompasses more than 1,570 hotel, resort, restaurant, and cruise ship operations in 81 countries. Lodging operations include more than 810 locations in 63 countries. Restaurant operations include more than 753 locations in 55 countries, and cruise operations include six luxury ships with an additional vessel under construction.

These hospitality group brands and services, combined with sister companies, Carlson Marketing Group, Carlson Wagonlit Travel, and other travel industry companies and consumer incentive programs provide employment for more than 190,000 people around the world.

In addition to global business success, Carlson Companies is also recognized as a top employer. Both *Fortune* and *Working Mother* magazines have rated the company as one of their "100 Best Places to Work in America."

Marilyn is a regular on *Fortune* magazine's list of the "Most Powerful Women in Business" and has been selected by *Business Week* as one of the "Top 25 Executives in Business." Marilyn has been ranked by *Travel Agent* magazine as the "Most Powerful Woman in Travel" annually. She has served as chair of the National Women's Business Council. The council serves as an independent source of advice and counsel to the president, Congress, the U.S. Small Business Administration, and the Interagency Committee on Women's Business.

Marilyn has also served as national chair of the Travel Industry Association of America and is a member of the Council if the World Economic Forum and serves on the forum's board of governors for travel and tourism.

Among the hospitality industry–related honors she has received are the Cutting Edge Award by American Hotel & Lodging Association and the Stephen W. Brener Lodging Hospitality. Silver Plate Award presented at the Annual New York University Hospitality Industry Investment Conference. She has been named Hospitality Executive of the Year by the Penn State Hotel and Restaurant Society.

Marilyn graduated from Smith College with a degree in international economics and attended the Sorbonne in Paris and the Institute des Hautes Etudes Economiques Politiques in Geneva, Switzerland, studying political science and international economics.

www.carlson.com/press_07_29_05cfm, cited August 20, 2006.

▶ Check Your Knowledge

1. List five attributes, traits, and characteristics of a leader.
2. What is the Malcolm Baldrige National Quality Award?

The Disney Approach to Guest Service

The Disney mission statement is simple: "We create Happiness." Disney is regarded as one of the excellent corporations throughout the text. The following discussion, adapted from a presentation given by Susan Wilkie to the Pacific chapter of the Council on Hotel Restaurant and Institutional Education (CHRIE) conference outlines their approach to guest service.

When conceiving the idea to build Disneyland, Walt Disney established a simple philosophical approach to his theme park business, based on the tenents of quality, service, and show. The design, layout, characters, and magic of Disneyland grew out of Walt's successful experience in the film industry. With Disneyland, he saw an opportunity to create a whole new form of entertainment: a three-dimensional live show. He wanted Disneyland to be a dynamic, ever-changing experience.

To reinforce the service concept, Disney has *guests*, not *customers*, and *cast members*, not *employees*. These terms set the expectations for how guests will be served and cared for while at the park or resort. This commitment to service means

- Disney clearly understands its product and the meaning of its brand.
- It looks at the business from the guests' perspective.
- It considers creating an exceptional experience for every individual who enters its gates to be its responsibility.

Disney executives say that "our inventory goes home at night." Disney's ability to create a special brand of magic requires the talents of thousands of people fulfilling many different roles. But the heart of it is the frontline cast members. So, what is it that makes the service at Disney so great? The key elements of Disneyland guest services include the following:

- Hiring, developing, and retaining the right people
- Understanding its product and the meaning of the brand

- Communicating the traditions and standards of service to all cast members
- Training leaders to be service coaches
- Measuring guest satisfaction
- Recognizing and rewarding performance

Disney has used profile modeling but says it all comes down to a few simple things:

- Interpersonal relationship building skills
- Communication
- Friendliness

Disney uses a forty-five-minute team approach to interviewing called *peer interviews*. In one interview, there may be four candidates and one interviewer. The candidates may include a homemaker returning to the workforce, a teacher looking for summer work, a retiree looking for a little extra income, and a teenager looking for a first job. All four candidates are interviewed in the same session. The interviewer is looking for how they individually answer questions but also how well they interact with each other—a good indicator of their future onstage treatment of guests.

The most successful technique used during the forty-five-minutes is to *smile*. The interviewer smiles at the people being interviewed to see if they *return the smiles*. If they don't, it doesn't matter how well they interview—they won't get the job.

On the first day at work, every new Disney cast member participates in a one-day orientation program at the Disney University, "Welcome to Show Business." The main goal of this experience is to learn the Disney approach to helpful, caring, and friendly guest service.

How does this translate into action? When a guest stops a street sweeper to ask where to pick up a parade schedule and the sweeper not only answers the question but recites the parade times from memory, suggests the best viewing spots on the parade route, offers advice on where to get a quick meal before parade time, *and* ends the interaction with a pleasant smile and warm send-off, people can't help but be impressed. It also makes the sweepers feel their jobs are interesting and important—which they are!

I AM YOUR GUEST

We can all find inspiration from these anonymous words about people who make our business possible:

- ✓ *I am your guest.* Satisfy my needs, add personal attention and a friendly touch, and I will become a "walking advertisement" for your products and services. Ignore my needs, show carelessness, inattention, and poor manners, and I will cease to exist as far as you are concerned.
- ✓ *I am sophisticated.* Much more so than I was a few years ago. My needs are more complex. It is more important to me that you appreciate my business; when I buy your products and services I'm saying you are the best.

✓ *I am a perfectionist.* When I am dissatisfied, "take heed." The source of my discontent lies in something you or your products have failed to do. Find that source and eliminate it or you will lose my business and that of my friends as well. For when I criticize your products or services, I will talk to anyone who will listen.

✓ *I have other choices.* Other businesses continually offer "more for my money." You must prove to me again and again that I have made a wise choice in selecting you and your company above all others.

The Show is why people go to Disneyland. Each land tells a unique story through its theme and attention to detail, and the cast members each play a role in the Show. The most integral component of the training is the traditions and standards of guest service. The first of these is called the *Personal Touch*. The cast members are encouraged to use their own unique style and personality to provide a personal interaction with each guest. One of the primary ways Disney accomplishes this is through name tags. Everyone, regardless of position, goes by his or her first name. This tradition was started by Walt and continues today. It allows cast members to interact on a more personal level with guests. It also assists internally, by creating an informal environment that facilitates the flow of open communication and breaks down some of the traditional barriers.

Opening Disneyland

Imagine what Walt Disney had to overcome to open Disneyland. Disneyland opened on July 17, 1955, to the predictions that it would be a failure. And, in truth, everything that could go wrong did. Just to give an example, here is what happened on opening day:

- Plumbers went on strike.
- Tickets were duplicated.
- Attractions broke down.
- There was a gas leak in Fantasyland.
- The asphalt on Main Street, U.S.A. didn't harden in time, so in the heat of July, horses' hooves and women's high heels stuck in the street.

As Walt once said, "You may not realize it when it happens, but a kick in the teeth might be good for you." Walt had his fair share of challenges, one of which was obtaining financing to develop Disneyland—he had to deal with more than 300 banks.

Cinderella Castle soaring above tourists at Walt Disney World Resort, near Orlando

So what is the Disney service model?

It begins with a smile—This is the universal language of hospitality and service. Guests recognize and appreciate the cast members' warmth and sincerity.

Make eye contact and use body language—This means stance, approach, and gestures. For instance, cast members are trained to use *open* gestures for directions, not pointed fingers, because open palms are friendlier and less directive.

Respect and welcome all guests—This means being friendly, helpful, and going out of the way to *exceed* guests' expectations.

Value the magic—This means that when they're on stage, cast members are totally focused on creating the magic of Disneyland. They don't talk about personal problems or world affairs, and they don't mention that you can find Mickey in more than one place.

Initiate guest contact—Cast members are reminded to initiate guest contact actively. Disney calls this being aggressively friendly. It's not enough to be responsive when approached. Cast members are encouraged to take the first step with guests. They have lots of little tricks for doing this, such as noticing a guest's name on a hat and then using the name in conversation or kneeling to ask a child a question.

Creative service solutions—For example, one Disneyland Hotel cast member recently became aware of a little boy who had come from the Midwest with his parents to enjoy the park and then left early because he was ill. The cast member approached the supervisor with an idea to send the child chicken soup, a character plush toy, and a get-well card from Mickey. The supervisor loved the idea, and all cast members are now allowed to set up these arrangements in similar situations without a supervisor's approval.

End with a "thank you"—The phrases cast members use are important in creating a service environment. They do not have a book of accepted phrases; rather, through training and coaching, cast members are encouraged to use their own personality and style to welcome and approach guests, answer questions, anticipate their needs, thank them, and express with sincerity their desire to make the guest's experience exceptional.

Taken individually, these might sound pretty basic. But, taken together, they help define and reinforce the Disney culture. After initial cast member training is completed, these concepts must be applied and continually reinforced by leaders who possess strong coaching skills. Disney uses a model called the *Five Steps of Leadership* to lead the cast member performance.

Each step in the leadership model is equally important in meeting service and business goals. Each leader must do the following:

1. Provide clear expectations and standards.
2. Communicate these expectations through demonstration, information, and examples.
3. Hold cast members accountable for their feedback.
4. Coach through honest and direct feedback.
5. Recognize, reward, and celebrate success.

To supplement and reward the leadership team, Disney provides technical training to every new manager and assistant manager. In addition, the management team also participates in classes at the Disney University to learn the culture, values, and the leadership philosophy necessary to be successful in the Disney environment.

Disney measures the systems and reward process by distributing 1,000 surveys to guests as they leave Disneyland and 100 surveys to guests who stayed at each of the Disney hotels. The guests are asked to take the surveys home and mail them back to Disney. In return, their names are entered for a drawing for a family weekend package at the park and hotel.

Feedback from the surveys has been helpful in improving the guest experience. For example, as a result of the surveys, the entertainment division realized that the opportunity to interact with a character was a key driver to guest satisfaction. So, the entertainment team designed a brochure, "The Characters Today", which is distributed at the main entrance daily. This brochure allows guests to maximize their opportunity to see the characters. This initiative has already raised guest satisfaction by ten percentage points.

Cast members are also empowered to make changes to improve service. These measures are supplemented by financial controls and "mystery shoppers" (when people use the services like any other guest, but they are really employed to sample the service and report their findings) that allow Disney to focus resources on increasing guest satisfaction. The reward system does not consist of just the hard reward system we commonly think of, such as bonuses and incentive plans, important though they are. Recognition is not a one-size-fits-all system. Disney has found that noncash recognition is as powerful if not more powerful as a recognition tool in many situations. Some examples follow:

- Disney recognizes milestones of years of service. They use pins and statues and have a formal dinner for cast members and guests to reinforce and celebrate the value of their experience and expertise at serving Disney's guests.

- Throughout the year, Disney hosts special social and recreational events that involve the cast members and their families in the product.

- Disney invites cast members and their families to family film festivals featuring new Disney releases to ensure that they are knowledgeable about the latest Disney products.

- The Disneyland management team hosts the Family Christmas Party after hours in the park. This allows cast members to enjoy shopping, dining, and riding the attractions. Management dresses in costumes and runs the facilities.

Trends in Hospitality and Tourism

There is a healthy increase in hospitality and tourism not only in North America but around the world. We can identify a number of trends that are having and will continue to have an impact on the hospitality industry. Some, like diversity, have already been realized and are sure to increase in the future. Here, in no particular order, are some of the major trends that hospitality professionals indicate as having an influence on the industry. You will find these and others discussed in the chapters of this text.

- *Globalization.* We have become the global village that was described a few years ago. We may have the opportunity to work or vacation in other countries, and more people than ever travel freely around the world.

- *Safety and security.* Since September 11, 2001, we have all become more conscious of our personal safety and have experienced increased scrutiny at airports and federal and other buildings. But it goes beyond that; terrorists kidnap tourists from their resorts and hold them for ransom, thugs mug them, and others assault them. Two security experts have made valuable contributions to each chapter that follows by giving us the benefit of their experience and expertise. Security of all types of hospitality and tourism operations is critical and disaster plans should be made for each kind of threat. Personal safety of guests must be the first priority.

- *Diversity.* The hospitality industry is one of the most diverse of all industries; not only do we have a diverse employee population, but we also have a diverse group of guests. Diversity is increasing as more people with more diverse cultures join the hospitality workforce.

- *Service.* It is no secret that service is at the top of guests' expectations, yet few companies offer exceptional service. World-class service does not just happen; training is important in delivering the service that guests have come to expect.

- *Technology.* Technology is a driving force of change that presents opportunities for greater efficiencies and integration for improved guest service. However, the industry faces great challenges in training employees to use the new technology and in standardization of software and hardware design. Some hotels have several systems that do not talk to each other, and some reservation systems bounce between 7 and 10 percent of sales nationally.

- *Legal issues.* Lawsuits are not only more frequent, but they cost more if you lose and more to defend. One company spent several million dollars just to defend one case. Government regulations and the complexities of employee relations create increased challenges for hospitality operators.

- *Changing demographics.* The U.S. population is gradually increasing and the baby boomers are retiring. Many retirees have the time and money to travel and utilize hospitality services.

- *Price–value.* Price and value are important to today's more discerning guests.

- *Sanitation.* Sanitation is critical to the success of any restaurant and foodservice operation. Guests expect to eat healthy foods that have been prepared in a sanitary environment.

Deciding whether these and other ethical dilemmas are right or wrong is not simple. Three key categories of questions need to be answered when making decisions about actions and behaviors:

1. Is it legal? Will I be violating civil law or company policy? Also, will I get fired if I accept it, allow it, or do it?
2. Is it balanced? Is it fair to all concerned in both the short term and the long term? Does it promote win-win relationships?
3. How will it make me feel about myself? Will it make me proud? Would I feel good if my family knew about it?

Summary

1. The hospitality and tourism industries are the largest and fastest-growing industries in the world.
2. Now is a great time to be considering a career in the hospitality and tourism field because thousands of supervising managers are needed for this dynamic industry.
3. Common dynamics include delivery of services and guest impressions of them.
4. Hospitality businesses are open 365 days a year and 24 hours a day and are likely to require shift work.
5. One essential difference between the hospitality business and other businesses is that in hospitality we are selling an intangible and perishable product.
6. Corporate philosophy is changing from managers planning, organizing, implementing, and so on, to that of managers counseling associates, giving them resources, and helping them to think for themselves.
7. Corporate philosophy embraces the values of the organization, including ethics, morals, fairness, and equality. The philosophy of "do whatever it takes" is critical for success.
8. Corporate culture refers to the overall style or feel of the company or how people relate to one another and their jobs.
9. A mission statement is a statement of central purposes, strategies, and values of the company. It should answer "What business are we in?"
10. A goal is a specific target to be met; objectives or tactics are the actions needed to accomplish the goal.
11. Total quality management has helped improve service to guests by empowering employees to give service that exceeds guest expectations.

Key Words and Concepts

corporate philosophy
empowerment
front of the house
goal
guest satisfaction
heart of the house

hospitality
inseparability
intangible
National Restaurant
    Association (NRA)
perishability

total quality management
    (TQM)
tourism

Review Questions

1. On the Companion Website, look at the Horst Schulze feature. What are the steps of service he talks about?
2. On the Companion Website, what does Horst Schulze say we want to accomplish, and what should any organization be doing?
3. Why is service so critical in the hospitality and tourism industries?
4. Describe and give an example of the following:
   Mission statement
   Moment of truth
5. What is the Disney service model?
6. Explain why Ritz-Carlton won the Malcolm Baldrige award.

Internet Exercises

1. Organization: **World Travel and Tourism Council**
   Web site: **www.wttc.org**
   Summary: The World Travel and Tourism Council (WTTC) is the global business leaders' forum for travel and tourism. It includes all sectors of industry, including accommodation, catering, entertainment, recreation, transportation, and other travel-related services. Its central goal is to work with governments so that they can realize the full potential economic impact of the world's largest generator of wealth and jobs: travel and tourism.
   (a) Find the latest statistics or figures for the global hospitality and tourism economy.

2. Organization: **Ritz-Carlton Hotels**
   Web site: **www.ritzcarlton.com**
   Summary: The Ritz-Carlton is renowned for its elegance, sumptuous surroundings, and legendary service. With fifty-eight hotels worldwide, a majority of them award winning, the Ritz-Carlton reflects 100 years of tradition.
   (a) What is it about Ritz-Carlton that makes it such a great hotel chain?

3. Organization: **Disneyland and Walt Disney World**
   Web site: **disney.go.com** and **www.disney.com**
   (a) Compare and contrast Disneyland's and Walt Disney World's web sites.

Apply Your Knowledge

1. Write your personal mission statement.
2. Suggest ways to improve service in a hospitality business.
3. Go to the Companion Website and answer the sample test questions for this chapter.

Suggested Activities

1. Where are you going? Take a moment to think about your future career prospects. Where do you want to be in five, ten or twenty years?
2. Prepare some general hospitality and career-related questions, and interview two supervisors or managers in the hospitality industry. Share and compare the answers with your class next session.
3. Look on the Companion Website for scholarship information and make an application if you find one that is suitable for you.

Endnotes

1. Personal conversation with Charlotte Jordan, May 6, 2007.
2. Nathan Cobb, *Boston Globe Magazine*, June 4, 1989, as cited in John R. Walker, *The Restaurant from Concept to Operation*, 4th ed. (New York: John Wiley and Sons, 2005), 59.
3. Starbucks Coffee, "Starbucks Timeline and History," www.starbucks.com/aboutus/timeline.asp.
4. www.marriott.com/corporateinfo/culture/CoreValuesCulture.mi.
5. Marriott, "Marriott Culture," www.marriott.com/corporateinfo/culture/coreCulture.mi.
6. Karl Albrecht and Ron Zemke, *Service America!* (Homewood, IL: Dow Jones-Irwin, 1985), 2–18.
7. Karl Albrecht, *At America's Service* (New York: Warner Books, 1992), 13.
8. Albrecht, *At America's Service*, 27.
9. You can view this list at http://money.cnn.com/magazines/moneymag/moneymag_archive/1987/10/01/84068/index.htm.
10. John R. Walker and Jack E. Miller, *Supervision: Leading Hospitality Human Resources,* 6th Ed. (New York: John Wiley and Sons, 2010), 22.

CHAPTER 2

Tourism

Highlights of Tourism

It is difficult to determine when tourism be star because, centuries ago, very few people traveled for pleasure or business as they do today. We do know that:

- In the fourth century B.C. (before Christ), work started on the Great Wall of China and it continued for centuries until the1600s. Although not exactly a tourist destination or attraction back then, it certainly is today.

- In 776 B.C., athletic games were held on the plain of Olympia in Greece (now the Olympic Games), and presumably people traveled there to participate or to watch.

- The Romans liked to visit the Bay of Naples, so they built a road from Rome in A.D. 312 (after Christ). The road was 100 miles long and took four days by litter to get there (in which a nobleperson sat on a platform and was carried by some unfortunate servants).

- Religious pilgrimages to Rome and the Holy Land (now Israel) began in the 1200s, so inns sprang up to feed and accommodate the pilgrims.

- Marco Polo became the first noted business traveler as he pioneered trade routes from Europe to China, staying at primitive inns called *khans* along the way, from 1275 to 1292.

- In the 1600s, during the age of horse-drawn coach travel in England, posthouses were set up to feed and shelter travelers and change the teams of horses every few miles. The journey from London to Bristol took three days—it now takes less than three hours by rail.

- In 1841, Thomas Cook organized a group tour for 570 people to a religious meeting in England.

- In the 1850s, Monaco (a principality in the south of France) decided to cure its economic woes by becoming a winter haven for the rich as a health resort and a casino.

- Cruising began in the 1840s with the Cunard Lines crossing the Atlantic between England and North America.

- In the 1840s, the Peninsula and Oriental Steam Navigation Company (P&O) cruised the Mediterranean.

- During the age of the grand tour from 1880 through the 1930s, wealthy Europeans toured Europe as a part of their education.

- Rail travel began in the 1800s.

- Auto travel began in the 1900s.

- Air travel began in the 1900s.

- American Airlines' first transcontinental flight between New York and Los Angeles was introduced in 1959.

- In 1970, the Boeing 747 began flying 450 passengers at a time across the Atlantic and Pacific Oceans.

- In the 1970s, ecotourism and sustainable tourism became important topics.

- In the 1980s, cruising became popular

- In 1986, the United States established the Visa Waiver Program to eliminate unnecessary barriers to travel to the United States. Currently, twenty-seven countries are part of the program.

- In the 2000s, tourism temporarily declined as a result of the September 11 attacks, severe acute respiratory syndrome (SARS), bird flu, and war. However, tourism is now increasing at a rate of about 4.6 percent a year, according to the World Travel and Tourism Council.

What Is Tourism?

Tourism is a dynamic, evolving, consumer-driven force and is the world's largest industry, or collection of industries, when all its interrelated components are placed under one umbrella: tourism, travel; lodging; conventions, expositions, meetings, events; restaurants, managed services; assembly, destination and event management; and recreation. Tourism plays a foundational role in framing the various services that hospitality companies perform.

The leading international organization in the field of travel and tourism, the **World Tourism Organization (WTO)**, is vested by the United Nations with a central and decisive role in promoting the development of responsible, sustainable, and universally accessible tourism, with the aim of contributing to economic development, international understanding, peace, prosperity, and universal respect for and observance of human rights and fundamental freedoms. In pursuing this aim, the organization pays particular attention to the interests of the developing countries in the field of tourism. The World Tourism Organization's definition of tourism is "Tourism comprises the activities of persons traveling to and staying in places outside their usual environment for not more than one consecutive year for leisure, business, and other purposes."[1]

The WTO plays a catalytic role in promoting technology transfers and international cooperation, stimulating and developing public–private sector partnerships, and encouraging the implementation of the Global Code of Ethics for Tourism. The WTO is dedicated to ensuring that member countries, tourist destinations, and businesses maximize the positive economic, social, and cultural effects of tourism and fully reap its benefits, while minimizing its negative social and environmental impacts. *Francesco Frangialli, secretary-general of the World Tourism Organization writes:*

> *The Global Code of Ethics for Tourism sets a frame of reference for the responsible and sustainable development of world tourism. It draws inspiration from many similar declarations and industry codes that have come before*

and it adds new thinking that reflects our changing society at the beginning of the 21st century.

With international tourism forecast to nearly triple in volume over the next 20 years, members of the World Tourism Organization believe that the Global Code of Ethics for Tourism is needed to help minimize the negative impacts of tourism on the environment and on cultural heritage while maximizing the benefits for residents of tourism destinations.

The Global Code of Ethics for Tourism is intended to be a living document. Read it. Circulate it widely. Participate in its implementation. Only with your cooperation can we safeguard the future of the tourism industry and expand the sector's contribution to economic prosperity, peace and understanding among all the nations of the world.[2]

Through tourism, the WTO aims at stimulating economic growth and job creation, providing incentives for protecting the environment and cultural heritage, and promoting peace, prosperity, and respect for human rights. Membership includes 143 countries, 7 territories, and some 350 affiliate members representing the private sector, educational institutions, tourism associations, and local tourism authorities. Unfortunately, the United States is not a member, but it may soon be.

The World Tourism Organization and the World Travel and Tourism Council (WTTC) declare the travel and tourism industry to have the following characteristics:[3]

- A 24-hour-a-day, 7-day-week, 52-week-a-year economic driver
- Responsible for 10.2 percent of world gross domestic product (GDP)
- Employer of 214 million people, or 7.8 percent of the global workforce
- Creation of more than 5.5 million travel and tourism jobs per year during the 2000s
- Spending on tourism in the United States is $72.3 billion
- Leading producer of tax revenues
- Forecasted 4.6 percent growth between 2006 and 2015.

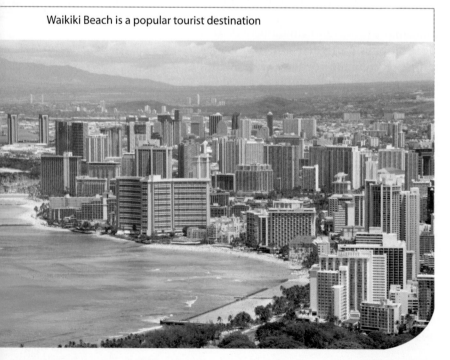

Waikiki Beach is a popular tourist destination

Given the declining manufacturing and agricultural industries, and in many countries the consequent rise in unemployment, world leaders should turn to the service industries for real strategic employment gains. For many developing nations, tourism represents a large percentage of gross national product and a way of gaining a positive balance of trade with other nations.

▶ Check Your Knowledge

1. What role does the WTO play in the tourism industry?
2. Describe the characteristics of tourism.
3. How is tourism sometimes categorized?

Benefits of Tourism

Tourism is firmly established as the number one industry in many countries and the fastest-growing economic sector in terms of foreign exchange earnings and job creation. International tourism is the world's largest export earner and an important factor in the balance of payments of most nations.

Tourism has become one of the world's most important sources of employment. It stimulates enormous investment in infrastructure, most of which helps to improve the living conditions of residents as well as tourists. It provides governments with substantial tax revenues. Most new tourism jobs and businesses are created in the developing countries, helping to equalize economic opportunities and keep rural residents from moving to overcrowded cities. Intercultural awareness and personal friendships fostered through tourism are powerful forces for improving international understanding and contributing to peace among all the nations of the world.

The World Tourism Organization encourages governments, in partnership with the private sector, local authorities, and nongovernmental organizations, to play a vital role in tourism. The WTO helps countries throughout the world to maximize the positive impacts of tourism, while minimizing its possible negative consequences on the environment and societies. Tourism is a collection of industries, or segments, that when combined, form the world's largest industry. Tourism offers the greatest global employment prospects. This trend is caused by the following factors:

1. The opening of borders: Despite security concerns, we can travel to more countries now than ten years ago. The United States has a visa waiver program with twenty-eight European countries, meaning citizens of these countries with machine-readable passports do not require a visa to visit the United States.
2. An increase in disposable income and vacation taking.
3. Reasonably affordable airfares.
4. An increase in the number of people with more time and money to travel.
5. More people with the urge to travel.

According to the World Travel and Tourism Council—the industry's business leaders' forum—tourism and travel generate, directly and indirectly, 10.2 percent of global gross domestic product (GDP), investment, and employment. The industry is forecast to grow strongly in real terms during the next ten years. This means growth in jobs in the United States and abroad.

Long-Term Prospects: Tourism 2020 Vision

Despite the terrorism attacks and a weak economic recovery, the long-term prospects for tourism appear to be good. *Tourism 2020 Vision* is the World Tourism Organization's long-term forecast and assessment of the development of tourism for the first twenty years of the new millennium. An essential outcome of the Tourism 2020 Vision is quantitative forecasts covering a twenty-five-year period, with 1995 as the base year and forecasts for 2000, 2010, and 2020 (Figure 2–1).

WTO's Tourism 2020 Vision forecasts that international arrivals are expected to reach more than 1.56 billion by the year 2020. Of these, 1.2 billion will be intraregional and 0.4 billion will be long-haul travelers.

The total tourist arrivals by region show that by 2020 the top three receiving regions will be Europe (717 million tourists), East Asia and the Pacific (397 million), and the Americas (282 million), followed by Africa, the Middle East, and South Asia.

The fact that tourism is expected to grow rapidly presents both tremendous opportunities and challenges. The good news is the variety of exciting career prospects for today's hospitality and tourism graduates. Tourism, although a mature industry, is a young profession. Careful management of tourism and travel will be necessary to avoid repercussions and negativism toward the "pesky" tourist, which is already happening to some extent in Europe, where the sheer number of tourists overwhelms attractions and facilities.

There is an **interdependency** between the various segments of tourism, travel, lodging, foodservice, and recreation. Hotel guests need to travel to reach the

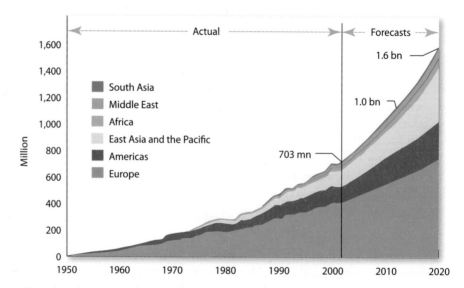

Figure 2–1 • Actual and Forecast Tourism Arrivals 1950–2020.
(*Source:* World Tourism Organization.)

hotel. They eat in nearby restaurants and visit attractions. Each segment is, to an extent, dependent on another for business.

The Five Ages of Tourism

The historical development of tourism has been divided into five distinct ages (or periods),[5] four of which paralled the advent of a new means of transportation.

Pre–Industrial Revolution (prior to 1840)

The railway age

The automobile age

The jet aircraft age

The cruise ship age

Pre-Industrial Revolution

As early as 5,000 years ago, some ancient Egyptians sailed up and down the Nile River to visit and construct the pyramids. Probably the first journey ever made for the purposes of peace and tourism was made by Queen Hatshepsut to the Land of Punt (believed to be on the east coast of Africa) in 1480 B.C. Descriptions of this tour have been recorded on the walls of the temple of Deir el-Bahri at Luxor.[6] These texts and bas-reliefs are among the world's rarest artworks and are universally admired for their wondrous beauty and artistic qualities. The Colossi of Memnon at Thebes have on their pedestals the names of Greek tourists of the fifth century B.C.[7] The Phoenicians were among the first real travelers in any modern sense. In both the Mediterranean and the Orient (now called Southeast Asia), travel was motivated by trade. Later, the Roman Empire provided safe passage for travelers via a vast road system that stretched from Egypt to Britain. Wealthy Romans traveled to Egypt and Greece, to baths, shrines, and seaside resorts.[8] The Romans were as curious as are today's tourists. They visited the attractions of their time, trekking to Greek temples and places where Alexander the Great slept, Socrates lived, Ajax committed suicide, and Achilles was buried; the pyramids; the Sphinx; and the Valley of the Kings—just as today's tourists do.[9] The excavated ruins of the Roman town Pompeii, which was buried by the volcanic eruption of Mount Vesuvius, revealed some twenty-plus restaurants, taverns, and inns that tourists visit even today.

The first Olympic Games for which we still have written records were held in 776 B.C. (though it is generally believed that the games had been going on for many years already).[10] Thus, sports has been a motivation for tourism for a long time.

Medieval travel was mostly for religious or trade reasons. People made pilgrimages to various shrines: Moslems to Mecca and Christians to Jerusalem and Rome. The Crusades (which began in 1195 and lasted for the next two hundred years) stimulated a cultural exchange that was in part responsible for the Renaissance.

Marco Polo (1254–1324) traveled the Silk Road, which was anything but a road as we know it, from Venice to Beijing. He was the first European to journey all the way across Asia to Beijing, China, and his journey, which lasted twenty-four years, and the tales from it became the greatest travelogue.[11]

The journey was both difficult and dangerous (excerpts can be read at the several Marco Polo web sites). One time, to make sure the Polo brothers would be given every assistance on their travels, Kublai Khan presented them with a golden tablet (or *paiza*, in Chinese, *gerege*, in Mongolian) a foot long and three inches wide inscribed with the words "By the strength of the eternal Heaven, holy be the Khan's name. Let him that pays him not reverence be killed." The golden tablet was a special VIP passport, authorizing the travelers to receive throughout the Great Khan's dominions such horses, lodging, food, and guides as they required.[12] This was an early form of passport.

▶ Check Your Knowledge

1. Describe the benefits of tourism
2. How many arrivals are forecast for 2010?
3. What are the five ages of tourism?

The Hall of Supreme Harmony in Beijing's Forbidden City

Rail, Automobile, and Coach Travel

Changes in the technology of travel have had widespread implications for society. In the United States, rail travel influenced the building of towns and cities, caused hotels to be built near rail depots, and opened up the West, among other things. Likewise, auto travel produced the motel and a network of highways, and the commercial jet created destination resorts in formerly remote and exotic locations, made the rental car business a necessity, and changed the way we look at geography. Although long-distance travel has always been fairly comfortable for the wealthy, it was not until the development of the railroad in the 1830s that travel became comfortable and cheap enough to be within reach of the masses.

[handwritten note: 4rail travel influenced develop of tourist cities + caused hotels to be built near rail posts.]

Traveling by Train

Coast to coast, the United States has a lot of land with a fair share of mountains, canyons, forests, deserts, rivers, and other natural barriers to travel. One of the main factors that led to the development of railroads in the United States was the need to move goods and people from one region of the country to another. Farmed goods needed to be transported to industrial areas, and people wanted a quicker route to the West, especially after the discovery of gold in California. Those who already lived at the frontier wanted the same conveniences as their neighbors in the East, such as efficient postal service.

[handwritten note: 4auto → motels / 4jet → destination resorts]

The train made mass travel possible for everyone. Long-distance travel became both cheaper and faster, making the horse and ship seem like "overpriced snails." The vast rail networks across North America, Asia, Australia, and Europe made the train station a central part of nearly every community. Naturally, entrepreneurs soon built hotels conveniently close to train stations.

[handwritten note: 4rails made travel cheaper + faster / 4made - factor of development of rails / 4rail - mass travel / 4rail ↓ due to auto and bus, + great depression]

Although hugely important and popular for many years, the popularity of rail travel started to decline as early as the 1920s. Why did people stop using the train? For two main reasons: the bus and the car. In addition, the Great Depression of the 1930s certainly deterred travelers. Although World War II brought a new surge in passenger numbers, people were seldom traveling for pleasure, and at the close of the war, the decline continued. Automobiles were again available, and people had

[handwritten note: 4WWII → new surge in passenger #s]

The Aerodynamic Amtrak ACELA train speeding along between Washington, D.C., and New York City reaches its destination in 2 hours 45 minutes the money to buy them. By 1960, airplanes had taken over much of the long-distance travel market, further reducing the importance of the train.

Facing a possible collapse of passenger rail services, Congress passed the *Rail Passenger Service Act* in 1970 (amended in 2001). Shortly after, the *National Railroad Passenger Corporation* began operation as a semipublic corporation established to operate intercity passenger trains, a move in the direction of semi-nationalization of U.S. railroads. The corporation is known today as Amtrak.

Rail Travel Abroad

While the United States tries to rejuvenate rail travel under the direction of Amtrak, rail service in other parts of the industrialized world is far ahead in progress. Taking the train makes good sense in densely populated areas such as those in western Europe and parts of Asia, and high-speed networks are already well developed, often drawing most of the traffic that formerly went by air. One good example is the Eurostar, connecting the United Kingdom with mainland Europe via the 31-mile-long underwater Channel Tunnel. France's TGV (Trains à Grande Vitesse) trains are perhaps the best known of them all, serving more than 150 cities in France and Europe, and traveling at about 186 mph (although they have the capacity of running at 250 mph). The TGV's most spectacular feature is the smoothness of the ride: It is like sitting in your armchair at home. Because of their importance, all trains—high speed or not—run frequently and on time. Fares are generally reasonable, and service levels are high.

Japan's Shinkansen, the bullet train system, makes the 550-mile run between Tokyo and Osaka in 3 hours and 10 minutes, down from the former rail time of 18 hours. In addition, it provides a ride so smooth that a passenger can rest a coffee cup on the windowsill and not a drop will spill, just like the TGV.

Do you dream of exploring Europe? As a student, you have probably heard of the famous Eurail Pass. Several European nations have banded together to offer visitors unlimited first-class rail service for a reduced lump sum. However, if you want to use Eurail, be sure to purchase a pass before you leave home because the pass is sold only outside of Europe. When visiting Europe, you can choose to travel in one country, in a few selected ones, or in all with Eurail; it's up to you to choose between the different passes available. In other parts of the world, Australia offers the Austrailpass, India the Indrail Pass, Canada the Canrail Pass, and Canada and the United States the North American Rail Pass. The new rail line in China linking Beijing to Nepal is interesting not only because it is one of the longest and one of the highest rail lines in the world, but also it is, according to some, going to dilute the Tibetan culture. This is one of the dilemmas of tourism: Some see this as economic and social development, and others want to leave things as they are.

Does the Train Have a Future?

For long trips, flying is obviously a lot faster than taking the train is. Therefore, long-distance train service is generally used only by those afraid to fly, or those who enjoy train travel as an experience in itself. But, as we explored in the case of Amtrak, rail travel may make a comeback in the United States. As airports and roads become more congested, as road travel becomes more time-consuming, and parking a rare luxury, a train ride becomes more appealing. With the necessary improvements and the development of high-speed links, trains may become more time-efficient.

The Maglevs are also coming. Not aliens from outer space, but superfast trains suspended in the air and propelled by magnetic force. Maglevs can travel at speeds of more than 300 miles per hour, lifted off the ground on a cushion formed by magnetic forces and pulled forward by magnets. They run more quietly and smoothly and can climb steeper grades than the conventional train can. Maglevs are more energy efficient, have lower maintenance costs, and require fewer staff than does comparable transportation; however, given the high cost of construction, the concept may not prove viable. China, on the other hand, does not seem to worry about the steep cost of the Maglev. The city of Shanghai has chosen Transrapid as its partner to build a twenty-mile Maglev link connecting the new airport to the Shanghai business district. If successful, an 800-mile link will be installed from Shanghai to Beijing. So, is the Maglev really feasible? Opponents of the idea claim that the Maglev is far too expensive to be worth the investment, considering that current high-speed trains can travel at speeds exceeding 200 mph if given the right conditions.

Traveling by Car

The internal combustion engine automobile was invented in Germany but quickly became America's obsession. In 1895, there were about 300 "horseless carriages" of one kind or another in the United States, including gasoline buggies, electric cars, and steam cars. Even during the Great Depression, almost two-thirds of American families had automobiles. Henry Ford's development of the assembly line and construction of good, solid roads helped make the automobile the symbol of American life that it is today.

The auto changed the American way of life, especially in the leisure area, creating and satisfying people's urge to travel. The automobile remains the most convenient and rapid form of transportation for short and medium distances. Without question, it has made Americans the most mobile people in history and has given them options not otherwise possible. Whereas many Europeans ride their bikes or use the bus or train to get to school or work, Americans cannot

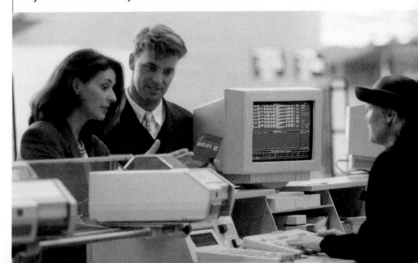

Rental cars offer business and leisure travelers the convenience of fly–drive or drive-only to facilitate tourists' needs

seem to function without their cars. In fact, it is not uncommon for an American to drive 20,000 miles a year.

Road trips are a must for most Americans—college students, families, and retirees alike. Travel by car is by far the largest of all segments in the ground transportation sector of the travel and tourism industry. So, it is no wonder that the highways and byways of the United States and Canada play such important roles in tourism. The advantages of car travel are that the car brings you to places that are otherwise inaccessible. Mountain resorts, ski destinations, dude ranches, and remote beaches are just a few examples. This travel generates millions of dollars, and in certain places the local economy depends on the car tourist.

Rental Cars

Some 5,000 rental car companies operate in the United States. Waiting at nearly every sizable airport in the world are several highly competitive rental car agencies, a significant segment of the travel/tourism business. About 75 percent of their sales take place at airport counters that are leased from the airport, the cost of which is passed on to the customer. The larger companies do 50 percent or more of their business with large corporate accounts, accounts that receive sizable discounts under contract. The hurried business traveler is likely to rent a car, speed out of the airport, do his or her business in a day or two, return to the airport, and hop on a plane to return home. The pleasure traveler, however, is more likely to rent a small car for a week or more. This group constitutes about 30 percent of the rental car market. The top four rent-a-car company agencies in the United States are Hertz, Avis, National, and Budget. The agencies maintain approximately 625,000 rental cars that are usually new and are sold after six months to reduce maintenance costs and help avoid breakdowns.

Traveling by Bus

Although the scheduled bus routes aren't as competitive as scheduled service for airlines, buses still play an important role in the travel and tourism industry, especially with regards to their charter and tour services. Some bus companies even offer services such as destination management, incentive programs, and planning of meetings, events, and conferences. Several companies to check out are Gray Line Worldwide, Contiki Tours, and Canadian Tours International.

The major reasons for selecting the bus over other modes of travel are convenience and economy. Many passengers are adventurous college students from the United States and abroad or senior citizens, both with limited funds but plenty of time on their hands. Most people don't choose bus travel for long trips, however, because a flight is much quicker and often just as economical. However, in places such as the heavily populated northeast corridor, regular bus service between most sizable communities in New England and New York often makes it easier and safer for travelers to ride the bus than to drive their cars into the city. Anyone who has experienced New York City traffic will probably agree.

Another reason why buses are popular is because they allow the leisure traveler to sit back, relax, and enjoy the scenery. In addition, they are hassle free and provide an opportunity to make new friends and stop along the way. Long-distance buses offer a variety of amenities similar to an airplane, with an extra benefit of almost door-to-door service! Buses travel to small and large communities, bringing with them tourist dollars and thus a boost to the local economy.

Types of Bus Service

In addition to routes between towns and cities, bus travel includes local route service, charter, tour, special services, commuter service, airport service, and urban and rapid transit service. The largest and most recognized of all of the specialized travel services is Gray Line. Founded in 1910, Gray Line is a franchise operation based in Colorado. The company assembles package tours and customized tours, arranges rail and air transfers, and even provides meeting and convention services. Its major service, however, is sightseeing trips by bus. When a traveler arrives at a destination and wishes to see the town and the major tourist attractions, Gray Line is usually ready to serve. The 150-member organization carries about 28 million passengers a year at more than 200 destinations. Their trips are widely diversified, such as "around-the-town" in Paris and "around-the-country" in Thailand. In the United States, Gray Line's biggest market is Los Angeles, followed by San Francisco, and then Manhattan.

▶ Check Your Knowledge

1. In what locations does rail travel make the most sense?
2. What is the future of rail travel?
3. Who are the major users of buses?

Airlines

Air travel has made it possible to build great resorts on remote islands, it has fostered multinational enterprises, and it has broadened the horizons of hundreds of millions of people. Without the airplane, most resort destinations would have been virtually impossible to build. The number of international travelers would be far fewer because of the time, money, and difficulty involved in travel. The airplane makes travel easier and more convenient because even the most remote location is just a few hours away by plane, and reasonable airfares make it possible for more people to travel by air.

Air transport has become an integral factor in the travel and tourism industry. Hotels, car rental agencies, and even cruise lines depend heavily on airplanes for profits. For instance, lower airfares result in more passengers, and hence a higher occupancy at hotels. Whole towns and cities can and do benefit from this concept by receiving more taxes from tourists, which leads to better public facilities, better schools, and even lower local and property taxes.

In the United States, there are, at any one time, about 4,500 airplanes in the skies. On top of that, by 2012, total passenger traffic between the United States and the rest of the world is projected to reach 1 billion flights annually. The expansion of the airline industry was tremendous in the 1990s, and even though many U.S. airlines are currently facing financial problems, the number of flights is back to pre–September 11, 2001, levels, and the industry growth is expected to continue in the future, with additional security measures both in airports and on board flights. In recent years the airline has become the preferred means of travel for the long haul. The jet aircraft has made previously inaccessible places such as Bali, Boracay, and Bangkok easily accessible and for a reasonable price. Today millions of Americans travel within the United States and abroad, and millions more visit the United States because of air travel.

Over the past few years—with the exception of Southwest, AirTran, and Jet Blue—major U.S. airlines have lost billions of dollars. One reason is competition from low-cost domestic and international airlines.

Since September 11, 2001, business travelers continue to spend less, and airlines' pension, fuel, and security costs have risen. The major airlines have laid off employees, delayed delivery of new jets, and closed some hubs, reservations, and maintenance centers in efforts to reduce costs. Several of the major U.S. airlines have been and are in financial trouble, so they are charging an additional fuel surcharge on tickets just so that they can stay in the air. Other strategies are needed to keep airlines viable.

For example, in efforts to promote passenger loyalty and operating effectiveness, the major U.S. airlines have formed strategic alliances with partner airlines to provide passengers with easier ticket purchases and transportation to destinations in countries not served by U.S. airlines, for example, Tampa, Florida, to Hong Kong; American Airlines to Los Angeles or New York; and Cathay Pacific to Hong Kong and beyond. Alliances of this nature will allow airlines access to each other's feeder markets and to resources that will enable them to compete in what will ultimately be a worldwide deregulation. A *feeder market* is a market that provides the source—in this case, passengers for the particular destination. Ultimately, any major European airline without a strategic alliance in the United States will only limit its own horizons and lose market share.

Another example is South West Airlines. Southwest operates more efficiently than the competition does despite the fact that its workforce is unionized. Southwest gets more flight time from its pilots than does American Airlines—672 hours a year versus 371—and racks up 60 percent more passenger

American Airlines and its thirteen One World partner airlines go just about anywhere. The One World partners include British Airways, Cathy Pacific, Japan Airlines

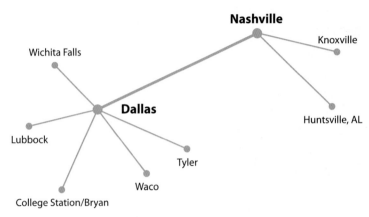

Figure 2–2 • The Hub-and-Spoke System.

miles per flight attendant. These efficiencies have resulted in annual profits for thirty consecutive years as a result of Southwest's dedication to a low-cost, high-customer-satisfaction strategy.

Carriers such as Southwest, AirTran, Ted (short for United), Song (Delta), and Jet Blue have lower operating costs because they use only one type of aircraft, fly point to point, and offer a no-frills service. Their lower fares have forced many larger airlines to retreat.

To reduce losses brought about by deregulation and high labor, pension plan, and fuel costs, major carriers have eliminated unprofitable routes, often those serving smaller cities. New airlines began operating shuttle services between the smaller cities and the nearest larger or hub city. This created the hub-and-spoke system (see Figure 2–2).

The Hub-and-Spoke System To remain efficient and cost effective, major U.S. airlines have adopted a **hub-and-spoke system**, which enables passengers to travel from one smaller city to another smaller city via a hub or even two hubs. Similarly, passengers may originate their travel from a small city and use the hub to reach connecting flights to destinations throughout the world.

The hub-and-spoke system has two main benefits: (1) Airlines can service more cities at a lower cost, and (2) airlines can maximize passenger loads from small cities, thereby saving fuel. The airlines have also used deregulation to their advantage to save money whenever possible. For instance, cutting nonprofitable routes from some smaller cities.

New Airplanes

Boeing's first new airplane model in several years takes advantage of huge advances made in aviation technology in the past decade and is capable of flying long-haul routes using up to 20 percent less fuel than today's similar-sized airplanes. Up to 50 percent of the primary structure of the plane, including the fuselage and wing, is made of components such as carbon fiber, which reduces the weight of the plane.[13]

Able to fly up to 9,700 miles without refueling, the Boeing 787 Dreamliner could easily manage a flight between New York and Moscow, Manila, or Sao Paulo or between Boston and Athens. Richard Aboulafia, chief analyst with Teal Group, comments, "If you look at it from an airline standpoint: you don't have a choice. If you don't have a 787-class aircraft and your competitor does, he can under price you and out-profit you."[14]

The giant double-decker Airbus A380 can carry up to 500 passengers for a distance of up to 8,000 miles. Singapore Airlines is due to begin service of this aircraft later this year between Singapore and the United States and Europe.

The new Boeing 787 Dreamliner is able to fly up to 9,700 miles without stopping

Components of Airline Profit and Loss

Have you ever wondered why air travel is so expensive? You might find some answers in this section where we look at the different costs included when you buy an air ticket. Airlines have both fixed and variable costs. *Fixed costs* are constant and do not change regardless of the amount of business. Examples are the lease of airplanes, the maintenance of airline-owned or leased terminals, interest on borrowed money, insurance, and pensions. *Variable costs* tend to rise and fall with the volume of sales or number of flights. They include wages and salaries, advertising and promotion, fuel costs, passenger food and drink, and landing fees.

The biggest single cost for airline operation is labor, which is typically 30 to 45 percent of total operating costs. Senior pilots for airlines such as United and Delta receive as much as $150,000 or more a year. Flight attendant jobs receive as much as $60,000 or more a year plus several fringe benefits.[15] Additionally, landing and takeoff charges charged to airlines by airports can add up to thousands of dollars per plane, depending on the airport and time of day. Passenger servicing costs such as reservations, ticketing, food, baggage handling, and an amount for additional security and fuel must also be accounted for in the ticket price. Once a schedule is set and the breakeven point is reached, selling tickets to extra passengers produces large profits for airlines. Being able to offer just the right amount of discount tickets that may be needed to fill a plane then becomes highly important. Capacity control is one yield management technique for maximizing sales income by lowering the price of seats according to expected demand.

The Load Factor A key statistic in analyzing an airline's profitability is the **load factor**, which means the percentage of seats filled on all flights, including

*[handwritten margin notes: 4 biggest cost 4 airlines — labour

Load Factor — % of Seats filled on all flights]*

planes being flown empty to be in position for the next day's schedule. The load factor, like the occupancy rate of a hotel, is an indicator of efficient or inefficient use. The current U.S. Commercial Air Carrier load factor is usually around 70 percent, an increase caused mainly by capacity plans of large carriers. The break-even point, the point at which carriers neither lose money nor make a profit, is likely to be unique on any given flight. This point is determined by the rate structure in effect, the length of the flight, the time spent on the ground, and other costs such as wages and salaries. An airline with a long-haul high-density route, for example, from New York to Los Angeles, has a decided cost advantage over another airlines' short-haul, low-density routes. The cost of flying a plane is sharply reduced once it reaches cruising altitude. A short flight thus costs more per mile than a long one does because a greater proportion of flight time and fuel is consumed in climbing to and descending from the cruising altitude.

[handwritten margin note: ↳ cost of flying decreases sig when it reaches cruising pt; a longer trip may be cheaper on a per mile/km basis]

In busy airports such as O'Hare, Los Angeles, Atlanta, and Kennedy, planes may spend much time waiting to take off or land. Every minute's wait adds dollars to personnel, fuel, and other costs. To keep costs down, the airlines have shifted to newer two-engine planes such as the B 767, which enables them to reduce fuel consumption by as much as 30 percent. Aircraft have also reconfigured seat arrangements to include more seats, but this results in seats that are smaller and have less leg room for passengers. Claustrophobic? You'd better travel business class! A few years ago, American Airlines removed some rows of seats to give more leg room by spacing the remaining seats farther apart. This has been a popular decision ever since, and many others have followed in creating a new business class for travel.

Cruise Ships

More than 200 cruise lines offer a variety of wonderful vacations, from a Carnival cruise to freighters that carry only a few passengers. Travelers associate a certain romance with cruising to exotic locations and being pampered all day.

Being on a cruise ship is like being on a floating resort. For example, the *Diamond Princess* is a "Super Love Boat" weighing in at 116,000 tons with 18 docks costing $400 million. This ship is longer than two football fields and capable of carrying up to 2,670 passengers.[16] Accommodations range from luxurious suites to cabins that are even smaller than most hotel rooms. Attractions and distractions range from early-morning workouts to fabulous meals, with nightlife consisting of dancing, cabarets, and sometimes casinos. Day life might involve relaxation, visits to the hair salon or spa, organized games, or simply reclining in a deck chair by the pool. Nonstop entertainment includes language lessons, charm classes, port-of-call briefings, cooking, dances, bridge, table tennis, shuffleboard, and more.

The cruise market has increased dramatically in recent years. About 9.0 million Americans cruise each year. Rates vary from a starting point of about $95 per person per day on Carnival Cruise Lines to $850 on the *Radisson Diamond*. Rates typically are quoted per diem (per day) and are cruise-only figures based on double occupancy. Some 215 ships provide lake and river, cruises, but most cruises are oceangoing. Casual ships cater to young couples, singles, and families

4 largest income:
BEVERAGE's

4 most cruise
ships are
"foreign owned"
due to:
1. lower labour
   costs
2. gambling
   permits
3. lower constr.
   costs.
4. few/less/no
   taxes

with children. At the other end of the spectrum, ships that appeal to the upscale crowd draw a mature clientele that prefers a more sedate atmosphere, low-key entertainment, and dressing up for dinner. The spectacular new ships with multideck atriums and razzle-dazzle entertainment cater to the tourist market who have a median income of $50,000 a year.

Carnival Cruise Lines is the most financially successful, netting about 20 percent of sales. It targets adults between the ages of twenty-five and fifty-four and expects to attract close to 3 million passengers with its spectacular atriums and round-the-clock activities. Its largest income, other than the fare itself, is from beverage service. Casino income is also high, and its casinos are the largest afloat. Carnival hopes that passengers will enjoy buying drinks and putting quarters, or preferably dollars, into the shipboard slot machines. They also hope their passengers will not mind their small cabins because the activities on the ship occupy passengers' waking hours and much of the night.

In 2007 alone, about 11 million passengers vacationed on a ship. To date, approximately 16 percent of the U.S. population target market have ever cruised, but millions more intend to cruise in the next few years. Many passengers are remarkably loyal to their particular vessel; as many as half of the passengers on a cruise may be repeat guests. Most cruise ships sail under foreign flags because they were built abroad for the following reasons.[17]

1. U.S. labor costs for ships, officers, and crew, in addition to maritime unions, are too high to compete in the world market.
2. U.S. ships are not permitted to operate casino-type gambling.
3. Many foreign shipyards are government subsidized to keep workers employed, thereby lowering construction costs.

Take a Cruise for a Great Vacation

A DAY IN THE LIFE OF RICHARD SPACEY

Cruise Director, Royal Caribbean International

Voyager of the Seas, one of the largest and most innovative cruise ships ever built, has a total guest capacity of 3,700 with 1,200 crew members. *Voyager of the Seas* is truly a revolution in the cruising industry. A virtual city in itself, she features the world's first floating ice skating rink, a rock climbing wall, an inline skating track, and the largest and most technically advanced theater afloat. There is a four-story Royal Promenade shopping and entertainment boulevard spanning the length of the ship that acts as a hub for the ship's vast array of activities and entertainment. Cruise director Richard Spacey was instrumental in implementing the unique entertainment and activities program aboard with a support staff of 130 people. What follows is an account of a day in the life of the cruise director of one of the largest cruise ships in the world.

Monday—First Day at Sea

7:30–8:30am – Yesterday we embarked 3,650 guests in Miami and headed for our first port of call, Labadee, our own private island on the coast of Hispaniola. Before most of the guests are up for the day, I plan and submit our daily activities schedule for the rest of the voyage to our hotel director for his approval. All of the cruise director's staff management team have submitted their reports after our staff meeting at embarkation yesterday. Scheduling of the twelve activities staff for the week is handled by the assistant cruise director, who also submits the payroll and overtime hours for my approval. Our cruise programs administrator says that three couples were married in the wedding chapel yesterday, and they are included in the 108 couples that have chosen to spend their honeymoon with us. A special party will be held later on in the week to celebrate this happy occasion. The youth activities manager reports that there are more than 600 children aboard, ranging in age from three to seventeen. The youth activities manager and her team of thirteen are responsible for providing age-appropriate activities for our junior cruisers. We offer a special deck and pool area/arcade for children in addition to our extensive youth facilities, which include a teen disco.

Fourteen hundred international guests are aboard and they consist of sixty different nationalities. The international ambassador (who speaks five languages) provides translations of our daily program and acts as the cruise director's liaison for all of our international guests.

A large part of our business is group and incentive business. The group coordinator appropriates lounges and facilities for these special group events under the auspices of the cruise director. There will be seminars, group meetings, presentations, and cocktail parties. We have a state-of-the-art conference center/executive boardroom/screening room in addition to a large convention facility named "Studio B," which doubles as the ice rink. A retractable floor over the ice rink makes this a great space for large conventions. The shore excursion manager reports that tour sales are good for this voyage among the fifty land-based excursions that we offer. All of this information is consolidated into a report to the hotel director that is submitted on a daily basis.

8:45–9:30am – Hotel director's meeting. All of the division heads in the Hotel Department meet to discuss the daily operation of this floating hotel. Today's agenda includes a monthly safety meeting. Each division head presents his or her monthly report on safety and environmental protection. Hospitality and the safety of our guests and crew are our top priorities.

9:45am – The start of my public duties. I give a daily announcement and rundown of all the activities and entertainment happenings around the ship.

continued

A DAY IN THE LIFE OF RICHARD SPACEY (continued)

10:00am – Morning walkaround. Time to kick off the first session of Jackpot Bingo for the week. On my way through the promenade, I encounter our interactive performers hamming it up with our guests. This is a troupe of two highly skilled performers. (Some of them are former Ringling Brothers' clowns.) They play different characters throughout the voyage and add quite a lot to the guest experience. I also stop by the Royal Caribbean Online Internet center, which is quite busy. We also offer an in-stateroom hookup of personal computers for unlimited Internet access (for a fee).

10:30am – The Studio B ice rink is busy with guests skating at our first All Skate session. There are several sessions throughout the day. The ice skating cast (ten individuals) are responsible for running the sessions as well as skating in our Ice Show.

11:00am – Time to change out of my day uniform into a business suit and put on stage makeup for the taping of our onboard talk and information show, "Voyager Live." I produce this segment from the Royal Promenade. We have three video programmers and an interactive television technician. Interactive TV allows our guests to order room service, excursions, and movies with the click of a button in the privacy of their staterooms.

I am one of the main sources for revenue promotion on board. The television programming is a great asset in a small floating city of this size. Thirty-seven channels offer safety information, music, shopping tips, CNBC, CNN, ESPN, and free movies in several languages.

12:00noon – Noon Lunch with the staff in the Officers and Staff Dining Room.

1:00pm – Change out of the business suit into shorts and a Polo shirt to emcee the Belly Flop Competition at 1:30 poolside. Always a "big" event among our guests. Quite a few laughs. This is followed by horse racing, cruising style. We pick six jockeys who move six wooden horses by a roll of the dice. The betting is fierce as the guests cheer their favorite horses on. I become the track announcer for three races and horse auctioneer. Today we auction off the six horses for our Voyager Derby later in the week. The horses go to the highest bidder, and then the "owners" run them in a race later on in the week for all the money. The six horses go for $2,100. A nice pot for one lucky winner.

2:30pm – I stop by the Sports Court to check out the action. The sports court is full of families enjoying our Family Hour activities with the youth staff. We offer a nine-hole miniature golf course, golf driving simulator, full-court basketball/volleyball, inline skating, Ping-Pong, and a rock climbing wall that rises up the smokestack 200 feet above sea level—the best view in the Caribbean. By the end of the day, 125 people will have climbed the wall.

3:00–4:30pm – POWER NAP TIME. The day will not end until about 12:30 A.M. Being "on stage" and available practically twenty-four hours a day can take its toll. This nap will carry me through until the end of the evening.

6:00pm – Back to the office to catch up on e-mail and general administrative business. It is also time to work on budget and revenue forecasting for the upcoming year.

7:30pm – Off to the Royal Promenade deck to mingle with the guests at the Welcome Aboard reception. The captain gives his welcome speech and then we send them off to their dinner or the show at 8:30.

8:30pm – Meet in the Champagne Bar with the hotel director before dinner. Tonight we will entertain guests who are on their fiftieth cruise and also a representative from an insurance company who is thinking of booking 700 guests on a future cruise with us.

9:00pm – On my way to the dining room, I introduce our production show in the La Scala Theater for the main-seating guests.

10:45pm – After dessert, I introduce the show for second-seating guests and watch the show for quality control.

11:45pm – After the show finishes, I do a final walk around the lounges on the ship with my assistant. Karaoke has just finished in one of the secondary lounges and we have music playing everywhere. We have thirty-five musicians comprising several bands featuring all varieties of music (string quartet, jazz ensemble, piano bar, Calypso, Latin, Top 40). The disco is lively with singles' night tonight and there are a few couples enjoying light jazz in the Jazz Club.

12:30am – A full day. Definitely a far cry from Julie on the *Love Boat*! Time for bed because I have to be on the gangway at 8:00 A.M. to welcome our guests to Labadee.

In addition, cruise ships sail under foreign flags (called flags of convenience) because registering these ships in countries such as Panama, the Bahamas, and Liberia means fewer and more lax regulations and little or no taxation.

Employment opportunities for Americans are mainly confined to sales, marketing, and other U.S. shore-based activities, such as reservations and supplies. Onboard, certain positions such as cruise director and purser, are sometimes occupied by Americans.

The reasons that few Americans work onboard cruise ships are because the ships are at sea for months at a time with just a few hours in port. The hours are long and the conditions for the crew are not likely to be acceptable to most Americans. No, you don't get your own cabin! Still interested? Try www.crewunlimited.com.

The Cruise Market

There are marked differences between the segments of the cruise industry.

Mass Market—Generally, people with incomes in the $35,000 to $74,000 range, interested in an average cost per person of between $95 and $195 per day, depending on the location and size of the cabin.

Middle Market—Generally, people with incomes in the $75,000 to $99,000 range, interested in an average cost per person of $175 to $350 per day. These ships are capable of accommodating 750 to 1,000 passengers. The middle-market ships are stylish and comfortable, with each vessel having its own personality that caters to a variety of different guests. Among the cruise lines in the middle market are Princess Cruises, Norwegian Cruise Lines, Royal Caribbean, Holland America Lines, Windstar Cruises, Cunard Lines, and Celebrity Cruises.

Luxury Market—Generally, people with incomes higher than $100,000, — interested in an average cost per person of more than $400 per day. In this market, the ships tend to be smaller, averaging about 700 passengers, with superior appointments and service. What constitutes a luxury cruise is partly a matter of individual judgment, partly a matter of advertising and public relations. The ships that received the top accolades from travel industry writers and others who assign such ranks cater only to the top 5 percent of North American income groups. Currently, the ships considered to be in the very top category are *Seabourn Spirit, Seabourn Legend, Seabourn Pride, Crystal Cruises Crystal Harmony, Radisson Diamond,* and *Silversea Silver Wind.* These six-star vessels have sophisticated cuisine, excellent service, far-reaching and imaginative itineraries, and highly satisfying overall cruise experiences.

4 rising demand has changed cruises to become more resort like
4 w more ammenities + activities.

The rising demand for cruising means larger ships with resort-like design, numerous activities, and amenities such as "virtual golf," pizzerias, and caviar bars. Significant growth opportunities still exist for the industry. With only about 10 percent of the cruise market tapped and with an estimated market potential of billions, the cruise industry is assured of a bright future.

▶ Check Your Knowledge

1. Why are the major U.S. airlines struggling financially?

2. Why do most cruise ships sail under foreign flags?

3. Describe the cruise market.

The Sacre-Coeur and Notre Dame de Lorette from Montmarte

An Exciting Destination

Now, let's visit one of the world's most popular and exciting cities.

Think of the excitement of planning a trip to the city of Paris, which is for many the most fabulous city in the world. Known as the City of Light, it is also one of the most romantic cities. Paris is a city of beautiful buildings, boulevards, parks, markets, and restaurants and cafes. Paris has excitement. So, for tourists, what to see first is the often-asked question over morning coffee and, of course, a croissant. There are city tours, but the best way to see Paris is on foot, especially if you want to avoid the hoards of tourists hovering around the popular attractions! Take your pick from the many places of interest: You could begin with the Eiffel Tower or the Cathedral of Notre Dame, the Louvre and the Muse d'Orsay, the Ile de la Cite, or simply a stroll down the Champs-Elysees.

Paris began as a small village on an island called Île de la Cité, in the middle of the river Seine. In time, Paris grew onto the Left Bank (Rive Gauche) where the University of the Sorbonne was founded with instruction in Latin—so, it became known as the Quartier Latin or Latin Quarter. The Latin Quarter has a Bohemian intellectual character with lots of small cafes and wine bars similar to Greenwich Village and Soho in New York. Nearby is Montparnasse, an area that is popular with today's artists and painters. On the Right Bank (Rive Droit) of the river Seine are many attractions; one favorite is the area of Montmartre, with the diminutive St. Pierre Church, the domes of Sacré-Coeur, and the Place du Tertre. Just walking along the winding streets up to Sacré-Coeur gives one a feel of the special nature of Paris. To savor the sights of the little markets with an array of fresh fruits, vegetables, and flowers; catch the aromas wafting out from the cafes; and see couples walking arm in arm in a way that only lovers in Paris do add to the ambiance that captivates all who go there and provides wonderful memories.

Close-up, Sacré-Coeur is a magnificent building in gleaming white. It towers over Paris, with its five bulb-like domes resembling a Byzantine church. The view from there, one of the highest parts of Paris, is spectacular, especially at sunset.

The Cathedral of Notre-Dame is the most famous Gothic cathedral in the world. The thirteenth-century cathedral is adorned with ornate stone carvings depicting the Virgin Mary, signs of the Zodiac, the Last Judgment, Vices and Virtues, Christ and his Apostles, and Christ in Triumph after the Resurrection. A portal above these and other stone carvings are the gargoyles immortalized in Victor Hugo's *The Hunchback of Notre Dame* as Quasimodo's den.

The Eiffel Tower was built more than 100 years ago for a World's Fair and has become one of the most recognizable buildings in the world and a symbol of Paris. On a clear day, at the top of the tower, you can see for up to forty miles.

Of the many fashionable boulevards and avenues, the Boulevard des Champs-Elysées, the main boulevard of Paris, stands out as one of the most grand. The Arc de Triomphe, the world's largest, commemorates Napoleon's victories.

The Louvre, the former residence of King Louis XIV, is the world's largest palace and largest museum. It is here that priceless works of art are displayed for public view. The *Mona Lisa* and *Venus de Milo* are the star attractions of exten-sive collections of Chinese, Egyptian, Greek, Roman, French, and European art, sculpture, and ceramics. In the courtyard of the Louvre is the controversial Plexiglas pyramid that was built to ease overcrowding at the entrance—but perhaps in part because of its striking contrast with the palace, the lines of museum visitors are now even longer than they were before. Other museums in Paris house collections of the best works of art by the greatest painters the world has known. They represent various periods of art throughout the centuries.

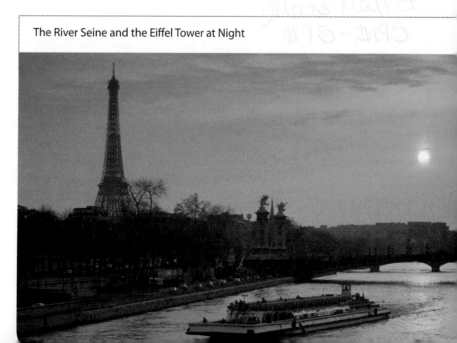

The River Seine and the Eiffel Tower at Night

The Economic Impact of Tourism

The World Travel and Tourism Council, a Brussels-based organization, commissioned a study on the economic impact of tourism[18] by the Wharton Economic Forecasting Association. The report suggests that the total demand for travel and tourism will be $2,571 billion by 2010, or more than 10 percent of the world's gross national product (GNP). (See Figure 2–3.) Tourism, says the study, grows about twice as fast as world GNP. Of the industry's total world spending, about 31 percent takes place in the European Community and 30 percent on the North American continent.

World international arrivals, according to the WTO, will reach 1 billion in 2010, and 1.6 billion by 2020, more than triple the 475 million people who traveled abroad in 1992. Nearly every state publishes its own tourism economic impact study indicating billions of dollars in tourism revenue. The Tourism Industry Association's annual "The Tourism Work for America Report"[19] indicates that travel and tourism are one of the nation's leading sectors. Statistics include the following:

- International travelers spend about $94 billion on travel-related expenses (e.g., lodging, food, and entertainment) in the United States annually.

- 20.8 million people are directly employed in the travel industry, making travel and tourism the nation's second largest employer, after health services.

- Travel generates about $100 billion a year in tax receipts. If it were not for tourism, each U.S. household would have to pay $898 more per year in taxes.

**International Tourism Receipts
(US $ billion)**

Rank		2006
1	United States	85.7
2	Spain	50.1
3	France	42.9
4	Italy	38.1
5	China	33.9
6	United Kingdom	33.7
7	Germany	32.8
8	Australia	17.8
9	Turkey	16.9
10	Austria	16.7

Source: World Tourism Organization (WTO)©.

Figure 2–3 • Worlds' Top Ten Tourism Earners. Notice that China now features prominently as a leading tourism nation.

- Spending by international visitors in the United States is about $21 billion more than travel-related spending by Americans outside the United States.

- Approximately 46 million international travelers visit the United States each year.

- Just a 1 percent increase in the world market would mean 7.6 million more visitors, which would create 150,000 jobs and contribute $2 billion in new tax revenue.

By employing approximately one out of every ten workers, travel and tourism is the world's largest employer and is the largest industry. The estimates are that in the year 2012 there will be 249 million travel- and tourism-related jobs, accounting for 8.6 percent of total employment, which is 1 in every 11.7 jobs.

The Multiplier Effect

Tourists bring new money into the economy of the place they are visiting, and this has effects beyond the original expenditures. When a tourist spends money to travel, to stay in a hotel, or to eat in a restaurant, that money is recycled by those businesses to purchase more goods, thereby generating further use of the money. In addition, employees of businesses who serve tourists spend a higher proportion of their money locally on various goods and services. This chain reaction, called the **multiplier effect**, continues until there is a leakage, meaning that money is used to purchase something from outside the area. Figure 2–4 illustrates the multiplier effect.

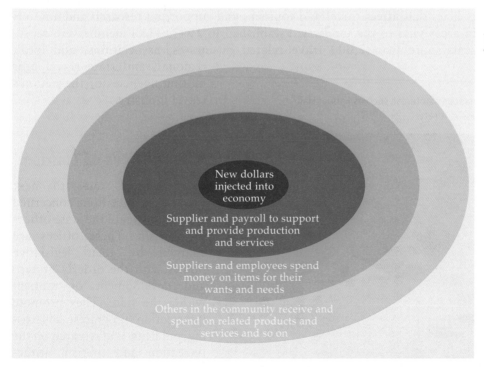

Figure 2–4 • The Multiplier Effect

In most economic impact studies to date, developed economies have a multiplier effect between 1.5 and 2.0.[20] This means that the original money spent is used again in the community between 1.5 and 2.0 times. If tourism-related businesses spend more money on locally produced goods and services, it benefits the local economy.

Promoters of Tourism

The **Pacific Area Travel Association (PATA)** represents thirty-four countries in the Pacific and Asia that have united behind common goals: excellence in travel, and tourism growth. PATA's accomplishments include shaping the future of travel in the Asia/Pacific region; it has had a remarkable record of success with research, development, education, and marketing.

Many countries have a minister of tourism, which is a cabinet-level position that can advocate tourism development, marketing, and management through the National Tourism Organization (NTO). Unfortunately, the United States does not have even a senior-level government official for tourism. Instead, an organization known as the Travel Industry of America (TIA) is the main body for the promotion and development of tourism in the United States. It speaks for the common interests and concerns of all components of the U.S. travel industry. Its mission is to benefit the whole U.S. travel industry by unifying its goals, coordinating private sector efforts to encourage and promote travel to and within the United States, monitoring government policies that affect travel and tourism, and supporting research and analysis in areas vital to the industry. Established in 1941, TIA's membership represents more than 2,000 travel-related businesses, associations, and local, regional, and state travel promotion agencies of the nation's travel industry.

State offices of tourism promote places of interest, such as Fanuel Hall and Quincy Market, in Boston, Massachusetts

State Offices of Tourism

In the United States, the next level of organizations concerned with tourism are the state offices of tourism. These offices are charged by their legislative bodies with the orderly growth and development of tourism within the state. They promote information programs, advertising, publicity, and research on the recreation and tourism attractions in the state.

City-Level Offices of Tourism and Convention Centers

Cities have also realized the importance of the "new money" that tourism brings. Many cities have established **convention and visitors bureaus (CVBs)**, whose main function is to attract and retain visitors to the city. The convention and visitors bureaus are staffed by representatives of the city's attractions, restaurants, hotels and motels, and transportation system. These bureaus are largely funded by the transient occupancy tax (TOT) that is charged to hotel guests. In most cities, the TOT ranges from 8 to 18 percent. The balance of funding comes from membership dues and promotional activities. In recent years, convention centers have sprung up in a number of large and several smaller cities. Spurred on by expectations of economic and social gain, cities operate both convention and visitors bureaus and convention centers. Both convention and visitors bureaus and convention centers are discussed in detail in Chapter 12.

[handwritten margin note: CVBs promote attract + retain visitors to the city; funded via TOT (transient occupancy tax) 8-18%]

Tour Operators

Tour operators promote tours and trips that they plan and organize. A *tour* is a trip taken by an individual or group of people who travel together with a professional tour manager/escort and follow a preplanned itinerary. Most tours include travel, accommodations, meals, land transportation, and sightseeing. The tour operator negotiates discounted travel, accommodation, and meals and sightseeing, and then adds a markup before advertising the package. Tour operators also offer **vacation packages** to people traveling alone. Vacation packages include a combination of two or more travel services—hotel, car rental, and air transportation—offered at a package price. Most vacation packages offer a choice of components and options, allowing the client to customize his or her package to personal interests and budget.

Travel Agencies

A *travel agent* is a middleperson who acts as a travel counselor and sells travel services on behalf of airlines, cruise lines, rail and bus transportation companies, hotels, and auto rental companies. Agents may sell individual parts of the overall system or several elements, such as air and cruise tickets. The agent acts as a broker, bringing together the client (buyer) and the supplier (seller). Agents have quick access to schedules, fares, and advice for clients about various destinations.

The American Society of Travel Agents (ASTA) is the world's largest travel trade association, with more than 20,000 members in more than 165 countries. Agents use computer reservation systems (CRSs) to access service availability and make bookings. In the United States, the main vendors of CRSs are Sabre, Apollo, Worldspan, System One, and Galileo.

A travel agent is more than a ticket seller. Agents serve their clients in the following ways:

- Arranging transportation by air, sea, rail, bus, car rental, and so on
- Preparing individual itineraries, personally escorted tours, group tours, and prepared package tours

[handwritten margin note: travel agent acts a travel counsellor; ASTA - largest travel trade assoc; CRS - comp res system; ex: Apollo, Sabre, Galileo]

- Arranging for hotel, motel, and resort accommodations; meals; sightseeing tours; transfers of passengers and luggage between terminals and hotels; and special features such as tickets for music festivals, the theater, and so forth

- Handling and advising on many details involved with travel, such as insurance, traveler's checks, foreign currency exchange, documentary requirements, and immunizations and other inoculations needed

- Using professional know-how and experience (e.g., schedules of air, train, and bus connections, rates of hotels, quality of accommodations)

- Arranging reservations for special-interest activities, such as group tours, conventions, business travel, gourmet tours, and sporting trips

However, the travel business has changed, resulting in a sharp decline in the number of travel agents, because there is less need for the traditional travel agent in the age of the Internet. Internet travel services such as Travelocity, and Expedia have changed the way we book travel. As you know, it is quick and easy to go online and select travel dates, times, and fares. In fact, tourism services are among the top online purchases. As consumers, we can shop for the best price and most convenient schedule and purchase e-tickets by entering our credit card numbers and billing information over a secure connection.

Commission Caps

Travel agents once gained most of their income from airline and cruise line commissions. However, travel agencies have seen air travel commissions, their primary source of income, decline since commission caps were first imposed. The airlines have now eliminated commissions, so agencies are charging travelers a fee for their services to offset the costs involved in providing those services.

Out of necessity, travel agents have become more specialized to make up for the loss of commission revenue from the airlines. Some have specialized in the booking of cruises because cruise lines still pay commissions of between 10 and 15 percent of the price of the cabin booked. Others have expanded their product offerings by including meeting and event planning and management. Another way of gaining more commission is simply to charge clients an extra amount for their tickets. There are still business and leisure travelers who do not have the time or inclination to book their

[handwritten margin note: 4 make money: -commissions -branching into meetings & conventions -charging clients]

Travel agents have knowledge of destinations and can make air, ground, and hotel reservations for clients to visit popular destinations such as Venice, Italy own trips online. For them, the travel agent can provide a hassle-free service and be there when needed.

Tour Wholesalers and Consolidators

Tour suppliers provide the package components for tour operators via the services of hotels, attractions, restaurants, airlines, cruise lines, railroads and sightseeing which are packaged into a tour that is sold through a sales channel to the public.[21] Tour wholesaling came into prominence years ago because airlines had vacant seats, which, like hotel rooms, are perishable. Airlines naturally wanted to sell as many seats as possible and found that they could sell blocks of seats to wholesalers close to departure dates. These tickets are for specific destinations around which tour wholesalers build a tour. Wholesalers then sell their tours directly through retail agents.

Consolidators work closely with airlines to purchase discounted seats that they then sell to consumers for a price that is generally about 20 percent lower than the price offered by airlines or an online service company such as Travelocity. For example, The price of a consolidator's fare for a round trip to Bali from New York is $975, but the airline or Travelocity fare can be double that. So, consolidators are the place to call or e-mail when you are interested in booking an airfare.

National Offices of Tourism

National offices of tourism (NOTs) seek to improve the economy of the country they represent by increasing the number of visitors and consequently their spending in the country. Connected to this function is the responsibility to oversee and ensure that hotels, transport systems, tour operators, and tour guides maintain high standards in the care and consideration of the tourist. The main activities of NOTs are as follows:

- Publicizing the country
- Assisting and advising certain types of travelers
- Creating demand for certain destinations
- Supplying information
- Ensuring that the destination is up to expectations
- Advertising[22]

Destination Management Companies

A *destination management company* (DMC) is a service organization in the visitor industry that offers a host of programs and services to meet clients' needs. Initially, a destination management sales manager concentrates on selling the destination to meeting planners and performance improvement companies (incentive houses).

The needs of such groups may be as simple as an airport pickup or as involved as hosting an international sales convention with theme parties. DMCs

INTRODUCING PATTI ROSCOE

Chairperson, Patti Roscoe and Associates (PRA) and Roscoe/Coltrell Inc. (RCI)

Patricia L. Roscoe landed in California in 1966, charmed by the beautiful San Diego sun compared to the cold winters in Buffalo, New York, her hometown. She was a young, brilliant middle manager who was to face the challenges of a time period when women were expected to become either nurses or teachers. She became involved with the hotel industry, working for a large private resort hotel, the Vacation Village. Those were the years to be remembered. She gained a very thorough knowledge of southern California tourism, as well as the inherent mechanisms of the industry. With the unforgettable help and guidance of her manager, she began to lay the foundations of her future career as a very successful leader in the field. The outstanding skills that she learned are, in fact, the very basis of her many accomplishments.

The list of her awards and honors is astounding: the prestigious CITE distinction (Certified Incentive Travel Executive), San Diego Woman of Accomplishment, and San Diego's Allied Member of the Year. The U.S. Small Business Administration gave her the Wonder Woman Award for her outstanding achievements in the field, and the San Diego Convention and Visitors Bureau has conferred on her the prestigious RCA Lubach Award for her contributions to the industry.

She is also extremely involved in civic and tourism organizations, including the Rotary Club, the American Lung Association of San Diego and Imperial Counties, and the San Diego Convention and Visitors Bureau.

The key to her success perhaps lies in her remarkable skills of interacting with people. It is the human resources, in fact, that represent the major strength of PRA. Its employees are experienced, dedicated, and service oriented. But what makes them so efficient is their dedication to working together as a team. Patti Roscoe guides, inspires, and motivates these teams. She is a self-admitted "softy," a creative and emotional leader who enjoys training her employees and following their growth step by step, to eventually give them the power of initiative they deserve, as a tool to encourage their creativity and originality. She constantly seeks to balance the concept of teamwork with the individual goals and private lives of her employees. It is through the achievement of such a balance that a profitable, healthy community is preserved. PRA is a bit more than a community, however: It is a family, and just like a mother, Patti's formula is discipline and love. At the same time, Patti's leading efforts are aimed at training her employees to "think outside of the box," and "keep one's view as broad as possible," which is the only way to rise above the commonplace, the rhetorical, and the trivial, to escape provincialism, and thus become unique individuals.

That's how the magic is done. PRA excels in creating "something that becomes exclusively yours—that has never been done before." PRA is decentralized into service teams to foster an entrepreneurial environment in which initiative and creativity can be boosted to the fullest. Therefore, PRA staff design personalized, unique events to give their customers an unforgettable time.

Since its opening in 1981, PRA has become one of the most successful destination management companies in the country, providing personal, caring service characterized by flexibility and creativity.

work closely with hotels; sometimes DMCs book rooms, and other times hotels request the DMC's know-how on organizing theme parties.

Patricia Roscoe, chairperson of Patti Roscoe and Associates (PRA), says that meeting planners often have a choice of several destinations and might ask, "Why should I pick your destination?" The answer is that a DMC does everything, including providing airport greetings, transportation to the hotel, and VIP check-in; organizing theme parties; sponsoring programs; organizing competitive sports events, and so on, depending on the budget.

Sales managers associated with DMCs obtain leads, which are potential clients, from the following sources:

- Hotels
- Trade shows
- Convention and visitors bureaus
- Cold calls
- Incentive houses
- Meeting planners

Each sales manager has a staff or team that includes people in the following positions:

- Special events manager, who has expertise in sound, lighting, staging, and so on
- Accounts manager, who is an assistant to the sales manager
- Operations manager, who coordinates everything, especially on-site arrangements, to ensure that what is sold actually happens

For example, Patti Roscoe's destination management company organized meetings, accommodations, meals, beverages, and theme parties for 2,000 Ford Motor Company dealers in nine groups over three days per group.

Roscoe also works closely with incentive houses, such as Carlson Marketing or Maritz Travel. These incentive houses approach a company and offer to evaluate and set up incentive plans for the sales team, including whatever it takes to motivate them. Once approved, Carlson contacts a destination management company and asks for a program.

In conclusion, thousands of companies and associations hold meetings and conventions all over the country. Many of these organizations use the services of professional meeting planners, who in turn seek out suitable destinations for the meetings and conventions. Some larger hotels and resorts now have a destination management department to handle all the arrangements for groups and conventions.

▶ Check Your Knowledge

1. Describe the economic impact of tourism.

2. Is it better to have a higher or lower multiplier effect and why?

3. Describe the promoters of tourism.

Why People Travel

There are many reasons why people travel, but the two main reasons are for pleasure and for business. Research indicates that when consumers are asked what they associate most with success and accomplishment, the number one response is travel for pleasure.

Among the reasons people travel for pleasure are the following:

- Visiting friends and relatives
- Health
- Enlightenment, education
- Beauty, nature, and national parks
- Religion
- Indulgence
- Sports
- Festivals
- Shopping
- Fun of the trip
- Gaming
- Adventure
- Heritage
- Ecotourism
- Attractions

Leisure / Pleasure Travel

Eighty-two percent of domestic travel is **leisure/pleasure travel** (leisure, recreation, holidays, and visiting friends and relatives—VFR). Approximately 670 million person-trips are taken for pleasure, according to the United States Travel Data Center's (USTDC) national travel survey. Nearly half of all the pleasure travelers visited friends and relatives.

When surveyed, people tend to list the following reasons for travel:

- To experience new and different surroundings
- To experience other cultures
- To rest and relax
- To visit friends and family
- To view, or participate in, sporting/recreational activities

Travel is likely to increase in the coming years, which will have a significant impact on tourism. Some reasons for the anticipated increases are as follows:

↳ 82% of dom travel is due to leisure + VFR.

↳ almost 1/2 of pleasure visit friends + relatives.

- *Longer life span.* The average person in the United States now has a life expectancy of about seventy-five years. In fact, in just a few years, many baby boomers will retire.

- *Flexible working hours.* Today, many people work four 10-hour days and have longer weekends. Of course, many others, especially in the hospitality and tourism industries, work on weekends and have leisure time during the week.

- *Early retirement.* Increasingly, people are being given the opportunity to retire at age fifty-five. This early retirement is generally granted to employees with thirty years of service to their company or government agency.

- *Greater ease of travel.* Today, it is easier to travel on holidays and weekends, for both business and leisure purposes. Each mode of travel affords increasing opportunities to take advantage of the additional leisure time.

- *Tendency to take shorter, more frequent trips.* People now tend to take shorter but more frequent minivacations rather than taking all their vacation time at once. Europeans generally take much longer vacations than North Americans do. For Europeans, four weeks is the normal vacation benefit of new employees, and six weeks is typical after a few years of employment.

- *Increase in the standard of living.* More people in many developing countries have increased their income and wish to travel. China, with its newfound enterprise zones, is producing hundreds of thousands of entrepreneurs who will soon be traveling to foreign countries. Millions of east European residents of the former Soviet Bloc countries now have the capability and the right to travel. And finally, an additional 300 million people from China and India will soon have passports.

Stanley Plog, a respected social scientist, has suggested that travelers can be separated into two extremes: (1) psychocentrics, who prefer familiar travel destination, and (2) allocentrics, who prefer new and different destinations.

Most travelers fall into a large bell-shaped curve between these two extremes. Figure 2–5 illustrates the types of destinations that psychocentrics and allocentrics are likely to visit. Psychocentrics, as the figure illustrates, prefer travel to well-known destinations that have been visited by millions before. These destinations tend to be constant and predictable. Allocentric personalities tend to be more adventurous, curious, energetic, and outgoing; they will usually be attracted to novel destinations like the South Pacific, Asia, and Africa. Generally, twice as many people are inclined to be allocentric. This has an effect on small-scale tourist areas. First visited by allocentrics, the area (be it a village, town, or resort) then becomes more popular and is forced into becoming more commercialized. Waikiki Beach on Oahu is an example of this—as few as thirty years ago, there were no high-rise hotels there.

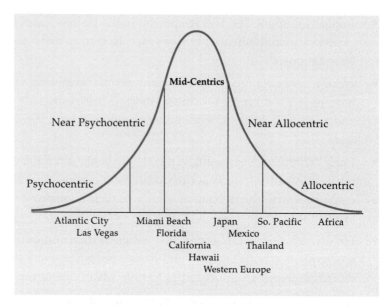

Figure 2–5 • Psychocentric and Allocentric Types of Destinations.
[Adapted from Stanley Plog, "Why Destination Areas Rise and Fall in Popularity," a paper presented to the southern California Chapter of the Travel Research Association, October 10, 1972, as cited in Edward Mayo and Lance Jarvis, *The Psychology of Leisure Travel* (Boston: CBI Publishing Company, 1981),118.]

Push/Pull Model

An interesting way of modeling travel motivations is to divide them into factors that pull, that is, attractions, and those that push, that is, personal needs. Arlin Epperson, a travel consultant, proposes the push/pull model. He lists push factors as the intangible desires that are generated from within the person.

Disney World attracts those motivated by a pull factor. A relaxing week on a Caribbean beech is probably inspired by a push factor. Much travel is likely motivated to some degree by both push and pull factors. For example, a vacation in an isolated mountain cabin would allow for escape, self-discovery, and rest, while at the same time providing scenic beauty.

Different Places for Different People

Obviously, travelers select destinations for different reasons—climate, history or culture, sports, entertainment, shopping facilities, and so forth. The major appeal of England for Americans seems to be history and culture. American Express surveyed people going to several destinations—Florida, California, Mexico, Hawaii, the Bahamas, Jamaica, Puerto Rico, the Virgin Islands, and Barbados. Almost half of the respondents were professionals, generally middle-aged and well educated. Many were wealthy travelers who took frequent vacations outside the United States. These respondents ranked the appeals of travel in descending order of importance:

- Scenic beauty
- Pleasant attitudes of local people

- Suitable accommodations
- Rest and relaxation
- Airfare cost
- Historical and cultural interests
- Cuisine
- Water sports
- Entertainment (e.g., nightlife)
- Shopping facilities
- Sports (golfing and tennis)

Four basic considerations emerged as factors influencing travel: entertainment, purchase opportunities, climate for comfort, and cost. Even within a group, of course, different factors apply. One individual may select a destination primarily because of opportunities for challenging golf and tennis, another because of the friendly local people, and another because the place offers rest and relaxation. Most of the group would, however, be influenced by airfare costs.

Expectation and Reality

Karen Smith and Claudia Green of New York and Pace Universities comment: With the growth in international tourism, challenges have emerged for the traveler as well as the destination location.[23] Travelers often have culturally based expectations for the travel experience that may or may not be met by international travel. Current research focuses on the impact of the traveler's culture on expectations for service, as well as ways to assess customer expectations and evaluate customer satisfaction. Service providers in destination locations are making efforts to meet the needs of diverse populations of travelers.

Satisfaction, or dissatisfaction, with the travel experience, of course, depends on how it is viewed by the traveler. A glorious sunset and majestic mountain may be seen as a great bore if an individual is highly gregarious and alone on the trip. The best service in a restaurant with the finest food and decor is meaningless if the

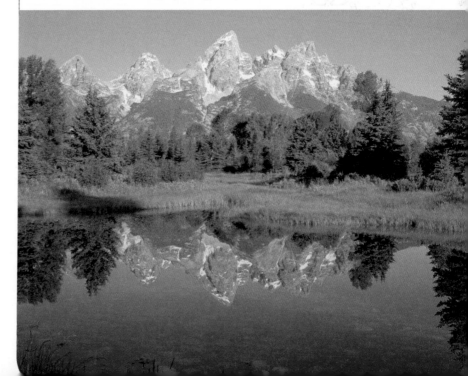

One of the most beautiful places in the United States is Jackson Lake, Grand Teton National Park, Wyoming

[Handwritten margin notes: "↳because it is a service industry and experiences are subjective — some ppl may ♡ it while some hate it"]

[Handwritten margin notes: "↳it all depends on the ind's expectations + what they're reality is"]

person is dyspeptic at the moment. One traveler loves the rain, another despises it. Mountains are one person's delight, heights make another person dizzy. The anthropologist revels in the remote village, the citydweller finds the same place dull. So much depends on what the person expects of the experience and how he or she actually experiences it.

Travel is an experience, not a tangible object. It results in psychic reward or punishment. It creates pleasant anticipation or aversion, excitement and challenge or fatigue and disappointment. The anticipation, the experience, and the memory occur in the mind, leaving no tangible evidence as to why travel was undertaken and why the same trip is experienced in so many different ways by different people. Travel literature and films often falsify reality or are shot so selectively that the actual environment is not recognizable by the visitor. The phony shot that makes the pool look longer than it is, the colors that never exist in nature, the lavish buffet that was rigged especially for the photograph, the glorious sunset that occurs once a year—all of this creates expectations that cannot be realized and leads to disappointment.

[Handwritten note: "↳sometimes when ppl falsely advertise → makes it worse"]

Business Travel

[Handwritten margin notes: "↳business travellers spend more money tend to be younger but don't stay as long"]

[Handwritten margin notes: "↳they are probably frequent travellers though."]

In recent years, business travel has declined due to[27] the general economic climate, increase in airfares terrorism, and businesses reducing their travel budgets have negatively affected business travel.

Yet, a high percentage of the guests who check into upscale hotels around the world are traveling for business reasons. Much **business travel** is hard work, whether it is travel in one's own automobile or in the luxury of a first-class seat aboard an airplane. A good portion of business travel is, however, mixed with pleasure.

Counted as business travelers are those who travel for business purposes, such as for meetings; all kinds of sales, including corporate, regional, product, and others; conventions; trade shows and expositions; and combinations of more than one of these purposes. In the United States, meetings and conventions alone attract millions of people annually. Sometimes the distinction between business and leisure travel becomes blurred. If a convention attendee in Atlanta decides to stay on for a few days after the conference, is this person to be considered a business or leisure traveler? Business travelers, when compared to leisure travelers, tend to be younger, spend more money, travel farther, and travel in smaller groups, but they do not stay as long as leisure travelers do.

An ecotourist admires Temple 11 (Temple of the Masks) in the Great Plaza at Tikal

Tourism Safety

Lynne Christen

Before September 11, 2001, travelers rarely gave much thought to safety. Tourism marketers directed their market positioning to tangibles such as beautiful beaches, lavish spas, spacious and well-decorated rooms, and more amenities than the competition. Since the terrorist attacks, travel safety has become an integral part of travel planning. Tourists are saying, "I don't think it's safe to go there," and "I'm not ready to start flying again." Concerns are reinforced by frequent upgrades and downgrades of the national threat level. This is the new reality of travel and a challenge for the entire tourism industry.

The bad news is that this fear of travel has a negative impact on virtually every segment of the travel industry. The good news is that, according to studies by the Travel Industry Association of America (TIA), in spite of the concerns, both business and leisure travel are again beginning to show steady growth.

Travel agents, hospitality managers, air and cruise lines, and tour operators must take proactive steps to monitor and manage the safety and security segments of their operations. They must shift from previous approaches of downplaying potential safety problems. Successful tourism providers will prominently position safety, making it an integral and visible part of marketing strategies. Educating customers and helping them to become more confident make them safer travelers.

It is important to note that the odds of a tourist being killed or injured by terrorism are extremely low. The biggest threat to tourist safety is everyday street crime, theft, and medical emergencies. Granted, hotel fires and cruise ship disasters occur (usually with major publicity), but they are rare. Statistics show that a sprinklered hotel or cruise ship is safer than the average home.

One way to begin educating the tourism consumer is in basic crime prevention. Crime safety and security brochures are excellent educational tools and can easily be made available in airports, hotels, cruise ships, and tour buses. Tourists should be provided Internet web sites, books, magazines, and media safety resources and encouraged to research their safety concerns.

It is equally important for all tourism professionals to be aware of resources available to travelers. International travelers should begin their trip planning by researching their destination countries and checking U.S. State Department travel warnings (**www.state.gov**). Travel warnings are issued when a country becomes unsafe, usually as a result of war, terrorism, or potential unrest.

The Central Intelligence Agency (CIA) also publishes an excellent document called *The CIA World Factbook* (**www.cia.gov**). This book has detailed information on demographics, climate, geography, economy, politics, and more for every country in the world.

Researching a country's medical facilities is often overlooked as a key safety element. This is especially important for travelers who have special or chronic medical needs. Hospitals and clinics, taken for granted in the United States and western Europe, may not be available in other parts of the world. Other medical issues to consider include the availability of prescription medications, air evacuation, and insurance coverage. Many tourists are not aware that Medicare coverage and many private insurance policies do not apply outside the United States. The Centers for Disease Control and prevention (**www.cdc.gov**) provides up-to-date, accurate medical travel information, including disease warnings and vaccination recommendations.

Filing a travel plan is also an overlooked component of travel safety. Tourists should print several detailed copies of their travel schedule and various accommodation addresses and telephone numbers and provide them to friends and family. Tourists in foreign countries should notify the appropriate U.S. embassy or consulate when they are staying in the country for two weeks or more. This notification includes contact information in the event of a travel warning or the need for evacuation.

▶ Check Your Knowledge

1. Are you a more psychocentric or allocentric tourist?
2. Describe the push/pull model.
3. What are the main reasons for leisure and business travel?

Social and Cultural Impact of Tourism

From a social and cultural perspective, tourism can have both positive and negative impacts on communities. Undoubtedly, tourism has made significant contributions to international understanding. World tourism organizations recognize that tourism is a means of enhancing international understanding, peace, prosperity, and universal respect for and observance of human rights and fundamental freedom for all without distinction as to race, sex, language, or religion. Tourism can be a very interesting sociocultural phenomenon. Seeing how others live is an interest of many tourists, and the exchange of sociocultural values and activities is rewarding.

Provided that the number of tourists is manageable and that they respect the host community's sociocultural norms and values, tourism provides an opportunity for a number of social interactions. A London pub or a New York café are examples of good places for social interaction. Similarly, depending on the reason for the tourist visit, myriad opportunities are available to interact both socially and culturally with local people. Even a visit to another part of the United States can be both socially and culturally stimulating. For example, New Orleans has a very diverse social and cultural heritage. Over the years, the city has been occupied by Spanish, French, British, and Americans, so the food, music, dance, and social norms are unique to the area.

The competitiveness of international destinations is based on such attributes as service quality, as well as on value for the price, safety, security, entertainment, weather, infrastructure, and natural environment.[24] Political stability is also important in determining the desirability of a destination for international tourism. Imagine the feelings of an employee in a developing country who earns

Beaches at the Cote d'Azur, southern France may have standing room only

Handwritten margin notes:
1) tourism has the potential to bridge social + cultural gaps as long as visitors are respectful to the host deot's values, norms, ethics etc.
2) WTO's oversees this + its part of their mandate
3) Tourism is an excellent way to learn abt other cultures

CORPORATE PROFILE

G. A. P Adventures

If you are tired of the one-week-in-the-Florida-sun vacation and want to do something exciting and off the beaten path, then G. A. P Adventures is the perfect company to turn to. They provide more than 600 different itineraries in more than 100 countries and have, during the last years, given more than 20,000 travelers the adventure of their lifetime. This year, approximately 1.5 million more people are expected to visit their web site, some of them to change their lives forever.

G. A. P Adventure's CEO Bruce Poon Tip has been honored with the Entrepreneur of the Year Award, sponsored by NASDAQ, Ernst & Young, and the National Post. G. A.P Adventures has also been named one of Canada's 50 best managed companies and top 100 employers. Furthermore, they have greatly helped to improve the conditions in the many countries they visit.

Their philosophy "The Freedom of Independent Travel with the Security of a Group" has been practiced since the start. They respect their travelers as individuals, and there is no requirement to be athletic to embark on one of their trips. The only thing needed is to have the spirit of adventure and the desire to experience a world totally different from what you are accustomed to.

Also, the concept of responsible tourism is very important to G.A.P Adventures, and they come and go and interact with the local populations, leaving behind them only footprints. Their commitment is to support local people and communities and to protect the environment they travel in. To that end, G. A. P. Adventures developed Planeterra—the G. A. P Adventures Foundation that gives back to the people and communities their passengers visit on their trips.

They hire people in different departments, including Operations, Product, Sales and Marketing, Finance, HR, and Tour Leading. G. A. P Adventures employs more than 300 staff worldwide. All current postings can be found under the career section of their web site.

Maybe the most obvious choice for you is the position as a G.A.P tour leader. In this position, your main task is to make people's holiday dreams come true and make sure all passengers have an enjoyable time abroad.

Most of the time, the local hostel where you spend the night is your home, and your office is your backpack.

On your way to work you might have to hike the Inca Trail or canoe down the Amazon River. If you are interested in meeting and really interacting with people from different cultures, and like to show your passion to passengers of different backgrounds, ages, and interests, this is the perfect job for you.

Some of the requirements to work as a G. A. P tour leader include fluency in English and Spanish, a passion for travel, a love for Latin America (which is their main area of operations), and excellent people skills. No matter what happens and how bad your day has been, you always have to be the happy and helpful leader. Additional skills needed include awareness of, and commitment to, sustainable tourism, both environmentally

continued

CORPORATE PROFILE *(continued)*

and culturally, as well commitment to an eighteen-month contract. It takes time to become the perfect adventure tour leader, and once you have learned it, the company may decide to renew your contract. You also need to be resourceful, which here means being able to solve any kind of problem that might arise, expected or unexpected. Because of the nature of the work, you also need to have good health, first-aid certification, and an average level of computer literacy (Internet/e-mail/Microsoft Word/Microsoft Excel). If you have seen the world, or want to see it, in a truly interactive way, and you have leadership skills and are adventurous and brave, then this might be the perfect job for you. Why not give it a try?

Note: To apply to be a tour leader, you must complete the online application form found on the web site.

Source: This Focus draws on G. A. P Adventures web site: www.gapadventures.com

perhaps $5 per day when he or she sees wealthy tourists flaunting money, jewelry, and a lifestyle not obtainable.

Just imagine what will happen when another 300 million people become tourists by virtue of increasing standards of living and the ability of more people to obtain passports. Currently, only about 21.7 percent of the U.S. population has passports, although that may increase because everyone returning to the United States from Mexico and Canada must now have a passport. The population of eastern Europe and the new rich of the Pacific Rim countries will substantially add to the potential number of tourists. So, its no surprise that travel tourism is expected to double by 2015.

Ecotourism

Ecotourism is focused more on individual values; it is "tourism with a conscience," sharing many of the same aspirations as sustainable tourism (described next). The International Ecotourism Society (TIES) defines *ecotourism* as "responsible travel to natural areas that conserves the environment and improves the well-being of local people." This means that those who implement and participate in ecotourism activities should follow the following principles:

- Minimize impact.
- Build environmental and cultural awareness and respect.
- Provide positive experiences for both visitors and hosts.
- Provide direct financial benefits for conservation.
- Provide financial benefits and empowerment for local people.
- Raise sensitivity to host countries' political, environmental, and social climate.
- Support international human rights and labor agreements.[25]

Most ecotourism destinations can be found in developing countries with natural surroundings and plentiful flora and fauna. Places such as deserts, tropical rain forests, coral reefs, and ice glaciers are prime locations. Also important in ecotourism is the presence of a culture that is unique. The focus of ecotourism is to provide tourists with new knowledge about a certain natural area and the culture that is found in it, along with a little bit of adventure. As for the natives, ecotourism aims to help improve the local economy and conservation efforts. All parties are to gain a new appreciation for nature and people.

Generally, most of the more popular ecotourism destinations are located in underdeveloped and developing countries. As vacationers are becoming more adventurous and are visiting remote, exotic places, they are participating in activities that should affect nature, host communities, and themselves in a positive manner. And because of the growing interests of travelers, many developed countries are following the trend and developing ecotourism programs. Ecotourism can be a main source of worldwide promotion of sustainable development geared toward tourists and communities in all countries.

Thus far, ecotourism projects tend to be developed on a small scale. It is much easier to control such sites, particularly because of limits that are normally set on the community, the local tourism business, and the tourists. Limitations may include strict control of the amount of water and electricity used, more stringent recycling measures, regulation of park and market hours, and, more important, limiting the number of visitors to a certain location at one time and limiting the size of the business. Another reason ecotourism projects are kept small is to allow more in-depth tours and educational opportunities.

Sustainable Tourism

The increasing number of tourists visiting destinations has heightened concern about the environment, physical resources of the place, and sociocultural degradation. The response of tourism officials has been to propose that all tourism be sustainable. The concept of **sustainable tourism** places a broad-based obligation on society especially those involved in making tourism policy; planning for development; and harmonizing tourism and tourism development by improving the quality of a place's environment and resources, physical and sociocultural. According to the World Tourism definition, sustainable tourism development and management refer to the environmental and socio-cultural aspects of tourism, with the establishment of a suitable balance between these three dimensions to guarantee its long-term sustainability.

The United National Environment Program (UNEP) says that sustainability principles refer to the environmental, economic, and socio-cultural aspects of tourism. Sustainable tourism should (1) make optimal use of environmental resources that constitute a key element in tourism development; (2) respect the socio-cultural authenticity of host communities, conserve their built and living cultural heritage and traditional values, and contribute to inter-cultural understanding and tolerance; and (3) ensure viable, long-term economic operations, providing socio-economic benefits to all stakeholders that are fairly distributed, including stable employment and income-earning opportunities and social services to host communities, and contributing to poverty alleviation.

The two key factors are community-based tourism and quality tourism. Community-based tourism ensures that a majority of the benefits go to locals and not to outsiders. Quality tourism basically offers tourists "good value for their money." This also serves as a protection of local natural resources and as an attraction to the kinds of tourists who will respect the local environment and society. All tourism should be sustainable, but the problem is that all too frequently it is not. Let's look around the world and see how the concept of sustainable tourism is applied.

Europe has been criticized for lack of sustainability, but apart from the congested areas of, for example, London, Rome, and Paris, there are plenty of destinations focusing on sustainable tourism. In particular, tours to explore the ancient ruins, architecture, and cultures of Turkey and Greece are a popular choice. Also, the largely untouched nature and distinctive culture of the Scandinavian countries are growing in recognition and importance.

If you want to explore Asia, join an ecotour to the snow-capped Himalayas in Nepal or the sultry jungles of Thailand. More and more places, such as Malaysia, Thailand, and the Philippines, are developing their tourism programs based on environmental conservation and protection. Looking for Shangri-la? The former hidden kingdom of the Hunza Valley in Pakistan has been opened for ecotourism, allowing a select number of tourists to see the 700-year-old Hunza Fort and village. The project has been internationally acclaimed as an outstanding example of sustainable tourism.

More adventures await you in Africa, where the tourism industry, especially ecotourism, has been growing tremendously over the past years. The most popular activity is the safari, which lets you get up close and personal with exotic wildlife such as elephants, gazelles, lions, tigers, cheetahs, and countless others. Kenya is an important destination for safaris, as are Tanzania, South Africa, Botswana, and Malawi.

Australia is home to an impressive variety of eco-friendly places. The Great Barrier Reef is perhaps the most famous spot. The "Leave No Trace" program, originally an American initiative, ensures that visitors to the reef act in a responsible manner. As a visitor to the Great Barrier Reef, you can enjoy activities such as snorkeling, fishing, diving, hiking, camping, and much more with many certified eco-friendly companies. Also, the massive glaciers of Antarctica are subject to increasing interest and attention. These days, many regions of the world are designating their attractions as ecotourism sites. Vacationers are becoming more adventurous and are visiting remote, exotic places. They are participating in activities that hopefully affect nature, host communities, as well as themselves, in a positive manner.

From Yellowstone National Park in the United States to the Mayan Ruins of Tikal in Guatemala; from the Amazon River in Brazil to the vast safari lands of Kenya; from the snow-capped Himalayas in Nepal to the sultry jungles of Thailand; from the Great Barrier Reef in Australia to the massive ice glaciers in Antarctica, it seems that sustainable tourism is taking place in all corners of the world. Quite frankly, some sort of ecotourism activity is happening in almost every country.

Other Great Ways to Be a Sustainable Tourist [26]

Being a travel and tourism student, we assume that you love to travel. However, as we explored earlier in this chapter, different people have different motivations for traveling, and therefore different perspectives on how to behave when on a trip. Because of the huge differences between destinations in terms of cultural, natural, and other resources, there is really no universal best way to behave when traveling. The proper way to behave and ensure sustainability when traveling in Thailand will obviously not be the same as when visiting Uzbekistan, Albania, Swaziland, Suriname, or England.

Many destinations suffer from the number of tourists that flock in, whether it be in terms of environmental or cultural damage and change. For example, much of the coastline in southern Spain has been taken over by resort development functioning as a home away from home for several European charter tourists. Thailand has been on almost every backpacker's itinerary for decades and is just now beginning to do something about the damage that has resulted from overuse. In many countries, tourists are being attacked by angry locals who are fed up with foreigners' "ego-tours" and disrespect for their place and customs. These are some of the results of *un*sustainable travel.

So, let's give a thought to the future of tourism. Think about the coming generations, your own retirement travel plans, and your kids' opportunity to see the world. *You* might not be able to do the travel you want in the way that you want if *we* don't make travel and tourism sustainable *now*. Sustainable tourism should be the natural choice for anyone that cares about the world and the future. Check out these pointers to see if your travels are moving in the right direction toward sustainability:

Are you a **TRAVELER**?

T means **Tolerance** for the people you have the privilege of meeting.

R means **Respect** for local culture and customs.

A means **Adventure** of a lifetime, not doing enough damage for a lifetime.

V means **Viability** of your actions in the long term.

E means **Endorsement** of local businesses, not large corporations.

L means **Learning** about the culture of your hosts, not just about their beer selection.

E means **Environmental** consideration, awareness, and responsibility.

R means **Representing** your own country in the best possible way.

Cultural, Heritage, Nature, and Volunteer Tourism

Tourism has developed to the point that there are now several special-interest areas. *Culture* and *heritage* are "our legacies from the past, what we live with today, and what we pass on to future generations. Our cultures and natural heritages are irreplaceable sources of life and inspiration." The **United Nations Educational, Scientific, and Cultural Organization (UNESCO)** has designated a number of World Heritage Sites worthy of protection and preservation because of the outstanding value to humanity of this natural and cultural heritage. There are nineteen U.S. sites on the World Heritage List, among them the Statue of Liberty and the Grand Canyon. Other places as unique and diverse as the wilds of East Africa's Serengeti, the pyramids of Egypt, the Great Barrier Reef in Australia, and the Baroque cathedrals of Latin America are also on the list. What makes the concept of world heritage exceptional is its universal application. World Heritage Sites belong to all the peoples of the world, no matter where they call home.[28]

Various examples of cultural heritage tourism, nature tourism, and volunteer tourism are as follows:

Cultural tourism. These trips are motivated by interest in cultural events such as feasts or festivals or activities such as theater, history, arts and sciences, museums, architecture, and religion. An example of **cultural tourism** is a visit to the Polynesian Center in Hawaii where you will find information on and examples of the lifestyles, songs, dance, costumes, and architecture of seven Pacific islands: Fiji, New Zealand, Marquesas, Samoa, Tahiti Tonga, and Hawaii.

Heritage tourism. This type of tourism is motivated by historic preservation—a combination of the natural, cultural, and architectural environment. An example of heritage tourism is a visit to the Alamo in Texas, a former battle-field that attracts 3 million visitors a year.

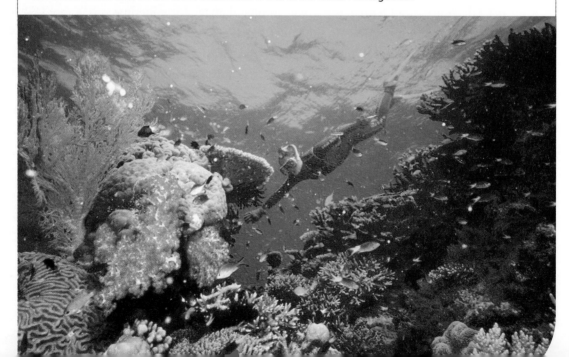

The Great Barrier Reef off the coast of Australia is one of the World Heritage sites

Nature tourism. These trips are motivated by nature, such as a visit to a national park. In recent years, aging baby boomers have increasingly become interested in nature tourism and include nature attractions as a part of or a reason for their trip. (Notice that there are some similarities among these tourism areas of special interest.)

Culinary tourism. Gastronomic tours of Europe and Asia in places like Florence, Italy, and Bangkok, Thailand, have an appeal to the "foodies" among us. If not the main reason for a trip, culinary adventures are certainly a contributing reason, and the appeal is growing stronger with the advent of such programs as Anthony Bourdain's "No Reservations."

Volunteer tourism. Dr. Stephen Wearing of the University of Technology in Sidney, Australia, and author of a book on **volunteer tourism** says:

> *One of the major attractions for those who volunteer for overseas aid projects is the opportunity to travel safely and cheaply. While volunteers provide material benefits for the host community in exchange for shelter, both have the opportunity to experience each other's cultural difference.*
>
> *Dr. Wearing believes volunteer tourism will rival the popularity of ecotourism this decade.*
>
> *College students, business people, and retirees are volunteering their time and expertise to help as volunturists. They go to both developing and developed countries, wherever they can be of assistance to a particular cause. Some people choose a vacation that suits their interests by contacting the Earthwatch Institute and joining with scientists on a range of projects.*[29]

Trends in Tourism and Travel

- Ecotourism, sustainable tourism, and heritage tourism will continue to grow in importance.

- Globally, the number of tourist arrivals will continue to increase by about 4 percent per year, topping 1 billion by 2010.

- Governments will increasingly recognize the importance of tourism not only as an economic force, but also as a social-cultural force of growing significance.

- More bilateral treaties are being signed, which will make it easier for tourists to obtain visas to visit other countries.

- The promotion and development of tourism will move even more from the public sector (government) to the private sector (involved industry segments).

- Technology will continue to advance, allowing even more information to be available more quickly to more places around the world.

- Marketing partnerships and corporate alliances will continue to increase.
- Employment prospects will continue to improve.
- Ticketless air travel will continue to increase.
- Travel and tourism bookings via the Internet will continue to increase rapidly.
- As an ever-increasing number of tourists visit destinations, managing these destinations will continue to be a challenge.
- Low-cost, no-frills airlines, such as Jet Blue, ATA, Ted (as in United), and, of course, Southwest, will continue to gain an increased market share at the expense of the six main U.S. airlines.
- Airlines will try to entice travelers to book their trips via the airline's web site rather than through Expedia and similar sites.
- Automatic airport check-ins will become more popular.
- The cruise industry will continue to expand.
- There will be more alternative cruises.
- There will be increased concern for the health and safety of travel and tourism.
- Nature, culinary, and volunteer tourism will continue to increase.

CASE STUDY

Congratulations! You have just been appointed to your city's council. You discover that a hot topic soon to be presented to the council is the construction of a convention center. Your initial research shows that several midsized cities are considering the convention center as a way to increase economic activity, including job creation. The challenge these cities face is how to finance the convention center; projected costs are $100 million. Voters may resist a ballot to increase local taxes (either property or sales), but there is still the transient occupancy tax (TOT)—that is, taxes paid by people staying in local hotels—to consider. However, that tax is already earmarked for various local charities, and as we all know, good politicians want to get reelected, so voting against several worthy causes would not be popular. How can the center be financed and built? The city could float a bond on the market or could raise the TOT, but that might dissuade some groups from coming to your city because other cities have lower TOTs.

What would you do? What information do you need to decide whether to support or oppose the convention center?

Summary

1. Tourism can be defined as the idea of attracting, accommodating, and pleasing groups or individuals traveling for pleasure or business. It is categorized by geography, ownership, function, industry, and travel motive.

2. Tourism involves international interaction and, therefore, government regulation. Several organizations, such as the World Tourism Organization, promote environmental protection, tourism development, immigration, and cultural and social aspects of tourism.

3. Tourism is a collection of industries that, when combined, form the world's largest industry and employer. It affects other industry sectors, such as public transportation, foodservice, lodging, entertainment, and recreation. In addition, tourism produces secondary impacts on businesses that are affected indirectly, which is known as the multiplier effect.

4. Travel agencies, tour operators, travel managers, wholesalers, national offices of tourism, and destination management companies serve as middlepersons between a country and its visitors.

5. Physical needs, the desire to experience other cultures, and an interest in meeting new people

are some of the motives of travelers. Because of flexible work hours, early retirement, and the easy accessibility of traveling, tourism is constantly growing.

6. From a social and cultural perspective, tourism can further international understanding and economically improve poorer countries. However, it can also disturb a culture by presenting it with mass tourism, and the destruction of natural sites. A trend in avoiding tourism pollution is ecotourism.

7. Business travel has increased in recent years as a result of the growth of convention centers in several cities. As a result, business travelers have given a boost to hotels, restaurants, and auto rental companies. The number of female business travelers is rising as well.

8. Ecotourism is tourism with a conscience, or responsible travel to natural areas that conserves the environment and improves the well-being of the local people.

9. The concept of sustainable tourism places a broad-based obligation on society, especially those involved with tourism policy, planning, and development.

Key Words and Concepts

business travel
convention and visitors bureaus
cultural tourism
ecotourism
hub-and-spoke system
interdependency
leisure/pleasure travel
load factor

multiplier effect
Pacific Area Travel Association (PATA)
sustainable tourism
tourism
United Nations Educational, Scientific, and Cultural Organization (UNESCO)

vacation package
volunteer tourism
World Tourism Organization (WTO)

Review Questions

1. Look at Chapter 2 material on the Companion Website. What career opportunities does Virginia Haley describe?
2. On the Companion Website, what suggestions does Virginia Haley have for students?
3. Give a broad definition of tourism and explain why people are motivated to travel.
4. Give a brief explanation of the economic impact of tourism. Name two organizations that influence or further the economic impact of tourism.
5. Choose a career in the tourism business and give a brief overview of what your responsibilities would be.
6. Discuss the positive and negative impacts that tourism can have on a country in relation to tourism pollution and ecotourism.

Internet Exercises

1. Organization: **World Tourism Organization**
   Web site: **www.world-tourism.org/**
   Summary: The WTO is the only intergovernmental organization that serves in the field of travel and tourism and is a global forum for tourism policy and issues. It has about 138 member countries and territories. Its mission is to promote and develop tourism as a significant means of fostering international peace and understanding, economic development, and international trade.
   (a) How much is spent on international tourism?
   (b) What does the *Tourism: 2020 Vision* predict?
2. Organization: **World Travel and Tourism Council**
   Web site: **www.wttc.org**
   Summary: The World Travel and Tourism Council is the forum for business leaders in the travel and tourism industry. With chief executives of some 100 of the world's leading travel and tourism companies as its members, WTTC has a unique mandate and overview on all matters related to travel and tourism.
   (a) What is your opinion of the "Blueprint for New Tourism"?

Apply Your Knowledge

1. Analyze your family's and friends' recent or upcoming travel plans and compare them to the examples in the text for reasons why people travel.
2. Suggest some ecotourism activities for your community.
3. How would you promote or improve tourism in your community?
4. Answer the sample test questions on the Companion Website.

Suggested Activities

1. Go online and get prices for an airline round trip ticket between two cities for a flight that is:
   a. More than 60 days out
   b. 30–59 days out
   c. 15–29 days out
   d. 7–14 days out
   e. for tomorrow
2. Compare the prices and share the results with your class.
3. Read and comment on the career advice contained on the Companion Website.

Endnotes

1. www.world_tourism.org
2. Ethics in Tourism, "Background," www.unwto.org/code_ethics/eng/global.htm.
3. www.wttc.org
4. World Tourism Organization. "About the World Tourism Organization (UNWTO-OMT)," www.world-tourism.org/aboutwto/eng/menu.html.
5. Charles R. Goeldner and J. R. Brent Ritchie, *Tourism: Principles and Practices*, 9th ed. (New York: John Wiley and Sons, 2003), 42–48.
6. Goeldner and Ritchie, *Tourism: Principles and Practices*, 43.
7. Goeldner and Ritchie, *Tourism: Principles and Practices*, 43.
8. Donald E. Lundberg, *The Tourist Business*, 6th ed. (New York: Van Nostrand Reinhold, 1990), 16.
9. Lundberg, *Tourist Business*, 17.
10. http://ancienthistory.about.com/cs/olympics/a/aa021798.htm
11. www.silk-road.com/art/marcopolo.html
12. Ibid.
13. "Boeing Unveils Ambitious 787 Dreamliner Passenger Jet," *Philippine Star*, July 10, 2007, B8.
14. "Boeing Unveils Ambitious 787 Dreamliner," B8.
15. Salary.com, "Salary Wizard," www.salary.com/.
16. Princess Cruises, "Diamond Princess," www.princess.com/learn/ships/di/index.html. and www.cruisecritic.com/reviews/review.cfm?shipID=296
17. www.cruising.org/press/overview%202006/2.cfm
18. www.wttc.org/economic_research/kystats.htm
19. www.world_tourism.org/market_research/facts
20. Personal conversation with Dr. D.Chang, September 27, 2007. http://tia.org/pubs/pubs.asp?publicationID=33
21. http://ntaonline.com
22. Personal correspondence with Karen Smith and Claudia Green, June 28, 2005.
23. Personal correspondence with Karen Smith and Claudia Green, June 28, 2005.
24. Personal conversation with Dr. Greg A. Dunn September 14, 2007
25. www.ecotourism.org/webmodules/webartidosnet/templates/eco_template.aspx?articleid=95&zoneid=2
26. This section is from http://uneptie.org/pc/tourism/sus-tourism/home.htm
27. Personal correspondence with Edward Inskeep, June 4, 2007.
28. United Nations Educational, Scientific, and Cultural Organization, "World Heritage," whc.unesco.org/en/about.
29. www.uts.edu.au/new/releases/2002/January/22.html

PART II

Lodging

CHAPTER 3

The Hotel Business

OBJECTIVES

After reading and studying this chapter, you should be able to:

- Describe hotel ownership and development via hotel franchising and management contracts.

- Classify hotels by type, location, and price.

- Discuss the concept and growth of vacation ownership.

- Name some prestigious and unusual hotels.

Hotel Development and Ownership

Franchising and management contracts are the two main driving forces in the development and operation of the hotel business. After the potential of franchising caught on, there was no stopping American ingenuity. In about a half century, the hotel business was changed forever, and here is how it happened.

Franchising

Franchising in the hospitality industry is a concept that allows a company to expand more rapidly by using other people's money than if it had to acquire its own financing. The company or franchisor grants certain rights to the franchise, for example, the rights to use its trademark, signs, proven operating systems, operating procedures and possibly reservations system, marketing know-how, purchasing discounts, and so on, for a fee. In return, the franchisee agrees by signing the franchise contract to operate the restaurant, hotel, or franchised outlet, in accordance with the guidelines set by the franchisor. Franchising is a way of doing business that benefits both the franchisor—who wants to expand the business rapidly—and the franchisee—who has financial backing but lacks specific expertise and recognition. Some corporations franchise by individual outlets and others franchise by territory. North America is host to more than 180 hotel brand extensions and franchised hotel brands.

Franchising hotels in the United States began in 1907, when the Ritz Development Company franchised the Ritz-Carlton name in New York City.[1] Howard Johnson began franchising his hotels in 1927. This allowed for rapid expansion, first on the East Coast and later in the Midwest and finally, in the mid-1960s, into California. Today, there are more than 900 restaurants in the chain.

Holiday Inns (now a part of InterContinental Hotels Group, one of the largest lodging enterprises in the world) also grew by the strategy of franchising. In 1952, Kemmons Wilson, a developer, had a disappointing experience while on a family vacation when he had to pay for an extra room for his children. Therefore, Wilson decided to build a moderately priced family-style hotel. Each room was comfortably sized and had two double beds; this enabled children to stay for free in their parents' rooms. In the 1950s and early 1960s, as the economy grew, Holiday Inns grew in size and popularity. Holiday Inns eventually added restaurants, meeting rooms, and recreational facilities. They upgraded the furnishings and fixtures in the bedrooms and almost completely abandoned the original concept of being a moderately priced lodging operation.

One of the key factors in the successful development of Holiday Corporation was that they were one of the first companies to enter the midprice range of the market. These inns, or motor hotels, were often located away from the expensive downtown sites, near important freeway intersections and the more reasonably priced suburbs. Another reason for their success was the value they offered: comfort at a reasonable price, avoiding the expensive trimmings of luxury hotels.

About this time, a new group of budget motels emerged. Motel 6 (so named because the original cost of a room was $6 a night) in California slowly spread across the country, as did Days Inn and others. Cecil B. Day was in the construction business and found Holiday Inns too expensive when traveling on vacation with his family. He bought cheap land and constructed buildings of no more than two stories to keep the costs down. These hotels and motels, primarily for commercial travelers and vacationing families, were located close to major highways and were built to provide low-cost lodging without frills. Some of these buildings were modular constructions. Entire rooms were built elsewhere, transported to the site, and placed side by side.

It was not until the 1960s that Hilton and Sheraton began to franchise their names. Franchising was the primary growth and development strategy of hotels and motels during the 1960s, 1970s, and 1980s. However, franchising presents two major challenges for the franchisor: maintenance of quality standards and avoidance of financial failure on the part of the franchisee.

The Colorful Hotel Indigo Lobby, a Franchised Hotel InterContinental Concept

It is difficult for the franchise company to state in writing all the contingencies that will ensure that quality standards are met. Recent franchise agreements are more specific in terms of the exterior maintenance and guest service levels. Franchise fees vary according to the agreements worked out between the franchisor and the franchisee; however, an average agreement is based on 3 or 4 percent of room revenue.

The world's largest franchisor of hotels, with 5,200 hotels, is Wyndham Worldwide of Parsippany, New Jersey. Choice Hotels International, ranked second with 4,545 franchised hotels, is a subsidiary of the Blackstone Group that now owns Hilton. InterContinental Hotels and Resorts is now the third largest franchisor with 3,200 hotels. Figure 3–1 shows franchised hotels among the top ten corporate chains. Interestingly, in February 2007, Four Seasons Hotels. agreed to a takeover by a group that included Bill Gates's Cascade Investments, and Saudi Prince Alwaleed bin Talal.

Franchising provides both benefits and drawbacks to the franchisee and franchisor. The benefits to the franchisee are as follows:

- A set of plans and specifications from which to build
- National advertising
- Centralized reservation system
- Participation in volume discounts for purchasing furnishings, fixtures, and equipment
- Listing in the franchisor's directory
- Low fee percentage charged by credit card companies

The drawbacks to the franchisee are as follows:

- Franchisees must pay high fees, both to join and ongoing.
- Central reservations generally produces between 17 and 26 percent of reservations.
- Franchisees must conform to the franchisor's agreement.
- Franchisees must maintain all standards set by the franchisor.

Company	Number of Guest Rooms	Hotels Franchised	Total Hotels
InterContinental Hotels Group (Intercontinental Hotels & Resorts, Crowne Plaza Hotels & Resorts, Hotel Indigo, Holiday Inn Hotels & Resorts, Holiday Inn Express, Staybridge Suites, Candlewood Suites)	556,000	3,158	3,700
Wyndham Worldwide [formerly Cendant] (Super 8, Days Inn, Ramada, Wyndham Hotels & Resorts, Baymont Inn & Suites, Wingate Inn, Travelodge, Howard Johnson, AmeriHost Inn, Knights Inn)	543,000	6,000	6,344
Marriot International (Marriot Hotels & Resorts, JW Marriot Hotels & Resorts, Renaissance Hotels & Resorts, Courtyard, Residence Inn, Fairfield Inn, Marriot Conference Centers, TownePlace Suites, SpringHill Suites, The Ritz-Carlton Hotel Company LLC)	513,832	1,700	2,832
Hilton Hotels Corporation (Conrad, Doubletree, Embassy Suites, Hampton Hotels, Hilton, Hilton Garden Inn, Homewood Suites, Scandic, Waldorf-Astoria Collection)	495,000	2,134	2,817
Choice Hotels International (Comfort Inn, Comfort Suites, Quality, Sleep Inn, Clarion, Cambria Suites, MainStay Suites, Econo Lodge, Rodeway Inn, Suburban Extended Stay Hotel)	437,385	5,376	5,897
Accor (Sofitel, Red Roof Inn, Motel 6, Studio 6, Novotel, Suitehotel, Ibis, Etap)	475,433	1,000	4,000
Best Western International	316,095	0	4,200
Starwood Hotels & Resorts Worldwide (St. Regis, The Luxury Collection, Sheraton, Westin, Four Points by Sheraton, Le Meridien, W Hotels, aloft)	258,000	337	850
Carlson Hospitality Worldwide (Regent Hotels & Resorts, Radisson Hotels & Resorts, Park Plaza Hotels & Resorts, Country Inns & Suites by Carlson, Park Inn Hotels)	147,129	518	938
Global Hyatt Corporation (Hyatt Hotels & Resorts, Hyatt Place, Hyatt Summerfield Suites, Park Hyatt, Grand Hyatt, Hyatt Regency)	134,296		731

Figure 3–1 • Franchised Hotels among the Top Ten Largest Corporate Chains.

Sources: Karyn Strauss and Mary Scoviak, "Hotels 325," *Hotels*, July 2006, www.hotelsmag.com/archives/2006/07/sr/; Lodging Hospitality, "Top Brands," March 2007, www.ehonline.com/article/16515; company web sites.

The benefits to the franchise company are as follows:

- Increased market share and recognition
- Up-front fees

The drawbacks to the franchise company are as follows:

- The need to be very careful in the selection of franchisees
- Difficulty in maintaining control of standards

Franchising continues to be a popular form of expansion both in North America and the rest of the world. However, there are always a few properties that lose their right to franchise by not maintaining standards.

Is There a Franchise in Your Future?[2]

Many of you may not realize the pervasiveness of franchised operations in the United States. Predictions are that more than 50 percent of all retail sales in the United States (including restaurants) will soon be transacted through franchised units. Further, franchises are available not only in the hotel, restaurant, travel, and recreation industries, but also in a large variety of other businesses that might interest you. These businesses include automotive tires and parts, retailing of all kinds, mail and copy services, janitorial and decorating services, personnel agencies, and so on. Today, many franchises can be operated from home by those interested in lifestyle changes.

If you end up working for a hospitality-related organization after graduation, chances are that your career will be influenced by franchising. You may work directly for a franchisor (the company that sells a franchised concept to an entrepreneur), whether on the corporate staff (e.g., training, franchise consulting) or in an operations position in a franchisor-owned unit. Many franchisors own their own units to test new operational or marketing ideas and to demonstrate the viability of the business to potential franchisees (the entrepreneurs who buy the franchised unit).

Alternatively, you may work for a franchisee. Some franchisees are small businesses, owning only one or a few units. Other franchisees are large corporations, owning hundreds of units and doing hundreds of millions of dollars in sales every year. For instance, RTM, Inc., owns and operates more than 600 Arby's restaurants. Additionally, it owns and franchises two midsized chicken restaurants, Lee's Famous Recipe Chicken and Mrs. Winner's Chicken and Biscuits. Working for a company as large as RTM would be similar to working for a large franchisor.

A third way that franchising may involve you is through ownership. Rather than starting your own independent business after college, you may want to consider buying a franchise. Several advantages can result. First, by working with a larger company you get the benefits of its experience in running the business that you have chosen to enter. Many of the mistakes that a new entrepreneur may make have already been overcome by your franchisor. The company might provide cash flow. The company might also provide other support services at little or no cost, such as marketing and advertising, site selection, construction plans,

CORPORATE PROFILE

Avis Budget (formerly Cendant) Group

The Avis Budget Group (formerly Cendant) is an empire consisting of businesses and brands under three major names: Wyndham Worldwide, Realogy (the real estate branch) and Avis Budget, (Avis Rent a Car and Budget Rent a Car vehicle rental). Included under Wyndham Worldwide are Wyndham, Days Inn, Howard Johnson, Ramada, Knights Inn, Super 8, Travelodge, Villager Lodges and Wingate Inn totaling 539,000 rooms. Realogy includes Century 21, ERA (Electronic Realty Associates), Coldwell Banker, Avis Rent A Car, and PHH Corp. Combined, these businesses account for approximately half a million hotel rooms in the United States, Canada, Latin America, and Europe, and more than 11,500 franchised real estate offices with more than 190,000 brokers in the United States, Mexico, Canada, Puerto Rico, Europe, Africa, and the Asia-Pacific region.

Although clearly in the consumer services industry, its clients include other businesses and corporations—not individual consumers. As a franchisor, the company licenses the owners and operators of independent businesses to use Cendant's brand names, without taking on big business risks and expenses. Cendant does not operate hotels or real estate brokerage offices, but instead provides coordination and services that allow franchisees to retain local control of their activities. At the same time, they benefit from the economies of scale of widely promoted brand names and well-established standards of service, national and regional direct marketing, co-marketing programs, and volume purchasing discounts. All brands share "extensive market research, use well-developed technology, such as proprietary reservation systems and, in the case of lodging, a room inventory tracking system, which is extremely technology intensive and eliminates waste."[1] By monitoring quality control and extensively promoting the brand names, Cendant offers its independent franchise owners franchise fees that are relatively low compared to the increased profitability they gain.

Through franchising, the company limits its own risks and is able to keep overhead costs low. Chief Financial Officer Michael P. Monaco says the company "limits the volatility in the business as best as we can because fees come from revenue, not the franchisee's profitability.[2] A further advantage of being a franchiser of such dimension is that the company is even more protected from the cyclical nature of the economy than are other franchise ventures.

The critical mass created by all the businesses working together makes it more valuable as a whole than as the sum of its parts, gives it outstanding purchasing power and market control, and makes it extremely effective in selling to a wide audience.

The wave of baby boomers consists of 76 million people who are soon to retire, and this trend will continue for a few more years. This clientele consumes primarily two things: travel and residential real estate. In light of this trend, diversification from the hotel market into real estate, mortgage companies, and timeshare operators makes sense.

The synergy of Cendant is realized by providing travel, accommodation, and related services.[3] Services such as Cheap Tickets, Lodging.com, Rates To Go, HotelClub.com, Cendant Travel and Galileo, a travel distribution service are used by 44,000 travel agencies. WizCom supplies its customers with electronic distribution and e-commerce solutions for Internet global distribution services (GDS's) and other travel reservations systems, offering the industry's first switching service. WizCom enables global distribution systems and Internet connectivity, as well as central reservations (CRS) and information services to the hotels, car rental, and tour industries.[4]

[1]Todd Pitock, "The Artful Acquirer," *Journal of Business Strategy* 18, no. 2, (March/April 1997): 19.

[2]Pitock, "Artful Acquirer," 19.

[3]Personal conversation with Kenneth E. Crocker, March 14, 2004.

[4]Cendant, "Cendant," www.cendant.com/about-cendant/travel_distribution.services/supplier-seminars.html.

[handwritten margin notes: 4 expectations may not be met. b) freedom restricted. A) must conform. b) franchisor not doing well.]

assistance with financing, and so on. All this assistance leads to a second key reason for buying a franchise—reducing your risk of failure. Franchising is probably less risky than is starting your own business from scratch.

Consider the following factors that many franchisors seek. Are you strongly motivated to succeed and do you have a past history of business success, even if it is in a different business? Do you have a significant sum of money as well as access to credit? Are you willing to accept the franchisor's values, philosophy, and ways of doing business, as well as its technical assistance? Do you have the full support of your immediate family as you develop your business? Are you willing to devote substantially all of your working time to the business?

Franchising does have some disadvantages, as noted by many former franchisees. Your expectations of success may not be met. Perhaps the business did not have the potential that you expected, or perhaps you were not willing to invest the time needed. In a few cases, an overzealous or dishonest franchisor representative has misled franchisees.

As a franchisee, your freedom is somewhat restricted. You must operate within the constraints set out by your franchise agreement and the operational standards manual. Although there may be some room for you to express your creativity and innovation, it is generally limited. This may mean that, over time, the work might become monotonous and unchallenging, yet you have a long-term commitment to the company because of the franchise agreement that you signed. Your failure to consistently follow the franchisor's methods for running the business could result in the termination of your contract and your forced removal from the business.

Finally, the franchisor may not be performing well, thereby hurting your local business. Also, they may allow other franchisees to open units so near to your operation that your business is adversely affected.

Buying a franchise can be a very rewarding business experience in many ways. But like any other business venture, it requires research and a full discussion with family, friends, and business advisors, such as your accountant and attorney. You should carefully weigh whether or not you are psychologically suited to be a franchisee. Perhaps you perform more effectively in a corporate structure as an employee. Perhaps you are better suited to starting your own business from scratch. A careful analysis can help you make an informed decision. Buying a franchise such as Subway, Cold Stone Creamery, or Sea Master cruises is a lot cheaper—as in a few thousand dollars—compared to one million-plus for a hotel or even a McDonald's. A key question to

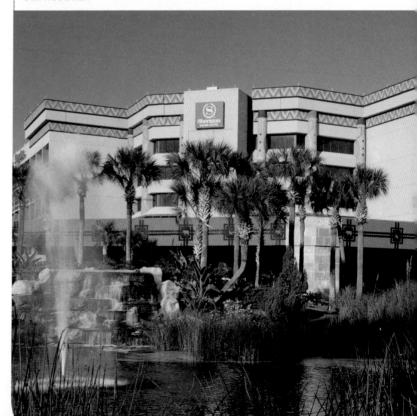

The Sheraton Safari Hotel and Resort, Orlando, Florida, is a part of the Starwood REIT

Independent hotels join the association for a fee & they have central res.

be answered before you buy a franchise is whether you are better suited to being a franchisee or an independent entrepreneur.

Referral Associations

Referral associations offer similar benefits to properties as do franchises, albeit at a lower cost. Hotels and motels with a referral association share a centralized reservation system and a common image, logo, or advertising slogan. In addition, referrals may offer group buying discounts to members, as well as management training and continuing education programs. Each independent hotel refers guests to each of the other member hotels. Hotels and motels pay an initial fee to join a referral association. Size and appearance standards are less stringent than those in a franchise agreement; hence, guests may find more variation between the facilities than between franchise members.

Preferred Hotels and Resorts Worldwide is a consortium of 105 independent, luxury hotels and resorts united to compete with the marketing power of chain operations. It promotes the individuality, high standards, hospitality, and luxury of member hotels. It also provides marketing support services and a reservation center.

With the decrease in airline commissions, referral organizations, especially those at the luxury end of the market, are well placed to offer incentives to agents to book clients with the referral group's hotels. An example is awarding trips to the property for every ten rooms booked. Another is when the referral hotels offer, for instance, a 20 percent commission to travel agents during slow periods. Three luxury Boston-area preferred properties—the Boston Harbor Hotel, the Bostonian Hotel, and the Charles Hotel in Cambridge, Massachusetts—joined in promoting a St. Patrick's Day weekend package. Preferred Hotels in Texas—the Mansion on Turtle Creek and Hotel Crescent Court in Dallas, La Mansion Del Rio South in San Antonio, and the Washington Hotel in Fort Worth—launched a major, year-long promotion that includes a tie-in with major retail, credit card, and airline partners.

In addition to regional marketing programs, the referral associations that handle reservations for members have joined Galileo International's Inside Availability Service. This gives agents access to actual rates and room availability that is not always available information on the standard central reservation system (CRS) databases.

Leading Hotels of the World (LHW) was set up in 1928 as Luxury Hotels of Europe and Egypt by 38 hotels, including the London Savoy; the Hotel Royal in Evian, France; and the Hotel Negresco in Nice, France; each was interested in improving its marketing. The organization worked by having hotels advise their guests to use the establishments of fellow members. It then opened a New York office to make direct contact with wealthy American and Canadian travelers wishing to visit Europe and Egypt.

LHW, which is controlled by its European members, acts as an important marketing machine for its members, especially now, with offices around the world providing reservations, sales, and promotional services. All the hotels and offices are connected by a central computer reservation system called ResStar. The number of reservations members receive from Leading Hotel members varies from place to place, but with more than 100 hotels waiting to join, it must be beneficial.

Like LHW, Small Luxury Hotels of the World (SLH) is another marketing consortium in which seventy-nine independently owned and managed hotels and resorts are members. For more than thirty-five years, it has sought to market and sell its membership to the travel industry and to provide an interhotel networking system for all members. Each hotel is assessed and regularly checked to ensure that it maintains the very highest standards.

Management Contracts

Management contracts have been responsible for the hotel industry's rapid boom since the 1970s. They became popular among hotel corporations because little or no up-front financing or equity is involved. Hotel management companies often form a partnership of convenience with developers and owners who generally do not have the desire or ability to operate the hotel. The management company provides operational expertise, marketing, and sales clout, often in the form of a centralized reservation system (CRS). Some companies manage a portfolio of properties on a cluster, regional, or national basis. Even if the hotel corporation is involved in the construction of the hotel, ownership generally reverts to a large insurance company or other large corporation. This was the case with the La Jolla, California, Marriott Hotel. Marriott Corporation built the hotel for about $34 million, and then sold it to Paine Webber, a major investment-banking firm, for about $52 million on completion. Not a bad return on investment!

The management contract usually allows for the hotel company to manage the property for a period of five, ten, or twenty years. For this, the company receives as a management fee, often a percentage of gross and/or net operating profit, usually about 2 to 4.5 percent of gross revenues. Lower fees in the 2 percent range are more prevalent today, with an increase in the incentive fee based on profitability. Some contracts begin at 2 percent for the first year, increase to 2.5 the second, and 3.5 the third and for the remainder of the contract.[3] Today, many contracts are for a percentage of sales and a percentage of operating profit. This is normally 2 + 2 percent. Increased competition among management companies has decreased the management contract fees in the past few years. In recent years, hotel companies increasingly have opted for management contracts because considerably less capital is tied up in managing as compared with owning properties. This has allowed for a more rapid expansion of both the U.S. and international markets. The ten largest management companies are listed in Figure 3–2.

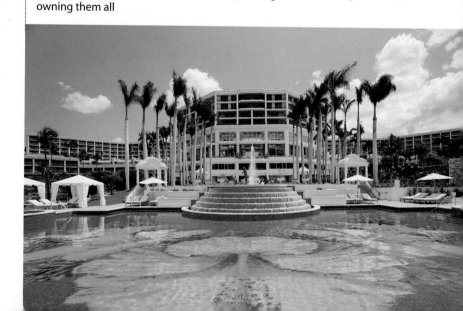

Hyatt Hotels operates some of its hotels by management contract, rather than owning them all

Company	Hotels Managed	Hotels
1. Marriott International	934	2,741
2. Accor	525	4,065
3. Extended Stay Hotels	672	672
4. Vantage Hospitality Group	610	610
5. InterContinental Hotels	504	3,606
6. Starwood Hotels and Resorts	378	845
7. Westmont Hospitality Group	360	360
8. Tharaldson Enterprises	349	349
9. Hilton Hotels	332	2,817
10. Société du Louvre (Starwood Capital Group)	321	819

Figure 3–2 • Ten Largest Management Companies.
(*Source:* Company websites.)

Recent management contracts have called for an increase in the equity commitment on the part of the management company. In addition, owners have increased their operational decision-making options to allow them more control over the property. General managers have increased responsibility to owners who also want their share of profit.

Today, hotel management companies exist in an extremely competitive environment. They have discovered that the hotel business, like most others, has changed and they are adapting accordingly. Today's hotel owners are demanding better bottom-line results and reduced fees. Management companies are seeking sustainability and a bigger share of the business. With international expansion, a hotel company entering the market might actively seek a local partner or owner to work within a form of joint venture.

▶ Check Your Knowledge

1. What main factor changed the nature of the hotel industry? What impact does it have today?
2. In your own words, define *franchising* and *management contracts*.

Real Estate Investment Trust

Real estate investment trusts (REITs) have existed since the 1960s. In those early days, they were mostly mortgage holders. But in the 1980s, they began to own property outright, often focusing on specific sectors such as hotels, office buildings, apartments, malls, and nursing homes. A REIT must have at least 75 percent of its assets in real estate. Today, about 300 REITs, with a combined market value of $70 billion, are publicly traded. Investors like them because they do not pay corporate income tax and instead are required to distribute at least 95 percent

INTRODUCING CONRAD HILTON AND HILTON HOTELS CORPORATION

"King of Innkeepers" and Master of Hotel Finance

Hilton's success was attributed to two main strategies: (1) hiring the best managers and letting them have total autonomy, and (2) being a careful bargainer who, in later years, was careful not to overextend his finances. Conrad Hilton had begun a successful career in the banking business before he embarked on what was to become one of the most successful hotel careers ever.

In 1919, while on bank business in Cisco, Texas, he bought the Mobley Hotel with an investment of $5,000. Hilton rented rooms to oil industry prospectors and construction workers. Because of high demand for accommodations and very little supply, Hilton rented rooms in eight-hour shifts, for 300 percent occupancy. On some occasions, he even rented out his own room and slept in a lobby chair.

Because Hilton knew the banking business well and had maintained contacts who would lend him money for down payments on properties, he quickly expanded to seven Texas hotels. Hilton's strategy was to borrow as much money as possible to expand as rapidly as possible. This worked well until the Great Depression of the early 1930s. Hilton was unable to meet the payments on his properties and lost several but did not declare bankruptcy.[1]

Hilton, like many great leaders, even during the Depression years had the determination to bounce back. To reduce costs, he borrowed money against his life insurance and even formed an alliance with the National Hotels Corporation.

Hilton's business and financial acumen is legendary. The *New York Times* described Conrad Hilton as "a master of finance and a cautious bargainer who was careful not to overfinance" and someone who had "a flawless sense of timing."[2]

Hilton was the first person to notice vast lobbies with people sitting in comfortable chairs but not spending any money. So, he added the lobby bar as a convenient meeting place and leased out space for gift shops and newsstands. Most of the additional revenue from these operations went directly to the bottom line. Today, Hilton Hotels Corporation includes Conrad Hotels, Doubletree, Embassy Suites Hotels, Hampton Inn and Hampton Inns & Suites, Hilton Hotels, Hilton Garden Inn, Hilton Grand Vacation, Homewood Suites by Hilton, and the Waldorf-Astoria Collection. These brands total thousands of hotels in cities all over the world, and "Be my guest" is still the gracious and warm way guests are received. There are 2,300 Hilton brand hotels today, and they are being bought by the Blackstone Group.[3]

[1]Paul R. Dittmer and Gerald G. Griffen, *The Dimensions of the Hospitality Industry: An Introduction.* (New York: Van Nostrand Reinhold, 1993), 91–92; and Conrad Hilton, *Be My Guest,* New York: Prentice Hall Press 1957, 184–199.

[2]Joan Cook, "Conrad Hilton, Founder of Hotel Chain, Dies at 92," *New York Times,* January 5, 1979, sec. 11, 5.

[3]www.hilton.com, July 30, 2007 and CNN July 12, 2007.

Source: Hospitality Industry Archives, University of Houston.

of net income to shareholders. In addition, because they trade as stocks, they are much easier to get into or out of than are limited partnerships or the direct ownership of properties. In the hotel industry, REITs are clearly where the action is. As with any investment, the investor is looking for a reasonable return on the investment. Anyone can buy stocks of REITs or other publically traded companies; first, it is wise to ensure that the company is well managed and financially sound before putting any money down. The leading REIT corporations are Patriot American Hospitality, Wyndham Hotels, and Starwood Lodging Trust.

The hip style of Hotel Indigo is a lifestyle concept hotel

New Hotel Construction

New hotels are built as a business venture by a developer, and because the developer expects to make a reasonible return on this substantial investment, a feasibility study is done to assess the viability of the project. Obviously, there needs to be a gap in the market in which a segment is currently not being served (for example, the hip, lifestyle boutique hotels such as Hotel Indigo), plus, a new hotel is expected to take some business away from existing properties if the room rates are close in price. There are two views on new hotels versus remodeled hotels as far as room rates and profits are concerned. It is often difficult for a new property to make a profit for a few years because of the higher cost of construction and the need to become known and gain a good market share. On the other hand, a remodeled hotel has the cost of remodeling to pay for plus higher operating costs for energy and maintainence, so they tend to cancel each other out.

Today, many larger hotels are developed as part of a mixed-use project. The hotel could be near or next to a convention center, business, or attraction. The hotel may also have a residential component (as in residencies if it's a Ritz Carlton or a condotel) and may include a spa.

Older hotels are generally renovated about every seven years. This is bacause they become dated and would otherwise lose market share, which equals profit. Older hotels have an advantage over new ones—or should have an advantage as a result of positive recognition in the market. Additionally, much or all of their mortgage may be paid off, so their debt service is likely easier on the cash flow than it is for a new hotel. Older hotels may have more charm, but they are more expensive to maintain. Older hotels should have built up repeat business through guest loyalty, something a new hotel has to do.

Classification of Hotels

According to the American Hotel & Lodging Association (AH&LA), the U.S. lodging industry consists of 46,000 hotels and motels, with a total of 3.3 million rooms. The gross volume of business generated from these rooms is $93.1 billion. Unlike many other countries, the United States has no formal government classification of hotels. However, the American Automobile Association (AAA) classifies hotels by diamond award, and the Mobile Travel Guide offers a five-star award.

The AAA has been inspecting and rating the nation's hotels since 1977. Less than 2 percent of the 41,000 properties inspected annually throughout the United States, Canada, and Mexico earned the five-diamond award, which is the association's highest award for excellence. In 2000, the five-diamond award was bestowed on 79 lodgings in the United States, Canada, and Mexico. Twelve of the properties received both the five-diamond and the five-star awards.

AAA uses descriptive criteria to evaluate the hotels that it rates annually in the United States, Canada, Mexico, and the Caribbean (see Figure 3–3).

	◇	◇◇	◇◇◇	◇◇◇◇	◇◇◇◇◇
General	Simple roadside appeal Limited landscaping	Average roadside appeal Some landscaping	Very good roadside appeal Attractive landscaping	Excellent roadside appeal Professionally planned landscaping	Outstanding roadside appeal Professional landscaping with a variety of foliage and stunning architecture
Lobby	Adequate size with registration, front desk, limited seating, and budget art, if any	Medium size with registration, front desk, limited seating, carpeted floors, budget art, and some plants	Spacious with front desk, carpeted seating area arranged in conversation groupings, good-quality framed art, live plants, luggage carts, and bellstation	Spacious or consistent with historical attributes; registration and front desk above average with solid wood or marble; ample seating area with conversation groupings and upscale appointments including tile, carpet, or wood floors; impressive lighting fixtures; upscale framed art and art objects; abundant live plants; background music; separate check-in/-out; bellstation	Comfortably spacious or consistent with historical attributes; registration and front desk above average; ample seating with conversation groupings and upscale appointments; impressive lighting fixtures; variety of fine art; abundant plants and fresh floral arrangements; background music; separate check-in/-out; bellstation that may be part of concierge area; concierge desk
Guestrooms	May not reflect current industry standards	Generally reflect current industry standards	Reflect current industry standards	Reflect current industry standards and provide upscale appearance	Reflect current standards and provide luxury appearance
Service	Basic attentive service	More attentive service	Upgraded service levels	High service levels and hospitality	Guests are pampered by flawless service executed by professional staff

Figure 3–3 • Summary of AAA Diamond Rating Guidelines.
(Courtesy of Hotel and Lodging Management.)

- One-diamond properties have simple roadside appeal and the basic lodging needs.
- Two-diamond properties have average roadside appeal, with some landscaping and a noticeable enhancement in interior decor.
- Three diamonds carry a degree of sophistication through higher service and comfort.
- Four diamonds have excellent roadside appeal and service levels that give guests what they need before they even ask for it.
- Five-diamond properties have the highest service levels, sophistication, and offerings.

Hotels may be classified according to location, price, and type of services offered. This allows guests to make a selection on these as well as personal criteria. Following is a list of hotel classifications:

City center. Luxury, first-class, midscale, economy, suites

Resort. Luxury, midscale, economy suites, condominium, time-share, convention

Airport. Luxury, midscale, economy, suites

Freeway. Midscale, economy suites

Casino. Luxury, midscale, economy

Full service.

Convention.

Economy.

Extended stay.

Bed and breakfast.

Alternatively, the hotel industry may be segmented according to price. Figure 3–4 gives an example of a national or major regional brand-name hotel chain in each segment.

City Center Hotels

City center hotels, by virtue of their location, meet the needs of the traveling public for business or leisure reasons. These hotels could be luxury, midscale, business, suites, economy, or residential. They offer a range of accommodations and services. Luxury hotels offer the ultimate in decor, butler service, concierge and special concierge floors, secretarial services, the latest WiFi or in-room technology, computers, fax machines, beauty salons, health spas, 24-hour room service, swimming pools, tennis courts, valet service, ticket office, airline office, car rental, and doctor/nurse on duty or on call. Generally, they offer a signature restaurant, coffee shop, or an equivalent recognized name restaurant; a lounge; a named bar; meeting and convention rooms; a ballroom; and possibly a fancy night spot. The Drake Hotel in Chicago is an example of a city center luxury hotel. An example of a midpriced hotel in New York City is the Ramada Hotel; an economy hotel is the Day's Inn; a suites property is the Embassy Suites.

Economy $49–$69	Midprice $69–$125	Upscale $125–$225	Luxury $150–$450	All-Suites $109–$225
Holiday Inn Express	Holiday Inn Fairfield Inn		Crowne Plaza	
Fairfield Inn	Courtyard Inn Residence Inn	Courtyard Inn Marriott Residence Inn	Marriott Marquis Ritz-Carlton	Marriott Suites
Days Inn		Omni	Renaissance	
EconoLodge	Radisson Inn	Radisson		Radisson Suites
Ramada Limited	Ramada Inn	Ramada		Ramada Suites
	Sheraton Inn Four Points	Sheraton	Sheraton Grande	Sheraton Suites
Sleep Inn	American Inn	Hyatt	Hyatt Regency Hyatt Park	Hyatt Suites
Comfort Inn	Quality Inn Wingate	Clarion Hotels		Quality Suites Comfort Suites
Extended Stay America	Hilton Inn	Hilton	Hilton Towers	Hilton Suites
Thrift Lodge	Doubletree Club	Doubletree		Doubletree Suites
Travelodge Hotels	Travelodge Hotels	Forte Hotels	Forte Hotels	
	Country Inn & Suites	Westin	Westin	Spring Hill Suites
Super 8	La Quinta			
	Red Roof Inn			Homewood Suites by Hilton
	Best Western			Hampton Suites
	Hampton Inn			Embassy Suites

Note: Some brands' price ranges may overlap because of location and seasonal pricing.

Figure 3–4 • Hotels by Price Segment.

Resort Hotels

Resort hotels came of age with the advent of rail travel. Increasingly, citydwellers and others had the urge to vacation in locations they found appealing. Traveling to these often more exotic locations became a part of the pleasure experience. In the late 1800s, luxury resort hotels were developed to accommodate the clientele that the railways brought. Such hotels include the famous Greenbrier at White Sulphur Springs, West Virginia; the Hotel del Coronado near San Diego, California; the Breakers in Florida; and the Homestead at Hot Springs, Virginia.

The leisure and pleasure travelers of those days were drawn by resorts, beaches, or spectacular mountain scenery. At first, many of these grand resorts were seasonal. However, as automobile and air travel made even the remote resorts more accessible and an increasing number of people could afford to visit, many resorts became year-round properties.

Resort communities sprang up in the sunshine belt from Palm Springs to Palm Beach. Some resorts focus on major sporting activities such as skiing, golf, or fishing; others offer family vacations. Further improvements in both air and automobile travel brought exotic locations within the reach of the population. Europe, the Caribbean, and Mexico became more accessible. As the years passed, some of the resorts suffered because the public's vacation plans changed.

The traditional family month-long resort vacation gave way to shorter, more frequent getaways of four to seven days. The regular resort visitors became older; in general, the younger guests preferred the mobility of the automobile and the more informal atmosphere provided by the newer and more informal resorts.

Hyatt hotels have organized a program consisting of a variety of activities for children, thereby giving parents an opportunity either to enjoy some free time on their own or join their children in fun activities. Many resort hotels began to attract conventions, conferences, and meetings so that they could maintain or increase occupancy, particularly during the low and shoulder seasons.

Guests go to resorts for leisure and recreation. They want a good climate—summer or winter—in which they can relax or engage in recreational activities. Because of the remoteness of many resorts, guests are a kind of "captured clientele," who may be on the property for days at a time. This presents resort managers with some unique operating challenges. Another operating challenge concerns seasonality: Some resorts either do not operate year-round or have periods of very low occupancy. Both present challenges in attracting, training, and retaining competent staff.

Many guests travel considerable distances to resorts. Consequently, they tend to stay longer than they do at transient hotels. This presents a challenge to the food and beverage manager to provide quality menus that are varied and are presented and served in an attractive, attentive manner. To achieve this, resorts often use a

A Ski Lodge in British Columbia

cyclical menu that repeats itself every fourteen to twenty-one days. Also, they provide a wide variety and number of dishes to stimulate interest. Menus are now more health conscious—lighter and low in saturated fats, cholesterol, salt, and calories.

The food needs to be presented in a variety of ways. Buffets are popular because they give guests the opportunity to make choices from a display of foods. Barbecues, display cooking, poolside dining, specialty restaurants, and reciprocal dining arrangements with nearby hotels give guests even more options.

With increased global competition, not only from other resorts but also from cruise lines, resort managers are challenged to both attract guests and to turn those guests into repeat business, which traditionally has been the foundation of resort viability.

To increase occupancies, resorts have diversified their marketing mix to include conventions, business meetings, sales meetings, incentive groups, sporting events, additional sporting and recreational facilities, spas, adventure tourism, ecotourism, and more.

Because guests are cocooned in the resort, they expect to be pampered. This requires an attentive, well-trained staff; hiring, training, and retaining a competent staff present a challenge in some remote areas and in developing countries.

There are a number of benefits to operating resorts. The guests are much more relaxed in comparison to those at transient hotels, and the resorts are located in scenically beautiful areas. This frequently enables staff to enjoy a better quality of life than do their transient hotel counterparts. Returning guests tend to treat associates like friends. This adds to the overall party-like atmosphere, which is prevalent at many of the established resorts.

Airport Hotels

Many airport hotels enjoy high occupancy because of the large number of travelers arriving and departing from major airports. The guest mix in airport hotels consists of business, group, and leisure travelers. Passengers with early or late flights may stay over at the airport hotel, whereas others rest while waiting for connecting flights.

Airport hotels are generally in the 200- to 600-room size and are full service. To care for the needs of guests who may still feel as if they are in different time zones, room service and restaurant hours may be extended or even offered around the clock. More moderately priced hotels have vending machines.

As competition at airport hotels intensified, some added meeting space to cater to businesspeople who want to fly in, meet, and fly out. Here, the airport hotel has the advantage of saving the guests from having to go downtown. Almost all airport hotels provide courtesy van transportation to and from the airport.

Convenient locations, economical prices, and easy and less costly transportation costs to and from the airport are some reasons why airport hotels are becoming intelligent choices for business travelers. Airport hotels can mean a bargain for groups, especially considering that the transportation to the hotel and back from the airport is usually free or is very inexpensive, says Brian Booth, director of sales and marketing at the Dallas Hyatt Regency Airport Hotel. One of the most conveniently located hotels in the country is the Miami International Airport Hotel, which is located within the airport itself.

FOCUS ON SECURITY

Hotel Security

Hank Christen, MPA, EMT, Director of Emergency Response Operations for Unconventional Concepts and consultant to the Department of Defense.

In today's world, hotel guests consider safety a prime concern. Travelers expect and demand a secure facility. Perceived threats or fears are not limited to terrorism; hotels must have an all-hazard safety and security plan that addresses crime, natural disasters, accidents, and medical emergencies.

Use these top ten aspects of hospitality safety and security as a cornerstone for an effective program.

1. An effective program has to be visible. The visibility deters threats and creates a sense of safety for guests.

2. Create and maintain a proactive, all-hazard emergency plan. Start by conducting a thorough facility security inspection and potential threat assessment. Examine past records for natural disasters at your locale. For example, hurricanes are an issue in Florida and earthquakes are a California consideration. In any location, hospitality guests may be vulnerable to theft, assault, and rape. Local emergency agencies offer invaluable planning expertise and resources at little or no cost.

3. Security must be everyone's job, not just the responsibility of management.

4. Look inside your organization for potential security problems. A thorough background check of all new employees is an essential component of security programs.

5. Recognize the risks of workplace violence. Hotels often have large staffs from culturally diverse backgrounds. Working under stress in close proximity, internal disputes can easily erupt into workplace violence. Supervisors should be trained to recognize the early precursors to these disputes and react proactively to prevent them from escalating into safety and security problems.

6. Develop a crisis response team. A major crisis is rare, but when one occurs, a crisis response team plays a significant role in minimizing consequences and repairing damage. During disasters, the team is the liaison element between the hotel and emergency first-responder agencies.

7. Every staff member must be trained and prepared for medical emergencies. Employees should be trained to recognize, report, and respond to medical incidents. Emergency plans should address responsibilities for summoning emergency medical services (EMS) and other emergency agencies.

8. Include guest education in your security plan. Provide safety and security information. Distribute security tips on brochures. Encourage guests to share their concerns with safety surveys or questionnaires. Guest education prevents many potential safety and security problems.

9. Make safety and security programs an ongoing priority. Conduct security exercises. Don't limit training to a once-a-year safety video and expect the staff to make it their personal priority. Constant emphasis reinforces the importance of staying alert and aware of security at all times.

10. Recognition and rewards create buy-in from team members. Studies show that as much as 80 percent of all behavior is determined by reward systems. Set safety and security goals and reward results for all employees.

INTRODUCING VALERIE FERGUSON

Regional Vice President of Loews Hotels

Past Chair of the American Hotel & Lodging Association and Regional Vice President of Loews Hotels

To most, "making it big" seems like a regular statement and a task easily achieved. To Valerie Ferguson, well, it comes with a lot of work, dedication, and heart. She speaks often about seizing opportunities and adding self-interest to what you do for your career.

For this African American female, life wasn't always easy. As the managing director of Loews Philadelphia Hotel and regional vice president of Loews Hotels, she has a lot to say about what got her where she is now.

One of her most important role models was her father, Sam Ferguson. She says, "My father and I had a great relationship in which he supported me, but in which he never put any images in front of me about what I should shoot for."

After high school, Valerie applied to and was accepted at the University of San Francisco, where she earned a degree in government. Eventually realizing that law wasn't where her heart was, she decided to move out to Atlanta where she got a job as a nighttime desk clerk at the Hyatt Regency. She fell in love with the hotel industry and saw it as a challenge. Soon enough, though, she realized that the challenges she was really facing were issues of race and gender. She explains, "I was raw in my approach to the business world, but I soon came to realize that it takes more than working hard. To succeed, a person must be able to proclaim his or her goals."

Her success comes from being out there and connecting with people and society. Valerie is past chair of the American Hotel & Lodging Association (AH&LA) board and still serves on the Diversity Committee. She is also past associate director of the National Restaurant Association. She is a director on the boards of the Pennsylvania Travel Council, Philadelphia Workforce Investment, Communities in Schools, and the Educational Institute.

Valerie was nominated general manager of the year for the Hyatt Hotels Corporation. Through the years, she has managed several hotels for Hyatt and Ritz-Carlton. Her outstanding work and devotion to the hospitality and lodging industry have not gone unrewarded. She was named one of the Top 100 Black Women in Corporate America by *Ebony* magazine. She was named one of the Top 100 Black Women of Influence by the Atlanta Business League Pioneers. She was also named one of the 100 Most Influential Women in Travel by *Travel Agent* magazine. Other honorary awards for her work in the lodging industry were the 1998 National Association for the Advancement of Colored People (NAACP) Southeast Region Trailblazer Award for Business, the Martin Luther King Jr. Drum Major for Justice Award from Coretta Scott King and the Women of the Southern Christian Leadership Conference (SCLC). Ed Rabin, executive vice president of Hyatt and an early Ferguson mentor, says, "From the get-go, she demonstrated an ability and willingness to understand and learn the business and win over guests, colleagues, and peers in the process."

When Loews was being opened, Valerie was thrilled with the adventure of being with a still-growing company. President and CEO of Loews Jonathan Tisch became a close friend as they served together on the board of the American Hotel and Lodging Association (AHLA). In 1994, Valerie ran for a seat on the AHLA's executive committee and eventually succeeded Tisch as chair. She was the first African American and second woman to serve as AHLA chair.

She comments on the hospitality industry, "The hospitality industry is one of the last vestiges of the American dream, where you can enter from very humble beginnings and end up a success." The great relationship she has with people has been a great contribution to her well-deserved success.

Ferguson has come a long way in her career. She is proud of what she is doing and doesn't believe that she has stopped climbing the ladder of success. She is fighting to make other women and minority members realize that there is a whole world of opportunities out there and they should set their goals high. She believes that equality of opportunity "should not come as the result of a mandate of the federal government or as the result of pressure from groups outside this industry. The impetus for change must come from within the hearts and souls of each of us."

Sources: Lodging 23, no. 5 (January 1998); www.loewshotels.com; www.ahma.com/about/officers/ferguson.htm; www.findarticles.co/cf_0_/mv0VOU/1998_July_30/50216477/pl/article.jhtml; www.hotel-online.com/Neo/SpecialReports1998/Nov98_Ferguson.html.

Freeway Hotels and Motels

Freeway hotels and motels came into prominence, with the help of the Interstate Highway Act, in the 1950s and 1960s. They are smaller than most hotels—usually fewer than fifty rooms—and are frequently mom-and-pop establishments or franchised (such as Motel 6). As Americans took to the open road, they needed a convenient place to stay that was reasonably priced with few frills. Guests could simply drive up, park outside the office, register, rent a room, and park outside the room. Over the years, more facilities were added: lounges, restaurants, pools, soft drink machines, game rooms, and satellite TV.

Motels are often clustered near freeway off ramps on the outskirts of towns and cities. Today, some are made of modular construction and have as few as eleven employees per hundred rooms. These savings in land, construction, and operating costs are passed on to the guest in the form of lower rates.

Casino Hotels

The casino hotel industry is now coming into the financial mainstream, to the point that, as a significant segment of the entertainment industry, it is reshaping the U.S. economy. The entertainment and recreation sector has become a very important engine for U.S. economic growth, providing a boost to consumer spending, and thus creating tremendous prosperity for the industry. The fastest-growing sector of the entertainment field is gaming, which is discussed in Chapter 11.

Casino hotels are leaning toward making their hotels into "family-friendly" hotels. The gaming business is strictly for adults; however, these hotels realize that making their hotels family friendly will attract more families to spend a day or two in their hotels. Circus Circus in Las Vegas pioneered the concept more than a decade ago. Various other casino hotels are following suit. They have baby-sitters available at any time of the day, children's attractions ranging from parks to circuses and museums, and kids menus in restaurants. For adults, in addition to gaming, a multinational cuisine for dining, health spas for relaxation, dance clubs, and dazzling shows are available.

Casino hotels are now marketing themselves as business hotels. They include in their rooms work space, a fax, a copier, and computer data ports. Other amenities include a full-service business center, travel bureau, and room service. Larger casino hotels also attract conventions, which represent a lucrative business. There are now more than 150 hotels in Native American tribal land. They cater to an increasing number of guests who want to stay and be entertained as well as gamble.

Convention Hotels

Convention hotels provide facilities and meet the needs of groups attending and holding conventions. Apart from this segment of the market, convention hotels also attract seasonal leisure travelers. Typically, these hotels exceed 500 guest rooms and include larger public areas to accommodate hundreds of people at any given time. Convention hotels have many banquet areas within and around the hotel complex. These hotels have a high percentage of double occupancies, and rooms have double queen-sized beds. Convention hotels may also offer a concierge floor to cater to individual guest needs. Round-the-clock room service, an in-house laundry, a business center, a travel desk, and an airport shuttle service are other amenities found in convention hotels.

The Universal Portofino Bay Hotel in Orlando is a popular convention hotel modeled after Portofino, Italy

Full-Service Hotels

Another way to classify hotels is by the degree of service offered: full-service, economy, extended-stay, and all-suite hotels. Full-service hotels offer a wide range of facilities, services, and amenities, including many that were mentioned under the luxury hotel category: multiple food and beverage outlets including bars, lounges, and restaurants; both formal and casual dining; and meeting, convention, and catering services. Business features might include a business center, secretarial services, fax, in-room computer hookups, and so on.

Most of the major North American cities have hotel chain representation, such as Doubletree, Four Seasons, Hilton, Holiday Inn, Hyatt, Marriott, Omni, Ramada, Radisson, Ritz-Carlton, Loews, Le Meridian, Sheraton, and Westin. Some of these chains are positioning themselves as basic full-service properties. An example of this strategy is Marriott's Courtyard hotels, which have small lobbies and very limited food and beverage offerings. The resulting savings are passed on to the guests in the form of more competitive rates. Thus, the full-service market may also be subdivided into upscale and midpriced hotels.

Economy/Budget Hotels

After enjoying a wave of growth for most of the last twenty years, the economy hotel segment may be close to the saturation point. There are about 25,000 properties in this segment with many markets. The economic law of supply and demand rules: If an area has too many similar properties, then price wars usually break out as they try to attract guests. Some will attempt to differentiate themselves and stress value rather than discounting. This adds to the fascination of the business.

An economy or budget hotel offers clean, reasonably sized and furnished rooms without the frills of full-service hotels. Chains such as Travelodge, Motel 6, Microtel, Days Inn, and La Quinta became popular by focusing on selling beds, not meals or meetings. This enabled them to offer rates about 30 percent lower than the midpriced hotels can. Economy properties, which represent about 15 percent of total hotel rooms, have experienced tremendous growth.

Motel 6, so named because rooms rented for $6 a night when this chain opened, is now owned by Accor Hotels of France

More recent entrants to this market sector are Promus's Hampton Inns, Marriott's Fairfield, and Choice's Comfort Inns. These properties do not have restaurants or offer substantial food and beverages, but they do offer guests a continental breakfast in the lobby.

Boutique Hotels

Boutique hotels offer a different lodging experience compared to mid- to large chain hotels. Boutique hotels have a unique architecture, style, decor, and size. They are smaller than their chain competitors, with about 25 to 125 rooms and a high level of personal service. Some examples of boutique hotels are the trendy South Beach retro types and the avant-garde hotel George in Washington, D.C.

A good example of a chain boutique hotel is Hotel Indigo, an Intercontinental Hotel Company. Hotel Indigo provdies an oasis where guests can escape the hectic pace of travel and think more clearly, work more productively, rest more refreshingly. It offers an environment that doesn't just shelter guests, but inspires and reenergizes them. That's the idea behind Hotel Indigo.[4]

Le Germaine

Extended-Stay Hotels

Some hotels cater to guests who stay for an extended period. They do, of course, take guests for a shorter time when space is available; however, the majority of guests are long term. Guests take advantage of a reduction in room rates based on the length of their stay. The mix of guests is mainly business and professional/technical, or relocating families.

Residence Inns and Homewood Suites are market leaders in this segment of the lodging industry. These properties offer full kitchen facilities and shopping services or a convenience store on the premises. Complimentary continental breakfast and evening cocktails are served in the lobby. Some properties offer a business center and recreational facilities.

Residence Inn

All-Suites Extended-Stay Hotels

All-suites extended-stay hotels typically offer approximately 25 percent more space for the same amount of money as the regular hotel in the same price range. The additional space is usually in the form of a lounge and possibly a kitchenette area.

Residence Inn.

Embassy Suites, owned and operated by the Promus Corporation; Residence Inns, Fairfield Suites, and Town-Place Suites, all by Marriott; Extended Stay America; Homewood Suites; and Guest Quarters are the market leaders in the all-suites, extended-stay segment of the lodging industry. Several of the major hotel chains have all-suites extended-stay subsidiaries, including Radisson, Choice Hotels (which dominate the economy all-suites segment with Comfort and Quality Suites), Sheraton Suites, Hilton Suites, Homegate Studios, and Suites by Wyndham Hotels. These properties provide a closer-to-home feeling for guests who may be relocating or attending seminars or who are on work-related projects that necessitate a stay of greater than about five days.

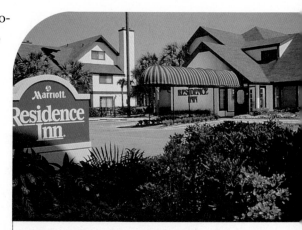

Residence Inn is a market leader in the extended-stay segment of the lodging industry

There are now almost 1,500 all-suites extended-stay properties. Many of these properties have business centers and offer services such as grocery shopping and laundry/dry cleaning. The designers of extended-stay properties realize that guests prefer a homelike atmosphere. Accordingly, many properties are built to encourage a community feeling, which allows guests to interact informally.

Condotels

As the word suggests, a condotel is a combination of a hotel and condominium. Developers build a hotel and sell it as condo units, which the owners can pool for use as hotel rooms and suites. The hotel operating company gets a cut of the money from renting the units and so does the owner. The owner of the condo unit may have exclusive right to the use of the unit for a fixed period of time (usually one month); other than that, the hotel operating company knows that it can rent out the condos.

Mixed-Use Hotels

Some new hotels are developed as mixed-use properties, meaning that a hotel may also have "residences"—real condos that people use, so they are not for renting like condotel—a spa, and sports facilities. Mixed-use hotels can also be a part of a major urban or resort development, which may include office buildings, convention centers, sporting facilities, or shopping malls.

Bed and Breakfast Inns

Bed and breakfast inns, or B&Bs as they are familiarly known, offer an alternative lodging experience to the normal hotel or motel. According to *Travel Assist Magazine,* B&B is a concept that began in Europe and started as overnight lodging in a private home. A true B&B is an accommodation with the owner, who lives on the premises or nearby, providing a clean, attractive accommodation and breakfast, usually a memorable one. The host also offers to help the guest with directions, restaurants, and suggestions for local entertainment or sightseeing.

A Bed and Breakfast in Yorkshire, England

There are many different styles of B&Bs with prices ranging from about $30 to $300 or more per night. B&Bs may be quaint cottages with white picket fences leading to gingerbread houses, tiny and homey, with two or three rooms available. On the other hand, some are sprawling, ranch-style homes in the Rockies; multistoried town homes in large cities; farms; adobe villas; log cabins; lighthouses; and many stately mansions. The variety is part of the thrill, romance, and charm of the B&B experience.[5]

There are an estimated 25,000 bed and breakfast places in the United States alone. Bed and breakfast inns have flourished for many reasons. Business travelers are growing weary of the complexities of the check-in/checkout processes at some commercial hotels. With the escalation of transient rates at hotels, an opportunity has been created to serve a more price-sensitive segment of travelers. Also, many leisure travelers are looking for accommodation somewhere between a large, formal hotel and staying with friends. The B&Bs offer a homelike atmosphere. They are aptly called "a home away from home." Community breakfasts with other lodgers and hosts enhance this feeling. Each B&B is as unique as its owner. Décor varies according to the region of location and the unique taste of its owner. The owner of the bed and breakfast often provides all the necessary labor, but some employ full- or part-time help.

▶ Check Your Knowledge

1. What characteristics do the following hotel segments encompass?
    a. City center hotels
    b. Resort hotels
    c. Airport hotels
    d. Freeway hotels and motels
    e. Full-service hotels
    f. Economy/budget hotels
    g. Extended-stay hotels
    h. Bed and breakfast inns

Best, Biggest, and Most Unusual Hotels and Chains

So, which is the best hotel in the world? The answer may depend on whether you watch the Travel Channel or read polls taken by a business investment or travel magazine. The Oriental Hotel in Bangkok, Thailand, has been rated number one in the world; so, too, has the Regent of Hong Kong, the Mandarin Oriental of Hong Kong, and the Connaught of London. Each "list" picks other hotels. The largest hotel in the world was the 5,505-room MGM Grand in Las Vegas. This, however, has been surpassed by the new Venetian Hotel, also in Las Vegas, which contains 6,172 rooms.

[handwritten margin note: The Oriental Hotel in Bangkok.]

[handwritten margin note: MGM Grand largest.]

The Best Hotel Chains

The Ritz-Carlton and the Canadian-owned and operated Four Seasons are generally rated the highest-quality chain hotels. The Ritz-Carlton Hotel Company has received all the major awards the hospitality industry and leading consumer organizations can bestow. It has received the Malcolm Baldrige National Quality Award, from the United States Department of Commerce—the first and only hotel company to win the award; the first and only service company to win the award two times: 1999 and 1992. Ritz-Carlton has long been recognized as the best luxury hotel chain in the industry.

*[handwritten margin note: *Ritz Carlton + 4 Seasons]*

The Most Unusual Hotels

Among the world's most unusual hotels are ones like The Treetops Hotel in one of Kenya's wild animal parks—literally in the treetops. The uniqueness of the hotel is that it is built on the tops of trees overlooking a wild animal watering hole in the park.

[handwritten margin note: 4 Ice hotel & treetop hotel]

Another magnificent spectacle is the Ice Hotel, situated on the shores of the Torne River in the old village of Jukkasjäsvi in Swedish Lapland. The Ice Hotel is built from scratch on an annual basis with a completely new design, new suites, new departments, even the "Absolute Ice Bar," a bar carved in ice with ice glasses and ice plates. The Ice Hotel can accommodate more than 100 guests with each room having its own distinct style. The hotel also has an Ice Chapel, an ice art exhibition hall, and, believe it or not, a cinema.

Australia boasts an underwater hotel at the Great Barrier Reef, where guests have wonderful underwater views from their rooms.

Bedroom in the Aurora Ice Hotel, Chena Hot Springs, Alaska

Japan has several unusual hotels. One is a cocoonlike hotel, called Capsule Hotel, in which guests do not have a room as such. Instead, they have a space of about 4 feet by 7 feet. In this space is a bed and a television—which guests almost have to operate with their toes! Such hotels are popular with people who get caught up in the obligatory late-night drinking with the boss and with visiting professors that find them the only affordable place to stay in expensive Tokyo.

The highest hotel in the world, in terms of altitude, is nestled in the Himalayan mountain range at an altitude of 13,000 feet. Weather permitting, there is a marvelous view of Mount Everest. As many as 80 percent of the guests suffer from nausea, headaches, or sleeplessness caused by the altitude. No wonder the hottest-selling item on the room-service menu is oxygen—at $1 a minute.

Vacation Ownership

From its beginnings in the French Alps in the late 1960s, **vacation ownership** has become the fastest-growing segment of the U.S. travel and tourism industry, increasing in popularity at the rate of about 15 percent each year.

Vacation ownership offers consumers the opportunity to purchase fully furnished vacation accommodations in a variety of forms, such as weekly intervals or in points-based systems, for a percentage of the cost of ownership. For a one-time purchase price and payment of a yearly maintaince fee, purchasers own their vacation either in perpetuity (forever) or for a predetermined number of years. Owners share both the use and cost of upkeep of their unit and the common grounds of the resort property. Vacation ownership purchases are typically financed through consumer loans of five to ten years duration, with terms dependent on the purchase price and the amount of the buyer's down payment. The average cost of a vacation ownership is about $12,500.

Vacation clubs, or point-based programs, provide the flexible use of accommodations in multiple resort locations. With these products, club members purchase points that represent either a travel and use membership or a deed real estate product. These points are then used like money to purchase accommodations during a season, for a set number of days at a participating resort. The number of points needed to access the resort accommodation varies by the members' demand for unit size, season, resort location, and amenities.

Henry Silverman of Avis Budget, which owns the Indianapolis, Indiana-based Resort Condominiums International (RCI), says that a timeshare is really a two-bedroom suite that is owned, rather than a hotel room that is rented for a transient night. A vacation club, on the other hand, is a "travel-and-use"

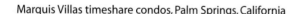

Marquis Villas timeshare condos, Palm Springs, California

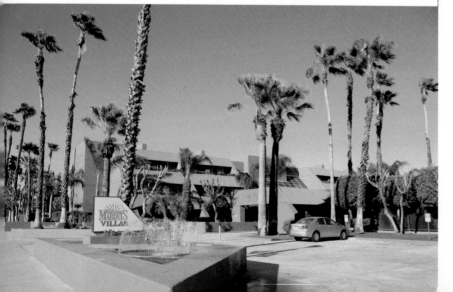

[handwritten margin note: → time sharing ppl have the opp to buy properties for x amount of time "more owning than renting a hotel suite"]

product. Consumers do not buy a fixed week, unit size, season, resort, or number of days to vacation each year. Instead, they purchase points that represent currency, which is used to access the club's vacation benefits. An important advantage to this is the product's flexibility, especially when tied to a point system. Disney Vacation Club is one major company that uses a point system. General manager Mark Pacala states, "The flexibility of choosing among several different vacation experiences is what sets the Disney Vacation Club apart from many similar plans. The vacation points system allows members to select the type of vacation best suited to their needs, particularly as those needs change from year to year." Each year, members choose how to use their vacation points, either for one long vacation or a series of short getaways.[6]

The World Tourism Organization has called timeshares one of the fastest-growing sectors of the travel and tourism industry. Hospitality companies are adding brand power to the concept with corporations such as Marriott Vacation Club International, the Walt Disney Company, Hilton Hotels, Hyatt Hotels, Promus's Embassy Suites, InterContinental, and even the Ritz-Carlton and Four Seasons participating in an industry that has grown rapidly in recent years. Still, only about 3 percent of all U.S. households own vacation ownership. RCI estimates that the figure could rise to 10 percent within the next decade for households with incomes of more than $50,000. It is not surprising that hotel companies have found this to be a lucrative business.

RCI, the largest vacation ownership exchange (that allows members to exchange vacations with other locations), has more than 2.8 million member families living in 200 countries. Three thousand seven hundred participating resorts and members can exchange vacation intervals for vacations at any participating resort, and, to date, RCI has arranged exchange vacations for more than 54 million people.[7] Vacation ownership is popular at U.S. resorts from Key West in Florida to Kona in Hawaii and from New York City and Las Vegas to Colorado ski resorts.

Interval World is a vacation exchange network made up of more than 2,000 resorts and more than 1.6 million member families worldwide. Interval does not own or manage any of the resorts, but rather provides members—vacation owners from around the world—with a variety of exchange services to enhance their vacation experiences. Members can exchange a stay at their home resort for a stay at one of the timeshares supported by Interval World.

By locking in the purchase price of accommodations, vacation ownership helps ensure future vacations at today's prices at luxurious resorts with amenities, service, and ambiance that rival any of the world's top-rated vacation destinations. Through vacation exchange programs, timeshare owners can travel to other popular destinations around the world. With unparalleled flexibility and fully equipped condominiums that offer the best in holiday luxury, vacation ownership puts consumers in the driver's seat, allowing them to plan and enjoy vacations that suit their lifestyle.

Timeshare resort developers today include many of the world's leading hoteliers, publicly held corporations, and independent companies. Properties that combine vacation ownership resorts with hotels, adventure resorts, and gaming resorts are among the emerging timeshare trends. The reasons for purchasing most frequently cited by current timeshare owners are the high standards of quality accommodations and service at the resorts where they own and exchange, the flexibility offered through the vacation exchange opportunities, and the cost effectiveness of vacation ownership. Nearly one-third of vacation owners purchase additional intervals after experiencing ownership. This trend is even stronger among long-time owners: More than 40 percent of those who have owned for eight years or longer have purchased additional intervals within the timeshare.

Travel the World through Exchange Vacations

Vacation ownership offers unparalleled flexibility and the opportunity for affordable worldwide travel through vacation ownership exchange. Through the international vacation exchange networks, owners can trade their timeshare intervals for vacation time at comparable resorts around the world. Most resorts are affiliated with an exchange company that administers the exchange service for its members. Typically, the exchange company directly solicits annual membership. Owners individually elect to become members of the affiliated exchange company. To exchange, the owner places his or her interval into the exchange company's pool of resorts and weeks available for exchange and, in turn, chooses an available resort and week from that pool. The exchange company charges an exchange fee, in addition to an annual membership fee, to complete an exchange. Exchange companies and resorts frequently offer their members the additional benefit of saving or banking vacation time in a reserve program for use in a different year.

International Perspective

We are all part of a huge global economy that is splintered into massive trading blocks, such as the European Union (EU) and the North American Free Trade Agreement (NAFTA) among Canada, the United States, and Mexico, with a total population of 350 million consumers.

The EU, with a population of more than 400 million people in twenty-five nations, is an economic union that has removed national restrictions not only on trade but also on the movement of capital and labor. The synergy developed between these fifteen member nations is beneficial to all and is a form of self-perpetuating development. As travel, tourism, commerce, and industry have increased within the European Economic Community (EEC), which is soon to expand by another ten nations, and beyond, so has the need for hotel accommodations.

NAFTA will likely be a similar catalyst for hotel development in response to increased trade and tourism among the three countries involved. But Argentina, Brazil, Chile, and Venezuela may also join an expanded NAFTA, which would become known as the Americas Trading Bloc.

It is easy to understand the international development of hotels given the increase in international tourism trade and commerce. The growth in tourism in Pacific Rim countries is expected to continue at the same rate as in recent years. Several resorts are planned in Indonesia, Malaysia, Thailand, and Vietnam. Further international hotel development opportunities exist in eastern Europe, Russia, and the other republics of the former Soviet Union, where some companies have changed their growth strategy from building new hotels to acquiring existing properties.

In Asia, Hong Kong's growth has been encouraged by booming economies throughout Southeast Asia and the kind of tax system for which supply-siders hunger. The Hong Kong government levies a flat 16.5 percent corporate tax, a 15 percent individual income tax, and no tax on capital gains or dividends. Several hotel corporations have their headquarters in Hong Kong. Among them are Mandarin Oriental, Peninsula, and Shangri-La, all world-renowned for their five-star status. They are based in Hong Kong because of low corporate taxation and the ability to bring in senior expatriate executives with minimal bureaucratic difficulty.[8]

In developing countries, once political stability has been sustained, hotel development quickly follows as part of an overall economic and social progression. An example of this is the former eastern European countries and former Soviet republics that for the past few years have offered development opportunities for hotel corporations.

Sustainable Lodging

Today, of necessity, developers are more environmentally conscious because it can cost far more not only to build a lodging facility but also to run it if it is not sustainable. By using local materials, a new hotel or resort can save money on the cost of materials plus the cost of transporting those materials from a distance, or even importing them. Given the weak U.S. dollar, it increases costs if materials must be imported.

The cost of energy has increased so much in recent years that lodging construction now incorporates ways of using natural lighting and building energy-efficient buildings. Energy-efficient buildings require far less air-conditioning than do conventional buildings because they use materials such as darkened glass and lower-wattage lighting that produces lower temperatures.

Raffles Singapore, a World-Famous Classic Hotel

Trends in Hotel Development

Trends
⇨ Capacity cntrl
⇨ Safety + security
  (terrorism)
⇨ Assets + capital
⇨ Technology
⇨ New mgmt
⇨ Globalization
⇨ Consolidation
⇨ Diversification
⇨ Rapid growth in
  vacation
    ownership
⇨ ↑ in # of spas +
  treatment offered
⇨ Gaming hotels

- *Capacity control.* Refers to who will control the sale of inventories of hotel rooms, airline seats, auto rentals, and tickets to attractions. Presently, owners of these assets are in control of their sale and distribution, but increasingly control is falling into the hands of those who own and manage global reservation systems and/or negotiate for large buying groups. Factors involved in the outcome will be telecommunications, software, available satellite capacity, governmental regulations, limited capital, and the travel distribution network.

- *Safety and security.* Important aspects of safety and security are terrorism, the growing disparity between the haves and have-nots in the world, diminishing financial resources, infrastructure problems, health issues, the stability of governments, and personal security.

- *Assets and capital.* The issues concerning assets and capital are rationing of private capital and rationing of funds deployed by governments.

- *Technology.* An example of the growing use of *expert systems* (a basic form of artificial intelligence) would be making standard operating procedures available online, twenty-four hours a day, and establishing yield management systems designed to make pricing decisions. Other examples include increasing numbers of smart hotel room and communications ports to make virtual office environments for business travelers and the impact of technology on the structure of corporate offices and individual hotels.

- *New management.* The complex forces of capacity control, safety and security, capital movement, and technology issues will require a future management cadre that is able to adapt to rapid-paced change across all the traditional functions of management.

- *Globalization.* A number of U.S. and Canadian chains have developed and are continuing to develop hotels around the world. International companies are also investing in the North American hotel industry.

- *Consolidation.* As the industry matures, corporations are either acquiring or merging with each other.

- *Diversification within segments of the lodging industry.* The economy segment now has low-, medium-, and high-end properties. The extended-stay market has a similar spread of properties as do all the other hotel classifications.

- *Rapid growth in vacation ownership.* Vacation ownership is the fastest-growing segment of the lodging industry and is likely to continue growing as the baby boomers enter their fifties and sixties.

- *An increase in the number of spas and the treatments offered.* Wellness and the road to nirvana are in increasing demand as guests seek release from the stresses of a fast-paced lifestyle.

- *Gaming.* An increasing number of hotels are coming online that are related to the gaming industry.

- *Mixed-use properties.* An increasing number of hotels are being developed as multiuse properties, meaning hotels with residences (condominiums), spas, and recreational facilities.

- *Sustainable lodging development.* There is increasing development of lodging facilities with environmentally designs, construction, and operating procedures.

Factors propelling franchise growth include these:

- Fresh looks (curb appeal)
- Location near highways, airports, and suburbs
- Expansion in smaller cities throughout the United States
- New markets located in proximity to golf courses and other attractions
- Foreign expansion and a move to increase brand awareness

CASE STUDY

In recent years, several new lodging brands have been introduced by leading hotel chains to the market. Among the names of these brands are DoubleTree, Candlewood Suites, Homewood Suites, Mainstay, Spring Hill Suites, and so on. In addition, there is Hyatt, which recently purchased AmeriSuites, which it has renovated and now call Hyatt Place.

A hot trend in lodging development is condo hotels. With condo hotels, a developer can more quickly raise the funds necessary from investors than from other traditional sources such as banks and finance houses. As a result, it makes sense for developers to encourage investors by offering an arrangement for owners to have exclusive use of the unit for a fixed number of days a year (typically 30–60 days) and for the hotel company to rent out the units/rooms for the remainder of the year. The cost of development is high and ranges from an average of $800 to $900 per square foot up to $1,400. Projects such as the Residences at MGM Grand Las Vegas, which sold more than $1 billion, or the Hard Rock Hotel and Casino, also in Las Vegas, which launched 1,300 units in less than ten weeks are amazing. Other areas of the United States are good existing or potential markets for condo hotel development.

Despite the rave reviews on Wall Street for condo hotels, there are some unresolved issues. With time, who will develop and pay for the replacement of furniture fixtures and equipment (FF&E)? What are the association dues and what form will the relationship take between owners, the developer, and the hotel company? There are the additional complexities for the hotel operator—such as space for meetings, restaurants, and recreation—and how many rooms will be available on any given night. Yet, the payoffs for both individual investor–owners and hotel operating companies are good to great. With 78 million baby boomers ready to retire, the prospects look very good to all concerned.

Discussion Questions

1. So what is in a name? Is Hyatt right to use the name Hyatt Place?
2. Is Intercontinental or Hilton wrong not to include their name, as in Hilton Hampton Inn or Hampton Inn by Hilton? What is your opinion?
3. Which other areas of the United States are good potential locations for condo hotels and why?
4. Will condo hotels split into various segments like other lodging properties have?

Summary

1. Improved transportation has changed the nature of the hotel industry from small, independently owned inns to big hotel and lodging chains that are operated using concepts such as franchising and management contracts.
2. Hotels can be classified according to location (city center, resort, airport, freeway), types of services offered (casino, convention), and price (luxury, midscale, budget, and economy). Hotels are rated by Mobil and AAA Awards (five-star or five-diamond rankings).
3. Vacation ownership offers consumers the opportunity to purchase fully furnished vacation accommodations, similar to condominiums, sold in a variety of forms, such as weekly intervals or point-based systems, for only a percentage of the cost of full ownership. According to the WTO, timeshares are one of the fastest-growing sectors of the travel and tourism industry.
4. Every part of the world offers leisure and business travelers a choice of unusual or conservative accommodations that cater to personal ideas of vacation or business trips.
5. The future of tourism involves international expansion and foreign investment, often in combination with airlines, and with the goal of improving economic conditions in developing countries. It is further influenced by increased globalization, as evidenced by such agreements as NAFTA.

Key Words and Concepts

franchising	real estate investment trusts	referral associations
management contracts	(REITs)	vacation ownership

Review Questions

1. On the Companion Website, what advice does Ritz-Carlton General Manager Jim McManemon give hospitality students?
2. On the Companion Website, what is Robert Steele III's path to hotel general manager? What is it like to be president of the American Hotel and Lodging Association? What advice does he have for students?
3. What are the advantages of (a) management contracts and (b) franchising? Discuss their impacts on the development of the hotel industry.
4. Explain how hotels cater to the needs of business and leisure travelers in reference to the following concepts: (a) resorts, (b) airport hotels, and (c) vertical integration.
5. Explain what vacation ownership is. What are the different types of timeshare programs available for purchase?

Internet Exercises

1. Organization: **Hilton Hotels**
   Web site: **www.hilton.com**
   Summary: Hilton Hotels Corporation and Hilton International, a subsidiary of Hilton Group plc, have a worldwide alliance to market Hilton. Hilton is recognized as one of the world's best-known hotel brands. Collectively, Hilton offers more than 2,500 hotels in more than fifty countries,

truly a major player in the hospitality industry.

    (a) What are the different hotel brands that can be franchised through Hilton Hotels Corporation?

    (b) What are your views on Hilton's portfolio and franchising options?

Click the "Franchise Development" icon. Now click "All HHC Franchise Brands."

2. Organization: **HOTELS Magazine**
Web site: **www.hotelsmag.com**

Summary: *Hotels* magazine is a publication that offers vast amounts of information on the hospitality industry with up-to-date industry news, corporate trends, and nationwide developments.

    (a) What are some of the top headlines currently being reported in the industry?

    (b) Click the "Hotels Giants" icon. Browse through the Corporate Rankings and Industry Leaders. List the top five hotel corporations and note how many rooms each one has.

Apply Your Knowledge

1. From a career perspective, what are the advantages and disadvantages of each type of hotel?

2. If you were going into the lodging sector, which type of property would you prefer to work at and why?

3. Complete the sample test questions on the Companion Website.

Suggested Activities

1. Identify which kind of hotel you would like to work at and give reasons why.

2. Comment on the career advice provided on the Companion Website.

Endnotes

1. New York Architecture Images, "The Plaza Hotel," www.nyc-architecture.com/MID/MID056.htm.
2. This section is courtesy of Robert Kok, Professor, Johnson and Wales University.
3. Personal conversation with Bruce Goodwin, May 4, 2005.
4. www.ichotelsgroup.com/n/d/in/1/en/home?firstpoint=dcb1
5. TravelASSIST Magazine, "What Is a Bed an Breakfast Inn?" www.travelassist.com/mag/a88.html.
6. Lynn Sheldon, "Timeshare Concept Adopted by the Hotel Industry," Rhode Island Roads magazine, riroads.com/archive/timesharehotels.htm.
7. RCI, "RCI Milestone," www.rci.com/RCIW/RCIW_index?body=RCIW_Milestone&action=aboutrci.
8. Personal conversation with Leonard Gordon, March 15, 2006.

CHAPTER 4

Rooms Division Operations

OBJECTIVES

After reading and studying this chapter, you should be able to:

- Outline the duties and responsibilities of key executives and department heads.

- Draw an organizational chart of the rooms division of a hotel and identify the executive committee members.

- Describe the main functions of the rooms division departments.

- Describe property management systems and discuss yield management.

- Calculate occupancy percentages, average daily rates, and actual percentage of potential rooms revenue.

- Outline the importance of the reservations and guest services functions.

- List the complexities and challenges of the concierge, housekeeping, and security/loss prevention departments.

This chapter examines the function of a hotel and the many departments that constitute a hotel. It also helps to explain why and how the departments are interdependent in successfully running a hotel.

The Functions and Departments of a Hotel

The primary function of a hotel is to provide lodging accommodation. A large hotel is run by a general manager and an executive committee that consists of the key executives who head major departments: rooms division director, food and beverage director, marketing and sales director, human resources director, chief accountant or controller, and chief engineer or facility manager. These executives generally have a regional or corporate counterpart with whom they have a reporting relationship, although the general manager is their immediate superior.

A hotel is made up of several businesses or revenue centers and cost centers. A few thousand products and services are sold every day. Each area of specialty requires dedication and a quality commitment for each department to get little things right all the time. Furthermore, hotels need the cooperation of a large and diverse group of people to perform well. Godfrey Bler, the general manager (GM) of the elegant 800-room General Eisenhower Hotel, calls it "a business of details."

Hotels are places of glamour that may be awe inspiring. Even the experienced hotel person is impressed by the refined dignity of a beautiful hotel like a Ritz-Carlton or the artistic splendor of a Hyatt. The atmosphere of a hotel is stimulating to a hospitality student. Let us step into an imaginary hotel to feel the excitement and become a part of the rush that is similar to show business, for a hotel is live theater and the GM is the director of the cast of players.

Hotels, whether they are chain affiliated or independent properties, all exist to serve and enrich society and at the same time make a profit for the owners. Frequently, hotels are just like pieces of property on a Monopoly board. They often make or lose more money with equity appreciation or depreciation than through operations. Hotels have been described as "people palaces." Some are certainly palatial, and others are more functional. Hotels are meant to provide all the comforts of home to those away from home.

The Grand Hall in the Willard InterContinental, Washington, D.C. It was at this hotel that the term *lobbyist* was coined when then President Grant would retire after dinner to an armchair in the lobby. People would approach him and try to gain his support for their causes

Management Structure

Management structure differs among larger, midscale, and smaller properties. The midscale and smaller properties are less complex in their management structures than are the larger ones. However, someone must be responsible for each of the key result areas that make the operation successful. For example, a small property may not have a director of human resources, but each department head will have general day-to-day operating responsibilities for the human resources function. The manager has the ultimate responsibility for all human resources decisions. The same scenario is possible with each of the following areas: engineering and maintenance, accounting and finance, marketing and sales, food and beverage management, and so on.

Role of the Hotel General Manager

Hotel general managers have a lot of responsibilities. They must provide owners with a reasonable return on investment, keep guests satisfied and returning, and keep employees happy. This may seem easy, but because there are so many interpersonal transactions and because hotels are open every day, all day, the complexities of operating become challenges that the general manager must face and overcome. The GM not only focuses on leading and operating the hotel departments but also on aspects of the infrastructure, from room atmosphere to security.

Larger hotels can be more impersonal. Here, the general manager may only meet and greet a few VIPs. In the smaller property, it is easier—though no less important—for the GM to become acquainted with guests to ensure that their stay is memorable and to secure their return. One way that experienced GMs can meet guests, even in large hotels, is to be visible in the lobby and food and beverage

(F&B) outlets at peak times (checkout, lunch, check-in, and dinner time). Guests like to feel that the GM takes a personal interest in their well-being. Max Blouet, who was general manager of the famous George V Hotel in Paris for more than thirty years, was a master of this art. He was always present at the right moment to meet and greet guests during the lunch hour and at the evening check-in. Hoteliers always remember they are hosts.

The GM is ultimately responsible for the performance of the hotel and the employees. The GM is the leader of the hotel. As such, she

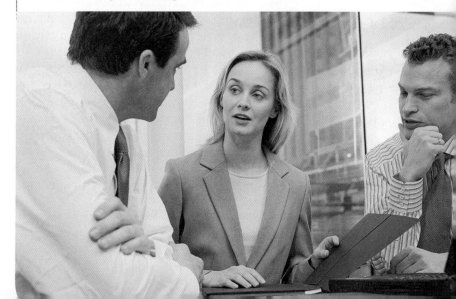
A General Manager Discussing the "Forecast" with a Rooms Division Director

or he is held accountable for the hotel's level of profitability by the corporation or owners.

To be successful, GMs need to have a broad range of personal qualities. Among those most often quoted by GMs are the following:

- Leadership ✳
- Attention to detail
- Follow-through—getting the job done
- People skills
- Patience
- Ability to delegate effectively

INTRODUCING CESAR RITZ

Cesar Ritz was a legend in his own time; like so many of the early industry leaders, he began at the bottom and worked his way up through the ranks. In his case, it did not take long to reach the top because he quickly learned the secrets of success in the hotel business. His career began as an apprenticed hotel keeper at the age of fifteen. At nineteen, he was managing a Parisian restaurant. Suddenly, he quit that position to become an assistant waiter at the famous Voisin restaurant. There he learned how to pander to the rich and famous. In fact, he became so adept at taking care of the guests—remembering their likes and dislikes, even their idiosyncrasies—that a guest would ask for him and would only be served by him.

At twenty-two, he became manager of the Grand National Hotel in Lucerne, Switzerland, one of the most luxurious hotels in the world. The hotel was not very successful at the time Ritz became manager, but with his ingenuity and panache, he was able to attract the "in" crowd to complete a turnaround. After eleven seasons, he accepted a bigger challenge: the Savoy Hotel in London, which had only been open a few months and which was not doing well. Cesar Ritz became manager of one of the most famous and luxurious hotels in the world at the age of thirty-eight.

Once again, his flair and ability to influence society quickly made a positive impression on the hotel. To begin with, he made the hotel a cultural center for high society. Together with Escoffier as executive chef, he created a team that produced the finest cuisine in Europe in the most elegant of surroundings. He made evening dress compulsory and introduced orchestras to the restaurants. Cesar Ritz would spare no expense to create the lavish effect he sought. On one occasion, he converted a riverside restaurant into a Venetian waterway, complete with small gondolas and gondoliers singing Italian love songs.[1]

Ritz considered the handling of people as the most important of all qualities for a hotelier. His imagination and sensitivity to people and their wants contributed to a new standard of hotel keeping. The Ritz name remains synonymous with refined, elegant hotels and service.[2] However, Ritz drove himself to the point of exhaustion, and at age fifty-two, he suffered a nervous breakdown.

1. Richard A. Wentzel, "Leaders of the Hospitality Industry or Hospitality Management," *An Introduction to the Industry,* 6th ed. (Dubuque, IA: Kendall/Hunt, 1991), 29.

2. Donald E. Lundberg, *The Hotel and Restaurant Business,* 4th ed. (New York: Van Nostrand Reinhold, 1984), 33–34.

A successful GM selects and trains the best people. A former GM of Chicago's Four Seasons Hotel deliberately hired division heads who knew more about what they were hired for than he did. The GM sets the tone—a structure of excellence—and others try to match it. Once the structure is in place, each employee works to define the hotel's commitment to excellence. General managers need to understand, empathize, and allow for the cultures of both guests and employees. Progressive general managers empower associates to do anything legal to delight the guest.

The Executive Committee

The general manager, using input from the **executive committee** (Figure 4–1), makes all the major decisions affecting the hotel. These executives, who include the directors of human resources, food and beverage, rooms division, marketing and sales, engineering, and accounting, compile the hotel's occupancy forecast together with all revenues and expenses to make up the budget. They generally meet once a week for one or two hours—although the Ritz-Carlton has a daily lineup at 9 A.M.— and might typically cover some of the following topics:

Guest satisfaction

Employee satisfaction

Total quality management

Occupancy forecasts

Sales and marketing plans

Training

Major items of expenditure

Renovations

Ownership relations

Energy conservation

Recycling

New legislation

Profitability

Directors of departments:
- HR
- F&B
- Rooms Division
- DOS
- Engineering
- Accounting

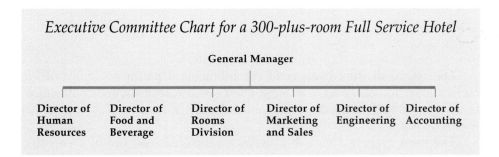

Executive Committee Chart for a 300-plus-room Full Service Hotel

General Manager

Director of Human Resources	**Director of Food and Beverage**	**Director of Rooms Division**	**Director of Marketing and Sales**	**Director of Engineering**	**Director of Accounting**

Figure 4–1 • Executive Committee Chart.

Some GMs rely on input from the executive committee more than others do, depending on their leadership and management style. These senior executives determine the character of the property and decide on the missions, goals, and objectives of the hotel. For a chain hotel, this will be in harmony with the corporate mission.

In most hotels, the executive committee is involved with the decisions, but the ultimate responsibility and authority rests with the GM. One major role of the committee is communicator, both up and down the line of authority. This helps build interdepartmental cooperation. Not all lodging operations will have an executive committee—obviously, there is no need for one at a small motel, lodge, or a B&B.

▶ Check Your Knowledge

1. What is the role of the general manager?
2. Who is a member of the executive committee and what topics does this person deal with?

The Departments

In larger hotels, the rooms division has several departments that all work together to please guests. In midsize and smaller properties, those departments may be reduced in size and number, but they still need to serve guests.

Rooms Division

The rooms division director is held responsible by the GM for the efficient and effective leadership and operation of all the rooms division departments. They include concerns such as the following:

Financial responsibility for rooms division

Employee satisfaction goals

Guest satisfaction goals

Guest services

Guest relations

Security

Gift shop

The **rooms division** consists of the following departments: front office, reservations, housekeeping, concierge, guest services, security, and communications. Figure 4–2 shows the organizational chart for a 300-plus-room hotel rooms division.

The guest cycle in Figure 4–3 shows a simplified sequence of events that takes place from the moment a guest calls to make a reservation until he or she checks out.

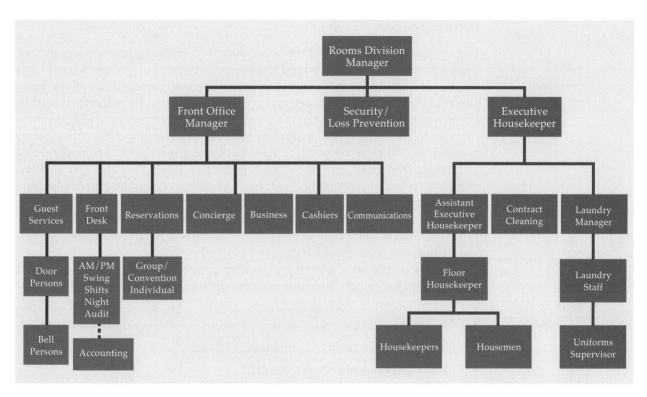

Figure 4–2 • Rooms Division Organizational Chart.

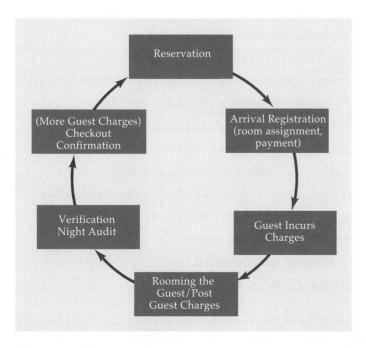

Figure 4–3 • The Guest Cycle.

FOM:
to enhance
guest services

Front Office

The front office manager's (FOM) main duty is to enhance guest services by constantly developing services to meet guest needs. An example of how some FOMs practice enhancing guest services is to have a guest service associate (GSA) greet guests as they arrive at the hotel, escort them to the front desk, and then personally allocate the room and take the guest and luggage to the room. This innovative way of developing guest services looks at the operation from the guest's perspective. There is no need to have separate departments for doorperson, bellperson, front desk, and so on. Each guest associate is cross-trained in all aspects of greeting and rooming the guest. This is now being done in smaller and midsized properties as well as at specialty and deluxe properties. Guest service associates are responsible for the front desk, concierge, communications/PBX (The term PBX is still widely used; it stands for Private Brand Exchange), bellpersons, valet, and reservations.

During an average day in a hotel—if there is such a thing—the front office manager and his or her associates perform the following duties:

- Check night clerk report.
- Review previous night's occupancy.
- Review previous night's average rate.
- Look over market mix and determine what rooms to sell at what price.
- Handle checkouts and check-ins.
- Check complimentary rooms.
- Verify group rooms to be picked up for the next thirty days.
- Review arrivals and departures for the day.
- Politely and efficiently attend to guest inquiries.
- Review the VIP list and prepare preregistration.
- Organize any room changes guests may request and follow up.
- Arrange preregistrations for all arrivals.
- Attend rooms divisions and operations meeting.
- Advise housekeeping and room service of flowers/fruit for VIPs.
- Review arrivals and departures for the next day.
- Make staffing adjustments needed for arrivals and departures.
- Note any important things in the log book.
- Check issuing and control of keys.
- Review scheduling (done weekly).
- Meet with lead GSAs (done daily).

In some hotels, the reservations manager and associates report to the director of sales. These positions report to the chief accountant: night auditor, night audit associates, and cashiers.

The front office has been described as the hub or nerve center of the hotel. It is the department that makes a first impression on the guest and one that the guest relies on throughout his or her stay for information and service. Positive first impressions are critical to the successful guest experience. Many guests arrive at the hotel after long, tiring trips. They want to be met by someone with a warm smile and a genuine greeting. If a guest should have a negative experience when checking into a hotel, he or she will be on guard in encounters with each of the other departments. The position description for a guest service agent details the work performed. Position descriptions for the three main functions of the front office are as follows:

1. *To sell rooms.* The hotel departments work like a team in a relay race. Sales or reservations staff make up room sales until the evening before the guest's arrival. At 6:00 P.M., when the reservations office closes, all the expected arrivals and available rooms are then handed over to the front desk P.M. shift. Reservations calls after 6:00 P.M. may either be taken by the front desk staff or the 1-800 number. The front desk team will try to sell out (achieve 100 percent occupancy) by selling the remaining rooms to call-in or walk-in guests—and of course the frantic calls from preferred guests who need a favor!

   Upselling occurs when the guest service agent/front desk clerk suggestively sells the features of a larger room, a higher floor, or perhaps a better view. Yield management originated in the airline industry where demand also fluctuates. Basically, a percentage of guests who book and send in a deposit in advance will be able to secure a room at a more reasonable price than can someone booking a room with just three days' notice. The price will be even higher for the booking at three days' notice if demand is good.

   Many other factors influence the hotel's ability to sell out. Chief among these are *demand*—the number of people needing rooms—and *supply*—the number of available rooms. A good example is the New York Hotel Convention. This event takes place in a city that has a high demand for hotel rooms in proportion to its inventory (number of available rooms). Because there is a fairly constant demand for rooms in New York, special events tend to increase demand to a point that forces up **room rates.** (See Figure 4–4.) Another example comes from the airline industry, which always seems to raise prices at the peak travel times (Thanksgiving, Christmas, Easter, and the summer vacation times). They only offer special fares when school is in session. Revenue management is explained in more detail later in this chapter.

A Front Office Manager Taking Care of a Guest Request

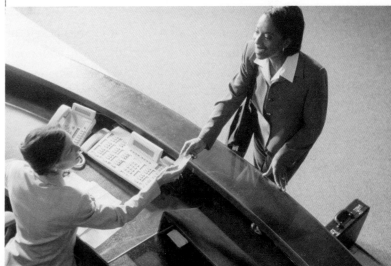

FOCUS ON ROOMS DIVISION

How to Have Fun Working at the Front Desk and Be Successful at the Same Time

William B. Martin, *California State, Monterey Bay*

If you are currently working at a front desk as a service provider or if you plan to do so in the near future, here are a few handy hints about being successful. Note that this list is only a beginning. By no means is it totally complete or does it cover all contingencies.

1. Get plenty of sleep the night before your shift. Arrive at work well rested.
2. Come to work early, in plenty of time to get all the change of shift information that you will need.
3. Approach each shift with a positive frame of mind.
4. Remember that when you are interacting with guests, you *are* the hotel.
5. Always keep in mind that delivering quality guest services is your first priority.
6. Smile a lot when interacting with guests and fellow service providers.
7. Keep in mind that your job is to service not only external customers (guests) but also internal customers—those people who also work at the hotel but who rely on you to get things done and perform your job well.
8. Remember that practicing quality guest service requires that you are good at procedural service as well as personal service. One is not sacrificed for the sake of the other. Both are emphasized and practiced.
9. Be genuinely enthusiastic about being a service provider. If you can't be, find another job.
10. Stay flexible. Be open to new demands and experiences.
11. When a large family checks into one room, anticipate that they may need extra towels or perhaps a hide-a-bed.
12. Take care of all requests for room repair and maintenance immediately.
13. Be willing to learn and open to learning new ways of doing things.
14. Try to tell a guest what you can do, not what you can't do. Keep it positive.
15. Always greet a guest with a smile.
16. When you are tired, don't show it, especially in front of guests.
17. Be an attitude catalyst. Infect others with your positive attitude.
18. Refer to a guest by name whenever and wherever you can. Especially during check-in, call the guest by name at least two or three times.
19. After check-in is complete, say, "Thank you, Mr./Ms. Doe. Have a great stay."
20. When passing a guest outside the front desk, in the hallway, or out on the patio, always smile and say hello.
21. Pre–room assign large tour groups and delegate key distribution to the tour director.
22. Always, always keep in constant touch with housekeeping, and say "thank you" to them a lot.
23. Look for cues such as age, attire, group mix, body language, or verbal abilities to determine any possible service needs a guest may have.

24. When booking reservations, get all needed information and ask about any special needs the guest may have.
25. Avoid the five forbidden phrases: "I don't know." "We can't do that." "You'll have to. . ." "Hang on a second. I'll be right back." Saying "no" at the beginning of a sentence.
26. Anticipate guest needs. Be one step ahead of them so that you can provide service without them having to ask.
27. Have plenty of toiletry supplies for guest emergencies available.
28. Genuinely enjoy working with guests, other service providers, and managers. Be a people person. If this is not you, find another job.
29. Remain guest focused. Constantly work toward understanding what it is that they need and helping them to feel welcome, comfortable, and important.
30. Smile, smile, smile!

Major hotel chains offer a number of different room rates, including the following:

rack rate
corporate
association rate
government
encore
cititravel
entertainment cards
AAA
AARP (American Association of Retired Persons)
wholesale
group rates
promotional special

The rack rate is the rate that is used as a benchmark quotation of a hotel's room rate. Let us assume that the Hotel California had a rack rate of $135. Any discounted rate may be offered at a percentage deduction from the rack rate. An example would be a corporate rate of $110, an association rate of $105, and AARP rate of $95—certain restrictions may apply. Group rates may range from $95 to $125 according to how much the hotel needs the business.

Throughout the world there are three main plans on which room rates are based:

AP/American Plan—room and three meals a day
MAP/Modified American Plan—room plus two meals
EP/European Plan—room only, meals extra

Figure 4–4 • The Types of Room Rates Offered by Hotels.

2. *To maintain balanced guest accounts.* This begins with advance deposits, opening the guest folio (account), and posting all charges from the various departments. Most hotels have property management systems (PMS) (property management systems are explained in more detail later in this chapter) and point-of-sale terminals (POS), which are online to the front office.

This means that guest charges from the various outlets are directly debited to the guest's folio. Payment is either received on guest checkout or transferred to the **city ledger** (a special account for a company that has established credit with the hotel). This means that the account will be sent and paid within a specified time period.

3. *To offer services such as handling mail, faxes, messages, and local and hotel information.* People constantly approach the front desk with questions. Front desk employees need to be knowledgeable about the various activities in the hotel. The size, layout, and staffing of the front desk will vary with the size of the hotel. The front desk staff size of a busy 800-room city center property will naturally differ from that of a country inn. The front desk is staffed throughout the twenty-four hours by three shifts.

The evening shift duties are the following:

1. Check the log book for special items. (The log book is kept by guest contact; associates at the front office note specific and important guest requests and occurrences such as requests for room switches or baby cribs.)

2. Check on the room status, number of expected checkouts still to leave, and arrivals by double-checking registration cards and the computer so that they can update the forecast of the night's occupancy. This will determine the number of rooms left to sell. Nowadays, this is all part of the capability of the PMS.

3. Handle guest check-ins. This means notifying the appropriate staff of any special requests guests may have made (e.g., nonsmoking room or a long bed for an extra-tall guest).

4. Take reservations for that evening and future reservations after the reservations staff have left for the day.

Night Auditor

A hotel is one of the few businesses that balances its accounts at the end of each business day. Because a hotel is open twenty-four hours every day, it is difficult to stop transactions at any given moment. The **night auditor** waits until the hotel quiets down at about 1:00 A.M., and then begins the task of balancing the guests' accounts receivable. The process of night auditing is as follows:

1. The night audit team runs a preliminary reconciliation report that shows the total revenue generated from room and tax, banquets and catering, food and beverage outlets, and other incidentals (phone, gift shop, etc.).

2. All errors on the report are investigated.

3. All changes are posted and balanced with the preliminary charges.

4. A comparison of charges is carried out, matching preliminary with actual charges.

5. Totals for credit card charges, rooms operations, food and beverages, and incidentals are verified.

6. The team "rolls the date"—they go forward to the next day.

Other duties of the night audit staff include the following:

1. Post any charges that the evening shift was not able to post.
2. Pass discrepancies to shift managers in the morning. The room and tax charges are then posted to each folio and a new balance shown.
3. Run backup reports so that if the computer system fails, the hotel will have up-to-date information to operate a manual system.
4. Reconcile point-of-sale and PMS to guest accounts. If this does not balance, the auditor must balance it by investigating errors or omissions. This is done by checking that every departmental charge shows up on guest folios.
5. Complete and distribute the daily report. This report details the previous day's activities and includes vital information about the performance of the hotel.
6. Determine areas of the hotel where theft could potentially occur.

Larger hotels may have more than one night auditor, but in smaller properties these duties may be combined with night manager, desk, or night watchperson duties.

CORPORATE PROFILE

Hyatt Hotels

When Nicholas Pritzker emigrated with his family from the Ukraine to the United States, he began his career by opening a small law firm. His outstanding management skills led to the expansion of the law firm, turning it into a management company. The Pritzkers gained considerable financial support, which allowed them to pursue their goals of expansion and development. These dreams came into reality with the opening of the first Hyatt Hotel, on September 27, 1957.

Today Hyatt is an international brand of hotels within the Global Hyatt Corporation a multi-billion-dollar hotel management and development company. It is among the leading chains in the hotel industry, with close to 8 percent of the market share.[1] Hyatt has earned worldwide fame as the leader in providing luxury accommodations and high-quality service, targeting especially the business traveler, but strategically differentiating its properties and services to identify and market to a very diverse clientele. This differentiation has resulted in the following types of hotels:

1. The *Hyatt Regency Hotels* represent the company's core product. They are usually located in business city centers and are regarded as five-star hotels.
2. *Hyatt Resorts* are vacation retreats. They are located in the world's most desirable leisure destinations, offering the "ultimate escape from everyday stresses."

(continued)

CORPORATE PROFILE *(continued)*

3. The *Park Hyatt Hotels* are smaller, European-style, luxury hotels. They target the individual traveler who prefers the privacy, personalized service, and discreet elegance of a small European hotel.

4. The *Grand Hyatt Hotels* serve culturally rich destinations that attract leisure business as well as large-scale meetings and conventions. They reflect refinement and grandeur, and they feature state-of-the-art technology and banquet and conference facilities of world-class standard.

5. *Hyatt Vacation Club* offers vacation ownership, vacation rentals, and mini vacations

6. *U.S. Franchise Systems, Inc.,* franchises Hawthorne Suites, Microtel, and Best Inns.

7. Hyatt has also acquired the upscale, limited-service *AmeriSuites hotel chain*, which is being repositioned under a new Hyatt brand called Hyatt Place.

Hyatt Hotels Corporation has been recognized by the *Wall Street Journal* as one of the sixty-six firms around the world poised to make a difference in industries and markets. The effective management that characterized the company in its early years with the Pritzker family has continued through time. Hyatt Hotels Corporation is characterized by a decentralized management approach, which gives the individual general manager a great deal of decision-making power, as well as the opportunity to use personal creativity and, therefore, stimulate differentiation and innovation. The development of novel concepts and products is perhaps the key to Hyatt's outstanding success. For example, the opening of the Hyatt Regency Atlanta, Georgia, gave the company instant recognition throughout the world. Customers were likely to stare in awe at the twenty-one-story atrium lobby, the glass elevators, and the revolving rooftop restaurant. The property's innovative architecture, designed by John Portman, revolutionized the common standards of design and spacing, thus changing the course of the lodging industry. The atrium concept introduced there represented a universal challenge to hotel architects to face the new trend of grand, wide-open public spaces.

A further positive aspect of the decentralized management structure is the fact that the individual manager is able to be extremely customer responsive by developing a thorough knowledge of the guests' needs and thereby providing personalized service—fundamental to achieving customer satisfaction. This is, in fact, the ultimate innkeeping purpose, which Hyatt attains at high levels.

The other side of Hyatt's success is the emphasis on human resources management. Employee satisfaction, in fact, is considered to be a prerequisite to external satisfaction. Hyatt devotes enormous attention to employee training and selection. What is most significant, however, is the interaction among top managers and operating employees.

[1]The company operates 213 hotels and resorts in forty-three countries worldwide.

The **daily report** contains key operating ratios such as **room occupancy percentage (ROP),** which is the number of rooms occupied divided by the number of rooms available:

$$\text{ROP} = \frac{\text{Rooms Occupied}}{\text{Rooms Available}}$$

Thus, if a hotel has 850 rooms and 622 are occupied, the occupancy percentage is $622 \div 850 = 73$ percent.

The **average daily rate** is calculated by dividing the rooms revenue by the number of rooms sold:

$$\frac{\text{Rooms Revenue}}{\text{Rooms Sold}}$$

If the rooms revenue is $75,884 and the number of rooms sold is 662, then the ADR is $114.63. The ADR is, together with the occupancy percentage, one of the key operating ratios that indicates the hotel's performance. See Figure 4–5 for an example of a daily report.

Room Occupancy Percentage (ROP):

If total available rooms are	850
And total rooms occupied are	622

73%

Then:

Occupancy percentage = (622 / 850) × 100 = 73%

Average Daily Rate:

If rooms revenue is	$75,884
And total number of rooms sold is	622

$122.

Then:

Average daily rate = $\dfrac{75,884}{662}$ = $ 114.63

A more recently popular ratio to gauge a hotel rooms division's performance is the percentage of potential rooms revenue, which is calculated by determining potential rooms revenue and dividing the actual revenue by the potential revenue.

▶ Check Your Knowledge

1. What is the rooms division director responsible for?

2. Describe the duties performed by the front office manager (FOM).

3. What is the Rack Rate and what other types of room rates are there?

4. How do you calculate the room occupancy percentage and the average daily rate?

Hotel Information Technology Systems

Information technology has helped hotels reach one of the main goals of a hotel: to deliver exceptional guest satisfaction. Some hotels have utilized technology for many years. The first hotel to use a computer was the New York Hilton in 1963. This was the first computer-automated guest room management system, but it was very inefficient because front desk clerks had to use key punch cards to record information, and then process these cards in a batch at a later time.[1] Fortunately, hospitality information technology has progressed, and today several efficient systems are fast becoming industry standards.

Clarion Hotel Bayview

Daily Management Report Supplement
January 2007

Daily Report
January 2007

Occupancy%	Today	Avg or %	M–T–D Avg or %		Y–T–D Avg or %	
Rack Rooms	9	2.9%	189	3.37	189	3.37
Corporate Rooms	0	0.0%	103	1.83	103	1.83
Group Rooms	274	87.8%	2,379	42.36	2,379	42.36
Leisure Rooms	3	1.0%	395	7.03	395	7.03
Base Rooms	23	7.4%	348	6.14	345	6.14
Government Rooms	2	0.6%	32	.57	32	.57
Wholesale Rooms	1	0.3%	121	2.15	121	2.15
No-Show Rooms		0.0%	0	.00	0	.00
Comp Rooms	0	0.0%	37	.66	37	.66
Total Occ Rooms & Occ %	312	100%	3,601	64.12	3,601	64.12
Rack	$1,011	$112.33	17,207	91.04	17,207	91.04
Corporate	$0	ERR	8,478	82.31	8,478	82.31
Group	$22,510	$82.15	178,066	74.85	178,066	74.85
Leisure	$207	$69.00	24,985	63.25	24,985	63.25
Base	$805	$35.00	12,063	34.97	12,063	34.97
Govt	$141	$70.59	2,379	74.34	2,379	74.34
Wholesale	$43	$43.00	5,201	42.98	5,201	42.98
No-Show/Comp/Allowance	$0		–914	–24.69	–914	–24.69
Total Rev & Avg Rate	$24,717	$79.22	247,466	68.72	247,466	68.72

Hotel Revenue

Rooms	$24,717		247,466	77.46	247,466	77.46
Food	$1,400		37,983	11.89	37,983	11.89
Beverage	$539		9,679	3.03	9,679	3.03
Telephone	$547		5,849	1.83	5,849	1.83
Parking	$854		11,103	3.48	11,103	3.48
Room Svc II	$70		1,441	.45	1,441	.45
Other Revenue	$1,437		963	1.87	963	1.87
Total Revenue	$29,563		319,484	100.00	319,484	100.00

Figure 4–5 • A Hotel Daily Report.

Clarion Hotel Bayview

Daily Management Report Supplement
January 2007

Daily Report
January 2007

Cafe 6th & K	Today	Avg or %	M–T–D	Avg or %	Y–T–D	Avg or %
Cafe Breakfast Covers	88	57.1%	1,180	47.12	1,180	47.12
Cafe Lunch Covers	43	27.9%	674	26.92	674	26.92
Cafe Dinner Covers	23	14.9%	650	25.96	650	25.96
Total Cafe Covers	154	100.0%	2,504	100.00	2,504	100.00
Cafe Breakfast	$608	$6.91	7,854	6.66	7,854	6.66
Cafe Lunch	$246	$5.72	5,847	8.67	5,847	8.67
Cafe Dinner	$227	$9.86	4,309	6.63	4,309	6.63
Gaslamp Lounge Food			2,431	3.74	2,431	3.74
Total Rev / Avg Check	$1,081	$7.02	20,440	8.16	20,440	8.16

Banquets

	Today	Avg or %	M–T–D	Avg or %	Y–T–D	Avg or %
Banquet Breakfast Covers	0	ERR	154	13.24	154	13.24
Banquet Lunch Covers	0	ERR	134	11.52	134	11.52
Banquet Dinner Covers	0	ERR	254	21.84	254	21.84
Banquet Coffee Break Covers	0	ERR	621	53.40	621	53.40
Total Banquet Covers	0	ERR	1,163	100.00	1,163	100.00
Banquet Breakfast	$0	ERR	980	6.36	980	6.36
Banquet Lunch	$0	ERR	2,997	22.36	2,997	22.36
Banquet Dinner	$0	ERR	4,530	17.84	4,530	17.84
Banquet Coffee Break	$0	ERR	1,093	1.76	1,093	1.76
Total Rev / Avg Check	$0	ERR	9,600	8.25	9,600	8.25

Room Service

	Today	Avg or %	M–T–D	Avg or %	Y–T–D	Avg or %
Room Service Breakfast Covers	13	40.6%	324	48.00	324	48.00
Room Service Lunch Covers	3	9.4%	53	7.85	53	7.85
Room Service Dinner Covers	16	50.0%	298	44.15	298	44.15
Total Covers	32	100.0%	675	100.00	675	100.00
Room Service Breakfast	$119	$9.13	2,665	8.22	2,665	8.22
Room Service Lunch	$29	$9.77	418	7.89	418	7.89
Room Service Dinner	$171	$10.67	2,907	9.75	2,907	9.75
Total Rev / Avg Check	$319	$9.96	5,990	8.87	5,990	8.87

Figure 4–5 • A Hotel Daily Report. *(continued)*

(handwritten margin notes)
PMS:
4 fosse
4 manages
    reservations,
guest folios,
arrivals, deps,
reports.

- Room mngmt
    module:
4 keeps FO &
4 Hsk informed
    of room status

- Guest Accting
    module:
4 folios,

Property Management Systems

The **property management system (PMS)** is the center of information processing in a hotel. A property management system is a computer-based lodging information system that relates to both the front- and back-office activities. Property management systems are used to help complete many tasks within a short period of time. Hotels with a large number of guests and employees to serve and inform predominantly use these systems. A PMS will aid a property to become more efficient with time, which is an important factor for guests who demand personal attention and fast service.

The property management system can interact with many other modules and applications. One application of the PMS in the front office is the **room management module,** which keeps the front office and housekeeping informed about the status of rooms. The hotel room master in the PMS contains data on each room such as room number, room type, room features, room rates, locations, and the status of each room. Knowing the status of each room definitely helps the housekeeping department know what work has to be done, what work is in progress, and what work has been completed.

Another front office module is a **guest accounting module.** A guest accounting module increases the hotel's control over guest accounts, makes them easily available at any time, and significantly shortens the night audit procedure. Other functions of a PMS are electronic locking systems, energy management systems, and call accounting systems.

There are many potential users of a PMS. Any manager making strategic decisions could utilize the information provided by a PMS. Some property management systems even offer microcomputer interfaces so that the information from the PMS can be downloaded onto a personal computer to be utilized by a number of business applications.

Some hotels use an express check-in process that allows guests to conveniently check in and out without associate assistance by using a touch screen that interfaces with the hotel's property management system. A booth in the lobby allows guests to input their reservation details or provide data from an inserted card or touch-screen selections. Based on the information given, after obtaining an electronic signature, an electronic room key is then encoded and dispensed. A printout of guest stay information, including room type, rate, and departure date, is printed.[2] Guests may also use the booth to check out. Guest preferences are noted for future use, and even airline boarding passes can now be issued.

The PMS system interfaces with the Internet to allow guests the capability to book rooms online. Hotels are now attempting to drive bookings to "their" web sites rather than pay commission to companies such as Hotels.com, Travelocity, and Expedia.

Perhaps the ultimate in guest convenience is the wireless curbside guest check-in made possible by the VingCard system. This recent technological advance allows guests to go right to their rooms from curbside. The system is capable of interfacing with existing PMS systems to fully integrate property management, reservations, and guest service functions. With a portable keycard encoder and MICROS's OPERA Palm, a wireless handheld device with

A Popular Property Management System

real-time database access, the system works seamlessly to provide the ultimate in guest convenience.[3]

Some property management systems use Microsoft Windows to move data between applications and to share information, a process called *information sharing*. Information sharing permits menu-driven interface with other systems, such as advanced reservations, room inventory, self-check-in/out, night audit, guest accounting, city ledger, group handling, and travel agency accounting.[4] All these systems are designed to improve guest service. But beware: Management needs to ensure that the front desk associate doesn't just look down while keying in the guest name and other details without ever really looking up at the customer. The hotels that will be successful in the next few years are the ones that go out of their way to make guests really feel welcome and offer high-tech yet high-touch service.

Hotel guests expect their rooms to be a home away from home, an office, a retreat, and even a playroom. High-speed Internet access (HSIA) is becoming a necessity. Hotels and restaurants that don't offer HSIA lose guests, as happened at one Holiday Inn Express that had not upgraded; guests moved across the street where their technology needs were met. Naturally, it did not take long for the Holiday Inn to install WiFi. Starbucks was the first restaurant chain to offer WiFi to guests, who can now enjoy a latté with their e-mail. Even some McDonald's have gone WiFi.

High-speed Internet access is a given, but it is a challenge for hotel operators to select a service provider. Some of the older hotels have selected to go totally wireless using RoomLinx (**www.roomlinx.com**), a choice that gives guests high-speed Internet access not just from their rooms but also throughout the hotel, including meeting rooms.

Moderately priced Wingate Inns partners with Lodge Net (**www.lodgenet .com**) to offer guests high-speed Internet access in every room and a full array of entertainment options: movies, video games, and music. MGM Grand selected Cox Communications Hospitality Network (**www.cox.com**) to deploy what will be the largest hotel wireless Internet network in the nation. Guests can purchase WiFi access or use the existing hospitality network wired Internet service from the convenience of their own rooms.

Web-enabled personal digital assistants (PDAs) allow companies such as Hyatt Hotels to offer its Gold Passport guests a PDA-based program from Portable Internet (**www.portableinternet.com**) to deliver driving directions as well as shopping, restaurants, and entertainment information. Guests can access descriptions of the properties and their facilities and advanced reservations. At the Venetian Casino Resort in Las Vegas, guests can check in with their PDAs as soon as they walk in the door and can also make table reservations via Open Table. They may also select the in-room temperature and the room service menu.

Energy Management Systems

Technology is used to extend guest in-room comfort by means of an energy management system. Passive infrared motion sensors and door switches can reduce energy consumption by 30 percent or more by

VingCard Vision is a full-featured, functionally rich access control system that allows guests to self-check-in

automatically switching off lights and air-conditioning, thus saving energy when the guest is out of the room. Additional features include the following:

- Room occupancy status reporting
- Automatic lighting control
- Minibar access reporting
- Smoke detector alarm reporting
- Central electronic lock control
- Guest control amenities

Because of increasing energy costs, some operators are installing software programs that will turn off nonessential equipment during the peak billing times of day (utility companies' charges are based on peak usage). Hospitality operators can save money by utilizing this type of energy-saving software to reduce their energy costs.

Call Accounting Systems

Call accounting systems (CAS) track guest room phone charges. Software packages can be used to monitor where calls are being made and from which phones on the property. To track this information, the CAS must work in conjunction with the PBX (telephone) and the PMS. Call accounting systems today can be used to offer different rates for local guest calls and long-distance guest calls. The CAS can even be used to offer discounted calling during off-peak hours at the hotel.

Guest Reservation Systems

Before hotels started using the Internet to book reservations, they received reservations by letters, telegrams, faxes, and phone calls. Airlines were the first industry to start using **global distribution systems (GDS)** for reservations (Figure 4–6). Global distribution systems are electronic markets for travel, hotel, car rental, and attraction bookings.

A **central reservation system (CRS)** houses the electronic database in the **central reservation office (CRO)**. Hotels provide rates and availability information to the CRO usually by data communication lines. This automatically updates the CRS so that guests get the best available rate when they book through the central reservation office. Guests instantly receive confirmation of their reservation or cancellation. The hotel benefits from using a central reservation system. With such a system, hotels can avoid overselling rooms by too large a margin. The CRS database can also be used as a chain or individual property marketing tool because guest information can easily be stored. A CRS can also provide yield management information for a hotel. The more flexible a central reservation system is, the more it will help with yield management. For example, when demand is weak for a hotel, rates will need to

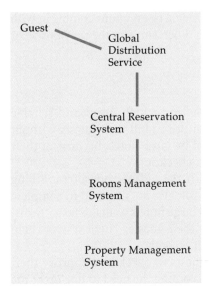

Figure 4–6 • The Sequence and Relationships of a Hotel Guest Reservation.

drop to increase reservations and profitability. When demand is higher, the hotel can sell room rates that are closer to the rack rate (*rack rate* is the highest rate quoted for a guestroom, from which all discounts are offered).

A CRS can be used in several areas of a hotel. If a hotel has a reservations department, the terminals or personal computers in that department can be connected to the central reservation system. It is also important for front desk employees to have access to the CRS so that they know what the hotel has available because they may need to book rooms for walk-ins who don't have reservations. Constant communication back and forth is needed between the central reservation system and the front office and reservations department. Managers who are the decision makers in the hotel will also use the system to forecast and set pricing for rooms and different amenities.

Hotels can use other forms of technology to facilitate reservation systems. Several companies offer an **application service provider (ASP)** environment that can deliver a complete booking system tied to the hotel's inventory in real time via the Web. One operator, Paul Wood of the El Dorado Hotel in Santa Fe, New Mexico, says that he simply went to the ASP's web site and put in a promotional corporate

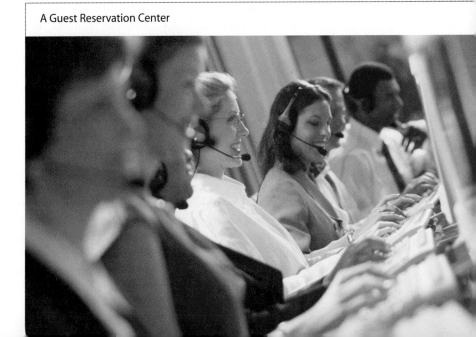

A Guest Reservation Center

rate for the summer, and the same day he started seeing reservations coming in with that code. After a few months, bookings were up 3 percent over the previous year.

Billing Guests

Hospitality businesses today seek to obtain the most high-speed and reliable computer systems they can afford that they can use to bill their guests without delay. Fast access to guests' accounts is required by large hotels because of their high priority of guest satisfaction (no lineups at checkout).

Billing guests has become much easier with the aid of computers. Billing guests can be a long process if information technologies are not used to complete transactions. Property management systems aid large hotels to make faster transactions and provide a more efficient service to their guests. These systems help the hospitality associates bill their guests within seconds.

Some hotels utilize software that enables guests to check and approve their bills by using the TV and remote control, thus avoiding the need to line up at the cashier's desk to check out. A copy of the final bill is then mailed to the guest's home address.

Security

Each business in the hospitality industry offers some sort of security for their guests and employees. Peace of mind that the hotel or restaurant is secure is a key factor in increasing guest satisfaction. Security is one of the highest concerns of guests who visit hospitality businesses. Hospitality information technology systems include surveillance systems in which cameras are installed in many different areas of the property to monitor the grounds and help ensure guest safety. These cameras are linked directly to computers, televisions, and digital recorders, which helps security teams keep an eye on the whole property.

Recent technological advances have produced electronic door locking systems, some of which even offer custom configurations of security and safety. Guest room locks are now capable of managing information from both magstripe and smart cards simultaneously. From the hotel's point of view, a main advantage of this kind of key is that the hotel knows who has entered the room and at what time because the system can trace anyone entering the room.

In-room safes can now be operated by key cards. Both systems are an improvement on the old metal keys. Even smarter safes use biometric technology such as the use of thumbprints or retina scans to verify a user's identity.

Guest Comfort and Convenience

Hotels provide guest comfort and convenience to maintain a home-away-from-home feeling for their guests. Hotels receive recognition when they provide many additional in-room services and amenities for their guests, such as dining, television, telephones, Internet connections, minibars, and hygiene products. These amenities help provide a cozy experience for the guest. Many other services can be provided outside of the rooms, such as swimming pools, massages, fine dining, postal services, and meeting space. Other services are provided to suit the demands of all types of guests; a concierge and business center, for example.

Hotels communicate with many entities to provide services for their guests. Some companies offer creative solutions to hotels for enhanced in-room services for guests. Sprint InSite with KoolConnect Interactive Media has created a product that provides many services to the guest from just one supplier. Services include Internet access and e-mail; movies, music, and games on demand; hotel and concierge services; special promotions; advertising; travel planning; feedback from guests; and customer support. All these services aid hotels in fulfilling guest demands. Sprint states, "Build loyalty and promote business retention by enhancing the overall quality-of-visit for your guest."[5] Play Stations and video games are also a part of the technology-based guest amenities.

Revenue and Yield Management

Revenue management is used to maximize room revenue at the hotel. It is based on the economics of supply and demand, which means that prices rise when demand is strong and drop when demand is weak. Naturally, management would like to sell every room at the highest rack rate. However, this is not a reality, and rooms are sold at discounts from the rack rate. An example is the corporate or group rate. In most hotels, only a small percentage of rooms are sold at rack rate. This is because of conventions and group rates and other promotional discounts that are necessary to stimulate demand.

What **yield management** does is allocate the right type of room to the right guest at the right price so as to maximize revenue per available room.[6] Thus, the purpose of yield management is to increase profitability. Generally, the demand for room reservations follows the pattern of group bookings, which are made months or even years in advance of arrival, and individual bookings, which

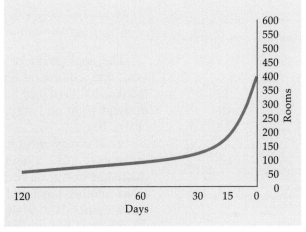

Figure 4–7 • Individual Room Booking Reservations Curve.
(*Source:* Personal correspondence with Jay R. Schrock, May 18, 2007.)

Figure 4–8 • Group Booking Curve.

mostly are made a few days before arrival. Figures 4–7 and 4–8 show the pattern of group and individual room reservations. Yield management examines the demand for rooms over a period of a few years and determines the extent of demand for a particular room each night. This includes busy period, slow periods, and holidays. The computer program figures out a model of that demand, which is then used to guestimate future demand so that management can determine pricing levels to set.

Because group reservations are booked months, even years, in advance, yield management systems can monitor reservations and, based on previous trends and current demand, determine the number and type of rooms to sell at what price to obtain the maximum revenue.

The curve in Figure 4–7 indicates the pattern of few reservations being made 120 days prior to arrival. Most of the individual room bookings are made in the last few days before arrival at the hotel. The yield management program monitors the demand and supply and recommends the number and type of rooms to sell for any given day, and the price for which to sell each room.

With yield management, not only will the time before arrival be an important consideration in the pricing of guest rooms, but also the type of room to be occupied. For example, there could be a different price for a double, queen, or king room when used for single occupancy. This rate could be above the single rack rate. Similarly, double and multiple room occupancy would yield higher room rates. It works as follows:

Suppose a hotel has 300 rooms and a rack rate of $150. The average number of rooms sold is 200 per night at an average rate of $125. The yield for this property is

$$\text{Room occupancy percentage} = 200 \div 300 = 66.6\%$$

The rate achievement factor is

$$\$125 \div \$150 = 0.833$$

and the yield is

$$0.666 \times 0.833 = 55.5\%$$

The application of yield management in hotels is still being refined to take into consideration factors such as multiple nights' reservations and incremental food and beverage revenue. If the guest wants to arrive on a high-demand night and stay through several low-demand nights, what should the charge be?

Yield management has some disadvantages. For instance, if a businessperson attempts to make a reservation at a hotel three days before arrival and the rate quoted to maximize revenue is considered too high, this person may decide to select another hotel and not even consider the first hotel when making future reservations.

Revenue per available room, or **rev par,** was developed by Smith Travel Research. It is calculated by dividing room revenue by the number of rooms available. For example, if room sales are $50,000 in one day for a hotel with

400 available rooms, then the formula is $50,000 divided by 400, or $125. Hotels use rev par to see how they are doing compared to their competitive set of hotels. Owners use rev par to gauge who they want to run their hotels.

▶ Check Your Knowledge

1. What functions does the property management system perform?
2. What is revenue management? How is revenue management applied in the hotel industry?

Reservations

The reservations department is headed by the reservations manager who, in many hotels today, is on the same level as the front office manager and reports directly to the director of rooms division or the director of sales. This emphasizes the importance of the sales aspects of reservations and encompasses yield management. Reservations is the first contact for the guest or person making the reservation for the guest. Although the contact may be by telephone, a distinct impression of the hotel is registered with the guest. Because of this, exceptional telephone manners and telemarketing skills are necessary. Because some guests may be shopping for the best value, it is essential to sell the hotel by emphasizing its advantages over the competition.

The reservation department generally works from 8:00 A.M. to 6:00 P.M. Depending on the size of the hotel, several people may be employed in this important department. The desired outcome of the reservations department is to exceed guest expectations when they make reservations. This is achieved by selling all of the hotel rooms for the maximum possible dollars and avoiding possible guest resentment of being overcharged. Reservations originate from a variety of sources:

1. Telephone to the same property
    a. Fax
    b. Letter
    c. Cable
2. Corporate/1-800 numbers
3. Travel agents
4. The Internet
5. Meeting planners
6. Tour operators
7. Referral from another company property
8. Airport telephone
9. Walk-in

Clearly, reservations are of tremendous importance to the hotel because of the potential and actual revenue realized. Many hotel chains have a 1-800 number that a prospective guest may call without charge to make a reservation at any of the company properties in the United States and internationally. The corporate central reservations system allows operators to access the inventory of room availability of each hotel in the chain. Once a reservation has been made, it is immediately deducted from the inventory of rooms for the duration of the guest stay. The central reservations system interfaces with the hotel's inventory and simultaneously allows reservations to be made by the individual hotel reservations personnel. A number of important details need to be recorded when taking reservations.

Confirmed reservations are reservations made with sufficient time for a confirmation slip to be returned to the client by mail or fax. Confirmation is generated by the computer printer and indicates confirmation number, dates of arrival and departure, type of room booked, number of guests, number of beds, type of bed, and any special requests. The guest may bring the confirmation slip to the hotel to verify the booking.

Guaranteed reservations are given when the person making the reservation wishes to ensure that the reservation will be held. This is arranged at the time the reservation is made and generally applies in situations when the guest is expected to arrive late. The hotel takes the credit card number, which guarantees payment of the room, of the person being billed. The hotel agrees to hold the room for late arrival. The importance of guaranteed reservations is that the guest will more likely cancel beforehand if unable to show up, which gives more accurate inventory room count and minimizes no-shows.

Another form of guaranteed reservations is advance deposit/advance payment. In certain situations, for example, during a holiday, to protect itself against having empty rooms (no-shows), the hotel requires that a deposit of either one night or the whole stay be paid in advance of the guest's arrival. This is done by obtaining the guest's credit card number, which may be charged automatically for the first night's accommodation. This discourages no-shows. Corporations that use the hotel frequently may guarantee all of their bookings so as to avoid any problems in the event a guest arrives late, remembering that in cities where the demand is heavy, hotels release any nonguaranteed or nonpaid reservations at 4:00 P.M. or 6:00 P.M. on the evening of the guest's expected arrival.

Communications CBX or PBX

The communications CBX or PBX includes in-house communications; guest communications, such as pagers and radios; voice mail; faxes; messages; and emergency center. Guests often have their first contact with the hotel by telephone. This underlines the importance of prompt and courteous attention to all calls because first impressions last.

The communications department is a vital part of the smooth running of the hotel. It is also a profit center because hotels generally add a 50 percent charge to all long-distance calls placed from guest rooms. Local calls cost about $0.75 to $1.25, plus tax.

Communications operates twenty-four hours a day, in much the same way as the front office does, having three shifts. It is essential that this department be staffed with people who are trained to be calm under pressure and who follow emergency procedures.

Guest Services/Uniformed Services

Because first impressions are very important to the guest, the guest service or uniformed staff has a special responsibility. The guest service department or **uniformed staff** is headed by a guest services manager who may also happen to be the bell captain. The staff consists of door attendants and bellpersons and the concierge, although in some hotels the concierge reports directly to the front office manager.

Door attendants are the hotel's unofficial greeters. Dressed in impressive uniforms, they greet guests at the hotel front door, assist in opening/closing automobile doors, removing luggage from the trunk, hailing taxis, keeping the hotel entrance clear of vehicles, and giving guests information about the hotel and the local area in a courteous and friendly way. People in this position generally receive many gratuities (tips); in fact, years ago, the position was handed down from father to son or sold for several thousand dollars. Rumor has it that this is one of the most lucrative positions in the hotel, even more lucrative than the general manager's.

[handwritten margin note:]
4 door attendants
4 bell person
4 concierge
4

INTRODUCING RYAN ADAMS

Guest Services Manager, Hotel del Coronado, San Diego, California

I have been in the industry now for eleven years and I am always amazed at the magnetic draw this industry has on you. I always tell people, "It's not the job that is so hard, that is rudimentary; it is people that really make the challenge worth undertaking." I wake up at 6:00 A.M. every morning and prepare myself mentally before I go to work on how I am going to tackle the day.

My automatic coffee maker wakes me up and I establish my bearings as I proceed to take my shower and then turn on ESPN to catch sport highlights. I pour myself a cup of coffee and sit on the couch trying to figure out what I missed and memorize scores from the previous night's game. I then switch over to CNN to catch up on politics and headline news just in case there actually might be something of interest to my isolated world.

I usually arrive at work about 7 A.M. so that I can see the night shift bellman for a half hour, and then the morning valet and cashiers. You learn a lot from the night crew. They see a lot of the nonsense that happens over the midnight hour. I touch base with the front desk and the concierge to see if they have any challenges starting off the day. I then retreat to my office.

As I get into my office, it never fails that I have at least five voice mails and ten e-mails. I listen to my voice mails and print my e-mails and look at my calendar in Microsoft Outlook to see what meetings I have

(continued)

INTRODUCING RYAN ADAMS (continued)

dedicated my time to. I then make a list of what I need to respond to and work on the pile of papers on my desk. I usually have a pile of papers from the night before because I get a lot of mail. I look at my fourteen-day forecast to see what events or groups we have in house and touch base with my bell phone receptionist who usually has good insight into the day's events.

My responsibilities are to oversee the functions of the bellman, elevator operators, doorman, valet runners, kiosk cashiers, mass transportation, parking control, and the concierge. I have two assistant guest services managers that come in at 11 A.M. and 2:30 P.M. to cover the other shifts. I also have a parking operations supervisor and a cashier supervisor. We hold a weekly meeting so that I can share the vision of the company and my own. After all, I am not just a manager; I am a leader who has to take people somewhere where they would not have gone otherwise.

I spend most of my day in meetings. On Tuesdays, I attend the operations meetings. Our managing director and general manager speak to us about financial position and goals for the quarter. They also bring up special highlights or events. We hear from sales and convention management regarding groups and then catering for events. Room reservations personnel update us on their budget and how many rooms are going to be occupied for the next two weeks and then compare that to the forecasted level of occupancy. We then hear from accounting facilities, recreation, retail, guest services, and signature services. It is a very informative meeting and it also gives you a good read on the mood of upper management.

I try to spend as much face time with my associates as possible, getting feedback and safety suggestions and to let them vent frustrations as I try to win them over to the big picture. I spend a little time "shmoozing" clients who have porterages and deliveries to ensure my team is doing their best to impress. I attend their pre-convention meetings to discover what the clients are about. We identify their needs and fulfill them with the kind of guest service that leaves their jaws dropped.

The funny thing about modern technology is how dependent you become on it. Gone are the days of the good ole boy network when all you had to do was ask. Now you have to set up a meeting in Microsoft Outlook, send e-mails, fill out tons of paperwork, and constantly check your voice mails and e-mails. The company has made it a little easier by supplying me with a Nextel phone, or "the leash" as we call it. This phone has walkie-talkie capability and allows the executive team to communicate on a network.

I know what you're thinking: sounds tedious and problematic. Well it is. The challenge of making it all come together is what is so appealing to me. I usually get so involved that I forget to eat lunch, unless one of my teammates pulls me away for a bite and engages me in some endless banter about work. I stock my office refrigerator with candy bars and various beverages because I usually don't make the time to eat; it just gets too busy.

My days typically end about 5 P.M. or 6 P.M. I have by then passed on all information the night crews will need and delegated responsibilities to the two assistant guest services managers. I still have a big stack of papers to go through and file for tomorrow. I hop on my bicycle, ride by security to check in my keys, and then I am off to go home and see my lovely wife. This is the day in a life of a guest services manager.

The bellperson's main function is to escort guests and transport luggage to their rooms. Bellpersons also need to be knowledgeable about the local area and all facets of the hotel and its services. Because they have so much guest contact, they need a pleasant, outgoing personality. The bellperson explains the services of the hotel and points out the features of the room (lighting, TV, air-conditioning, telephone, wake-up calls, laundry and valet service, room service and restaurants, and the pool and health spa).

Concierge

The concierge is a uniformed employee of the hotel who has her or his own separate desk in the lobby or on special concierge floors. The concierge is a separate department from the front office room clerks and cashiers.

Luxury hotels in most cities have concierges. New York's Plaza Hotel has 800 rooms and a battery of ten concierges who serve under the direction of Thomas P. Wolfe. The concierge assists guests with a broad range of services such as the following:

- Tickets to the hottest shows in town, even for the very evening on the day they are requested. Naturally, the guest pays up to about $150 per ticket.

- A table at a restaurant that has no reservations available.

- Advice on local restaurants, activities, attractions, amenities, and facilities.

- Airline tickets and reconfirmation of flights.

- VIP's messages and special requests, such as shopping.

Less frequent requests are:

- Organize a wedding on two days' notice

- Arrange for a member of the concierge department to go to a consulate or embassy for visas to be stamped in guests' passports

- Handle business affairs

What will a concierge do for a guest? Almost anything, *Condé Nast Traveler* learned from concierges at hotels around the world. Among the more unusual requests were the following:

Concierges assist guests with a variety of services

1. Some Japanese tourists staying at the Palace Hotel in Madrid decided to bring bullfighting home. Their concierge found bulls for sale, negotiated the bulls' purchase, and had them shipped to Tokyo.

2. After watching a guest pace the lobby, the concierge of a London hotel, now operating the desk at the Dorchester, asked the pacer if he could help. The guest was to be married within the hour, but his best man had been detained. Because he was dressed up anyway, the concierge volunteered to substitute.

3. A guest at the Hotel Plaza Athenee in Paris wanted to prevent her pet from mingling with dogs from the "wrong side" of the boulevard while walking. Madame requested that the concierge buy a house in a decent neighborhood so that her pampered pooch might stroll in its garden unsullied. Although the dog continued to reside at the hotel, Madame's chauffeur shuttled him to the empty house for his daily constitutional.

Concierges serve to elevate a property's marketable value and its image. They provide the special touch services that distinguish a "top property." To make sure they can cater to a guest's precise needs, concierges should make sure that they know precisely what the guest is looking for budget-wise, as well as any other parameters. Concierges must be very attentive and must anticipate guest needs when possible. In this age of highly competitive top-tier properties and well-informed guests, only knowledgeable concierge staff can provide the services to make a guest's stay memorable. As more properties try to demonstrate enhanced value, a concierge amenity takes on added significance.

The concierge needs not only a detailed knowledge of the hotel and its services, but also of the city and even international details. Many concierges speak several languages; most important of all, they must want to help people and have a pleasant, outgoing personality. The concierges' organization, which promotes high professional and ethical standards, is the (Union Professionelle des Portiers des Grand Hotels (UPPGH)), more commonly called the *Clefs d' Or* (pronounced clays-dor) because of the crossed gold-key insignia concierges usually wear on the lapels of their uniforms.

Housekeeping

The largest department in terms of the number of people employed is housekeeping. Up to 50 percent of the hotel employees may work in this department. Because of the hard work and comparatively low pay, employee turnover is very high in this essential department. The person in charge is the executive housekeeper or director of services. Her or his duties and responsibilities call for exceptional leadership, organization, motivation, and commitment to maintaining high standards. The logistics of servicing large numbers of rooms on a daily basis can be challenging. The importance of the housekeeping department is underlined by guest surveys that consistently rank cleanliness of rooms number one.

The four major areas of responsibilities for the executive housekeeper are as follows:

1. Leadership of people, equipment, and supplies
2. Cleanliness and servicing the guest rooms and public areas
3. Operating the department according to financial guidelines prescribed by the general manager
4. Keeping records

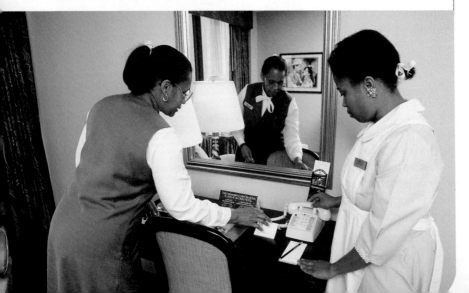

An executive housekeeper checks the desk in a hotel room. Attention to detail is important in maintaining standards

An example of an executive housekeeper's day might be as follows:

7:45 A.M. Walk the lobby and property with the night cleaners and supervisors

Check the housekeeping logbook

Check the forecast house count for number of checkouts

Check daily activity reports, stayovers, check-ins, and VIPs to ensure appropriate standards

Attend housekeepers' meeting

Meet challenges

Train new employees in the procedures

Meet with senior housekeepers/department managers

Conduct productivity checks

Check budget

Approve purchase orders

Check inventories

Conduct room inspections

Review maintenance checks

Interview potential employees

6:00 P.M. Attend to human resource activities, counseling, and employee development

Perhaps the biggest challenge of an executive housekeeper is the leadership of all the employees in the department. Further, these employees are often of different nationalities. Depending on the size of the hotel, the executive housekeeper is assisted by an assistant executive housekeeper and one or more housekeeping supervisors, who in turn supervise a number of room attendants or housekeeping associates (see Figure 4–9). The assistant executive housekeeper manages the housekeeping office. The first important daily task of this position is to break out the hotel into sections for allocation to the room attendants' schedules.

The rooms of the hotel are listed on the floor master. If the room is vacant, nothing is written next to the room number. If the guest is expected to check out, then SC will be written next to the room number. A stayover will have SS, on hold is AH, out of order is OO, and VIPs are highlighted in colors according to the amenities required.

If 258 rooms are occupied and 10 of these are suites (which count as two rooms), then the total number of rooms to be allocated to room attendants is 268 (minus any no-shows). The remaining total is then divided by 17, which is the number of rooms that each attendant is expected to make up.

Total number of rooms occupied	258
Add 10 for the suites	10
Total number of rooms and suites occupied	268
Less any no-shows	3
	$265 \div 17 = 16$

Therefore, sixteen attendants are required for that day.

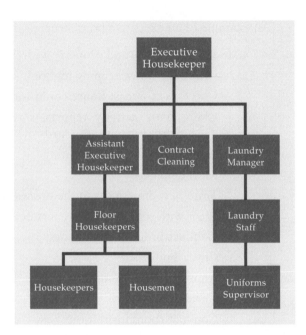

Figure 4–9 • Housekeeping
Department Organization Chart.

Figure 4–10 shows a daily attendant's schedule. To reduce payroll costs and encourage room attendants to become "stars," a number of hotel corporations have empowered the best attendants to check their own rooms. This has reduced the need for supervisors. Notice in Figure 4–10 how the points are weighted for various items. This is the result of focus groups of hotel guests who explained the things about a room that are important to them. The items with the highest points were the ones that most concerned the guests.

The housekeeping associates clean and service between fifteen and twenty rooms per day, depending on the individual hotel characteristics. Servicing a room takes longer in some older hotels than it does in some of the newer properties. Also, service time depends on the number of checkout rooms versus stayovers because servicing checkouts takes longer. Housekeeping associates begin their day at 8:00 A.M., reporting to the executive or assistant executive housekeeper. They are assigned a block of rooms and given room keys, for which they must sign and then return before going off duty.

The role of the executive housekeeper may vary slightly between the corporate chain and the independent hotel. An example is the purchasing of furnishings and equipment. A large independent hotel relies on the knowledge and experience of the executive housekeeper to make appropriate selections, whereas the chain hotel company has a corporate purchase agent (assisted by a designer) to make many of these decisions.

The executive housekeeper is responsible for a substantial amount of record keeping. In addition to the scheduling and evaluation of employees, an inventory of all guest rooms and public area furnishings must be accurately maintained with the record of refurbishment. Most of the hotel's

Housekeepers Guest Room Self–Inspection Rating
Inspection Codes:

P – POLISH	R – REPLACE	E – WORK ORDER	S – SOAP SCUM	SM – SMEAR
SA – STAIN	H – HAIR	D – DIRT	DU – DUST	M – MISSING

PART I – GUEST ROOM		S			U	COMMENTS
Entry, door, frame, threshold, latch			1			
Unusual odor OR smoke smell			3			
CLOSET, doors, louvers–containing			1			
Hangers, 8 suits, 4 skirts, 2 bags w/ invoices			2			
Two (2) robes, with info card			2			
Extra TP & FACIAL			1			
One (1) luggage rack			1			
Current rate card			1			
VALET	Shoe Horn & Mitt		2			
DRESSER	LAMP/ SHADE/ BULB		2			
	ICE BUCKET, LID, TRAY		2			
	TWO (2) WINE GLASSES		2			
	Room Service MENU		2			
MINIBAR	TOP, FRONT, 2 Wine glasses/ price list		1			
SAFE	KEY IN SAFE, SIGN		5			
CHECK BEHIND DRESSER			2			
DRAWERS	BIBLE AND BUDDHIST BOOK		1			
	PHONE BOOKS, ATT DIRECTORY		1			
TELEVISION	ON & OFF, CH 19 BEHIND		1			
COFFEE TABLE	REMOTE CONTROL/TEST 1		2			
	T.V. LISTINGS/BOOK MARK		1			
	GLASS TOP/LA JOLLA BOOK		1			
CARPET	VACUUM, SPOTS?		2			
SOFA	UNDER CUSHION/ BEHIND		2			
3 W LAMP	BULB, SHADE, & CORD		1			
WINDOWS	GLASS, DOOR, LATCH—C BAR?		2			
CURTAINS	Pull — check seams		1			
PATIO	2 CHAIRS, TABLE & DECK		3			
DESK	2 CHAIRS, TOP, BASE, & LAMP/SHADE		5			
	GREEN COMPENDIUM		3			
	Waste paper can		1			
BED	Tight, Pillows, bedspread		5			
	Check Under/SHEETS, PILLOWS		3			
HVAC	Control, setting, vent		1			
SIDE TABLES	Lamps & shade		2			
	Telephone, MESSAGE LIGHT		1			
	Clock Radio CORRECT TIME?		1			
MIRRORS	LARGE MIRROR OVER DRESSER		1			
PICTURES	ROOM ART WORK		1			
WALLS	Marks, stains, etc.		3			

Numbers in rating column range from 1 (least important) to 5 (most important).

Figure 4–10 • Housekeepers Guest Room Self-Inspection Form.

Housekeepers Guest Room Self–Inspection Rating

Inspection Codes:

P – POLISH	R – REPLACE	E – WORK ORDER		S – SOAP SCUM	SM – SMEAR
SA – STAIN	H – HAIR	D – DIRT		DU – DUST	M – MISSING

PART II – BATHROOM		S			U		COMMENTS
BATH TUB/SHOWER							
	GROUT / TILE & EDGE			2			
	ANTISLIP GRIDS			2			
	SIDE WALLS			1			
	SHOWER HEAD			1			
	WALL SOAP DISH			1			
	CONTROL LEVER			1			
	FAUCET			1			
	CLOTHESLINE			1			
	SHOWER ROD, HOOKS			1			
	SHOWER CURTAIN/ LINER			2			
VANITY	TOP, SIDE, & EDGE			1			
	SINK, TWO FAUCETS			3			
	3 GLASSES, COASTERS			2			
	WHITE SOAP DISH			1			
	FACIAL TISSUE & BOX			1			
AMENITY BASKET							
	1 SHAMPOO			1			
	1 CONDITIONER			1			
	1 MOISTURIZER			1			
	2 BOXED SOAP			1			
	1 SHOWER CAP			1			
MIRROR	LARGE & COSMETIC			2			
WALLS, CEILING, & VENT				2			
TOILET	TOP, SEAT, BASE, & LIP			2			
OTHER	TOILET PAPER, fold			1			
	SCALE AND TRASH CAN			2			
	FLOOR, SWEPT AND MOPPED			3			
	TELEPHONE			1			
BATH LINENS, racks							
	THREE (3) WASH CLOTHS			1			
	THREE (3) HAND TOWELS			1			
	THREE (3) BATH TOWELS			1			
	ONE (1) BATH MAT			1			
	ONE (1) BATH RUG			1			
LIGHT SWITCH				1			
DOOR	FULL LENGTH MIRROR			1			
	HANDLE/LOCK			1			
	THRESHOLD			1			
	PAINTED SURFACE			1			

Figure 4–10 • Housekeepers Guest Room Self-Inspection Form. *(continued)*

maintenance work orders are initiated by the housekeepers who report the maintenance work. Many hotels now have a computer linkup between house-keeping and engineering and maintenance to speed the process. Guests expect their rooms to be fully functional, especially at today's prices. Housekeeping maintains a perpetual inventory of guest room amenities, cleaning supplies, and linens.

Amazingly, it took about 2,000 years, but hotels have figured out that guests spend most of their stay on a bed, so they are introducing wonder beds and heavenly beds to allow guests to enjoy sweet dreams—but hopefully not miss that pesky wake-up call. Around the country, guest rooms are getting a makeover that includes new mattresses with devices that allow one side to be set firmer than the other side or on an incline. Other room amenities include new high-definition or plasma TVs, WiFi services, and room cards that activate elevators.

Productivity in the housekeeping department is measured by the person-hours per occupied room. The labor costs per person-hour for a full-service hotel ranges from $2.66 to $5.33, or twenty minutes of labor for every occupied room in the hotel. Another key ratio is the labor cost, which is expected to be 5.1 percent of room sales. Controllable expenses are measured per occupied rooms. These expenses include guest supplies such as soap, shampoo, hand and body lotion, sewing kits, and stationery. Although this will vary according to the type of hotel, the cost should be about $2.00 per room. Cleaning supplies should be approximately $0.50 and linen costs $0.95, including the purchase and laundering of all linen. These budgeted costs are sometimes hard to achieve. The executive housekeeper may be doing a great job controlling costs, but if the sales department discounts rooms, the room sales figures may come in below budget. This would have the effect of increasing the costs per occupied room.

Another concern for the executive housekeeper is accident prevention. Insurance costs have skyrocketed in recent years, and employers are struggling to increase both employee and guest safety. It is necessary for accidents to be carefully investigated. Some employees have been known to have an accident at home but go to work and report it as a work-related injury to be covered by workers' compensation. To safeguard themselves to some extent, hotels keep sweep logs of the public areas; in the event that a guest slips and falls, the hotel can show that it does genuinely take preventative measures to protect its guests.

The **Occupational Safety and Health Administration (OSHA),** whose purpose it is to ensure safe and healthful working conditions, sets mandatory job safety and health standards, conducts compliance inspections, and issues citations when there is noncompliance. Additionally, the U.S. Senate Bill 198, known as the **Employee Right to Know,** has heightened awareness of the storage, handling, and use of

A Room at the Mauna Lani Resort on the Kohala Coast Ready for Guests

dangerous chemicals. Information about the chemicals must be made available to all employees. Great care and extensive training is required to avoid dangerous accidents.

The executive housekeeper must also minimize loss prevention. Strict policies and procedures are necessary to prevent losses from guest rooms. Some hotels require housekeeping associates to sign a form stating that they understand they may not let any guest into any room. Such action would result in immediate termination of employment. Although this may seem drastic, it is the only way to avoid some hotel thefts.

Green Hotel Initiatives

The environmentally conscious companies are not only helping to avoid further environmental degradation but are also saving themselves money while being good corporate citizens. Operationally, hotels have been recycling for years and saving water and chemicals by leaving cards in guest rooms saying that sheets will be changed every third day unless otherwise requested. Some hotels move the top sheet down to the bottom on the second or third day. Likewise, a card in the bathroom explains to guests that if they want a towel changed to leave it on the floor. Hotels have been quick to realize that the life of sheets and towels has been greatly extended, thus increasing savings.

The wattage of lighting has been reduced and long-life and florescent bulbs are saving thousands of dollars a year per property. Air-conditioning units can now control the temperature of a room through body-motion sensing devices that even pick up people's breathing. These devices can automatically shut off the air-conditioning unit when guests are out of their rooms. Savings are also being made with low-flow toilets and showerheads that have high-pressure low-volume flows of water.

Laundry

Increasingly, hotels are operating their own laundries. This subdepartment generally reports to the executive housekeeper. The modern laundry operates computerized washing/drying machines and large presses. Dry cleaning for both guests and employees is a service that may also come under the laundry department. Hotels are starting to get away from in-house dry cleaning because of environmental concerns.

▶ Check Your Knowledge

1. Describe the different types of reservations that guests make at hotels.

2. What is the role played by uniformed services?

3. Explain the responsibilities of an executive housekeeper.

Security/Loss Prevention

Providing guest protection and loss prevention is essential for any lodging establishment regardless of size. Violent crime is a growing problem, and protecting guests from bodily harm has been defined by the courts as a reasonable expectation from hotels. The security/loss division is responsible for maintaining security alarm systems and implementing procedures aimed at protecting the personal property of guests and employees and the hotel itself.

A comprehensive security plan must include the following elements:

Security Officers
- These officers make regular rounds of the hotel premises, including guest floors, corridors, public and private function rooms, parking areas, and offices.
- Duties involve observing suspicious behavior and taking appropriate action, investigating incidents, and cooperating with local law enforcement agencies.

Equipment
- Two-way radios between security staff are common.
- Closed-circuit television cameras are used in out-of-the-way corridors and doorways, as well as in food, liquor, and storage areas.
- Smoke detectors and fire alarms, which increase the safety of the guests, are a requirement in every part of the hotel by law.
- Electronic key cards offer superior room security. Key cards typically do not list the name of the hotel or the room number. So, if lost or stolen, the key is not easily traceable. In addition, most key card systems record every entry in and out of the room on the computer for further reference.

Safety Procedures
- Front desk agents help maintain security by not allowing guests to reenter their rooms once they have checked out. This prevents any loss of hotel property by guests.
- Security officers should be able to gain access to guest rooms, store rooms, and offices at all times.
- Security staff develop **catastrophe plans** to ensure staff and guest safety and to minimize direct and indirect costs from disaster. The catastrophe plan reviews insurance policies, analyzes physical facilities, and evaluates possible disaster scenarios, including whether they have a high or low probability of occurring. Possible disaster scenarios may include fires, bomb threats, earthquakes, floods, hurricanes, and blizzards. The well-prepared hotel develops formal policies to deal with any possible scenario and trains employees to implement chosen procedures should they become necessary.

Identification Procedures
- Identification cards with photographs should be issued to all employees.
- Name tags for employees who are likely to have contact with guests not only project a friendly image for the property, but are also useful for security reasons.

Trends in Hotel and Rooms Division Operations

- *Diversity of work force.* All the pundits are projecting a substantial increase in the number of women and minorities who will not only be taking hourly paid positions, but also supervising and management positions as well.
- *Increase in use of technology.* Reservations are being made by individuals over the Internet. Travel agents are able to make reservations at more properties. There is increasing simplification of the various property management systems and their interface with POS systems. In the guest room, increasing demand for high-speed Internet access, category 5 cables, and in some cases equipment itself is anticipated.
- *Continued quest for increases in productivity.* As pressure mounts from owners and management companies, hotel managers are looking for innovative ways to increase productivity and to measure productivity by sales per employee.
- *Increasing use of revenue management.* The techniques of revenue management will increasingly be used to increase profit by effective pricing of room inventory.
- *Greening of hotels and guest rooms.* Recycling and the use of environmentally friendly products, amenities, and biodegradable detergents will increase.
- *Security.* Guests continue to be concerned about personal security. Hotels are constantly working to improve guest security. For example, one hotel has instituted a women-only floor with concierge and security. Implementation of security measures will increase.
- *Diversity of the guest.* More women travelers are occupying hotel rooms. This is particularly a result of an increase in business travel.
- *Compliance with the ADA.* As a result of the Americans with Disabilities Act (ADA), all hotels must modify existing facilities and incorporate design features into new constructions that make areas accessible to persons with disabilities. All hotels are expected to have at least 4 percent of their

parking space designated as "handicapped." These spaces must be wide enough for wheelchairs to be unloaded from a van. Guest rooms must be fitted with equipment that can be manipulated by persons with disabilities. Restrooms must be wide enough to accommodate wheelchairs. Ramps should be equipped with handrails, and meeting rooms must be equipped with special listening systems for those with hearing impairments.

- *Use of hotels' web sites.* Hotel companies will continue to try to persuade guests to book rooms using the hotel company web site rather than via an Internet site such as Hotels.com because the hotel must pay about $20 for each room booking from such sites.

- *In-room technology.* Hotels are upgrading in-room technology.

CASE STUDY

Checking Out a Guest

A guest walked up to the front desk agent in an upscale hotel, ready to check out. As she would usually do when checking out a guest, the agent asked the guest what his room number was. The guest was in a hurry and showed his anxiety by responding, "I stay in a hundred hotel rooms and you expect me to remember my room number?"

The agent then asked for the guest's name, to which he responded, "My name is Mr. Johnstein." After thanking him, the agent began to look for the guest's last name, but the name was not listed in the computer. Because the man had a heavy accent and the agent assumed that she had misunderstood him, she politely asked the guest to spell his last name. He answered, "What? Are you an idiot? The person who checked me in last night had no problem checking me in." Again, the agent looked on the computer to find the guest.

The guest, becoming even more frustrated, said, "I have a plane to catch and it is ridiculous that it has to take this long to check me out. I also need to fax these papers off, but I need to have them photocopied first." The agent responded, "There is a business center at the end of the counter that will fax and photocopy what you need." The guest replied, "If I wanted your opinion, I would have asked you for it. Haven't you ever heard of customer service? Isn't this a five-star hotel? With your bad attitude, you should be working in a three-star hotel. I can't believe they let you work here at the front desk. Haven't you found my name yet?"

The agent, who was beginning to get upset, asked the guest again to spell out his full name. The guest only replied, "Here are my papers I want faxed if you are capable of faxing them." The agent reached to take the papers, and the guest shouted, "Don't grab them from my hand! You have a bad attitude, and if I had more time, I would talk to someone about getting you removed from your position to a hotel where they don't require such a level of customer service." The agent was very upset, but kept herself calm to prevent the guest from getting angrier.

The agent continued to provide service to the guest, sending the faxes and making the photocopies he had requested. Upon her return, the agent again asked the guest to repeat his last name because he had failed to spell it out. The guest replied by spelling out his name, "J-o-h-n-s-t-o-n-e." The agent was finally able to find his name on the computer and checked him out while he continued to verbally attack her. The agent finished by telling the guest to have a nice flight.

Discussion Questions

1. Is it appropriate to have the manager finish the checkout? Or should the front desk agent just take the heat?
2. Would you have handled the situation in the same manner?
3. What would you have done differently?

CASE STUDY

Overbooked: The Front-Office Perspective

Overbooking is an accepted hotel and airline practice. Many question the practice from various standpoints, including ethical and moral. Industry executives argue that there is nothing more perishable than a vacant room. If it is not used, there is no chance to regain lost revenue. Hotels need to protect themselves because potential guests frequently make reservations at more than one hotel or are delayed and, therefore, do not show up.

The percentage of no-shows varies by hotel and location but is often around 5 percent. In a 400-room hotel, that is 20 rooms, or an average loss of approximately $2,600 per night. Considering these figures, it is not surprising that hotels try to protect themselves by overbooking.

Hotels look carefully at bookings: Whom they are for, what rates they are paying, when they were made, whether they are for regular guests or from a major account (a corporation that uses the hotel frequently), and so on.

Jill Reynolds, the front-office manager at the Regency La Jolla, had known for some time that the 400-room hotel would be overbooked for this one night in October. She prepared to talk with the front-desk associates as they came on duty at 7:30 in the morning, knowing it would be a challenge to sell out without "walking" guests. Seldom does a hotel sell out before having to walk a few guests.

The hotel's policy and procedure on walking guests enables the front desk associates to call nearby hotels of a similar category to find out if they have rooms available to sell. If it is necessary to walk a guest, the associate explains to the guest that, regrettably, no rooms are available because of fewer departures than expected. The associate must explain that suitable accommodations have been reserved at a nearby hotel and that the hotel will pay for the room and transportation to and from the hotel. Usually, guests are understanding, especially when they realize that they are receiving a free room and free transportation.

On this particular day, the house count indicates that the hotel is overbooked by thirty rooms. Three or four nearby, comparable hotels had rooms available to sell in the morning. Besides walking guests, Jill considers other options—in particular "splitting" the fifteen suites with connecting parlors. If the guests in the suites do not need the parlor, it is then possible to gain a few more "rooms" to sell separately; however, rollaway beds must be placed in the rooms. Fortunately, eight parlors were available to sell.

Discussion Question

1. If you were in the same situation, what would you do?

CASE STUDY

Overbooked: The Housekeeping Perspective

It is no secret that in all hotels the director of housekeeping must be able to react quickly and efficiently to any unexpected circumstances that arise. Stephen Rodondi, executive housekeeper at the Regency in La Jolla, California, usually starts his workday at 8:00 A.M. with a department meeting. These morning meetings help him and the employees to visualize their goals for the day. On this particularly busy day, Rodondi arrives at work and is told that three housekeepers have called in sick. This is a serious challenge for the hotel because it is overbooked and has all its 400 rooms to service.

Discussion Question

1. What should Stephen do to maintain standards and ensure that all the guest rooms are serviced?

Source: Courtesy of Stephen Rodondi, Executive Housekeeper, Hyatt Regency, La Jolla, California.

Summary

1. A big hotel is run by a general manager and an executive committee, which is represented by the key executives of all the major departments, such as rooms division, food and beverage, marketing, sales, and human resources.
2. The general manager represents the hotel and is responsible for its profitability and performance. Because of increased job consolidation, he or she also is expected to attract business and to empathize with the cultures of both guests and employees.
3. The rooms division department consists of front office, reservations, housekeeping, concierge, guest services, and communications.
4. The front desk, as the center of the hotel, sells rooms and maintains balanced guest accounts, which are completed daily by the night auditor. The front desk constantly must meet

guests' needs by offering services such as mailing, faxing, and messages.
5. Property management systems centralized reservations, and yield management have enabled hotels to work more efficiently and to increase profitability and guest satisfaction.
6. The communications department, room service, and guest services (such as door attendants, bellpersons, and the concierge) are vital parts of the personality of a hotel.
7. Housekeeping is the largest department of the hotel. The executive housekeeper is in charge of inventory, cleaning, employees, and accident and loss prevention. The laundry may be cleaned directly in the hotel or by a hired laundry service.
8. The electronic room key and closed-circuit television cameras are basic measures provided to protect the guests and their property.

Key Words and Concepts

application service provider (ASP)
average daily rate (ADR)
call accounting systems (CAS)
catastrophe plans
central reservation office (CRO)
central reservation system (CRS)
city ledger
concierge
confirmed reservations
daily report
Employee Right to Know
executive committee
global distribution systems (GDS)
guaranteed reservations

guest accounting module
night auditor
Occupational Safety and Health Administration (OSHA)
productivity
property management systems (PMS)
revenue management
rev par
room management module
room occupancy percentage (ROP)
room rates
rooms division
uniformed staff
yield management

Review Questions

1. Briefly define the purpose of a hotel. Why is it important to empathize with the culture of guests?
2. List the main responsibilities of the front office manager.
3. Look at the Companion Website clip of Chris Bryant. What are his duties as guest services manager?
4. How did Michelle Riesdorf become general manager of a Spring Hill Suites property?
5. What are the advantages and disadvantages of yield management?
6. Why is the concierge an essential part of the personality of a hotel?
7. Explain the importance of accident and loss prevention. What security measures are taken to protect guests and their property?

Internet Exercises

1. Organization: **Global Hyatt Corporation**
   Web site: www.hyatt.com
   Summary: Global Hyatt Corporation is a multi-billion-dollar hotel management company. Together with Hyatt International, the company has about 8 percent of the hotel industry market share. Hyatt is recognized for its decentralized management approach, in which general managers are given a great deal of the management decision-making process.
   Click the "Careers" icon and take a look at the Management Training Program that Hyatt has to offer.

   (a) What is Hyatt's management training program?
   (b) What requisites must applicants meet to qualify for Hyatt's management training program?

2. Organization: **Hotel Jobs**
   Web site: www.hoteljobs.com
   Summary: Hoteljobs.com is a web site that offers information to recruiters, employers, and job seekers in the hospitality industry.

   (a) What different jobs are being offered under "Job Search" and which one, if any, interests you?
   (b) Post your résumé online.

Apply Your Knowledge

1. If you were on the executive committee of a hotel, what kinds of things would you be doing to ensure the success of the hotel?
2. Your hotel has 275 rooms. Last night 198 were occupied. What was the occupancy percentage?
3. Answer the sample test questions on the Companion Website.

Suggested Activities

1. Go to a hotel's web site and find the price of booking a room for a date of your choice. Then, go to one of the web sites (Hotels.com, Expedia, Travelocity, etc.) that "sell" hotel rooms and see how the price compares.
2. Comment on the career advice section on the Companion Website.

Endnotes

1. Personal conversation with Rollie Teves, July 20, 2007.
2. The author greatfully acknowledges the cooperation and professional courtesy extended by Louise Casamento of Micros systems. www.micros.com
3. VingCard press kit. July 24, 2007. The author greatfully acknowledges the professional courtesy of VingCards.
4. Personal conversation with David Chang, Ph.D., November 10, 2007.
5. Personal conversation with Bruce Loockwood, March 16, 2006.
6. Personal correspondence with Jay R. Schrock, Ph.D., July 18, 2007.

CHAPTER 5

Food and Beverage Operations

OBJECTIVES

After reading and studying this chapter, you should be able to:

- Describe the duties and responsibilities of a food and beverage director and other key department heads.

- Describe a typical food and beverage director's day.

- State the functions and responsibilities of the food and beverage departments.

- Perform computations using key food and beverage operating ratios.

Food and Beverage Management

In the hospitality industry, the food and beverage division is led by the **director of food and beverage.** She or he reports to the general manager and is responsible for the efficient and effective operation of the following departments:

* Kitchen/catering/banquet

* Restaurants/Room Service/Minibars

* Lounges/Bars/Stewarding

Figure 5–1 illustrates a food and beverage organization chart.

The position description for a director of food and beverage is both a job description and a specification of the requirements an individual needs to do the job. In recent years, the skills needed by a food and beverage director have grown enormously, as shown by the following list of responsibilities:

* Exceeding guests' expectations in food and beverage offerings and service

* Leadership

* Identifying trends

* Finding and keeping outstanding employees

* Training

* Motivation

* Budgeting

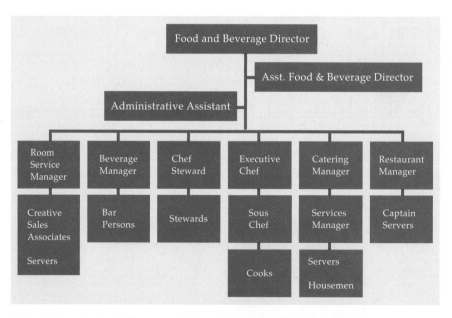

Figure 5–1 • Food and Beverage Division Organization Chart for a Large Hotel.

- Cost control

- Finding profit from all outlets

- Having a detailed working knowledge of the front-of-the-house operations

These challenges are set against a background of stagnant or declining occupancies and the consequent drop in room sales. Therefore, greater emphasis has been placed on making food and beverage sales profitable. Traditionally, only about 20 percent of the hotel's operating profit comes from the food and beverage divisions. In contrast, an acceptable profit margin from a hotel's food and beverage division is generally considered to be 25 to 30 percent. This figure can vary according to the type of hotel. For example, according to Pannell Kerr Forster, an industry consulting firm, all-suite properties achieve a 7 percent food and beverage profit (probably because of the complimentary meals and drinks offered to guests).

A typical food and beverage director's day might look like the following:

8:30 A.M.	Check messages and read logs from outlets and security. Tour outlets, especially the family restaurant (a quick inspection).
	Check breakfast buffet, reservations, and shift manager.
	Check daily specials.
	Check room service.
	Check breakfast service and staffing.
	Meet executive chef and purchasing director.
	Meet executive steward's office to ensure that all equipment is ready.
	Meet banquet service office to check on daily events and coffee break sequence.
10:00 A.M.	Work on current projects: new summer menu, pool outlet opening, conversion of a current restaurant with a new concept, remodeling of ballroom foyer, installation of new walk-in freezer, analysis of current profit-and-loss (P&L) statements. Plan weekly food and beverage department meetings.
11:45 A.M.	Visit kitchen to observe lunch service and check the "12:00 line," including banquets.
	Confer with executive chef.
	Check restaurants and banquet luncheon service.
1:00 P.M.	Have working lunch in employee cafeteria with executive chef, director of purchasing, or director of catering.
1:30 P.M.	Meet with human resources to discuss current incidents.
2:30 P.M.	Check messages and return calls. Telemarket to attract catering and convention business.
	Conduct hotel daily menu meeting.
3:00 P.M.	Go to special projects/meetings.
5:30 P.M.	Tour cocktail lounges.

	Check for staffing.
	Review any current promotions.
	Check entertainment lineup.
6:00 P.M.	Check special food and beverage requests/requirements of any VIPs staying at the hotel.
	Tour kitchen.
	Review and taste.
8:00 P.M.	Review dinner specials.
	Check the restaurant and lounges.

A food and beverage director's typical day starts at 8:00 A.M. and ends at 8:00 P.M., unless early or very late events are scheduled, in which case the working day is even longer. Usually, the food and beverage director works Monday through Saturday. If there are special events on Sunday, then she or he works on Sunday and takes Monday off. In a typical week, Saturdays are used to catch up on reading or specific projects.

The director of food and beverage eats in his or her restaurants at least twice a week for dinner and at least once a week for breakfast and lunch. Bars are generally visited with clients, at least twice per week. The director sees salespersons regularly because they are good sources of information about what is going on in the industry and they can introduce leads for business. The director attends staff meetings, food and beverage meetings, executive committee meetings, interdepartmental meetings, credit meetings, and P&L statement meetings.

To become a food and beverage director takes several years of experience and dedication. One of the best routes is to gain work experience or participate in an internship in several food and beverage departments while attending college. This experience should include full-time, practical kitchen work for at least one to two years, followed by varying periods of a few months in purchasing, stores, cost control, stewarding, and room service. Stewarding is responsible for back-of-the-house areas such as dishwashing and issuing and inventorying china, glassware, and cutlery. Stewarding duties include maintaining cleanliness in all areas. Additionally, a year spent in each of the following work situations is helpful: restaurants, catering, and bars. After these departmental experiences, a person would likely serve as a department manager, preferably in a different hotel from the one in which the departmental experience was gained. This prevents the awkwardness of being manager of a department in which the person was once an employee and also offers the employee the opportunity to learn different things at different properties.

▶ Check Your Knowledge

1. What are the skills and responsibilities of a food and beverage director?

2. Describe a food and beverage director's day.

INTRODUCING GEORGE GOLDHOFF

Vice President of Food and Beverage, Bean Rivage Resort and Casino, Biloxi, Mississippi

Being hired as the pot washer for the Old Homestead Country Kitchen at the early age of fifteen hardly seemed to herald the beginnings of an auspicious career in the hospitality industry. But to George Goldhoff, with his high energy and natural leadership skills, he had found the perfect environment in which to excel. The sense of family and camaraderie between the staff members and the interaction with guests, mixed with the intensity of performance and deadlines, have never lost their appeal. Excellence in service would become his lifelong pursuit.

Fast-forward twenty years. As director of food and beverage at Bellagio of MGM/Mirage, Inc., in Las Vegas, George is responsible for the quality assurance, personnel development, and financial performance of seventeen restaurants and ten bars, with 3,000 employees and more than $200 million in revenues. His responsibilities may have increased since his pot washer days, but the core message in his service training remains intact: sincerity toward the guest and anticipation of guest needs. His approach to service is simple: Greet all guests with a smile, make sure they are comfortable, offer them something to eat and drink. These service basics, simple instructions given to him as a five-year-old by his parents, have stayed with him. Playing host at one of his parents' dinner parties, he learned early the power of a sincere smile and the rewarding experience of pleasing others. Little did he or his parents intuit that one day his child's play would evolve into a rewarding career in hospitality.

As one of the original members of the opening team for the Bellagio, George drew from his extensive and varied food and beverage background to make the Bellagio's opening a success. In 1983 George graduated from Schenectady County Community College as a dean's list student and recipient of an athletic scholarship award. He continued on to the University of Massachusetts where he earned his B.S. degree in hotel, restaurant, and travel administration. His acceptance to these two institutions, after having dropped out of high school, instilled in George the self-confidence in his abilities and the technical skills necessary to achieve his goals. For a young man without a high school diploma who was often characterized as wild and rebellious, it was a revelation, an awakening to his potentials and the realization that he could accomplish great things. His introduction to corporate culture was as an assistant front office manager and Hyatt corporate trainee in Savannah, Georgia.

Upon completion of his training, he moved to beautiful Tahoe in 1988, where he was able to combine his love for restaurants and sports. An all-around athlete, adhering to the work hard, play hard principle, he pursued speed skiing competitions at the highest levels. He stayed on as general manager of Rosie's Café for two and a half years. However, growing tired of the small town confines of Tahoe City and with the singular challenges of Rosie's Café becoming undemanding, George acted on a friend's advice, contacted a mutual friend, and took a job on a 750-foot merchant ship. For the next six months George sailed around the world cooking breakfast, lunch, and dinner for a crew of twelve, while visiting ports in Gibraltar, Malta, Egypt, the United Arab Emirates, Kuwait, and Saudi Arabia. In 1990, aspiring to be a major player not just in skiing, but in the restaurant arena as well, he sought grander, more sophisticated restaurants to manage.

George's ambitions led him to the Plaza Hotel in New York, where he started as an assistant beverage director. George immersed himself in his new position with his usual high-voltage energy and infectious enthusiasm, earning him nicknames such as the Golden Boy and Mr. Hollywood. It did not take long for George to be recognized for his positive attitude and management abilities. Within six months, he was promoted to manager of the stately Oak Room, the youngest manager in the restaurant's ninety-year history. Within a two-year period, he was promoted to managing four of the Plaza Hotel's five à la carte restaurants.

Holding to his personal belief that "you are the company you keep," he has always endeavored to associate with the highest quality restaurateurs and organizations. In 1993, he realized one of his dreams—the opportunity

(continued)

INTRODUCING GEORGE GOLDHOFF *(continued)*

to work with the legendary Joe Baum—managing the famous Rainbow Room in Rockefeller Center. His commitment to service, the evident pride he takes in his work, and his high standard of ethics earned George praise from Joe Baum as being his best maître d' ever. Such a high compliment could have gone to his head. However, George is not one to sit back and take it easy. Instead, he set even higher standards and focused his energies on new goals. He quotes his old boss and industry idol Joe Baum as saying, "Values and standards are those you make for yourself. You don't have to be as good as the other guy. You have to be better—a lot better."

Against the advice of well-meaning family and peers, he left the Rainbow Room in 1997 to enroll in the MBA program at Columbia University. This was no easy decision, considering George was happily married at this point, with one child and another on the way. However, he has never been afraid to take risks, and is not one to fear taking on new challenges. In fact, his adventurous and go-getter nature revels in change. With the same self-confidence, resourcefulness, and ability to focus on multiple tasks, not surprisingly, he took first place in Columbia's Business Plan competition and was the recipient of the prestigious Eugene Lang Entrepreneurial Initiative Fund. Armed with his MBA degree and newly acquired business skills, he was ready for his next adventure.

Even before he had graduated, he was tapped by Stephen Rushmore, founder and president of Hospitality Valuation Services, to work with him as a consultant and valuation analyst. Here he was afforded the opportunity to incorporate his academic learning, fresh ideas, and extensive hotel background into his work. He created the 1996 Hotel Valuation Index (HVS), which was later published in the *Cornell Quarterly*. Ever the entrepreneur, he left HVS in 1997 to establish his own venture, The Irish Coast, Inc., creating and implementing the Guinness Irish pub concept. He jumped into the task of perfecting the Irish pub ambience of warmth, comfort, and congeniality, the heart of hospitality. Hence, it was only a matter of time before he would find himself in Las Vegas, the "Hospitality Capital of the World." In 1998, he signed on with Mirage Resorts to open the ultimate luxury resort and casino, Bellagio.

For George, it's all about service. Excellence in customer satisfaction and a genuine concern for his staff and coworkers have been his guiding principles. Characterized by colleagues as a dreamer, he has the rare ability to communicate his vision and to motivate and inspire others into executing that vision, making it a reality. The ability to instill in those around him the desire to strive beyond and stretch past their comfort zones is just one of his leadership characteristics. His motivational secret is to "constantly remind the staff that their job is precious, even if they've been doing it year after year." He maintains that the key to service is to "know one's job and to remember that a little kindness goes a long way to making people happy. A guest always knows if someone doesn't care."

In addition to starting up and overseeing the entire food and beverage operations for the hotel, he was chosen to represent Mirage Resorts in Focus Las Vegas, a leadership development program of the Las Vegas Chamber of Commerce. Making a difference in others' lives has always been one of the appealing factors of being in the hospitality field. He has always felt personally rewarded when he can give back to others, such as promoting a new busperson, building up someone else's self-esteem, watching people gain confidence in themselves and take pride in their work. He concedes he did not reach his position on his own, but with the assistance of many caring mentors. Always mindful and appreciative of those who have helped him throughout his career, he enjoys helping others discover their own potential. He considers human relations to be one of his strengths and regards staff development to be one of his greatest priorities as a leader. Empowering frontline employees is essential to maintaining a restaurant's competitive edge: "Give them the tools and let them do the job."

George has great expectations for himself and those around him and is not afraid of hard work. In fact, he works with a passion. The long hours and the intensity do not faze him. His adaptability to different situations, his ability to relate to a variety of personalities and temperaments, and his keen sense of humor serve him well both in front and back of the house. With his winning smile and straightforward demeanor, he sets his sights on a promising future and the many adventures ahead.

Kitchen

A hotel kitchen is under the charge of the **executive chef** or chef in smaller and medium-sized properties. This person, in turn, is responsible to the director of food and beverage for the efficient and effective operation of kitchen food production. The desired outcome is to exceed guests' expectations in the quality and quantity of food, its presentation, taste, and portion size, and to ensure that hot food is served hot and cold food is served cold. The executive chef operates the kitchen in accordance with company policy and strives to achieve desired financial results.

Some executive chefs are now called **kitchen managers;** they even serve as food and beverage directors in midsized and smaller hotels. This trend toward "right-sizing," observed in other industries, euphemistically refers to restructuring organizations to retain the most essential employees. Usually, this means cutting labor costs by consolidating job functions. For example, Michael Hammer is executive chef and food and beverage director at the 440-room Hilton La Jolla in Torrey Pines, California. Mike is typical of the new breed of executive chefs: His philosophy is to train his sous chefs, *sous* being a French word meaning "under," to make many of the operating deci-sions. He delegates ordering, hiring, and firing decisions; sous chefs are the ones most in control of the production and the people who work on their teams. By delegating more of the operating decisions, he is developing the chefs de partie (or stations chefs) and empowering them to make their own deci-sions. As he puts it, "No decision is wrong—but in case it is unwise, we will talk about it later."

The executive chef of a very large hotel manages the kitchen and may not do much cooking

Mike spends time maintaining morale, a vital part of a manager's responsi-bilities. The kitchen staff is under a great deal of pressure and frequently works against the clock. Careful cooperation and coordination are the keys to success. He explains that he does not want his associates to "play the tuba"—he wants them to conduct the orchestra. He does not hold food and beverage department meetings; instead he meets with groups of employees frequently, and problems are handled as they occur. Controls are maintained with the help of software that costs their standard recipes, establishes **perpetual inventories,** and calculates potential food cost per outlet. Today, executive chefs and food and beverage directors look past food cost to the actual profit contribution of an item. For example, if a pasta dish costs $3.25 and sells for $12.95, the contribution mar-gin is $9.70. Today, there are software programs such as ChefTec that offer soft-ware solutions for purchasing, ordering, inventory control, and recipe and menu costing; ChefTec Plus offers perpetual inventory, sales analysis, theoretical inventory reports, and multiple profit centers.

Controlling costs is an essential part of food and beverage operations and, because labor costs represent the most significant variable costs, staffing becomes an important factor in the day-to-day running of the food and beverage locations. Labor cost benchmarks are measured by covers-per-person-hour. For example, in stewarding, it should take no more than one person per hour to clean

37.1 covers. Mike and his team of outlet managers face interesting challenges, such as staffing for the peaks and valleys of guest needs at breakfast. Many guests want breakfast during the peak time of 7:00 to 8:30 A.M., requiring organization to get the right people in the right place at the right time to ensure that meals are prepared properly and served in a timely manner.

At the Hilton La Jolla–Torrey Pines, Executive Chef Hammer's day goes something like the following:

1. Arrive between 6:00 and 7:00 A.M. and walk through the food and beverage department with the night cleaners.
2. Check to make sure the compactor is working and the area is clean.
3. Check that all employees are on duty.
4. Ask people what kind of challenges they will face today.
5. Sample as many dishes as possible, checking for taste, consistency, feel, smell, and overall quality.
6. Check walk-ins.
7. Recheck once or twice a day to see where department stands production-wise—this helps reduce or eliminate overtime.
8. Approve schedules for food and beverage outlet.
9. Keep a daily update of food and beverage revenues and costs.
10. Forecast the next day's, week's, and month's business based on updated information.
11. Check on final numbers for catering functions.

Financial results are generally expressed in ratios, such as **food cost percentage**—the cost of food divided by the amount of food sales. In its simplest form, an example is the sale of a hamburger for $1.00. If the cost of the food is $0.30, then the food cost percentage is 30 percent, which is about average for many hotels. The average might be reduced to 27 percent in hotels that do a lot of catering. As discussed later in this section, in determining the food and beverage department's profit and loss, executive chefs and food and beverage directors must consider not only the food cost percentage, but also the **contribution margin** of menu items. The contribution margin is the amount contributed by a menu item toward overhead expenses and is the difference between the cost of preparing the item and its selling price.

Another important cost ratio for the kitchen is labor cost. The **labor cost percentage** may vary depending on the amount of convenience foods purchased versus those made from scratch (raw ingredients). In a kitchen, this may be expressed as a **food sales percentage**. For example, if food sales total $1,000 and labor costs total $250, then labor costs may be expressed as a percentage of food sales by the following formula:

$$\frac{\text{Labor Cost}}{\text{Food Sales}}, \quad \text{therefore} \quad \frac{\$250}{\$1,000} = 25\% \text{ labor cost}$$

Labor management is controlled with the aid of programs such as TimePro from Commeg Systems. TimePro is a time, attendance, and scheduling package that provides an analytical tool for managers and saves time on forecasting and scheduling.

CORPORATE PROFILE

Four Seasons Regent Hotels

In 1960, Isadore Sharp opened the first Four Seasons Hotel on Jarvis Street in downtown Toronto, Canada.[1] Today, Four Seasons Hotels and Resorts manage sixty-five hotels in twenty-nine countries, under the brand names Four Seasons and Regent.

Isadore Sharp's understanding of what modern travelers want from a hotel has positioned Four Seasons as the first choice of many business travelers. They can expect their check-in to be fast and efficient, the rooms to be luxurious, the laundry to be back on time, and the food to be very good. Genuinely caring about the needs of the guests has led to the introduction of many innovative services that have made Four Seasons a benchmark for quality and service. For example, the company was the first to introduce in-room amenities and company-wide concierge services.

Quality in every aspect of the business translates into excellent food and beverage. Each of the restaurants in all of the Four Seasons properties was designed to lead the local fine-dining market. Four Seasons successfully challenged the hotel food stigma. Its restaurants serve imaginative and attractive dishes that suit the tastes of both the local guests and the international clientele.

Once again, meeting the guests' needs was accomplished with the introduction of alternative cuisine—stylish and flavorful items prepared with an eye on proper nutrition—designed for the frequent business traveler who spends many nights in hotel rooms and would appreciate lighter menu options.

Alternative cuisine is a method of preparation that creates nutritionally balanced dishes with reduced levels of cholesterol and sodium, without sacrificing quality, originality, taste, or presentation. The principles of alternative cuisine are achieved by

- *Reducing fats* by using low-fat-content ingredients and avoiding high-fat dairy products, oils, mayonnaise, and so on
- *Reducing sodium* by reducing salt, and use of high-sodium foods such as olives, pickles, and Parma ham, and by avoiding any unnatural flavoring
- *Reducing cholesterol* by carefully limiting animal meats and avoiding organ meats, skin of poultry, egg yolks, and so on

Instead, Four Seasons chefs emphasize the use of foods containing animal protein (fish, poultry, and selected meats such as veal, flank steaks, game), complex carbohydrates (vegetables, salads, starch), simple carbohydrates (fruits), and fiber (whole-grain breads, rice, pasta, cereal). The results are pleasing to the health-conscious traveler. A typical two-course alternative cuisine lunch can have as few as 500 calories. A three-course dinner can count as little as 650.

These food and beverage innovations have contributed to Four Seasons–Regent Hotel restaurants ranking among the top restaurants in their respective cities. They reflect the company's single-minded commitment to quality and guest satisfaction in all aspects of the hotel experience.

The Four Seasons has recently won these awards:

- *Fortune* magazine ranked the Four Seasons "one of the best companies to work for in America." They came in forty-eighth.

(continued)

CORPORATE PROFILE *(continued)*

- Eighteen Four Seasons Hotels were awarded top honors in the AAA Diamond Awards.
- Eight different Four Seasons Hotels received the Mobile Five-Star Award.
- *Gourmet* magazine's annual reader's survey of "America's Top Tables" had a total of nine Four Season's restaurants rated in the top twenty listings of their respective cities.

This Corporate Profile drawns on information from the Four Seasons Hotels and Resorts web site, www.fourseasons.com.

[handwritten annotations: Exec. chef → sous chef → chef tournant → station chefs; assistant/under]

An executive chef has one or more **sous chefs.** Because so much of the executive chef's time is spent on administration, sous chefs are often responsible for the day-to-day running of each shift. Depending on size, a kitchen may have several sous chefs: one or more for days, one for evenings, and another for banquets.

Under the sous chefs is the **chef tournant.** This person rotates through the various stations to relieve the **station chef** heads. These stations are organized according to production tasks, based on the classic "brigade" introduced by Escoffier. The **brigade** includes the following:

Sauce chef, who prepares sauces, stews, sautes, hot hors d'oeuvres

Roast chef, who roasts, broils, grills, and braises meats

Fish chef, who cooks fish dishes

Soup chef, who prepares all soups

Cold larder/pantry chef, who prepares all cold foods: salads, cold hors d'oeuvres, buffet food, and dressings

Banquet chef, who is responsible for all banquet food

Pastry chef, who prepares all hot and cold dessert items

Vegetable chef, who prepares vegetables (this person may be the fry cook and soup cook in some smaller kitchens) Soup, cold larder, banquets, pastry, and vegetable chefs' positions may be combined in smaller kitchens.

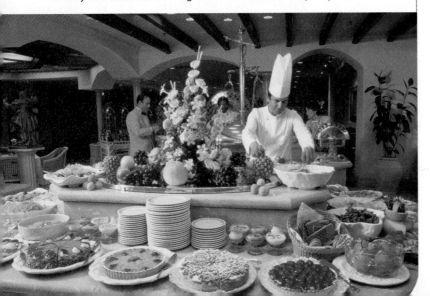

A Pastry chef adds the finishing touches to another fine pastry

▶ Check Your Knowledge

1. What is a food cost percentage and how is it calculated?
2. What is a contribution margin?
3. How is labor cost percentage calculated?

A DAY IN THE LIFE OF JIM GEMIGNANI

Executive Chef, Marriott Hotel

Jim Gemignani is executive chef at the 1,500-room Marriott Hotel in San Francisco. Chef Jim, as his associates call him, is responsible for the quality of food, guest, and associate satisfaction and for financial satisfaction in terms of results. With more than 200 associates in eight departments, Chef Jim has an interesting challenge. He makes time to be innovative by researching food trends and comparative shopping. Currently, American cuisine is in, as are free-standing restaurants in hotels. An ongoing part of American cuisine is the healthy food that Chef Jim says has not yet found a niche.

Hotels are building identity into their restaurants by branding or creating their own brand name. Marriott, for example, has Pizza Hut pizzas on the room service menu. Marriott hotels have created their own tiers of restaurants. JW's is the formal restaurant, Tuscany's is a northern Italian–themed restaurant, the American Grill has replaced the old coffee shop, and Kimoko is a Japanese restaurant. As a company, Marriott decided to go nationwide with the first three of these concepts. This has simplified menus and improved food quality and presentation, and yet regional specials allow for individual creativity on the part of the chef.

When asked about his personal philosophy, Chef Jim says that in this day and age, one needs to embrace change and build teams; the guest is an important part of the team. Chef Jim's biggest challenge is keeping guests and associates happy. He is also director of food service outlets, which now gives him a front-of-the-house perspective. Among his greatest accomplishments are seeing his associates develop—twenty are now executive chefs—retaining 96 percent of his opening team, and being voted Chef of the Year by the San Francisco Chef's Association.

Chef Jim's advice: "It's tough not to have a formal education, but remember that you need a combination of 'hands-on' and formal training. If you're going to be a leader, you must start at the bottom and work your way up; otherwise, you will become a superior and not know how to relate to your associates."

Food Operations

A hotel may have several restaurants or no restaurant at all; the number and type of restaurants varies as well. A major chain hotel generally has two restaurants: a signature or upscale formal restaurant and a casual coffee shop–type restaurant. These restaurants cater to both hotel guests and to the general public. In recent years, because of increased guest expectations, hotels have placed greater emphasis on food and beverage preparation and service. As a result, there is an increasing need for professionalism on the part of hotel personnel.

Hotel restaurants are run by **restaurant managers** in much the same way as other restaurants. **Restaurant managers** are generally responsible for the following:

- Exceeding guest service expectations
- Hiring, training, and developing employees

- Setting and maintaining quality standards
- Marketing
- Banquets
- Coffee service
- In-room dining, minibars, or the cocktail lounge
- Presenting annual, monthly, and weekly forecasts and budgets to the food and beverage director

Some restaurant managers work on an incentive plan with quarterly performance bonuses. Hotel restaurants present the manager with some interesting challenges because hotel guests are not always predictable. Sometimes they will use the hotel restaurants, and other times they will dine out. If they dine in or out to an extent beyond the forecasted number of guests, problems can arise. Too many guests for the restaurants results in delays and poor service. Too few guests means that employees are underutilized, which can increase labor costs unless employees are sent home early. A restaurant manager keeps a diary of the number of guests served by the restaurant on the same night the previous week, month, and year.

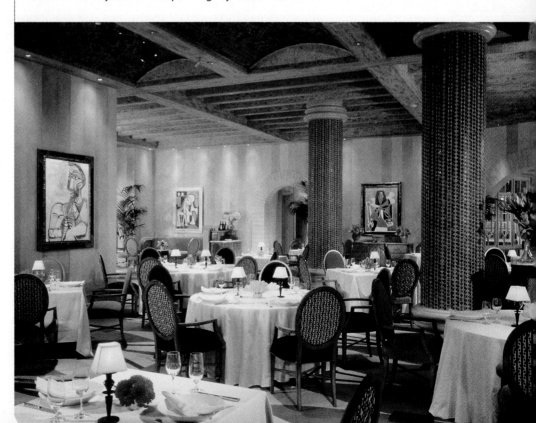

The dining room of the Bellagio Hotel's Picasso restaurant in Las Vegas features Mediterranean-style decor and paintings by Pablo Picasso

The number (house count) and type of hotel guest (e.g., the number of conference attendees who may have separate dining arrangements) should also be considered in estimating the number of expected restaurant guests for any meal. This figure is known as the **capture rate,** which, when coupled with historic and banquet activity and hotel occupancy, will be the restaurant's basis for forecasting the number of expected guests.

Most hotels find it difficult to coax hotel guests into the restaurants. However, many continuously try to convert foodservice from a necessary amenity to a profit center. The Royal Sonesta in New Orleans offers restaurant coupons worth $5 to its guests and guests of nearby hotels. Another successful strategy, adopted by the Plaza Athenee in New York, is to show guests the restaurants and explain the cuisine before they go to their rooms. This has prompted more guests to dine in the restaurant during their stay. At some hotels, the restaurants self-promote by having cooking demonstrations in the lobby: The "on-site" chefs offer free samples to hotel guests. Progressive hotels, such as the Kimco Hotel in San Francisco, ensure that the hotel restaurants look like freestanding restaurants with separate entrances.

FOCUS ON LODGING

Gracious Hospitality

Catherine Rabb, Johnson and Wales University

I find great pleasure in seeing a well-managed hotel handling full occupancy, special events, and busy dining rooms with seemingly effortless grace. How welcoming it is for the traveler or for the guest at a special event to be served by professionals who embody the true spirit of gracious hospitality.

What the guest doesn't see is the complex network of interlocking relationships and intensive training necessary behind the scenes to make each day successful at any hotel. It has been said that hotels need to be like ducks—appearing to glide effortlessly along the surface, while paddling like the devil underneath! Every person in our operation is a critical component of our business. We sell food and beverages in a variety of ways, but in hospitality operations the interaction with the guest becomes part of the product, with no room for returns if service is defective. We are only as good as our last meal, our last event, or our last contact with a guest. Service itself *is* the product.

As you will learn in this chapter, many different departments and people with diverse skills must work together efficiently. Hotels of different sizes and styles exist, so some operations need more people, and some need less; but for all hotels a dedication to providing the best available services and products is critical. This diverse group of people must work together to create a service product whose appearance is seamless. The coordination of people, talents, schedules, and needs is a complex ballet of intricate steps choreographed to create a seamless whole. A successful operation needs the talents of every member of the staff and welcomes the varied skills, energies, and ideas that their team brings to the table. Everyone, from the newest part-time employee to the manager, is needed to be at the top of their game to reach the goal of service excellence.

The term *multitasking* has perhaps been overused in recent years; however, nowhere is the term better suited than to describe the routine tasks done by so many industry professionals. Whether we are chefs, bar-
(continued)

tenders, stewards, catering managers, or food and beverage directors, we all need a wide variety of skills and abilities to be successful in this challenging industry. We need the technical skills necessary to do the job: correct service techniques, food preparation skills, the ability to mix a perfect drink, or to set a room properly for a special event. We must also possess the ability to interact with our team members, each of whom is responsible for a different set of tasks performed under pressure. It is critical that we understand and master the fact that our business must make a profit, and we work hard to blend effective budgets and cost controls with our service goals. We continuously provide extensive, thorough, effective, and ongoing training for ourselves and our staff so that our team is knowledgeable, trained, and empowered to act in the best interest of the guest and, ultimately, our operation. Our knowledge of the legalities of operating a business must be extensive so that our operations and our staff are protected. We are competitive because our market is changing and challenging, and we continually strive to position our businesses to be competitive. We must be strong because the physical demands of the business can be demanding, and we must be self-aware, for doing a challenging job well means that we are able to take care of ourselves and our lives outside the hotel. We lead by example to inspire our teammates to do the very best job they can, whatever the circumstances. Terrific service requires terrific people who possess the ability to integrate these characteristics into every workday.

What type of people are drawn to this business? People who love a challenge. People who enjoy other people. People who love their work and take pride in their ability to create a beautiful banquet, a perfect soup, or a well-designed training program. People with a work ethic, honesty, and integrity that make them an example to others. People who love to learn. People who enjoy the fact that every day is different and brings different challenges. Perhaps someone like you!

No matter what type of operation you might be in, the joy of working with, developing, and training strong teams filled with interesting, competent, and diverse people who can work together to create a service product that is truly special is the best part about our business. The guest may never be aware of the hard work from so many people that goes on behind the scenes at every hotel, but they are certainly aware when all our efforts succeed in providing outstanding service.

Compared with other restaurants, some hotel restaurants offer greater degrees of service sophistication. This necessitates additional food preparation and service skills and training. Compared to freestanding/independent restaurants, it is more difficult for hotel restaurants to operate at a profit. They usually are open from early morning until late at night and are frequently underpatronized by hotel guests who tend to prefer to eat outside the hotel at independent restaurants. Because of the complexities of operating food and beverage outlets and comparatively low profit margins, some hotels lease out their restaurant space. This presents another potential problem: how to maintain standards of quality and service.

Bars

Hotel bars allow guests to relax while sipping a cocktail after a hectic day. This opportunity to socialize for business or pleasure is advantageous for both guests and the hotel. Because the profit percentage on all beverages is higher than it is on food items, bars are an important revenue source for the food and beverage departments. The cycle of beverages from ordering, receiving, storing, issuing, bar stocking, serving, and guest billing is complex, but, unlike restaurant meals, a beverage can be held over if not sold. An example of a world-famous hotel bar is the King Cole Bar in the St. Regis Hotel in New York City. This bar has been a favored New York "watering hole" of the rich and famous for many years. The talking point of the bar is a painted mural of Old King Cole, the nursery rhyme character.

Bars are run by bar managers. The responsibilities of a bar manager include the following:

- Supervising the ordering process and storage of wines
- Preparing a wine list
- Overseeing the staff
- Maintaining cost control
- Assisting guests with their wine selection
- Proper service of wine
- Knowledge of beers and liquors and their service

Bar efficiency is measured by the **pour/cost percentage.** Pour cost is obtained by dividing the cost of depleted inventory by sales over a period of time. Food and beverage directors expect a pour cost of between 16 and 24 percent. Generally, operations with lower pour costs have more sophisticated control systems and a higher-volume catering operation. An example of this is an automatic system that dispenses the exact amount of beverage requested via a pouring gun, which is fed by a tube from a beverage store. These systems are expensive, but they save money for volume operations by being less prone to pilferage, overpouring, or other tricks of the trade. Their greatest savings comes in the form of reduced labor costs; fewer bartenders are needed to make the same amount of drinks. However, the barperson may still hand pour premium brands for show.

Hotel bars are susceptible to the same problems as other bars. The director of food and beverage must set strict policy and procedure guidelines and see to it that they are followed. In today's litigious society, the onus is on the operator to install and ensure **responsible alcoholic beverage service,** and all beverage service staff should receive training in this important area because it might limit the bar's liability. (The NRA offers Serve Safe alcohol.) If a guest becomes intoxicated and is still served alcohol or a minor is served alcohol and is involved in an accident involving someone else, then the server of the beverage, the barperson, and the manager may be liable for the injuries sustained by the person who was harmed, the third party.

Another risk bars encounter is **pilferage.** Employees have been known to steal or tamper with liquor. They could, for example, dilute it with water or colored liquids, sell the additional liquor, and pocket the money. There are several other ways to defraud a bar. One of the better known ways is to overcharge guests for beverages. Another is to underpour, which gives guests less for their money. Some bartenders overpour measures to receive larger tips. The best way to prevent these occurrences is to have a good control system, which should include **shoppers**—people who are paid to use the bar like regular guests, except they are closely watching the operation.

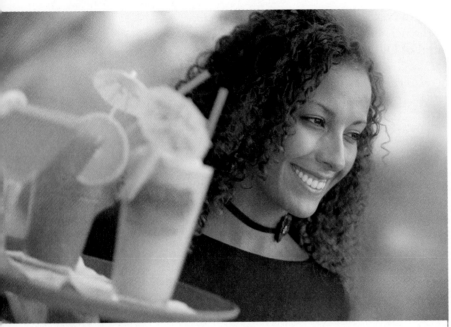

A server brings drinks at an outdoor bar

Types of bars:
↳ Lobby
↳ Restaurant
↳ Service bars
↳ catering + bang.
↳ pool bars
↳ minibars
↳ night clubs
↳ sports bars
↳ casino bars

In a large hotel there are several kinds of bars:

Lobby bar. This convenient meeting place was popularized when Conrad Hilton wanted to generate revenue out of his vast hotel lobby. Lobby bars, when well managed, are a good source of income.

Restaurant bar. Traditionally, this bar is away from the hubbub of the lobby and offers a holding area for the hotel's signature restaurant.

Service bar. In some of the very large hotels, restaurants and room service have a separate backstage bar. Otherwise, both the restaurant and room service are serviced by one of the regular beverage outlets, such as the restaurant bar.

Catering and banquet bar. This bar is used specifically to service all the catering and banquet needs of the hotel. These bars can stretch any operator to the limit. Frequently, several cash bars must be set up at a variety of locations; if cash wines are involved with dinner, it becomes a race to get the wine to the guest before the meal, preferably before the appetizer. Because of the difficulties involved in servicing a large number of guests, most hotels encourage inclusive wine and beverage functions in which the guests pay a little more for tickets that include a predetermined amount of beverage service. Banquet bars require careful inventory control. The bottles should be checked immediately after the function, and, if the bar is very busy, the bar manager should pull the money just before the bar closes. The breakdown of function bars should be done on the spot if possible to help prevent pilferage.

The banquet bar needs to stock not only large quantities of the popular wines, spirits, and beers but also a selection of premium spirits and after-dinner liqueurs. These are used in the ballroom and private dining rooms in particular.

Pool bars. Pool bars are popular at resort hotels where guests can enjoy a variety of exotic cocktails poolside. Resort hotels that cater to conventions often put on theme parties one night of the convention to allow delegates to kick back. Popular themes that are catered around the pool might be a Hawaiian luau, a Caribbean reggae night, Mexican fiesta, or Country and Western events. Left to the imagination, one could conceive of a number of theme events.

Minibars. Minibars or honor bars are small, refrigerated bars in guest rooms. They offer the convenience of having beverages available at all times. For security, they have a separate key, which may be either included in the room key envelope at check-in or withheld according to the guest's preference. Minibars are typically checked and replenished on a daily basis. Charges for items used are automatically added to the guest folio.

Night clubs. Some hotels offer guests evening entertainment and dancing. Whether formal or informal, these food and beverage outlets offer a full beverage service. Live entertainment is very expensive. Many hotels are switching to operations with a DJ or where the bar itself is the entertainment (e.g., sports bar). Directors of food and beverage are now negotiating more with live bands, offering them a base pay (below union scale) and a percentage of a cover charge.

Sports bars. Sports bars have become popular in hotels. Almost everyone identifies with a sporting theme, which makes for a relaxed atmosphere that complements contemporary lifestyles. Many sports bars have a variety of games such as pool, football, bar basketball, and so on, which, together with satellite-televised sporting events, contribute to the atmosphere.

Casino bars. Casino bars and beverage service are there to keep people gambling by offering low-cost or free drinks. Some have lavish entertainment and light food offerings, which entice guests to enjoy the gaming experience, even when sustaining heavy losses.

Different types of bars produce revenue according to their location in the hotel and the kind of hotel in which they are located. Nightclubs, sports bars, and the banqueting department see bulk consumption of alcoholic beverages; and restaurant bars usually see more alcohol consumption than minibars and lounge bars.

▶ Check Your Knowledge

1. What departments does the food and beverage director oversee?
2. What are the responsibilities of a food and beverage director on a day-to-day basis?
3. Explain how the pour/cost percentage is used in a bar to measure efficiency.

Stewarding Department

The **chief steward** is responsible to the director of food and beverage for the following functions:

- Cleanliness of the back of the house (all the areas of the backstage that hotel guests do not see)
- Maintaining clean glassware, china, and cutlery for the food and beverage outlets
- Maintaining strict inventory control and monthly stock check
- Maintenance of dishwashing machines

A Chief Steward checking the silver inventory

- Inventory of chemical stock
- Sanitation of kitchen, banquet aisles, storerooms, walk-ins/ freezers, and all equipment
- Pest control and coordination with exterminating company
- Forecasting labor and cleaning supplies

In some hotels, the steward's department is responsible for keeping the kitchen(s) clean. This is generally done at night to prevent disruption of the food production operation. A more limited cleaning is done in the afternoon between the lunch and dinner services. The chief steward's job can be an enormous and thankless task. In hotels, this involves cleaning up after several hundred people three times a day. Just trying to keep track of everything can be a headache. Some hotels have different patterns of glasses, china, and cutlery for each outlet. The casual dining room frequently has an informal theme, catering and banqueting a more formal one, and the signature restaurant, very formal place settings. It is difficult to ensure that all the pieces are returned to the correct places. It is also difficult to prevent both guests and employees from taking souvenirs. Strict inventory control and constant vigilance help keep pilferage to a minimum.

Catering Department

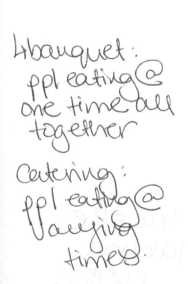

Throughout the world's cultural and social evolution, numerous references have been made to the breaking of bread together. Feasts or banquets are one way to show one's hospitality. Frequently, hosts attempted to outdo one another with the extravagance of their feasts. Today, occasions for celebrations, banquets, and catering include the following:

- State banquets, when countries' leaders honor visiting royalty and heads of state
- National days
- Embassy receptions and banquets
- Business and association conventions and banquets
- Gala charity balls
- Company dinner dances
- Weddings

The term *catering* has a broader scope than does *banquets*. **Banquets** refers to groups of people who eat together at one time and in one place. **Catering** includes a variety of occasions when people may eat at varying times. However, the terms are often used interchangeably.

For example, catering departments in large, city-center hotels may service the following events in just one day:

- A Fortune 500 company's annual shareholders meeting
- An international loan-signing ceremony
- A fashion show
- A convention
- Several sales and board meetings
- Private luncheons and dinner parties
- A wedding or two

[handwritten note: 4 BEO: CEO: — Banquet/conf event order]

Naturally each of these requires different and special treatment. Hotels in smaller cities may cater the local chamber of commerce meeting, a high school prom, a local company party, a regional sales meeting, a professional workshop, and a small exhibition.

Catering may be subdivided into on-premise and off-premise. In off-premise catering, the event is catered away from the hotel. The food may be prepared either in the hotel or at the event. The organization chart in Figure 5–2 shows how the catering department is organized. The dotted lines show cooperative reporting relationships, and continuous lines show a direct reporting relationship. For example, the banquet chef reports directly to the executive chef, but must cooperate with the director of catering and the catering service manager.

The **director of catering** (**DOC**) is responsible to the food and beverage director for selling and servicing, catering, banquets, meetings, and exhibitions in a way that exceeds guests' expectations and produces reasonable profit. The director of catering has a close working relationship with the rooms division manager because the catering department often brings conventions, which require rooms, to the hotel. There is also a close working relationship with the executive chef. The chef plans the banqueting menus, but the catering manager must ensure that they are suitable for the clientele and practical from a service point of view. Sometimes they work together in developing a selection of menus that will meet all the requirements, including cost and price.

The director of catering must be able to do the following:

1. Sell conventions, banquets, and functions.
2. Lead a team of employees.
3. Together with input from team members, make up departmental goals and objectives.
4. Set individual and department sales and cost budgets.
5. Set service standards.
6. Ensure that the catering department is properly maintained.

A Marriott catering manager reviews an event order. Attention to detail is critical to ensure complete guest satisfaction.

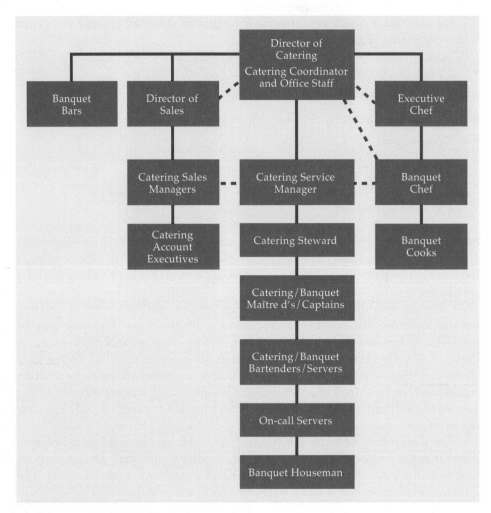

Figure 5–2 • Organization of the Catering Department.

7. Be extremely creative and knowledgeable about food, wine, and service.
8. Be very well versed in the likes, dislikes, and dietary restrictions of various ethnic groups, especially Jewish, Middle Eastern, and European.

Position Profile

The director of catering is required to have a variety of skills and abilities, including the following:

Technical

• A thorough knowledge of food and beverage management, including food preparation and service

• Ability to sell conventions, functions, and banquets

- Ability to produce a profit
- Ability to develop individual and department sales and cost budgets

Leadership

- Lead a team of employees.
- Set departmental mission, goals, and objectives.
- Train the department members in all facets of operations.
- Set service standards.
- Ensure that the catering department is properly maintained.

The catering department is extremely complex and demanding; the tempo is fast and the challenge to be innovative is always present. The director of catering in a large city hotel should, over the years, build up a client list and an intimate knowledge of the trade shows, exhibitions, various companies, groups, associations, and social, military, education, religious, and fraternal market (SMERF) organizations. This knowledge and these contacts are essential to the director of catering's success, as is the selection of the team members.

The main sales function of the department is conducted by the director of catering (DOC) and catering sales managers (CSMs). Their jobs are to optimize guest satisfaction and revenue by selling the most lucrative functions and exceeding guests' food and beverage and service expectations.

The DOC and catering sales managers obtain business leads from a variety of sources, including the following:

Hotel's director of sales. She or he is a good source of event bookings because she or he is selling rooms, and catering is often required by meetings and conventions.

General managers. These are good sources of leads because they are very involved in the community.

Corporate office sales department. If, for example, a convention were held on the East Coast one year at a Marriott hotel, and by tradition the association goes to the West Coast the following year, the Marriott hotel in the chosen city can contact the client or meeting planner. Some organizations have a selection of cities and hotels bid for major conventions. This ensures a competitive rate quote for accommodations and services.

Convention and visitors bureau. Here is another good source of leads because its main purpose is to seek out potential groups and organizations to visit that city. To be fair to all the hotels, they publish a list of clients and brief details of their requirements, which the hotel catering sales department may follow up on.

Reading the event board of competitive hotels. The event board is generally located in the lobby of the hotel and is frequently read by the competition. The CSM then calls the organizer of the event to solicit the business the next time.

Rollovers. Some organizations, especially local ones, prefer to stay in the same location. If this represents good business for the hotel, then the DOC and GM try to persuade the decision makers to use the same hotel again.

Cold calls. During periods of relative quiet, CSMs call potential clients to inquire if they are planning any events in the next few months. The point is to entice the client to view the hotel and the catering facilities. It is amazing how much information is freely given over the telephone.

The most frequent catering events in hotels are the following:

- Meetings
- Conventions
- Dinners
- Luncheons
- Weddings

For meetings, a variety of room setups are available, depending on a client's needs. The most frequently selected meeting room setups are as follows:

Theater style. Rows of chairs are placed with a center group of chairs and two aisles. Figure 5–3 shows a **theater-style room seating** setup with equipment centered on an audiovisual platform. Sometimes multimedia presentations, requiring more space for reverse image projections, reduce the room's seating capacity.

Classroom style. As the name suggests, tables, usually slim 18-inch ones, are used because meeting participants need space to take notes. **Classroom-style seating** usually takes about three times as much space as theater style and takes more time and labor to set up and break down. Figure 5–4 shows a classroom-style setup.

Horseshoe style. **Horseshoe-style room seating** (Figure 5–5) is frequently used when interaction is sought among the delegates, such as training sessions and workshops. The presenter or trainer stands at the open end of the horseshoe with a black or white board, flip chart, overhead projector, and video monitor and projector.

Room setups:
- Theater
- Classroom
- Horseshoe
- Dinner style
- Boardroom

Figure 5–3 • Theater-Style Seating.

Figure 5–4 • Classroom-Style Seating.

Figure 5–5 • Horseshoe-Style Seating.

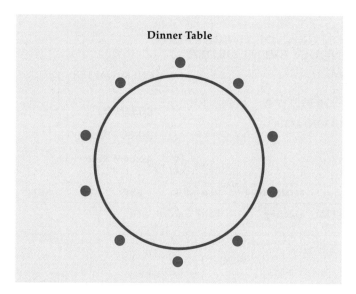

Figure 5–6 • Dinner-Style Seating.

Dinner style. Dinners are generally catered at round tables of eight or ten persons for large parties and on boardroom-style tables for smaller numbers. Of course, there are variations of the **dinner-style room seating setup** (see Figure 5–6).

Catering Event Order

A **catering event order (CEO),** which may also be called a **banquet event order (BEO),** is prepared/completed for each function to inform not only the client but also the hotel personnel about essential information (what needs to happen and when) to ensure a successful event.

The CEO is prepared based on correspondence with the client and notes taken during the property visits. Figure 5–7 shows a CEO and lists the room's layout and decor, times of arrival, if there are any VIPs and what special attention is required for them, that is, reception, bar times, types of beverages and service, cash or credit bar, time of meal service, the menu, wines, and service details. The catering manager or director confirms the details with the client. Usually, two copies are sent, one for the client to sign and return and one for the client to keep.

An accompanying letter thanks the client for selecting the hotel and explains the importance of the function to the hotel. The letter also mentions the guaranteed-number policy. This is the number of guests the hotel will prepare to serve and will charge accordingly. The guaranteed number is given about seven days prior to the event. This safeguards the hotel from preparing for 350 people and having only 200 show up. The client, naturally, does not want to pay for an extra 150 people—hence the importance of a close working relationship with the client. Contracts for larger functions call for the client to notify the hotel of any changes to the anticipated number of guests in increments of ten or twenty.

Experienced catering directors ensure that there will be no surprises for either the function organizer or the hotel. This is done by calling to check on how

SHERATON GRANDE TORREY PINES
BANQUET EVENT ORDER

WELCOME BREAKFAST
MEETING
CROCKER AND ASSOCIATES
41 MAIN ST
BOWLING GREEN, OHIO 43218

PHONE: (619) 635-4627
FAX: (619) 635-4528
GROUP CONTACT: Dr. Ken Crocker
ON-SITE-CONTACT: same

CHERI WALTER

BILLING:

DIRECT BILL

Amount Received:

DAY	DATE	TIME	FUNCTION	ROOM	EXP	GTE	SET	RENT
Wed	January 25, 2007	7:30 AM – 12:00 PM	Meeting	Palm Garden	50			250.00

BAR SET UP:

N/A

MENU:

7:30 AM CONTINENTAL BREAKFAST

Freshly Squeezed Orange Juice, Grapefruit Juice, and
　Tomato Juice
Assortment of Bagels, Muffins, and Mini Brioche
Cream Cheese, Butter, and Preserves
Display of Sliced Seasonal Fruits
Individual Fruit Yogurt
Coffee, Tea, and Decaffeinated Coffee

PRICE:_____

11:00 AM BREAK

Refresh Beverages as needed

WINE:

FLORAL:

MUSIC:

AUDIO VISUAL:
–OVERHEAD PROJECTOR/SCREEN
–FLIPCHART/MARKERS
–VCR/MONITORS

PARKING:

HOSTING PARKING, PLEASE PROVIDE VOUCHERS

LINEN:
HOUSE

SETUP:
–CLASSROOM-STYLE SEATING
–HEAD TABLE FOR 2 PEOPLE
–APPROPRIATE COFFEE BREAK SETUP
–(1) 6' TABLE FOR REGISTRATION AT ENTRANCE
　WITH 2 CHAIRS, 1 WASTEBASKET

All food and beverage prices are subject to an 18% service charge and 7% state tax. Guarantee figures, cancellations, changes must be given 72 hours prior or the number of guests expected will be considered the guarantee. To confirm the above arrangements, this contract must be signed and returned.

ENGAGOR SIGNATURE _____ DATE _____

BEO # 003069

Figure 5–7 • Catering Event Order (Courtesy of Sheraton Grande Torrey Pines.)

the function planning is going. One mistake catering directors sometimes make is accepting a final guest count without inquiring as to how that figure was determined. This emphasizes the fact that the catering director should be a consultant to the client. Depending on the function, the conversion from invitations to guests is about 50 percent. Some hotels have a policy of preparing for about 3 to 5 percent more than the anticipated or guaranteed number. Fortunately, most events have a prior history. The organization may have been at a similar hotel in the same city or across the country. In either case, the catering director or manager will be able to receive helpful information from the catering director of the hotel where the organization's function was held previously.

The director of catering holds a daily or weekly meeting with key individuals who will be responsible for upcoming events. Those in attendance should be the following:

Director of catering

Executive chef and/or banquet chef

Beverage manager or catering bar manager

Catering managers

Catering coordinator

Director of purchasing

Chief steward

Audiovisual representative

The purpose of this meeting is to avoid any problems and to be sure that all the key staff know and understand the details of the event and any special needs of the client.

Catering Coordinator

The **catering coordinator** has an exacting job in managing the office and controlling the "bible" or function diary now on computer. She or he must see that the contracts are correctly prepared and check on numerous last-minute details, such as whether flowers and menu cards have arrived.

Web-enabled technology tools such as Newmarket International's Delphi System (which is used at more than 4,000 properties) is a leader in delivering group, sales, catering, and banquet software for global travel and entertainment groups. One of the latest hotels to adopt the Delphi System is the Wynn Las Vegas, which installed the sales and catering systems Delphi Diagrams, MeetingBroker, and e-Proposal. The Delphi System can keep inventory current in real time because of its ability to interface with the property management system. The suite of Delphi products allows function space to be clearly and concisely managed, which increases guest satisfaction and profitability.

An Elegant Banquet Room

Catering Services Manager

The **catering services manager (CSM)** has the enormous responsibility of delivering higher-than-expected service levels to guests. The CSM is in charge of the function from the time the client is introduced to the CSM by the director of catering or catering manager. This job is very demanding because several functions always occur simultaneously. Timing and logistics are crucial to the success of the operation. Frequently, there are only a few minutes between the end of a day meeting and the beginning of the reception for a dinner dance.

The CSM must be liked and respected by guests and at the same time be a superb organizer and supervisor. This calls for a person of outstanding character and leadership—management skills that are essential for success. The CSM has several important duties and responsibilities, including the following:

- Directing the service of all functions
- Supervising the catering housepersons in setting up the room
- Scheduling the banquet captains and approving the staffing levels for all events
- Cooperating with the banquet chef to check menus and service arrangements
- Checking that the client is satisfied with the room setup, food, beverages, and service
- Checking last-minute details
- Making out client bills immediately after the function.
- Adhering to all hotel policies and procedures that pertain to the catering department, including responsible alcoholic beverage service and adherence to fire code regulations
- Calculating and distributing the gratuity and service charges for the service personnel
- Coordinating the special requirements with the DOC and catering coordinator

▶ Check Your Knowledge

1. What is the difference between banquets and catering?
2. What does SMERF stand for?
3. Where do the director of catering and the catering sales manager obtain their information?
4. What are the various styles used when setting up a meeting room? Give examples of when each style might be used.

Room Service/In-Room Dining

The term **room service** has for some time referred to all service to hotel guest rooms. Recently, some hotels have changed the name of room service to *in-room dining* to present the service as more upscale. The intention is to bring the dining experience to the room with quality food and beverage service.

A survey of members of the American Hotel & Lodging Association showed that 56 percent of all properties offer room service and that 75 percent of airport properties provide room service. Generally, the larger the hotel and the higher the room rate, the more likely it is that a hotel will offer room service.

Economy and several midpriced hotels avoid the costs of operating room service by having vending machines on each floor and food items such as pizza or Chinese food delivered by local restaurants. Conversely, some hotels prepare menus and lower price structures that do not identify the hotel as the provider of the food. As a result, the guests may have the impression that they are ordering from an "outside" operation when they are in fact ordering from room service.

The level of service and menu prices will vary from hotel to hotel. The Hilton at Torrey Pines, California, has butler service for all guest rooms without additional charge.

A few years ago, room service was thought of as a necessary evil, something that guests expected, but which did not produce profit for the hotel. Financial pressures have forced food and beverage directors to have this department also contribute to the bottom line. The room service manager has a difficult challenge running this department, which is generally in operation between sixteen and twenty-four hours a day. Tremendous effectiveness is required to make this

Room Service Being Delivered at a South Seas Tropical Resort

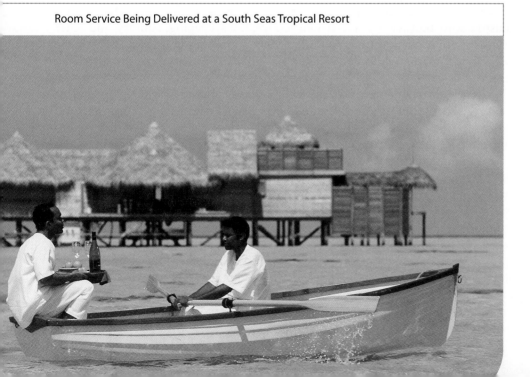

department profitable. Nevertheless, it can be done. Some of the challenges in operating room service are as follows:

Delivering orders on time—this is especially important for breakfast, which is by far the most popular room service meal

Making room service a profitable food and beverage department

Avoiding complaints of excessive charges for room service orders

There are many other challenges in room service operation. One is forecasting demand. Room service managers analyze the front-desk forecast, which gives details of the house count and guest mix—convention, group, and others for the next two weeks. The food and beverage forecast will indicate the number of covers expected for breakfast, lunch, and dinner. The convention résumés will show where the convention delegates are having their various meals. For example, the number of in-house delegates attending a convention breakfast can substantially reduce the number of room service breakfast orders. Experience enables the manager to check if a large number of guests are from different time zones, such as the West or East Coasts or overseas. These guests have a tendency to either get up much earlier or much later than the average guest. This could throw room service demands off balance. Demand also fluctuates between weekdays and weekends; for example, city hotels may cater to business travelers, who tend to require service at about the same time. However, on weekends, city hotels may attract families, who will order room service at various times.

To avoid problems with late delivery of orders, a growing number of hotels have dedicated elevators to be used only by room service during peak periods. At the 565-room Stouffer Riviera Chicago, director of food and beverage Bill Webb has a solution: Rapid action teams (RAT) are designated food and beverage managers and assistants who can be called on when room service orders are heavy.

Westin Hotels recently introduced Service Express, an innovation that allows a customer to address all needs (room service, housekeeping, laundry, and other services) with a single call. In addition, new properties are designed with the room service kitchen adjacent to the main kitchen so that a greater variety of items can be offered.

Meeting the challenge of speedy and accurate communication is imperative to a successful room service operation. This begins with timely scheduling and ends with happy guests. In between is a constant flow of information that is communicated by the guest, the order taker, the cook, and the server.

Another challenge is to have well-trained and competent employees in the room service department. From the tone of voice of the order taker and the courteous manner with which the order is taken to the panache of the server for the VIP dinners, training makes the difference between ordinary service and outstanding service. With training, which includes menu tasting with wine and suggestive selling, an order taker becomes a room service salesperson. This person is now able to suggest cocktails or wine to complement the entree and can entice the guest with tempting desserts. The outcome of this is to increase the average guest check. Training also helps the setup and service personnel hone their skills to enable them to become productive employees who are proud of their work.

Trends in Lodging Food and Beverage Operations

- The use of branded restaurants instead of hotels operating their own restaurants.
- Hotels opting not to offer food and beverage outlets. These are usually smaller to midsized properties that may have restaurants on the same lot nearby.
- Making restaurants and beverage outlets more casual.
- Using themes for a restaurant. For example, one major hotel chain has adopted a Northern Italian theme in all its restaurants.
- Standardized menus for all hotel restaurants in a chain.
- Many hotels are converting one of the beverage outlets into a sports-themed bar.
- Technology is being used to enhance guest services and control costs in all areas of a hotel, including guest ordering and payment, food production, refrigeration, marketing, management control, and communication.
- More low-fat low-carb menu items.

CASE STUDY

Ensuring Guest Satisfaction

The Sunnyvale Hotel is operated by a major hotel management corporation. To ensure guest satisfaction, 300 survey forms each containing sixty-five questions are mailed to guests each month. Usually, about seventy of the forms are returned. The hotel company categorizes the guest satisfaction scores obtained into colored zones, with green being the best, then clear and yellow, and red being the worst. Scores can be compared with those of equivalent hotels.

The most recent survey indicated a significant decline for the Sea Grill Restaurant with scores in the red zone. Guests' concerns were in the following areas: hostess attentiveness, spread of service, and quality of food.

Upon investigation, the director of food and beverage also realized that the name of the restaurant, Sea Grill, was not appropriate for the type of restaurant being operated. When asked, some guests commented that "it's a bit odd to eat breakfast in a fish place."

Discussion Question

1. What would you do, as director of food and beverage, to get the guest satisfaction scores back into the clear or green zones?

CASE STUDY

Friday Evening at the Grand Hotel's Casual Restaurant

Karla Gomez is the supervisor at the Grand Hotel's casual restaurant. Karla's responsibilities include overseeing five servers and two busers, seating guests, and taking reservations. One Friday evening, the restaurant was very busy—all twenty tables were occupied, there was a substantial wait-list, and there were people on standby. The service bar was almost full of guests and most of the seated guests in the dining area had finished their entrees or were just beginning their desserts. They were not leaving, however, in part because of cold, rainy weather outside. The guests did not seem to be in a rush to leave the restaurant, but several of the guests waiting for tables were complaining about the long wait.

Discussion Question

1. What can Karla do to solve the problem?

Summary

1. The food and beverage department division is led by the director of food and beverage, who is responsible for the efficient operation of kitchen, catering, restaurants, bars, and room service; in addition, the director has to keep up with trends and preplan for special events.

2. A hotel kitchen is the responsibility of the executive chef, who is in charge of the quality and quantity of food, organization of the kitchen and his or her sous chefs, administrative duties, and careful calculation of financial results.

3. A hotel usually has a formal and a casual restaurant, which are either directly connected to the hotel or operated separately.

4. Bars are an important revenue source for a hotel, but they must adhere to strict guidelines to be profitable. Commensurate with its size, a hotel might have several kinds of bars, such as a lobby bar, restaurant bar, minibar, or even a night club.

5. The chief steward has the often unrewarded job of cleaning the kitchen, cutlery, plates, glasses, and backstage of the hotel and is in charge of pest control and inventory.

6. Catering is subdivided into on-premise and off-premise occasions, which may include meetings, conventions, dinners, luncheons, and weddings. According to the occasion, the type of service and room setup may vary. Catering involves careful planning and the interaction and cooperation of many people.

7. Room service offers the convenience of dining in the room, with quality food and beverage service, at a price acceptable to both the guest and the hotel.

Key Words and Concepts

banquet
banquet event order (BEO)
brigade
capture rate
catering
catering coordinator
catering event order (CEO)
catering services manager (CSM)
chef tournant
chief steward
classroom-style seating
contribution margin
dinner-style room seating
director of catering (DOC)
director of food and beverage
executive chef

food cost percentage
food sales percentage
horseshoe-style room seating
kitchen manager
labor cost percentage
perpetual inventory
pilferage
pour/cost percentage
responsible alcoholic beverage service
restaurant manager
room service
shopper
sous chef
station chef
theater-style room seating

Review Questions

1. On the Companion Website, what excellent advice does Food & Beverage Director Bob Weil give?
2. What is Bob Weil's management style?
3. Briefly describe the challenges a food and beverage director faces on a daily basis.
4. List the measures used to determine the food and beverage department's profit and loss.
5. Explain the problems a hotel faces in making the following departments profitable: restaurants, bars, and room service.
6. Explain the importance of the catering department for a hotel and list the responsibilities of a catering sales manager.

Internet Exercises

1. Organization: **Foodservice**
   Web site: www.foodservice.com
   Summary: Foodservice.com is a web site that focuses on the foodservice industry. It has links to employment, industry resources, foodservice, technology innovations, and much more.
   (a) Click the "Forums and Chat" icon. Go to the "Chef and Cooks Corner" and take a look at some of the latest articles. Bring your favorite one to the table (discuss in class).
   (b) Look at the most current articles on food safety. What are the major concerns being addressed?

2. Organization: **National Restaurant Association**
   Web site: www.restaurant.org
   Summary: The National Restaurant Association is an organization devoted to representing, educating, and promoting the restaurant/hospitality industry.
   (a) Look under the "Education" icon. What does it mean to be "FMP Certified" and what are the eligibility requirements?
   (b) What are some of the upcoming events and what do they have to offer?

Apply Your Knowledge

1. Complete the sample test questions on the Companion Website.
2. If a casual dining restaurant in a four-star hotel forecasts 100 covers, how many servers, busers, hosts, and assistant managers would you schedule on that particular day? Calculate the labor cost of these associates for that day if the manager(s) work from 1:00 to 11:00 P.M., the server(s) work from 4:00 to 11:00 P.M., the buser(s) work from 4:30 to 11:30 P.M., and the host(s) works from 4:00 to 11:00 P.M.

Use minimum wage of $5.75 for calculations. Use the rate of $12 per hour for the assistant manager(s) and $6.50 for hosts.

3. Kitchen labor costs are an important ratio used to determine the efficiency of the food and beverage department. The labor cost for a banquet meal is $126.45 and the revenue for the banquet is $505.80. What is the labor cost percentage?
4. Comment on the careers advice section of the Companion Website.

Suggested Activities

1. Contact a bar manager in your area. Discuss with him or her how to monitor pilferage and overpouring. Ask what the expected and actual pouring cost percentages are and how the manager deals with any variances.

2. Visit a hotel restaurant in your area. Make a note of how busy the establishment is. Does it seem to be staffed with the appropriate number of employees? Are guests being served in a timely manner? Think about why this specific restaurant may be overly crowded or overly vacant. What could or should be done differently? What seems to be working well?

PART III

Restaurants, Managed Services, and Beverages

CHAPTER 6

The Restaurant Business

OBJECTIVES

After reading and studying this chapter, you should be able to:

- Describe the different characteristics of chain and independent restaurants.

- Identify some of the top chain and independent restaurants.

- List the classifications of restaurants.

- Differentiate characteristics of chain and independent restaurants.

The Restaurant Business

Restaurants are a vital part of our everyday lifestyles; because we are a society on the go, we patronize them several times a week to socialize, as well as eat and drink. Restaurants offer a place to relax and enjoy the company of family, friends, colleagues, and business associates, to restore our energy level before heading off to the next class or engagement. Actually, the word *restaurant* derives from the word *restore*. Today there are more than 925,000 restaurants in the United States with 12.5 million employees (marking the restaurant business the largest employer apart from the government!). The restaurant industry's share of the food dollar has risen to 47.5 percent. On a typical day more than 130 million people in the United States are guests in restaurants and foodservice operations.[1]

As a society we spend an increasing amount, approaching 50 percent, of our food dollar away from home. Restaurants are a multi-billion-dollar industry that provides employment and contributes to the nation's social and economic well-being. No discussion of restaurants can continue with talking about the main ingredient: food. So, let's take a brief look at our culinary heritage.

Classical Cuisine

North America gained most of its culinary legacy from France. Two main events were responsible for our culinary legacy coming from France. First was the French Revolution in 1793, which caused the best French chefs of the day to lose their employment because their bosses lost their heads! Many chefs came to North America as a result, bringing with them their culinary talents. The second event was when Thomas Jefferson, who in 1784 spent five years as envoy to France, and brought a French chef to the White House when he became president. This act stimulated interest in French cuisine and enticed U.S. tavern owners to offer better-quality and more interesting food.

No mention of classical cuisine can be made without talking about the two main initiators: Mari-Antoine Careme (1784–1833), who is credited as the founder of classical cuisine, and Auguste Escoffier, who is profiled later in this chapter. Careme was abandoned on the streets of Paris as a child, and then worked his way up from cook's helper to become the chef to the Prince de Talleyrand and the Prince Regent of England. He also served as head chef to the future King George 1V of England, Tsar Alexander of Russia, and Baron de Rothschild. His goal was to achieve "lightness," "grace," "order," and "perspicuity" of food. Careme dedicated his career to refining and organizing culinary techniques. His many books contain the first really systematic account of cooking principles, recipes, and menu making.[2]

The other great contributor to classical cuisine, August Escoffier (1846–1935), unlike Careme, never worked in an aristocratic household. Instead, he held forth in the finest hotels of the time: the Place Vendome in Paris and the Savoy and Carlton hotels in London. Escoffier is noted for his many contributions to cuisine, including simplifying the Grand Cuisine of Careme by reducing the number of flavors and garnishes and even simplifying the number of sauces to five "mother" or leading sauces. Escoffier brought simplicity and harmony to refine the Grand Cuisine. His many cookbooks are still in use today: *La Guide Culinaire* (1903) is a collection of more than five thousand classic cuisine recipes; in *Le Liver des Menus* (1912), he compares a great meal to a symphony; and *Ma Cuisine* (1934). All of his books emphasize the importance of mastering the techniques of cooking.[3]

This is an exciting time to be involved in the culinary arts and restaurant industry. Not only are new restaurant concepts and themes to fit a variety of tastes and budgets appearing on the scene, but the culinary arts are being developed by several creative and talented chefs. It is important to realize that in this industry, we are never far from food. So, let's take a look at the recent development of **culinary arts.**

The main "ingredient" in a restaurant is cuisine, and one of the main foundations

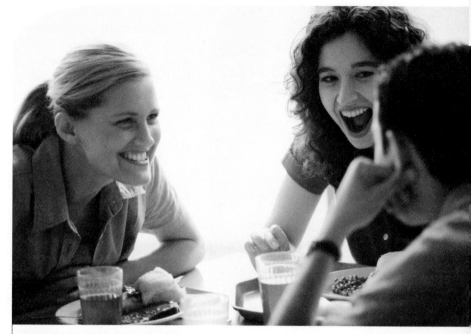

A group of friends enjoy a fine dining experience

of classical French cooking, on which much of American cuisine is based, is the five **mother sauces:** bechamel, velouté, espagnole, tomato, and hollandaise. These elaborate sauces were essential accompaniments for the various dishes on the menu. Until about 1900, all menus were written in French—some still are— and regardless of whether a person was dining in a good hotel or restaurant in London or Lisbon, the intention was that the dish should be prepared in the same manner and taste similar to the French version. The travelers of the day either spoke French or had a knowledge of menu French.

Classical French cuisine was popular until the late 1960s and early 1970s when **nouvelle cuisine** became popular. Nouvelle cuisine is a lighter cuisine than is the classical French and is based on simpler preparations—with the aid of processors, blenders, and juicers—using more natural flavors and ingredients. Instead of thickening a sauce with a flour-based **roux,** a **purée** of vegetables could be used instead. Fresh is in, and this includes herbs for flavor. Nouvelle cuisine combines classical techniques and principles with modern technology and scientific research. "Simpler quicker" quickly became more stylish, with plate presentation becoming a part of the chef's art. North American cooking had arrived. The bounties of Canada and the United States provided the basis for regional cuisine to flourish nationally. **Fusion,** the blending of flavors and techniques from two cuisines, became popular. For example, New England and Italian or Californian and Asian cuisines can be blended. For example, a Japanese recipe might be blended with a Mexican one to create a new hybrid recipe.

Many great chefs have influenced our recent culinary development. Among them are Julia Child, whose television shows did much to take the mystique out of French cooking and encourage a generation of homemakers to elevate their cooking techniques and skills, and more recently Anthony Bourdain on the Travel Channel with his excellent program titled *No Reservations,* and Emeril "Bam" Lagasse and Bobby Flay, who have popularized cooking via the Food Network on TV.

Chef Emeril Lagasse

Charlie Trotter, One of America's Finest Restaurant Chef–Owners and King of Fusion

Culinary schools have done an excellent job of producing a new generation of chefs who are making significant contributions to the evolving culinary arts, including chefs such as Alice Waters, who at Chez Panice, her restaurant in Berkeley, California, is credited with the birth of California cuisine. Waters uses only fresh produce bought from local farmers. Paul Prudhomme is another contemporary chef who has energized many aspiring chefs with his passion for basic cooking, especially cajun style.

Charlie Trotter, chef–owner of Charlie Trotter's in Chicago, who is considered by many to be America's finest chef–owner and king of fusion, said in one of his books:

After love there is only cuisine! It's all about excellence, or at least working towards excellence. Early on in your approach to cooking—or in running a restaurant—you have to determine whether or not you are willing to commit fully and completely to the idea of the *pursuit of excellence*. I have always looked at it this way: if you strive for perfection—an all out assault on total perfection—at the very least you will hit a high level of excellence, and then you might be able to sleep at night. To accomplish something truly significant, excellence has to become a life plan.[4]

Chef Trotter brings his knowledge and exposure together into a coherent view on what the modern fine dining experience could be. He says, "I thought the blend of European refinement regarding the pleasures of the table, American ingenuity and energy in operating a small enterprise, Japanese minimalism and poetic elegance in effecting a sensibility, and a modern approach to incorporating health and dietary concerns would encompass a spectrum of elements through which I could express myself fully. Several years later, I find I am even more devoted than ever to this approach."[5]

Food Trends and Practices

As the level of professionalism rises for the chef of the twenty-first century, chefs will need a strong culinary foundation with a structure that includes multiculture cooking skills and strong employability traits, such as passion, dependability, cooperation, and initiative. Additional management skills include strong supervisory training, sense of urgency, accounting skills, sanitation/safety knowledge, nutritional awareness, and marketing/merchandising skills.

Not only are trans fats banned from many cities menus but, according to the National Restaurant Association's research, nearly three out of four Americans say they are trying to eat more healthfully in restaurants than they did two years ago. The HealthyDiningFinder.com web site is a great resource for those

INTRODUCING AUGUSTE ESCOFFIER (1846–1935)

"Emperor of the World's Kitchens"

Auguste Escoffier is considered by many to be the patron saint of the professional cook. Called the "emperor of the world's kitchens," he is considered a reference point and a role model for all chefs. His exceptional culinary career began at the age of thirteen, when he apprenticed in his uncle's restaurant, and he worked until 1920, and retired to die quietly at home in Monaco in 1935. Uneducated, but a patient educator and diligent writer, he was an innovator who remained deeply loyal to the regional and bourgeois roots of French cookery. He exhibited his culinary skills in the dining rooms of the finest hotels in Europe, including the Place Vendome in Paris and the Savoy and Carlton hotels in London.

When the Prince of Wales requested something light but delicious as late dinner after a night in the casino in Monte Carlo, Auguste Escoffier responded with *poularde Derby,* a stuffed chicken served with truffles cooked in champagne, alternating with slices of butter-fried *foie gras,* its sauce basted with the juices from the chicken and truffles. Another interesting anecdote regarding the chef's originality in making sauces tells of a special dinner for the Prince of Wales and Kaiser Wilhelm. Escoffier was asked to create a special dish to honor such an occasion. Struggling with an apparent loss of creativity until the night before the event, the chef finally noticed a sack of overripe mangos, from which he created a sauce that he personally came out from the kitchen to serve. As he placed the plate on the table, he looked at the Kaiser and with a wicked smile said, "*zum Teufel*"—to the devil. Thus was born Sauce Diabla, today a favorite classic sauce. Escoffier's insistence on sauces derived from the cooking of main ingredients was revolutionary at the time and in keeping with his famous instruction: *faités simple*—keep it simple.

In fact, in his search for simplicity, Escoffier reduced the complexity of the work of Careme, the "cook of kings and king of cooks," and aimed at the perfect balance of a few superb ingredients. In *Le Livre des Menus* (1912), Escoffier makes the analogy of a great dinner as a symphony with contrasting movements that should be appropriate to the occasion, the guests, and the season. He was meticulous in his kitchen, yet wildly imaginative in the creation of exquisite dishes. In 1903, Escoffier published *Le Guide Culinaire,* an astounding collection of more than five thousand classic cuisine recipes and garnishes. Throughout the book, Escoffier emphasizes technique, the importance of a complete understanding of basic cookery principles, and ingredients he considers to be essential to the creation of great dishes.

Escoffier's refinement of Careme's *grand cuisine* was so remarkable it developed into a new cuisine referred to as *cuisine classique.* His principles have been used by successive generations, most emphatically by the *novelle cuisine* brigade. Francois Fusero, *chef de cuisine* at the Hotel Hermitage, Monte Carlo, and many others, regards Escoffier as his role model.

looking to make smart choices when dining out.[6] Among the early program members are Arby's, P. F. Chang, Buca di Beppo, Cracker Barrel, Round Table Pizza, El Pollo Loco, and Famous Dave's.

The term *back-to-basic cooking* has been redefined to mean taking classical cooking methods and infusing modern technology and science to create healthy and flavorful dishes. Some examples of this include the following:

- Thickening soups and sauces by processing and using the food item's natural starches instead of traditional thickening methods

- Redefining the basic mother sauces to omit the béchamel and egg-based sauces and add or replace them with coulis, salsas, or chutneys

- Pursuing more cultural culinary infusion to develop bold and aggressive flavors
- Experimenting with sweet and hot flavors
- Taking advantage of the shrinking globe and disappearance of national borders to bring new ideas and flavors to restaurants
- Evaluating recipes and substituting ingredients for better flavor; that is, flavored liquid instead of water, infused oils and vinegars instead of nonflavored oils and vinegars
- Substituting herbs and spices for salt
- Returning to one-pot cooking to capture flavors
- Offering more healthy dining choices in restaurants

Today, being a chef is considered a profession that offers a variety of opportunities in every segment of the hospitality industry and anywhere in the world.

Culinary Practices

In this new millennium, we are seeing culinary education setting the pace for dining exploration.[7] As you prepare for a career in the hospitality industry, you will find it imperative that you develop a strong culinary foundation. Within the structure of this you will need to develop cooking skills, strong employability traits, people skills, menu development skills, nutrition knowledge, sanitation/safety knowledge, accounting skills, and computer skills.

Before you can become a successful chef, you have to be a good cook. To be a good cook, you have to understand the basic techniques and principles of cooking. The art of cooking has not changed much in thousands of years. And, although the concept of cooking has not changed, science and technology have allowed us to improve the methods of food preparation. We still use fire to cook with: Grilling, broiling, and simmering are still popular methods of cooking.

To become a successful chef, you will need to learn all of the basic cooking methods in order to understand flavor profiles. As you look at recipes to cook, try to enhance the basic ingredient list to improve the flavor. As an example, always try to substitute a flavored liquid if water is called for in a recipe. It is also important to understand basic ingredient flavors so that you can improve flavor. The idea behind back-to-basic cooking means you evaluate your recipe and look for flavor improvement with each item.

Employability traits are those skills that focus on attitude, passion, initiative, dedication, sense of urgency, and dependability. These traits are not always traits that can be taught, but a good chef can demonstrate them by example. Most of the employers with job opportunities for students consider these skills to be more important than technical skills. The belief is that if you have strong employability traits, your technical skills will be strong.

One of the most important things to realize about the restaurant industry is that *you can't do it alone.* Each person in your operation has to work together for

INTRODUCING RICHARD MELMAN

Chairman of the Board and Founder, Lettuce Entertain You Enterprises, Inc.

Richard Melman is founder and chairman of Lettuce Entertain You Enterprises, a Chicago-based corporation that owns and licenses seventy restaurants nationwide and in Japan.

The restaurant business has been Melman's life work, beginning with his early days in a family-owned restaurant, and later as a teenager working in fast-food eateries and a soda fountain, and selling restaurant supplies. After realizing that he wasn't cut out to be a college student and failing to convince his father that he should be made a partner in the family business, Melman met Jerry A. Orzoff, a man who immediately and unconditionally believed in Melman's ability to create and run restaurants. In 1971, the two opened R. J. Grunts, a hip burger joint that soon became one of the hottest restaurants in Chicago. Here, Melman and Orzoff presented food differently and with a sense of humor, creating the youthful and fun restaurant that was a forerunner in the trend toward dining out as entertainment that swept this country in the early 1970s.

Melman and Orzoff continued to develop restaurant concepts together until Orzoff's death in 1981. Through his relationship with Orzoff, Melman formulated a philosophy based on the importance of partners, of sharing responsibilities and profits with them, and of developing and growing together.[1]

To operate so many restaurants well, Lettuce has needed to hire, train, and develop people, and then keep them happy and focused on excellence. Melman's guiding philosophy is that he is not interested in being the biggest or the best known—only in being the best he can be. He places enormous value on the people who work for Lettuce Entertain You Enterprises and feels tremendous responsibility for their continued success. Today, he has forty working partners, most of whom came up through the organization, and has five thousand people working for him. Over the years, Melman has stayed close to the guests by using focus groups and frequent-diner programs. The group's training programs are rated among the best in the business, and Melman's management style is clearly influenced by team sports. He says, "There are many similarities between running a restaurant and a team sport. However, it's not a good idea to have ten all-stars; everybody can't bat first. You need people with similar goals—people who want to win and play hard."[2]

Melman's personal life revolves around his family. He and his wife Martha have been married for thirty years and have three children.[3]

[1]Marilyn Alva, "Does He Still Have It?" *Restaurant Business* 93, no. 4 (March 1, 1994), 104–111.

[2]Personal communication with Richard Melman, June 8, 2004.

[3]www.leye.com, August 1, 2007.

you to be successful. The most important ingredient in managing people is to *respect them.* Many words can be used to describe a manager (coach, supervisor, boss, mentor), but whatever term is used, you have to be in the game to be effective. Managing a kitchen is like coaching a football team—everyone must work together to be effective. The difference between a football team and a kitchen is that chefs/managers cannot supervise from the sidelines; they have to be in the game. One of my favorite examples of excellent people management skills is that of the general manager of a hotel who had the ware-washing team report directly to him. When asked why, he indicated that they are the people who know what is

[handwritten margin note: kitchen needs 2 work together like a football team]

being thrown in the garbage, they are the people who know what the customers are not eating, and they are the people most responsible for the sanitation and safety of an operation. There are many components to managing people—training, evaluating, nurturing, delegating, and so on—but the most important is respect.

▶ **Check Your Knowledge**

1. From what country did North America gain most of its culinary legacy?
2. Define fusion cuisine and give an example.

Developing a Restaurant

[handwritten margin notes: factors affecting a restaurants success:]
[↳ operating philosophy]
[↳ restaurant market]

Developing a restaurant may be the ultimate entrepreneurial dream. In which other industry can you get into a business like a restaurant for only a few thousand dollars? Of course, you need to have acquired the knowledge and skills along the way by getting experience in the kind of restaurant you intend to open. Yes, independent restaurants are a rush for the owners—they are one of the few places where guests use all of their senses to enjoy the experience. Through taste, sight, smell, hearing, and touch all employes and guests can savor the food, service, and atmosphere of the restaurant. The successful operation of a restaurant is dependent on a number of factors. Let's examine the factors that make for a successful restaurant development, from the operating philosphy to controls, and all the functions in between.

[handwritten margin notes: ↳ restaurant concept]
[↳ restaurant location]
[↳ rest. ambience]
[↳ menu planning]
[↳ needs + desires of guests]
[↳ capability of chefs]
[↳ $]
[↳ equipment, layout, flow]
[↳ consistency in everything]

Operating Philosophy, Mission, Goals, and Objectives

At the heart of an enterprise is the philosophy of the owner. The philosophy represents the way the company does business. It is an expression of the ethics, morals, and values by which the company operates. Many companies have formal mission statements that explain their reason for being in business. Danny Meyer of Union Square Hospitality calls it "*enlightened hospitality*—meaning if your staff is happy your guests will be, too." Meyer gives each of his 450 employees a voucher to dine in one of the restaurants every month. They have to write a report on the experience; Meyer enjoys reading them. Ever the coach and teacher, he says that it's better to have your staff tell you what's wrong than for you to have to tell them. No wonder his restaurants like Union Square Cafe, Gramercy Tavern, Eleven Madison Park, Tabla, Blue Smoke, and others are the top rated in New York.

Restaurant Market

The market is composed of those guests who will patronize the restaurant. A respective restaurant owner will analyze the market to determine whether

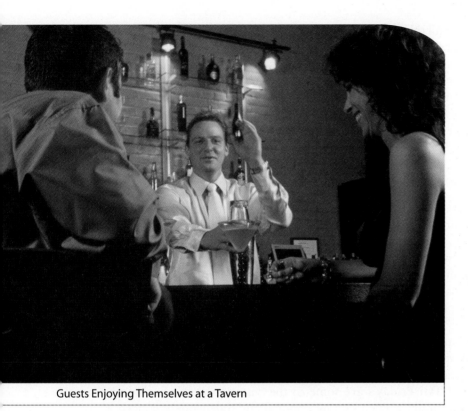

Guests Enjoying Themselves at a Tavern

sufficient demand exists in a particular market niche, such as Italian or Southern cuisine. A **niche** is a marketing term used to describe a specific share or slot a of a certain market. A good indication of the size of the market can be ascertained by taking a radius of from one to five miles around the restaurant. The distance will vary according to the type and location of the restaurant. In Manhattan, it may only be a few blocks, whereas in rural West Virginia it may be a few miles. The area that falls within the radius is called the **catchment area**. The demographics of the population within the catchment area is analyzed to reveal age, number of people in various age brackets, sex, ethnicity, religion, income levels, and so on. This information is usually available from the chamber of commerce or data at the local library or real estate offices.

One yardstick used to determine the potential viability of a restaurant is to divide the number of restaurants in the catchment area by the total population. The average number of people per restaurant in the United States is about 500. Perhaps this kind of saturation is one of the reasons for the high failure rate of restaurants. Obviously, each area is different; one location may have several Italian restaurants but no Southern restaurant. Therefore, a Southern restaurant would be unique in the market and, if properly positioned, may have a competitive advantage. If someone in the catchment area wanted to eat Italian food, he or she would have to choose among the various Italian restaurants. In marketing terms, the number of potential guests for the Italian restaurant would be divided by the number of Italian restaurants to determine **fair market share** (the average number of guests that would, if all other things went equal, eat at any one of the Italian restaurants). *Figure 6–1* shows a thousand potential guests. If they all decided to eat Italian in the fair market share scenario, each restaurant would receive 100 guests. In reality, we know this does not happen—for various reasons, one restaurant becomes more popular. The number of guests that this and the other restaurants receive then is called the **actual market share**. *Figure 6–2* shows an example of the actual market share that similar restaurants might receive.

Restaurant Concept

Successful restaurant concepts are created with guests in mind. All too frequently someone thinks it would be a good idea to open up a particular kind of restaurant, only to find there are insufficient guests to make it viable.

For the winners, creating and operating a restaurant business is fun—lots of people coming and going, new faces, old friends. Restaurants provide a social gathering place where employees, guests, and management can get their adrenaline flowing in positive ways. The restaurant business is exciting and challenging; with the right location, food, atmosphere, and service it is possible to extract the market and make a good return on investment.

There are several examples of restaurant concepts that have endured over the past few decades. Applebee's, Chart House, Hard Rock Café, Olive Garden, Red Lobster, and TGI Friday's are some of the better-known U.S. chain restaurant concepts. Naturally, there are more regional and independent concepts.

The challenge is to create a restaurant concept and bring it into being, a concept that fits a definite market, a concept better suited to its market than that presented by competing restaurants.[8] Every restaurant represents a concept and projects a total impression or an image. The image appeals to a certain market—casual, formal, children, adults, ethnic, and so on. The concept should fit the location and reach out to its target market. A restaurant's concept, location, menu, and decor should intertwine.[9]

In restaurant lingo, professionals sometimes describe restaurants by the net operating percentage that the restaurant makes. TGI Friday's restaurants, for

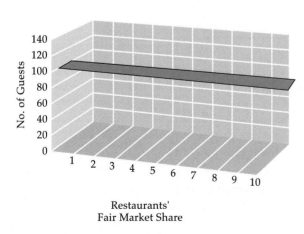

Figure 6–1 • Fair Market Share.

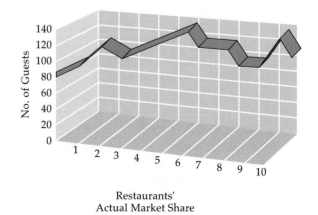

Figure 6–2 • Actual Market Share.

example, are usually described as 20 percent restaurants. A local restaurant may be only a 10 percent restaurant.

In order for the operation of a restaurant to be successful, the following factors need to be addressed:

- Mission

- Goals

- Objectives

- Market

- Concept

- Location

- Menu planning

- Ambiance

- Lease

- Other occupational costs

The odds in favor of becoming a big restaurant winner are good. Thousands of restaurants do business in the United States. Each year, thousands of new ones open and thousands more close, and many more change ownership. The restaurant business is deceptively easy to enter, but it is deceptively difficult to succeed in it.[10]

Restaurant concept is undoubtedly one of the major components of any successful operation. Some restaurants are looking for a concept; some concepts are searching for a restaurant.

Restaurant Location

The restaurant concept must fit the location, and the location must fit the concept (see Figure 6–3). The location should appeal to the target market (expected interests). Other things being equal, prime locations cost more, so operators must either charge more for their menu items or drive sufficient volume to keep the rent/lease costs to between 5 and 8 percent of sales.

Key location criteria include the following:

- Demographics—how many people are there in the catchment area?

- The average income of the catchment area population

- Growth or decline of the area

- Zoning, drainage, sewage, and utilities

- Convenience—how easy is it for people to get to the restaurant?

- Visibility—can passersby see the restaurant?

- Accessibility—how accessible is the restaurant?

- Parking—Is parking required? If so, how many spaces are needed and what will it cost?

- Curbside appeal—how inviting is the restaurant?

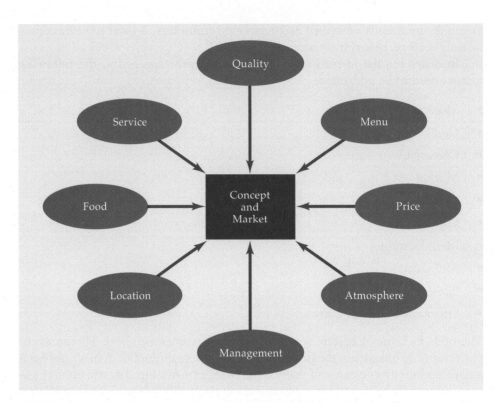

Figure 6–3 • Concept and Market (Reprinted with permission from John R. Walker and Donald E. Lundberg, The Restaurant from Concept to Operation, 3rd ed. New York: John Wiley and Sons, 2001, p. 62.)

- Location—how desirable is the neighborhood?

  Several popular types of restaurant locations include the following:

- Stand-alone restaurants
- Cluster or restaurant row
- Shopping mall
- Shopping mall—free standing
- Downtown
- Suburban

Restaurant Ambiance

The **atmosphere** that a restaurant creates has both immediate conscious and unconscious effects on guests. The immediate conscious effect is how guests react to the **ambiance** on entering the restaurant—or even more importantly as an element in the decision-making process used in selecting a restaurant. Too noisy? Are the tables too close? The subconscious is affected by mood, lighting, furnishings, and music; these play an important role in leaving a subtle impression on guests.

Today, atmospherics are part of the theme and have an immediate sensory impact on customers.

Perhaps the most noticeable atmospheric restaurants are those with a theme. The theme will use color, sound, lighting, decor, texture, and visual stimulation to create special effects for patrons. Among restaurants with good atmospherics are Macaroni Grill, Panera Bread, Outback, Hard Rock Cafe, and Chart House.

▶ Check Your Knowledge

1. Imagine you are starting your own restaurant. In the process, you realize you need a mission statement. Write a mission statement for your new restaurant.
2. Define the following terms and briefly describe the role they play:
   a. Market
   b. Concept
   c. Ambiance

Menu Planning

The menu may be the most important ingredient in a restaurant's success. A restaurant's menu must agree with the concept; the concept must be based on what the guest in the target market expects; and the menu must exceed those expectations. The type of menu will depend on the kind of restaurant being operated.

There are six main types of menus:

A la carte menus. Offer items that are individually priced.

Table d'hôte menus. Offer a selection of one or more items for each course at a fixed price. This type of menu is used more frequently in hotels and in Europe. The advantage is the perception guests have of receiving good values.

Du jour menus. List the items "of the day."

Tourist menus. Are used to attract tourists' attention. They frequently stress value and food that is acceptable to the tourists.

California menus. Are so named because, in some California restaurants, guest may order any item on the menu at any time of the day.

Cyclical menus. Repeat themselves over a period of time.

A menu generally consists of perhaps six to eight appetizers, two to four soups, a few salads—both as appetizers and entrees—eight to sixteen entrees, and about four to six desserts.

The many considerations in menu planning attest to the complexity of the restaurant business. Considerations include the following:

- Needs and desires of guests
- Capabilities of cooks
- Equipment capacity and layout

- Consistency and availability of menu ingredients
- Price and pricing strategy (cost and profitability)
- Nutritional value
- Accuracy in menu
- Menu analysis (contribution margin)
- Menu design
- Menu engineering
- Chain menus.[11]

Needs and Desires of Guests

In planning a menu, the needs and desires of the guests are what is important—not what the owner, chef, or manager thinks. If it is determined that there is a niche in the market for a particular kind of restaurant, then the menu must harmonize with the theme of the restaurant.

The Olive Garden restaurants are a good example of a national chain that has developed rapidly during the past few years. The concept has been positioned and defined as middle of the road with a broad-based appeal. During the concept development phase, several focus groups were asked their opinions on topics from dishes to decor. The result has been extremely successful.

Several other restaurants have become successful by focusing on the needs and desires of the guest. Among them are Hard Rock Cafe, TGI Friday's, Red Lobster, and Applebee's.

Capabilities of Cooks

The capabilities of the cooks must also harmonize with the menu and concept. An appropriate level of expertise must be employed to match the peak demands and culinary expertise expected by the guests. The length and complexity of the menu and the number of guests to be served are both factors in determining the extent of the cooks' capabilities.

The equipment capacity and layout affect the menu and the efficiency with which the cooks can produce the food. Some restaurants have several fried or cold items on the appetizer menu simply to avoid use of the stoves and ovens, which will be needed for the entrees. A similar situation occurs with desserts; by avoiding the use of the equipment needed for the entrees, cooks find it easier to produce the volume of meals required during peak periods.

One of the best examples of effective utilization of menu and equipment is in Chinese restaurants. At the beginning of many Chinese restaurant menus, there are combination dinners. The combination dinners include several courses for a fixed price. Operators of Chinese restaurants explain that about 60 to 70 percent of guests order those combinations. This helps the cooks because they can prepare for the orders and the food is produced quickly, which pleases the guests. It would create havoc if everyone ordered à la carte items because the kitchen and the cooks could not handle the volume in this way.

Equipment Capacity and Layout

All restaurant menus should be developed with regard to the capacity and layout of the equipment. Anyone who has worked in a busy kitchen on Friday or Saturday night and been "slammed" will realize that part of the problem may have been too ambitious a menu (too many items requiring extensive preparation and the use of too much equipment).

If the restaurant is already in existence, it may be costly to alter the kitchen. Operators generally find it easier to alter the menu to fit the equipment. The important thing is to match the menu with the equipment and production scheduling. A menu can be created to use some equipment for appetizers; for this one reason, the appetizers selections on the menu often include one or two cold cuts, possibly a couple of salads, but mostly some deep-fried items or soups. This keeps the stove and grill areas free for the entrees. The desserts, if they are not brought in, are mostly made in advance and served cold or heated in the microwave. Other considerations include the projected volume of sales and the speed of service for each menu item.

Most chefs are sufficiently adaptable to be able to prepare quality meals with the equipment provided. Some may prepare a more detailed *mise an place* (everything in place to prepare a menu item), and others will go further to partially cook items so that they can be furnished to order. Of course, there is always the old standby—the daily special—that can take the pressure off the production line.

Consistency and Availability of Menu Ingredients

In the United States, most ingredients are available year-round. However, at certain times of the year, some items become more expensive. This is because they are out of season—in economic terms, the demand exceeds the supply so the price goes up. An example of this is when a storm in the Gulf of Mexico disrupts the supply of fresh fish and shellfish and causes an increase in price. To offset this kind of situation, some operators print their menus daily. Others may purchase a quantity of frozen items when the prices are low.

Price and Pricing Strategy

The target market and concept will, to a large extent, determine the menu price ranges. An example might be a neighborhood restaurant where the appetizers are priced from $3.25 and $6.95 and entrees are in the $6.95 and $11.95 price range. The selling price of each item must be acceptable to the market and profitable to the restaurateur. Factors that go into this decision include the following:

- What is the competition charging for a similar item?
- What is the item's food cost?
- What is the cost of labor that goes into the item?
- What other costs must be covered?
- What profit is expected by the operator?
- What is the contribution margin of the item?[12]

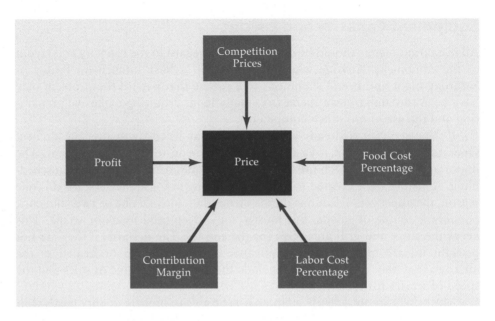

Figure 6–4 • Factors That Influence a Restaurant's Menu Prices.

Figure 6–4 illustrates the factors that influence a restaurant's menu prices. There are two main ways to price menus. A comparative approach analyzes the price ranges of the competition and determines the price range for appetizers, entrees, and desserts. The second method is to cost the individual dish item on the menu and multiply it by the ratio amount necessary to achieve the desired food cost percentage. For example, to achieve a 30 percent food cost for an item priced at $6.95 on the menu, the food cost would have to be $2.09. Beverage items are priced the same way. This method will result in the same expected food cost percentage for each item. It would be great if we lived in such a perfect world. The problem is that if some items were priced out according to a 30 percent food cost, they might appear to be overpriced according to customers' perceptions. For example, some of the more expensive meat and fish would price out at $18 to $21 when the restaurant would prefer to keep entree prices under $15. To balance this, restaurants lower the margin on the more expensive meat and fish items—as long as there are only one or two of them—and raise the price on the some of the other items, such as soup, salad, chicken, and pasta. This approach is called the **weighted average,** whereby the factors of food cost percentage, contribution margin, and sales volume are weighted.

Nutritional Value

A more health-conscious customer has promoted most restaurant operators to make changes not only to the menu selections but also to the preparation methods. Restaurant operators are using more chicken, fish, seafood, and pasta items on the menus today compared with a few years ago. Beef is more lean than ever before. All of these items are being prepared in more healthful ways such as broiling, poaching, braising, casseroling, or rotisserieing instead of frying.

Increasingly, restaurants are publishing the nutritional value of their food. McDonald's has taken a leadership role in this. Other restaurants are utilizing a heart-healthy symbol to signify that the menu item is suitable for guests with concerns about heart-healthy eating. Many restaurants are changing the oil used from the saturated fat, which is high in cholesterol, to 100 percent vegetable oil or canola oil, which is cholesterol free.

Accuracy in Menu

Laws prohibit misrepresentation of items being sold. In the case of restaurants the so-called truth-in-menu laws refer to the fact that descriptions on the menu must be accurate. Prime beef must be prime cut, not some other grade, fresh vegetables must be fresh, not frozen, and Maine lobster had better actually come from Maine. Some restaurants have received sizable fines for violations of accuracy in menu.

Menu Analysis

One of the earliest approaches to menu analysis was developed by Jack Miller. He called the best-selling items *winners;* they not only sold more but were also at a lower food cost percentage. In 1982, Micheal Kasavana and Donald Smith developed menu engineering, in which the best items are called *stars*—those that have the highest contribution margin and the highest sales. Later, David Paresic suggested that a combination of three variables—**food cost percentage** (percentage of the selling price of an item that must be spent to purchase the raw ingredients), **contribution margin**, and **sales volume**—should be used.

Another key variable in menu analysis is labor costs. A menu item may take several hours to prepare, and it may be difficult to precisely calculate the time a cook spends in preparation of the dish. Operators add the total food and labor costs together to determine prime cost, which should not exceed about 60 to 65 percent of sales. The remaining 35 to 40 percent is for overhead and profit.

Menu Engineering

Menu engineering is a sophisticated approach to setting menu prices and controlling costs. It operates on the principle that the food cost percentage of each menu item is not as important as the total contribution margin of the menu as a whole. Usually this means that the food cost percentage of a menu item could be larger than desired, yet, the total contribution margin of the menu will increase. Through menu engineering, menu items that should be repositioned, dropped, repriced, or simply left alone can be identified.

Menu Design and Layout

Basic menus can be recited by the server. Casual menus are sometimes written on a chalk or similar type board. Quick-service menus are often illuminated above the order counter. More formal menus are generally single page, or folded with three or more pages. Some describe the restaurant and type of food offered; most have beverage suggestions and a wine selection. The more upscale American-Continental restaurants have a separate wine list.

Some menus are more distinctive than others, with pictures of the items or at least enticing descriptions of the food. Research indicates that there is a focal point at the center of the right-hand page; this is the spot in which to place the star or signature item.[13]

Like a brochure for the hotel, a menu is a sales tool and motivational device. A menu's design can affect what guests order and how much they spend. The paper colors, and artwork all play an important role in influencing guest decisions and help to establish a restaurant's image and ambiance.

As you can see, a number of factors make for a successful restaurant. Help is available from the U.S. Small Business Association (www.sba.gov/services/training/newcourses/index.html) which has several courses and other information for those interested in developing a business plan for a restaurant. Now, let's look at the classifications of restaurants.

Classifications of Restaurants

There is no single definition of the various classifications of restaurants, perhaps because it is an evolving business. Most experts would agree, however, that there are two main categories: **independent restaurants (indies)** and **chain restaurants.** Other categories include designations as *fine dining, casual restaurants*, and *quick-service restaurants.* Some restaurants may even fall into more than one category—for instance, a restaurant can be both ethnic and quick service, such as Taco Bell.

The National Restaurant Association's figures indicate that Americans are spending an increasing number of food dollars away from home at various food-service operations. Americans are eating out more than ever—up to five times a week—and on special occasions such as birthdays, anniversaries, Mother's Day, and Valentine's Day. The most popular meal eaten away from home is lunch, which brings in approximately 50 percent of fast-food restaurant sales.[14]

Individual restaurants (also called indies) are typically owned by one or more owners, who are usually involved in the day-to-day operation of the business. Even if the owners have more than one store (restaurant-speak for a "restaurant"), each usually functions independently. These restaurants are not affiliated with any national brand or name. They offer the owner independence, creativity, and flexibility, but are generally accompanied by more risk. For example, the restaurant may not be as popular as the owners hoped it would be, or the owners lacked the knowledge and expertise necessary for success in the restaurant business, or the owners did not have the cash flow to last several months before a profit could be made. You only have to look around your neighborhood to find examples of restaurants that failed for one reason or another.

Chain restaurants are a group of restaurants, each identical in market, concept, design, service, food, and name. Part of the marketing strategy of a chain restaurant is to remove uncertainty from the dining experience. The same menu, food quality, level of service, and atmosphere can be found in any one of the restaurants, regardless of location. Large companies or entrepreneurs are likely chain restaurant owners. For example, Applebee's is a restaurant chain; some stores are company owned but the majority are franchised by territory.

Full-Service Restaurants

Restaurant types included in this category are fine dining, casual, theme, celebrity, steak houses, and some ethnic restaurants.

Fine Dining

A **fine dining restaurant** is one where a good selection of menu items is offered; generally at least fifteen or more different entrees can be cooked to order, with nearly all the food being made on the premises from scratch using raw or fresh ingredients. Full-service restaurants may be formal or casual and may be further categorized by price, decor/atmosphere, level of formality, and menu. Most fine dining restaurants may be cross-referenced into other categories, as mentioned previously. Many of these restaurants serve **haute cuisine** (pronounced *hote*), which is a French term meaning "elegant dining," or literally "high food." Many of the fine restaurants in the United States are based on French or northern Italian cuisine, which, together with fine Chinese cuisine, are considered by many Western connoisseurs to be the finest in the world.

Most fine dining restaurants are independently owned and operated by an entrepreneur or a partnership. These restaurants are in almost every city. In recent years fine dining has become more fun because creative chefs offer guests fine cuisine as an art. At places like Union Square Café and Gramercy Tavern in New York, Danny Meyer is looking for guests who want spectacular meals without the fuss. Many cities have independent fine dining restaurants that offer fine dining for an occasion—a birthday, an "expense account" (business entertaining), or other celebration.

Marco Maccioni, son of Sirio Maccioni of the famed Le Cirque, says that the sons did not want to simply clone Le Cirque. For the menu, they sought inspiration from Mama's home cooking—pizza, pasta, and comfortable, braised dishes.

Many cities have independent fine dining restaurants that pursue those who are not content with wings and deep-fried cheese. Chefs are therefore making approachable, yet provocative food; each course is expertly prepared and may be served with wine. The top independent restaurant in terms of sales is the Tavern on the Green in New York City, which opened in 1976. Tavern on the Green is one of the most financially successful restaurants. It has sales of approaching $40 million from 1,500 seats—including banquets with an average dinner check of $72.72—and serves 550,000 people a year. Now that's cooking![15]

Several types of restaurants are included in the fine dining segment: various steakhouses; ethnic, celebrity, and theme

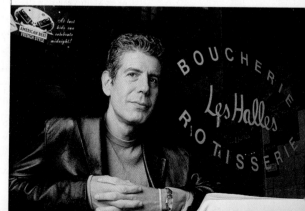

Anthony Bourdain, owner and chef of Les Halles Restaurant, sits at one of its tables. Bourdain is the top-selling author of *Kitchen Confidential* and *A Cook's Tour*

FOCUS ON RESTAURANTS

Restaurant Operations: The Challenge of the Intangibles

William B. Martin, *Cal Tech—Monterey Bay*

Does this situation sound familiar? You are sitting at home (studying, of course) and a friend or relative suggests that you should go out for dinner. That sounds good to you, so you say, "Okay." That is the easy part.

Next comes the more difficult part. Where should you go? And so you ask, "Where do you want to go?" Your friend (or relative) responds, "I don't know. Where do you want to go?" And so it goes, back and forth until finally you arrive at a decision as to where you will go.

Some time later, you arrive at your chosen destination. You experience whatever the restaurant has to offer. Afterward, consciously or unconsciously, you decide whether you will return to that particular restaurant.

As we can see from this common scenario, from a customer's point of view, dining out involves three critical questions: (1) To eat out or not? (2) Where to go? and (3) Whether to return?

Let's take a closer look at typical restaurant consumer responses to each of these questions and see what we can learn.

To Eat Out or Not?

Why do people choose to dine out? What are the reasons? Multiple consumer surveys over the years have consistently reflected the following reasons. The rank order of importance may vary from survey to survey, but the reasons, themselves, remain fairly constant.

The top ten reasons consumers tend to dine out in a full-service restaurant include to celebrate a special occasion, relax, avoid cooking, have a family night out, be waited on, enjoy the atmosphere, enjoy a familiar place, have menu choices, meet friends, and try foods not eaten at home.

The reasons consumers tend to dine out in a fast-food restaurant are surprisingly similar with two variations: to eat inexpensively and to eat quickly. All the other reasons for dining at a full-service restaurant are also cited for dining at a fast-food restaurant.

Now, let's take a minute and look carefully at this list of reasons for dining out—whether fast food or full service. What *don't* you see on this list? What is missing?

What is missing is that the reason for dining out is "to eat." What does this tell us? What it tells us is that people choose to dine out for lots of reasons in addition to the need to eat. Eating comes along with the experience, but the choice to dine out in the first place is made for more complicated reasons—most of which are psychological and social reasons: to celebrate, to meet friends, to enjoy, to experience something new, to relax, and so forth.

How can we interpret this? What can we learn? First, we have to distinguish between tangibles and intangibles because in the restaurant business we deal with both, and both are very important to our success.

Tangibles are those things that can be seen, smelled, touched, poked, prodded, weighed, or otherwise physically inspected. Food, of course, fits into this category.

Intangibles, on the other hand, can't be so easily weighed and measured. They deal with human characteristics such as emotions, physiological states of mind, and sociological and cultural influences. They are indeed varied and complex—and often elusive because we can't inspect them, touch them, or smell them to know whether they are "right" or "wrong." Now here's the punch line: *The reasons that people decide whether or not to dine out are predominately intangible in nature.* As you can see from the list, the reasons tend to be primarily psychologically and sociologically based.

Where to Go?

You have decided to go out. Now, how do you choose a restaurant? How it looks? Type of food? Location? The amount of money in your pocket (or purse)? Reputation? A recommendation? An advertisement?

The answer is probably any one, all, or a combination of the preceding. If you have been to a restaurant before, you may choose to return for a combination of liking the food, the ambience, the value (what you get for your money), and the service. Choosing a restaurant for the first time usually involves a different set of criteria, which usually includes type of food, location, and perceived pricing.

Whereas the reasons for choosing a particular restaurant are varied and complex, the type of *food* desired plays an important role, if not *the* role, in making a choice. Whether it is fast food or full service, we tend to choose a particular restaurant because we want to eat the style or type of food that the restaurant serves.

Whether to Return?

So, you have made a choice of where to eat. Among other factors, the type of food that is served has attracted you. Now, what determines whether you will return—or not?

Think about the last time you went out to eat in a restaurant. Once there, what happened? Was it a positive experience? How was the food? The service? The ambience? Did you have a good time? Would you go back? Why or why not?

If you had a bad or disappointing food experience, most likely you would tend not to go back. No doubt about it, food is a critical factor. But, there is more—much more. Let's go back to those *intangibles* that have influenced your decision to dine out in the first place. The decision to return is greatly influenced by how well your intangible expectations were met. Did you have a good time? Did you enjoy yourself? Were you treated well? These are questions that go way beyond food. They address your *total dining experience*. Simply put, when that *total* experience is positive, you tend to return. When it is not, you don't.

In short, a restaurant is much more than about food. Restaurant success is about creating a total positive atmosphere and dining experience.

We have addressed three questions: To eat out or not? Where to go? And whether to return? In two of the three questions, intangibles remain *the* critical decisive factor. That is why in the restaurant business managing the intangibles is just as important as managing the tangibles. As you can readily see, in the restaurant business it's the intangibles that can make or break you.

restaurants. The upscale steakhouses, such as Morton's of Chicago, Ruth Chris's, and Houston's, continue to attract the expense account and "occasion" diners. Naturally, they are located near their guests and in cities with convention centers or attractions that draw big crowds.

A few ethnic restaurants are considered fine dining—most cities have a sampling of Italian, French, and other European, Latin, and Asian restaurants. Some even have fusion (a blend of two cuisines, for example, Italian and Japanese). Fusion restaurants must pay particular attention when blending two unique ethnic flavors. If successful, the dish could turn out to be the latest craze; if unsuccessful, it could be disastrous!

Celebrity chef–owned fine dining restaurants of interest are operated by Wolfgang Puck, co-owner of Spago and Chinois in Los Angeles, and Alice Waters of Chez Panisse in Berkeley, California. Both have done much to inspire a new generation of talented chefs. Alice Waters has been a role model for many female chefs and has received numerous

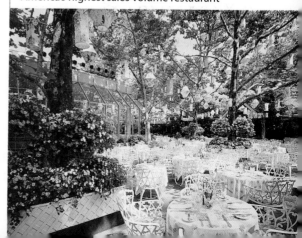

Tavern on the Green in New York's Central Park is America's highest sales volume restaurant

One famous restaurant in New Orleans is the Court of the Two Sisters. It has the names of prisoners from various wars inscribed on the walls of the entrance way

awards and published several cookbooks, including one for children.

The level of service in fine dining restaurants is generally high, with a hostess or host to greet and seat patrons. Captains and food servers advise guests of special items and assist with the description and selection of dishes during order taking. If there is no separate sommelier (wine waiter), the captain or food server may offer a description of the wine that will complement the meal and can assist with the order taking. Some upscale or luxury full-service restaurants have table-side cooking and French service from a gueridon cart.[16] The decor of a full-service restaurant is generally compatible with the overall ambiance and theme that the restaurant is seeking to create. These elements of food, service, and decor create a memorable experience for the restaurant guest.

Theme Restaurants

Many **theme restaurants** are a combination of a sophisticated specialty and several other types of restaurants. They generally serve a limited menu but aim to wow the guest by the total experience. Of the many popular theme restaurants, two stand out. The first highlights the nostalgia of the 1950s, as done in the T-Bird and Corvette diners. These restaurants serve all-American food such as the perennial meatloaf in a fun atmosphere that is a throwback to the seemingly more carefree 1950s. The mostly female food servers appear in short polka-dot skirts with gym shoes and bobby socks.

The second popular theme restaurant is the dinner house category; among some of the better known national and regional chains are TGI Friday's, Houlihan's, and Bennigan's. These are casual American bistro-type restaurants that combine a lively atmosphere created in part by assorted bric-a-brac to decorate the various ledges and walls. These restaurants have remained popular over the past twenty years. In a prime location, they can do extremely well.

People are attracted to theme restaurants because they offer a total experience and a social meeting place. This is achieved through decoration and atmosphere and allows the restaurant to offer a limited menu that blends with the theme. Throughout the United States and the world, numerous theme restaurants stand out for one reason or another. Among them are decors featuring airplanes, railway, dining cars, rock and roll, 1960s nostalgia, and many others.

INTRODUCING SARAH STEGNER

Chef–Owner, Prairie Grass Café

Sarah Stegner opened Prairie Grass Café in Northbrook, Illinois, with her partner, former executive chef George Bumbaris of the Ritz-Carlton Chicago, in 2004. A little history . . .

Stegner, an Evanston, Illinois, native, grew up in a family devoted to food. Her grandmother was a caterer "before women did those kinds of things," and her grandfather was an avid backyard vegetable gardener. The table was the center of the family and was where Stegner's passion for food emerged.

After a year spent studying classical guitar at Northwestern University, Stegner followed her heart and enrolled at the Dumas Pere Cooking School. She graduated with a chef's certificate one year later and was hired as an apprentice at the Ritz-Carlton Chicago.

In 1990, after six years of working in various culinary capacities (including a first job of cleaning fish for twelve hours a day), Stegner was promoted to chef of the Dining Room. She worked for years under the guiding hands of Fernand Gutierrez, former executive chef and director of food and beverage at the Ritz-Carlton Chicago, and current food and beverage director at Four Seasons Mexico City. Since then, Stegner has distinguished herself as one of America's most creative young chefs.

As a result of her talents, she has captured many national honors. Chef Stegner was named Best Chef of the Midwest in 1998 by the prestigious James Beard Foundation and the Dining Room was named one of the top five restaurants in Chicago in 1999 by *Gourmet* magazine, and it received four stars from the *Chicago Tribune*. In addition, it was rated best hotel dining room in Chicago in 1999 by the prestigious Zagat Chicago Restaurant Guide and was named Best Restaurant in Chicago in 1996 by *Gourmet;* one of the top thirteen hotel dining rooms in the United States in 1996 by *Bon Appétit;* and one of the top ten hotel restaurants in the world in 1996 by *Hotels* magazine.

Chef Stegner is recipient of the 1995 Robert Mondavi Culinary Award of Excellence and captured the national title of 1994 Rising Star Chef of the Year in America by the James Beard Foundation. She also holds the title of Prix Culinaire International Pierre Taittinger 1991 U.S. Winner, where she represented the United States in the finals in Paris and was the only female chef present at the global competition.

In recent years, Chef Stegner has enjoyed periodic training in France, under the expertise of Chef Pierre Orsi at his two-star Michelin Pierre Orsi Restaurant in Lyon, France, and with chefs Bertolli and Berard Bessin in Paris.

She also finds time to donate her talents to charitable causes. Six years ago, she founded the Women Chefs of Chicago, comprising the city's top female chefs who donate cuisine for numerous events throughout the city to raise money for charity. Under her direction. The Women Chefs of Chicago have helped raise more than $500,000 for Chicagoland charities in the past few years.

Sarah's support of her state's agriculture is reflected in her food: she uses the finest seasonal produce from Midwest vegetable farmers and cheesemakers. She works with her husband, Rohit Nambiar, who manages the front of house at Prairie Grass Café. Her mother, Elizabeth Stegner, makes the pies served at Prairie Grass Café. Sarah feels right at home in her new restaurant.

Celebrity Restaurants

Celebrity-owned restaurants have been growing in popularity. Some celebrities, such as Wolfgang Puck, come from a culinary background, whereas others, such as Naomi Campbell, Claudia Schiffer, and Elle Macpherson (owners of the Fashion Café), do not. A number of sports celebrities also have restaurants.

Wolfgang Puck and Wife Barbra Lazaroff at Spago, Known for Its Innovative Cuisine and Stunning Dining Rooms Designed by Barbra

Among them are Michael Jordan, Dan Marino, Junior Seau, and Wayne Gretzky. Television and movie stars have also gotten into the act. Oprah Winfrey was part owner of the Eccentric in Chicago for a number of years. Dustin Hoffman and Henry Winkler are investors in Campanile, a popular Los Angeles restaurant. Dive, in Century City (Los Angeles), is owned by Steven Spielberg; House of Blues, by Denzel Washington. Musicians Kenny Rogers and Gloria Estefan are also restaurant owners.

Celebrity restaurants generally have an extra zing to them—a winning combination of design, atmosphere, food, and perhaps the thrill of an occasional visit by the owner(s). For example, Fashion Café in New York invites the guest to literally step through the lens of a camera into the glamorous world of fashion. Guests are seated in the Milan, Paris, or New York rooms, where they are entertained with daily fashion shows.

Steak Houses

The steak restaurant segment is quite buoyant despite nutritional concerns about red meat. The upscale steak dinner houses, such as Flemming's of Chicago, Ruth's Chris, and Houston's, continue to attract the expense account and "occasion" diners. Some restaurants are adding additional value-priced items such as chicken and fish to their menus to attract more guests. Steak restaurant operators admit that they are not expecting to see the same customer every week but hopefully every two or three weeks. The Chart House chain is careful to market its menu as including seafood and chicken, but steak is at the heart of the business, with most of its sales from red meat.

Outback Steakhouse, which is profiled in this chapter, owns and operates about a thousand Outback restaurants and about thirty Flemming's Prime Steakhouse and Wine Bars. Metromedia Restaurant Group operates and franchises more than 800 casual dining restaurants, including Bonanza and Ponderosa family steakhouses and Steak and Ale eateries, plus the 300-unit Bennigan's Irish American Grill and Tavern chain.[17] Other restaurants in this segment include Stewart Anderson's Black Angus, Golden Corral, Western Sizzlin', and Ryan's Family Steak Houses, which all have sales of more than $300 million each. In fact, chains have the biggest share of the segment.

Casual Dining and Dinner House Restaurants

The types of restaurants that can be included in the casual dining restaurants category are as follows:

Midscale casual restaurants. Romano's Macaroni Grill, the Olive Garden
Family restaurants. Cracker Barrel, Coco's Bob Evans, Carrow's
Ethnic restaurants. Flavor Thai, Cantina Latina, Panda Express

CORPORATE PROFILE

Outback Steakhouse

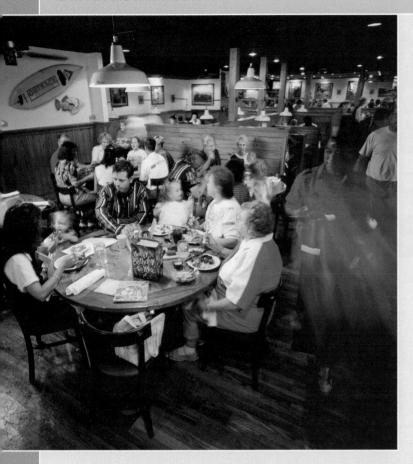

The founders of Outback Steakhouse have proved that unconventional methods can lead to profitable results. Such methods include opening solely for dinner, sacrificing dining-room seats for back-of-the-house efficiency, limiting servers to three tables each, and handing 10 percent of cash flow to the restaurants' general managers.

March 1988 saw the opening of the first Outback Steakhouse. Outback's founders, Chris Sullivan, Robert Basham, and Senior Vice President Tim Gannon, know plenty about the philosophy "No rules, just right" because they have lived it since day one. Even the timing of their venture to launch a casual steak place came when many pundits were pronouncing red meat consumption dead in the United States.

The chain went public and has since created a track record of strong earnings. It was evident that the three founders were piloting one of the country's hottest restaurant concepts. The trio found themselves with hundreds of restaurants, instead of the five they originally envisioned.

Robert Basham, cofounder, president, and chief operating officer at Outback Steakhouse, was given the Operator of the Year award at the Multi-Unit Foodservice Operators Conference (MUFSO). He helped expand the chain, a pioneer in the steak house sector of the restaurant business, to more than a thousand restaurants with some of the highest sales per unit in the industry despite the fact that they serve only dinner.

Perhaps the strongest indication of what this company is about lies in its corporate structure, or lack thereof. Despite its rapid growth, the company has no public relations department, no human resources department, and no recruiting apparatus. In addition, the Outback Steakhouse headquarters is very different from that of a typical restaurant company. There is no lavish tower—only modest office space in an average suburban complex. Instead of settling into a conservative chair and browsing through a magazine-lined coffee table (as is the case in most reception areas), at Outback you must belly up to an actual bar, brass foot rail and all, to announce your arrival.

Also, Outback's dining experience—large, highly seasoned portions of food for moderate prices—is so in tune with today's dining experience that patrons in many of its restaurants experience hour-long dinner waits seven nights a week. The friendly service is notable, from the host who opens the door and greets guests, to the well-trained servers, who casually sit down next to patrons in the booths and explain the house specialties featured on the menu.

Using such tactics and their "No rules, just right" philosophy, the founders have accomplished two main goals: discipline and solid growth. Good profits and excellent marketing potentials show just how successful the business has become. Outback also owns and operates Bonefish Grill, Flemming's Prime Steakhouse, Caraba's Italian Grill, Roy's, and Cheeseburger in Paradise.

Hard Rock Café offers first-rate, moderately priced casual American fare with, of course, a side of rock and roll

As implied, **casual dining** is relaxed and could include restaurants from several classifications: chain or independent, ethnic, or theme. Hard Rock Café, TGI Friday's, the Olive Garden, Houston's, Romano's Macaroni Grill, and Red Lobster are good examples of casual dining restaurants.

Houston's is a leader in the casual restaurant segment with about $5.5 million in average per unit sales in its thirty-five restaurants. The menu is limited to about forty items and focuses on American cuisine, with a $16 average per-person ticket for lunch and a cost of $35 to $45 for dinner. While encouraging local individuality in its restaurants and maintaining exceptional executive and unit general manager stability, it succeeds with no franchising and virtually no advertising.

Over the past few years, the trend in **dinner house restaurants** has been toward more casual dining. This trend merely reflects the mode of society. Dinner house restaurants have become fun places to let off steam. A variety of restaurant chains call themselves dinner house restaurants. Some of them could even fit into the theme category.

Many dinner house restaurants have a casual, eclectic decor that may promote a theme. Chart House, for example, is a steak and seafood chain that has a nautical theme. Friday's is an American bistro dinner house with a full menu and a decor of bric-a-brac that contributes to the fun atmosphere. Friday's is a chain that has been in operation for nearly forty years, so the concept has stood the test of time. Friday's is featured in Chapter 7, "Restaurant Operations," as a corporation of excellence.

Family Restaurants

Family restaurants evolved from the coffee shop style of restaurant. In this segment, most restaurants are individually or family operated. Family restaurants are generally located in or with easy access to the suburbs. Most offer an informal setting with a simple menu and service designed to please all the family. Some of these restaurants offer alcoholic beverages, which mostly consist of beer, wine, and perhaps a cocktail special. Usually, there is a hostess/cashier standing near the entrance to greet and seat guests while food servers take the orders and bring the plated food from the kitchen. Some family restaurants have incorporated salad and dessert bars to offer more variety and increase the average check.

The lines separating the various restaurants and chains in the family segment are blurring as operators upscale their concepts. Flagstar's acquisition of Coco's and Carrow's family restaurant brands has created the high-end niche of family dining—somewhere between traditional coffee shops and the casual dining segment. The value-oriented operator in the family dining segment is Denny's, also owned by Flagstar. The more upscale family concepts include Perkins, Marie Callender's, and Cracker Barrel, all of which are sometimes referred to as the "relaxed" segment. These chains tend to have higher check averages than do traditional and value-oriented family chains, and compete not only with them, but also with moderately priced, casual-themed operators, such as Applebee's and TGI Friday's.

Karen Brennan, vice president of marketing for the Coco's concept, says that people's use of restaurants is very different from five years ago. Consumers are thinking in terms of "meal solutions." The operators in this segment are seeking to capitalize on two trends affecting the industry as a whole: the tendency of families to dine out together more often, and the quest among adults for higher-quality, more flavorful food offerings.

Ethnic Restaurants

The majority of **ethnic restaurants** are independently owned and operated. The owners and their families provide something different for the adventurous diner or a taste of home for those of the same ethnic background as the restaurant. The traditional ethnic restaurants sprang up to cater to the taste of the various immigrant groups—Italian, Chinese, and so on.

Perhaps the fastest-growing segment of ethnic restaurants in the United States, popularity-wise, is Mexican. Mexican food has a heavy representation in the southwestern states, although, because of near-market saturation, the chains are spreading east. Taco Bell is the Mexican quick-service market leader with a 60 percent share. This *Fortune 500* company has achieved this incredible result with a value-pricing policy that has increased traffic in all units. There are more than 7,000 units with sales of about $5 billion. Other large Mexican food chains are Del Taco, Chi-Chi's, La Salsa, and El Torito. These Mexican food chains can offer a variety of items on a value menu. Our cities offer a great variety of ethnic restaurants, and their popularity is increasing.

Quick-Service Fast-Food Restaurants

Quick-service restaurants (QSRs) consist of diverse operating facilities whose slogan is "quick food." The following types of operations are included under this category: hamburger, pizza, chicken, pancakes, sandwich shops, and delivery services.

The quick-service sector is the one that really drives the industry. Recently, the home-meal replacement and fast casual concepts have gained momentum. (see Figure 6–5.)

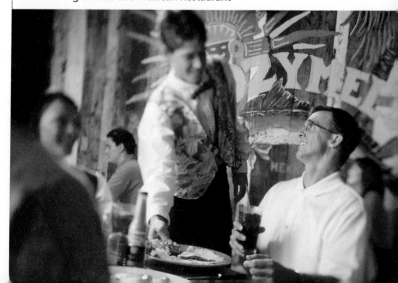
Guests Being Served at a Mexican Restaurant

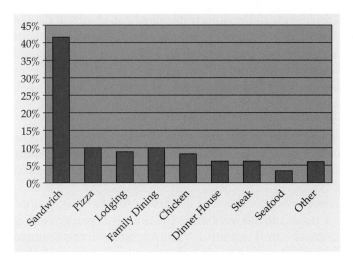

Figure 6–5 • Approximate Market Share of Restaurant Segments.

Quick-service or fast-food restaurants offer limited menus featuring food such as hamburgers, fries, hot dogs, chicken (in all forms), tacos, burritos, gyros, teriyaki bowls, various finger foods, and other items for the convenience of people on the go. Customers order their food at a counter under a brightly lit menu featuring color photographs of food items. Customers are even encouraged to clear their own trays, which helps reduce costs. The following are examples of the different types of quick-service/fast-food restaurants:

Hamburger. McDonald's, Burger King, Wendy's

Pizza. Pizza Hut, Domino's, Godfather's

Steak. Bonanza, Ponderosa

Seafood. Long John Silver's

Chicken. KFC, Church's, Boston Market, Kenny Roger's, Popeye's

Sandwich. Subway

Mexican. Taco Bell, El Torito

Drive-thru-in/delivery. Domino's, Pizza Hut

Quick-service restaurants have increased in popularity because of their location strategies. They are found in very convenient locations in every possible area. Their menus are limited, which makes it easy for customers to make quick decisions on what to eat. The world equates time with money these days, and most people do not want to spend time trying to look through long menus to make an eating decision. These restaurants deliver fast service and usually include self-service facilities, too. Such restaurants also use cheaper, processed ingredients, which allow them to have extremely low, competitive prices. Quick-service restaurants also require minimum use of both skilled and unskilled labor, which increases the profit margins.

In an attempt to raise flat sales figures, more quick-service restaurant (QSR) chains are using cobranding at stores and nontraditional locations, including highway plazas and shopping centers. It is hoped that the traffic-building combos will increase sales among the separate brands, such as Carl's Jr. and Green Burrito, as well as concepts like Triarc's Arby's, Zu Zu, P.T. Noodles, and T.J. Cinnamon brands. Many QSR chains are targeting international growth, mostly in the larger cities in a variety of countries.

Hamburgers

McDonald's is the giant of the entire quick-service/fast-food segment and serves nearly 54 million people daily.[18] This total is amazing because it is more than the next three megachains combined—Burger King, KFC, and Pizza Hut. McDonald's has individual product items other than the traditional burger—for

INTRODUCING RAY KROC

Founder of McDonald's

The world's greatest fast-food success story is undoubtedly McDonald's. Back in the 1950s, Ray Kroc was selling soda fountains. He received an order from Mr. McDonald for two soda fountains. Ray Kroc was so interested in finding out why the McDonald brothers' restaurant needed two machines (everyone else ordered one) that he went out to the restaurant. There he saw the now-familiar golden arches and the hamburger restaurant. Ray persuaded the McDonalds to let him franchise their operation. Billions of burgers later, the reason for the success may be summarized as follows: quality, speed, cleanliness, service, and value. This has been achieved by systemizing the production process and by staying close to the original concept—keeping a limited menu, advertising heavily, being innovative with new menu items, maintaining product quality, and being consistent.

Of all hospitality entrepreneurs, Ray Kroc has been the most successful financially. In 1982, he was senior chairman of the board of McDonald's, an organization intent on covering the earth with hamburgers. Among the remarkable things about Kroc is that it was not until age 52 that he embarked on the royal road to fame and fortune.

The original McDonald's concept was created by two brothers, Richard and Maurice, who had no interest in expanding. The McDonald brothers were content with their profitable yet singular restaurant in San Bernardino, California. However, the golden arches impressed Kroc, as did the cleanliness and simplicity of the operation.

Kroc's organizational skills, perseverance, and incredible aptitude for marketing were his genius. His talent also extended to selecting close associates who were equally dedicated and who added financial, analytical, and managerial skills to the enterprise. Kroc remained the spark plug and master merchandiser until he died in 1984, leaving a multi-million-dollar legacy.

Much of Kroc's $400 million has gone to employees, hospitals, and the Marshall Field Museum. It is distributed through Kroc's own foundation. Most important, Kroc developed several operational guidelines, including the concepts of "KISS"—keep it simple, stupid—and QSC&V—quality, service, cleanliness, and value. Kroc's "Never Be Idle a Moment" motto was also incorporated into the business.

Enterprises such as McDonald's are not built without ample dedication, and Ray Kroc certainly had a wealth of dedication. Today, an average McDonald's franchise can net more than $1 million annually thanks to Kroc's ingenious marketing strategies. In fact, McDonald's Corporation has become so affluent that it was named *Entrepreneur* magazine's number one franchise.

example, chicken McNuggets and burritos as well as salads and fish, which all aim to broaden customer appeal. Customer appeal has also been broadened by the introduction of breakfast and by targeting not only kids but seniors. Innovative menu introductions have helped stimulate an increase in per-store traffic.

In recent years, because traditional markets have become saturated, McDonald's has adopted a strategy of expanding overseas. It is embarking on a rapid expansion in the world's most populous nation, China, with more than 12,000 restaurants nationwide. The reason for this expansion in China is a rapidly developing middle class with a growing appetite for Western culture and food. McDonald's is now in 119 countries and has a potential audience of 3.2 billion people. Of the company's roughly 32,000 restaurants, some 8,600 are outside the United States, serving 47 million people each day.

It is interesting to note that about 50 percent of total profits come from outside of the United States. More than two-thirds of new restaurants added by McDonald's are outside of the United States. McDonald's also seeks out nontraditional locations in the U.S. market, such as on military bases or smaller-sized units in the high-rent districts or gas stations.

McDonald's is taking another step toward being the most convenient foodservice operation in the world by striking deals with gasoline companies Chevron, U.S. Petroleum Star Enterprise, and Mobil Oil Corporation to codevelop sites.

It is very difficult to obtain a McDonald's franchise in the United States because they have virtually saturated the primary markets. It often costs between $1 million and $2 million to open a major brand fast-food restaurant. Franchises for lesser-known chains are available for less money (about $35,000) plus the 4 percent of sales royalty fee and 4 percent fee for advertising, but an entrepreneur needs about $125,000 liquid and $400,000 net worth for an upscale, quick-service outlet, not counting land costs.

Each of the major hamburger restaurant chains has a unique positioning strategy to attract their target markets. Burger King hamburgers are flame broiled, and Wendy's uses fresh patties. Some smaller regional chains are succeeding in gaining market share from the big-three burger chains because they provide an excellent burger at a reasonable price. In-N-Out Burger, Sonic, and Rally's are good examples of this.

Pizza

The pizza segment continues to grow. By some estimates, it is now a $21 billion market, with much of the growth fueled by the convenience of delivery. There are several chains: Pizza Hut, Domino's, Godfather's, Papa John's, and Little Caesar's. Pizza Hut, with 12,600 units and system-wide sales of 2,600 million,[19] has broken into the delivery part of the business over which, until recently, Domino's had a virtual monopoly. Pizza Hut has now developed system-wide delivery units that also offer two pizzas at a reduced price.

In response to the success of Pizza Hut's Stuffed Crust Pizza, Domino's highlights its Ultimate Deep Dish Pizza and its new Pesto Crust Pizza. It is currently stressing the quality of its advertising. With twelve toppings to choose from, people can have fun designing their own pizza.

Chicken

Chicken has always been popular and is likely to remain so because it is relatively cheap to produce and readily available and adaptable to a variety of preparations. It also is perceived as a healthier alternative to burgers.

KFC, with a worldwide total of more than 12,000 units and annual sales of more than $10.3 billion, dominates the chicken segment. Even though KFC is a market leader, the company continues to explore new ways to get its products to consumers. More units now offer home delivery, and in many cities KFC is teaming up with sister restaurant Taco Bell, selling products from both chains in one convenient location. KFC continues to build menu variety as it focuses on providing complete meals to families. Amazingly, there are now more than a thousand KFC restaurants in China.

Church's Chicken, with 1,500 units, is the second largest chicken chain. It offers a simple formula consisting of a value menu featuring Southern-style chicken, spicy chicken wings, okra, corn on the cob, coleslaw, biscuits, and other items. Church's focused on becoming a low-cost provider and the fastest to market. To give customers the value they expect day in and day out, it is necessary to have unit economies in order. System-wide, Church's now registers 34 percent in food costs and 25.9 percent labor costs.

Popeye's is another large chain in the chicken segment, with 1,818 units in twenty seven international markets. It is owned by AFC, the same parent company as Church's. Popeye's is a New Orleans–inspired "spicy chicken" chain operating more than 300 restaurants in Texas and Louisiana that is expanding into eleven markets around the country. The chain hopes to increase average unit sales to $1 million.

There are a number of up-and-coming regional chains, such as El Pollo Loco, of Irvine, California. It focuses on a marinated, flame-broiled chicken that is a unique, high-quality product. Kenny Rogers and Cluckers are also expanding rotisserie chains.

Sandwich Restaurants

Indicative of America's obsession with the quick and convenient, sandwiches have achieved star status. Recently, menu debuts in the sandwich segment have outpaced all others. Classics, such as melts and club sandwiches, have returned with a vengeance—but now there are also wraps and panini.

A sandwich restaurant is a popular way for a young entrepreneur to enter the restaurant business. The leader in this segment is Subway, which operates more than 27,943 units in eighty-seven countries.[20] Cofounder Fred Deluca parlayed an initial investment of $1,000 into one of the largest and fastest-growing chains in the world. Franchise fees are $12,500, with a second store fee of $2,500.

The Subway strategy is to invest half of the chain's advertising dollars in national advertising. Franchise owners pay 2.5 percent of sales to the marketing fund. As with other chains, Subway is attempting to widen its core eighteen- to thirty-four-year-old customer base by adding Kids Packs and Value 4-inch Round sandwiches aimed at teens and women. Sandwich restaurants stress the health value of their restaurants.

Bakery Café

The bakery café sector is headed up by Panera Bread, a 1,027-unit chain in thirty-eight states, with the mission of "a loaf in every arm" and the goal of making specialty bread broadly available to consumers across the United States. Panera focuses on the art and craft of breadmaking with made-to-order sandwiches, tossed-to-order salads, and soup served in bread bowls.[21]

▶ Check Your Knowledge

1. Describe the different types of restaurants, and give examples of each. Highlight some of the characteristics that make up the specific restaurant types.

Trends in the Restaurant Business

- *Demographics.* As the baby boomers move into middle age and retirement, a startling statistic is emerging: forty-five- to sixty-four-year-olds (the age group with the highest income) will make up almost one-third of the U.S. population. Simply put, the largest demographic group will have the most money and will offer opportunities for restaurants that meet their needs.

- *Branding.* Restaurant operators are using the power of branding, both in terms of brand-name recognition from a franchising viewpoint and in the products utilized.

- *Alternative outlets.* Restaurants face increased competition from convenience ("c-stores") and home meal replacement outlets.

- *Globalization.* Continued transnational development of restaurants crossing borders.

- *Diversification.* Continued diversification within the various dining segments.

- *Shared locations.* More twin and multiple locations; restaurants such as Pizza Hut and KFC will share locations.

- *Points of service.* More points of service (e.g., Taco Bell at gas stations).

- *Las Vegas.* Several restaurants and nightclubs have opened recently, such as the Strip House, CUT, RubBBQ, Blush, The Bank; plus French chef Joel Robuchon at the MGM Grand was recently awarded a coveted three-star rating by Michelin Guide.

Summary

1. Restaurants offer the possibility of excellent food and social interaction. In general, restaurants strive to surpass an operating philosophy that includes quality food, good value, and gracious service.
2. To succeed, a restaurant needs the right location, food, atmosphere, and service to attract a substantial market. The concept of a restaurant has to fit the market it is trying to attract.
3. The location of a restaurant has to match factors such as convenience, neighborhood, parking, visibility, and demographics. Typical types of locations are downtown, suburban, shopping mall, cluster, or stand-alones.
4. The menu and pricing of a restaurant must match the market the restaurant wants to attract, the capabilities of the cooks, and the existing kitchen equipment.
5. The main categories of restaurants are fine dining and specialty, independent, and chain. Further distinctions can be made: quick-service, ethnic, dinner house, occasion, and casual. In general, most restaurants fall into more than one category.

Key Words and Concepts

actual market share
ambience
atmosphere
casual dining
catchment area
celebrity-owned restaurant
chain restaurant
contribution margin
culinary arts
dinner house restaurant
ethnic restaurant
fair market share
family restaurant
fine dining restaurant

food cost percentage
fusion
haute cuisine
independent restaurant (indie)
fusion
mother sauces
niche
nouvelle cuisine
purée
quick-service restaurant (QSR)
roux
sales volume
theme restaurant
weighted average

Review Questions

1. Watch the video on the Companion Website and describe John Mayer's typical workday.
2. From the Companion Website, what is Bonefish Grill's concept?
3. Describe the evolution of American culinary arts.
4. What are the five mother sauces?
5. Name some of America's finest chefs.
6. How are restaurants classified?
7. Explain why there is no single definition of the various classifications of restaurants; give examples.

Internet Exercises

1. Organization: **Charlie Trotter**
   Web site: charlietrotters.com/restaurant
   Summary: Charlie Trotter is regarded as one of the finest chefs in the world. Chef Trotter's restaurant has received numerous awards, yet chef Trotter is always seeking new opportunities.
   (a) What are Chef Trotter's recent activities?
2. Organization: **Olive Garden Restaurant**
   Web site: www.olivegarden.com
   Summary: The Olive Garden is a multiunit chain that primarily serves exquisite Italian food. It is currently operated by Darden Restaurants and has about 534 restaurants in the United States and Canada. Olive Garden strives to create a feeling of warmth and caring for every guest, which extends beyond the walls of the restaurants into the community. Olive Garden participates in civic community service, such as delivering meals during times of crisis, sponsoring charity events, and hosting school tours of the restaurants.
   (a) What kind of restaurant does the name Olive Garden represent?
   (b) What is the Garden Fare? How is its menu different from the design and layout of the lunch menu?

Apply Your Knowledge

In groups, evaluate a restaurant and write out a list of weaknesses. Use the headings outlined in the restaurant chapters. Then, for each of the weaknesses, decide on which actions you would take to exceed guest expectations.

Suggested Activities

1. On the Companion Website, what advice does John Mayer give students?
2. Identify a restaurant in your neighborhood and identify its catchment area. How many potential guests live and work in the catchment area?
3. Search the Web for examples of four great restaurant web sites. Compare them and share your findings in class.

Endnotes

1. National Restaurant Association, *Restaurant Industry Fact Sheet 2007.*
2. Sarah R. Labensky and Alan M. Hause, *On Cooking,* 4th ed. (Upper Saddle River, NJ: Prentice Hall, 2007), 6–7.
3. Labensky and Hause, *On Cooking,* 6–7.
4. Charlie Trotter, *Charlie Trotter* (Berkeley, CA: Ten Speed Press, 1994), 11.
5. Trotter, *Charlie Trotter,* 12.
6. "NRA Joins Healthy Dining to Promote Healthful Menu Choices," Fast Casual, July 18, 2006, www.fastcasual.com/article.php?id=5393.
7. This section is courtesy of Chef Michael Zema, Elgin Community College Elgin, IL.
8. John Walker, *The Restaurant from Concept to Operation,* 5th ed. (Hoboken, NJ: Wiley, 2008), 5.
9. Walker, *The Restaurant from Concept to Operation,* 5.
10. Walker, *The Restaurant from Concept to Operation,* 5.
11. Walker, *The Restaurant from Concept to Operation,* 208.
12. Walker, *The Restaurant from Concept to Operation,* 211.
13. Walker, *The Restaurant from Concept to Operation,* 230.
14. Personal conversation with Jay R. Schrock.
15. www.en.wikipedia.org/wiki/Tavern–on–the–Green and www.tavernonthegreen.com/factsheet.asp?headinfo=abouttavern&subhead=factsheet
16. A gueridon cart is a wheelable cart that is used to add flair to tableside service. It is also used for flambé dishes.
17. www.metromediarestaurants.com/about.htm
18. www.en.wikipedia.org/wiki/McDonald's
19. www.hoovers.com/pizza-hut/—ID_89521—/free-co-factsheet.xhtml
20. www.en.wikipedia.org/wiki/subway_%28restaurant%29
21. www.panerabread.com/about/company/ and Subway Web Team (2007). Official Subway Restaurants Website. Subway Restaurants. Retrieved September 23, 2007.

CHAPTER 7

Restaurant Operations

OBJECTIVES

After reading and studying this chapter, you should be able to:

- Describe restaurant operations for the front of the house.

- Explain how restaurants forecast their business.

- Outline back-of-the-house operations.

- Identify key elements of an income statement.

- Name the key restaurant operating ratios.

- Outline the functional areas and tasks of a restaurant manager's job.

Front of the House

Restaurant operations are generally divided between what is commonly called **front of the house** and **back of the house**. The front of the house includes anyone with guest contact from the hostess to the busperson. The sample organization chart in Figure 7-1 shows the differences between the front- and back-of-the-house areas.

The restaurant is run by the general manager, or restaurant manager. Depending on the size and sales volume of the restaurant, there may be more managers with special responsibilities, such as kitchen manager, bar manager, and dining room manager. These managers are usually cross-trained to relieve each other.

In the front of the house, restaurant operation begins with creating and maintaining what is called **curbside appeal**, or keeping the restaurant looking attractive and welcoming. Ray Kroc of McDonald's once spent a couple of hours in a good suit with one of his restaurant managers cleaning up the parking lot of one of his restaurants. Word soon got around to the other stores that management begins in the parking lot and ends in the bathrooms. Most restaurant chains have checklists that each manager uses. In the front of the house, the parking lot, including the flower gardens, need to be maintained in good order. As guests approach the restaurant, hostesses may hold the door open and welcome them to the restaurant. At the 15th Street Fisheries restaurant in Ft. Lauderdale, hostesses welcome the guests by assuring them that "we're glad you're here!"

Once inside, the **hostess**, or as T.G.I. Friday's calls them, "smiling people greeters" (SPGs), greets guests appropriately, and, if seating is available, escorts them to a table. If there is a wait, the hostess will take the guests' names and ask for their table preference.

Aside from greeting the guests, one critical function of the hostess is to rotate arriving guests among the sections or stations. This ensures an even and timely distribution of guests—otherwise one section may get overloaded. Guests are sometimes asked to wait a few minutes even if tables are available. This is done to help spread the kitchen's workload.

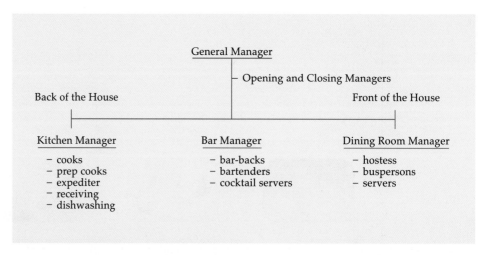

Figure 7–1 • Restaurant Organization Chart.

The hostesses maintain a book, or chart, showing the sections and tables so that they know which tables are occupied. Hostesses escort guests to the tables, present menus, and may explain special sales promotions. Some may also remove excess covers from the table.

In some restaurants, servers are allocated a certain number of tables, which may vary depending on the size of the tables and the volume of the restaurant. Usually, five is the maximum. In other restaurants, servers rotate within their section to cover three or four tables.

The server introduces himself or herself, offers a variety of beverages and/or specials, or invites guests to select from the menu. This is known as suggestive selling. The

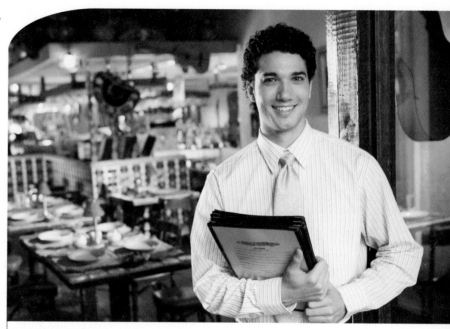

A Front Door Greeter

server then takes the entree orders. Often, when taking orders, the server begins at a designated point and takes the orders clockwise from that point. In this way, the server will automatically know which person is having a particular dish. When the entrees are ready, the server brings them to the table. He or she checks a few minutes later to see if everything is to the guests' liking and perhaps asks if they would like another beverage. Good servers are also encouraged, when possible, to prebus tables.

Busers and servers may clear the entree plates, while servers suggestively sell desserts by describing, recommending, or showing the desserts. Coffee and after-dinner cocktails are also offered. Suggestions for steps to take in table service include the following:

1. Greet the guests.
2. Introduce and suggestively sell beverages.
3. Suggest appetizers.
4. Take orders.
5. Check to see that everything is to the guests' liking within two bites of the entrees.
6. Ask if the guests would like another drink.
7. Bring out dessert tray and suggest after-dinner drinks and coffee.

In addition to the seven steps of the table service, servers are expected to be NCO—neat, clean, and organized—and to help ensure that hot food is served hot, and cold food is served cold.

For example, during the lunch hour, servers may be scheduled to start at 11:00 A.M. The opening group of two or three people is joined by the closing group of the same number at around 11:45 P.M. If the restaurant is quiet, servers may be phased out early. When the closing group comes in, there is a quick shift meeting, or "alley rally." This provides an opportunity to review recent sales figures, discuss any promotions, and acknowledge any items that are "86'ed"— the restaurant term for a menu item that is not available. Recognition is also given to the servers during the meetings, serving as morale boosters.

Restaurant Forecasting

Most businesses, including restaurants, operate by formulating a budget that projects sales and costs for a year on a weekly and monthly basis. Financial viability is predicted on sales, and sales budgets are forecasts of expected business.

Forecasting restaurant sales has two components: guest counts, or covers, and the average guest check. **Guest counts**, or **covers**, are the number of guests patronizing the restaurant over a given time period—a week, month, or year. To forecast the number of guests for a year, the year is divided into 13 periods: twelve 28-day and one 29-day accounting period. This ensures that accounting procedures are able to compare equal periods rather than months of unequal days. The accounting periods are then broken down into four 7-day weeks. Restaurant forecasting is done by taking into consideration meal period, day of week, special holidays, and previous forecast materializations.

In terms of number of guests, Mondays usually are quiet; business gradually builds to Friday, which is often the busiest day. Friday, Saturday, and Sunday frequently provide up to 50 percent of revenue. This, however, can vary according to type of restaurant and its location.

The **average guest check** is calculated by dividing total sales by the number of guests. Most restaurants keep such figures for each meal. The number of guests forecast for each day is multiplied by the amount of the average food and beverage check for each meal to calculate the total forecast sales. Each day, actual totals are compared with the forecasts. Four weekly forecasts are combined to form one accounting period; the thirteen accounting periods, when totaled, become the annual total.

Restaurant forecasting is used not only to calculate sales projections but also for predicting staffing levels and labor cost percentages. Much depends on the accuracy of forecasting. Once sales figures are determined, all expenditures, fixed and variable, have to be deducted to calculate profit or loss.[1]

Service

More than ever, what American diners really want when they eat out is good service. Unfortunately, all too often, that is not on the menu. With increased competition, however, bad service will not be tolerated in American restaurants. Just as American cuisine came of age in the 1970s and 1980s, service is showing signs of maturing in the twenty-first century.

A new American service has emerged. A less formal—yet professional— approach is preferred by today's restaurant guests. The restaurants' commitment

FOCUS ON THE RESTAURANT BUSINESS

The Manager's Role

John T. Self, California State Polytechnic University, Pomona

It seems like only yesterday that I was walking into my first restaurant as a new manager trainee fresh from college. I found the restaurant industry perfect for me. It had plenty of variety, energy, and opportunity that matched my personality. I loved the fact that I would not have to just sit behind a desk doing the same thing every day. As a restaurant manager, your day will include accounting, human resources, marketing, payroll, purchasing, personal counseling, and many more functions that will challenge you.

You will be part of a management team that is the foundation of any restaurant, regardless of whether it is a chain or an independent. Managers have a huge sphere of influence, including customer service, sales, and profitability. You will be part of a management team responsible for a multimillion dollar operation.

When you first become a manager, it is easy to be overwhelmed. You will probably feel that you will never be able to understand all the moving parts of a restaurant. However, as you grow in your management position, you will not only understand how it all works, but you will also understand how you influence each part.

Being a restaurant manager offers the opportunity to grow as an individual because you will deal with so many types of people, including employees, peers, supervisors, vendors, and customers. You will learn how to excite and motivate your team to share common goals. You will find it very rewarding to teach others about the culture of the business and you will find many opportunities to make a positive impact on your staff.

The restaurant industry is the epicenter of the people business, and management is at the heart of the restaurant industry. Motivating people, delegating responsibility to people, and leading people is what we are about and what we do.

Although any company you eventually join will present a slightly different environment, career path, hours, days, responsibilities, and opportunities, they all share a common core of food and people.

Courtesy of John Self

to service is evidenced by the fact that most have increased training for new employees. For example, at Splendido in San Francisco's Embarcadero, the amount of time new servers spend in training has increased from 40 to 100 hours. Servers are not merely order takers; they are the salespeople of the restaurant. A server who is undereducated about the menu can seriously hurt business. One would not be likely to buy a car from a salesperson who knew nothing about the car; likewise, guests feel uneasy ordering from an unknowledgeable server.

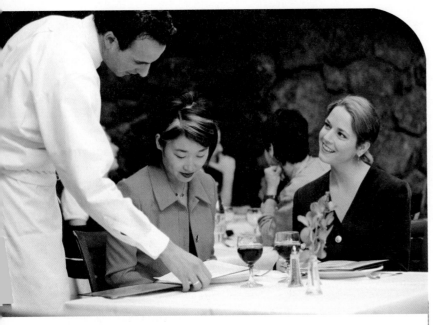

A Server as a Salesperson, Explaining a Dish on the Menu to a Guest

Restaurants in the United States and Canada and many other parts of the world all use American service, in which the food is prepared and appealingly placed onto plates in the kitchen, carried into the dining room, and served to guests. This method of service is used because it is quicker and guests receive the food hot as presented by the chef.

At Posterio, servers are invited to attend a one-and-a-half-hour wine class in the restaurant; about three-quarters of the fourty-member staff routinely benefit from this additional training. The best employees are also rewarded with monthly prizes and with semiannual and annual prizes, which range from $100 cash, a limousine ride, dinner at Posterio, or a night's lodging at the Prescott Hotel to a week in Hawaii.

Servers at other San Francisco restaurants role-play the various elements of service such as greeting and seating guests, suggestive selling, correct methods of service, and guest relations to ensure a positive dining experience. A good food server in a top restaurant in many cities can earn $50,000 or more a year.

Good servers quickly learn to gauge the guests' satisfaction levels and to be sensitive to guests' needs; for example, they check to ensure guests have everything they need as their entree is placed before them. Even better, they anticipate guests' needs. For example, if the guest had used the entree knife to eat the appetizer, a clean one should automatically be placed to the right side of the guest's plate. In other words, the guest should not receive the entree and then realize he or she needs another knife.

Another example of good service is when the server does not have to ask everyone at the table who is eating what. The server should either remember or do a seating plan so that the correct dishes are automatically placed in front of guests.

Danny Meyer, owner of New York City's celebrated Union Square Cafe and recipient of both the Restaurant of the Year and Outstanding Service Awards from the James Beard Foundation, gives each of the restaurant's employees—from busperson to chef—a $600 annual allowance ($50 each a month) to eat in the restaurant and critique the experience.[2]

At the critically acclaimed Inn at Little Washington in Washington, Virginia, servers are required to gauge the mood of every table and jot a number (one to ten) and sometimes a description ("elated, grumpy, or edgy") on each ticket. Anything below a seven requires a diagnosis. Servers and kitchen staff work together to try to elevate the number to at least a nine by the time dessert is ordered.

Suggestive Selling

Suggestive selling can be a potent weapon in the effort to increase food and beverage sales. Many restaurateurs cannot think of a better, more effective, and easier way to boost profit margins. Servers report that most guests are not offended or uncomfortable with suggestive selling techniques. In fact, customers may feel special that the server is in tune with their needs and desires. It may be that the server suggests something to the guest that he or she has never considered before. The object here is to turn servers into sellers. Guests will almost certainly be receptive to suggestions from competent servers.

On a hot day, for example, servers can suggest frozen margaritas or daiquiris before going on to describe the drink specials. Likewise, servers who suggest a bottle of fumé blanc to complement a fish dish or a pinot noir or cabernet sauvignon to go with red meat are likely to increase their restaurant's beverage sales.

Upselling takes place when a guest orders a "well" drink like a vodka and tonic. In this case, the server asks if the guests would like a Stoli and tonic. (Stoli is short for Stolichnaya, a popular brand of vodka.)

An example of the benefits of upselling is a server who describes a menu item like this: "Our special tonight is a slow-roasted aged prime Angus beef ribroast, served with roasted potatoes and a medley of fresh vegetables." Now, if this entrée cost $10 more than another beef dish on the menu, and the same thing happens with suggestions for guests to select from fish, seafood, and other meat or vegetarian items, the table's check will increase by $50 to $75. We know that a server receives about 15 percent in tips and does four or five tables that can turn twice each per night. You do the math: 15% of $50 = $7.50, and say the server does four tables = $4 \times \$7.50 \times 2$ = an additional $60 in tips.

▶ Check Your Knowledge

1. What is considered the front of the house?
2. Define curbside appeal.
3. Suggest methods for remembering who ordered what on a table for a large party.
4. Name some of the responsibilities and duties of an assistant restaurant manager.
5. Briefly explain American service.

Front-of-the-House Restaurant Systems

Point-of-Sale Systems

Point-of-sale (POS) systems are very common in restaurants and other foodservice settings, such as stadiums, theme parks, airports, and cruise ships. These systems are used by hotel properties that have food and beverage and retail outlets. They are used to track food and beverage charges and other retail charges that may occur at a hotel or restaurant. A point-of-sale system is made up of a

A Popular Point-of-Sale System

number of POS terminals that interface with a remote central processing unit. A POS terminal may be used as an electronic cash register, too.

MICROS, a leading software, hardware, and enterprise systems provider, offers Restaurant 3000, a modular suite of applications that encompasses front-of-the-house, back-of-the-house, and enterprise systems. The popular 3700 POS is a Microsoft Windows-based touch-screen system where client terminals are networked to a central POS server. Transactions are rung at the terminal and posted into the database for later analysis and reporting. The 3700 POS will support a network of kitchen printers so that orders can be presented to line cooks and chefs for food preparation. This POS system also supports use of a wireless personal digital assistant as an order-taking device so that servers can take orders directly from the guest tableside. Mobile handheld devices can greatly speed the processing of orders to the kitchen and ultimately increase revenues as a result of faster table turns.

Kitchen Display Systems

Kitchen display systems further enhance the processing of orders to and in the kitchen. Printers in the kitchen are replaced with video monitors and present orders to kitchen associates along with information on how long orders are taking to be prepared. Orders change color or flash on the monitor, which alerts kitchen associates to orders that are taking too long. Kitchen monitors are widely used in quick-service restaurants but are also gaining momentum in table service restaurants. Kitchen video systems also post order preparation times to a central data base for later reporting and analysis by management to determine how the kitchen is performing.

Guest Services Solutions

Guest services solutions are applications that are designed to help a restaurateur develop a dining relationship with guests. Applications include a frequent-diner management program, delivery management with caller ID interface, and guest accounts receivable to manage home accounts and gift certificate management. All these applications are accessed through the POS system and give restaurateurs the opportunity to offer their guests convenience, while allowing the restaurateurs to track who their best customers are. Guest activity is posted into the central database and management can develop targeted marketing programs based on this information.

▶ Check Your Knowledge

1. What do front-of-the-house systems entail?
2. Briefly define guest services solutions.

Back-of-the-House Restaurant Systems

Back-of-the-house systems are also known as product management systems and include inventory control and food costing, labor management, and financial reporting features. SoftCafe develops software for restaurants and foodservice operations, allowing them to create menus on personal computers. SoftCafe MenuPro creates professional menus at a fraction of the cost of print shop menus, with more than a thousand predesigned menu styles, hundreds of food illustrations, menu backgrounds, more than fifty font types, and a culinary spelling checker.[3] Beverage inventory systems are discussed in Chapter 9.

Restaurant Magic, based in Tampa, Florida, has several excellent restaurant management solutions: Data.Central is delivered to a desktop as an enterprise-quality, secure and reliable, centralized business management solution to deliver powerful, user-friendly forms and reports to any Web-connected Windows PC in a restaurant organization. Data.Central is a technological breakthrough in centralized application and database management because it is written entirely in the Visual C# language and deployed as a Microsoft .NET Framework solution. Access to information is specified at the login level and applications, reports, and important data are updated once available to all users automatically.[4] For a restaurant chain such as Outback Steakhouse, "secure centralized management of enterprise data is more than a best practice, it is a necessity."[5] The benefits of programs such as Data.Central are clear: Multistore managers can now view data for the enterprise. Store-level managers can view data for their store, or any group of stores they choose.

Restaurant Magic's Profit and Loss Reporting delivers profit and loss information on demand, consolidating information from purchasing to produce accurate cost of goods sold. All the key data is collected from point of sale to track all revenues and forms of payments and complementary activity, from time clocks to collect labor costs and integrate it with all other data to produce profit and loss reporting daily, weekly, and multiperiod. The Profit and Loss Reporting allows a collaborative P&L budgeting system where the store and regional managers work together to build budgets and assess results quickly.[6]

Wireless POS Systems

Peter Perdikakis is the owner of two Skyline fast-casual restaurants in Cincinnati. The restaurants are unusual in that the kitchen is open and visible to diners. Servers used to simply yell the orders across the steam table. Peter says, "You eat off china and have silverware, but it's very fast—typically you get your order about two minutes after it's ordered. Other POS systems slowed this process down because the servers had to go over to a terminal and write down the order," which is why Peter became interested in wireless. When he wanted to expand his operations, he selected a Pocket POS system from PixelPoint, consisting of two primary fixed terminals (one at a drive-through window and one at the checkout station), three handheld units for use on the dining floor, and another fixed unit for the back office.

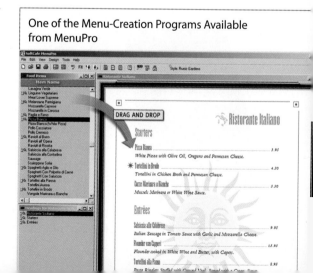

One of the Menu-Creation Programs Available from MenuPro

The PixelPoint wireless POS system allows the servers to use a handheld personal digital assistant (PDA), which operates on the Windows CE platform, to send orders to the kitchen. Given that wireless POS systems speed up orders, their use in restaurants is likely to increase.

Labor Management

Most front-of-the-house systems have the ability to track employee working time. A back-of-the-house labor management package adds the ability to manage all of a restaurant's payroll and human resource information. A labor management system includes a human resources module to track hiring, employee personal information, vacation, I-9 status, security privileges, tax status, availability, and any other information pertinent to employees working at the restaurant. A labor management system would also include scheduling capability so that managers can create weekly schedules based on forecasted business. Schedules can then be enforced when employees check in and out so that labor costs can be managed.

The labor management package also presents actual work time and pay rates to a payroll processor so that paychecks can be cut and distributed. It also collates tips data and receipt data from the front of the house so that proper tip allocations can be reported according to IRS guidelines.

Financial Reporting

Back-of-the-house and front-of-the-house systems post data into a relational database located on the central server. The restaurant manager uses these data for reporting and decision making. Profit and loss reports, budget variances, end-of-day reports, and other financial reports are generated from the central database. Financial management reporting needs to be flexible so that restaurant operators can manipulate it in ways that are useful to them. It is also important to get reports during the day in real time as the day unfolds so that restaurateurs can make decisions before profit is lost. Some reporting packages provide a graphical representation of the financial data displayed continuously on a monitor so that critical restaurant data are always available. This type of reporting provides restaurants with a real-time "heartbeat" for their operations.

Both back-of-the-house and front-of-the-house systems must be reliably linked so that POS food costs, labor costs, service times, and guest activity can be analyzed on the same reports. Restaurant management can then make critical business decisions armed with all necessary information. Technology is also used to collect data throughout the day for real-time budget control and "on-the-fly" management of labor effectiveness. Budgets are tight, and this is a way for management to watch, in real time, where their labor costs are at all times.

Pocket PC Used in Restaurants

Personal Digital Assistants

Personal digital assistants (PDAs) help hospitality businesses stay effective and efficient by improving time management and helping with faster service. For example, computer systems are used today in restaurants to transmit orders to the kitchen and to retrieve and post guest payments. These actions took extra time in the past, when the computer systems were placed at a distance from the server. PDAs have been created to allow servers to control their business with their fingertips.

One leading software provider to restaurant operators is Restaurant Technology, Inc. (RTI). RTI was founded by two restaurant owners who understand the accounting applications that operate from a central platform known as the

Restaurant Financial System. Working together, their accounting programs form an integrated system, with these modules:

- Accounts payable
- Check reconciliation
- Daily store reporting
- General ledger
- Payroll
- Time keeping

PDAs can also be used in the hotel setting. Often, PDAs can be integrated with a property management system (PMS) to give housekeepers real-time information about which rooms need to be cleaned and which rooms are not occupied. In the same way, as housekeepers complete the cleaning of a room, they can send a wireless signal to the front desk to affirm that the room is ready to be occupied.

▶ Check Your Knowledge

1. Explain in what ways advances in technology aid the inventory process in restaurants.
2. What are back-of-the-house systems also known as?
3. What are the benefits of using a PDA?

Back of the House

The back of the house is generally run by the kitchen manager and refers to all the areas that guests do not typically come in contact with. This includes purchasing, receiving, storing/issuing, food production, stewarding, budgeting, accounting, and control.

One of the most important aspects to running a successful restaurant is having a strong back-of-the-house operation, particularly in the kitchen. The kitchen is the backbone of every full-service restaurant; thus, it must be well managed and organized. Some of the main considerations in efficiently operating the back of the house include staffing, scheduling, training, food cost analysis, production, management involvement, management follow-up, and employee recognition.

Food Production

Planning, organizing, and producing food of a consistently high quality are no easy tasks. The kitchen manager, cook, or chef begins the production process by determining the expected volume of business for the next few days. The same period's sales from the previous year will give a good indication of the expected volume and the breakdown of the number of sales of each menu item. As described earlier,

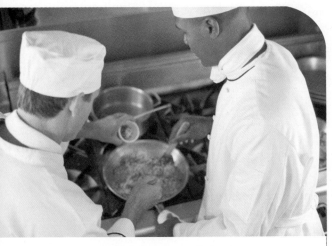

Chefs Working Together as a Team

ordering and receiving will have already been done for the day's production schedule.

The **kitchen manager** checks the head line cook's order, which will bring the prep (preparation) area up to the par stock of prepared items. Most of the prep work is done in the early part of the morning and afternoon. Taking advantage of slower times allows the line cooks to do the final preparation just prior to and during the actual meal service.

The kitchen layout is set up according to the business projected as well as the menu design. Most full-service restaurants have similar layouts and designs for their kitchens. The layout consists of the back door area, walk-ins, the freezer, dry storage, prep line, salad bar, cooking line, expediter, dessert station, and service bar area.

The **cooking line** is the most important part of the kitchen layout. It might consist of a broiler station, window station, fry station, salad station, saute station, and pizza station—just a few of the intricate parts that go into the setup of the back of the house. The size of the kitchen and its equipment are all designed according to the sales forecast for the restaurant.

The kitchen will also be set up according to what the customers prefer and order most frequently. For example, if guests eat more broiled or sautéed items, the size of the broiler and sauté must be larger to cope with the demand.

Teamwork, a prerequisite for success in all areas of the hospitality and tourism industry, is especially important in the kitchen. Because of the hectic pace, pressure builds, and unless each member of the team excels, the result will be food that is delayed, not up to standard, or both.

Although organization and performance standards are necessary, it is helping each other with the prepping and the cooking that makes for teamwork. "It's just like a relay race; we can't afford to drop the baton," says Amy Lu, kitchen manager of China Coast restaurant in Los Angeles. Teamwork in the back of the house is like an orchestra playing in tune, each player adding to the harmony.

Another example of organization and teamwork is T.G.I. Friday's five rules of control for running a kitchen:

1. Order it well.
2. Receive it well.
3. Store it well.
4. Make it to the recipe.
5. Don't let it die in the window.

It is amazing to see a kitchen line being overloaded, yet everyone is gratified when the team succeeds in preparing and serving quality food on time.[7]

A number of chefs are joining the green hospitality movement by encouraging the purchase of sustainable farming produce. More than 1,100 American Culinary Federation chefs are emphasizing organic and locally grown produce, whole-grain breads, and grass-fed meat products. Sustainable farming is making

A DAY IN THE LIFE OF JAMES LORENZ

Kitchen Manager, T.G.I. Friday's, La Jolla, California

7:00am – Arrive. Check the work of cleaning crew (such as clogs in burners, stoves/ovens, etc.) for total cleanliness.

7:15–7:40am – Set production levels for all stations (broiler/hot sauce/expediter, cold sauce, vegetable preparation, baker preparation, line preparation: sauté/noodles, pantry, fry/seafood portioning).

8:00am – The first cooks begin arriving; greet them and allocate production sheets with priority items circled.

9:00am – On a good day, the produce arrives at 9:00 A.M. Check for quality, quantity, accuracy (making sure the prices match the quotation sheet), and that the produce is stored properly.

9:30–11:00am – Follow up on production. The sauté cook, who is last to come in, arrives. He or she is the closing person for the morning shift.

- Follow up on cleanliness, recipe adherence, production accuracy.
- Check the stations to ensure the storage of prepped items (e.g., plastic draining inserts under poultry and seafood), the shelf life of products, general cleanliness, and that what is in the station is prepared correctly (e.g., turkey diced to the right size and portioned and dated correctly).

10:45am – Final check of the line and production to ensure readiness. Did everyone prepare enough?

11:00–2:30pm – All hands on deck. Jump on the first ticket. Pretoast buns for burgers and hold in heated drawers. Precook some chicken breasts for salads. Monitor lunch until 2:30 P.M.
- Be responsible for cleanliness.
- Determine who needs to get off the clock.
- Decide what production is left for the remainder of the day.
- Focus on changing over the line, change the food pan inserts (BBQ sauce, etc.).

2:30–3:15pm – Complete changeover of the line and check the stocking for the P.M. crew:
- Final prep portioning.
- Check the dishwasher area and prep line for cleanliness.
- Check that the product is replaced in the store walk-in or refrigerator.
- Reorganize the produce walk-in. Check the storage of food, labels, and day dots, lids on.
- Thank the A.M. crew and send them home.

4:00–4:15pm – Welcome the P.M. crew
- Place produce order (as a double-check, ask the P.M. crew what they might need).

5:00pm – Hand over to P.M. manager.

such a wave in the restaurant industry as a whole that the National Restaurant Association began work on a multiyear plan to guide the restaurant and foodservice industry toward environmentally sound practices and develop policy initiatives focusing on sustainability. The NRA's goal is to identify practices that can reduce costs for restaurants while encouraging the creation and use of sustainable materials and alternative energy sources. As an example of a leadership role in the growth of sustainable food usage is Chipotle Mexican Grill with 600 restaurants that sell about 30 million pounds of grass-fed meat each year. Plus, about 55 percent of the chain's chicken is naturally raised. Chipotle's "Food with Integrity" mission is the cornerstone of everything they do.[8]

Kitchen/Food Production

Staffing and Scheduling

Practicing proper staffing is absolutely crucial for the successful running of a kitchen. It is important to have enough employees on the schedule to enable the restaurant, as a whole, to handle the volume on any given shift. Often it is better to overstaff the kitchen, rather than understaff it, for two reasons. First, it is much easier to send an employee home than it is to call someone in. Second, having extra employees on hand allows for cross-training and development, which is becoming a widely used method.

Problems can also be eliminated if a staffing plan is created to set needed levels. These levels should be adjusted according to sales trends on a monthly basis.

Also crucial to the smooth running of the kitchen is having a competent staff. This means putting the best cooks in the appropriate stations on the line, which will assist in the speed of service, the food quality, and the quality of the operations.

Training and Development

Implementing a comprehensive training program is vital in the kitchen because of a high turnover rate. Trainers should, of course, be qualified and experienced in the kitchen. Often, the most competent chefs are used to train new hires. Such trainings are usually done on the job and may include study material. Some restaurants may even require new hires to complete a written test, evaluating the skills acquired through the training process.

Ensuring adequate training is necessary because the success of the business lies in the hands of the trainer and the trainee. If employees are properly trained when they begin their employment, little time and money will need to be spent on correcting errors. Thorough training also helps in retaining employees for longer periods of time.

Training, however, does not stop after the new hire passes a test. Developing the skills of all the employees is critical to the growth and success of the kitchen and, ultimately, the restaurant. A development program may consist of delegating duties or projects to the staff, allowing them to expand their horizons within the kitchen and the restaurant business. Such duties include projections of sales, inventory, ordering, schedule writing, and training.

This will help management get feedback on the running of the kitchen and on how well the development program works in their particular operation. Also, this allows for internal growth and promotion.

Production Procedures

Production in the kitchen is key to the success of a restaurant because it relates directly to the recipes on the menu and how much product is on hand to produce the menu. Thus, controlling the production process is crucial. To undertake such a task, **production control sheets** are created for each station, for example, broiler, sauté, fry, pantry, window, prep, dish, and dessert. With the control sheets, levels are set up for each day according to sales. Figure 7–2 shows a production sheet for a popular seafood restaurant.

The first step in creating the production sheets is to count the products on hand for each station. After the production levels are determined, the amount of product required to reach the level for each recipe is decided. After these calculations are completed, the sheets are handed to the cooks. It is important to make these calculations before the cooks arrive, considering the amount of prep time that is needed to produce before business is conducted. For instance, if a restaurant is open only for lunch and dinner, enough product should be on hand by 11:00 A.M. to ensure that the cooks are prepared to handle the lunch crowd.

When determining production, par levels should be changed weekly according to sales trends. This will help control and minimize waste levels. Waste is a large contributor to food cost; therefore, the kitchen should determine the product levels necessary to make it through only one day. Products have a particular shelf life, and if the kitchen overproduces and does not sell the product within its shelf life, it must be thrown away. More important, this practice allows for the freshest product to reach the customers on a daily basis.

After the lunch rush, the kitchen checks to see how much product was sold and how much is left for the night shift. (Running out of a product is unacceptable and should not happen. If proper production procedures are followed, a restaurant will not have to "86" anything on the menu.) After all production is completed on all stations, the cooks may be checked out. It is essential to check out the cooks and hold them accountable for production levels. If they are not checked out, they will slide on their production, negatively affecting the restaurant and the customer.

The use of production sheets is critical, as well, in controlling how the cooks use the products because production plays a key role in food cost. Every recipe has a particular "spec" (specification) to follow. When one deviates from the recipe, quality goes down, consistency is lost, and food cost goes up. That is why it is important to follow the recipe at all times.

Management Involvement and Follow-Up

As in any business, management involvement is vital to the success of a restaurant. Management should know firsthand what is going on in the back of the house. It is also important that they be "on the line," assisting the staff in the preparation of the menu and in the other operations of the kitchen, just as they should be helping when things are rushed. When management is visible to the staff, they are prone to do what they need to be doing at all times, and food quality is more apparent and consistent. Managers should constantly be walking and talking food cost, cleanliness, sanitation, and quality. This shows the staff how serious and committed they are to the successful running of the back of the house.

ITEM	PAR	ON HAND	PREP	INITIAL
FRESH CATCH				
Add Island Sauce to any fish				
BBQ Shrimp				
Casino				
Coconut Lobster				
Fried Lobster				
Ritz Crusted				
Seafood Kabob				
Stuffed Salmon				
SNAPPER				
Almondine				
Anna				
Broiled				
Fingers				
Stuffed				
FLOUNDER				
Allmondine				
Fried, Baked				
Stuffed				
GROUPER				
Baked				
Casino				
Coconut				
Coconut				
Floribean				
Fried Nutty				
Mexical				
Nuggets				
Nutty				
Potato Crusted				
Ritz				
Stuffed				
Wisconsin				
Holiday Specials				
DAILY APPETIZERS				
Oysters Maria (3 ea)				
Mozzereal Cheese Sticks (5 ea)				
Jammers, Jalapeno (4ea)				
Jammers, Seafood (10ea)				
Clam Strip Basket (6oz)				
Buffalo Shrimp (5ea)				
BBQ Shrimp (1 Skewer 5 Shrimp)				
Gator Gites (6oz)				

ITEM	PAR	ON HAND	PREP	INITIAL
WRAPS				
Ham or Turkey				
Ham & turkey				
Shrimp Salad				
Chicken Caesar				
Chicken Salad				
BLT Wrap				
DAILY SALADS				
Seafood or Chicken Salad				
Shrimp				
Chicken Mediterrarean				
PIZZA				
Shrimp or B.B.Q. Chicken				
Portabello				
SOUP & SAND				
Clamwich, Mini Grouper				
Crab Cake, Chicken Salad				
EXTRA DAILY SPECIALS				
Monday AUCE Fish				
Tues Lobster				
Wed AUCE Popcorn\Crabby Night				
Thur Prime Rib				
Beef Tips and Noodles				
Chicken Pot Pie				
Salisbury Stk				
Ham & Mac & Cheese				
Chicken Oscar				
Stone Crab Mustard Sauce				
Corn Salsa				
SPECIALS ITEMS FOR CATERING				
Pull From Freezer				
Item	Par	On Hand	Pull	Initial
				08/25/2003
				01/12/04

Figure 7–2 • A Production Sheet for a Popular Seafood Restaurant.

(*Source:* Anna Maria Oyster Bar, Inc.)

As management spends more time in the kitchen, more knowledge is gained, more confidence is acquired, and more respect is earned. Employee–management interaction produces a sense of stability and a strong work ethic among employees, resulting in higher morale and promoting a positive working environment. To ensure that policies and standards are being upheld, management follow-up should happen on a continual basis. This is especially important when cooks are held accountable to specifications and production and when other staff members are given duties to perform. Without follow-up, the restaurant may fold.

Employee Recognition

Employee recognition is an extremely important aspect of back-of-the-house management. Recognizing employees for their efforts creates a positive work environment that motivates the staff to excel and to ultimately produce consistently better-quality food for the guests.

Recognition can take many different forms, from personally commending a staff person for his or her efforts to recognizing a person in a group setting. By recognizing employees, management can make an immediate impact on the quality of operations. This can be a great tool for building sales, as well as assisting in the overall success of the restaurant.

▶ Check Your Knowledge

1. Explain the following terms: guest counts/covers, product specification, production control sheets.
2. Discuss TGI Friday's five rules for running a kitchen.

INTRODUCING CHRIS DELLA–CRUZ, GENERAL MANAGER OF SUSO RESTAURANT

Expectations of the General Manager

The expectations of the general manager are different in each restaurant; however, there are certain commonalities as well. Some of these commonalities are as follows:

- General managers answer directly to the owner or to regional directors for major corporations.
- General managers are expected to run good numbers for the periods. The numbers analyzed are food cost, labor cost, beverage cost. These areas are controlled to produce sufficient profit for the restaurant.
- General managers promote good morale and teamwork in the restaurant. Having a positive environment in the restaurant is of utmost importance. This will not only keep the employees happy, but it will also contribute to providing better service to the guests.

continued

INTRODUCING CHRIS DELLA–CRUZ, GENERAL MANAGER OF SUSO RESTAURANT *(continued)*

Duties and Responsibilities

The general manager of a restaurant is directly in charge of all the operations in the restaurant. General managers are also in charge of the floor managers, kitchen manager, and all the remaining employees in the restaurant.

The general manager should always check on the floor managers to ensure that all policies and regulations are being met. This will keep operations running smoothly.

Another important duty is to organize and control the staffing of the restaurant. The floor managers usually write the employee schedule; however, the general manager is still directly responsible for proper staffing for the period. This will help keep labor costs to about 20 percent of sales. The general manager is also in charge of conducting employee reviews and training.

Qualifications for a General Manager

To be hired as a general manager, the following qualifications are necessary:

- The general manager should be very knowledgeable in the restaurant business.
- He or she should have previously worked all the stations in a restaurant and be very familiar with them.
- The general manager should be able to get along with all people, be fair with all employees, and not discriminate.
- Having a degree is not the most important thing in becoming a general manager. However, a degree is very useful in moving up the ladder in a company to regional manager, regional director, and so on.

Budgeted Costs in a Restaurant

Running a good pace in the restaurant is of absolute importance. Every restaurant has different numbers to make. The following numbers came from Chris's restaurant. These numbers reflect their goals versus actual numbers run for a given week.

	Goal(%)	Actual(%)	Variance
Food Cost	27.0	27.2	+0.2
Labor Cost	19.9	20.8	+0.9
Beverage Cost	19.0	18.2	−0.8

As can be seen, this restaurant did well with the beverage cost; however, the food cost and the labor cost are two areas to focus on for the upcoming week.

Making good percentages for the restaurant is the most important focus simply because this is where the restaurant makes or does not make a profit. When the general manager runs good numbers, then he or she will receive a large bonus check for contributing to the profit of the restaurant. This is why it is so important to focus on these three key areas.

Scheduling the Restaurant

Appropriate scheduling plays a key role in the success of the restaurant. For one thing, overscheduling and underscheduling have a direct effect on the labor cost. If there are too many employees working on a shift for the business acquired, then the labor cost will be high. In contrast, if there are not enough employees working, then the service will suffer and overtime will increase the labor cost.

Purchasing

Purchasing for restaurants involves procuring the products and services that the restaurant needs to serve its guests. Restaurant operators set up purchasing systems that determine the following:

- Standards for each item (**product specification**)
- Systems that minimize effort and maximize control of theft and losses from other sources
- The amount of each item that should be on hand (par stock and reorder point)
- Who will do the buying and keep the purchasing system in motion
- Who will do the receiving, storage, and issuing of items[9]

It is desirable for restaurants to establish standards for each product, called product specification. When ordering meat, for example, the cut, weight, size, percentage of fat content, and number of days aged are all factors that are specified by the purchaser.

Establishing systems that minimize effort and maximize control of theft may be done by computer or manually. However, merely computerizing a system does not make it theft-proof. Instead, employing honest workers is a top priority because temptation is everywhere in the restaurant industry.

An efficient and effective system establishes a stock level that must be on hand at all times. This is called a **par stock**. If the stock on hand falls below a specified reorder point, the computer system automatically reorders a predetermined quantity of the item.

In identifying who will do the buying, it is most important to separate task and responsibility between the person placing the order and the person receiving the goods. This avoids possible theft. The best way to avoid losses is to have the chef prepare the order; the manager or the manager's designee place the order; and a third person, responsible for the stores, receive the goods together with the chef (or the chef's designee).

Commercial (for-profit) restaurant and foodservice operators who are part of a chain may have the menu items and order specifications determined at the corporate office. This saves the unit manager from having to order individually; specialists at the corporate office can not only develop the menu but also the specifications for the ingredients to ensure consistency. Both chain and independent restaurants and foodservice operators use similar prepurchase functions (Figure 7–3).

Figure 7–3 • Food Cost Control Process.

- Plan menus.

- Determine quality and quantity needed to produce menus.

- Determine inventory stock levels.

- Identify items to purchase by subtracting stock levels from the quantity required to produce menus.

- Write specifications and develop market orders for purchases.

Professor Stefanelli at the University of Nevada, Las Vegas, suggests a formal and an informal method of purchasing that includes the following steps.[10]

Formal	*Informal*
Develop purchase order	Develop purchase order
Establish bid schedule	Quote price
Issue invitation to bid	Select vendor and place order
Tabulate and evaluate bids	
Award contract and issue delivery order	
Inspect/receive deliveries, inventory stores, and record transactions in inventory	Receive and inspect deliveries, store, and record transaction
Evaluate and follow up	Evaluate and follow up
Issue food supplies for food production and service	Issue food supplies for food production and service

The formal method is generally used by chain restaurant operators and the informal one by independent restaurant operators.

A **purchase order** comes as a result of the product specification. As it sounds, a purchase order is an order to purchase a certain quantity of an item at a specific price. Many restaurants develop purchase orders for items they need on a regular basis. These are then sent to suppliers for quotations, and samples are sent in for product evaluations. For example, canned items have varying amounts of liquid. Typically, it is the drained weight of the product that matters to the restaurant operator. After comparing samples from several vendors, the operator can choose the supplier that best suits the restaurant's needs.

Receiving

When placing an order, the restaurant operator specifies the day and time (for example, Friday, 10:00 A.M. to 12:00 noon) for the delivery to be made. This prevents deliveries from being made at inconvenient times.

Receiving is a point of control in the restaurant operation. The purpose of receiving is to ensure the quantity, quality, and price are exactly as ordered. The quantity and quality relate to the order specification and the standardized recipe. Depending on the restaurant and the type of food and beverage control system, some perishable items are issued directly to the kitchen, and most of the nonperishable items go into storage.

Storing/Issuing

Control of the stores is often a problem. Records must be kept of all items going into and out of the stores. If more than one person has access to the stores, it is difficult to know where to attach responsibility in case of losses.

Items should be issued from the stores only on an authorized requisition signed by the appropriate person. One restaurateur who has been in business for many years issues stores to the kitchen on a daily basis. No inventory is kept in the production area and there is no access to the stores. To some, this may be overdoing control, but it is hard to fault the results: a good food cost percentage. All items that enter the stores should have a date stamp and be rotated using the first in–first out (FIFO) system.

First in–first out is a simple but effective system of ensuring stock rotation. This is achieved by placing the most recent purchases, in rotation, behind previous purchases. Failure to do this can result in spoilage.

Obviously, restaurants should maintain strict controls. Among the better-known controls are taking inventory regularly; calculating food and beverage cost percentages; having receiving done by a person other than the person who orders; using a par stock reordering system; using one entrance/exit for employees and not permitting employees to bring bags into the restaurant with them; employing a good accountant; and, yes, checking the garbage!

Budgeting

Budgeting costs fall into two categories: fixed and variable. **Fixed costs** are constant regardless of the volume of business. Fixed costs are rent/lease payments, interest, and depreciation. **Variable costs** fluctuate with the volume of business. Variable costs include controllable expenses such as payroll, benefits, direct operating expense, music and entertainment, marketing and promotion, energy and utility, administrative, and repairs and maintenance.

Regardless of sales fluctuations, variable or controllable expenses vary in some controllable proportion to sales. For example, if a restaurant is open on a Monday, it must have a host, server, cook, dishwasher, and so on. The volume of business and sales total may be $750. However, on Friday that sales total might be $2,250 with just a few more staff. The controllable costs increased only slightly in proportion to the sales, and the fixed costs did not change.

Restaurant managers also need to spend time with staff members

Restaurant Accounting

To operate any business efficiently and effectively, it is necessary to determine the mission, goals, and objectives. One of the most important goals in any enterprise is a fair return on investment, otherwise known as profit. In addition, accounting for the income and expenditures is a necessary part of any business enterprise. The restaurant industry has adopted a uniform system of accounts.

The **uniform system of accounts** for restaurants (USAR) outlines a standard classification and presentation of operating results. The system allows for easy comparison among restaurants because each expense item has the same schedule number.

Balance Sheet

A **balance sheet** for a restaurant, or any business, reflects how the assets and liabilities relate to the owner's equity at a particular moment in time. The balance sheet is mainly used by owners and investors to verify the financial health of the organization. Financial health may be defined in several ways—for example, liquidity, which means having a sufficient amount of cash available to pay bills when they are due, and debt leverage, which is the percentage of a company's assets owned by outside interests (liabilities).

CORPORATE PROFILE

T.G.I. Friday's Restaurant

In the spring of 1965, Alan Stillman, a New York perfume salesman, opened a restaurant located at First Avenue and 63rd Street. The restaurant boasted striped awnings, a blue exterior, and yellow supergraphics reading T.G.I. Friday's. Inside were wooden floors covered with sawdust, Tiffany-style lamps, bentwood chairs, red-and-white tablecloths, and a bar area complete with brass rails and stained glass.

T.G.I. Friday's was an immediate success. The restaurant on Manhattan's upper east side became the meeting place for single adults. In fact, *Newsweek* and the *Saturday Evening Post* called the opening of T.G.I. Friday's "the dawn of the singles' age."

In 1971, franchisee Dan Scoggin opened a T.G.I. Friday's in Dallas and in four other sites around the country. The success was instant; thus, began the company that is Friday's today.

By 1975, there were ten T.G.I. Friday's in eight states, but the great success that the company had seen was starting to diminish. Dan Scoggin began a countrywide tour to visit each restaurant; he talked with employees, managers, and customers to isolate the roots of successes and failures. This was the critical turning point for the company. The focus shifted from being just another restaurant chain to giving guests exactly what they wanted. The theories and philosophies Scoggin developed are the principles by which Friday's now does business.

T.G.I. Friday's goal was to create a comfortable, relaxing environment where guests could enjoy food and drink. Stained glass windows, wooden airplane propellers, racing sculls, and metal advertising signs comprised the elegant clutter that greeted guests when they entered a T.G.I. Friday's. Nothing was left to chance. Music, lights, air-conditioning, decor, and housekeeping were all designed to keep guests comfortable. Employees were encouraged to display their own personalities and to treat customers as they would guests in their own homes.

As guests demanded more, T.G.I. Friday's provided more—soon becoming the industry leader in menu and drink selection. The menu expanded from a slate chalkboard to an award-winning collection of items representing every taste and mood.

T.G.I. Friday's also became the industry leader in innovation—creating the now-famous Jack Daniel's Grill. This was the first restaurant chain to offer stone-ground whole-wheat bread, avocados, bean sprouts, and Mexican appetizers across the country. As guests' tastes continued to change, T.G.I. Friday's introduced pasta dishes, brunch items, and fettucine.

America owes the popularization of frozen and ice cream drinks to T.G.I. Friday's, where smooth, alcoholic and nonalcoholic drinks were made with fresh fruit, juices, ice cream, and yogurt. These recipes were so precise that T.G.I. Friday's drink glasses were scientifically designed for the correct ratio of each ingredient. These specially designed glasses have since become popular throughout the industry.

Through the years, T.G.I. Friday's success has been phenomenal. More than 750 restaurants have opened in forty nine states and fifty five countries. With average gross revenues of $3.5 million per year at each location, it has the highest per unit sales volume of any national casual dining chain.

T.G.I. Friday's is privately owned by Carlson Companies, Inc., of Minneapolis—one of the largest privately held companies in the country. Today, T.G.I. Friday's has come to be known as a casual restaurant where family and friends meet for great food, fun, and conversation. Everyone looks forward to T.G.I. Friday's!

What does it take to be successful in the restaurant business, and what does it take to be a leader? The answers to these questions are crucial to success as a restaurant company. The essentials of success in business are as follows:

1. Treat everyone with respect for their dignity.
2. Treat all customers as if they are honored guests in your home.
3. Remember that all problems result from either poor hiring, lack of training, unclear performance expectations, or accepting less than excellence.
4. Remember that management tools are methods, not objectives.

As you can see, these are principles to guide decision making as opposed to step-by-step actions. However, if these principles are not followed, then actions have very short-term effects. And if you do choose to follow them, they form a base on which you can easily decide which specific actions are necessary in any given situation.

The basics of leadership are as follows:

1. Hire the right people.
2. Train everyone thoroughly and completely.
3. Be sure that everyone clearly understands the performance expectations.
4. Accept only excellence.

Here are the very basics of how to provide strong, clear leadership. However, once again these are only the minimum requirements, not all the qualities necessary to be a good leader. Individual success and that of a company such as T.G.I. Friday's are predicated on understanding and following the essentials of success in business and the basics of leadership. Whether an hourly employee or a manager, it is critical that each employee manage his or her part of the business using these philosophies.

continued

CORPORATE PROFILE *(continued)*

The Guest Focus

At most companies, it appears that senior management runs the company. The employees consider senior management to be the most important people with whom they interact. As a result, decisions are made in an effort to please senior management, and decisions that affect people lower in the hierarchy are viewed as less important. T.G.I. Friday's success is dependent on inverting the typical management pyramid. Guests are the most important element in the organization; immediately following them are the employees who are closest to the guests—those people who have the greatest impact on the guests' experience. The livelihood of each employee depends on one group of people: guests. It is critical to determine what guests' needs are and fill those needs. To the extent that this objective is accomplished, the needs of each person in the pyramid will be fulfilled. Every decision at T.G.I. Friday's is made with guests in mind.

One thing that makes T.G.I. Friday's unique is the philosophies and theories. These are principles that each employee understands to ensure that everyone stays focused on the same goals. T.G.I. Friday's philosophies and theories were first conceived in the mid-1970s. They are used to solve existing problems and enable management to be proactive to problems experienced in the past.

The "Five Easy Pieces Theory" stresses T.G.I. Friday's deep concern for the guests' satisfaction. T.G.I. Friday's will always cheerfully go out of their way to serve a quality product prepared to individual tastes. In the movie titled *Five Easy Pieces,* the star, Jack Nicholson, goes to a restaurant and orders a side order of whole-wheat toast. The waitress makes it clear that they do not serve whole-wheat toast. Nicholson notes on the menu that the chicken salad sandwich comes on whole-wheat bread. The annoyed waitress points to a sign in the restaurant that reads "No substitutions" and "We reserve the right to refuse service to anyone." Jack Nicholson orders a chicken salad sandwich on whole-wheat toast, but tells the waitress to hold the mayo, hold the lettuce, hold the chicken salad, and just bring him the whole-wheat toast. Unwisely, she asks where she should hold the chicken salad. Nicholson sarcastically responds, "Between your knees!" On that note, he leaves, a very dissatisfied guest. T.G.I. Friday's managers and employees are responsible for honoring any guest request within realistic possibilities. Many managers take a guest's request even further and get them exactly what they want—even if the ingredients are not in the restaurant.

The "Triangle Theory" explains the need to balance and expand upon the goals of the guest, employee, and company, and maximize the results to each. Managers make many decisions and must always consider the effect of those decisions on all three sides of the triangle—the guest, the employee, and the company. Some decisions can cause one side of the triangle to prosper (temporarily) at the expense of the other two. For example, if a company overprices its menu items, it can greatly improve the bottom line. However, guests will object to being cheated and will not return. This will ultimately result in lower staffing and will eventually kill the company. Management's responsibility is to balance the results among the three sides so that all sides thrive. But this is only the first step. To grow and expand the business, decisions must be made that maximize or expand all three sides of the triangle at the same time.

These are just a few of the philosophies and theories on which T.G.I. Friday's is based.

Restaurants are one of the few, fortunate types of businesses to operate on a cash basis for income receivables. There are no outstanding accounts receivable because all sales are in cash—even credit cards are treated as cash because of their prompt payment. Typically, restaurants invest significant funds in assets, such as equipment, furniture, and building (if they own it). The balance sheet will reflect how much of the cost of these assets has been paid for, and are thus owned by the company (owner's equity), and how much is still due to outsiders (liability). Furthermore, the balance sheet will show the extent to which the company has

8. Interview vendors who wish to sell products to establishment.

9. Check finished product quality and act to correct problems.

10. Work as expediter to get meals served effectively.

11. Inspect dining area, kitchen, rest rooms, food lockers, storage, and parking lot.

12. Check daily reports for indications of internal theft.

13. Instruct employees regarding the control of waste, portion sizes, and so on.

14. Prepare forecast for daily or shift food preparation.

Service

1. Receive and record table reservations.

2. Greet familiar customers by name.

3. Seat customers.

4. Talk with customers while they are dining.

5. Monitor service times and procedures in the dining area.

6. Observe customers being served to correct problems.

7. Ask customers about quality of service.

8. Ask customers about quality of the food product.

9. Listen to and resolve customer complaints.

10. Authorize complimentary meals or beverages.

11. Write letters in response to customer complaints.

12. Telephone customers in response to customer complaints.

13. Secure and return items left by customers.

Sanitation and Safety

1. Accompany local officials on health inspections on premise.

2. Administer first aid to employees and customers.

3. Submit accident, incident, and OSHA reports.

4. Report incidents to police.

5. Observe employee behavior and establishment conditions for compliance with safety and security procedures.

Recycling

At the end of the night at most restaurants, leftover food, paper, bottles, and cardboard typically are put in a Dumpster in the back alley, destined for a landfill. Separating garbage is dirty; it requires people and time to do it. But several operators say making minor changes reduces trash and helps budgets. Zero waste is how Nomad Café in Berkeley, California, prefers to operate its business. It saves more than $10,000 every year by recycling and composting. Making simple changes to its daily routine of throwing out garbage also aided Scoma's in San Francisco. It color-coded the system and got staff into the habit of recycling. Scoma's saves an average of $2,000 per month.[12]

Trends in Restaurant Operations

- More flavorful food.
- Increased takeout meals, especially at lunch, and more home meal replacement (for dinner).
- Increased food safety and sanitation.
- Guests becoming more sophisticated and needing more things to excite them.
- More food court restaurants in malls, movie theater complexes, and colleges and universities where guests line up (similar to a cafeteria), select their food (which a server places on a tray), and pay a cashier.
- Steak houses becoming more popular.
- With more restaurants in each segment, the segments increasingly split into upper, middle, and lower tiers
- Twin and multirestaurant locations.
- Quick-service restaurants (QSRs) in convenience stores.
- Difficulty in finding good employees.

CASE STUDY

Short Staffed in the Kitchen

Sally is the general manager of one of the best restaurants in town, known as The Pub. As usual, at 6:00 P.M. on a Friday night, there is a forty-five-minute wait. The kitchen is overloaded, and they are running behind in check times, the time that elapses between the kitchen getting the order and the guest receiving his or her meal. This is critical, especially if a complaint is received because a guest has waited too long for a meal to be served.

Sally is waiting for her two head line cooks to come in for the closing shift. It is now 6:15 P.M. and she receives phone calls from both of them. Unfortunately, they are both sick with the flu and are not able to come to work.

As she gets off the phone, the hostess tells Sally that a party of fifty is scheduled to arrive at 7:30 P.M. Sally is concerned, knowing that they are currently running a six-person line with only four cooks. The productivity is very high, but they are running extremely long check times. How can Sally handle the situation?

Discussion Questions

1. How would you handle the short-staffing issue?
2. What measures would you take to get the appropriate cooks in to work as soon as possible?
3. What would you do to ensure a smooth, successful transition for the party of fifty?
4. How would you manipulate your floor plan to provide great service for the party of fifty?
5. How would you immediately make an impact on the long check times?
6. What should you do to ensure that all the guests in the restaurant are happy?

CASE STUDY

Shortage in Stock

It is 9:30 Friday morning at The Pub. Product is scheduled to be delivered at 10:00. Sally specifically ordered an exceptional amount of food for the upcoming weekend because she is projecting it to be a busy holiday weekend. Sally receives a phone call at 10:30 from J&G Groceries, stating that they cannot deliver the product until 10:00 A.M. on Saturday morning. She explains to the driver that it is crucial that she receives the product as soon as possible. He apologizes; however, it is impossible to have delivery made until Saturday morning.

By 1:00 P.M., they are beginning to run out of product, including absolute necessities such as steaks, chicken, fish, and produce. The guests are getting frustrated because the staff are beginning to 86 a great deal of product. In addition, if they do not begin production for the P.M. shift soon, they will be in deep trouble.

On Friday nights, The Pub does in excess of $12,000 in sales. However, if the problem is not immediately alleviated, the restaurant will lose many guests and a great amount of profits.

Discussion Questions

1. What immediate measures would you take to resolve the problem?
2. How would you produce the appropriate product as soon as possible?
3. Who should you call first, if anyone, to alleviate the problem?
4. What can you do to always have enough product on hand?
5. Is it important to have a backup plan for a situation like this? If so, what would it be?

Summary

1. Most restaurants forecast on a weekly and monthly basis a budget that projects sales and costs for a year in consideration of guest counts and the average guest check.
2. To operate a restaurant, products need to be purchased, received, and properly stored.
3. Food production is determined by the expected business for the next few days. The kitchen layout is designed according to the sales forecasted.
4. Good service is very important. In addition to taking orders, servers act as salespersons for the restaurant.
5. The front of the house deals with the part of the restaurant having direct contact with guests, in other words, what the guests see—grounds maintenance, hosts/hostesses, dining and bar areas, bartenders, busers, and so on.
6. The back of the house is generally run by the kitchen manager and refers to all areas guests usually do not come in contact with. This includes purchasing, receiving, storing/issuing, food production, stewarding, budgeting, accounting, and control.

Key Words and Concepts

average guest check	income statement
back of the house	kitchen manager
balance sheet	labor costs percentage
beverage cost percentage	net profit
budgeting costs	operating ratios
contribution margin	par stock
controllable expense	personal digital assistants (PDAs)
cooking line	point-of-sale (POS) systems
covers	prime cost
curbside appeal	product specification
employee recognition	production control sheets
first in–first out	purchase order
fixed costs	receiving
food cost percentage	restaurant forecasting
front of the house	suggestive selling
gross profit	uniform system of accounts
guest counts	variable costs
hostess	

Review Questions

1. On the Companion Website, what advice do chef Gray Colpits and chef Suzanne Marquette give?
2. On the Companion Website, what suggestions does John Horne make for those who may want to open a restaurant?
3. Briefly describe the two components of restaurant forecasting.
4. Explain the key points in purchasing, receiving, and storing.
5. Why is the kitchen layout an important aspect of food production?
6. Explain the purpose of suggestive selling. What characteristics make up a good server?
7. Accounting is important to determine the profitability of a restaurant. Briefly describe the following terms:
   a. Controllable expenses
   b. Uniform system of accounts
   c. Prime cost
8. What is the point-of-sales system, and why is a control system important for a restaurant operation?
9. What are the differences between the back of the house and the front of the house?
10. What steps must one take in preparing production sheets?

Internet Exercises

1. Organization: **National Restaurant Association (NRA)**
   Web site: www.restaurant.org
   Summary: The NRA is the business association of the food industry. It consists of 400,000 members and more than 170,000 restaurants. Member restaurants represent table service and quick-service operators, chains, and franchises. The NRA helps international restaurants receive the benefits of

the association and gives guidance for success to nonprofit members.

(a) List the food-borne diseases listed on the NRA site. Find out about each disease and how the National Restaurant Association suggests you can prevent it.

(b) What kinds of careers are available in the restaurant and hospitality industry?

(c) What legal issues does this site advise you on if you want to start your own restaurant?

2. Organization: **Chili's Grill and Bar**
   Web site: chilis.com

Summary: Chili's is a fun and exciting place to have burgers, fajitas, margaritas, and chili. Established in 1975 in Dallas, the chain now has more than 637 restaurants in the United States and twenty other countries.

(a) What requirements must you meet to open a Chili's franchise? From what you have learned about the issues involved in starting your own business, how is setting up your own business different from having a franchise?

(b) What is the "Chilihead culture"?

Apply Your Knowledge

In a casual Italian restaurant, sales for the week of September 15 are as follows:

Food sales	$10,000
Beverage sales	2,500
Total	$12,500

1. If the food cost is 30 percent, how much did the food actually cost?
2. If the beverage cost is 25 percent of beverage sales, how much did the beverages cost?
3. If the total labor cost is 28 percent, how much money does that represent and how much is left over for other costs and profit?

Suggested Activities

1. On the Companion Website, which restaurants does John Horne respect?
2. From the Companion Website, what qualities does John Horne say make a good restauranteur?
3. Divide into groups of two and assign the roles of guest and server. Role-play using the concept of suggestive selling and upselling.
4. Create an income statement for an imaginary restaurant.

Endnotes

1. This section draws from John R. Walker, *The Restaurant from Concept to Operation*, 5th ed. (Hoboken, NJ: John Wiley and Sons, 2008), 86–87.
2. Personal conversation with Danny Meyer, January 14, 2004.
3. SoftCafé, "Design and Print Your Menu in Minutes!—with MenuPro," www.softcafe.com/menupro.htm.
4. Personal correspondence with restaurant Magic Software, Tampa, Florida, July 29, 2007.
5. Dusty Williams, "Information Technologists," www.restaurantmagic.com/informationTech.php.
6. Data Central, "Welcome to Data Central," www.restaurantmagic.com/home.php.
7. Personal correspondence with James Lorenz, May 16, 2007.
8. Richard Slawsky, "Sustainable Farming Grows on Chefs," QSR Web, March 8, 2007, www.qsrweb.com/article.php?id=7025.
9. This section draws from Walker, *Restaurant from Concept to Operation*, 275.
10. Walker, *Restaurant from Concept to Operation*, 275.
11. Personal conversation with bobby Hays, general manager, Chart House Restaurant, Solana Beach, California, January 1994.
12. Jamie Popp, "Trash Talk," *Restaurants and Institutions* 116, no. 9 (May 1, 2006): 75.

CHAPTER 8

Managed Services

OBJECTIVES

After reading and studying this chapter, you should be able to:

- Outline the different managed services segments.

- Describe the five factors that distinguish managed services operations from commercial ones.

- Explain the need for and trends in elementary and secondary school foodservice.

- Describe the complexities in college and university foodservice.

- Identify characteristics and trends in health care, business and industry, and leisure and recreation foodservices.

Overview

Managed services consists of foodservice and related operations including the following:

- Airlines
- Military
- Elementary and secondary schools
- Colleges and universities
- Health care facilities
- Business and industry
- Leisure and recreation organizations
- Conference centers
- Airports
- Travel plazas

Companies and organizations such as educational or health care organizations decide if the want to operate their foodservice and related operations themselves or whether they want to contract that out to a managed services company. If they decide to operate their own foodservice, they may realize some cost savings, but if they lack the expertise, they may prefer to invite contractors to submit proposals. The company or organization can then invite contractors to make a presentation and formally discuss and finalize all contractual details.

Several features distinguish managed services operations from **commercial foodservices** such as restaurants:

- In a restaurant, the challenge is to please the guest. In managed services, it is necessary to meet both the needs of the guest and the client (i.e., the institution itself).

- In some operations, the guests may or may not have alternative dining options available to them and are a captive clientele. These guests may be eating at the foodservice operation only once or on a daily basis.

- Many managed operations are housed in host organizations that do not have foodservice as their primary business.

- Most managed services operations produce food in large-quantity batches for service and consumption within fixed time periods. For example, **batch cooking** means to produce a batch of food to serve at 11:30 A.M., another batch to serve at 12:15 P.M., and a third batch to serve at 12:45 P.M., rather than putting out all the food for the whole lunch period at 11:30 A.M. This gives the guests who come to eat later in the serving period as good a quality meal as those who came to eat earlier.

- The volume of business is more consistent and therefore easier to cater. Because it is easier to predict the number of meals and portion sizes, it is easier to plan, organize, produce, and serve meals; therefore, the atmosphere is less hurried than that of a restaurant. Weekends tend to be quieter than weekdays in managed services and, overall, the hours and benefits may be better than those of commercial restaurants.

A company or organization might contract its food- or other services for the following reasons:

- Financial
- Quality of program
- Recruitment of management and staff
- Expertise in management of service departments
- Resources available: people, programs, management systems, information systems
- Labor relations and other support
- Outsourcing of administrative functions[1]

Airlines and Airports

In-Flight and Airport Foodservice

When airlines do provide meals, foodservice either comes from their own *in-flight* business or they have the service provided by a contractor. In-flight food may be prepared in a factory mode at a facility close to but outside of the airport. In these cases, the food is prepared and packaged; then, it is transported to the departure gates for the appropriate flights. Once the food is loaded onto the aircraft, flight attendants take over serving the food and beverages to passengers.

In-flight foodservice is a complex logistical operation: The food must be able to withstand the transport conditions and the extended hot or cold holding period from the time it is prepared until the time it is served. If a food item is to be served hot, it must be able to rethermalize well on the plate. The meal should also look appetizing and taste good. Finally, all food and beverage items must be delivered on time and correctly to each departing aircraft.

Gate Gourmet International is the largest in-flight foodservices provider, operating in twenty-seven countries on six continents from more than 140 catering facilities and producing more than 250 million meals on average annually. It is estimated that sales will exceed $2 billion supported by more than 26,000 employees. Another major player in the in-flight food service market is Sky Chefs, headquartered in Dallas, Texas. The in-flight foodservice management operators plan the menus, develop the product specifications, and arrange the purchasing contracts. Each airline has a representative who oversees one or more locations and checks on the quality, quantity, and delivery times of all food and beverage items. Airlines regard in-flight foodservice as an expense that needs to be controlled. To trim costs, most domestic airlines now sell snacks instead of meals on a number of short flights and even flights that span main meal times.

Airport restaurants from quick service to casual fine dining have seen an upswing in business as a result of the airlines cutback on in-flight foodservice. Encounter is a restaurant at LAX (Los Angeles International Airport)

International airlines try to stand out by offering superior food and beverages in hopes of attracting more passengers, especially the higher-paying business and first-class passenger. Others reduce or eliminate foodservice as a strategic decision to support lower fares. Because of the length of the flight, and the higher price paid for the ticket, international flights have better-quality food and beverage service.

On board, each aircraft has two or three categories of service, usually coach, business, and first class. First- and business-class passengers usually receive free beverages and upgraded meal items and service. These meals may consist of such items as fresh salmon or filet mignon; the rest of us get those "carry-on doggie-bags"!

A number of smaller regional and local foodservice operators contract to a variety of airlines at hundreds of airports. Most airports have caterers or foodservice contractors who compete for airline contracts. With several international and U.S. airlines all using U.S. airports, each airline must decide whether to use its own foodservice (if it has one) or to contract with one of several independent operators.

As airlines have decreased their in-flight foodservice, airport restaurants have picked up the business. Popular chain restaurants such as T.G.I. Friday's and Chili's are in several terminals, along with the quick-service restaurants such as Pizza Hut. These restaurants supplement airport foodservice offered by local restaurants.

▶ Check Your Knowledge

1. What are managed services?
2. Why would companies use contract management?

Military

Military foodservice is a large and important component of managed services. There are about 1.5 million soldiers, sailors, and aviators on active duty in the United States. Even with the military downsizing, foodservice sales top $6 billion per year. Base closings have prompted many military foodservice

*[handwritten margin notes: service, quality + quantity of food is determined by:
- economy/bus/1st class
- type of flight int'l/domestic
- no mills?]*

CORPORATE PROFILE

Sodexho

Sodexho is a North American leading food and facilities management services company. This company is also a member of the international Sodexho Alliance that was founded in 1966 by a Frenchman named Pierre Bellon with its first service provider in Marseille, France. Primarily serving schools, restaurants, and hospitals, the company soon became internationally successful by signing deals with Belgian foodservice contractors. In 1980, after considerable success in Europe, Africa, and the Middle East, Sodexho Alliance decided to expand its reach into North and South America. In 1997, the company joined with Universal Ogden Services, a leading U.S. remote-site service provider. The empire grew a year later when Sodexho Alliance and Marriott Management Services merged. The merger created a new company called Sodexho Marriott Services. Listed on the New York Stock Exchange, the new company became the market leader in food and management services in the United States. At that time, Sodexho Alliance was the biggest shareholder, holding 48.4 percent of shares on the company's capital. In 2001, however, Sodexho Alliance acquired 53 percent of the shares in Sodexho Marriott Services, which changed its name to simply Sodexho.

Today, Sodexho Alliance has more than 313,000 employees at 24,900 sites in seventy-six countries. In the United States, there are 120,000 employees. The goal of Sodexho is to improve the quality and life of customers and clients all over the United States and Canada. They offer outsourcing solutions to the health care, corporate, and education markets. This includes the following services: housekeeping, groundskeeping, foodservice, plant operation and maintenance, and integrated facilities management.

Sodexho's mission is to create and offer services that contribute to a more pleasant way of life for people wherever and whenever they come together. Its challenge is to continue to make its mission and values come alive through the way in which employees work together to serve the clients and customers. The values of Sodexho are service spirit, team spirit, and spirit of progress.

A leading provider of food and facilities management services in North America, Sodexho provides their services at more than 6,000 locations, including corporations, colleges and universities, health care organizations, and school districts. They are always looking to develop talent. Sodexho offers internships in foodservice and facilities management businesses as well as in staff positions such as finance, human resources, marketing, and sales. Sodexho believes that workforce diversity is essential to the company's growth and long-term success. By valuing and managing diversity at work, Sodexho can leverage the skills, knowledge, and abilities of all employees to increase employee, client, and customer satisfaction.

Source: This feature draws on the Sodexho USA home page, www.sodexhousa.com/about_us.html.

organizations to rediscuss services and concepts to better meet the needs of their personnel.

Recent trends in military foodservice call for services such as officers' clubs to be contracted out to foodservice management companies. This change has reduced military costs because many of the officers' clubs lost money. The clubs now have moved the emphasis from fine dining to a more casual approach with family appeal. Many clubs are renovating their base concept even further, restyling according to theme concepts, such as sports or country western, for example. Other cost-saving measures include menu management, such as the use of a single menu for lunch and dinner (guests seldom eat both meals at the clubs). With proper plating techniques and portion size manipulation, a single menu (the same menu) can be created for lunch and dinner, meaning one inventory for both meals and less stock in general. To make this technique work successfully, the menu features several choices for appetizers, entrees, and desserts.

Another trend is the testing of prepared foods that can be reheated and served without much labor. Technological advances mean that field troops do not eat out of tin cans anymore; instead, they receive their food portions in plastic-and-foil pouches called meals ready-to-eat (MREs). Today, mobile field kitchens can be run by just two people, and bulk food supplies have been replaced by preportioned, precooked food packed in trays, which then are reheated in boiling water.

Feeding military personnel includes feeding troops and officers in clubs, dining halls, and military hospitals, as well as in the field. As both the budget and the numbers of personnel decrease, the military is downsizing by consolidating responsibilities. With fewer people to cook for, fewer cooks are required.

A model for such downsizing is the U.S. Marine Corps, which contracts out foodservice. With smaller numbers, they could not afford to take a marine away from training to work in the dining facilities without affecting military operations. Sodexho has the contract for the U.S. Marine Corps Serving on seven bases in fifty-five barracks, plus clubs and other related services. In addition, fast-food restaurants such as McDonald's and Burger King have opened on well over 150 bases; they are now installing Express Way kiosks on more bases. The fast-food restaurants on base offer further alternatives for military personnel on the move. One problem that may arise as a result of the downsizing and contracting out of military foodservice is that it is not likely that McDonald's could set up on the front line in a combat situation. The military will still have to do their own food-service when it comes to mobilization.

Elementary and Secondary Schools

The United States government enacted the National School Lunch Act in 1946. The rationale was that if students received good meals, the military would have healthier recruits. In addition, such a program would make use of the surplus food that farmers produced.

Each day, millions of children are fed breakfast or lunch, or both, in approximately 98,000 schools.[2] Many challenges currently face elementary and secondary school foodservice. One major challenge is to balance salability with good nutrition. Apart from cost and nutritional value, the broader social issue of the universal free meal arises. Proponents of the program maintain that better nourished children have a better attention span, are less likely to be absent from school, and will stay in school longer. Offering free meals to all students also removes the poor kid stigma from school lunch. Detractors from the universal program say that if we learned anything from the social programs that were implemented during the 1960s, it was that throwing money at problems is not always the best answer. Both sides agree that there is serious concern about what young students are eating. It's probably no surprise that the percentage of children who eat one serving or less of fruits and vegetables each day (excluding french fries) is as high as it is. The results are shown in Figure 8–1. One example of a school system "encouraging" a healthier meal program is in Texas where fried chicken will no longer be a lunchtime staple and deep-fat-frying is being eliminated. Instead, all potatoes, including french fries, must be oven baked and no food item can exceed 28 grams of fat. Fruits and vegetables, preferably fresh, must be offered every day for lunch and breakfast. Sodas will not be offered during the school day in middle school. The aim is to provide a healthy environment for children to grow.[3]

The preparation and service of school foodservice meals varies. Some schools have on-site kitchens where the food is prepared and dining rooms where the food is served. Many large school districts operate a central commissary that prepares the meals and then distributes them among the schools in that district. A third option is for schools to purchase ready-to-serve meals that require only assembly at the school.

Schools may decide to participate in the **National School Lunch Program** (NSLP) or operate on their own. In reality, most schools have little choice because participating in the program means that federal funding is provided in the amount of approximately $2.19 per meal per student. Contract companies such as ARAMARK and Sodexho are introducing more flexibility in choices for students.

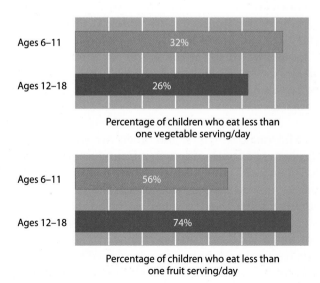

Ages 6–11   32%

Ages 12–18   26%

Percentage of children who eat less than one vegetable serving/day

Ages 6–11   56%

Ages 12–18   74%

Percentage of children who eat less than one fruit serving/day

Figure 8–1 • Numbers of Servings of Fruit and Vegetables That Children Eat.
(*Source:* National Center Institute.)

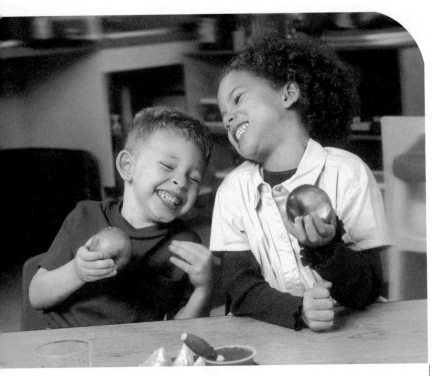

Getting kids to eat proper food is a challenge

Meeting dietary guidelines is also an important issue. Much work has gone into establishing the nutritional requirements for children. It is difficult to achieve a balance between healthy food and costs, taking children's eating habits into account. Under the NSLP regulations, students must eat from what is commonly known as the type A menu. All the items in the type A menu must be offered to all children at every meal. The children have to select a minimum of three of the five meal components for the school to qualify for funding. However, USDA regulations have established limits on the amount of fat and saturated fat that can be offered. Fat should not exceed 30 percent of calories per week, and saturated fat was cut down to 10 percent of calories per week.

The government-funded NSLP, which pays in excess of $7 billion per year for the meals given or sold at a discount to schoolchildren, is a huge potential market for fast-food chains. Chains are extremely eager to penetrate into the elementary and secondary school markets, even if it means a decrease in revenues. "We do reduce the price of our product, and we do make less margin than in our normal operations," says Joy Wallace, national sales director/nontraditional sales for Pizza Hut. However, they believe that it is to their benefit to introduce Pizza Hut to young people very early—in other words, the aim is to build brand loyalty. For example, in Duluth, Minnesota, James Bruner, foodservice director for the city schools, was forced into offering branded pizza in several junior high and high schools. The local principals, hungry for new revenue, began offering Little Caesar's in direct competition to the cafeteria's frozen pizzas.

Taco Bell is in nearly 3,000 schools, Pizza Hut is in 4,500, and Subway is in 650. Domino's, McDonald's, Arby's, and others are well established in the market as well. Despite the positives, although it is not hard to convince the children, chains need to convince the adults. Much debate has arisen as to whether chains should enter the schools. Many parents feel that the school environment should provide a standard example of what sound nutrition should be, and they believe that with fast food as an option, that will not be the case.

At a school lunch challenge at the American Culinary Federation (ACF) conference, chefs from around the country developed nutritious menus geared to wean children away from junk food to healthy foods. An 80-cent limit on the cost of raw ingredients was placed on the eleven finalists. Innovation and taste, as well as healthfulness, were the main criteria used to evaluate the winning entry: turkey taco salad, sausage pizza bagel, and stuffed potatoes.

[Handwritten margin notes:]

- chains want to enter more schools as it will create brand loyalty @ a young age

- parents dispute this as they want to educate children abt sound nutrition

- Nutrition edu progs are now part of school lunch progs

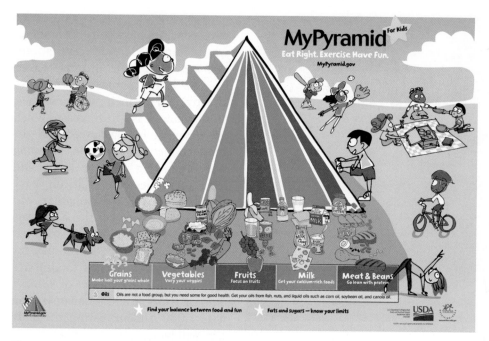

Figure 8–2 • Food Pyramid.
(*Source:* Comstock Almay Images Royalty Free.)

Nutrition Education Programs

Nutrition education programs are now a required part of the nation's school lunch program. As a result of this program, children are learning to improve their eating habits, which, it is hoped, will continue for the rest of their lives. To support the program, nutritional education materials are used to decorate the dining room halls and tables. Perhaps the best example of this is the food pyramid called MyPyramid developed by the Food and Nutrition Service of the U.S. Department of Agriculture. Figure 8–2 shows this food pyramid, which illustrates what to eat each day to follow a healthy diet.

Colleges and Universities

College and university foodservice operations are complex and diverse. Among the various constituents of foodservice management are residence halls, sports concessions, conferences, cafeterias/student unions, faculty clubs, convenience stores, administrative catering, and outside catering.

On-campus dining is a challenge for foodservice managers because, as you well know, the clients live on campus and eat most of their meals at the campus dining facility. If the manager or contractor is not creative, students, staff, and faculty will quickly become bored with the sameness of the surroundings and menu offerings. Most campus dining is cafeteria style, offering cyclical menus that rotate every 10 or 14 days.

College Foodservice

However, a college foodservice manager does have some advantages when compared with a restaurant manager. Budgeting is made easier because the on-campus students have already paid for their meals and their numbers are easy to forecast. When the payment is guaranteed and the guest count is predictable, planning and organizing staffing levels and food quantities are relatively easy and should ensure a reasonable profit margin. For instance, the **daily rate** is the amount of money required per day from each person to pay for the foodservice. Thus, if foodservice expenses for one semester of 98 days amount to $650,000 for an operation with 1,000 students eating, the daily rate will be

$$\frac{\$650,000 \div 98 \text{ days}}{1000 \text{ students}} = \$6.63$$

College foodservice operations now offer a variety of meal plans for students. Under the old board plan, when students paid one fee for all meals each day—whether they ate them or not—the foodservice operator literally made a profit from the students who did not actually eat the meals they had paid for. More typically now, students match their payments to the number of meals eaten: Monday through Friday, breakfast, lunch, dinner; dinner only; and prepaid credit cards that allow a student to use the card at any campus outlet and have the value of the food and beverage items deducted from his or her credit balance.

Leaders of the National Associations of College Auxiliary Services (NACAS), which represents 1,200 member institutes, have noticed that on-campus services and activities are undergoing continuous change. The environment has become a critical part of policy and implementation that transcends parochial interests for those that best meet the needs of the institution and, ultimately, its students.

The driving forces of change on campuses are the advent and growth of branded concepts, privatization, campus cards, and computer use. A college foodservice manager today must have greater skills in retail marketing and merchandizing as students are given more discretion in how they may spend their money for food on campus.

Student Unions

As you know, the college student union offers a variety of managed services that caters to the needs of a diverse student body. Among the services offered are

INTRODUCING MANUEL LORENZO

Sodexho Food Services

Manuel Lorenzo is a supervisor for Sodexho Food Services and arrives at Alliant International University (AIU) to begin his shift at 9:00 A.M. Manuel's first duty is to check the catering board, where he will find a list of scheduled catering events for the day. Manuel then plans the food preparation and starts gathering the necessary equipment.

By 10:00 A.M., Manuel goes around to all the foodservice outlets that are open during the night hours and collects money and receipts. The cash must then be immediately transported to the bank of deposit. The figures must also be entered into the company computer.

After Manuel completes handling the money, he talks with Richard Nargi, the general manager of foodservices at AIU. He keeps him abreast of information for the day. This is the time any problems or concerns can be addressed. At 11:00 A.M., Manuel walks around to make sure the cafeteria is ready to serve lunch. Manuel supervises the lunch operation until it ends at 1:30. After lunch, he continues working on catering functions and makes sure everything flows and is ready for dinner.

Before leaving for the day, Manuel must check to see that all catering vehicles are tanked and running properly. Then the storerooms must be cleaned and organized. The general manager will also have a list of projects for Manuel to complete. These tasks usually consist of maintaining sanitation standards. Last, Manuel checks staffing levels for the rest of the week and deals with basic human resource functions.

Manuel sees time management as one of the major challenges of his career. Events are constantly pending, and he has only a very limited amount of time to plan, organize, and carry out those functions. Manuel contends that the only way to be successful, in this respect, is to be highly organized. Manuel says that success requires one to be a "people-person." This skill helps him deal with employees effectively and helps him understand the people he serves, so that he can serve them better.

Keeping the customer satisfied is an other challenge for Manuel. University foodservice operations have the unique and difficult task of keeping long-term boarding residents happy with food quality. Manuel solves this problem by serving a wide variety of entrees, yet keeping consistent with daily staples.

Each catering event is different because of the variety in food served. With each new function, Manuel learns something about food and/or culture. Mr. Lorenzo admits that this is one of the most interesting, exciting, and rewarding aspects of his job.

cafeteria foodservice, beverage services, branded quick-service restaurants, and take-out foodservice.

The cafeteria foodservice operation is often the "happening" place in the student union where students meet to socialize as well as to eat and drink. The cafeteria is generally open for breakfast, lunch, and dinner. Depending on the volume of business, the cafeteria may be closed during the nonmeal periods and weekends, and the cafeteria menu may or may not be the same as the residence foodservice facility. Offering a menu with a good price value is crucial to the successful operation of a campus cafeteria.

On campuses at which alcoholic beverage service is permitted, beverage services mainly focus on some form of a student pub where beer and perhaps wine and spirits may be offered. Not to be outdone, the faculty will undoubtedly have a lounge that also offers alcoholic beverages. Other beverages may be served at various outlets such as a food court or convenience store. Campus beverage service provides opportunities for foodservice operators to enhance profits.

In addition, many college campuses have welcomed branded, quick-service restaurants as a convenient way to satisfy the needs of a community on the go. Such an approach offers a win-win situation for colleges. The experience and brand recognition of chain restaurants such as Pizza Hut, McDonald's, Subway, and Wendy's attract customers; the restaurants pay a fee, either to the foodservice management company or the university directly. Obviously, there is a danger that the quick-service restaurant may attract customers that the cafeteria might then lose, but competition tends to be good for all concerned.

Take-out foodservice is another convenience for the campus community. At times, students—and staff—do not want to prepare meals and are thankful for the opportunity to take meals with them. And it is not just during examination time that students, friends, and staff have a need for the take-out option. For example, tailgate parties prior to football and basketball games or concerts and other recreational/sporting events allow entrepreneurial foodservice operators to increase revenue and profits. The type of contract that a managed services operator signs varies depending on the size of the account. If the account is small, a fee generally is charged. With larger accounts, operators contract for a set percentage (usually about 5 percent) or a combination of a percentage and a bonus split. Figure 8–3 shows a typical college menu for the dining hall where students usually eat on campus.

As with all types of contract services, there are advantages and disadvantages. Here are both from a client's (that would be your college) perspective:

Advantages	Disadvantages
• Experience in size and types of foodservice operations	
• Use contracted department as a model for rest of institution	Potential for lost contracts, meaning foodservice contracts are generally for a period of five years after which bids are requested for another contract. So, the operator must maintain the service and pricing that please the client (the college/ university).
• Variety of services	
• Resource and support available	
• Hold contractor to a higher level of performance	

Responsibilities in Managed Services

A foodservice manager's responsibilities in a small or midsize operation are frequently more extensive than those of managers of the larger operations. This is because larger units have more people to whom certain functions can be

WEEK 1

	MONDAY	TUESDAY	WEDNESDAY	THURSDAY	FRIDAY
Breakfast - Cold cereal, fruit and yogurt bar, toast, juices, milks, coffee, tea, hot chocolate and fresh fruit					
Bakery:	Quick Coffee Cake	Assorted Danish	Cinnamon Coffee Cake	Sticky Top Roll	Banana Nut Muffins
Hot Cereal:	Oatmeal	Malt-O-Meal	Cream of Wheat	Grits	Oatmeal
Entrees:	Buttermilk Pancakes	Waffles	French Toast	Oatmeal Pancakes	Waffles w/Peaches
	Scrambled Eggs	Scrambled Eggs	Scrambled Eggs	Scrambled Eggs	Scrambled Eggs
	Sausage Gravy	Egg O'Muffin w/Bacon	Ham & Cheese	Chorizo & Eggs	Egg Burrito
	& Biscuits	Hearty Fried Potatoes	Omelette	Cottage Fries	Home Fries
	Cottage Fries	Bacon	Hash Browns	Sausage Links	

Lunch - Salad Bar, Rice & Chili Bar, Cereal, Build-Your-Own-Sandwich Bar & Fresh Fruit					
Soup:	Beef Barley	Italian Minestrone	Chicken Gumbo	Chicken Noodle	New England Clam Chowder
Entrees:	Baked Seafood & Rice	Chicken Tortilla	Fishwich	Cheesy Mushroom	BBQ Ham Sandwich
	Grilled Ham & Cheese	Casserole	Spanish Macaroni	Burger	Ground Beef &
	Potato Salad	Patty Melt	Ranch Beans	Hamburger	Potato Pie
	Wax Beans	French Fries	Italian Green Beans	Grilled Cheese	Whipped Potatoes
	Mixed Vegetables	Hominy	Braised Carrots &	Onion Rings	Italian Green Beans
		Spinach	Celery	Carrots	Beets
				Oriental Veg. Blend	
Dessert:	Chocolate Pudding	Applesauce Cake	Peanut Butter	Coconut Cake	Vanilla Pudding
	Soft Serve Ice Cream	Soft Serve Ice Cream	Cookies		

Dinner - Salad Bar, Cereal, & Fresh Fruit (Tortillas served at Breakfast & Dinner)					
Soup:	Beef Barley	Italian Minestrone	Chicken Gumbo	Chicken Noodle	New England Clam Chowder
Entrees:	Oven Broiled Chicken	Beef Fajitas	Roast Turkey w/Gravy	Egg Roll Over Rice	Pizza! Pizza! Pizza!
	Grilled Liver & Onions	Fried Perch	Old Fashion Beef Stew	Grilled Pork Chop	Curly Fries
	Parsley Potatoes	Spanish Rice	Whipped Potatoes	Rice	Broccoli
	Corn	Asparagus	Corn Cobbettes	Beets	Mixed Vegetables
	Zucchini	Carrots	Brussel Sprouts	Cauliflower au Gratin	
Dessert:	Chocolate Chip	Spicy Whole	Chocolate Mayo	Peach Cobbler	Best Ever Cake
	Cookies	Wheat Bar	Cake		

Figure 8–3 • Sample College Menu.
(Courtesy of Sodexho Foodservice Management.)

CORPORATE PROFILE

ARAMARK

In the 1950s, Davre Davidson and Bill Fishman, both in the vending business, realized that they shared the same dreams and hopes of turning vending into a service and combining it with foodservice. The two entrepreneurs joined forces to become the first truly national vending and foodservice company. Automatic Retailers of America (ARA) was born in 1959. Fishman and Davidson had the management skills, the capital, and the expertise to expand. And this they did! ARAMARK is the world's leading provider of quality managed services. It operates in all 50 states and in 19 foreign countries, offering a very diversified and broad range of services to businesses of all sizes, as well as to thousands of universities; hospitals; and municipal, state, and federal government facilities.

ARAMARK's emphasis on the quality of service management was evident from the very beginning of its operation. ARAMARK entered new markets by researching the best-managed local companies, acquiring them, and persuading key managers to stay with the company.

The company's vision statement in fact, describes ARAMARK as "a company where the best people want to work." Customers recommend ARAMARK to others because the company constantly exceeds expectations. In this case, success is measured in the growth of the company, its earnings, and its employees themselves. This is one fundamental constant in ARAMARK's early success: It grew its business by focusing on growing its management. The company's guiding principles reaffirm such a concept: "Because we succeed through performance, we encourage the entrepreneur in each of us, and work always to improve our service. Because we thrive on growth, we seek new markets and new opportunities, and we innovate to get and keep new customers."

With the 1961 acquisitions of Slater System, Inc., the largest foodservice business in the country, ARAMARK began the diversification process and has continued to amplify the portfolio of services it offers. The focus on management skill at every level, especially the local level, gave ARAMARK an invaluable resource. In fact, with every acquisition, local managers were encouraged and rewarded for becoming multiskilled entrepreneurs. This approach to outsourcing, stated more simply, is the ability of the company to apply the best management skills to all the lines of business the company uses to diversify.

Among ARAMARK operations are the following:

- *Food, leisure, and support services:* The company provides food, specialized refreshments, dietary services, and operations support to businesses, educational facilities, government, and medical institutions. ARAMARK also manages food, lodging, hospitality, and support services at national parks and other recreational facilities that serve the general public.

- *Health and education services:* ARAMARK provides specialized management services for hospitals and medical services. It also specializes in providing early-childhood and school-age education services.
- *Uniform services:* ARAMARK Uniform and Career Apparel is a leading provider of uniform rental and leasing services to more than 200,000 customer accounts in 46 states from more than 200 service locations and distribution centers across the United States.

ARAMARK successfully manages the diversity of segment concepts under the guideline of one single purpose: to be the world leader in managed services. With annual revenues in excess of $12 billion in 2008, the company is among the market leaders in all of its businesses, and it is in an ideal position for further market growth. Joseph Neubauer, chairman and CEO, realizes this: "I am energized by the bright prospects for the journey ahead. . . . I can't wait to get started."

Source: Courtesy of ARAMARK.

delegated, such as human resources. For example, following are some of the responsibilities that the foodservice manager in a small or midsize operation might have in addition to strictly foodservice responsibilities:

Employee Relations

- Team development
- Rewards/recognition
- Drug alcohol abuse/prevention
- Positive work environment
- Coaching/facilitating vs. directing

Human Resource Management

- Recruitment/training/evaluating
- Wage/salary administration
- Benefits administration
- Compliance with federal/state laws/EEO/Senate Bill 198
- Harassment/OSHA
- Disciplinary actions/terminations
- Unemployment/wrongful disclosure

Financial/Budgeting

- Project budgets
- Actual vs. projected budget monitoring (weekly)
- Controlling food cost, labor, expenses, and so on
- Record keeping requirements/audit
- Monitoring accounts payable/receivable
- Billing/collecting
- Compliance with contracts
- Cash procedures/banking

Safety Administration

- Equipment training/orientation
- Controlling workers' compensation
- Monthly inspections/audits (federal/state/OSHA requirements/Senate Bill 198)

Safety Budget

- Work on the expensive injuries
- Reduce lost time frequency rate and injury frequency rate

Food Production/Service

- Menu/recipe development
- Menu mix vs. competition
- Food waste/leftovers utilization
- Production records
- Production control
- Presentation/merchandising

Sanitation/FBI Prevention

- FBI (food-borne illness) prevention
- Sanitation/cleaning schedule
- Proper food handling/storage
- Daily prevention/monitoring
- Monthly inspection
- Health department compliance

Purchasing/Recruiting

- Ordering/receiving/storage
- Food and beverage specifications/quality

- Inventory control
- Vendor relation/problems

Staff Training/Development

- On-the-job vs. structured
- Safety/sanitation/food handling and so on
- Food preparation/presentation
- Guest service

INTRODUCING REGYNALD G. WASHINGTON

Vice President and General Manager for Disney Regional Entertainment and
Vice President of New Business Initiatives for Walt Disney Parks and Resorts

For a student majoring in hotel and restaurant management, being a general manager, president, or even chief executive officer in the food industry is a goal to be achieved. For Regynald G. Washington, not only has it been a goal reached, but a dream realized. His bright smile spells success. As a child growing up in a middle-income family in the town of Marathon in the Florida Keys, working was mandatory. At the early age of thirteen, he was introduced to the food industry. His first job consisted of waiting on and busing tables and doing other chores in the Indies Inn Resort and Yacht Club. He took this on as an exciting and new challenge.

For Regynald, attitude is everything. His positive attitude toward being the best that he can be was derived from a phrase his parents used to repeat to him: "A chip on your shoulder earns a lack of respect from colleagues, friends, and family." His great energy and pride in his work is what makes him stand out among many other leaders in the food industry. He has a quality and people-oriented mind that keeps him focused on any task he wishes to accomplish.

Regynald graduated from Florida International University with a degree in hotel and restaurant administration. He continued to work for Indies Inn Resort, but by this time he was running the food and beverage operation. This was the beginning of the long career road for Regynald G. Washington.

In the years that followed, Regynald worked as a restaurant general manager and at Concessions International, an airport food and beverage, duty free, gifts, and magazine organization in Atlanta. He was promoted to executive vice president in 1990. He then formed Washington Enterprises and developed Sylvia's Restaurant in Atlanta, which turned out to be very successful.

A few years later, though, a major entertainment company executive recruiter offered Washington an opportunity to join the new and creative food and beverage approach that the company was aiming to develop.

Regynald's secret to managing 2,500 employees and satisfying Epcot's customers is simply organization and care. Having organization and direction in your work eliminates stress and makes time for fun. Making sure that all the staff know what they are doing and that they are doing it well and serving guests hot food hot and cold food cold is all it takes. He uses a back-to-basics formula, which requires that everything go well, from making guests happy to proper staffing. Not only has his ambition and energy helped him climb to the top, but he also has great concern for others and wants to help his employees learn new things and move

continued

INTRODUCING REGYNALD G. WASHINGTON *(continued)*

forward in their careers. He is very well focused on quality and precision in anything and everything he does. One of his number one concerns is food safety.

To make sure everything is intact and going well, Regynald and his support team perform unannounced inspections every quarter. A specific food and beverage facility is concentrated on and fully evaluated for its table turns, guest service, food quality, and training programs. Specialists act as the guests and observe and report anything that seems less than perfect. Epcot executive chefs check the kitchen food as well as the menu. In-house sanitarians evaluate the level of sanitation at the facility. The goal of these inspections is to make sure nothing is less than perfect. Excellence is the goal for Regynald. He admires and respects the people who work with him and has ranked them as being the best food and beverage people.

Regynald is a frequent guest lecturer in educational forums and has served on the advisory boards of a number of universities for their hospitality management programs. His board service includes being a trustee of the National Restaurant Association Educational Foundation.

Regynald believes that he has achieved a lot and has had many successes during his career. His career is exciting and motivating and he has the opportunity to make a difference in people's lives every single day. This is what he always wanted and now he has it. He says, "My parents really wanted me to become a lawyer, physician, or architect. They didn't believe you could reach the top and do exciting things in the restaurant industry."

Source: This profile draws on Whit Smyth, "Regynald Washington, EPCOT's Chief of Food and Beverage, Says Pleasing Customers Is No Mickey Mouse," *Nation's Restaurant News* 33, no. 4 (January 25, 1999): 28–30; personal correspondence with Regynald Washington, April 6, 2005.

A number of support staff positions offer career opportunities not only within managed services but also in all facets of hospitality operations and arrangements. They include sales, marketing, controller/audit, financial analysis, human resources, training and development, affirmative action/EEO compliance, safety administration, procurement/distribution, technical services (recipes, menus, product testing), labor relations, and legal aspects.

A sample operating statement is shown in Figure 8–4. It shows a monthly statement for a college foodservice operation.

▶ Check Your Knowledge

1. In your own words, define in-flight foodservice.
2. What are some of the challenges faced by in-flight foodservice operators? What can be done to solve these problems?
3. Name the foodservice operations that constitute managed services.
4. How is each foodservice operation characterized?
5. In small groups, discuss the differences between the foodservice operations; then, share with the class.

DESCRIPTION		%	STUDENT UNION	%	TOTAL	%
SALES						
FOOD REGULAR	$ 951,178				$ 951,178	
FOOD SPECIAL FUNCTIONS	40,000				40,000	
PIZZA HUT EXPRESS			$ 100,000		100,000	
BANQUET & CATERING	200,000				200,000	
CONFERENCE	160,000				160,000	
BEER			80,000		80,000	
SNACK BAR			300,000		30,000	
A LA CARTE CAFE	60,000				60,000	
** TOTAL SALES	$ 1,411,178		$ 480,000	100.0%	$ 1,891,178	100.0%
PRODUCT COST						
BAKED GOODS	$ 9,420		$ 4,700		$ 14,120	
BEVERAGE	10,000		8,000		18,000	
MILK & ICE CREAM	11,982		2,819		14,801	
GROCERIES	131,000		49,420		180,420	
FROZEN FOOD	76,045		37,221		113,266	
MEAT, SEAFOOD, EGGS, & CHEESE	129,017		48,000		177,017	
PRODUCE	65,500		26,000		91,500	
MISCELLANEOUS					0	
COLD DRINK	0		0		0	
** TOTAL PRODUCT COST	$ 432,964		$ 176,160	36.7%	$ 609,124	32.2%
LABOR COST						
WAGES	$ 581,000		$ 154,000		$ 735,000	
LABOR—OTHER EMPLOYEES	101,500		545,000		156,000	
BENEFITS + PAYROLL TAXES	124,794		50,657		175,451	
MANAGEMENT BENEFITS	58,320		6,000		64,320	
WAGE ACCRUALS	0				0	
** TOTAL LABOR COST	$ 865,614		$ 265,157	55.2%	$ 1,130,771	59.8%
FOOD OPERATING COST-CONTROLLABLE						
CLEANING SUPPLIES	$ 24,000		$ 6,000		$ 30,000	
PAPER SUPPLIES	9,000		46,000		55,000	
EQUIPMENT RENTAL					0	
GUEST SUPPLIES					7,000	
PROMOTIONS	4,500		2,500		40,000	
SMALL EQUIPMENT	35,000		5,000		0	
BUSINESS DUES & MEMBERSHIP					3,000	
VEHICLE EXPENSE	3,000				4,300	
TELEPHONE	3,600		700		$ 22,000	
	$ 17,000		$ 5,000			

Figure 8–4 • An Operating Statement.

(continued)

Health Care Facilities

Health care managed services operations are remarkably complex because of the necessity of meeting the diverse needs of a delicate clientele. Health care managed services are provided to hospital patients, long-term care and assisted living residents, visitors, and employees. The service is given by tray, cafeteria, dining room, coffee shop, catering, and vending.

The challenge of health care managed services is to provide many special meal components to patients with very specific dietary requirements. Determining which meals need to go to which patients and ensuring that they reach their destinations

DESCRIPTION		%	STUDENT UNION	%	TOTAL	%
LAUNDRY & UNIFORMS					0	
MAINTENANCE & REPAIRS	$ 1,200		$ 200		$ 1,400	
FLOWERS	10,000		4,000		140,000	
TRAINING					0	
SPECIAL SERVICES	18,000		3,000		21,000	
MISCELLANEOUS						
** TOTAL CONTROLLABLE SUPPLIES	$ 125,300	8.9%	$ 72,400	15.1%	$ 197,700	10.5%
OPERATING COSTS-NONCONTROLLABLE						
AMORTIZATION & DEPRECIATION	$ 13,500		$ 7,000		$ 20,500	
INSURANCE	55,717		14,768		70,485	
MISCELLANEOUS EXPENSE	12,400		4,100		16,500	
ASSET RETIREMENTS					0	
RENT/COMMISSIONS	48,000		40,000		88,000	
PIZZA HUT ROYALTIES			7,000		7,000	
PIZZA HUT —						
LICENSING MARKETING			7,000		7,000	
TAXES, LICENSE & FEES	5,000		500		5,500	
VEHICLE —						
DEPRECIATION & EXPENSE	4,000				4,000	
ADMINISTRATION & SUPERVISION						
** TOTAL NONCONTROLLABLE COST	$ 138,617	9.8%	$ 80,368	16.7%	$ 218,985	11.6%
** TOTAL COST OF OPERATIONS	$ 1,562,495	110.7%	$ 594,085	123.8%	$2,156,580	114.0%
EXCESS OR (DEFICIT)	(151,317)	(10.7%)	(114,085)	(23.8)	(265,402)	(14.0%)
PARTICIPATION-CONTRACTOR *** NET EXCESS OR (DEFICIT)						
STATISTICS						
CUSTOMER COUNT						
HOURS WORKED						
AVERAGE FOOD-SALES/CUSTOMER						

Figure 8–4 • An Operating Statement. (*continued*)

involve especially challenging logistics. In addition to the patients, health care employees need to enjoy a nutritious meal in pleasant surroundings in a limited time (usually thirty minutes). Because employees typically work five days in a row, managers must be creative in the development of menus and meal themes.

The main focus of hospital foodservice is the **tray line.** Once all the requirements for special meals have been prepared by a registered dietitian, the line is set up and menus color coded for the various diets. The line begins with the tray, a mat, cutlery, napkin, salt and pepper, and perhaps a flower. As the tray moves along the line, various menu items are added according to the color code for the particular patient's diet. Naturally, each tray is double- and triple-checked, first at the end of the tray line and then on the hospital floor. The line generally goes floor by floor at a rate of about five trays a minute; at this rate, a large hospital with 600 beds can be served within a couple of hours. This is time consuming for the employees because three meals a day represent up to six hours of line time. Clearly, health care foodservice is very labor intensive, with labor accounting for about 55 to 66 percent of operating dollars. In an effort to keep costs down, many operators have increased the number of help-yourself food stations, buffets, salads, desserts, and topping bars. They also focus on increasing revenues through catering and retail innovations. Operators must also contend with the fact that food costs are not totally covered by Medicare.

Hospital foodservice has evolved to the point where the need for new revenue sources has changed the traditional patient and nonpatient meal-service ratios at many institutions. This situation was imposed by the federal government when it narrowed the treatment-reimbursement criteria; originally 66 percent of a typical acute-care facility's foodservice budget went toward patients' meals, with the remainder allocated for feeding the employees and visitors. In the past few years, as cash sales have become more important, the 66/33 percent ratio has reversed.

Experts agree that because economic pressures will increase, foodservice managers will need to use a more high-tech approach, incorporating labor-saving sous-vide and cook–chill methods. This segment of the industry, which currently is dominated by self-operated managed services, will continue to see contract specialists, such as Sodexho, Compass, and ARAMARK Services, increase their market share at the expense of self-operated health care managed services. One reason for this is that the larger contract companies have the economy of scale and a more sophisticated approach to quantity purchasing, menu management, and operating systems that help to reduce food and labor costs. A skilled independent foodservice operator has the advantage of being able to introduce changes immediately without having to support layers of regional and corporate employees.

Another trend in health care managed services is the arrival of the major quick-service chains. McDonald's, Pizza Hut Express, Burger King, and Dunkin' Donuts are just a few of the large companies that have joined forces with the contract managed services operators. Using branded quick-service leaders is a win-win situation for both the contract foodservice operator and the quick-service chain.

The chains benefit from long-term leases at very attractive rates compared with a restaurant site. Chains assess the staff size and patient and visitor count to determine the size of unit to install. Thus far, they have found that weekday lunches and dinners are good, but the numbers on weekends are disappointing.

In contrast, several hospitals are entering the pizza-delivery business: They hook up phone and fax ordering

The All-Important Tray Line in Health Care Foodservice

A Business and Industry Account of Sodexho

lines, and they hire part-time employees to deliver pizzas made on the premises. This ties in with the increasing emphasis on customer service. Patients' meals now feature "comfort foods," based on the concept that the simpler the food is, the better—hence, the resurgence of meat loaf, pot pies, meat and potatoes, and tuna salad, which contributes to customer satisfaction and makes patients feel at home and comfortable.

Some hospitals have adopted a "room service menu" concept for patients whose diets are not restricted. Here patients are often contacted before they arrive at the hospital so that the foodservice professionals may find out the likes and requests of future patients.

Business and Industry

Business and industry (B&I) managed services is one of the most dynamic segments of the managed services industry. In recent years, B&I foodservice has improved its image by becoming more colorful, with menus as interesting as commercial restaurants.

There are important terms to understand in B&I foodservice:

1. *Contractors.* **Contractors** are companies that operate foodservice for the client on a contractual basis. Most corporations contract with managed services companies because they are in manufacturing or some other service industry. Therefore, they engage professional managed services corporations to run their employee dining facilities.

2. *Self-operators.* **Self-operators** are companies that operate their own foodservice operations. In some cases, this is done because it is easier to control one's own operation; for example, it is easier to make changes to comply with special nutritional or other dietary requests.

3. *Liaison personnel.* **Liaison personnel** are responsible for translating corporate philosophy to the contractor and for overseeing the contractor to make certain that he or she abides by the terms of the contract.[4]

Contractors have approximately 80 percent of the B&I market. The remaining 20 percent is self-operated, but the trend is for more foodservice operations to be contracted out. The size of the B&I sector is approximately 30,000 units. To adapt to corporate downsizing and relocations, the B&I segment has offered foodservice in smaller units, rather than huge full-sized cafeterias. Another trend is the necessity for B&I foodservice to break even or, in some cases, make a profit. An interesting twist is the emergence of multitenant buildings, the occupants of which may all use a central facility. However, in today's turbulent business environment, there is a high vacancy rate in commercial office space. This translates into fewer guests for B&I operators in multitenant office buildings.

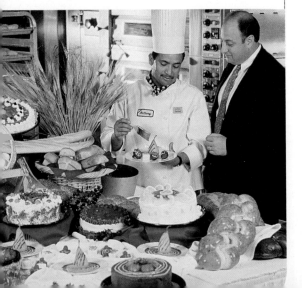

An ARAMARK Business and Industry Foodservice Account

As a result, some office buildings have leased space to commercial branded restaurants.

B&I managed services operators have responded to requests from corporate employees to offer more than the standard fast-food items of pizza and hamburgers; they want healthier food options offered, such as make-your-own sandwiches, salad bars, fresh fruit stations, and ethnic foods.

Most B&I managed services operators offer a number of types of service. The type of service is determined by the resources available: money, space, time, and expertise. Usually these resources are quite limited, which means that most operations use some form of cafeteria service.

B&I foodservice may be characterized in the following ways:

1. Full-service cafeteria with *straight line, scatter,* or *mobile systems*
2. *Limited-service cafeterias* offering parts of the full-service cafeteria, fast-food service, cart and mobile service, fewer dining rooms, and executive dining rooms

FOCUS ON MANAGED SERVICES

Mega-Event Management: The Olympics—Going for the Gold

Fred J. DeMicco, *Professor and ARAMARK Chair of Hotel, Restaurant and Institutional Management, University of Delaware, and Penn State Walter J. Conti Professor of HRIM*

ARAMARK is a world leader in providing global managed services, including food, facility, and other support services. ARAMARK has leadership positions serving the business, education, health care, sports, entertainment, and recreation management segments. Related to sports, entertainment, and food service is "serving the world" at the Olympics.

ARAMARK has a long and rich history with the Olympic Games, dating back to 1968 when it served at the Mexico City Summer Games, the largest in history at the time. Since then, the company has managed services at more Olympic Games than any other company, earning its own "gold medal" performance at both the summer and winter games over the past four decades, including the 1976 Summer Olympic Games in Montreal, Canada; the 1980 Winter Olympic Games in Lake Placid, New York; the 1984 Winter Olympic Games in Sarajevo, Yugoslavia; the 1984 Summer Olympic Games in Los Angeles, California; the 1988 Winter Olympic Games in Calgary, Canada; the 1988 Summer Olympic Games in Seoul, South Korea; the 1992 Summer Olympic Games in Barcelona, Spain; the 1994 Winter Olympic Games in Lillehammer, Norway; the 1996 Centennial Olympic Games in Atlanta, Georgia; the 1998 Winter Olympic Games in Nagano, Japan; the Summer Olympic Games in Sydney, Australia, in 2000; and the Summer Olympic Games in Athens, Greece.

ARAMARK chefs and nutritionists develop a World Menu with more than 550 recipes designed to meet the needs of athletes from 200 different countries, with different ethnic and religious backgrounds and varying nutritional needs, to help them achieve their best during their Olympic performances.

continued

FOCUS ON MANAGED SERVICES *(continued)*

For the third time, Mr. DeMicco is taking students to the Olympic Village to work for ARAMARK. In 1996, his students worked the summer games in Atlanta, and they traveled to Sydney to work in the 2000 summer games.

With 1,500 different menu items available, twenty-four hours a day, the students will have their work cut out for them. Some of the stranger dishes that appeared on athletes' plates during the 2000 Sydney Olympics included kangaroo prosciutto, smoked emu, grilled mako shark, and goat vindaloo.

"The exposure to this type of event provides more learning than any other foodservice venture," Jerome Bill, of ARAMARK, says. "Usually a small city is built, operated for approximately thirty-three days, and then is taken down just as fast. The logistics are tremendous."

ARAMARK recruits and trains more than 6,500 persons to prepare and serve more than 5 million meals during the thirty-three days the Olympics and Para-Olympics take place. The grocery list for such an event is enormous. In Atlanta in 1996, some of the major ingredients that ARAMARK used included 576,000 eggs, 34,000 pounds of rice, 32,800 pounds of margarine, and 9,057 pounds of shredded cheddar cheese.

"Where else can you welcome 15,000 of the best in the world into your home for dinner? It is truly the ultimate display of blending one's background, classroom experience, and human nature into an unforgettable learning environment. Students learn more than just serving and cooking; they reach the brink of fully understanding the true meaning of hospitality," said Marc Bruno, MBA ARAMARK.

The students were able to interact with elite athletes in the world in a fast-paced and constantly changing environment. They were able to be part of providing foodservice that met the unique cultural and nutritional needs of athletes from more than 200 countries. They went in every day knowing that their jobs were critical to each athlete's peak performance.

According to a student participant, "The Olympics allowed me to get an inside view of how a mega event was run, the problems that came up, and how they were overcome. Being in the Olympic Village introduced me to working with people of many different cultures. I am currently working for NBC Olympics in the Games Services department. I am really looking forward to being part of another Olympic Games."

▶ Check Your Knowledge

1. What roles other than those strictly related to foodservice does the foodservice manager perform?

2. Briefly explain some of the tasks the foodservice manager performs. What makes each task so important?

Managed Services Other Than Food

Many companies such as Sodexho have recognized the potential to increase their market opportunities by developing service capabilities beyond food. This also offers hospitality managers the opportunity to expand their career paths as well. Typically, hospitals, colleges, schools, and businesses outsource other service departments the same as they do food. Companies on the cutting edge are able to offer clients broader packages of services. These services often come under the area of facilities management[5] and offer the following services:

- Housekeeping/custodial/environment services
- Maintenance and engineering
- Grounds and landscaping
- Procurement and materials management
- Office and mail services
- Concierge services
- Patient transportation services (hospitals)

Many colleges and universities recognize that this is an area for career opportunities and are developing courses and programs surrounding the area of facilities management. Managers who work in the managed services segment of the industry have the advantage of learning about several disciplines. In doing so, they increase their career growth potential and can find career paths similar to those available in the lodging segment of the industry.

Leisure and Recreation

The leisure and recreation[6] segment of managed services may be the most unique and the most fun part of the foodservice industry in which to work.

Leisure and recreation foodservice operations include stadiums, arenas, theme parks, national parks, state parks, zoos, aquariums, and other venues where food and beverage are provided for large numbers of people. The customers are usually in a hurry, so the big challenge of the foodservice segment is to offer the product in a very short period of time. The average professional sporting event lasts for only two to three hours of time.

What makes this segment unique and fun is the opportunity to be part of a professional sporting event, a rock concert, a circus, or other event in a stadium or arena. There is also the choice of working in a national or state park and being part of the great outdoors. The roar of the crowd and the excitement of the event make this a very stimulating place to work. Imagine *getting paid* to see the Super Bowl versus *paying* to see the Super Bowl.

Stadium Points of Service

Leisure and recreation facilities usually have several points of service where food and beverage are provided. In the typical stadium, a vendor yells, "Here, get your hot dog here!" to the fans in the stands, while on the concourse other fans get their food and beverage from concession stands. These stands offer everything from branded—meaning well-known brands—foods to hot dogs hamburgers to local cuisine. For example, in Philadelphia the cheesesteak sandwich is popular, whereas in Baltimore crabcake sandwiches are favored by fans. Another place for people to get food is in a restaurant, which most stadiums have as a special area. In some cases, fans must be members of the restaurant; in other cases, fans can buy special tickets that provide them with access to this facility. These restaurants are like any other except that they provide unobstructed views of the playing area.

The other major point of service is the food and beverage offered in the premium seating areas known as superboxes, suites, and skyboxes. These premium seating areas are usually leased by corporations to entertain corporate guests and customers. In each of these areas, branded and gour metfood and beverage service is provided for the guests. These facilities are capable of holding thirty to forty guests and usually have an area where the food is set up buffet style and a seating area where the guests can see the sporting or other event. In a large, outdoor stadium, there could be as many as sixty or seventy of these superbox-type facilities.

In summary, a large stadium or arena could have vendors in the stands, concession outlets, restaurants, and superboxes all going at once and serving upward of 60,000 to 70,000 fans. Feeding all these people takes tremendous planning and organization on the part of the foodservice department. The companies that have many of the contracts for stadiums and arenas are ARAMARK, Fine Host, Sodexho, Compass Group, and Delaware North.

Other Facilities

Besides stadiums and arenas, food and beverage service is provided in several other types of facilities by the same major managed service companies that service stadiums. Most of the U.S. national parks are contracted to these companies. These parks have hotels, restaurants, snack bars, gift shops, and a myriad of other service outlets where tourists can spend their money. In addition to parks, other venues where food and beverage are offered include zoos, aquariums, tennis tournaments such as the U.S. Open in New York, and professional golf tournaments. All these events involve big numbers of people. For example, a professional golf event, which lasts a week including practice time, will have upward of 25,000 spectators per day watching the pros play. Tournament events are similar to stadium and arena foodservice operations because they also include concession stands, food and beverage areas for the fans, and "corporate tents" for special catering and company guests.

Advantages and Disadvantages

A foodservice career in this segment has several advantages, which include the unique opportunity to see professional and amateur sporting events to your heart's delight, to hear the roar of the crowd, to be in rural, scenic areas and enjoy the great outdoors, to provide a diverse set of services for the guests or fans, and to have a set work schedule.

The disadvantages of this segment include very large crowds of people to serve in a short time; a work schedule of weekends, holidays, nights; the chance to give only impersonal service; less opportunity to be creative with food; seasonal employment; and an on-season/off-season work schedule.

Leisure and recreation foodservice is a very exciting, unique part of the hospitality industry that offers employees very different opportunities from standard hotel and restaurant jobs. With the current trend toward building new stadiums and arenas around the country, this segment offers many new career openings.

Trends in Managed Services

- College and university foodservice managers face increasing challenges. *Restaurants and Institutions* magazine asked several managers to identify some of those challenges. In general, managers mentioned trying to balance rising costs with tighter dollars. Bill Rigan, foodservice center manager at Oklahoma State University, Stillwater, points out two main challenges: the reduction of revenues from board-plan sales in addition to increased costs such as food and utilities. He dealt with these challenges by recognizing that he could not change the utilities or hourly rates for employees, he would have to maximize purchasing potential. He also made optimal usage of "from scratch" cooking, convenience foods, and more efficient labor scheduling.

- Martha Willis, foodservice director at Tennessee Technological University, Cookesville, sees declining enrollment and a reduction in state funding as challenges. This translates to a cutback in services and more pressure to produce a bigger bottom line. Martha intends to achieve this by filling vacant full-time positions with part-time and student employees. The savings made by not paying full-time employee benefits can amount to 30 percent of a person's wage.

- Increased use of campus cards (declining balance or debit cards).

- Increased use of food-to-go—for instance, before sporting events.

- Increased use of foodservice carts at vantage points to provide service to students who may not be able to reach the main buildings in time for refreshments before the next class.

- Dueling demands for foodservice managers—From students who want more freshly prepared foods in convenient locations and from administrators who want more revenue from existing sources.

- Twenty-four-hour foodservice for those clients who need round-the-clock service.

- Increased business in health care and nursing homes. As the population ages, there is an increased need to provide services for this important and growing segment.

- Proliferation of branded concepts in all segments of managed services, including military, school and college, business and industry, health care, and airport.

- Development of home meal replacement options in each segment of the managed services sector, as a way to increase revenue.
- Increasing use of fresh product. People are more health conscious and want healthy produce.

CASE STUDY

Gas Leak

The kitchen at a major corporation's managed service business account includes several gas and electric stoves, ovens, broilers, steamers, grills, and other appliances. On average, the kitchen serves 500 lunches. At 10:15 A.M., on a Tuesday in December, a gas leak prompts the gas company to cut off the gas supply.

Discussion Question

1. What can be done to offer the best possible lunch food and service?

CASE STUDY

Chaos in the Kitchen

Jane is the foodservice director at an on-campus dining service that feeds 800 students per meal for breakfast, lunch, and dinner. Jane arrives at her office at 7:00 A.M. (half an hour before breakfast begins) only to find many problems.

After listening to her phone messages, she finds that her breakfast cashier and one of her two breakfast dishroom employees have called in sick. The cashier position is essential, and the second dishroom person is necessary at 8:15 A.M. when the students leave to go to their 8:30 A.M. classes.

Then, the executive chef tells Jane that one of their two walk-in refrigerators is not working properly, so some of the food is above the safe temperature of 40°F.

The lead salad person later comes to her, saying that one of the three ice machines is not working. Hence, there will not be enough ice to ice down the salad bars and to use for cold beverages at lunch.

Last, the catering supervisor tells Jane that he has just found out that there was a misunderstanding with the bakery that supplies their upscale desserts. The desserts were requested by the president of the university for a luncheon he is having that day; however, because the employee at the bakery wrote the wrong delivery date, the desserts would not be delivered. This will cause the president to be angry.

Discussion Questions

1. How should Jane handle being short a cashier and a dishroom person at breakfast?
2. What should Jane do with the food in the defective refrigerator? Should the food that is measured to be above 40°F be saved?
3. What are Jane's options concerning the ice shortage?
4. How should Jane handle the president's function, knowing that the requested desserts have not been delivered?
5. If the special dessert cannot be purchased in time, how should the catering supervisor approach this situation when speaking with the president's office?
6. What can be done to ensure that mistakes, such as the one made by the bakery employee, do not happen again?

Summary

1. Managed services operations include segments such as airlines, military, schools and colleges, health care facilities, and businesses.
2. Food has become scarce on short and median domestic flights. Most airlines have food prepared by a contractor, such as Dobbs International or Sky Chefs.
3. Service to the military includes feeding troops and officers in clubs, dining halls, and hospitals as well as out in the field. Direct vendor delivery, menu management, prepared foods, and fast-food chains located on the base have met new trends in military foodservice.
4. Schools are either equipped with on-site kitchens and dining rooms or receive food from a central commissary. They try to balance salability with good nutrition. Today, nutrition education is a required subject in school.
5. College and university managed services operations include residence halls, cafeterias,

student unions, faculty clubs, convenience stores, and catering.
6. The responsibilities of a foodservice manager are very complex. He or she is in charge of employee relations, human resource management, budgeting, safety administration, sanitation, and inventory.
7. Health care managed services operations need to provide numerous special meals to patients with very specific dietary requirements and nutritious meals in a limited time period for employees. The main areas of concern for health care managed services operations are tray lines and help-yourself food stations.
8. Business and industry managed services operations either operate with a full-service cafeteria or limited-service cafeteria. The type of service is determined by money, space, and time available.
9. Leisure and recreation foodservice offers yet more career opportunities. It is often available at several points of service.

Key Words and Concepts

batch cooking
commercial foodservice
contractors
daily rate
liaison personnel

managed services
National School Lunch Program (NSLP)
nutrition education programs
self-operators
tray line

Review Questions

1. From the Companion Website, what qualities does Adena Osika look for in graduates of hospitality programs?
2. What are managed services operations?
3. List and explain features that distinguish managed services operations from commercial ones.
4. Describe the issues that schools are currently facing concerning school food service.
5. Explain the term *National School Lunch Program* (NSLP).
6. Identify recent trends in college foodservice management.
7. What are the pros and cons concerning fast-food chains on campus?
8. Briefly explain the complex challenges for health care managed services operations.

Internet Exercises

1. Organization: **ARAMARK**
   Web site: www.aramark.com
   Summary: ARAMARK is "a global leader in managed services" according to its web site. ARAMARK is an outsourcing company that provides services ranging from everyday catering to corporate apparel.
   (a) Click the "Careers" link. Who is ARAMARK's star of the month? What is his or her position and responsibilities?
   (b) What are some of the characteristics that make a star of the month?

2. Organization: **Sodexho**
   Web site: www.sodexhousa.com
   Summary: Sodexho offers a full range of outsourcing solutions and is a leading food and facilities management services company in North America.
   (a) What corporate services does Sodexho offer?
   (b) Look at the current opportunities (at Sodexho or ARAMARK) within your area.

Apply Your Knowledge

1. From the sample operating statement (Figure 8–4), calculate the labor cost percentage by taking total labor cost and dividing by total sales × 100. Remember the formula:

$$\frac{\text{Cost}}{\text{Sales}} \times 100$$

2. Consider a retail operation at a local college where a grilled chicken combo, which consists of a grilled chicken breast, fries, and a 20-oz. soda, is on the menu. Find out the cost of the ingredients and write out everything needed for the combo, including its service. What is your cost price? How much would you charge customers for the item to make a reasonable profit?

Suggested Activity

Create a sample menu for a day at an elementary or high school. Then, compare your items to the food guide pyramid and the recommended daily servings. How does your menu measure up?

Endnotes

1. Personal conversation with Susan Pillmeier, ARAMARK, and John Lee, Sodexho, July 28, 2005.
2. United States Department of Agriculture Food and Nutrition Service, "Programs and Services," www.fns.usda.gov/fns/services.htm.
3. Sahra Bahari, "Students Can Expect Healthier Selection," *Fort Worth Star-Telegram*, August 12, 2007.
4. Personal correspondence with John Lee, director of college and external relations, Sodexho, September 13, 2005.
5. Personal correspondence with John Lee, September 13, 2005.
6. Courtesy of David Tucker.

CHAPTER 9

Beverages

OBJECTIVES

After reading and studying this chapter, you should be able to:

- List and describe the main grape varieties.

- Suggest appropriate pairings of wine with food.

- Identify the various types of beer.

- List the types of spirits and their main ingredients.

- Explain a restaurant's liability in terms of serving alcoholic beverages.

This chapter offers an overview of alcoholic and nonalcoholic beverages in the hospitality industry. Be sure that you realize the utmost importance of responsible beverage consumption and service. Arrange for a designated driver if you intend to have a drink. If you do drink alcoholic beverages, then stay with the same drink—don't mix them (two different types are grape and grain—that is, wine and spirits). That's when trouble really begins and hangovers are bad. Remember that moderation is the key to enjoying beverages, whether at a get-together with friends at a local restaurant or on a getaway for spring break. Examine the tragic alcohol-related auto and other accidents that too many people are involved in each year. Enjoy, but do not overindulge.

Serving beverages is traditional throughout the world. According to his or her culture, a person might welcome a visitor with coffee or tea—or bourbon. Beverages are generally categorized into two main groups: alcoholic and nonalcoholic. **Alcoholic beverages** *are further categorized as wines, beer, and spirits. Figure 9–1 shows these three categories.*

Wines

Wine is the fermented juice of freshly gathered ripe grapes. Wine may also be made from other sugar-containing fruits, such as blackberries, cherries, or elderberries. In this chapter, however, we will confine our discussion to grape wines. Wine may be classified first by color: red, white, or rose. Wines are further classified as light beverage wines, still wines, sparkling wines, fortified wines, and aromatic wines.

Light Beverage Wines

White, red, or rose table wines are "still" light beverage wines; such still table wines may come from a variety of growing regions around the world. In the United States,

Wine	Beer	Spirits
Still	Top fermenting	Grapes/fruit
Natural	Lager	Grains
Fortified	Bottom fermenting	Cactus
Aromatic	Ale	Sugar cane/molasses
Sparkling	Stout	
	Lager	
	Pilsner	
	Porter	

Figure 9–1 • Alcoholic Beverages.

the premium wines are named after the grape variety, such as chardonnay and cabernet sauvignon. This proved so successful that Europeans are now also naming their wines after the grape variety and their region of origin, such as Pouilly Fuisse and Chablis.

Sparkling Wines

Champagne, sparkling white wine, and sparkling rose wine are called the **sparkling wines**. Sparkling wines sparkle because they contain carbon dioxide. The carbon dioxide may be either naturally produced or mechanically infused into the wine. The best-known sparkling wine is champagne, which has become synonymous with celebrations and happiness.

Champagne became the drink of fashion in France and England in the seventeenth century. Originating in the Champagne region of France, the wine owed its unique sparkling quality to a second fermentation—originally unintentional—in the bottle itself. This process became known as *methode champenoise.*

The Benedictine monk, Dom Perignon (1638–1715), was the cellar master for the Abbaye Hautvilliers and an exceptional wine connoisseur. He was the first to experiment with blending different wines to achieve the

Bottles of champagne. Remember not to point the cork at anyone when opening the bottle; point it at the ceiling. In fact, a napkin should be placed over the cork, which is then held there and the bottle is gently twisted open. Champagne is served chilled in fluted glasses, which help keep the bouquet and effervescence longer

so-called *cuvee* (the basis of champagne production). He also revolutionized wine by retaining the resulting carbon dioxide in the bottles. Dom Perignon's methods were refined throughout the centuries and led to the modern method used in champagne production.

Champagne may, by law, only come from the Champagne region of France. Sparkling wines from other countries have *methode champenoise* written on their labels to designate that a similar method was used to make that particular sparkling wine.

Figure 9–2 explains how to handle and serve champagne.

▶ Check Your Knowledge

1. Why is champagne served in fluted glasses?
2. How are alcoholic beverages categorized?
3. Why should you avoid mixing grape (wine) and grain (spirits) drinks?
4. Where should you point the cork of a champagne bottle when opening it?

[handwritten margin notes:]
↳called sparkling due to CO₂
↳became drink of fashion in Fr & Eng.
↳methode champenoise: natural sparkles

Champagne should be stored horizontally at a temperature between fifty and fifty-five degrees Fahrenheit. However, it should be served at a temperature between forty-three and forty-seven degrees Fahrenheit. This is best achieved by placing the bottle in an ice bucket.

When serving champagne, there are some recommended steps to take to achieve the best results, as listed below.

1. If the bottle is presented in a champagne cooler, it should be placed upright in the cooler, with fine ice tightly packed around the bottle.
2. The bottle should be wrapped in a cloth napkin. Remove the foil or metal capsule to a point just below the wire, which holds the cork securely.
3. Hold the bottle firmly in one hand at a forty-five degree angle. Unwind and remove the wiring. With a clean napkin, wipe the neck of the bottle and around the cork.
4. With the other hand, grasp the cork so that it will not fly out. Twist the bottle and ease the cork out.
5. When the cork is out, retain the bottle at an angle for about five seconds. The gas will rush out and carry with it some of the champagne if the bottle is held upright.
6. Champagne should be served in two motions: pour until the froth almost reaches the brim of the glass. Stop and wait for the foam to subside. Then finish filling the glass to about three-quarters full.

Figure 9–2 ● Handling and Serving Champagne.

Fortified Wines

Sherries, ports, madeira, and marsala are **fortified wines**, meaning that they have had brandy or wine alcohol added to them. The brandy or wine alcohol imparts a unique taste and increases the alcohol content to about 20 percent. Most fortified wines are sweeter than regular wines. Each of the groups of fortified wines has several subgroups with myriad tastes and aromas.

Aromatic Wines

Aromatized wines are fortified and flavored with herbs, roots, flowers, and barks. These wines may be sweet or dry. Aromatic wines are also known as aperitifs, which generally are consumed before meals as digestive stimulants. Among the better-known brands of aperitif wines are Dubonnet Red (sweet), Dubonnet White (dry), vermouth red (sweet), vermouth white (dry), Byrrh (sweet), Lillet (sweet), Punt e Mes (dry), St. Raphael Red (sweet), and St. Raphael White (dry).

Sherry can be dry (fino), medium, or sweet. Pictured here are bottles of dry sherry with a glass. The lighter the color, the dryer the sherry

The History of Wine

Wine has been produced for centuries. The ancient Egyptians and Babylonians recorded using the fermentation process. The very first records about wine making date back about 7,000 years. The Greeks received the vine from the Egyptians, and later the Romans contributed to the popularization of wine in Europe by planting vines in the territories they conquered.

The wine produced during these times was not the cabernet or chardonnay of today. The wines of yesteryear were drunk when they were young and likely to be highly acidic and crude. To help offset these deficiencies, people added different spices and honey, which made the wine at least palatable. To this day, some Greek and German wines have flavoring added.

Handwritten note at top of page: Fing: filtering to stabilize + removing solids. Clarified: add egg white/bentonite

The making of good wine is dependent on the quality of the grape variety, type of soil, climate, preparation of vineyards, and method of wine making. Thousands of grape varieties exist, thriving in a variety of soil and climatic conditions. Different plants thrive on clay, chalky, gravelly, or sandy soil. The most important wine-making grape variety is the *Vitis vinifera*, which yields cabernet sauvignon, gamay, pinot noir, pinot chardonnay, and riesling.

Handwritten note: most imp varietal: Vitis Vinifera – cab sauv, gamay, pinot noir, pinot chard.

Making Wine

Port wines are generally red, fortified, and sweet. Vintage port is the most prized by port lovers. Port is typically served with cheese and biscuits at the end of a meal

Wine is made in six steps: crushing, fermenting, racking, maturing, filtering, and bottling. Grapes are harvested in the autumn, after they have been scientifically tested for maturity, acidity, and sugar concentration. The freshly harvested grapes are taken to pressing houses where the grapes are destemmed and crushed. The juice that is extracted from the grapes is called **must**.

Handwritten note: 1) Crushing 2) Fermenting 3) Racking 4) Maturing 5) Filtering 6) Bottling

The second step of the process is **fermentation** of the must, a natural phenomenon caused by yeasts on the skin of the grapes. Additional yeasts also are added either environmentally or by formula. When exposed to air in the proper environment, the yeast multiplies. Yeast converts the sugar in the grapes to ethyl alcohol, until little or no sugar remains in the wine. The degree of sweetness or dryness in the wine can be controlled at the end of the fermentation process by adding alcohol, removing the yeast by filtration, or adding sulphur dioxide.

Red wine gains its color during the fermentation process from the coloring pigments of the red grape skins, which are put back into the must.

White grapes make white wines, and the main white grapes are chardonnay, sauvignon blanc, riesling, pinot blanc, and gewürztraminer

After fermentation has ceased, the wine is transferred to racking containers, where it settles before being poured into oak barrels or large stainless steel containers for the maturing process. Some of the better wines are aged in oak barrels, from which they acquire additional flavor and character during the barrel aging. Throughout the aging process, red wine extracts tannin from the wood, which gives longevity to the wine. Some white wine and most red wine is barrel-aged for periods ranging from months to more than two years. Other white wines that are kept in stainless steel containers are crisp, with a youthful flavor; they are bottled after a few months for immediate consumption.

After maturing, the wine is filtered to help stabilize it and remove any solid particles still in the wine. This process is called **fining**. The wine is then **clarified** by adding either egg white or bentonite, which sinks to the bottom of the vat. The wine then is bottled.

Fine **vintage** wines are best drunk at their peak, which may be a few years—or decades—away. Red wines generally take a few more years to reach their peak than do white wines. In Europe, where the climate is more variable, the good years are rated as vintage. The judgment of experts determines the relative merits of each wine-growing district and awards merit points on a scale of 1 to 10.

Matching Wine with Food

The combination of food and wine is one of life's great pleasures. We eat every day, so a gourmet will seek out not only exotic foods and vintage wines, but also simple food that is well prepared and accompanied by an unpretentious, but quality wine.

Over the years, traditions have developed a how-to approach to the marrying of wines and food. Generally, the following traditions apply:

- White wine is best served with white meat (chicken, pork, or veal), shellfish, and fish.
- Red wine is best served with red meat (beef, lamb, duck, or game).
- The heavier the food, the heavier and more robust the wine should be.
- Champagne can be served throughout the meal.
- Port and red wine go well with cheese.
- Dessert wines best complement desserts and fresh fruits that are not highly acidic.
- When a dish is cooked with wine, it is best served with that wine.
- Regional food is best complemented by wines of the region.
- Wines should never accompany salads with vinegar dressings, or curries; the tastes will clash or be overpowering.
- Sweet wines should be served with foods that are not too sweet.

Figure 9–3 matches some of the better-known varietal wines with food.

Food and wine are described by texture and flavor. Textures are the qualities in food and wine that we feel in the mouth, such as softness, smoothness, roundness, richness, thickness, thinness, creaminess, chewiness, oiliness, harshness, silkiness, coarseness, and so on. Textures correspond to sensations of touch and temperature, which can be easy to identify—for example, hot, cold, rough, smooth, thick, or thin. Regarding the marrying of food and wine, light food with light wine is always a reliable combination. Rich food with rich wine can be wonderful as long as the match is not too rich. The two most important qualities to consider when choosing the appropriate wine are richness and lightness.

Flavors are food and wine elements perceived by the olfactory nerve as fruity, minty, herbal, nutty, cheesy, smoky,

Red grapes make red wine, and the main red grapes are cabernet sauvignon, merlot, merlot/cabernet sauvignon, pinot noir, and Shiraz

Sniffing the bouquet of the wine

Jay R. Schrock, *University of South Florida*

The combination of food and wine is as old as the making of wine. It is truly one of the great pleasures in life. Food and wine are natural accompaniments and enhance the flavor and enjoyment of each other. The flavor of a wine consumed by itself will taste different than when it is imbibed with food. Much of the wine taste experience is actually perceived from the nose; hence you will hear that "the wine has a good nose." In fact, wine experts, called *sommeliers,* say that 80 percent of the taste comes from the nose. The nose is where the flavors described as nuts, oak, fruits, herbs, spices, and all the others that describe wine come from. To improve the smell and taste of wine, we often decant it and serve it in stemware with large openings. The wine taster often swirls the wine to increase the aromas entering the nose.

Over the years, traditions have developed as to how to approach **wine and food pairing.** Remember these are traditions and that food and wine pairing is a highly subjective and an inexact process. The traditional rules basically state that red wines are served with red meat and white wines are served with fish and poultry. These rules are still generally valid; but they don't take into consideration the complexity of today's multiethnic fusion cuisines, with their wide range of flavors, and the corresponding wide range of wines from around the world that are now readily available to everyone. Today you are more likely to hear of food and wine pairing suggestions, rather than the hard and fast traditional rules of the past.

The new tradition has begun:

1. When serving more than one wine at a meal, it's best to serve lighter wines before full-bodied ones. The dryer wines should be served before sweeter wines. The exception is if a sweet-flavored food is served early in the meal. Serve wines with lower alcohol content before wines with higher alcohol content.
2. Pair light-bodied wines with lighter food and fuller-bodied wines with heaver, richer, or more flavorful foods. This is a restatement of the old red wine with red meat and white wine with fish and chicken.
3. Match flavors. A *Pinot Noir* goes well with duck, prosciutto, and mushrooms and *Gewürztraminer* is a well-suited accompaniment for ham, sausage, curry, and Thai and Indian food. Beware of pairing a wine with food that is sweeter than the wine. Most people agree that chocolate is the one exception. It seems to go with almost anything.
4. Delicately flavored foods that are poached or steamed should be paired with delicate wines.
5. Match regional wines with regional foods; they have been developed together and have a natural affinity for each other. The red sauces of Tuscany and the Chianti wines of the Tuscany region in Italy are an unbeatable combination.
6. Soft cheese such as Camembert and Brie pair well with a variety of red wine, including *cabernet sauvignon*, zinfandel, and red burgundy. Cabernet sauvignon also goes well with sharp, aged cheddar cheese. Pungent and intensely flavored cheeses, such as a blue cheese, are better with the sweeter *eis* wine or late-harvest dessert wines. Sheep and goat cheeses pair well with dry white wines, while red wine with fruit flavors goes best with milder cheeses.

Many of your restaurant guests may want to have wine with their dinner but are intimidated by the process or are afraid of the price. Set your guests' minds at ease when they are ordering wine. The know-it-all attitude will not work here; you are not trying to sell a used car or life insurance. You are trying to improve your guests' experience, the check average, and your tip. Make an honest suggestion, and try to explain the differences in wine choices. If guests are pondering two wines by the glass, do not just suggest the more expensive one; bring two glasses and let them taste. They will decide for themselves.

WINE	SMELL AND TASTE ASSOCIATED WITH WINE	FOOD PAIRING
Gewürztraminer (Alsace in France)	grapefruit, apple, nectarine, peach, nutmeg, clove, cinnamon	Thai, Indian, Tex-Mex, Szechwan, ham, sausage, curry, garlic
Chardonnay Chablis (Burgundy in France)	citrus fruit, apple, pear, pineapple, other tropical fruit	pork, salmon, chicken, pheasant, rabbit
Sauvignon Blanc Sancerre (Loire in France)	citrus fruit, gooseberry, bell pepper, black pepper, green olives, herbs	goat cheese, oysters, fish, chicken, pork, garlic
Pinot Blanc	citrus fruit, apple, pear, melon	shrimp, shellfish, fish, chicken
Pinot Noir Cote d' Or (Burgundy in France)	strawberry, cherry, raspberry, clove, mint, vanilla, cinnamon	duck, chicken, turkey, mushrooms, grilled meats, fish and vegetables, pork
Merlot Gamay (Beaujolais in France)	cherry, raspberry, plum, pepper, herbs, mint	beef, lamb, duck, barbecued meats, pork ribs
Cabernet Sauvignon Medoc (Bordeaux in France)	cherry, plum, pepper, bell pepper, herbs, mint, tea, chocolate	beef, lamb, braised, barbecued and grilled meats, aged cheddar, chocolate
Late harvest white wines	citrus fruit, apple, pear, apricot, peach, mango, honey	custard, vanilla, ginger, carrot cake, cheesecake, cream puffs, apricot cobbler

Figure 9–3 • Matching Wine with Food.
(Courtesy of Jay R Schrock.)

flowery, earthy, and so on. A person often determines flavors by using the nose as well as the tongue. The combination of texture and flavor is what makes food and wine a pleasure to enjoy; a good match between the food and wine can make occasions even more memorable. Figure 9–4 suggests the steps to be taken in **wine tasting.**

▶ Check Your Knowledge

1. What are the names of the main white and red grape varieties used to make wine?
2. Cabernet sauvignon is best served with _____.
3. Chardonnay is best served with _____.
4. Why does a wine taster swirl the wine around the glass before tasting it?
5. What is the general guideline for serving wine with food?

Many restaurants have introduced wine tastings as special marketing events to promote the restaurant itself, or a particular type or label of wine. Wine tasting is more than just a process—it is an artful ritual. Wine offers a threefold sensory appeal: color, aroma, and taste. Wine tasting, thus, consists of three essential steps.

1. Hold the glass to the light. The color of the wine gives the first indication of the wine's body. The deeper the color, the fuller the wine will be. Generally, wines should be clear and brilliant.
2. Smell the wine. Hold the glass between the middle and the ring finger in a "cup-like" fashion and gently roll the glass. This will bring the aroma and the bouquet of the wine to the edge of the glass. The bouquet should be pleasant. This will tell much about what the taste will be.
3. Finally, taste the wine by rolling the wine around the mouth and by sucking in a little air—this helps release the complexities of the flavors.

Figure 9–4 • Wine Tasting.

Major Winegrowing Regions

Europe

Germany, Italy, Spain, Portugal, and France are the main European wine-producing countries. Germany is noted for the outstanding Riesling wines from the Rhine and Moselle river valleys. Italy produces the world-famous Chianti. Spain makes good wine, but is best known for sherry. Portugal also makes good wine, but is better known for its port.

France is the most notable of the European countries, producing not only the finest wines but also champagne and cognac. The two most famous wine-producing areas in France are the Bordeaux and Burgundy regions. The vineyards, villages, and towns are steeped in the history of centuries devoted to the production of the finest quality wines. They represent some of the most beautiful countryside in Europe and are well worth visiting.

In France, wine is named after the village in which the wine is produced. In recent years, the name of the grape variety is also used. The name of the wine grower is also important; because the quality may vary, reputation understandably is very important. A vineyard might also include a chateau in which wine is made.

Within the Bordeaux region, wine growing is divided into five major districts: Medoc, Graves, St. Emilion, Pomerol, and Sauternes. The wine from each district has its own characteristics.

There are several other well-known wine-producing regions of France, such as the Loire Valley, Alsace, and Côtes du Rhône. French people regard wine as an important part of their culture and heritage.

Wine and Health

A glass of wine may be beneficial to health. This perspective was featured in the CBS news magazine program *60 Minutes*, which focused on a phenomenon called the French paradox. The French eat 30 percent more fat than Americans do, smoke more, and exercise less, yet they suffer fewer heart attacks—about one-third as many as Americans. Ironically, the French drink more wine than people of any other nationality—about 75 liters per person a year. Research

[handwritten margin notes:]

~wine clings to fatty deposits

~wine helps flush the fatty acids

↳ factual - wine good 4 health.

California's wine
↳climate - excellent
↳par w French wines
↳ Best in north + central cali.
↳ Napa + Sonoma Valley

Canada
↳ BC - Okanagan
+
Niagara.

indicates that wine attacks platelets, which are the smallest of the blood cells that cause the blood to clot, preventing excess bleeding. However, platelets also cling to the rough, fatty deposits on arterial walls, clogging and finally blocking arteries and causing heart attacks. Wine's flushing effect removes platelets from the artery wall. After the *60 Minutes* program was broadcast, sales of wine, particularly red wine, in the United States increased dramatically.

United States

In California, viticulture began in 1769 when Junipero Serra, a Spanish friar, began to produce wine for the missions he started. At one time the French considered California wines to be inferior. However, California is blessed with a near perfect climate and excellent vine-growing soil. In the United States, the name of the grape variety is used to name the wine, not the village or chateau as used by the French. The better-known varietal white wines in the United States are chardonnay, sauvignon blanc, riesling, and chenin blanc; varietal red wines are cabernet sauvignon, pinot noir, merlot, Syrah, and zinfandel.

California viticulture areas are generally divided into three regions:

1. North and central coastal region
2. Great central valley region
3. Southern California region

The north and central coastal region produces the best wines in California. A high degree of use of mechanical methods allows for efficient, large-scale production of quality wines. The two best-known areas within this region are the Napa and Sonoma Valleys. The wines of the Napa and Sonoma Valleys resemble those of Bordeaux and Burgundy. In recent years, the wines from the Napa and Sonoma Valleys have rivaled and even exceeded the French and other European wines. The chardonnays and cabernets are particularly outstanding.

The Napa and Sonoma Valleys are the symbols as well as the centers of the top-quality wine industry in California.

Several other states and Canadian provinces provide quality wines. New York, Oregon, and Washington are the other major U.S. wine-producing states. In Canada, the best wineries are in British Columbia's Okanagan Valley and southern Ontario's Niagara peninsula. Both of these regions produce excellent wines.

A Vineyard in Napa Valley

Australia

Australia has been producing wines for about 150 years, but it is only in the last half century that these wines have achieved the prominence and recognition they rightly deserve. Australian wine makers traveled to Europe and California to perfect the wine-making craft. Unlike France, with many rigid laws controlling wine growth and

INTRODUCING ROBERT MONDAVI

Founder of Robert Mondavi Winery

Since its founding in 1966, the Robert Mondavi Winery has established itself as one of the world's top wineries. The late Robert Mondavi, who passed away in 2008 at the age of 94, was wine's foremost spokesperson even into his nineties, and he contributed greatly to the wine industry throughout his successful life.

Robert Mondavi was born in 1913 to an Italian couple who had emigrated from the Marche region of Italy in 1910. His father, Cesare, became involved in shipping California wine grapes to fellow Italians. Extremely pleased with California, Cesare Mondavi decided to move to the Napa Valley and set up a firm that shipped fruit east. Robert Mondavi grew up among wines and vines and remained in his father's business.

Robert began by improving the family enterprise, adding to it the management, production, and marketing skills he learned at Stanford University, from which he graduated in 1936. Robert acknowledged the great business potential of the Napa Valley in the broader context of the California wine industry. He realized that the firm needed to be upgraded with innovations in technology in order to keep up with the changes in the overall business environment.

Mondavi had an ambitious dream that was realized when the Charles Krug Winery was offered for sale in 1943. He purchased the facility, and he knew that the strategy for success included well-planned marketing as well as the crucial wine-making expertise that the family already had.

Mondavi also understood the importance of the introduction of innovative processes that could place the winery in a competitive position. From the 1950s to the 1960s, he performed many experiments and introduced pivotal innovations. For example, Robert popularized new styles of wine, such as chenin blanc, which was previously known as white pinot and was not doing well in the market. Mondavi changed the fermentation, turning it into a sweeter, more delicious wine. The name was also changed, and sales increased fourfold the following year.

Robert Mondavi always aspired to create Napa Valley wines that would stand in the company of the world's finest. In 1966, he opened the Robert Mondavi Winery, which represented the fulfillment of his vision to build a facility that would enable him to produce truly world-class wines. In fact, since its establishment, the winery has led the industry, standing as an example of continuous research and innovation in wine making, as well as a "monument to persistence in the pursuit of excellence."

Among his many innovations at Robert Mondavi Winery was the creation of fumé blanc. American sauvignon blanc at the time was somewhat sweet and ordinary. Robert began producing it in a drier style, inspired by the wines of the Loire Valley. He called it fumé blanc, a play on the Loire's pouilly-fumé, and it became an immediate success. Although the winery's operations were successful, Mondavi was still looking to raise the bar. A trip to Europe whose purpose was to study the finest wineries' techniques convinced him to adopt a new, smaller type of barrel to age the wine, which he believed added a "wonderful dimension to the finished product." He also introduced cold fermentation techniques and a collaboration with NASA to study vineyard health.

Throughout the years, the winery's original vision has remained constant: to produce the best wines that are the perfect accompaniments to food and gracious living, and to provide the public with proper education about wine. In fact, the Robert Mondavi Winery sponsors several educational programs such as seminars on viticulture; a comprehensive tour program in the Napa Valley; the great chefs program; and the Taste conference, a celebration of wine, food, and art.

The Robert Mondavi Corporation has been acquired by Constellation Brands, a leading international producer and marketer of alcoholic beverages. The winery's winemaking and vineyard teams remain intact, with Director of Winemaking Genevieve Janssens at the helm since 1997.

*Australian wines
use high tech
to blend best
wines*

↳Hunter Valley.—

production, Australian wine makers use high technology to produce excellent wines, many of which are blended to offer the best characteristics of each wine.

Australia has about sixty wine-growing regions, with diverse climates and soil types, mostly in the southeastern part of the continent, in New South Wales, Victoria, and South Australia, all within easy reach of the major cities of Sidney, Melbourne, and Adelaide. There are about 1,120 wineries in Australia. One of the larger and more popular wineries is Lindemans, which regularly receives accolades for its consistent quality and value. The leading red wines are: cabernet sauvignon, cabernet-shiraz blends, cabernet-merlot blends, merlot, shiraz. The leading white wines are: chardonnay, semillon, sauvignon blanc, and semillon chardonnay. Among the better-known wine-growing areas is Hunter Valley in New South Wales, which produces semillon. When mature, this wine has a honey, nut, and butter flavor. The chardonnay is complex with a peaches-and-cream character. In recent years, Australian wines have shown exceptional quality and value, leading to increased sales in Europe, the United States, and Asia.

Wine also is produced in many other temperate parts of the world, most notably New Zealand, Chile, Argentina, and South Africa.

How to Read a Wine Label

*U.S.
↳ name of
vineyard
↳grape variety
↳ growing area
↳ vintage
↳producer*

Labeling requirements vary significantly from country to country. The local laws at the point of sale govern specific information that is required to be on the label where the wine is marketed, rather than where it is produced. This requirement often results in two different wine labels for the same wine. Then, if the wine is marketed where it was produced, it will have one wine label; if the wine is to be exported, it may have another version of the first wine label to meet the requirements of local laws. After the label is designed, it must be approved by the same government agency that controls wine production in that country, as well as the various government agencies that control the import and sale of the wine.[1]

In the United States, we label wines by their varietal grape and include the name of their region on the label. In Europe, wines tend to be labeled regionally rather than by varietal. The wine label on the front of the bottle generally has five headings:

1. The name of the vineyard
2. The grape variety
3. The growing area
4. The vintage
5. The producer

Wine labels are helpful in telling you a lot about what is in the bottle. Most wine bottles have two labels applied to each bottle. The front label is meant to attract your attention, while the back label may be used to provoke your senses. As an example, the label may state: "A wonderful aperitif, this smooth, elegant, wonderfully fruity wine . . ." The label may also include serving suggestions for pairing with food. These statements are not governed by law.[2]

Beer

Beer is a brewed and fermented beverage made from malted barley and other starchy cereals, and flavored with hops. *Beer* is a generic term for a variety of mash-based, yeast-fermented brewed malt beverages with an alcohol content mostly between 3.8 and 8 percent.[3] The term **beer** includes the following:

- Lager, the beverage that is normally referred to as beer, is a clear light-bodied refreshing beer.

- Ale is fuller bodied and more bitter than lager.

- Stout is a dark ale with a sweet, strong, malt flavor.

- Pilsner is not really a beer. The term *pilsner* means that the beer is made in the style of the famous beer brewed in Pilsen, Czech Republic.

The Brewing Process

Beer is brewed from water, **malt**, **yeast**, and **hops**. The brewing process begins with water, an important ingredient in the making of beer. The mineral content and purity of the water largely determine the quality of the final product. Water accounts for 85 to 89 percent of the finished beer.

Next, grain is added in the form of malt, which is barley that has been ground to a course grit. The grain is germinated, producing an enzyme that converts starch into fermentable sugar.

The yeast is the fermenting agent. Breweries typically have their own cultured yeasts, which, to a large extent, determine the type and taste of the beer.

Mashing is the term for grinding the malt and screening out any bits of dirt. The malt then goes through a hopper into a mash tub, which is a large stainless steel or copper container. Here the water and grains are mixed and heated.

The liquid is now called **wort** and is filtered through a mash filter or lauter tub. This liquid then flows into a brewing kettle, where hops are added and the mixture is boiled for several hours. After the brewing operation, the hop wort is filtered through the hop separator or hop jack. The filtered liquid then is pumped through a wort cooler and flows into a fermenting vat where pure-culture yeast is added for fermentation.[4] The brew is aged for a few days prior to being barreled for draught beer or pasteurized for bottled or canned beer.

Today, marketing and distribution partnerships promote an even greater choice of beers for consumers. Among those available from Anheuser-Busch distributors are: Fire Rock from Hawaii, Tiger, Harbin, Grölsch

In the process of making beer, hops are added to the wort in the brew kettle

[handwritten margin notes:
water ↓
Grain - Barley ↓
Mash ↓
'Liquid' wort ↓
brewing kettle where hops r added.]

from the Netherlands, Stavopramen, Tsingato from China, Harbin, and Landshark. Other interesting beverages include Michelob Ultra and Tuscan Orange Grapefruit. Michelob Ultra and Pomegranate Raspberry, and Michelob Ultra and Live Cactus.

Organic Beers

The U.S. Department of Agriculture (USDA) established the National Organic Program in 1997, opening the door for organic beer. The guidelines for organic beer are the same as for all organic foods: The ingredients must be grown without toxic and persistent pesticides or synthetic fertilizers and in soil that has been free from such chemicals for at least three years. No genetically modified (GMO) ingredients can be used in the brewing process. Studies show that organic farming reduces erosion and ground-water pollution and that it significantly reduces negative impacts on wildlife.[5]

Spirits

[handwritten margin notes:
Is made from a liquid that has been fermented + distilled.
is higher alcohol concentrate.]

A **spirit** or **liquor** is made from a liquid that has been fermented and distilled. Consequently, a spirit has a high percentage of alcohol, gauged in the United States by its proof content. **Proof** is equal to twice the percentage of alcohol in the beverage; therefore, a spirit that is 80 proof is 40 percent alcohol. Spirits traditionally are enjoyed before or after a meal, rather than with the meal. Many spirits can be consumed straight or neat (without ice or other ingredients), or they may be enjoyed with water, soda water, juices, or cocktail mixes.

[handwritten note: Proof - 2 time the % of alcohol in bev 80 proof is 40% alcohol]

INTRODUCING ROB WESTFALL

Bar Manager, The Speakeasy, Siesta Key, Florida

The Speakeasy has been a staple in Siesta Key's Village for over five years. Known for its exceptional variety of live music, it is also a place where locals feel right at home. Newly remodeled in November of 2004, The Speakeasy now features ice-cold air conditioning in a polished, clean environment. Smokers are welcome at our establishment and we provide premium cigar service. Located at the back of the room is our pool table with plenty of space to allow for professional play. Specialty drinks are another draw for patrons at The Speakeasy. Our menu is loaded with innovative cocktails that are tough to find in another establishment. Along with our extensive list of wines by the glass, we also offer many premium single-malt scotches, cognacs, bourbons, and a host of fine liqueurs. The Speakeasy is owned and operated by Café Gardens, which also owns the Daiquiri Deck located directly next door. For more information on The Speakeasy or the Daiquiri Deck, visit our website at www.daiquirideck.com.

A typical day for a manager at The Speakeasy goes like this:

9.45am – Arrive for manager meeting at the Daiquiri Deck. All Daiquiri Deck managers, the owners, and myself are present at this meeting. The meeting consists of a variety of issues. Typically, the first order of business is reviewing the numbers from the previous week. Numbers like net sales, cost of labor, cost of goods, and promotional costs are discussed. Additionally, budgets are a major concern every week. Budgets are set based on sales projections from the previous year and are very important to the success of the business. Next, we discuss any issues from the previous week. In the bar business, an "issue" could be just about anything from fights to vandalism. We find it extremely important to discuss all of these issues so that the management team is all one the same page. The meeting is adjourned after everyone around the table is given a chance to raise any issues they feel necessary. After everything has been discussed, it's time to go to work.

11.00am – Mondays are very important in the bar business. Inventory must be taken to ensure that costs are in line, and that you know what product you need. First, I take an inventory of all beverage products at The Speakeasy. Liquor, beer, wine, cigarettes, cigars, and mixers are all items that must be counted.

12.00pm – Upon completion of the inventory, it is time to put your orders together for the week. Knowing your usage is extremely important when placing an order. Buying in bulk is always superior to simply filling holes from week to week. Simply, it allows you more buying power and, essentially, more free goods. Bar supplies also need to be monitored. Straws, olive picks, stir sticks, bar glass cleaner and sanitizer, and bar napkins all need to be kept in stock. The absence of one item can often make or break a busy night at the bar.

1.00pm – Confirm band schedule. Booking bands and maintaining an entertainment schedule can sometimes be one of the most frustrating areas of the bar business. However, it can also be the most rewarding. The experience you gain from working with so many different types of entertainment is difficult to replace. The majority of bands show up on time and treat their job professionally, but there are a significant amount of them that do not. I call my bands to confirm their schedule on a weekly basis for this very reason. There is no worst feeling than walking into a potentially busy night and having your entertainment cancel.

2.00pm – Typically there is always some bar maintenance that needs to be addressed. I always take a walk around and check everything out to make sure that everything is working property. Smoke eaters, bathrooms, light bulbs, and bar cleanliness are all part of this maintenance.

3.00pm – Work on any upcoming promotions and ensure their success. Spirit tastings, holidays, Full Moon parties, and private parties are examples of these types of events. Planning is extremely important for the ultimate success of these events. I find that no matter how much you plan, you will have to improvise somewhere along the line, so the more planning you do, the less improvisation that is necessary.

4.00pm – Send memo to corporate office regarding what checks need to be written for entertainment that week. Ensure that each band has proper paperwork filled out for tax purposes.

5.00pm – Every day the staff needs to be reminded to step it up. Motivation comes from the top down. The bar business is a stage, and the bartenders are on a stage. The staff will typically need to be reminded of this on a consistent basis. Open lines of communication are very important and allow you to apply constructive criticism or accolades, as they are appropriate.

6.00pm – It's time to have a drink.

That's the management side of the bar. The nighttime is another animal entirely!

Fermentation of spirits takes place by the action of yeast on sugar-containing substances, such as grain or fruit. Distilled drinks are made from a fermented liquid that has been put through a distillation process.

Whiskies

Among the better-known spirits is whisky, which is a generic name for the spirit first distilled in Scotland and Ireland centuries ago. The word *whisky* comes from the Celtic word *visgebaugh*, meaning "water of life." Whisky is made from a fermented mash of grain to which malt, in the form of barley, is added. The barley contains an enzyme called diastase that converts starch to sugars. After fermentation, the liquid is distilled. Spirits naturally are white or pale in color, but raw whisky is stored in oak barrels that have been charred (burnt). This gives whisky its caramel color. The whisky is stored for a period of time, up to a maximum of twelve to fifteen years. However, several good whiskies reach the market after three to five years.

Most whiskies are blended to produce a flavor and quality that is characteristic of the brand. Not surprisingly, the blending process at each distillery is a closely guarded secret. There are four distinct whisky types that have gained worldwide acknowledgment throughout the centuries: Scotch whisky, Irish whisky, bourbon whisky, and Canadian whisky.

Scotch Whisky

Scotch whisky, or scotch, has been distilled in Scotland for centuries and has been a distinctive part of the Scots' way of life. From its origins in remote and romantic Highland glens, Scotch whisky has become a popular and international drink, its flavor appreciated throughout the world. Scotch became popular in the United States during the days of **Prohibition** (1919 to 1933) when it was smuggled into the country from Canada. It is produced like other whiskies, except that the malt is dried in special kilns that give it a smoky flavor. To be legally called Scotch whisky, the spirit must conform to the standards of the Scotch Whisky Act; only whisky made with this process can be called scotch whisky. Some of the better-known quality blended Scotch whiskies are Chivas Regal and Johnnie Walker Black, Gold, and Blue Labels.[6]

Irish Whisky

Irish whisky is produced from malted or unmalted barley, corn, rye, and other grains. The malt is not dried like it is in the production of scotch whisky, which gives Irish whisky a milder character, yet an excellent flavor. Two well-known Irish whiskies are Old Bushmill's Black Bush and Jameson's 1780.[7]

Bourbon Whisky

Liquor was introduced in America by the first settlers, who used it as a medicine. Bourbon has a peculiar history. In colonial times in New England, rum was the most popular distilled spirit. After the break with Britain, settlers of Scottish and Irish background predominated. They were mostly grain farmers

Checking the Color of Johnnie Walker scotch that is Maturing in Barrels

and distillers, producing whisky for barter. When George Washington levied a tax on this whisky, the farmers moved south and continued their whisky production. However, the rye crop failed, so they decided to mix corn, particularly abundant in Kentucky, with the remaining rye. The result was delightful. This experiment occurred in Bourbon County—hence the name of the new product.

Bourbon whisky is produced mainly from corn; other grains are also used, but they are of secondary importance. The distillation processes are similar to those of other types of whisky. Charred barrels provide bourbon with its distinctive taste. It is curious to note that barrels can only be used once in the United States to age liquor. Aging, therefore, occurs in new barrels after each distillation process. Bourbon may be aged up to six years to improve its mellowness. Among the better-known bourbon whiskies are Jack Daniels, Makers Mark, and George Dickle.

Canadian Whisky

Like bourbon, Canadian whisky is produced mainly from corn. It is characterized by a delicate flavor that nonetheless pleases the palate. Canadian whisky must be at least four years old before it can be bottled and marketed. It is distilled at 70 to 90 percent alcohol by volume. Among the better-known Canadian whiskies are Seagram's and Canadian Club.

White Spirits

Gin, rum, vodka, and tequila are the most common of the spirits that are called **white spirits**. Gin, first known as Geneva, is a neutral spirit made from juniper berries. Although gin originated in Holland, it was in London that the word *Geneva* was shortened to gin, and almost anything was used to make it. Often gin was made in the bathtub in the morning and sold in hole-in-the-wall dram shops all over London at night. Obviously, the quality left a lot to be desired, but the poor drank it to the point of national disaster.[8] Gin also was widely produced in the United States during Prohibition. In fact, the habit of mixing something else with it led to the creation of the cocktail. Over the years, gin became the foundation of many popular cocktails (e.g., martini, gin and tonic, gin and juice, and Tom Collins).

Rum can be light or dark in color. Light rum is distilled from the fermented juice of sugarcane, and dark rum is distilled from molasses. Rum comes mainly from the Caribbean Islands of Barbados (Mount Gay), Puerto Rico (Bacardi), and Jamaica (Myers). Rums are mostly used in mixed frozen and specialty drinks such as rum and Coke, rum punches, daiquiris, and piña coladas.

Tequila is distilled from the agave tequilana (a type of cactus), which is called *mezcal* in Mexico. Official Mexican regulations require that tequila be made in the area around the town of Tequila because the soil contains volcanic ash, which is especially suitable for growing the blue agave cactus. Tequila may be white, silver, or golden in color. The white is shipped unaged, silver is aged up to three years, and golden is aged in oak from two to four years. Tequila is mainly used in the popular margarita cocktail or in the tequila sunrise (made popular in a song by the Eagles rock group).

Vodka can be made from many sources, including barley, corn, wheat, rye, or potatoes. Because it lacks color, odor, and flavor, vodka generally is combined with juices or other mixers whose flavors predominate.

A Glass of Cognac

Other Spirits

Brandy is distilled from wine in a fashion similar to that of other spirits. American brandy comes primarily from California, where it is made in column stills and aged in white-oak barrels for at least two years. The best-known American brandies are made by Christian Brothers and Ernest and Julio Gallo. Their brandies are smooth and fruity with a touch of sweetness. The best brandies are served as after-dinner drinks, and ordinary brandies are used in the well for mixed drinks.

Cognac is regarded by connoisseurs as the best brandy in the world. It is made only in the Cognac region of France, where the chalky soil and humid climate combine with special distillation techniques to produce the finest brandy. Only brandy from this region may be called cognac. Most cognac is aged in oak casks from two to four years or more. Because cognacs are blends of brandies of various ages, no age is allowed on the label; instead, letters signify the relative age and quality.

Brandies labeled as *VSOP* must be aged at least four years. All others must be aged in wood at least five years. Five years, then, is the age of the youngest cognac in a blend; usually several others of older age are added to lend taste, bouquet, and finesse. About 75 percent of the cognac shipped to Canada and the United States is produced by four companies: Courvoisier, Hennessy, Martell, and Remy Martin.

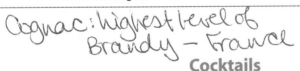

[handwritten note: Cognac: highest level of Brandy — France]

Cocktails

The first cocktails originated in England during the Victorian era, but it wasn't until the 1920s and 1930s that cocktails became popular.

Cocktails are usually drinks made by mixing two or more ingredients (wines, liquors, fruit juices), resulting in a blend that is pleasant to the palate, with no single ingredient overpowering the others. Cocktails are mixed by stirring, shaking, or blending. The mixing technique is particularly important to achieve the perfect cocktail. Cocktails are commonly divided into two categories according to volume: short drinks (up to 3.5 ounces) and tall drinks (generally up to 8.5 ounces).

The secret of a good cocktail lies in several factors:

- The balance of the ingredients.
- The quality of the ingredients. As a general rule, cocktails should be made from a maximum of three ingredients.
- The skill of the bartender. The bartender's experience, knowledge, and inspiration are key factors in making a perfect cocktail.

A good bartender should understand the effect and the "timing" of a cocktail. It is not a coincidence that many cocktails are categorized by when they are best served. There are aperitifs, digestifs, corpse-revivers, pick-me-ups, and so on. Cocktails can stimulate an appetite or provide the perfect conclusion to a fine meal.

▶ Check Your Knowledge

1. Describe the different types of beer.
2. Describe the various spirits.

A martini cocktail served in a martini glass

Nonalcoholic Beverages

Nonalcoholic beverages are increasing in popularity. In the 1990s and 2000s, a radical shift has occurred from the free love 1960s and the singles bars of the 1970s and early 1980s. People are, in general, more cautious about the consumption of alcohol. Lifestyles have become healthier, and organizations such as Mothers Against Drunk Driving (MADD) have raised the social conscience about responsible alcohol consumption. Overall consumption of alcohol has decreased in recent years, with spirits declining the most.

In recent years, several new beverages have been added to the nonalcoholic beverage list. From Goji juice to passion fruit green tea, the nonalcoholic beverage world has been innovative in creating flavored teas and coffees and an ever-increasing variety of juices to satisfy all our tastes.

Nonalcoholic Beer

Guinness, Anheuser-Busch, and Miller, along with many other brewers, have developed beer products that have the same appearance as regular beer but have a lower calorie content and approximately 95 to 99 percent of the alcohol removed, either after processing or after fermentation. The taste, therefore, is somewhat different from regular beer.

Coffee

Coffee is the drink of the present. People who used to frequent bars are now patronizing coffeehouses. Sales of specialty coffees exceed $4 billion a year. The Specialty Coffee Association of America estimates that there are more than 17,400 coffee cafés nationwide.[9]

Coffee first came from Ethiopia and Mocha, which is in the Yemen Republic. Legends say that Kaldi, a young Abyssinian goatherd, accustomed to his sleepy goats, noticed that after chewing certain berries, the goats began to prance about excitedly. He tried the berries himself, forgot his troubles, lost his heavy heart, and became the happiest person in "happy Arabia." A monk from a nearby monastery

[handwritten margin notes: Kaldis goats began eating berries & got energized - he then his brother tried & agreed - Pope baptized the drink which is when it became pop]

surprised Kaldi in this state, decided to try the berries too, and invited the brothers to join him. They all felt more alert that night during prayers![10]

In the Middle Ages, coffee found its way to Europe via Turkey but not without some objections. In Italy, priests appealed to Pope Clement VIII to have the use of coffee forbidden among Christians. Satan, they said, had forbidden his followers, the infidel Moslems, the use of wine because it was used in the Holy Communion and had given them instead his "hellish black brew." Apparently, the pope liked the drink, for his reply was, "Why, this Satan's drink is so delicious that it would be a pity to let the infidels have exclusive use of it!" So, his Holiness decided to baptize the drink, after which it quickly became the social beverage of Europe's middle and upper classes.[11]

In 1637, the first European coffeehouse opened in England; within thirty years, coffeehouses had replaced taverns as the island's social, commercial, and political melting pots.[12] The coffeehouses were nicknamed *penny universities,* where any topic could be discussed and learned for the price of a pot of coffee. The men of the period not only discussed business but actually conducted business. Banks, newspapers, and the Lloyd's of London Insurance Company began at Edward Lloyd's coffeehouse.

Coffeehouses were also popular in Europe. In Paris, Café Procope, which opened in 1689 and still operates today, has been the meeting place of many a famous artist and philosopher, including Rousseau and Voltaire (who are reputed to have drunk forty cups of coffee a day).

The Dutch introduced coffee to the United States during the colonial period. Coffeehouses soon became the haunts of the revolutionary activists plotting against King George of England and his tea tax. John Adams and Paul Revere planned the Boston Tea Party and the fight for freedom at a coffeehouse. This helped established coffee as the traditional democratic drink of Americans.

Brazil produces more than 30 percent of the world's coffee, most of which goes into canned and instant coffee. Coffee connoisseurs recommend beans by name, such as arabica and robusta beans. In Indonesia, coffee is named for the island on which it grows; the best is from Java and is rich and spicy with a full-bodied flavor. Yemen, the country in which coffee was discovered, names its best coffee for the port of Mocha. Its fragrant, creamy brew has a rich, almost chocolatey aftertaste. Coffee beans are frequently blended by the merchants who roast them; one of the best blends, mocha java, is the result of blending these two fine coffees.

Coffee may be roasted from light to dark according to preference. Light roasts are generally used in canned and institutional roasts, and medium is the all-purpose roast most people prefer. Medium beans are medium brown in color, and their surface is dry. Although this brew may have snappy, acidic qualities, its flavor tends to be flat. Full, high, or Viennese roast is the roast preferred by specialty stores, where balance is achieved between sweetness and sharpness. Dark roasts have a fancy rich flavor, with espresso the darkest of all roasts. Its almost black beans have shiny, oily surfaces. All the acidic qualities and specific coffee flavor are gone from espresso, but its pungent flavor is a favorite of espresso lovers.

Decaffeinating coffee removes the caffeine with either a solvent or water process. In contrast, many specialty coffees have

A casual coffeehouse offers coffee and related beverages and snacks

things added. Among the better-known specialty coffees are café au lait or caffe latte. In these cases, milk is steamed until it becomes frothy and is poured into the cup together with the coffee. Cappuccino is made with espresso, hot milk, and milk foam, which may then be sprinkled with powdered chocolate and cinnamon.[13]

Tea

Tea is a beverage made by steeping in boiling water the leaves of the tea plant, an evergreen shrub, or small tree, native to Asia. Tea is consumed as either a hot or cold beverage by approximately half of the world's population, yet it is second to coffee in commercial importance because most of the world's tea crop is consumed in the tea-growing regions. Tea leaves contain 1 to 3 percent caffeine. This means that weight for weight, tea leaves have more than twice as much caffeine as coffee beans. However, a cup of coffee generally has more caffeine than a cup of tea because one pound of tea leaves makes 250 to 300 cups of tea, whereas one pound of coffee makes only 40 cups.

Teopia

CORPORATE PROFILE

Starbucks Coffee Company

Operations

Starbucks Coffee Company (named after the first mate in Herman Melville's *Moby-Dick*) is the leading retailer, roaster, and brand of specialty coffee in North America. More than 7 million people visit Starbucks stores each week. In addition to its more than thousand retail locations, the company supplies fine dining, foodservice, travel, and hotel accounts with coffee and coffee-making equipment and operates a national mail-order division.

Locations and Alliances

Starbucks currently has thousands of stores in fifty U.S. states and in thirty-four countries. Starbucks Coffee Company and U.S. Office Products announced an agreement to distribute Starbucks fresh-roasted coffee and related products through U.S. Office Products extensive North American distributorship. Starbucks has strategic alliances with United Airlines and is now the exclusive supplier of coffee on every United flight.

In addition, Specialty Sales and Marketing supplies coffee to the health care, business and industry, college and university, and hotel and resort segments of the foodservice industry; to many fine restaurants throughout North America; and to companies such as Costco, Nordstrom, Starwood, Barnes and Noble, Hilton Hotels, Sodexho, ARAMARK, Compass, Wyndham, Borders, Radisson, Sysco, Safeway, Albertson's, Kraft Foods, Pepsico, and Marriott International.

continued

CORPORATE PROFILE *(continued)*

Starbucks Coffee Company

Product Line

Starbucks roasts more than thirty varieties of the world's finest arabica coffee beans. The company's retail locations also feature a variety of espresso beverages and locally made fresh pastries. Starbucks specialty merchandise includes Starbucks private-label espresso makers, mugs, plunger pots, grinders, storage jars, water filters, thermal carafes, and coffee makers. An extensive selection of packaged goods, including unique confections, gift baskets, and coffee-related items are available in stores, through mail order, and through a site in the Marketplace section of America Online.

Starbucks introduced Frappuccino blended beverages, a line of low-fat, creamy, iced coffee drinks. This product launch was the most successful in Starbucks history. The company also has a bottled version of Frappuccino, which is currently being distributed on a national basis and is available in grocery stores and in many Starbucks retail locations.

A long-term joint venture between Starbucks Coffee and Breyer's Grand Ice Cream dishes up a premium line of coffee ice creams, with national distribution of several different flavors to leading grocery stores. Starbucks has become the number one brand of coffee ice cream in the United States. Currently, ice cream lovers can choose from eight delectable flavors or two ice cream bars.

Starbucks and Capitol Records joined forces to produce Blue Note Blend, a compact disc featuring classic jazz recordings. It was played in Starbucks locations and was the first item to be sold to customers both over the counter and by mail order. The album was so successful that the company has subsequently released several other CDs, covering a wide range of tastes and moods, including Chicago blues, rhythm and blues, legendary female vocalists, an eclectic mix from the late 1960s and early 1970s, jazz, and opera.

Community Involvement

Starbucks contributes to a variety of organizations that benefit AIDS research, child welfare, environmental awareness, literacy, and the arts. The company encourages its partners (employees) to take an active role in their own neighborhoods.

Starbucks fulfills its corporate social responsibility mission by reducing its environmental footprint on the planet. The company addresses three high-impact areas: sourcing of coffee, tea, and paper; transportation of people and products; and design and operations (energy, water, waste reduction, and recycling). Starbucks has developed relations with organizations that support the people and places that grow their coffee and tea, such as Conservation International, CARE, Save the Children, and the African Wildlife Foundation. Additionally, Starbucks has entered into a partnership with the U.S. Agency for International Development (USAID) and Conservation International to improve the livelihoods of small-scale coffee farmers by private sector approaches within the coffee industry that are environmentally sensitive, socially responsible, and economically viable. In 2005, Starbucks received the World Environment Center's Gold Medal for International Corporate Achievement in Sustainable Development.

Starbucks has received numerous awards for quality innovation, service, and giving.

Source: Courtesy of Starbucks.

The following list shows where the different types of tea originate:

China—Oolong, orange pekoe
India—Darjeeling, Assams, Dooars
Indonesia—Java, Sumatra

Carbonated Soft Drinks and Energy

Coca-Cola and Pepsi have long dominated the carbonated soft drink market. In the early 1970s, Diet Coke and Diet Pepsi were introduced and quickly gained popularity. The diet colas now command about a 10 percent market share. Caffeine-free colas offer an alternative, but they have not, as yet, become as popular as diet colas.

Energy drinks are beverages that are designed to give the consumer a burst of energy by using a combination of methylaxanthines (including caffeine), B vitamins, and exotic herbal ingredients. Energy drinks commonly include caffeine, guarana (extracts from the guarana plant), taurine, various forms of ginseng, maltodextrin, inositol, carnitine, creatine, glucuronolactone, and ginkgo biloba. Some contain high levels of sugar, while most brands also offer an artificially sweetened version.[14] Red Bull is an example of a popular energy drink that originated in Thailand and has a Japanese heritage. It was adapted to Australian tastes and in only a few years has become popular around the world. The claims are that Red Bull vitalizes the body and mind by supplying tired minds and exhausted bodies with vital substances that have been lost, while reducing harmful substances. It provides immediate energy and vitamins to the consumer. Sales are more than 3 billion cans in more than 100 countries.[15]

Juices

Popular juice flavors include orange, cranberry, grapefruit, mango, papaya, and apple. Nonalcoholic versions of popular cocktails made with juices have been popular for years and are known as virgin cocktails.

Juice bars have established themselves as places for quick, healthy drinks. Lately, "smart drinks" that are supposed to boost energy and improve concentration have become popular. The smart drinks are made up of a blend of juices, herbs, amino acids, caffeine, and sugar and are sold under names such as Energy Plasma Blast and IQ Booster.

Other drinks have jumped on the healthy drink bandwagon, playing on the consumer's desire to drink something refreshing, light, and healthful. Often, these drinks are fruit flavored, giving the consumer the impression of drinking something healthier than sugar-filled sodas. Unfortunately, these drinks usually just add the flavor of the fruit and rarely have any nutritional value whatsoever.

Also, some drinks are created by mixing different fruit flavors to arrive at new, exotic flavors such as Passion-Kiwi-Strawberry and Mango-Banana Delight. Some examples of such drinks are Snapple and Tropicana Twister.

Sports enthusiasts also find drinks available in stores that professional athletes use and advertise. These specially formulated isotonic beverages help the body regain the vital fluids and minerals that are lost during heavy physical exertion. The National Football League sponsors Gatorade and encourages its use among its athletes. The appeal of being able to drink what the professionals drink is undoubtedly one of the major reasons for the success of Gatorade's sales and

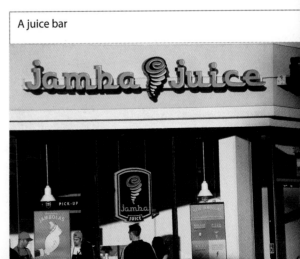

A juice bar

marketing. Other brands of isotonic beverages include Powerade and All Sport, which is sponsored by the National Collegiate Athletics Association.

Bottled Water

Bottled water was popular in Europe years ago when it was not safe to drink tap water. In North America, the increased popularity of bottled water has coincided with the trend toward healthier lifestyles.

In the 1980s, it was chic to be seen drinking Perrier (a sparkling water) or some other imported bottled water. Perrier, which comes from France, lost market share a few years ago when an employee tampered with the product. Now the market leader is Evian (a spring water), which is also French. Domestic bottled water is equally as good as imported and is now available in various flavors that offer the consumer a greater selection.

Bottled waters are available as sparkling, mineral, and spring waters. Bottled water is a refreshing, clean-tasting, low-calorie beverage that will likely increase in popularity as a beverage on its own or to accompany another beverage such as wine or whisky.

Bars and Beverage Operations

From an operating perspective, bar and beverage management follows much the same sequence as does food management, as shown in the following list:

- Forecasting
- Determining what to order
- Selecting the supplier
- Placing the order
- Receiving the order
- Storing
- Issuing
- Serving
- Accounting
- Controlling

Bar Setup

Whether a bar is part of a larger operation (restaurant) or a business in its own right, the physical setup of the bar is critical to its overall effectiveness. There is a need to design the area in such a way that it is not only pleasing to the eye but is also conducive to a smooth and efficient operation. This means that bar stations, where drinks are filled, are located in strategic spots, and that each station has everything it needs to respond to most, if not all, requests. All *well liquors* should be easily accessible, with popular call brands not too far out of reach. The brands that are less likely to be ordered (and more likely to be high priced) can be farther away from the stations. The most obvious place for the high-priced, premium brands is the back bar, a place of high visibility. Anyone sitting at the bar will be looking directly at it, giving the customers a chance to view the bar's choices.

As for beer coolers, their location depends on the relative importance of beer to the establishment. In many places, beer is kept in coolers under the bar or below the back bar, and sample bottles or signs are displayed for customers. However, in many places beer is the biggest seller, and bars may offer numerous brands from around the world. In such places, other setups may be used, such as standup coolers with glass doors so that customers can easily see all the varieties available. This is also true for draft beers.

Inventory Control

The beverage profitability of an organization is not a matter of luck. Profits result largely from the implementation and use of effective **inventory controls** by management and employees. Training is also important to ensure that employees treat inventory as cash and that they handle it as if it were their own money. Management's example will be followed by employees. If employees sense a lax management style, they may be tempted to steal. No control system can guarantee the prevention of theft completely. However, the better the control system, the less likely it is that there will be a loss.[16]

To operate profitably, a beverage operation manager needs to establish what the expected results will be. For example, if a bottle of gin contains twenty-five 1-ounce measures, it would be reasonable to expect twenty-five times the selling price in revenue. When this is multiplied for each bottle, the total revenue can be determined and compared to the actual revenue.

One of the critical areas of bar management is the design, installation, and implementation of a system to control possible theft of the bar's beverage inventory. Theft may occur in a number of ways including the following:

- Giving away drinks
- Overpouring alcohol
- Mischarging for drinks
- Selling a call liquor at a well price
- Outright stealing of bar beverages by employees

As is the case with food operations, anticipated profit margin is based on the ratio of sales generated to related beverage costs. Bar management must be able to account for any discrepancies between expected and actual profit margins.

All inventory control systems require an actual physical count of the existing inventory, which may be done on a weekly or monthly basis, depending on the needs of management. This physical count is based on units. For liquor and wine, the unit is a bottle, either 0.750 or 1.0 liter; for bottled beer, the unit is a case of twenty-four bottles; for draft beer, the unit is one keg. The results of the most current physical count are then compared to the prior period's physical count to determine the actual amount of beverage inventory consumed during the period. This physical amount is translated into a cost or dollar figure by multiplying the amount consumed for each item times its respective cost per unit. The total cost for all beverages consumed is compared to the sales generated to result in a profit margin that is compared to the expected margin.

Management should design forms that can be used to account for all types of liquor, beer, and wine available at the bar. The listing of the items should follow their actual physical setup within the bar to facilitate easy accounting of the inventory. The forms should also have columns where amounts of each inventory item can be noted. A traditional way to account for the amount of liquor in a bottle is by using the "10" count, where the level of each bottle is marked by tenths; thus, a half-full bottle of well vodka would be marked on the form as a ".5." Similarly, for kegs of draft beer, a breakdown of 25, 50, 75, and 100 percent may be used to determine their physical count.

Beverage Management Technology

Technology for beverage management has improved with products from companies such as Scannabar (**www.scanbar.com**), which offer beverage operators a system that accounts for every ounce, with daily, weekly, or monthly results. The ongoing real-time inventory allows viewing results at any time and place with tamperproof reliability interfaced with major POS systems.

The Scannabar liquor module has a bar-coded label on each bottle, making it easy to track bottles from purchase to recycle bin. Each bottle variety has the same ribbon, allowing for easy calibration. The bar-coded ribbon is used as a measuring tool to give accurate results. Inventory taking is done with a portable handheld radio-frequency bar code reader. Once the label is scanned, the level of alcohol in the bottle is recorded and the data are sent from the user's hand-held reader to the computer in the office for real-time results.[17]

The wine module keeps control of all wines by region, variety, or vintage. After the wines have been configured within the directory, the procedure is that, when a wine is received, the variety is identified by scanning the bar code already on the bottle or selected directly from the portable hand-held radio-frequency bar code reader. A bar-coded tag is placed around the collar, which creates a unique identity for each bottle. Once the bottle is ready to be served, either at the table or at the bar, the bar-coded tag is removed from the bottle and scanned out of inventory. Scanning the tag around the neck of the bottle accomplishes inventory taking.[18]

The beverage system from AZ Bar America (**www.azbaramerica.com**) offers a POS system that runs the operations behind the bar. It rings up the charge as the beverage is being poured while automatically removing the product from inventory.

Instead of holding up bottles and guessing what is left in them or even weighing each bottle at the end of shifts, the AZ2000 controller can at any time give a report of what was sold, who completed the transaction, how the system was used, and actual profits by brand, transaction, or product group. The system can be remotely monitored from home or other location by dialing into the bar location; this is handy for making price changes and monitoring sales activity.

[handwritten margin note: A system that helps owners keep tabs on the liquor consumption]

The AZ2000 is the heart of a dispensing system that interfaces with a variety of products: "spouts," a cocktail tower, beer, wine, juice, soft drink machines, and soda guns. The system even runs cocktail programming, so if the bartender does not know what goes into a certain drink, he on she can hit the cocktail button, and the system will tell the bartender what liquor bottle to pick up and control the recipe pour amounts.[19]

Personnel Procedures

Another key component of internal control is having procedures in place for screening and hiring bar personnel. Employees must be experienced in bartending and cocktail serving and also must be honest because they have access to the bar's beverage inventory and its cash.

Bar managers may also implement several other procedures to control inventory and reduce the likelihood of employee theft. One popular method is the use of *spotters,* who are hired to act like typical bar customers, but who are actually observing the bartenders and/or cocktailers for inappropriate behavior, such as not taking money from customers or overpouring. Another method for checking bar personnel is to perform a bank switch in the middle of the shift. In some cases, employees steal from the company by taking money from customers without ringing it up on the register. They keep the extra money in the cash drawer until the end of the shift when they are cashing out, at which point they retrieve the stolen funds. To do a bank switch, the manager must "z-out" a bartender's cash register, take the cash drawer, and replace it with a new bank. The manager then counts the money in the drawer, subtracts the starting bank, and compares that figure to the one on the register's tape. If there is a significant surplus of funds, it is highly likely that the employee is stealing. If there is less than what is indicated on the tape, the employee may be honest but careless when giving change or hitting the buttons on the register. Either way, there is a potential for loss.

Restaurant and Hotel Bars

In restaurants, the bar is often used as a holding area to allow guests to enjoy a cocktail or aperitif before sitting down to dinner. This allows the restaurant to space out the guests' orders so that the kitchen can cope more effectively; it also increases beverage sales. The profit margin from beverages is higher than the food profit margin.

In some restaurants, the bar is the focal point or main feature. Guests feel drawn to having a beverage because the atmosphere and layout of the restaurant encourages them to have a drink. Beverages generally account for about 25 to 30 percent of total sales. Many restaurants used to have a higher

The Banyan Court bar at the Moana Hotel is a perfect venue for a "sundowner"

percentage of beverage sales, but the trend toward responsible consumption of alcoholic beverages has influenced people to decrease their consumption.

Bars carry a range of each spirit, beginning with the *well* package. The well package is the least expensive pouring brand that the bar uses when guests simply ask for a "scotch and water." The *call* package is the group of spirits that the bar offers to guests who are likely to ask for a particular name brand. For example, guests may call for Johnnie Walker Red Label. An example of a premium scotch is Johnnie Walker Black Label, and a super premium scotch is Chivas Regal.

A popular method of costing each of the spirits poured is calculated according to the following example:

A premium brand of vodka such as Grey Goose costs $32.00 per liter and yields twenty-five $1\frac{1}{4}$-oz shots that each sell for $5.50. So, the bottle brings in $137.50. The profit margins produced by bars may be categorized as follows:

Liquor Pouring Cost % (approx.)	12
Beer	25
Wine	38

When combined, the sales mix may have an average pouring cost of 16 to 20 percent.

Most bars operate on some form of par stock level, which means that for every spirit bottle in use, there is a minimum par stock level of one, two, or more bottles available as a backup. As soon as the stock level falls to a level below the par level, more is automatically purchased.

Nightclubs

Nightclubs have long been a popular place to go to get away from the stresses of everyday life. From the small club in a suburban neighborhood to the world famous clubs of New York, Las Vegas, and Miami's South Beach, all clubs have one thing in common: People frequent them to kick back, relax, and, more often than not, enjoy a wild night of dancing and partying with friends and strangers alike.

Like restaurant ownership, starting up a nightclub is very risky business. But with the right education and proper planning, nightclub ownership can be a very profitable endeavor. As with most businesses in the hospitality industry, many believe that experience is more important than education and that you can learn as you go. However, when embarking on a journey as involved as owning a nightclub, a person with a degree and a high level of education is well ahead of the game.

The ability to read the market is key in developing a nightclub. When investing anywhere from $300,000 to $1 million in start-up costs, it is of utmost importance to be sure that the right spot is chosen and that a relevant market is within reach. Great nightclubs result from an accurate and calculated read of a marketplace, not by virtue of good luck. In fact, the number one cause of early nightclub failure stems from an inaccurate read on the marketplace. For example, if an entrepreneur is interested in opening up a country line dancing nightclub in an urban neighborhood, he or she may want to do extensive market research to be sure that members of the community even like country music.

When considering the prospect of a new nightclub, it is important to invest considerable time in the study of demographics, market attitude, and social dynamics of the proposed target. Many people tend to come up with a concept they are dead set on pursuing without really digging into the market. One should take all markets into account, even if the other markets may not seem relevant at the time. In the future it may be these same markets that are being divided to come to the newer clubs that have just opened.

A new and exciting concept is a highly important factor in creating a nightclub. Some people feel that if one nightclub is doing well down the street, they will open the same type and be equally successful. This is not true. Variety is one of the keys to successful business. By offering patrons a fresh new opportunity, one can draw clientele away from the old clubs and into the new club.

Budgeting is another big factor in developing a nightclub. Although such an undertaking can be very

Night clubs offer fun, excitement, and an atmosphere in which to socialize

costly, cutting corners in building and design will only hurt the business later. It is better to spend the money now and do it right than to have to spend more money for repairs later. Creating a budget should include all aspects of the operation, including, but not limited to, food and beverage costs, staffing and labor, licenses, building ramifications, décor, lighting, and entertainment.

Be sure to know all the legal issues that come with running a nightclub. For example, many laws exist on the sale and distribution of alcohol. In many instances, if a problem occurs involving a patron who was last drinking at the club, the problem can be considered the fault of the operation's management. Lawsuits can arise fairly easily, and it is highly important to be aware of such possibilities.

Nightclubs can be great experiences for both the patrons and the owner because revenues can be very high. However, it is important to remember the risks involved and work to minimize them.

Although this is only a brief discussion of the creation of a nightclub, the points given are quite important to successful operation. As with all business endeavors, the more one knows about the industry that he or she is getting involved with, the better off the business will be. For more information regarding the nightclub industry, go to **www.nightclub.com** or **www.nightclubbiz.com**.

Microbreweries/Brewpubs

Brewpubs are a combination brewery and pub or restaurant that brews its own fresh beer onsite to meet the taste of local customers. Microbreweries are craft breweries that produce up to 15,000 barrels (or 30,000 kegs) of beer a year. The North American microbrewery industry trend revived the concept of small breweries serving fresh, all-malt beer. Although regional breweries, microbreweries, and brewpubs account for only a small part of the North American brewing industry in terms of total beer production (less than 5 percent), they have a potentially large growth rate. One reason for the success of microbreweries and brewpubs is the wide variety of styles and flavors of beer they produce. On one

(handwritten margin note: educates public & easier to meet publics needs.)

hand, this educates the public about beer styles that have been out of production for decades and, on the other hand, helps brewpubs and restaurants meet the individual tastes and preferences of their local clientele.

Starting a brewpub is a fairly expensive venture. Although brewing systems come in a wide range of configurations, the cost of the equipment ranges from $200,000 to $800,000. Costs are affected by factors such as annual production capacity, beer types, and packaging. The investment in microbreweries and brewpubs is well justified by the enormous potential for returns. Microbreweries can produce a wide variety of ales, lagers, and other beers, the quality of which depends largely on the quality of the raw materials and the skill of the brewer. There are several regional brewpub restaurants of note, including Rock Bottom, which built its foundation on a tradition of fresh handcrafted beers and a diverse menu. It promotes itself as a place to gather with friends, drink the best beer around, enjoy a great meal, and share good times. John Harvard's has a famous selection of ales and lagers brewed on the premises according to the old English recipes brought to America in 1637 by John Harvard, after whom Harvard University is named. Gordon Biersch has several excellent brewery restaurants also offering handcrafted ales and beers along with a varied menu.

Sports Bars

Sports bars have always been popular but have become more so with the decline of disco and singles bars. They are places where people relax in the sporting atmosphere, so bar/restaurants such as Trophies in San Diego or Characters at Marriott hotels have become popular "watering holes." Satellite television coverage of the top sporting events helps sports bars to draw crowds. Sports bars have evolved over the years into much more than a corner bar that features the game of the week. In the past, sports bars were frequented by die-hard sports fans and rarely visited by other clientele. Today, the original sports bar is more of an entertainment concept and is geared toward a more diverse base of patrons.

Sports bars were originally no more than a gathering spot for local sports fans when the home team played on TV. Now such places have been transformed into mega-sports adventures, featuring musical entertainment, interactive games, and hundreds of TVs tuned in to just about every sport imaginable. "There are no more watering holes," says Zach Strauss, general manager of Sluggers World Class Sports Bar in Chicago. "Things have changed. People are more health conscious; nobody really drinks, drinks, drinks anymore. . . . You have to offer more than booze. People expect sports bars to have more personality, better food, and better service."[20]

Today's sports bars are attracting a much more diverse clientele. Now more women and families are frequenting these venues, which provides a new prospect for revenue for bar owners. Scott Estes, founding partner of Lee Roy Selmon's restaurant in Tampa, Florida, has recognized that women are an increasing revenue force in the industry and has made adjustments to his restaurant to be sure to capitalize on this rapidly expanding market. "A lot of women are very involved in sports, and we wanted women to feel comfortable coming here. Sports bars are also making changes in their establishments to become more family oriented. Lee Roy Selmon's main dining room, for example, is a television-free environment. Many families go into sports bars and request a room with no

TVs, so, recognizing that, an increasing number of owners have chosen to set aside a special place where families can eat uninterrupted by the noise of TV.

Another method of attracting bar patrons on slower nights is to offer games and family-friendly menus. Frankie's Food, Sports, and Spirits in Atlanta attracts families by hosting a sports-trivia game for teens. For the younger crowd, the restaurant provides a kids' menu every day and serves each pint-sized meal on upside-down Frisbees, which children can take home as souvenirs. Sports bars have also become the latest version of the traditional arcade. Many bars offer interactive video games where friends and families can compete against one another. Virtual reality games such as Indy 500 and other sports games are available at many establishments. Some venues have even gone a step farther and offer batting cages, bowling alleys, and basketball courts for their patrons to enjoy.

Another aspect of the sports bar that has changed drastically is the menu. Sports bars have a reputation for serving spicy chicken wings, hamburgers, and other typical bar fare. But just as sports bars have evolved in their entertainment offerings, so too have their menus. People's tastes have changed, causing sports bars to offer a more diverse menu. Today guests can dine on a variety of foods, from filet mignon, to fresh fish, to gourmet sandwiches and pizza. Now people frequent sports bars as much for the great meal they will have as for the entertainment. In the past, sports bars usually had a few TVs that showcased games that would appeal to the area and big games such as the Super Bowl. The sudden increase in technology and TV programming available has made game viewing very different. The popularity of satellites and digital receivers has allowed bars to tune in to virtually dozens of events at any given time. Bars now have hundreds of televisions, and fans can watch games featuring every sport, team, and level of play around the world at any time of the day or night.

Burbank, California–based ESPN Zone has about 200 televisions in each of its locations so that fans can catch all the action. A handful of televisions is placed in the restaurant's bathrooms because "we don't want you to miss a second," says Nina Roth, marketing manager for ESPN Zone in New York City. "If you have to go at the last minute, you're not going to miss the end of the game." The evolution of sports bars has turned the smoky corner bar into an exciting dining and sports experience. Customers who once rarely frequented the establishments, such as women and families, are now some of the biggest patrons, increasing both attendance and revenue at sports bars.

Coffee Shops   Barista.

New York Yankees fans celebrate in a sports bar

Another fairly recent trend in the beverage industry in the United States and Canada is the establishment of coffeehouses, or coffee shops. Coffeehouses originally were created based on the model of Italian bars, which reflected the deeply rooted espresso tradition in Italy. The winning concept of Italian bars lies in the ambiance they create, which is suitable for conversation of a personal, social, and business nature. A talk over a cup of coffee with soft background music and maybe a pastry is a typical scenario for Italians. Much of the same concept was re-created in the United States and Canada, where there was a niche in the beverage industry that was yet to be acknowledged and filled. The original concept was modified, however, to include a much wider variety of beverages and styles of coffee to meet the tastes of their consumers, who have a tendency to prefer a greater selection of products. Consequently, the typical espresso/cappuccino offered by Italian bars has been expanded in North America to include items such as iced mocha, iced cappuccino, and so forth.

Students as well as businesspeople find coffeehouses a place to relax, discuss, socialize, and study. The success of coffeehouses is reflected in the establishment of chains, such as Starbucks, as well as family-owned, independent shops.

Cyber cafés are a recent trend in the coffeehouse sector. Cyber cafés offer the use of computers, with Internet capability, for about $6 per hour. Guests can enjoy coffee, snacks, or even a meal while online. Reasonable rates allow regular guests to have e-mail addresses.

▶ Check Your Knowledge

1. Describe the bar setup.
2. How is inventory control conducted?
3. What is the average beverage pouring cost percentage?
4. What is a trend in sports bars?

Liquor Liability and the Law

Owners, managers, bartenders, and servers may be liable under the law if they serve alcohol to minors or to persons who are intoxicated. The extent of the liability can be very severe. The legislation that governs the sale of alcoholic beverages is called **dram shop legislation**. The dram shop laws, or civil damage acts, were enacted in the 1850s and dictated that owners and operators of drinking establishments are liable for injuries caused by intoxicated customers.

Some states have reverted back to the eighteenth-century common law, removing liability from vendors except in cases involving minors. Nonetheless, most people recognize that as a society we are faced with major problems of underage drinking and drunk driving.

To combat underage drinking in restaurants, bars, and lounges, a major brewery distributed a booklet showing the authentic design and layout of each state's driver's licenses. Trade associations, such as the National Restaurant Association and the American Hotel & Lodging Association, have, together with other major corporations, produced a number of preventive measures and programs aimed at responsible alcohol beverage service. The major thrust of these initiatives is awareness programs and mandatory training programs such as Serve Safe for Alcohol that promote responsible alcohol service. Serve Safe for Alcohol is sponsored by the National Restaurant Association and is a certification program that teaches participants about alcohol and its effects on people, the common signs of intoxication, and how to help customers avoid drinking too much.

Other programs for responsible alcohol service and consumption include designated drivers, who only drink nonalcoholic beverages to ensure that they can drive friends home safely. Some operators give free nonalcoholic beverages to the designated driver as a courtesy.

One positive outcome of the responsible alcohol service programs for operators is a reduction in the insurance premiums and legal fees for beverage establishments that had skyrocketed in previous years.

Trends in the Beverage Industry

- The comeback of cocktails
- Designer bottled water
- Microbreweries
- More wine consumption
- Increase in coffeehouses and coffee intake
- Increased awareness and action to avoid irresponsible alcoholic beverage consumption
- An increase in beverages to attract more female participation.
- An increase in the number and variety of "energy drinks."

CASE STUDY

Hiring Bar Personnel

As bar manager of a popular local night club, it is your responsibility to interview and hire all bar personnel. One of your friends asks you for a job as a bartender. Because he has experience, you decide to help him out and give him a regular shift. During the next few weeks, you notice that the overall sales for his shifts are down slightly from previous weeks when other bartenders worked that shift. You suspect he may be stealing from you.

Discussion Questions

1. What are your alternatives for determining whether your friend is, in fact, stealing?
2. If you determine that he has been stealing, how do you handle it?

CASE STUDY

Java Coffee House

Michelle Wong is manager of the Java Coffee House at a busy location on Union Street in San Francisco. Michelle says that there are several challenges in operating a busy coffeehouse, such as training staff to handle unusual circumstances. For example, one guest consumed a cup of coffee and ate two-thirds of a piece of cake and then said he didn't like the cake, so didn't want to pay for his order.

Another problem is suppliers who quote good prices to get her business and then, two weeks later, raise the price of some of the items.

Michelle says that the young employees she has at the Java Coffee House are her greatest challenge of all. According to Michelle, there are four kinds of employees—lazy; good, but not responsible; those who steal; and great ones who are no trouble.

Discussion Questions

1. What are some suggestions for training staff to handle unusual circumstances?
2. How do you ensure that suppliers are delivering the product at the price quoted?
3. What do you do with lazy employees?
4. What do you do with irresponsible employees?
5. How do you deal with employees who steal?

Summary

1. Beverages are categorized into alcoholic and nonalcoholic beverages. Alcoholic beverages are further categorized into spirits, wines, and beer.
2. Wine is the fermented juice of ripe grapes. It is classified as red, white, and rose, and we distinguish between light beverage wines, sparkling wines, and aromatic wines.
3. The six steps in making wine are crushing, fermenting, racking, maturing, filtering, and boiling. France, Germany, Italy, Spain, and Portugal are the main European wine-producing areas, and California is the main American wine-producing area.
4. Beer is a brewed and fermented beverage made from malt. Different types of beer include ale, stout, lager, and pilsner.

5. Spirits have a high percentage of alcohol and are served before or after a meal. Fermentation and distillation are parts of their processing. The most popular white spirits are rum, gin, vodka, and tequila.
6. Today people have become more health conscious about consumption of alcohol; nonalcoholic beverages such as coffee, tea, soft drinks, juices, and bottled water are increasing in popularity.
7. Beverages make up 20 to 30 percent of total sales in a restaurant, but managers are liable if they serve alcohol to minors. Programs such as designated driver and Responsible Alcholic Beverage Service and the serving of virgin cocktails have increased.

Key Words and Concepts

alcoholic beverage	must
beer	nonalcoholic beverage
brandy	Prohibition
champagne	proof
clarify	sparkling wine
cognac	spirit
dram shop legislation	vintage
fermentation	white spirits
fining	wine
fortified wines	wine and food pairing
hops	wine tasting
inventory control	wort
liquor	yeast
malt	
mashing	

Review Questions

1. On the Companion Website, what qualities does John Saputo look for in graduates?
2. From the Companion Website, what has Kellee Brockman done while working for Gold Coast Eagle Distributing?
3. What is the difference between fortified and aromatic wines? In what combination is it suggested to serve food wine and why?
4. Describe the brewing process of beer. What is the difference between a stout and a pilsner?
5. Name and describe the main types of spirits.
6. Why have nonalcoholic drinks increased in popularity, and what difficulties do bar managers face when serving alcohol?
7. Describe the origin of coffee.
8. Describe the proper procedure for handling and serving champagne.
9. Describe the origin of cocktails. What constitutes a cocktail?
10. Describe a typical bar setup.

Internet Exercises

1. Organization: **Clos Du Bois**
   Web site: www.closdubois.com
   Summary: Clos Du Bois is one of America's well-known and loved wineries and is a premier producer of wines from Sonoma County in California. The winery was started in 1974 and since then has acquired many more vineyards and a name for itself. It now sells about a million cases of premium wine annually.

   (a) Look at the detailed food and wine pairings. What can you serve with the Clos Du Bois Sonoma County sauvignon blanc? Compare it to what you already know about what to eat with sauvignon blanc.
   (c) The Clos Du Bois has been named Wine of the Year for nine years by *Wine & Spirits*. What is it about this wine that makes it so different from others?

2. Organization: **Siebel Institute of Technology**
   Web site: www.siebelinstitute.com
   Summary: Siebel Institute of Technology is recognized for its training and educational programs in brewing technology.

(a) What are some of the services that the Institute of Technology offers its students?
(b) List the career path options available through Siebel Institute of Technology.

Apply Your Knowledge

1. In groups, do a blindfold taste test with cans of Coke and Pepsi. See if your group can identify which is which and who likes Coke or Pepsi the most.
2. Complete a class survey of preference for Coke or Pepsi and share the results with your classmates.
3. Request a local wine representative to demonstrate the correct way of opening and serving a bottle of nonalcoholic wine. Then practice opening a bottle yourself.
4. What type of wine would be recommended with the following:
   a. Pork
   b. Cheese
   c. Lamb
   d. Chocolate cake
   e. Chicken

Suggested Activities

1. Search the Internet for underage drinking statistics and related highway deaths in your state.
2. Mothers Against Drunk Driving (MADD) is a nonprofit organization working to stop drunk drivers and support victims of drunk drivers. Find out what impact MADD has had on society.
3. Create an outline for a sports bar concept.

Endnotes

1. Personal correspondence with Jay R. Schrock, November 16, 2007.
2. *Ibid.*
3. Personnel conversation with Wayne Johnstone, November 16, 2007.
4. Budweiser Brewing Company presentation, University of South Florida, September 7, 2004.
5. Hottinger, Greg, "Organic Beer," O'Mama Report, Organic Trade Association, www.theorganicreport.com/pages/605_organic_beer.cfm.
6. Wikipedia, "Scotch Whiskey," en.wikipedia.org/wiki/Scotch_whiskey.
7. Wikipedia, "Scotch Whiskey," en.wikipedia.org/wiki/Scotch_whiskey.
8. C. Katsigiris and M. Porter, *The Bar and Beverage Book*, 3rd ed. (New York: John Wiley and Sons, 2002), 139.
9. Personal conversation with Susan Davis of the Specialty Coffee Association of America, August 26, 2005.
10. Ancora Coffee Roasters, "Goats Enjoy Coffee!" www.ancora-coffee.com/history-goats.asp.
11. Ancora Coffee Roasters, "Goats Enjoy Coffee!" www.ancora-coffee.com/history-goats.asp.
12. The Bean Shop, "History of Coffee," www.thebeanshop.com/beanshop/default.asp?p=31.
13. www.en.wikipedia.org/wiki/cappuccino.
14. Wikipedia, "Energy Drinks," en.wikipedia.org/wiki/Energy_drink.
15. Wikipedia, "Energy Drinks," en.wikipedia.org/wiki/Energy_drink.
16. www.restaurant.org/rusa/magArticle.cfm?ArticleID=515.
17. Scannabar, "Liquor Module," www.scanbar.com/eng/liquor.html.
18. Scannabar, "Wine Module," www.scanbar.com/eng/wine.html.
19. http://findarticles.com/p/articles/mi_MOBQF/is_5_16/ai_n14706433pg_4
20. Personal conversation with Zach Strauss, General Manager of Sluggers World Class Sports Bar in Chicago, May 4, 2007.

PART IV

Recreation, Theme Parks, Clubs, and Gaming Entertainment

CHAPTER 10

Recreation, Theme Parks, and Clubs

OBJECTIVES

After reading and studying this chapter, you should be able to:

- Discuss the relationship of recreation and leisure to wellness.

- Explain the origins and extent of government-sponsored recreation.

- Distinguish between commercial and noncommercial recreation.

- Name and describe various types of recreational clubs.

- Identify the major U.S. theme parks.

- Describe the operations of a country club.

Recreational activities include all kinds of sports, both team and individual. Baseball, softball, football, basketball, volleyball, tennis, swimming, jogging, skiing, hiking, aerobics, rock climbing, and camping are all active forms of recreation. Passive recreational activities include reading, fishing, playing and listening to music, gardening, playing computer games, and watching television or movies. **Recreation** *is an integral part of our nation's total social, economic, and natural resource environment. It is a basic component of our lives and well-being.*[1]

Recreation, Leisure, and Wellness

As postindustrial society has become more complex, life has become more stressed. The need to develop the wholeness of the person has become increasingly important. Compared to a generation ago, the stress levels of business executives are much higher. The term *burnout*—and indeed the word *stress*—has become a part of our everyday vocabulary only in recent years. Recreation is all about creating a balance, a harmony in life that will maintain wellness and wholeness.

Recreation allows people to have fun together and to form lasting relationships built on the experiences they have enjoyed together. This recreational process is called *bonding*. Bonding is hard to describe, yet the experience of increased interpersonal feeling for friends or business associates as a result of a recreational pursuit is common. These relationships result in personal growth and development.

The word *recreation* is defined as the use of time in a manner designed for therapeutic refreshment of one's body or mind.[2] Recreation is synonymous with lifestyle and the development of a positive attitude. An example of this is the increased feeling of well-being experienced after a recreational activity. Some people make the mistake of trying to pursue happiness as a personal goal. It is not enough for a person to say, "I want to be happy; therefore, I will recreate." Nathaniel Hawthorne wrote in the midnineteenth century: "Happiness in this world, when it comes, comes incidentally. Make it the object of pursuit, and it leads us on a wild goose chase, and it is never attained. Follow some other object, and very possibly we may find that we have caught happiness without dreaming of it."[3]

Recreation is a process that seeks to establish a milieu conducive to the discovery and development of characteristics that can lead to happiness. Happiness and well-being, therefore, are incidental outcomes of recreation. Thus, happiness may be enhanced by the pursuit of recreational activities. Personal recreational goals are equally as important as any other business or personal goals. These goals might include running a mile in under six minutes or maintaining a baseball batting average above 0.300. The fact that a person sets and strives to achieve goals requires personal organization. This helps improve the quality of life.

Windsurfing is definitely an active recreational activity

Leisure is best described as time free from work, or discretionary time. Some recreation professionals use the words *leisure* and *recreation* interchangeably, while others define leisure as the "productive," "creative," or "contemplative" use of free time. History shows again and again a direct link between leisure and the advancement of civilization. Hard work alone leaves no time for becoming civilized. Ironically, however, the opportunity to be at leisure is the direct result of increased technological and productivity advancements.

Hiking is a great exercise and an ideal way to get back to nature

Government-Sponsored Recreation

Various levels of government that constitute **government-sponsored recreation** are intertwined, yet distinct, in the parks, recreation, and leisure services. The founding fathers of America said it best when they affirmed the right to life, liberty, and the pursuit of happiness in the Declaration of Independence. Government raises revenue from income taxes, sales taxes, and property taxes. Additionally, government raises special revenue from recreation-related activities such as automobile and recreational vehicles, boats, motor fuels, **transient occupancy taxes (TOT)** on hotel accommodations, state lotteries, and others. The monies are distributed among the various recreation- and leisure-related organizations at the federal, state/provincial, city, and town levels. Recreation and leisure activities are extremely varied, ranging from cultural pursuits such as museums, arts and crafts, music, theater, and dance to sports (individual and team), outdoor recreation, amusement parks, theme parks, community centers, playgrounds, libraries, and gardens. People select recreational pursuits based on their interests and capabilities.

Park and recreation leaders confront daunting challenges at a time when leisure and recreational resources are highly valued community assets. Yet, securing adequate funding for staff and services can be a juggling act.[4] The following are some of the issues recreation professionals must deal with:

- Comprehensive recreation planning
- Land classification systems
- Federal revenue sharing
- Acquisition- and development-funding programs
- Land-use planning and zoning
- State and local financing
- Off-road vehicle impacts and policy
- Use of easements for recreation
- Designation of areas (such as wilderness, wild and scenic rivers, national trails, nature preserves)

- Differences in purposes and resources (of the numerous local, state/provincial, and federal agencies that control more than one-third of the nation's land, much of which is used for recreation)

National Parks in the United States

The prevailing image of a **national park** is one of grand natural playgrounds, such as Yellowstone National Park; but there is much more to parks than that.[5] The United States has designated 367 national park units throughout the country, including a rich diversity of places and settings. The **National Parks Service** was founded in 1916 by Congress to conserve park resources and to provide for their use by the public in a way that leaves them unimpaired for the enjoyment of future generations. In addition to the better-known parks such as Yellowstone and Yosemite, the Parks Service also manages many other heritage attractions, including the Freedom Trail in Boston, Independence Hall in Philadelphia, the Antietam National Battlefield in Sharpsburg, Maryland, and the USS *Arizona* Memorial at Pearl Harbor in Hawaii. The Parks Service is also charged with caring for myriad cultural artifacts, including ancient pottery, sailing vessels, colonial-period clothing, and Civil War documents.

The ever-expanding mandate of the Parks Service also calls for understanding and preserving the environment. It monitors the ecosystem from the Arctic tundra to coral atolls, researches the air and water quality around the nation, and participates in global studies on acid rain, climate change, and biological diversity. The idea of preserving exceptional lands for public use as national parks arose after the Civil War when America's receding wilderness left unique national resources vulnerable to exploitation. Recent years have seen phenomenal growth in the system, with three new areas created in the last twenty years. These include new kinds of parks, such as urban recreational areas, free-flowing rivers, long-distance trails, and historic sites honoring our nation's social achievements.

The system's current roster of 367 areas covers more than 80 million acres of land, with individual areas ranging in size from the 13-million-acre Wrangell–St. Elias National Park and Preserve in Alaska to the Thaddeus Kosciuszko National Memorial (a Philadelphia row house commemorating a hero of the American Revolution), which covers two one-hundredths of an acre.

More than 272 million visitors go to the parks each year and take advantage of the full range of services and programs. The focus once placed on preserving the scenery of the most natural parks has shifted as the system has

> There is nothing so American as our National Parks. . . . The fundamental idea behind the parks . . . is that the country belongs to the people.
>
> Franklin D. Roosevelt

The splendor of nature awaits us in our national parks

grown and changed. Today emphasis is placed on preserving the vitality of each park's ecosystem and on the protection of unique or endangered plant and animal species.

Public Recreation and Parks Agencies

During the early part of the nineteenth century in the United States, the parks movement expanded rapidly as a responsibility of government and voluntary organizations. By the early 1900s, fourteen cities had made provisions for supervised play facilities, and the playground movement gained momentum. Private initiative and financial support were instrumental in convincing city government to provide tax dollars to build and maintain new play areas.

Street basketball is a great team sport

About the same time, municipal parks were created in a number of cities. Boston established the first metropolitan park system in 1892. In 1898, the New England Association of Park Superintendents (predecessor of the American Institute of Park Executives) was established to bring together park superintendents and promote their professional concerns. Increasingly, the concept that city governments should provide recreation facilities, programs, and services became widely accepted. Golf courses, swimming pools, bathing beaches, picnic areas, winter sports facilities, game fields, and playgrounds were constructed.

▶ Check Your Knowledge

1. Name a few parks in the United States and in Canada. What are some characteristics that make the parks you named special?

2. Name your favorite park. Share with your classmates why it is your favorite.

Commercial Recreation / Eco-Adventure Tourism

Recreation management came of age in the 1920s and 1930s, when recreation and social programs were offered as a community service. Colleges and universities began offering degree programs in this area. Both public and private sector recreation management has grown rapidly since 1950.

Commercial recreation, often called eco- or adventure tourism, provides residents and visitors with access to an area's spectacular wilderness through a variety of guided outdoor activities. Specifically, commercial recreation is defined as outdoor recreational activities provided on a fee-for-service basis, with a focus on experiences associated with the natural environment.[6] Commercial recreation includes theme parks, attractions, and clubs.

Theme Parks

The idea of theme parks all began in the 1920s in Buena Park, California, with a small berry farm and tea room. As owner Walter Knott's restaurant business grew, different attractions were added to the site to keep waiting customers amused. After a gradual expansion, over eighty years after its humble beginnings, Knott's Berry Farm has become the largest independent theme park in the United States.

Today, Knott's Berry Farm is 150 acres of rides, attractions, live entertainment, historical exhibits, dining, and specialty shops. The park features six themes—Ghost Town, Indian Trails, Fiesta Village, the Boardwalk, Wild Water Wilderness, and Camp Snoopy, which is the official home of Snoopy and the Peanuts characters. In addition, the California Marketplace is located right outside the park, and offers fourteen unique shops and restaurants.

Knott's Berry Farm has truly been a great influence on the American theme park industry. Hundreds of parks, both independent and corporate owned, started to develop following the birth of Knott's. Creator Walter Knott may have figured out why amusement parks became so popular so quickly. He was quoted as saying, "The more complex the world becomes, the more people turn to the past and the simple things in life. We [the amusement park operators] try to give them some of those things."[7] Even with the ever-increasing competition, Knott's continues to attract guests with its authentic historical artifacts, relaxed atmosphere, emphasis on learning, famous food, varied entertainment, innovative rides, and specialty shopping.[8]

Knott' Berry Farm is now owned and operated by Cedar Fair Entertainment Company.

Size and Scope of the Theme Park Industry

Visiting **theme parks** has always been a favorite tourist activity. Theme parks attempt to create an atmosphere of another place and time, and they usually emphasize one dominant theme around which architecture, landscape, rides, shows, foodservices, costumed personnel, and retailing are orchestrated. In this definition, the concept of *themes* is crucial to the operation of the parks, with rides, entertainment, and food all used to create several different environments.[9]

Theme parks and attractions vary according to theme, which might be historical, cultural, geographical, and so on. Some parks and attractions focus on a single theme, such as the marine zoological Sea World parks. Other parks and attractions focus on multiple themes, such as King's Island in Ohio, a family entertainment center divided into six theme areas: International Street, October Fest, River-Town, Hanna-Barbera Land, Coney Mall, and Wild Animal Habitat. Another example is Great America in California, a 100-acre family entertainment center that evokes North America's past in five themes: Home Town Square, Yukon Territory, Yankee Harbor, Country Fair, and Orleans Place.[10]

An abundance of theme parks are located throughout the United States. These parks have a variety of attractions, from animals and sea life, to thrill rides and motion simulators. There are parks with

A seven-story water slide at Water Mania Theme Park in Kissimmee, Florida, is an example of a single-themed park

educational themes and parks where people go simply to have a good time.

Many of the country's most well known parks are located in Florida. Walt Disney World Resort, Sea World, Water Mania, Wet 'n Wild, and Universal Studios are just a few of the many parks located in Orlando. Busch Gardens and Adventure Island are both in Tampa.

Busch Gardens, located in both Tampa, Florida, and Williamsburg, Virginia, is perhaps the most well known of the animal-themed parks. Busch Gardens is like a zoo with a twist. It features equal amounts of thrill rides and animal attractions. Guests can take a train ride through the Serengeti Plains, where zebras and antelope run wild, hop aboard a giant tube ride through the Congo River rapids, or ride on one of the parks' many world-record-holding roller coasters.

Orcas entertain the crowds at Sea World

Many cities in the United States are well known for their festivals, which bring in droves of vacationers year after year. One of the most well known is Mardi Gras (Fat Tuesday) in New Orleans, Louisiana. Mardi Gras began more than a hundred years ago as a carnival and has evolved into a world-renowned party. Mardi Gras takes place every year in February, the day before Ash Wednesday, the beginning of Lent. The days leading up to Fat Tuesday are filled with wild parades, costume contests, concerts, and overall partying. The famous Bourbon Street is the scene for most of the partygoing crowd, and it is often too crowded to even walk around. Beads are big at Mardi Gras, and thousands are given out each year. The culture of New Orleans greatly adds to the festiveness of Mardi Gras, because traditional jazz and blues can always be heard on most street corners.

Another famous site of interest is the Grand Ole Opry in Nashville, Tennessee. The Grand Ole Opry is a live radio show in which country music guests are featured. Started more than seventy-five years ago, the Grand Ole Opry is what made Nashville "Music City." Since the Opry's start, Nashville has created a theme park, Opryland, and a hotel, the Opryland Resort. Famous musicians come from all over the world to showcase their talents, and tourists flock from everywhere to hear the sounds of the Opry and see the sites that Nashville has to offer.

Introducing Walt Disney: A Man with a Vision

In 1923, at the age of twenty-one, Walt Disney arrived in Los Angeles from Kansas City to start a new business. The first endeavor of Walt Disney and his brother Roy

Mardi Gras revelers crowd about a parade float in New Orleans was a series of shorts (a brief film shown before a feature-length movie) called *Alice Comedies,* which featured a child actress playing with animated characters. Realizing that something new was needed to capture the audience, Walt Disney conjured up the concept of a mouse character. In 1927, Disney began a series called *Oswald the Lucky Rabbit.* It was well received by the public, but Disney lost the rights as a result of a dispute with his distributor.

Mickey and Minnie Mouse first appeared in *Steamboat Willie,* which also incorporated music and sound, on November 18, 1928. Huge audiences were ecstatic about the work of the Disney Brothers, who became overnight successes.

> To all who come to this happy place: Welcome! Disneyland is your land; here, age relives fond memories of the past, and here youth may savor the challenge and promise of the future.
>
> Disneyland is dedicated to the hard facts that have created America, with the hope that it will be a source of joy and inspiration to all the world.
>
> Disneyland Dedication Plaque,
> July 17, 1955

During the next few years, Walt and Roy made many Mickey Mouse films, which earned them enough to develop other projects, including full-length motion pictures in Technicolor.

According to Disney, "Disneyland really began when my two daughters were very young. Saturday was always Daddy's Day, and I would take them to the merry-go-round and sit on a bench eating peanuts while they rode. And sitting there alone, I felt there should be something built, some kind of family park where parents and children could have fun together."[11]

Walt's original dream was not easy to bring to reality. During the bleak war years, not only was much of his overseas market closed, but the steady stream of income that paid for innovation dried up. However, even during the bleak years, Walt never gave up. Instead, he was excited to learn of the public's interest in movie studios and the possibility of opening the studios to allow the public to visit the birthplace of Snow White, Pinocchio, and other Disney characters.

After its creation, Disneyland had its growing pains—larger than expected opening day crowds, long lines at the popular rides, and a cash flow that was so tight that the cashiers had to rush the admission money to the bank to make payroll. Fortunately, since those early days, Disneyland and the Disney characters have become a part of the American dream.

By the early 1960s, Walt had turned most of his attention from film to real estate. Because he was upset when cheap motels and souvenir shops popped up around Disneyland, for his next venture, Walt Disney World, he bought 27,500 acres around the park. The center of Walt Disney World was to be the Experimental Prototype Community of Tomorrow (Epcot). Regrettably, Epcot and Walt Disney World were his dying dreams; Walt Disney succumbed to cancer in 1966.

However, Walt's legacy carries on. The ensuing years since Walt's death have included phenomenal Disney successes with Epcot, movies, a TV station, the Disney Channel, Disney stores, and Disney–MGM Studios (now Disney's Hollywood Studios) theme park. In April 1992, EuroDisneyland Resort, now Disneyland Paris Resort, opened near Paris. For a variety of reasons (location, cost, climate, and culture), it was initially a failure, until his Royal Highness Prince Al Waleed Bin Talal Bin Abdula of Saudi Arabia purchased 25 percent of the EuroDisney Paris Resort. Tokyo Disneyland Resort continues to be successful; since its opening in 1983, millions have enjoyed the happiest place on earth. Disneyland Hong Kong Resort, China, opened in 2005 and promises to draw millions if not billions to the magical kingdom.

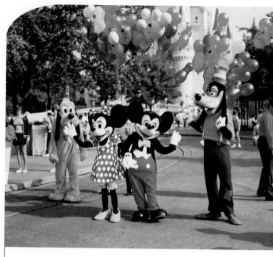

Walt Disney World

Both Walt Disney World Resort and Disneyland resort have excellent college programs that enable selected students to work during the summer months in a variety of hotel, foodservice, and related park positions. Disney has also introduced a faculty internship that allows faculty to intern in a similar variety of positions.

Walt Disney World Resort is composed of four major theme parks: Magic Kingdom, Epcot, Disney's Animal Kingdom, and Disney's Hollywood Studios, with more than 100 attractions, 22 resort hotels themed as faraway lands, spectacular nighttime entertainment, and vast shopping, dining, and recreation facilities that cover thousands of acres in this tropical paradise.

Walt Disney World Resort includes 25 lighted tennis courts, 99 holes of championship golf, marinas, swimming pools, jogging and bike trails, water skiing, and motor boating; 226 restaurants, lounges, and food courts; a starry-eyed tribute to 1930s Hollywood; and even bass fishing. Walt Disney World Resort is always full of new surprises: It now features the world's most unusual water adventure park, a "snow-covered" mountain with a ski resort theme called Blizzard Beach.

The Disney hotels are architecturally exciting and offer a number of amenities. The funfilled Disney's All-Star Sports Resort and Disney's colorful All-Star Music Resort are categorized as value-class hotels. Disney's Wilderness Lodge is one of the park's jewels, with its impressive tall-timber atrium lobby and rooms built around a Rocky Mountain geyser pool. For nighttime fun, there are the Pleasure Island nightclubs. In all, the park has a cast of 37,000 hosts, hostesses, and entertainers famous for their warm smiles and commitment to making every night an especially good one for Disney guests.

There is more to enjoy than ever in Epcot; INNOVENTIONS; the mind-blowing 3-D adventure, Honey, I Shrunk the Audience, in Future World; and, at the Disney's Hollywood Studios, the ultimate thriller, The Twilight Zone Tower of Terror.

Magic Kingdom Park

The heart of Walt Disney World Resort and its first famous theme park is the Magic Kingdom—the "happiest land on earth"—where "age relives fond memories" and "youth may savor the challenge and promise of the future." It is a giant theatrical stage where guests become part of exciting Disney adventures. It is also the home of Mickey Mouse, Snow White, Peter Pan, Tom Sawyer, Davy Crockett, and the Swiss Family Robinson.

More than forty major shows and ride-through attractions, not to mention shops and unique dining facilities, fill its seven lands of imagination. Each land carries out its theme in fascinating detail—architecture, transportation, music, costumes, dining, shopping, and entertainment are designed to create a total atmosphere where guests can leave the ordinary world behind. The seven lands include the following:

Main Street USA—Turn-of-the-century charm with horsedrawn streetcars, horseless carriages, Penny Arcade, and grand-circle tour on Walt Disney World Railroad

Adventureland—Explore with Pirates of the Caribbean, wild animal Jungle Cruise, Swiss Family Treehouse, Tropical Serenade by birds, flowers, and tikis

Frontierland—Thrills on Splash Mountain and Big Thunder Mountain Railroad, musical fun in Country Bear Jamboree, Shooting Gallery, Tom Sawyer Island caves and raft rides

Liberty Square—Steamboating on the Rivers of America, mystery in the Haunted Mansion, whooping it up in Diamond Horseshoe Saloon, viewing the impressive Hall of Presidents with the addition of President George W. Bush in a speaking role

Fantasyland—Cinderella Castle is the gateway to Peter Pan's Flight, Snow White's Scary Adventures, Dumbo the Flying Elephant, Alice's Mad Tea Party, musical cruise with doll-like dancers in "it's a Small World," and Cinderella's Golden Carrousel.

Mickey's Toontown Fair—Mickey's House, Grandma Duck's Farm, Mickey's Treehouse playground, and private photo session in Mickey's Dressing Room

Tomorrowland—Sci-fi city of the future, new whirling Astro-Orbiter, speedy Space Mountain, new production of Carousel of Progress, Grand Prix Raceway, elevated Transit tour, new Disney Character show on Tomorrowland Stage

Epcot

Epcot is a unique, permanent, and ever-changing world's fair with two major themes: Future World and World Showcase. Highlights include Illumi-Nations, a nightly spectacle of fireworks, fountains, lasers, and classical music.

Future World shows an amazing exposition of technology for the near future for home, work, and play in INNOVENTIONS. The newest consumer products are continually added. Major pavilions exploring past, present, and future are shown in the Spaceship Earth story of communications. The Universe of Energy giant dinosaurs help explain the origin and future of energy. There are also the World of

Motion soon-to-be test track, Journey into Imagination The Land, with spectacular agricultural research and environmental growing areas, and The Living Seas, the world's largest indoor ocean with thousands of tropical sea creatures.

Around the World Showcase Lagoon includes pavilions where guests can see world-famous landmarks and sample the native foods, entertainment, and culture of eleven nations:

The monorail zips past Spaceship Earth in Epcot at the Walt Disney World Resort near Orlando, Florida

Mexico—Mexico's fiesta plaza and boat trip on *Gran Fiesta Tour* plus San Angel Inn for authentic Mexican cuisine

Norway—Thrilling Viking boat journey and Akershus Royal Banquet Hall Restaurant

China—Wonders of China Circle-Vision 360 film tour from the Great Wall to the Yangtze River plus Nine Dragons Restaurant

Germany—Authentic Biergarten restaurant

Italy—St. Mark's Square street players and Tutto Italia Réstaurante

United States—The American Adventure's stirring historical drama

Japan—Re-creating an Imperial Palace plus Teppanyaki Dining Rooms

Morocco—Morocco's palatial restaurant Marrakesh

France—Impressions de France film tour of the French countryside, Les Chefs de France

United Kingdom—Shakespearean street players plus Rose & Crown Pub and Dining Room

Canada—Halifax to Vancouver Circle-Vision 360 tour

Each showcase has additional snack facilities and a variety of shops featuring arts, crafts, and merchandise from each nation.

Disney's Hollywood Studios

With fifty major shows, shops, restaurants, ride-through adventures, and backstage tours, Disney's Hollywood Studios combines real working motion picture, animation, and television studios with exciting movie attractions. The newest adventure in the Sunset Boulevard theater district is the Twilight Zone Tower of Terror, with a stunning thirteen-story elevator fall. The famous Chinese Theater on Hollywood Boulevard houses The Great Movie Ride.

Other major attractions include a Backstage Studio Tour of production facilities, Catastrophe Canyon, and New York Street; a tour of Walt Disney Animation Studios, Florida; exciting shows at Indiana Jones Epic Stunt Spectacular and Jim Henson's Muppet Vision 3D; plus a thrilling space flight on Star Tours.

Especially entertaining for movie and TV fans is Monster Sound Show, where audience members take part in performances. Favorite Disney films become entertaining stage presentations in the Voyage of The Little Mermaid theater and in Beauty and the Beast, a live, twenty-five-minute musical revue

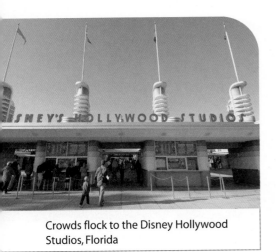
Crowds flock to the Disney Hollywood Studios, Florida

at Theater of the Stars. The best restaurants include the Hollywood Brown Derby, 50's Prime Time Cafe, Sci-Fi Dine-In Theater, Mama Melrose's Ristorante Italiano, and the ABC Commissary.

All this and much more are what help make Walt Disney World Resort the most popular destination resort in the world. Since its opening in 1971, more than 500 million guests, including kings and celebrities from around the world and all six U.S. presidents in office since the opening, have visited the parks. What causes the most comment from guests is the cleanliness, the friendliness of its cast, and the unbelievable attention to detail—a blend of showmanship and imagination that provides an endless variety of adventure and enjoyment.[12]

Disney's Animal Kingdom Park is the newest edition to Walt Disney World. The Animal Kingdom focuses on nature and the animal world around us. Guests can go on time-traveling rides and come face to face with animals from the prehistoric past to the present. Shows are put on featuring Disney's most popular animal-based films, such as *The Lion King* and *A Bug's Life*. Safari tours that bring guests up close and personal with live giraffes, elephants, and hippopotamuses are also offered at Disney's Animal Kingdom.

Walt Disney World Resort's two water parks are Blizzard Beach and Typhoon Lagoon. Blizzard Beach has a unique ski resort theme, while Typhoon Lagoon is based on the legend that a powerful storm swept through, leaving pools and rapids in its wake. Both parks offer a variety of slides, tube rides, pools, and moving rivers that drift throughout the parks.

Universal Studios

Universal Studios has been giving guided tours on its famous movie sets for more than thirty years, and tens of thousands of people visit Universal every day.[13] Since its founding, Universal Studios has become the most formidable competitor facing the Disney Corp.

In Orlando, Florida, Universal Studios has enjoyed huge success, despite encroaching on the "kingdom" of Disney. In addition to its Hollywood and Orlando parks, Universal has since expanded into Spain, China, and Japan. One reason for Universal's success is its adaptation of movies into thrill rides. Another is its commitment to guest participation. Guests get to help make sound effects and can participate in "stunts," making Universal Studios more than just a "look behind the scenes."

Universal Studios is also a good example of what is predicted to occur in the future with regards to amusement and theme parks. It is offering more realistic thrill rides by combining new technologies and state-of-the-art equipment. Also, the company has realized that visitors tend to go to theme parks just because they happen to be in the area. By greatly expanding the experience, NBC Universal is hoping that its improvements will make travelers want to visit Universal Studios as a one-stop destination.

Let's take a closer look at the Universal theme parks:

Universal Studios Hollywood was the first Universal park and boasts the title of the world's largest movie studio and theme park. As part of the new studio tour, visitors are taken into the tomb of the Mummy, feel the hot breath of King Kong, experience a major earthquake, and are right in the middle of a Hollywood movie shoot. Afterward, guests can "chill" at the Universal City Walk, a street that claims to offer the best in food, nightlife, shopping, and entertainment.

Universal Orlando is a destination in itself, with two theme parks, several themed resorts, and a bustling City Walk. In Universal Studios, like in the Hollywood park, you

The Dueling Dragons inverted roller coaster twists its way upside down over a loop at Universal Studios theme park, Orlando, Florida

can explore the exciting world of movie making. Its newest and most exciting park, *Islands of Adventure*, gives you the best in roller coasters and thrill rides, whereas *Wet 'n Wild* gives you the opportunity to enjoy a range of cool waterslides, among other things. If you're not already exhausted by the mere thought of it, why not check out City Walk for some food, shopping, and a taste of the hottest nightlife in town. Myriads of venues, popular with tourists and locals alike, offer an amazing variety of cool bars, hot clubs, and live music.

Universal Studios Experience in Beijing, China, gives the visitor a tantalizing taste of Hollywood and is known to be a fun and educational experience for the whole family. For the younger audience, the park also offers nightlife and entertainment, "American style"!

Universal Studios Japan is the newest addition and features eighteen rides and shows, some brand new and others old favorites, plus great dining and shopping.[14]

Anheuser-Busch Companies

Anheuser-Busch Companies is a St. Louis–based corporation with subsidiaries that include the world's largest brewing company and the second largest U.S. manufacturer of aluminum beverage containers. It is also the largest corporate-owned theme/animal park company in the United States.

Anheuser-Busch is a leader in conservation and education. The Anheuser-Busch Corporation animal parks not only offer guests from around the world the opportunity to see and experience the wonders of many marine and land animals, but they also have highly developed educational programs. These programs reach millions of people a year, in the parks, on TV, and over the Internet, informing them on topics such as endangered animals, the environment, and the wonders of the ocean. In addition, the Busch Entertainment Corporation is active in the areas of conservation, research, and wildlife assistance worldwide.

The company is dedicated to preserving marine life. It uses innovative programs to research various wildlife dilemmas. Busch Companies also participates in breeding, animal rescue, rehabilitation, and conservation efforts throughout the year. What Busch Companies does for the preservation of animals is important to the existence of its theme parks because the research and rescue programs are subsidized through guest revenue. Also, each park offers unique shows and attractions combining entertainment and education with a strong commitment to research and conservation.

Currently, Anheuser-Busch Companies run the following parks in the United States:

Sea World—The three Sea World parks are located in California, Florida, and Texas. Each park has various themes, marine and animal attractions, shows, rides, and educational exhibits. Sea World is based on the creatures of the sea. Guests can pet dolphins and other fish, watch shows featuring Shamu, the famous killer whale, and learn all about the mysteries of the sea. Several rides are also available at Sea World, and countless exhibits feature everything from stingrays to penguins.

Busch Gardens—These theme parks, located in both Tampa, Florida, and Williamsburg, Virginia, feature both exciting thrill rides and attractions in addition to large zoos and safari parks. The theme for the Williamsburg Park is that of the "Old Country." It re-creates the seventeenth-century charm of the Old World European atmosphere with a journey through nine authentically detailed European hamlets. "The Dark Continent" in Tampa has a distinctly African theme.

Adventure Island—Also located in Tampa, Adventure Island is the only splash park in the Tampa Bay area. It is also the only water theme park on Florida's west coast featuring several unique water play areas and thrilling splash rides. The water park comprises more than twenty-five acres of fun-filled water rides, cafés, and shops.

Water Country USA—Anheuser-Busch's other water theme park is located in Williamsburg. It is "the mid-Atlantic's largest water park, featuring state-of-the-art water rides and attractions, all set to a 1950s and 1960s surf theme plus live entertainment, shopping, and restaurants."[15] Like Adventure Island, Water Country has an educational atmosphere to help guests, especially children, learn water safety techniques. Everything in the park is set to the theme of the 1950s surfing era.

Sesame Place—This fourteen-acre park is located in Langhorne, Pennsylvania, and is dedicated totally to a Sesame Street theme. It was designed with the goal of stimulating children's natural curiosity to learn and explore, while building self-confidence as they interact with other children.

Discovery Cove—Adjacent to Sea World in Orlando, Florida, Busch's newest addition Discovery Cove is where you can immerse yourself in adventure. It offers up-close encounters with dolphins and other exotic sea life. Guests can swim with dolphins and snorkel through a coral reef, tropical river, waterfalls, and an amazing freshwater lagoon, among other things.[16]

Hershey's

What does the name Hershey bring to mind?[17] It was at the 1893 World's Columbian Exposition in Chicago that Hershey first became fascinated with the art of chocolate. Then Milton Hershey, a small-time candy manufacturer, decided he wanted to make chocolate to coat his caramels. He opened his new establishment in Lancaster, Pennsylvania, and named it Hershey Chocolate Company. In the 1900s, the company started to produce mass quantities of milk chocolate, which resulted in immediate success. Soon after, Hershey decided that there was a need to increase his production facilities. He built a new factory on the farmland of south-central Pennsylvania in Derry Township. The following decades brought many product-line expansions. In 1968, the company was renamed Hershey Foods Corporation. Today, the company is the leading manufacturer of chocolate, non-chocolate confectionery, and grocery products in North America. It exports to more than ninety countries and has approximately 13,700 employees and net sales in excess of $4 billion.

In 1907, Milton Hershey opened Hershey Park as a leisure park for employees of Hershey's Company. He wanted to create a place for his employees to relax and have some fun when they were not on the job. The park was small and simple, offering employees a place to picnic, canoe, and walk around the beautifully landscaped grounds. In 1908, the park started its soon-to-be huge expansion with the addition of a merry-go-round.

In the years to come, the park continued to add more rides and attractions. As the park continued to expand, the company decided to open the park's doors to the public. It became a small regional park with a pay-as-you-ride policy.

In 1971, the park underwent redevelopment to turn the small regional park into a large theme park. In addition, the company decided to add a one-time admission fee to eliminate the pay-as-you-ride policy and changed its name from Hershey Park to Hersheypark. Today, the park sits on more than 110 acres and is the home of in excess of sixty rides and attractions.

▶ Check Your Knowledge

1. What is Knott's Berry Farm?

2. Why did Walt Disney really create Disneyland?

3. Discuss your favorite theme park with your class. Explain why it is your favorite.

Regional Theme Parks

Dollywood

In 1961, a small attraction with a Civil War theme called Rebel Railroad opened its doors to the public.[18] In the 1960s, the name Rebel Road was changed to Goldrush Junction, and the theme was changed to resemble the Wild West. This attraction is now known all across the world as Dollywood. The name came about in 1986 when Dolly Parton became a co-owner of the park. The park sits on 125 acres in the foothills of the Great Smoky Mountains in Pigeon Forge, Tennessee. In addition to having all the rides of an amusement park, Dollywood is enriched with the culture of the Smoky Mountains. The park includes crafts such as blacksmithing, glass blowing, and wood carving. It also continues to host several festivals, concerts, and musical events. Today, Dollywood brings in more than 2.5 million visitors every year and continues to be Tennessee's number one tourist attraction.

LegoLand

LegoLand is a theme park owned and operated by the Lego Group.[19] In 1968, LegoLand, Billund, and has 1.6 million visitor annually. The parks are themed after—you guessed it—Lego's, the brightly colored plastic bricks, gears, minifigures, and other pieces that are assembled to create models of almost anything. The parks are marketed toward young families. This is emphasized in the rides: All the parks have roller coasters that are not quite as extreme as the roller coasters found in other theme parks. Today there are four LegoLand parks located in Windsor, England; Günzburg, Germany; Carlsbad, California; and Billund, Denmark. Each park features a miniland, which is made up of millions of bricks that create models of landmarks and scenes from all around the world. The Windsor Park is one of Britain's most popular attractions bringing 1.3 million visitors annually. The other parks (Californian, Danish, and German) all bring in approximately 1.4 million visitors annually. In 2005 a 70 percent interest in LegoLand's four theme parks was sold to the Blackstore group.[20]

GatorLand

GatorLand is a 110-acre theme park and wildlife preserve located in Orange County, Florida.[21] It all started when Owen Godwin built an alligator pit in his backyard. After World War II, Godwin bought a sixteen-acre plot located off of Florida's second most traveled highway. He decided that he wanted to build an attraction on his land that would provide a close-up view of Florida's animals in their native habitat. In 1949, Godwin opened the attraction's doors to the public under the name of the Florida Wildlife Institute, which he shortly after changed to the Snake Village and Alligator Farm. In 1954, Godwin once again changed the name of the attraction to its current name, GatorLand.

The 1960s brought growth to the tourism industry in Florida. As the industry grew, GatorLand continued to expand by adding a number of exhibits and attractions. Today, GatorLand features alligators, crocodiles, a breeding marsh, reptilian shows, a petting zoo, a swamp walk, educational programs, and train rides. In addition, it offers the following shows: Gator Jumparoo, which features alligators jumping four to five feet out of the water to retrieve food; Gator Wrestling, an alligator wrestling show in which wranglers catch an alligator by hand; and Upclose Animal Encounters, where visitors meet wildlife from around the globe. One of the oldest attractions in the area, GatorLand continues to be privately owned by Godwin's family today.

Wet 'n Wild

Wet 'n Wild was founded by George Millay in Orlando, Florida, in 1977.[22] George Millay is also known as the creator of Sea World. Wet 'n Wild is considered the first major water park opened in the United States. Millay received the first Lifetime Achievement Award from the World Waterpark Association for creation of Wet 'n Wild. The association named him the official "Father of the Waterpark."

Today, Wet 'n Wild is a chain of water parks with locations in Florida and North Carolina. The Wet 'n Wild North Carolina located in Greensboro features more than thirty-six rides and attractions that are classified "from mild to wild." Wet 'n Wild Orlando also offers something for everyone. The rides all fall into four categories: Thrill Rides, Multi Person Rides, Just For Kids, and Takin' It Easy. In 1998, Millay sold the Orlando Park to Universal Studios Recreation Group.

Clubs

Private clubs are places where members gather for social, recreational, professional, or fraternal reasons. Members enjoy bringing friends, family, and business guests to their club. Their club is like a second home, but with diverse facilities and staff to accommodate the occasion. Bringing guests to one's club can be more impressive than inviting them to one's home, and there is still a level of the same personal atmosphere as there would be if guests were invited home. Many of today's clubs are adaptations of their predecessors, mostly examples from England and Scotland. For example, the North American Country Club is largely patterned after the Royal and Ancient Golf Club of St. Andrews, Scotland, founded in 1758 and recognized as the birthplace of golf. Many business deals are negotiated on the golf course. A few years ago, country clubs were often considered to be bastions of the social elite.

Historically, the ambiance of these clubs attracted the affluent. The character of the clubs transcended generations. Member etiquette and mannerisms developed over years to a definable point by which members could recognize each other through subtleties, and those not possessing the desired qualities were not admitted.

Today there are more affluent people than ever, and their number continues to grow. The new rich are now targeted and recruited for a variety of new hybrid

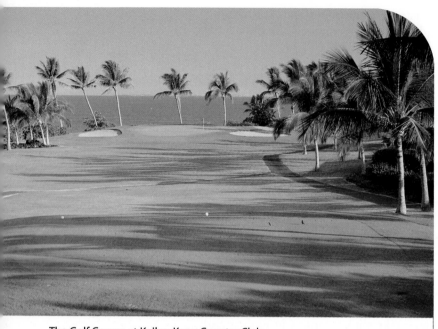

The Golf Course at Kailua-Kona Country Club

groups that also call themselves clubs. The newer clubs' cost of initiation and membership may be considerably less than some of the more established clubs. The stringent screening process and lengthy membership applications are now simplified, and cash is the key to admittance.

New clubs are born when a developer purchases a tract of land and builds a golf course with a clubhouse surrounded by homes or condominiums. The homes are sold and include a membership to the club. After all the homes are sold, the developer announces that the golf course and clubhouse will be sold to an investor who wishes to open it to the public. The homeowners rush to purchase the clubhouse and golf course to protect their investment. A board is formed, and the employees of the developer and all operations are usually transferred to and become the responsibility of the new owners or members.

Size and Scope of the Club Industry

There are approximately 14,000 private clubs in North America, including both country and city clubs. About 6,000 of these clubs are country clubs. When the total resources of all the clubs are considered such as land, buildings, equipment, along with thousands of employees and so on, clubs have billions of dollars of economic impact.

Club Management

Club management is similar in many ways to hotel management, both of which have evolved in recent years. The general managers of clubs now assume the role of chief operating officer, and in some cases chief executive officer of the corporation. They may also have responsibility for management of the homeowners' association and all athletic facilities, including the golf courses. In addition, they are responsible for planning, forecasting and budgeting, human resources, food and beverage operations, facility management, and maintenance. The main difference between managing a club and managing a hotel is that with clubs the guests feel as if they are the owners (in many cases they are) and frequently behave as if they are the owners. Their emotional attachment to the facility is stronger than that of hotel guests who do not use hotels with the same frequency that members use clubs. Another difference is that most clubs do not offer sleeping accommodations.

CORPORATE PROFILE

ClubCorp

Founded in 1957, Dallas-based Club-Corp is the world leader in delivering premier golf, private club, and resort experiences. Internationally, ClubCorp's affiliates own or operate nearly 170 golf courses, country clubs, private business, sports clubs, and resorts. ClubCorp has approximately $1.5 billion in assets. Among the company's nationally recognized golf properties are Pinehurst in the Village of Pinehurst, North Carolina (the largest golf resort in North America and site of the 1999 and 2005 U.S. Open); Firestone Country Club in Akron, Ohio (site of the 2003–2005 World Golf Championships—Bridgestone Invitational); the Homestead in Hot Springs, Virginia (America's first resort, founded in 1766); and Mission Hills Country Club in Rancho Mirage, California (home of the Kraft Nabisco Championship).

The more than sixty business clubs and business and sports clubs include the Boston College Club; City Club on Bunker Hill in Los Angeles; Citrus Club in Orlando, Florida; Columbia Tower Club in Seattle; Metropolitan Club in Chicago; Tower Club in Dallas; and the City Club of Washington, D.C. The company's 18,000 employees serve the nearly 200,000 member households and 200,000 guests who visit ClubCorp properties each year.

ClubCorp is in the business of building relationships and enriching lives. The extraordinary private club environments nourish relationships old and new, as well as create a world of privacy, luxury, and relaxation where guests' every need is anticipated and every expectation exceeded. Crafting fine, private club traditions for more than fifty years, ClubCorp has developed a signature philosophy of service that resonates with every encounter, every warm welcome, and every magic moment, joining to form the bedrock of all the clubs do.

Each club has its own distinctive personality and takes pride in creating the perfect settings for casual gatherings with friends to business meetings to formal celebrations. The clubs provide safe havens where members and their guests always are welcome. Whether looking for a country club experience or a professional retreat from which to conduct business affairs, our members are the beneficiaries of the ultimate in private club service and tradition.

ClubCorp clubs provide a variety of membership options and experiences for a range of lifestyle pursuits. In more than 170 private business and sports clubs, country clubs, golf courses, and golf resorts around the world, from Seattle to Mexico and from Boston to Beijing, ClubCorp provides for its members a haven of refuge, a home away from home, where every need is anticipated and every expectation surpassed.

Source: ClubCorp, "About Us," www.clubcorp.com.

Club members pay an initiation fee to belong to the club and annual membership dues thereafter. Some clubs also charge a set utilization fee, usually related to food and beverages, which is charged regardless of whether those services are used.

The Club Manager's Association of America (CMAA) is the professional organization to which many of the club managers of the 6,000 private country clubs belong. The association's goal is to advance the profession of club management by fulfilling the educational and related needs of the club managers. The association provides networking opportunities and fosters camaraderie among its member managers through meetings and conferences held locally and nationally. These gatherings keep managers abreast of current practices and procedures and new legislation. The general managers who join CMAA subscribe to a code of ethics.

Club Management Structure

The internal management structure of a club is governed by the corporation's articles of incorporation and bylaws. These establish election procedures, officer positions, a board of directors, and standing committees. Guidance and direction also are provided for each office and committee and how it will function. The general manager will usually provide an orientation for the new directors and information to help them in their new role. The members elect the officers and directors of the club. The officers represent the membership by establishing policies by which the club will operate. Many clubs and other organizations maintain continuity by having a succession of officers. The secretary becomes the vice president and the vice president becomes the president. In other cases, the person elected president is simply the person believed to be the most qualified to lead the club for that year. Regardless of who is elected president, the club's general manager must be able to work with that person and the other officers.

The president presides at all official meetings and is a leader in policy making. The vice president is groomed for the role of president, which is usually eminent, and will in the absence of the president perform the presidential duties. If the club has more than one vice president, the titles *first*, *second*, *third*, and so on, may be used. Alternatively, vice presidents may be assigned to chair certain committees, such as membership. Board members usually chair one or more committees.

Committees play an important part in the club's activities. If the committees are effective, the operation of the club is more efficient. The term of committee membership is specified, and committee meetings are conducted in accordance with Robert's Rules of Order, which are procedural guidelines on the correct way to conduct meetings. Standing committees include the following: house, membership, finance/budget, entertainment, golf, green tennis, pool, and long-range planning. The president may appoint additional committees to serve specific functions commonly referred to as ad hoc.

The treasurer obviously must have some financial and accounting background because an integral part of his or her duties is to give advice on financial matters, such as employing external auditors, preparing budgets, and installing control

INTRODUCING EDWARD J. SHAUGHNESSY

General Manager, Belleair Country Club

For Ed Shaughnessy, working in a country club is not just a job but a passion. Clubs feature great recreational facilities, including some fabulous golf courses, gourmet dining, the finest entertainment, and clientele who are more like family than customers. Shaughnessy has worked for three prestigious clubs in his career. He began working in clubs at the tender age of fourteen as a busboy. Shortly after graduating from high school, he accepted a full-time evening bar manager position at Sleepy Hollow Country Club in New York. He worked full time at nights while attending college full time until he received his AAS degree. Upon graduation, he was promoted to food and beverage manager, but continued his education, taking two or three courses every semester until he earned and received his BBA. He was subsequently promoted to assistant general manager.

After fourteen years at the same club and on his twenty-ninth birthday, he was offered and accepted the general manager's position at Belle Haven Country Club in Alexandria, Virginia. He began an active role in the National Capital Club Managers Association and was elected president. He continued his education and earned his Certified Club Manager (CCM) designation and his Certified Hospitality Educator (CHE) designation through the Club Manager's Association of America. He stayed at Belle Haven Country Club for eight years, but wanted to live closer to sunny beaches in a warmer climate.

An opportunity at the prestigious Belleair Country Club was brought to Shaughnessy's attention by John Sibbald, a top recruiter in the club industry, and in 1997 Ed Shaughnessy accepted the position of general manager/chief operating officer at the Belleair Country Club. He continued his education, earning his MBA in International Hotel and Tourism Management from Schiller International University, where he now teaches a variety of hospitality-related courses. Shaughnessy is still active with the Club Managers Association and serves on the Club Foundation Allocation Committee. This committee reviews scholarship and grant applications and recommends the awarding of funds to promote education. He also serves as the ethics chair for the Florida Chapter Club Managers Association.

Shaughnessy believes that there are two stages in life, growth and decay, and that we are all in one of these stages. For him, to be in the growth stage is preferred in life. He believes we are all given the choice to change our environment, and he enjoys catering to those with the highest expectations. It appears that people will always recognize and be willing to pay for great value and quality. Meticulous attention to detail and proactively providing what the customers desire before they have to ask is the key to success.

No two days are the same or predictable for a general manager. One day you could be developing a strategic plan, the next you may be invited to fly on a private Lear jet to see the Super Bowl. You have to make a conscious effort to balance work and family life. A general manager should remember that, although you can enjoy many of the same privileges as the elite, you are still an employee and must always set an exemplary role as a professional. A general manager's people skills are very important, as well as a comprehensive understanding of financial statements.

The challenge for the future is finding talented and service-oriented people who are needed to exceed the constantly increasing expectations of sophisticated and discriminating club members. Shaughnessy discovered some time ago that it may be necessary to grow one's own talent among his employees, and this gives him the confidence that he will be ready to serve his customers well. Shaughnessy has a high concern for the welfare of his loyal and dedicated employees. They could lose their jobs if the club is mismanaged. These people and their families count on him to operate the club efficiently. He also recognizes that he must take proactive steps to ensure the growth and success of his club. With two waterfront golf courses, a marina, and the amenities of a full-service country club, Ed Shaughnessy is taking steps to be sure he positions the club for continued success.

CMAA Code of Ethics

We believe the management of clubs is an honorable calling. It shall be incumbent upon club managers to be knowledgable in the application of sound principles in the management of clubs, with ample opportunity to keep abreast of current practices and procedures. We are convinced that the Club Managers Association of America best represents these interests and, as members thereof subscribe to the following CODE OF ETHICS.

We will uphold the best traditions of club management through adherence to sound business principles. By our behavior and demeanor, we shall set an example for our employees and will assist our club officers to secure the utmost in efficient and successful club operations.

We will consistently promote the recognition and esteem of club management as a profession and conduct our personal and business affairs in a manner to reflect capability and integrity. We will always honor our contractual employment obligations.

We shall promote community and civic affairs by maintaining good relations with the public sector to the extent possible within the limits of our club's demands.

We will strive to advance our knowledge and abilities as club managers, and willingly share with other Association members the lessons of our experience and knowledge gained by supporting and participating in our local chapter and the National Association's educational meetings and seminars.

We will not permit ourselves to be subsidized or compromised by any interest doing business with our clubs.

We will refrain from initiating, directly or through an agent, any communications with a director, member, or employee of another club regarding its affairs without the prior knowledge of the manager thereof, if it has a manager.

We will advise the National Headquarters, whenever possible, regarding managerial openings at clubs that come to our attention. We will do all within our power to assist our fellow club managers in pursuit of their professional goals.

We shall not be deterred from compliance with the law, as it applies to our clubs. We shall provide our club officers and trustees with specifics of federal, state and local laws, statutes, and regulations to avoid punitive action and costly litigation.

We deem it our duty to report to local or national officers any willful violations of the CMAA CODE OF ETHICS.

Source: Club Manager's Association of America.

systems. The general manager is responsible for all financial matters and usually signs or cosigns all checks.

It is the duty of the secretary to record the minutes of meetings and take care of club-related correspondence. In most cases, the general manager prepares the document for the secretary's signature. This position can be combined with that of treasurer, in which case the position is titled secretary–treasurer. The secretary may also serve on or chair certain committees.

The Club Managers Association of America (CMAA) has reexamined the role of club managers and, because of ever-increasing expectations, the role of the general manager has changed from the traditional managerial model to a leadership model. (This is discussed in more detail in Chapter 14.) The new CMAA model is based on the premise that general managers or chief operating officers (COOs) are more responsible for operating assets and investments and club culture.

Figure 10–1 shows the core competencies of a general manager or COO as private club management, food and beverage, accounting and financial management, human and professional resources, building and facilities management, external and governmental influences, management, marketing, and sports and recreation.

The second tier of the model is mastering the skills of asset management. Today's general manager or COO must be able to manage the physical property, the financial well-being, and the human resources of the club. These facets of the manager's responsibility are equally as important as managing the operations of the club.

The third and final tier of the new model is preserving and fostering the culture of the club, which can be defined as the club's traditions, history, and vision. Many managers or COOs intrinsically perform this function; however, it is often an overlooked and underdeveloped quality. A job description for club manager is given in Figure 10–2. The Club Management Competencies are shown in Figure 10–3. Additionally, you can see the overall organization of a country club in Figure 10–4.

Types of Clubs

Country Clubs

Nearly all **country clubs** have one or more lounges and restaurants, and most have banquet facilities. Members and their guests enjoy these services and can

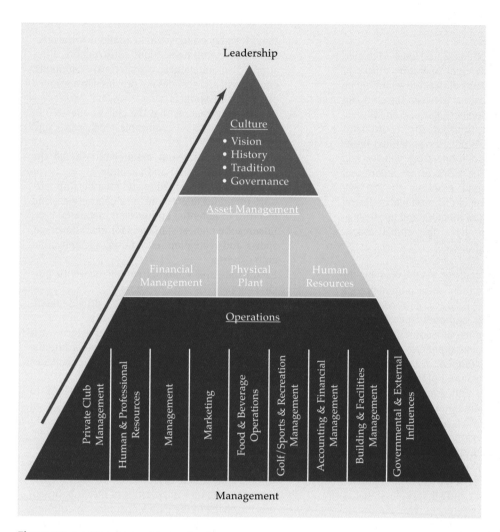

Figure 10–1 • Management to Leadership.

be billed monthly. The banquet facilities are used for formal and informal parties, dinners, dances, weddings, and so on, by members and their personal guests. Some country clubs charge what might seem to be an excessive amount for the initiation fee—as much as $250,000 in some cases—to maintain exclusivity.

Country clubs have two or more types of membership. Full membership enables members to use all the facilities all the time. Social membership allows members only to use the social facilities: lounges, bars, restaurants, and so on, and perhaps the pool and tennis courts. Other forms of membership can include weekday and weekend memberships.

Tiger Woods Teeing-Off During a Recent Tournament

I. **Position:** General Manager

II. **Related Titles:** Club Manager; Club House Manager

III. **Job Summary:** Serves as chief operating officer of the club; manages all aspects of the club including its activities and the relationships between the club and its board of directors, members, guests, employees, community, government, and industry; coordinates and administers the club's policies as defined by its board of directors. Develops operating policies and procedures and directs the work of all department managers. Implements and monitors the budget, monitors the quality of the club's products and services, and ensures maximum member and guest satisfaction. Secures and protects the club's assets, including facilities and equipment

IV. **Job Tasks (Duties):**

1. Implements general policies established by the board of directors; directs their administration and execution

2. Plans, develops, and approves specific operational policies, programs, procedures, and methods in concert with general policies

3. Coordinates the development of the club's long-range and annual (business) plans

4. Develops, maintains, and administers a sound organizational plan; initiates improvements as necessary

5. Establishes a basic personnel policy; initiates and monitors policies relating to personnel actions and training and professional development programs

6. Maintains membership with the Club Managers Association of America and other professional associations. Attends conferences, workshops, and meetings to keep abreast of current information and developments in the field

7. Coordinates development of operating and capital budgets according to the budget calendar; monitors monthly and other financial statements for the club; takes effective corrective action as required

8. Coordinates and serves as ex-officio member of appropriate club committees

9. Welcomes new club members; meets and greets all club members as practical during their visits to the club

10. Provides advice and recommendations to the president and committees about construction, alterations, maintenance, materials, supplies, equipment, and services not provided in approved plans and/or budgets

11. Consistently ensures that the club is operated in accordance with all applicable local, state, and federal laws

12. Oversees the care and maintenance of all the club's physical assets and facilities

13. Coordinates the marketing and membership relations programs to promote the club's services and facilities to potential and present members

14. Ensures the highest standards for food, beverage, sports and recreation, entertainment, and other club services

15. Establishes and monitors compliance with purchasing policies and procedures

16. Reviews and initiates programs to provide members with a variety of popular events

17. Analyzes financial statements, manages cash flow, and establishes controls to safeguard funds; reviews income and costs relative to goals; takes corrective action as necessary

18. Works with subordinate department heads to schedule, supervise, and direct the work of all club employees

19. Attends meetings of the club's executive committee and board of directors

20. Participates in outside activities that are judged as appropriate and approved by the board of directors to enhance the prestige of the club; broadens the scope of the club's operation by fulfilling the public obligations of the club as a participating member of the community

V. **Reports to:** Club President and Board of Directors

VI. **Supervises:** Assistant General Manager (Club House Manager); Food and Beverage Director; Controller; Membership Director; Director of Human Resources; Director of Purchasing; Golf Professional (Director of Golf); Golf Course Superintendent; Tennis Professional; Athletic Director; Executive Secretary

Source: Club Managers Association of America.

Figure 10–2 • A Job Description for a Club Manager.

City Clubs

City clubs are predominantly business oriented, although some have rules prohibiting the discussion of business and the reviewing of business-related documents in dining rooms. They vary in size, location, type of facility, and services offered. Some of the older, established clubs own their own buildings;

Private Club Management
History of Private Clubs
Types of Private Clubs
Membership Types
Bylaws
Policy Formulation
Board Relations
Chief Operating Officer Concept
Committees
Club Job Descriptions
Career Development
Golf Operations Management
Golf Course Management
Tennis Operations Management
Swimming Pool Management
Yacht Facilities Management
Fitness Center Management
Locker Room Management
Other Recreational Activities

Food and Beverage Operations
Sanitation
Menu Development
Nutrition
Pricing Concepts
Ordering/Receiving/Controls/Inventory
Food and Beverage Trends
Quality Service
Creativity in Theme Functions
Design and Equipment
Food and Beverage Personnel
Wine List Development

***Accounting and Finance
in the Private Club***
Accounting and Finance Principles
Uniform System of Accounts
Financial Analysis
Budgeting
Cash Flow Forecasting
Compensation and Benefit
  Administration
Financing Capital Projects
Audits
Internal Revenue Service
Computers
Business Office Organization
Long-Range Financial Planning

Human and Professional Resources
Employee Relations
Management Styles
Organizational Development
Balancing Job and Family
  Responsibilities
Time Management
Stress Management
Labor Issues
Leadership vs. Management

Building and Facilities Management
Preventive Maintenance
Insurance and Risk Management
Clubhouse Remodeling and
  Renovation

Contractors
Energy and Water Resource
  Management
Housekeeping
Security
Laundry
Lodging Operations

***External and Governmental
Influences***
Legislative Influences
Regulatory Agencies
Economic Theory
Labor Law
Internal Revenue Service
Privacy
Club Law
Liquor Liability
Labor Unions

Management and Marketing
Communication Skills
Marketing Through In-House
  Publications
Professional Image and Dress
Effective Negotiation
Member Contact Skills
Working with the Media
Marketing Strategies in a Private
  Club Environment

Source: Club Managers Association of
  America.

Figure 10–3 • The Club Management Competences.

others lease space. Clubs exist to cater to the wants and needs of members. Clubs in the city fall into the following categories:

- Professional
- Social
- Athletic
- Dining
- University
- Military
- Yachting
- Fraternal
- Proprietary

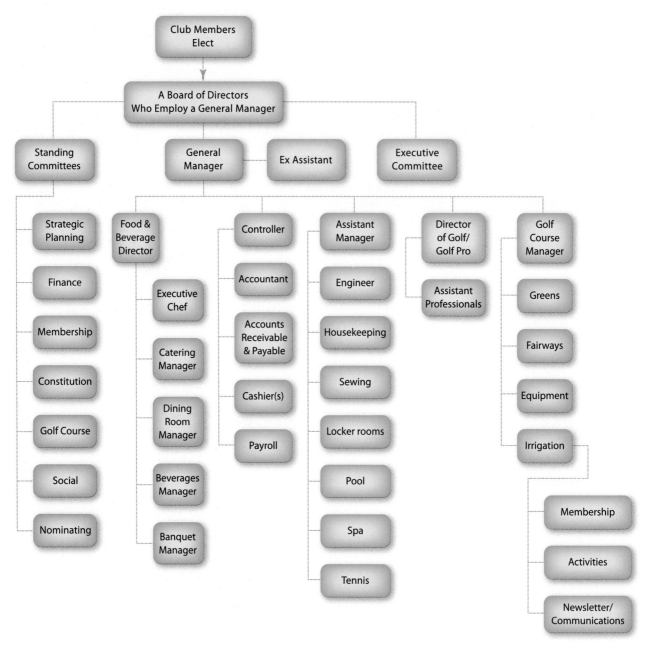

Figure 10–4 • The Organizational Chart of a Country Club.

Professional clubs, as the name implies, are clubs for people in the same profession. The National Press Club in Washington, D.C., the Lawyer's Club in New York City, and the Friars Club for actors and other theatrical people in Manhattan are good examples.

Social clubs allow members to enjoy one another's company; members represent many different professions, yet they have similar socioeconomic backgrounds. Social clubs are modeled after the famous men's social clubs in London, such as Boodles, St. James's, and White's. At these clubs, it is considered bad form to discuss business. Therefore, conversation and social interaction focus on companionship or entertainment unrelated to business.

The oldest social club in the United States is thought to be the Fish House in Philadelphia, founded in 1832. To ensure that the Fish House would always be socially oriented rather than business oriented, it was formed as a men's cooking club, with each member taking a turn preparing meals for the membership. Other social clubs exist in several major cities. The common denominator is that they all have upscale food and beverage offerings and club managers to manage them.

Athletic clubs give city workers and residents an opportunity to work out, swim, play squash and/or racquetball, and so on. Some of the downtown athletic clubs provide tennis courts and running tracks on the roof. Athletic clubs also have lounges, bars, and restaurants at which members may relax and interact socially. Some athletic clubs also have meeting rooms and even sleeping accommodations. The newest feature is known as the executive workout. This begins with a visit to the steam room, followed by a trip to the Jacuzzi, then sauna, a massage, and nap in the resting room before showering and returning to work.

Dining clubs are generally located in large city office buildings. Memberships are often given as an inducement to tenants who lease space in the office building. These clubs are always open for lunch and occasionally for dinner.

University clubs are private clubs for alumni. University clubs are generally located in the high-rent district and offer a variety of facilities and attractions focusing on food and beverage service.

Military clubs cater to both noncommissioned officers (NCOs) and enlisted officers. Military clubs offer similar facilities as do other clubs for recreation and entertainment and food and beverage offerings. Some military clubs are located on base. The largest membership club in the country is the Army Navy Country Club in Arlington, Virginia. The club has more than 6,000 members, 54 holes of golf, 2 clubhouses, and a host of other facilities. Many of these clubs in recent years have given over their club management to civilians.

Yacht clubs provide members with moorage slips, where their boats are kept secure. In addition to moorage facilities, yacht clubs have lounge, bar, and dining facilities similar to other clubs. Yacht clubs are based on a sailing theme and attract members with various backgrounds who have sailing as a common interest.

Fraternal clubs include many special organizations, such as the Veterans of Foreign Wars, Elks, and Shriners. These organizations foster camaraderie and often assist charitable causes. They generally are less elaborate than are other clubs, but have bars and banquet rooms that can be used for various activities.

Proprietary clubs operate on a for-profit basis. They are owned by corporations or individuals; individuals wanting to become members purchase a membership, not a share in the club. Proprietary clubs became popular with the real estate boom in the 1970s and 1980s. As new housing developments were planned, clubs were included in several of the projects. Households paid a small initiation fee and monthly dues between $30 and $50, allowing the whole family to participate in a wide variety of recreational activities.

Clearly, the opportunities for recreation and leisure abound. The goal must be to achieve a harmony between work and leisure activities and to become truly professional in both giving and receiving these services. The next few years will see a substantial increase in the leisure and recreational industries.

Hospitality and Recreation: Inextricably Intertwined

Bart Bartlett, Ph.D., Professor in Charge of Undergraduate Programs at Penn State University's School of Hospitality Management

Americans have more leisure time than ever before, and as leisure time has grown, leisure activities have evolved and grown as well. As this chapter points out, opportunities today for recreation and for careers in recreation management are vast and multifaceted. These include positions in commercial recreation (resorts, themed resorts, the ski industry), in noncommercial recreation (federal or state parks and community recreation), in clubs and sports venues, and in recreation with special populations.

Although the focus of this text is hospitality management, in many situations recreation and hospitality go hand in hand. When a ski trip incorporates recreation on the slopes with food and beverage services in the lodge or when a hotel guest uses the hotel's business services and the spa, recreation and hospitality are both involved. When a convention center hotel provides rooms, food, and beverage; coordinates meetings and breakout sessions; and also organizes recreation and group activities during the conference, hospitality and recreation begin to merge. In fact, because our guests' total experience often involves a combination of lodging, food and beverage, and recreation, we do not want to distinguish, but instead want to ensure guest satisfaction by seamlessly integrating these different elements into the total package.

As growth in leisure travel continues to outstrip growth in business travel, the growing leisure travel market will create an increasing emphasis on recreation as an integral part of hospitality. Furthermore, though hospitality and recreation may involve different emphases, the critical customer focus and customer service skills that we love about our industry are common to all aspects of hospitality and recreation.

Resorts and resort hotels are the prototypical combination of hospitality and recreation. A mega-resort such as Walt Disney World Resort provides an ideal example of a venue that integrates hospitality and recreation skills and services. On a Disney vacation, a family may enjoy lodging and food and beverage services provided by hotel staff and management trained in hospitality, go into the park itself to enjoy attractions and shows arranged and managed by a recreation specialist, take a break to enjoy foodservice provided by a hospitality provider, and at the end of the day enjoy dinner provided by the hospitality staff and entertainment or dancing arranged by a recreation professional.

The golf industry provides other examples. At a typical golf club, the director of golf operations is primarily involved with managing recreation activities, including scheduling and supervising play, course maintenance, and the pro shop. The clubhouse manager, meanwhile, is responsible for hospitality functions, including food and beverage operations, catering events, and membership. If either were missing, the club simply could not meet guests' and members' overall expectations.

Finally, because cruise ships are essentially floating resort hotels with many features of land-based resorts, both hospitality and recreation are required. On a cruise ship, the purser and food and beverage manager are responsible for hospitality functions, while the cruise director provides recreation programming. Both are critical parts of the cruise experience, thus providing the all-around good time guests desire and deserve.

Through this text, you are learning about hotels, restaurants, and managed services and about the knowledge and skills involved in managing these operations. This chapter talks about recreation and the opportunities to apply your hospitality skills in recreation settings. Across the spectrum, from business travelers to family vacationers, from golfing outings to business banquets, from backcountry adventures to haute cuisine dining, from white sand Caribbean beaches to black diamond ski slopes, customer service and a focus on customer satisfaction are constants, and both hospitality and recreation skills are critical to providing a memorable guest experience. The commonalities in settings, service, and focus on guest satisfaction indicate that hospitality and recreation are indeed inextricably intertwined!

▶ Check Your Knowledge

1. Name all types of clubs discussed here and briefly describe their functions.

2. List the important duties of a club manager.

3. Describe the operations of a country club.

Noncommercial Recreation

Noncommercial recreation includes voluntary organizations, campus, armed forces, and employee recreations, as well as recreation for special populations.

Voluntary Organizations

Voluntary organizations are nongovernmental, nonprofit agencies, serving the public-at-large or selected elements with multiservice programs that often include a substantial element of recreational opportunity. The best-known voluntary organizations include the Boy Scouts, Girl Scouts, YMCA, YWCA, and YM–YWHA.

In the early 1900s, YMCAs began to offer sporting facilities and programs. The Ys, though nonprofit, were pioneers in basketball, swimming, and weight training. Later, commercial health clubs also began to evolve, offering men's and women's exercise. As the sports and fitness movement grew, clubs appealed to special interests. Now clubs can be classified as follows: figure salons, health clubs, body-building gyms, tennis clubs, rowing clubs, swim clubs, racquetball centers, or multipurpose clubs.

A multipurpose club has more exclusive recreation programs than a health club does. Leagues, tournaments, and classes are common for racquet sports, and most clubs offer several types of fitness classes. Some innovative clubs offer automatic bank tellers, stock market quote services, computer matching for tennis competition, auto detailing, laundry and dry cleaning services, and wine-cellar storage.

Club revenue comes from membership fees, user fees, guest fees, food and beverage sales, facility rental, and so on. Human resources accounts for about 66 percent of expenses at most clubs.

It is amazing to realize that in the center of a city there may be several voluntary organizations, each serving a particular segment of the population. Richard Kraus writes that a study of the city of Toronto that examined various land uses and leisure programs in the city's core found the following organizations: a Boy's Club, a mission, the Center of the Metropolitan Association for the Retarded, a Catholic settlement house, a day care center, an Indian center, a YMCA and YWCA, a service center for working people, a Chinese center, a Ukrainian center, and several other organizations meeting special needs and interests. These were all in addition to public parks, recreation areas, and nineteen churches.

Campus, Armed Forces, and Employee Recreation

Campus Recreation

North America's colleges and universities provide a major setting for organized leisure and recreational programs with services involving millions of participants each year. The programs include involvement by campus recreation offices, intramural departments, student unions, residence staffs, or other sponsors. People spend much of their leisure time participating in a wide variety of organized recreational activities, such as aerobics, arts and crafts, the performing arts, camping, and sports. Recreation and fitness workers plan, organize, and direct these activities in local playgrounds and recreation areas, parks, community centers, health clubs, fitness centers, religious organizations, camps, theme parks, and tourist attractions. Increasingly, recreational and fitness workers also are found in workplaces, where they organize and direct leisure activities and athletic programs for employees of all ages.[23]

The various recreational activities help in maintaining good morale on campus. Some use recreational activities such as sports or orchestras or theater companies as a means of gaining alumni support. Students look for an exciting and interesting social life. For this reason, colleges and universities offer a wide range of recreational and social activities that may vary from campus to campus.

Armed Forces Recreation

It is the official policy of the Department of Defense to provide a well-rounded welfare and recreational program for the physical, social, and mental well-being of its personnel. Each service sponsors recreational activities under the auspices of the Morale, Welfare, and Recreation Program (MWR), which reports to the Office of the Assistant Secretary of Defense for Manpower, Reserve Affairs, and Logistics. MWR activities are provided to all military personnel and civilian employees at all installations.

MWR programs include the following types of activities:

- Sports, including self-directed, competitive, instructional, and spectator programs
- Motion pictures
- Service clubs and entertainment
- Crafts and hobbies
- Youth activities for children of military families
- Special-interest groups such as aero, automotive, motorcycle, and power boat clubs, as well as hiking, skydiving, and rod and gun clubs
- Rest centers and recreation areas
- Open dining facilities
- Libraries

Recreation is perceived as an important part of the employee benefits package for military personnel, along with the G.I. Bill, medical services, commissaries, and exchanges.

Employee Recreation

Business and industry have realized the importance of promoting employee efficiency. Human resource experts have found that workers who spend their free time at constructive recreational activities have less absenteeism resulting from emotional tension, illness, excessive use of alcohol, and so on. Employee recreation programs may also be an incentive for a prospective employee to join a company. So, remember to ask for a signing bonus if you are a softball star and the company you are about to join wants to win the tournament!

In the United States and Canada, almost all the leading corporations have an employee recreation and wellness program. Some companies include recreation activities in their team-building and management-development programs.

Recreation for Special Populations

Recreation for special populations involves professionals and organizations who serve groups such as those with mental illness, mental retardation, or physical challenges. In recent years, there has been increased recognition of the need to provide recreational programs for special populations. These programs, developed for each of the special population groups, use therapeutic recreation as a form of treatment.

One sports program for people with disabilities that has received considerable attention in recent years is the Special Olympics, an international year-round program of physical fitness, sports training, and athletic competition for children and adults with mental retardation. The program is unique because it accommodates competitors at all ability levels by assigning participants to competition divisions based on both age and actual performance.[24]

Today, the Special Olympics serves more than 1.4 million individuals in the United States and more than seventy other countries. Among the official sports are track and field events, swimming, diving, gymnastics, ice skating, basketball, volleyball, soccer, softball, floor hockey, bowling, Frisbee disk, downhill skiing, cross-country skiing, and wheelchair events. The National Parks and Recreation Association and numerous state and local agencies and societies work closely with Special Olympics in promoting programs and sponsoring competitions.[25]

Trends in Recreation and Leisure

- An increase in all fitness activities.
- A surge in travel and tourism.
- In addition to a continuation of traditional recreation and leisure activities, special programs targeted toward at-risk youths and latchkey children are also being developed.
- Several additional products in the commercial sector.
- Additional learning and adventure opportunities for the elderly, such as Elderhostel.

CASE STUDY

Service Proposal for Guests

You recently joined the front desk of a nice resort hotel in New England and your hotel manager has complimented you on your guest service ability. She has asked you to develop a walking/jogging trail for the guests.

Discussion Question

1. What would be some of the key elements to consider in developing a proposal for your hotel guests?

CASE STUDY

Overpopulation of National Parks

Our national parks are under serious threat from a number of sources, including congestion resulting from overvisitation, consequent environmental degradation, and pollution.

There are too many people and too many vehicles in the most popular national parks. Many visitors bring their city lifestyle, leaving garbage lying around, listening to loud music, and leaving the trails in worse shape.

Discussion Question

1. List the recommendations you have for the park superintendents to help save the parks.

Summary

1. Recreation is free time that people use to restore, rest, and relax their minds and bodies. Recreational activities can be passive or active, individual or group activities.

2. Recreational activities range from cultural pursuits such as museums or theaters, to sports or outdoor recreation such as amusement parks, community centers, playgrounds, and libraries. These services involve various levels of government.

3. National parks preserve exceptional lands for public use, emphasizing the protection of their ecosystems and endangered plant and animal species and honoring historical sites. Two of the best known of the current 367 parks in the United States include Yellowstone and Yosemite National Parks.

4. Today, city governments are increasingly expected to provide recreational facilities such as golf courses, swimming pools, picnic areas, and playgrounds as a community service.

5. Commercial recreation—for example, theme parks, clubs, and attractions—involves a profit for the supplier of the recreational activity.

6. Clubs are places where members gather for social, recreational, professional, or fraternal reasons. There are many different types of clubs such as country clubs and city clubs according to the interests they represent to their members.

7. Noncommercial recreation includes governmental and nonprofit agencies, such as voluntary organizations, campus, armed forces, employee recreation, and recreation for special populations, such as the physically challenged.

Key Words and Concepts

city clubs
club management
commercial recreation
country clubs
government-sponsored recreation
leisure
national parks
National Parks Service

noncommercial recreation
recreation
recreation for special populations
recreation management
theme parks
transient occupancy taxes (TOT)
voluntary organizations

Review Questions

1. Define recreation and its importance to human wellness. What factors affect an individual's decision to participate in recreational activities?

2. Describe the origin of government-sponsored recreation in consideration of the origin and purpose of national parks.

3. On the Companion Website, what opportunities does Jon Robinson say there are in the Park Service?

4. Briefly describe the difference between commercial and noncommercial recreation.

5. Briefly explain the purpose of a theme park and the purpose of clubs.

6. Explain the concept of recreation for special populations.

Internet Exercise

1. Organization: **Prestonwood Country Club**
   Web site: www.prestonwoodcc.com
   Summary: Prestonwood is a full-service
   country club that offers activities and fine
   food.

   (a) What kinds of activities are offered at
       the Prestonwood Country Club?
   (b) Parents may wish to take their kids on
       vacations. In these situations, what
       might this country club offer those kids?

Apply Your Knowledge

1. Create your own personal recreation goals and
   make a plan to reach them.

2. Describe the features of commercial versus
   noncommercial recreation.

Suggested Activities

1. Research the history of Mardi Gras on the
   Internet. Write a one-page description of the
   event and its cultural roots.

2. Look up your favorite theme park on the Web.
   Think about what kind of position you would
   like to have at the park. If the site has job
   listings, tell whether any of them appeal to you.

Endnotes

1. Personal correspondence with Jay Sullivan, August 4, 2007.
2. http://en.wikipedia.org/wiki/recreation
3. http://brainyquote.com/qnotes/author/n/nathaniel-hawthorne.html
4. Peopleassets, "The PeopleAssets/California Park & Recreation Society Leadership Competency Profile," www.peopleassets.net/cprs/reports/samplereport.htm.
5. This section draws on information supplied by the National Parks Service.
6. http://en.wikipedia.org/wiki/recreation
7. Personal correspondence with Knott's Berry Farms, April 2006.
8. Knott's Berry Farms website at www.knots.com/real/real.htm, accessed April 17, 2006.
9. Astrid Dorothea Ada Maria Kemperman, "Temporal Aspects of Theme Park Choice Behavior," 2000, http://alexandria.tue.nl/extra2/200013915.pdf.
10. Other prominent theme parks and attractions are Knott's Berry Farm, Universal Studios, and Six Flags across the United States.
11. savedisney.com/news/features/fe071505.1.asp (accessed July 29, 2007). Randy Bright, *Disneyland: Inside Story.* (New York: Abraus, 1987), 33.
12. Atlas Cruises and Tours, "Walt Disney World Vacation Packages," www.atlastravelweb.com/waltdisneyworldpackages.shtml.
13. http://en.wikipedia.org/wiki/universal_studios_Hollywood, accessed November 18, 2007.
14. www.nbcuni.com/about_NBC_Universal/Company_Overmen/ accessed February 10, 2007.
15. www.watercountryusa.com/wc/attractions_home.asp
16. www.discore.com/explore.aspx.covery.
17. www.hersheys.com/discover/melton/melton.asp
18. www.dollywoood.com/ndes_attractions
19. http://en.wikipedia.org/wiki/legoland
20. Ibid
21. www.gatorland.com/history/history.html.
22. CollegeGrad.com, "Career Information: Recreation Workers," http://en.wikipedia.org/wiki/wet_%27n_wild, www.collegegrad.com/careers/servi19.shtml.
24. Special Olympics, "About Us," www.specialolympics.org/special+olympics+public+website/English/About_us/default.htm.
25. Special Olympics, "About Us," www.specialolympics.org/special+olympics+public+website/English/About_us/default.htm.

CHAPTER 11

Gaming Entertainment

OBJECTIVES

After reading and studying this chapter, you should be able to:

- Outline the history of the gaming entertainment industry.

- Describe the various activities related to gaming entertainment.

- Explain how gaming entertainment converges with the hospitality industry.

- Discuss the different positions within the gaming industry.

One of the most significant developments in the hospitality industry during the past two decades has been the astounding growth of the casino industry and its convergence with the lodging and hospitality industries. What has emerged from this development is an entirely new arena of hospitality known as the gaming entertainment industry. With its rapid expansion in North America and throughout the world, new opportunities have been created for hospitality careers. This chapter explores the gaming entertainment industry and details exciting developments yet to come in this dynamic and controversial segment of the hospitality business.

Gaming Entertainment

For the purposes of this chapter, the term **gaming entertainment** refers to one subset of the gaming industry, that is, the casino industry. What used to be known as the casino business is now known as gaming entertainment. The dramatic growth of this part of the hospitality business has brought with it significant changes in how businesses in this industry operate and what they offer their guests. The changes have been so great that a new name needed to be created to accurately describe all the amenities this industry provides.

The gaming industry includes 445 casinos in eleven states.[1] The industry includes both land-based and riverboat casinos, card rooms, charitable games, lottery-operated games, and greyhound and horse races. The gaming industry as a whole is larger than most people can believe. Approximately $70 billion is *wagered*, or *bet*, on games or races every year.

That is more than seven times what is spent on movie tickets. The total amount bet is called the **handle** in the gaming industry, and it is often a misunderstood concept. When a customer places a bet in any type of gaming activity, sometimes that customer wins and sometimes he or she loses. The total amount of all bets is the handle, and the net amount of spending by the customer is termed **win** by the gaming industry.

What is the difference between gambling and gaming? **Gambling** is playing a game of risk for the thrill of the "action" and the chance of making money. True gamblers spend a great deal of time learning and understanding a favorite game of risk and enjoying its subtle attributes, and they find an enjoyable challenge in trying to "beat the house," or win more than they lose from a casino.

A Themed Gaming and Slot Machine Area in a Casino

It is true that the nearly 40 million visitors who visit Las Vegas and the more than 30 million in Atlantic City and the hundreds of thousands who frequent other casino operations love the green felt tables, the whirling roulette wheels, the feel of the chips, and the thrill of the game. The rows of colorful slot machines sounding out musical tones and flashing lights, the distant sounds of someone hitting a jackpot, and bells ringing and guests shouting create an environment of excitement and anticipation that can only be found on the casino floor. The gaming industry has exploded from just two jurisdictions in 1976 to include some form of legal gambling in forty-eight states.

Not long ago, the presence of a slot machine or a blackjack table was all that was needed to bring in the visitors. However, with the rapid spread of **casinos** throughout North America, this is no longer true. The competitive nature of the casino business has created a bigger, better product to meet the needs of guests. As Steve Wynn, owner of the Wynn Hotel and Resort, puts it, the casino floor is "a thing which people pass on their way to visit the things that really matter to them." The product that has evolved over the past decade is what is called *gaming entertainment*.

Gaming entertainment offers games of risk only as part of a total package of entertainment and leisure-time activities. Gaming entertainment serves a customer base of "social gamblers," customers who play a game of risk as a form of entertainment and a social activity, combining gambling with many other activities during their visit. Social gamblers, by this definition, are interested in many of the amenities of the gaming entertainment operation and take part in many diverse activities during a stay.

Gaming entertainment refers to the casino gaming business and all its aspects, including hotel operations, entertainment offerings, retail shopping, recreational activities, and other types of operations in addition to wagering on the gaming floor. It is a dynamic new tourism product that serves as a destination attraction. Gaming entertainment is the business of hospitality and entertainment with a core strength in casino gaming, also known as the global hospitality—gaming—entertainment market.

According to this definition, a gaming entertainment business always has a casino floor area that offers various games of risk and that serves as the focal point for marketing to and attracting guests. Next in importance to the guests is high-quality food and beverage operations.

Gaming entertainment is one of the last hospitality concepts to support the full-service, table-side gourmet restaurant, in addition to the lavish buffets that many casino locations offer. The number of foodservice concepts is wide and diverse—from signature restaurants featuring famous chefs, to ethnic offerings, to quick-service, franchised outlets. The gaming entertainment industry offers unlimited career opportunities in restaurant management and the culinary arts that were unheard of just a decade ago.

Gaming entertainment also goes hand in hand with the lodging industry because hotel rooms are part of the package. Full-service hotels are part and parcel of gaming entertainment. Rooms, food and beverage, convention services, banquet facilities, health spas, recreation, and other typical hotel amenities support gaming entertainment. Most of the largest and most complex hotels in the world are found in gaming entertainment venues, a number of which are described in detail later in this chapter.

So far, we have discussed gaming entertainment as a place to gamble on the casino floor, eat and drink, have a place to sleep and relax, and maybe do some business. But gaming entertainment offers much more. The entertainment offerings range from live performances by the most famous entertainers to production shows that use the latest high-tech wizardry. Gaming entertainment includes theme parks and thrill rides, museums, and cultural centers. The most popular gaming entertainment destinations are designed around a central theme that includes the hotel and casino operations.

Unlike its predecessor, the casino business, the gaming entertainment business has numerous revenue-generating activities. Gaming revenue is produced from casino win, or the money guests spend on the casino floor. The odds of any casino game favor the house, some more than others. Casino win is the cost of gambling to guests, who often win over the house in the short run, and are therefore willing to place bets and try their luck.

Nongaming revenue comes from sources that are not related to wagering on the casino floor. As the gaming entertainment concept continues to emphasize activities other than gambling, nongaming revenue is increasing in importance. This is what gaming entertainment is truly about—hospitality and entertainment based on the attraction of a casino.

Gaming entertainment takes different forms. The megaresorts of Las Vegas and Atlantic City garner the most publicity as the meccas of the gaming entertainment industry. However, there are smaller properties throughout Nevada and there are other casino-based businesses in forty-eight states and seven Canadian provinces. These casinos take the form of commercially operated businesses, both privately and publicly held. Some are land based, meaning the casinos are housed in regular buildings. Others are riverboats that cruise up and down a river, or barges that are moored in water and do not cruise, called dockside casinos.

Casinos are also operated by Native American tribes on their reservations and tribal lands. These are land-based casinos and are often as complex as any operation in Las Vegas. Gaming entertainment is also popular on cruise ships as part of the cruise vacation product or on what are called "cruises to nowhere," where gaming and entertainment on board the ship are the main attractions.

There is strong support for gaming in the marketplace as an entertainment activity. According to Harrah's Entertainment/TNS polling data, more than one-fourth or 54.1 million U.S. households gamble in casinos. U.S. households make 371 million visits annually to casinos.[2]

The demographic makeup of the typical gaming entertainment guest has remained consistent during the past several years. In comparison to the average American, casino players tend to have higher levels of income and education and are more likely to hold white-collar jobs. The customer profile of Las Vegas has gotten younger, and people who spend money want a total entertainment experience.

According to the latest Las Vegas Visitor Profile study, the average visitor to Las Vegas stays three to four nights; budgets $651 for gaming; and spends $107 per night on lodging (nonpackage visitors), $260 on food and drink, $68 on local transportation, $140 on shopping, $47 on shows, and $8.49 on sightseeing (www.lvcva.com/getfile/vps-2006).

Two decades ago, gambling in the United States was permitted in only two states. Today, only two states, Hawaii and Utah, do not permit some form of gambling!

Historical Review of Gaming Entertainment

Today, the precise original of gambling is still unknown. We know that gambling occurred in ancient Egypt. *Senet* was a game considered to be the forerunner of backgammon. A Senet board was found in the tomb of King Tutankhamen, but the oldest known record of Senet is shown in a tomb painting from the Third Dynasty, in the 27th century B.C.[3] Chinese records show that a game called Wei-gi was probably developed during the third millennium B.C. The Romans were also gamblers. They placed bets on chariot races, cockfights, and dice throwing.

In the seventeenth century, casino-style gaming clubs existed in England and central Europe. In England King Henry VIII, a gambler himself, outlawed gambling when he discovered that his soldiers spent more time gambling than improving their battle skills. A public gambling house was legalized for the first time in 1626 in Venice, Italy, and Baden Baden in Germany opened in 1748 and is still open today[4]. Soon the upper class met in so-called casinis to socialize and gamble. In the first half of the nineteenth century, organized gaming casinos started to develop.

Las Vegas—the name alone summons images of millions of neon lights, elaborate shows, outrageous performers, and bustling casinos—is a place where millions are won and lost every night. Las Vegas is all of that, and much more. The city represents the American dream. A dusty watering hole just over 100 years ago, it has been transformed into one of the most elaborate cities in the world and one of the hottest vacation spots for the entire family. Las Vegas is second only to Walt Disney World as the favorite vacation destination in the United States.

The gaming entertainment business has its roots in Las Vegas. From the early 1940s until 1976, Las Vegas had a monopoly on the casino business, not the gaming entertainment business. Casinos had no hotel rooms, entertainment, or other amenities. The hotels that existed were just a place to sleep when a guest was not on the casino floor.

Las Vegas is rich with tales of Benjamin Hymen Siegelbaum, better known as Bugsy Siegel. Bugsy was born February 28, 1906, in Brooklyn, New York, to a poor Austrian Jewish family. It is said that Siegel began his career by extorting money from pushcart peddlers, at a very young age. Eventually, he turned to a life of bootlegging, gambling rackets, and murder-for-hire operations. In 1931,

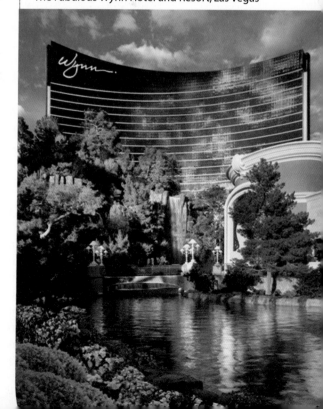

The Fabulous Wynn Hotel and Resort, Las Vegas

Bugsy was one of the four men that executed Joe "the Boss" Masseria. Several years later, he was sent West to develop rackets. In California, Siegel successfully developed gambling dens and ships. He also took part in narcotics smuggling, blackmail, and other questionable operations. After developing a nationwide bookmakers' wire service, Bugsy moved on to build the well-known Flamingo Hotel and Casino in Las Vegas. Upon completion, the casino ended up costing $6 million, which forced Siegel to skim profits. This angered the eastern bosses, and Bugsy died at his Beverly Hills home late in the evening of June 20, 1947, hit by a barrage of bullets fired through his living room window. At the same time, three henchmen walked into the Flamingo Hotel in Las Vegas and announced that they were the new owners.[5]

During the 1970s, Atlantic City was in an impoverished state. It was experiencing high amounts of crime and poverty. In an effort to revitalize the city, New Jersey voters in 1976 approved casino gambling for Atlantic City.[6] Following the referendum, casino gambling was legalized in the state of New Jersey by the Casino Control Act. The state looked to the casino hotel industry to invest capital, create jobs, pay taxes, and attract tourists, thus revitalizing the economy and creating a financial environment in which urban redevelopment could occur.

The act initiated a number of fees and taxes specific to the casino hotel business that would provide revenues to support regulatory costs, to fund social services for the disabled and the elderly throughout the state, and to provide investment funds for the redevelopment of Atlantic City. The Casino Control Act created the Casino Control Commission, whose purpose was not only to ensure the success and integrity of the Atlantic City casino industry, but also to carry out the objective of reversing the city's economic fortunes.[7]

Sensing that the objectives of the Casino Control Act were being fulfilled in New Jersey and wanting similar benefits for its state, but not wanting land-based casino gambling, Iowa legalized riverboat casinos thirteen years later. This was followed in rapid succession by legalization of gambling in Illinois, Mississippi, Louisiana, Missouri, and Indiana. With the spread of the casino industry throughout the United States and Canada, the competitive nature of the industry began to create a need for what is now known as gaming entertainment with the addition of noncasino attractions. Gaming entertainment is, therefore, a natural evolution of the casino industry.

Native American Gaming

In *California v. Cabazon Band of Mission Indians et al.* (1987), the Supreme Court decided 6 to 3 that once a state has legalized any form of gambling, the Native Americans in that state have the right to offer and self-regulate the same games, without government restrictions. The state of California and the county of Riverside had sought to impose local and state regulations on card and bingo clubs operated by the Cabazon and Morongo bands of Mission Indians. These court decisions were clear in their recognition of the rights of nations and tribes with regard to certain gaming activities.[8]

FOCUS ON GAMING

The Development of Two Corporate Cultures in Casinos

Kathryn Hashimoto, *East Carolina University*

In America, the history and evolution of casinos have created two very strong corporate cultures. A corporate culture could be described as the personality of the organization. Like a person, a business can be weak or strong, conservative or daring, or even stodgy or innovative. Corporate cultures are very important because they set the boundaries for behavior of managers and employees. The stronger the culture, the easier it is for employees to know what they should do when the formal rules are not available. In a casino, there are always new situations and problems that must be addressed, and a strong corporate culture sets the tone and guidelines for the problem solving and ultimate solution. In the case of casinos, the traditional casino culture is still evolving into a more corporate one.

Traditional Casino Culture

When casinos first developed in America, ownership was by a single individual who could lose that enterprise on a toss of the dice. It was the owner's "luck of the draw," not his management ability, that determined his length of stay. As a result, owners were superstitious and they trusted only their own instincts. This resulted in the "monopoly on brains" syndrome—the fact that only the owner, not employees, could make a great decision. Fear of management was what kept the employees honest. According to the traditional school of casino culture attitudes, employees should be constantly reminded that their jobs were a privilege, not a right. Their jobs could be taken away at any time. Therefore, promotion came to employees who were loyal to management. To prove their knowledge and loyalty, employees had to learn the trade from the ground up, starting as a dealer.

Employees showed their loyalty by doing whatever they could to help the owner. In some cases, employees were asked to violate rules and regulations to favor the house or accommodate a high roller's desires. Even though a guest might make unreasonable requests, operators would agree because the customer might take his or her business elsewhere. For example, at one casino a high roller requested that he have a male dealer instead of the woman who was currently at the table. The management complied, knowing that it was discriminatory. However, in their view it was cheaper to pay the class action suit that followed than to antagonize the player. Another example of the traditional casino culture was the emphasis on superstition and luck in decision making. Dealers were perceived to be personally responsible for the outcome of games. Any dealer who lost money had "bad karma" and was instantly fired—no questions asked. Without rational decision-making guidelines, superstition and one man's idea of common sense ruled the casino operation.

Shift to Corporate Culture in Casinos

During the 1960s and 1970s, there was a shift in casino management styles and decision making. Some say it was Howard Hughes who began this movement. The story goes that Hughes liked staying in the penthouse suite of the Desert Inn, so he paid his bill and lived there. However, the casino management was very concerned that he wasn't gambling enough, and they wanted the penthouse for a high roller, so they ordered him to vacate the premises. Hughes didn't want to leave. So, what did he do? He bought the casino and changed the rules. Under the new management, the casino began to function like a large corporation. Superstitions were replaced by well-researched facts. Teams of managers replaced the individual owner. The idea that a dealer was responsible for table losses was replaced by probability theory. The casino made money and this encouraged other corporate giants such as Baron Hilton to invest in casinos.

continued

FOCUS ON GAMING (continued)

These giants of corporate America started a new trend in casino management styles and corporate cultures. The casino was divided into two parts: the casino side and the administration side. The casino side revolved around what happened on the casino floor: the daily grind of securing the casino and tracking the money. The administration side handled the marketing, accounting, human resources, and the like. With this split, new emphasis was placed on education credentials such as MBAs. People with no background in gambling began to work on marketing plans and run the financial enterprise. Computers and statistics became the guiding decision makers. For example, the authority for "comping" decisions switched from floor people to computers. When this old school of traditional casino managers lost their "comping" privileges to a computer, it was a confusing time. How could a computer know who were the right people to comp? How could a machine build a rapport with the players so that they would come back? Old-time supervisors issued comps to whomever they pleased. It gave them power. But now the computer decided.

Two Cultures Collide

The clash of traditional culture versus new corporate culture was inevitable. The traditional casino culture was characterized by statements like, "The guys upstairs don't know the business" and "How can an MBA know anything about the way a casino works?" By the same token, the new culture examined these traditional views and found them lacking. The new corporate culture became characterized by statements like, "The traditional managers want to micromanage and keep everything to themselves" and "Managers do not want anyone else to know what is going on" and "What does a dealer know about marketing or accounting?" The collision between these two cultures would lead to inevitable changes.

However, it wasn't just the ownership switch that altered the traditional corporate culture. When Las Vegas and Atlantic City found themselves inundated with new kinds of gaming venues, the competition for employees became intense. Finding trained employees was a big problem. Anyone with any qualifications or experience quickly climbed the corporate ladder. Employees always had the enticement from the next casino or riverboat for higher wages. There were too many jobs and not enough workers. As a result, the casino employment department changed into human resources to reflect an emphasis on improving employee–employer relationships. Instead of hiring, disciplining, and firing, their responsibility shifted to keeping employees. "Employee satisfaction" became the new buzzwords. Now retention and motivation have become the new service management foci. Empowering, educating, and recognizing workers improve the chances for a company to build employee loyalty and reduce the costs of turnover.

Instead of the traditional casino view that "your job is a privilege," the new corporate culture view is that a casino should strive to "be the place of choice." Instead of looking for abilities, the new corporate culture searches for personality first: someone who is friendly, personable, and stable. A person can learn many skills, but he or she cannot be taught to be outgoing and friendly. These new views in corporate culture reflect the emphasis on the satisfied employee. As researchers study the best corporations, they are finding that good service management pays. There is a strong relationship between employees who like their jobs and customers who are treated with both enthusiasm and awareness of bottom-line profits. Understanding this connection is the key to winning a competitive slot in today's business environment.

Congress, which some observers say was alarmed by the prospect of tribal gaming going out of control, responded to these court decisions by passing the **Indian Gaming Regulatory Act of 1988 (IGRA)**. The IGRA provides a framework by which games are conducted to protect both the nations and tribes and the general public. For example, the IGRA outlines criteria for approval of casino management contracts entered into by nations or tribes and establishes civil penalties for violation of its provisions. The act clearly is a compromise in that it balances the rights of sovereign tribal nations to conduct gaming activities with the rights of the federal and state governments to regulate activities within their borders.[9]

The three objectives of the IGRA are to (1) provide a statutory basis for the operation of gaming by Native American tribes as a means of promoting tribal economic development, self-sufficiency, and strong tribal governments; (2) provide a statutory basis for the regulation of gaming by a Native American tribe adequate to shield it from organized crime and other corrupting influences; and (3) establish an independent regulatory authority, the National Indian Gaming Commission (NIGC), for governing gaming activity on Native American lands.[10]

IGRA defines three different kinds, or classes, of Native American gaming activities: (1) class I gaming, consisting of social games played solely for prizes of minimum value or traditional forms of Native American gaming; (2) class II gaming, consisting of bingo, games similar to bingo, and card games explicitly authorized by the laws of the state; and (3) class III gaming, consisting of all forms of gaming that are neither class I nor class II gaming, and therefore including most of what are considered casino games.[11]

The significance of the definition of class III gaming activity is that it defines the games that (1) must be located in a state that permits such gaming for any purpose by any person, organization, or entity and (2) are conducted in conformance with a compact that states are required to negotiate "in good faith" with the tribes.

Often tribes give local governments voluntary payments in recognition of services the tribe receives, and some pay revenues in exchange for permission to maintain a casino gambling monopoly in a state. In Michigan, Connecticut, and Louisiana, tribes have agreed to make payments to the state as part of their comprehensive compacts for casino gambling. In almost all the states, the tribes make payments to the state for state costs incurred in the process of regulation of the casinos as provided for in the negotiated agreements.

There are 354 gaming facilities on reservation lands in twenty-eight states, and Native American gaming has been the fastest-growing sector of casino gaming in the United States. Cherokee in North Carolina has been voted Travel Attraction of the Year by the Southeast Tourism Society. Not only is there a new casino but the natural attraction of the Smokey Mountains and all the thousands of years of rich culture of the Cherokee nation. Additional Native American gaming is also conducted by the First Nations Bands of Canada.[12]

Gamblers Playing Poker at the Foxwoods Resort Casino in Mashantucket, Connecticut

▶ **Check Your Knowledge**

1. Define the following:
   a. Bet
   b. Handle
   c. Win

2. Briefly describe the history of the gaming industry.

3. Where and when does the first official account of gaming practice date back to?

4. What does the Indian Gaming Regulatory Act of 1988 consist of?

Size and Scope of Gaming Entertainment

Why is the gaming entertainment industry growing so quickly? Basically, because people like to wager and, historically, there has been more demand than supply for wagering opportunities. As public acceptance of legalized gaming has grown, and state and local governments have permitted gaming entertainment establishments to open, supply is beginning to meet demand.

The gaming entertainment industry pays billions of dollars per year in gambling privilege taxes to state governments. Casino development has been credited with revitalizing economies through new capital investment, job creation, new tax revenue, and increased tourism.

Casino gaming has created thousands of direct and indirect jobs with billions paid in wages. When unemployment is high and an area is in economic despair, casinos create jobs. Casino gaming companies pay an average of 12 percent of total revenues in taxes. Casino gaming companies contribute to federal, state, and local governments through gaming-related and other taxes. Direct taxes include property, federal/state income, and construction sales and use taxes, which all industries pay, and gaming taxes, which are levied only on the gaming industry at rates ranging from 6.25 to 20 percent of gaming revenues.[13]

Key Players in the Industry

Today, there are only three industry giants: MGM Mirage, Harrah's, and Boyd Gaming. Changes in the industry happen in the wink of an eye. They all have diverse property portfolios, solid business practices, and are well respected by Wall Street.

MGM Mirage, one of the world's leading and most respected hotel and gaming companies, owns several casino resorts in Nevada, Mississippi, Michigan, and Australia. Recently, it bought out Mandalay Resorts Group (which owned Mandalay Bay, Luxor, Excalibur, Monte Carlo, and Circus Circus). The acquisition of Mandalay Resort Groups put MGM Mirage on top in Las Vegas. It now controls half of the Las Vegas strip. MGM Mirage has an impressive portfolio of properties that includes the Bellagio, MGM Grand Las Vegas, the Mirage, Treasure Island, New York New York Boardwalk Hotel and Casino, and several others.[14]

MGM Mirage prides itself on operating the world's largest hotel/casino. The MGM Grand Hotel, located on 113 acres along the Las Vegas strip, has more than 5,034 rooms and a 171,500-square-foot casino with some 3,700 slot machines, about 160 table games, some 50 shops, a theme park, and a special-events center featuring superstar acts. Across the strip is the MGM Mirage's 2,000-room New York New York Hotel and Casino. The New York New York Hotel and Casino includes an 84,000-square-foot casino containing more than 80 gaming tables and more than 2,000 slot machines. The Bellagio's lobby ceiling contains a breathtaking display of 2,000 hand-blown glass flowers created by world-renowned artist Dale Chihuly. A water fountain ballet in front of the resort offers viewers a musical and visual spectacle. MGM Mirage also runs a hotel/casino in northern Australia that caters to Asian gamblers. The company has agreed to develop casinos in Atlantic City, New Jersey, and South Africa.[15]

In 2009, MGM Mirage anticipates the opening of CityCenter Hotel and Casino. CityCenter will include 4,000 rooms in addition to three 400-room boutique hotels. It will be located in the heart of the Las Vegas Strip between the Bellagio and the Monte Carlo. In addition to the hotels and casino, the center will include 650 condominium-hotel units and 550,000 square feet of retail, dining, and entertainment space.[16]

Harrah's Entertainment and Caesars Entertainment have paired up to dominate the gaming industry. They are now the world's biggest casino operator. Harrah's Entertainment operates forty casinos in three countries, under the Harrah's, Caesars, and Horseshoe brand names. Harrah's Entertainment is the premier name in casino entertainment. The Harrah's brand was born in Reno, Nevada, in the late 1930s and has since grown to become the largest casino entertainment company in North America. Harrah's history is a rich combination of casino expertise and quality, which was launched in northern Nevada and expanded across the continent. Today, Harrah's is a $1.5 billion company, publicly traded on the New York Stock Exchange.

Boyd Gaming operates eighteen gaming and hotel facilities in six states. The company's twelve properties located in or close to Las Vegas are the Stardust Resort and Casino; Barbary Coast Hotel and Casino; Main Street Station Hotel, Casino, and Brewery; the Orleans Hotel and Casino; Suncoast Hotel and Casino; South Coast Hotel and Casino; Sam's Town Hotel and Gambling Hall; the Eldorado Casino; the Joker's Wild Casino; the California Hotel and Casino; Gold Coast Hotel and Casino; and the Fremont Hotel and Casino. Outside Nevada, Boyd operates the Sam's Town Hotel and Gambling Hall, a dockside gaming and entertainment complex in Tunica County, Mississippi; Blue Chip Casino Hotel in northwest Indiana; Sam's Town Casino, a Kansas City, Missouri, casino complex; Par-A-Dice Hotel Casino docked on the Illinois River; Delta Downs Racetrack Casino and Hotel, Sam's Town Hotel and Casino Shreveport, the Treasure Chest Casino all located in Louisiana; and the Borgata Hotel, Casino, and Spa in New Jersey.[17]

INTRODUCING STEPHEN A. WYNN

Chairman of the Board and CEO, Wynn Resorts

Casino developer Stephen A Wynn is widely credited with transforming Las Vegas from a gambling venue for adults into a world-renowned resort and convention destination. As chairman of the board, president, and chief executive officer of Mirage Resorts, Mr. Wynn envisioned and built the Mirage, Treasure Island, and Bellagio—boldly conceived resorts that set progressibvely higher standards for quality luxury and entertainment. As chairman of the board and chief executive officer of Wynn Resorts, Limited, Mr. Wynn developed Wynn Las Vegas, among the world's preeminent luxury hotel resorts. Mr. Wynn also developed the Wynn Macau, a flagship Asian casino resort in Macau, China, where his company has been awarded a twenty-year concession by the Macau government.

Mr. Wynn began his career in 1967 as part owner, slot manager, and assistant credit manager of the Frontier Hotel. Between 1968 and 1972 he also owned and operated a wine and liquor importing company. But it was an entrepreneurial real estate deal with Howard Hughes in 1971 that produced sufficient profits for a major investment in the landmark Golden Nugget Casino. He transformed an establishment that was once known only as a "gambling joint" into a Four Diamond resort, known for elegance and personal service. By 1973, at age thirty-one, Mr. Wynn controlled the property and began developing the Golden Nugget as a complete resort hotel. In 1978, he used the profits from the Golden Nugget in Las Vegas to build the Golden Nugget Hotel and Casino on the Boardwalk in Atlantic City. The resort became known for its elegant facilities, TV ads featuring Frank Sinatra, and impressive lineup of superstar entertainment. From its opening in 1979 until its sale in 1986, the Atlantic City property dominated the market in revenues and profits despite its smaller size.

In 1987, Mr. Wynn sold the Atlantic City Golden Nugget, which had cost $160 million, to Bally for $450 million and turned his creativity to developing the elegant Mirage Resort, which opened in 1989. With its imaginative erupting volcano and South Seas theme, the Mirage Resort ignited a $12 billion building boom that catapulted Las Vegas to America's number one tourist destination and fastest growing city. In 1991, Golden Nugget Incorporated was renamed Mirage Resorts Incorporated.

Following his staggering success at the Mirage, in 1993 Wynn opened Treasure Island, a Four Diamond property with a romantic tropical theme indoors and a full-size pirate ship used in the daily reenactment of the Battle of the Buccaneer Bay outdoors. He raised the bar again in 1998 when he opened the opulent $1.6 billion Bellagio, one of the world's most spectacular hotels. Visitors line the street in front of the hotel to watch the Dancing Waters, shooting fountains choreographed to music on the hotel's 8.5-acre manmade lake. He then brought Mirage Resorts' standard of style to historic Biloxi, Mississippi, with the 1835-room Beau Rivage, blending Mediterranean beauty and Southern hospitality.

In June 2000, Mr. Wynn sold Mirage Resorts Incorporated to MGM for $6.6 billion and purchased Las Vegas's legendary Desert Inn Resort and Casino. The Desert Inn was closed in August 2000, and on the site Mr. Wynn began developing Wynn Las Vegas, a 2700-room luxury destination resort that has inspired yet another wave of development on the strip.

For every property he develops, Wynn is known for assembling a dream team of highly motivated employees who keep guestrooms and public spaces impeccable, according to industry analysts. His properties are always exceptional, drawing a commanding share of a demanding market with an exceptionally high occupancy. He is confident that both his projects and Las Vegas will continue to thrive.

In October 2006 President George W. Bush appointed Mr. Wynn to serve on the Board of Trustees for the world-renowned John F. Kennedy Center for the Performing Arts in Washington, D.C., and in November 2006 he was inducted into the American Gaming Association's (AGA) Hall of Fame. Mr. Wynn is a member of the International Advisory Council for the Moran Eye Center and has received honorary degrees from the University of Nevada-Las Vegas, Siena College, The Culinary Institute of America, and Johnson & Wales.

Source: Courtesy Stephen A. Wynn.

▶ Check Your Knowledge

1. Why is the gaming entertainment industry growing so quickly?
2. Who are the top key players in the gaming industry?

Positions in Gaming Entertainment

Careers in the gaming entertainment industry are unlimited. Students of the industry who understand the multidisciplinary needs of the business find five initial career tracks in hotel operations, food and beverage operations, casino operations, retail operations, and entertainment operations.

Hotel Operations

The career opportunities in gaming entertainment hotel operations are much like the career opportunities in the full-service hotel industry, with the exception that food and beverage can be a division of its own and not part of hotel operations. The rooms and guest services departments offer the most opportunities for students of hospitality management. Because gaming entertainment properties have hotels that are much larger than nongaming hotels, department heads have a larger number of supervisors reporting to them and more responsibilities. Reservations, front desk, housekeeping, valet parking, and guest services can all be very large departments with many employees.

Food and Beverage Operations

Gaming entertainment has a foundation of high-quality food and beverage service in a wide variety of styles and concepts. Some of the best foodservice operations in the hospitality industry are found in gaming entertainment operations. There are many career opportunities in restaurant management and the culinary arts. As with hotel operations, gaming entertainment properties are typically very large and contain numerous food and beverage outlets, including a number of restaurants, hotel room service, banquets and conventions, and retail outlets. Many establishments support gourmet, high-end signature restaurants. It is not unusual to find many more executive-level management positions in both front- and back-of-the-house food and beverage operations in gaming entertainment operations than in nongaming properties.

Casino Operations

Casino operations jobs fall into five functional areas. Gaming operations staff include slot machine technicians (approximately one technician for every forty machines), table-game dealers (approximately four dealers for each table game), and table-game supervisors. Casino service staff includes security, purchasing, and maintenance and facilities engineers. Marketing staff includes public relations, market research, and advertising professionals. Human resources staff includes employee relations, compensation, staffing, and training specialists. Finance and administration staff includes lawyers, accounts payable, audit, payroll, and income control specialists.[18]

Although there was little organized dealer training as recently as a decade ago, the explosive growth of the gaming industry has increased the need for trained dealers skilled at working a variety of table games including **blackjack, craps, roulette, poker,** and **baccarat**. Now, through the use of textbooks and videotapes combined with hands-on training at a mock casino, future dealers learn the techniques and fine points of dealing at classes offered by both colleges and private schools.

Retail Operations

The increased emphasis on nongaming sources of revenues in the gaming entertainment business demands an expertise in all phases of retail operations, from store design and layout to product selection, merchandising, and sales control. Negotiating with concession subcontractors may also be a part of the overall retail activities. Retail operations often support the overall theme of the property and can often be a major source of revenue; however, retail management careers are often an overlooked career path in the gaming entertainment industry.

Entertainment Operations

Because of the increased competition, gaming entertainment companies are creating bigger and better production shows to turn their properties into destination attractions. Some production shows have climbed into the $30 to $90 million range, with special entertainment venues built for superstars such as Celine Dion.

Trends in the Gaming Entertainment Industry

- Gaming entertainment is depending less on casino revenue and more on room, food and beverage, retail, and entertainment revenue for its profitability and growth.

- The gaming entertainment industry and lodging industry are converging as hotel room inventory is rapidly expanding in gaming entertainment properties.

- Gaming entertainment, along with the gaming industry as a whole, will continue to be scrutinized by government and public policymakers as to the net economic and social impact of its activities.

CORPORATE PROFILE

Harrah's Entertainment Inc.

Harrah's Entertainment was founded in 1937 by William F Harrah as a small bingo parlor in Reno, Nevada. Today Harrah's is the largest gaming company in the world, with a portfolio of 48 casinos totaling four million square feet of gaming, which it owns or manages in three countries, under the Harrah's, Caesars, and Horseshoe brand names.[1] Harrah's has 28 land-based and 12 riverboat or dockside casinos, plus golf courses and combination racetrack and casinos in several states, including Nevada, Louisiana, New Jersey, Mississippi, Kansas, and Missouri. Harrah's grew by new property development, expansions, and acquisitions, and it now employs some 85,000 people, with the vision that "Each of our brands will be the overwhelming first choice for casino entertainment of its targeted customers."[2] Harrah's Entertainment is focused on building loyalty and value with its customers through a unique combination of guest service, excellent products, unsurpassed distribution, operational excellence, and technology leadership.[3] The marketing strategy is designed to appeal to those who are avid players, especially those who play in more than one market.[4]

In December of 2006, the company's board of directors voted to accept a buyout offer from Apollo Management and Texas Pacific Group for $17 billion, or $90 per share.[5] The corporation's shareholders approved the proposed buyout in April 2007 and approval by regulators is in progress.[6]

[1] http://finance.yahoo.com/q/pr?s=het
[2] www.harras.com/harrahs-corporate/about-us.html
[3] www.harrahs.com/harrahs-corporate/index.html
[4] www.investords.com/cgi-bin/stocksymbol.cgi?ticker=het
[5] Las Vegas Sun, December 19, 2006. as cited by http://en.wilipedia.org/Harrah%27s_Entertainment.
[6] The Sun Herald, April 5, 2007. as cited by http://en.wilipedia.org/Harrah%27s_Entertainment.

- As the gaming entertainment industry becomes more competitive, exceptional service quality will become an increasingly important competitive advantage for success.

- The gaming entertainment industry will continue to provide management opportunities for careers in the hospitality business.

CASE STUDY

VIP

A frequent guest of the casino makes a last-minute decision to travel to your property for a weekend stay. The guest enjoys gaming as a leisure activity and is one of the casino's better customers. When he arrives at the casino, he is usually met by a casino host and treated as a very important person because of his level of wagering at the blackjack tables. This guest is worth approximately $50,000 in casino win per year to the hotel. As a result of his last-minute arrangements, however, the guest cannot notify a casino host that he is on his way to the hotel. Upon arriving, he finds a very busy registration desk. He must wait in line for twenty minutes, and when he tries to check in, he is told that the hotel is full. The front-desk clerk acts impatient when the guest says that he is a frequent customer. In a fit of frustration, the would-be guest leaves the hotel and makes a mental note that all casinos have similar odds at the blackjack table and maybe another property will give him the respect he deserves.

Discussion Question

1. What systems or procedures could you institute to make sure this type of oversight does not happen at your property?

CASE STUDY

Negotiating with Convention Groups

Your convention sales department receives a call from a trip director for a large convention group. The group will use many function rooms for meetings during the day and will generate a substantial amount of convention services revenue. Likewise, their food and beverage needs are quite elaborate and will be great for the food and beverage department budget. However, the group is very sensitive concerning room price and is willing to negotiate the time of week for their three-night stay.

Discussion Question

1. What are the considerations that a gaming entertainment property must take into account when determining room rates for convention groups?

Summary

1. The casino industry has developed into a new business called gaming entertainment with the introduction of full-service hotels, retail, and entertainment offerings.
2. To operate gaming entertainment businesses, it is necessary to understand the relationship between the casino and other departments in the operation.
3. Gaming entertainment is strictly regulated by state governments, and the integrity developed over time by these regulations is necessary for the survival of the industry.
4. Nongaming revenue is increasing as a percentage of total revenue of gaming entertainment businesses.
5. Native American gaming entertainment businesses are a means for economic self-development by tribal people.

Key Words and Concepts

baccarat
blackjack
casino
craps
gambling
gaming entertainment

handle
Indian Gaming Regulatory Act of 1988 (IGRA)
poker
roulette
win

Review Questions

1. Briefly describe the history of legalized gaming in the United States.
2. What defines a gaming entertainment business?
3. Explain the attraction of gaming entertainment to the destination of a tourist.
4. Why is it necessary for strict regulations to be in force on the casino floor?
5. How are hotel operations in a gaming entertainment business different from hotel operations in a nongaming environment?

Internet Exercises

1. Organization: **Wynn Las Vegas**
   Web site: www.wynnlasvegas.com
   Summary: Located on the Las Vegas Strip, the Wynn Las Vegas has a lot to offer. From gaming and concerts, to hosting some of the biggest conventions, the Wynn Las Vegas will certainly keep visitors busy.
   (a) What are some of the gaming features that attract customers to the Wynn Las Vegas?
   (b) What are the benefits to the different packages available under special offers?
2. Pick a casino in Las Vegas and look it up on the Internet. What does it offer that sets it apart from other casinos in Las Vegas and from other casinos in the United States? In what areas is it similar to other casinos?

Apply Your Knowledge

1. Name the major gaming entertainment hotels in Las Vegas.

2. Give examples of nongaming revenue.

Suggested Activity

Research careers in the gaming entertainment industry. Are there more opportunities than you realized? What careers in the industry interest you the most?

Endnotes

1. American Gaming Association, "Industry Information FAQ," www.americangaming.org/industry/faq_index.cfm.
2. American Gaming Association, "Industry Information FAQ," www.americangaming.org/industry/faq_index.cfm. assets/files/aga-2007_sos.pdf pg. 7 of 49.
3. http://gamblingorigins.com/gambling-history-egypt.shtml
4. www.gypsware.com/gamblinghistory.html
5. Wikipedia, "Bugsy Siegel," en.wikipedia.org/wiki/Bugsy_Siegel.
6. Wikipedia, "Atlantic City, New Jersey," en.wikipedia.org/wiki/Atlantic_city.
7. Wikipedia, "Atlantic City, New Jersey," en.wikipedia.org/wiki/Atlantic_city.
8. Julia Glick, "Cabin Indian Leader Who Pursued Gaming Rights Dies," *Press-Enterprise*, Riverside, CA. January 4, 2007.
9. www.nigc.gov/Laws Regulations/IndianGamingRegulatoryAct/tabid/605/Default/aspx
10. www.nicg.gov/LawsRegulations/IndianGamingRegulatoryAct/table/605/Default.aspx
11. www.nicg.gov/LawsRegulations/IndianGamingRegulatoryAct/table/605/Default.aspx
12. www.nicg.gov/LawsRegulations/IndianGamingRegulatoryAct/table/605/Default.aspx
13. American Gaming Association, "Casino Gaming in America: Key Findings of the National Gambling Impact Study Commission (1997–99)," www.americangaming.org/assets/files/studies/aga_casino_gaming_2005.pdf.
14. MGM Mirage, "Company Overview," www.mgmmirage.com/companyoverview.asp.
15. MGM Mirage, "Company Overview," www.mgmmirage.com/companyoverview.asp.
16. MGM Mirage, "Company Overview," www.mgmmirage.com/companyoverview.asp.
17. Boyd Gaming, "About Us: Company History," www.boydgaming.com/about/.
18. Harrah's Entertainment, "Community," www.harrahs.com/harrahs-corporate/about_us/community-relations/IPImpacts.pdf

PART V

Assemblies and Event Management

CHAPTER **12**

Meetings, Conventions, and Expositions

OBJECTIVES

After reading and studying this chapter, you should be able to:

- Know about the major players in the convention industry.

- Describe destination management companies.

- Describe the different aspects of being a meeting planner.

- Describe the different types of contractors.

- Explain the different types of meetings, conventions, and expositions.

- Know the various venues for meetings, conventions, and expositions.

Development of the Meetings, Conventions, and Expositions Industry

People have gathered to attend **meetings, conventions,** and **expositions** since the ancient times, mainly for social, sporting, political, or religious purposes. As cities became regional centers, the size and frequency of such activities increased, and various groups and associations set up regular expositions.

Associations go back many centuries to the Middle Ages and before. The guilds in Europe were created during the Middle Ages to secure proper wages and maintain work standards. Associations began in the United States at the beginning of the eighteenth century, when Rhode Island candle makers organized themselves.

Meetings, incentive travel, conventions, and exhibitions (MICE) represent a segment of the tourism industry that has grown in recent years. The MICE segment of the tourism industry is very profitable. Industry statistics point to the fact that the average MICE tourist spends about twice the amount of money that other tourists spend.

Size and Scope of the Industry

Today, according to the American Society of Association Executives (ASAE), in the United States with 23,000 members, about 6,000 associations operate at the national level, and a hundred thousand more function at the regional, state, and local levels. The association business is big business. Associations spend billions holding thousands of meetings and conventions that attract millions of attendees.

The hospitality and tourism industries consist of a number of associations, including the following:

- The American Hotel & Lodging Association
- The National Restaurant Association
- The American Culinary Federation
- The International Association of Convention and Visitors Bureaus
- Hotel Sales and Marketing Association International
- Meeting Planners Association
- Club Managers Association of America
- Professional Convention Management Association

Associations are the main independent political force for industries such as hospitality, offering the following benefits:

- Governmental/political voice
- Marketing avenues

- Education
- Member services
- Networking

Thousands of associations hold annual conventions at various locations across North America and the rest of the world. Some associations alternate their venues from east to central to west; others meet at fixed locations, such as the National Restaurant Association (NRA) show in Chicago or the American Hotel & Lodging Association (AH&LA) convention and show in New York.

> " Meetings, conventions, and expositions provide attendees and personnel in specialized areas an opportunity to discuss important issues and new developments with their peers. "
>
> Laurel Ebert,
> The Boylston Convention Center,
> Boylston, Maryland

Key Players in the Industry

The need to hold face-to-face meetings and attend conventions has grown into a multi-billion-dollar industry. Many major and some smaller cities have convention centers with nearby hotels and restaurants.

The major players in the convention industry are **convention and visitors bureaus (CVBs)**, meeting planners and their clients, the convention centers, specialized services, and exhibitions. The wheel diagram in Figure 12–1 shows the number of different people and organizations involved with meetings, conventions, and expositions.

Convention and visitors bureaus are major participants in the meetings, conventions, and expositions market. The International Association of Conventions and Visitors Bureaus (IACVB) describes a CVB as a not-for-profit umbrella organization that represents an urban area that tries to solicit business- or

> " Meetings provide managers the opportunity to give positive feedback to their employees, address employee concerns, and to emphasize projects and/or goals. "
>
> Lianne Wilhoitte,
> Wilhoitte & Associates,
> Baltimore, Maryland

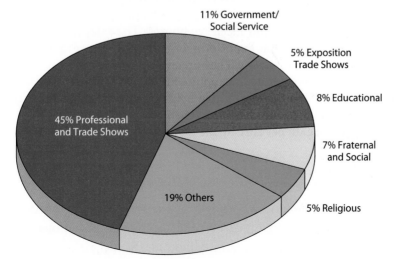

Convention Center Utilization by Market Sector

- 11% Government/Social Service
- 5% Exposition Trade Shows
- 8% Educational
- 7% Fraternal and Social
- 5% Religious
- 19% Others
- 45% Professional and Trade Shows

Figure 12–1 • Major Players in the Convention Industry.

pleasure-seeking visitors. The convention and visitors bureau comprises a number of visitor industry organizations representing the various industry sectors:

- Transportation
- Hotels and motels
- Restaurants
- Attractions
- Suppliers

The bureau represents these local businesses by acting as the sales team for the city. A bureau has *five* primary responsibilities:

1. To enhance the image of tourism in the local/city area
2. To market the area and encourage people to visit and stay longer
3. To target and encourage selected associations and others to hold meetings, conventions, and expositions in the city
4. To assist associations and others with convention preparations and to give support during the convention
5. To encourage tourists to partake of the historic, cultural, and recreational opportunities the city or area has to offer

The outcome of these five responsibilities is for the city's tourist industry to increase revenues. Bureaus compete for business at trade shows, where interested visitor industry groups gather to do business. For example, a tour wholesaler who is promoting a tour will need to link up with hotels, restaurants, and attractions to package a vacation. Similarly, meeting planners are able to consider several locations and hotels by visiting a trade show. Bureaus generate leads (prospective clients) from a variety of sources. One source, associations, have national/international offices in Washington, D.C. (so that they can lobby the government) and Chicago.

A number of bureaus have offices or representatives in these cities or a sales team who will make follow-up visits to the leads generated at trade shows. Alternatively, they will make cold calls on potential prospects, such as major associations, corporations, and incentive houses. The sales manager will invite the meeting, convention, or exposition organizer to make a **familiarization (FAM) trip** to do a site inspection. The bureau assesses the needs of the client and organizes transportation, hotel accommodations, restaurants, and attractions accordingly. The bureau then lets the individual properties and other organizations make their own proposals to the client. Figure 12–2 shows the average expenditure per delegate per stay by the convention type.

▶ Check Your Knowledge

1. According to the American Society of Association Executives (ASAE), in the United States how many associations operate at the national level?
2. What are the five primary responsibilities of a bureau?
3. What is the purpose of a familiarization (FAM) trip?

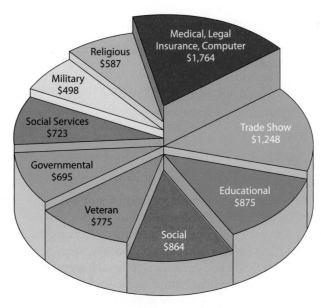

Average length of stay is 3.50 days

Figure 12–2 • Average Expenditure per Delegate per Stay by the Convention Type.
The significance of these amounts is that given an attendance of several hundred to thousands of guests the economic impact quickly adds up and benefits the community in a variety of ways.

Destination Management Companies

A destination management company (DMC) is a service organization within the visitor industry that offers a host of programs and services to meet clients' needs. Initially, a destination management sales manager concentrates on selling the destination to meeting planners and performance improvement companies (incentive houses).

The needs of such groups may be as simple as an airport pickup or as involved as an international sales convention with theme parties. DMCs work closely with hotels; sometimes DMCs book rooms, and other times hotels request the DMC's know-how on organizing theme parties. Patricia Roscoe, chairperson of Patti Roscoe and Associates (PRA), says that meeting planners often have a choice of several destinations and might ask, "Why should I pick your destination?" The answer is that a DMC does everything, including airport greetings, transportation to the hotel, VIP check-in, theme parties, sponsoring programs, organizing competitive sports events, and so on, depending on budget. Sales managers associated with DMCs obtain leads, which are potential clients, from the following sources:

- Hotels
- Trade shows
- Convention and visitors bureaus
- Cold calls
- Incentive houses
- Meeting planners

Each sales manager has a staff or team that can include the following:

- Special events manager, who will have expertise in sound, lighting, staging, and so on

- Accounts manager, who is an assistant to the sales manager

- A theme-events creative director

- Audiovisual specialist

- Operations manager, who coordinates everything, especially on-site arrangements, to ensure that what is sold actually happens.

For example, Patti Roscoe's destination management company organized meetings, accommodations, meals, beverages, and theme parties for 2,000 Ford Motor Company dealers in nine groups over three days for each group.

Roscoe also works closely with incentive houses, such as Carlson Marketing and Maritz Travel. These incentive houses approach a company and offer to set up incentive plans for companies' employees, including whatever it takes to motivate them. Once approved, Carlson contacts a destination management company and asks for a program.

In conclusion, thousands of companies and associations hold meetings and conventions all over the country. Many of these organizations use the services of professional meeting planners, who in turn seek out suitable destinations for the meetings and conventions. Meetings and conventions are now more international with several cities being popular in drawing large numbers of attendees.

Meeting Planners

Meeting planners may be independent contractors who contract out their services to both associations and corporations as the need arises or they may be full-time employees of corporations or associations. In either case, meeting planners have interesting careers. According to the International Convention Management Association (ICMA), about 212,000 full- and part-time meeting planners work in the United States.

The professional meeting planner not only makes hotel and meeting bookings but also plans the meeting down to the last minute, always remembering to check to ensure that the services contracted for have been delivered. In recent years, the technical aspects of audiovisual and simultaneous translation equipment have added to the complexity of meeting planning. The meeting planner's role varies from meeting to meeting, but may include some or all of the following activities:

Premeeting Activities

- Estimate attendance
- Plan meeting agenda
- Establish meeting objectives
- Set meeting budget

- Select city location and hotel/convention site
- Negotiate contracts
- Plan exhibition
- Prepare exhibitor correspondence and packet
- Create marketing plan
- Plan travel to and from site
- Arrange ground transportation
- Organize shipping
- Organize audiovisual needs

On-Site Activities

- Conduct pre-event briefings
- Prepare VIP plan
- Facilitate people movement
- Approve expenditures

Postmeeting Activities

- Debrief
- Evaluate
- Give recognition and appreciation
- Plan for next year

As you can see, this is quite a long list of activities that meeting planners handle for clients.

Service Contractors

Service contractors, exposition service contractors, general contractors, and *decorators* are all terms that have at one time or another referred to the individual responsible for providing all of the services needed to run the facilities for a trade show. Just as a meeting planner is able to multitask and satisfy all the demands in meeting planning, a general exposition contractor must be multitalented and equipped to serve all exhibit requirements and creative ideas.

The service contractor is hired by the exposition show manager or association meeting planner. The service contractor is a part of the facilities management team and, to use the facility, the sponsor must use their service contractor. In other situations, the facility may have an exclusive contract with an outside contractor, and they may require all expositions to deal with this contractor. Today there are Internet service companies that can take reservations, prepare lists, and provide all kinds of services via the Internet for meeting planners.

▶ Check Your Knowledge

1. What is a destination management company?
2. What are the primary responsibilities of professional meeting planners?

CORPORATE PROFILE

Las Vegas Convention and Visitors Authority

The Las Vegas Convention and Visitors Authority (LVCVA) is one of the top convention and visitors bureaus, charged with the following mission: To attract visitors by promoting Las Vegas as the world's most desirable destination for leisure and business travel.

The Las Vegas Convention and Visitors Authority hosts hundreds of conventions attended by more than a million delegates. The LVCVA is organized as follows: State law establishes the number, appointment, and terms of the authority's board of directors. A fourteen-member board provides guidance and establishes policies to accomplish the LVCVA mission.

Eight members are elected officials of the county, and each represents one of the incorporated cities therein; the remaining six members are nominated by the Las Vegas Chamber of Commerce or the Nevada Resort Association and represent different segments of the business industry. The board is one of the most successful public/private partnerships in the country. Under the presidency of Rossi Ralenkotter, the Las Vegas Convention and Visitors Authority and its board of directors have received numerous awards.

The Las Vegas Convention and Visitors Authority's organizational structure is shown in the accompanying diagram. The board of directors employs a president (executive) to serve as chief executive officer. Other members of the executive staff are senior vice president marketing, senior vice president operations, vice president facilities, vice president of strategic planning, vice president of human resources, vice president of convention sales, vice president of information technology, vice president of finance, vice president public affairs and vice president international brand strategy and legal counsel. The marketing division's first priority is to increase the number of visitors to Las Vegas and southern Nevada. The division is composed of eight teams that specialize in various market segments to increase the number of visitors and convention attendance. The teams are also shown in the diagram.

The destination services team is responsible for providing visitor services, including registration, convention housing, hotel/motel reservations, and visitor information. The Internet marketing and research team oversees the LVCVA's trade and consumer website strategies and tracks the dynamics of the Las Vegas and Clark County's tourism marketplace, along with the competitive gaming and tourism trade shows held in Las Vegas. The housing department receives and processes hotel and motel housing forms from convention and trade show delegates, forwarding the reservations to participating hotels daily. The reservations department operates toll-free telephone lines, transferring the calls of travel agents, tourists, conventioneers, and special event attendees to hotels and motels within a requested location and price range.

Five visitor centers operate in Primm, Boulder City, Mesquite, Laughlin, and Las Vegas seven days a week and serve more than 38,000 visitors a month. A brochure room supports the visitor centers by answering thousands of telephone calls and letters requesting a variety of information on Las Vegas, including recreation, weddings, entertainment, and special events. The staff sends out posters, brochures, and other information.

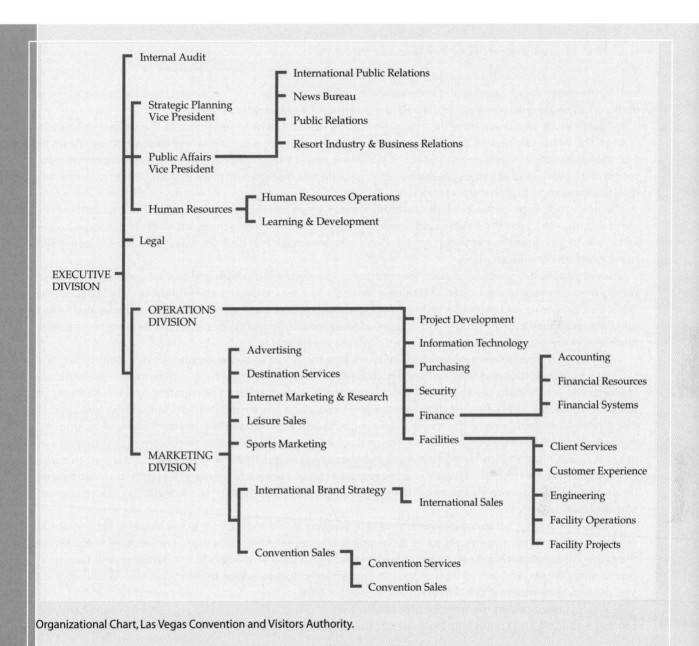

Organizational Chart, Las Vegas Convention and Visitors Authority.

The convention sales team coordinates convention sales efforts at the authority and contributes to the successes of convention sales citywide by providing sales leads to the hotels. Sales managers travel throughout the United States and the world, meeting with association meeting planners to sell the benefits of holding conventions in Las Vegas. Members of the team also attend numerous conventions and trade shows, where they host or sponsor special events and functions to entice conventions and trade shows to Las Vegas.

With a market share of 82 percent of leisure travelers visiting Las Vegas, travel promotion is vital to the LVCVA. The tour and travel team is responsible for positioning Las Vegas as a full-service resort destination, as

continued

CORPORATE PROFILE *(continued)*

well as the preeminent gaming and entertainment capital of the world. The leisure sales team aggressively markets Las Vegas with travel agents, wholesalers, and online travel portals.

In recent years wholesale travel has been one of the fastest growing segments of the Las Vegas tourism market. The wholesale market continues to increase, so the leisure sales team works to position Las Vegas as a destination without limits on the variety of packages and activities than can be arranged. To provide education on the variety of activities offered by Las Vegas, the wholesaler team plans and implements several annual familiarization tours for wholesalers.

Familiarization trips for travel agents are conducted by team members to generate enthusiasm and excitement around Las Vegas bookings. Travel agents' presentations are also scheduled in both primary and selected secondary airline market cities. Similar events are scheduled for Laughlin, which also advertises a 1-800 number for tourism information.

The corporate and incentive markets are traditionally considered the high end of the travel industry. These buyers are extremely sophisticated and value-conscious and are looking for the highest quality facilities and amenities. Corporate and incentive team members attend various trade shows throughout the United States and Canada, as well as selected cities in Europe and Asia, promoting Las Vegas as a complete, value-oriented, flexible, and accessible resort destination for corporate meetings.

With the goal of increasing international visitation in the midst of an expanding global marketplace, the LVCVA's international brand strategy team is charged with maintaining a high profile in the international marketplace, positioning Las Vegas and southern Nevada as the preferred destination and the gateway to the American Southwest. Twelve international offices manage Las Vegas' promotional efforts in a total of 75 countries worldwide, from the major markets of Canada, Mexico, and the United Kingdom, to primary markets of the European Union, Ireland, South Korea, Japan, and Australia, to the emerging markets of Brazil, Russia, China, and India. In addition to increasing Las Vegas brand and product awareness through sales, marketing, and public relations efforts in each of these markets, team members provide information, brochures, and sales material in foreign languages emphasizing Las Vegas as a world-class, full-service resort destination.

In recent years, special event planners have also showed increased interest in Las Vegas and Laughlin as event destinations. Team members travel to several special event trade shows and conferences to maximize the opportunities for special events to be held in Las Vegas. The team works in cooperation with Las Vegas Events and the Laughlin Marketing Partners to aggressively pursue events that provide television exposure and draw large numbers of participants, spectators, and visitors.

Travelers responded to the popular advertising theme "What Happens in Vegas, Stays in Vegas," and the Las Vegas tourism and convention business continues to flourish.

Advertising Team: The advertising team is responsible for developing the general marketing strategy that provides a blueprint for the development of specific marketing initiatives, advertisements, and public relations efforts. These strategies are incorporated into each division of the marketing department.

Public Affairs Department: The public affairs department includes public relations, the Las Vegas News Bureau, and resort industry and business relations. Public relations provides information about Las Vegas and southern Nevada through direct contact with domestic and international members of print and broadcast media. The News Bureau also maintains a complete photographic collection of Las Vegas, depicting the resort and entertainment growth of the area over a period of almost fifty years.

Resort industry and business relations serves as the community voice of the LVCVA to the organizations and numerous industry stakeholders throughout the region.

Operations Division: The operations division provides accounting and administrative support services to the marketing and executive divisions, as well as facilities management for the Las Vegas Convention Center and Cashman Center and security for the entire authority.

Finance: The finance division maintains a general accounting system for the authority to ensure accountability in compliance with legal provisions and in accordance with generally accepted accounting principles. Finance is composed of financial services, accounting, and payroll activities. Additional responsibilities include the preparation of the authority's annual financial report (CAFR) and the annual budget. The CAFR has received the Government Finance Officers Associate (GFOA) Excellence in Financial Reporting Award a number of times in recent years.

Purchasing: Purchasing supports the marketing, operations, and facilities divisions by providing for purchasing of materials, services, and goods needed to meet its goals and objectives. It is responsible for the storage and distribution of various supply items through an extensive warehousing program, as well as through printing and mail distribution.

Security: The security department provides protection of Authority property, equipment, employees, and convention attendees 24 hours a day, 365 days a year, and also oversees paid parking and fire safety functions. The team patrols both the convention center and Cashman Field properties and is trained in first aid assistance. Several officers have been recognized by the authority board and convention organizations for providing life-saving measures to convention attendees.

Information Technology: The information technology division (ITD) is responsible for efficiently and effectively meeting the automation and information needs of the authority. ITD sustains a staff of technically competent professionals to design, maintain, implement, and operate the systems necessary to support the goals of the authority.

Community Grants Program: The LVCVA has awarded more than $32 million in grants to local government entities and chambers of commerce since 1965.

The grant program serves the dual purpose of helping local agencies develop, promote, and increase tourism to Southern Nevada through various special events. Additionally, the grant program assists local chambers of commerce in promoting their destination through assistance in website funding, visitor information centers, and other tourism support programs.

The LVCVA has historically provided grant funds to programs and events that promote tourism to and within the destination. Originally founded as the Clark County Fair and Recreation Board, the LVCVA has maintained its commitment to the region through this program.

The LVCVA's primary source of revenue is provided by room taxes. All hotel, motel, and other transient lodging establishments in Clark County are assessed a room tax. The total tax on rooms in Clark County averages 9 percent. The room tax is collected from the individual lodging property by the governmental jurisdiction in which the property is located. The governing entity of that jurisdiction then distributes the proceeds among the LVCVA and various governmental organizations throughout the county and state. The LVCVA receives less than half of the available room tax money. Most of it is used to fund schools, parks, roads, and other infrastructure in Clark County.

Courtesy of Las Vegas Convention and Visitors Authority.

Types of Meetings, Conventions, and Expositions

Meetings

Meetings are conferences, workshops, seminars, or other events designed to bring people together for the purpose of exchanging information. Meetings can take any one of the following forms:

- *Clinic.* A workshop-type educational experience in which attendees learn by doing. A clinic usually involves small groups interacting with each other on an individual basis.

- *Forum.* An assembly for the discussion of common concerns. Usually, experts in a given field take opposite sides of an issue in a panel discussion, with liberal opportunity for audience participation.

- *Seminar.* A lecture and a dialogue that allow participants to share experiences in a particular field. A seminar is guided by an expert discussion leader, and usually thirty or fewer persons participate.

- *Symposium.* An event at which a particular subject is discussed by experts and opinions are gathered.

- *Workshop.* A small group led by a facilitator or trainer. It generally includes exercises to enhance skills or develop knowledge in a specific topic.

The reason for having a meeting can range from the presentation of a new sales plan to a total quality management workshop. The purpose of meetings is to affect behavior. For example, as a result of attending a meeting, a person should know or be able to do certain things. Some outcomes are very specific; others may be less so. For instance, if a meeting were called to brainstorm new ideas, the outcome might be less concrete than for other types of meetings. The number of people attending a meeting can vary. Successful meetings require a great deal of careful planning and organization. In a major convention city, convention delegates spend approximately $423 per day, almost twice that of vacation travelers. Figure 12–3 shows convention delegates' spending in a convention city.

Meetings are set up according to the wishes of the client. The three main types of meeting setups are theater style, classroom style, and boardroom style.

- Theater style generally is intended for a large audience that does not need to make a lot of notes or refer to documents. This style usually consists of a raised platform and a lectern from which a presenter addresses the audience.

- Classroom setups are used when the meeting format is more instructional and participants need to take detailed notes or refer to documents. A workshop-type meeting often uses this format.

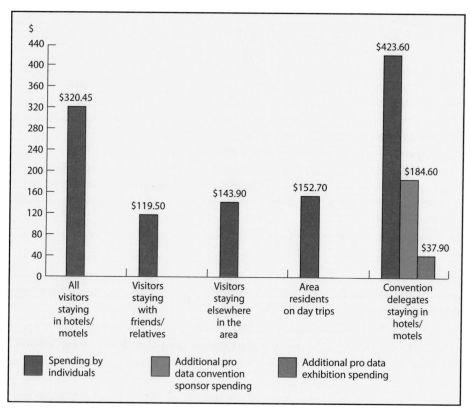

Figure 12–3 • Convention Delegates' Spending in Convention City San Francisco.

- Boardroom setups are made for small numbers of people. The meeting takes place around one block rectangular table.

Association Meetings

Every year there are thousands of association meetings that spend millions of dollars sponsoring many types of meetings, including regional, special interest, education, and board meetings. The things that are on the top of the list of places for an association meeting planner to choose from include the destination's availability of hotel and facilities, ease of transportation, distance from attendees, transportation costs, and food and beverage. Members attend association meetings voluntarily, so the hotel should work with meeting planners to make the destination seem as appealing as possible.

Associations used to be viewed as groups that held annual meetings and conventions with speeches, entertainment, an educational program, and social events. They have changed in activity and perception.

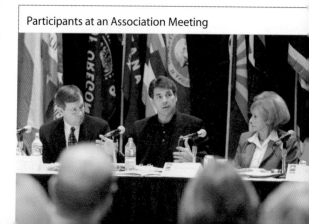

Participants at an Association Meeting

FOCUS ON SECURITY

Meeting and Conference Safety

Hank and Lynne Christen

Corporations and organizations spend millions of dollars each year on conferences, meetings, trade shows, and other special events, and both organizers and attendees expect and demand a safe and secure environment for their event.

Although terrorism is a continuing national and international concern, criminal incidents, accidents, fires, and natural disasters are more common risks that create enormous liability for the facility hosting an event. Although these liabilities cannot be completely eliminated, there are considerations and precautions that lower the risks and minimize the consequences if an unforeseen problem occurs.

The following are some important steps for improving conference and meeting security at your hospitality facility:

- Safety and security are key parts of conference or event proposals and preplanning. It is critical that initial meetings and preconference security specifications clearly detail who, what, when, where, why, and how organizers and attendees will be protected.
- Once a conference or meeting is scheduled, develop a specific two-part crisis plan for the event. Begin by addressing preparation and prevention. The second part of the plan should focus on "what-if" scenarios and establish contingency plans and strategies for reducing the impact of incidents on the guests and the event.
- Consider the international, national, and local political climate during an event. What is the national alert level? Is there local unrest or planned demonstrations? What is the current union-labor climate?
- Appoint a meeting and conference security specialist as the liaison between your facility and the meeting planners or organizers. If a problem or crisis occurs, leadership and communication are critical factors in handling the situation effectively.
- Provide attendees with personal safely guidelines and commonsense information that guests tend to overlook. Briefly outline emergency evacuation and bomb threat procedures.
- Remember that security extends beyond the actual event hours. Setup, breakdown, and overnight security are areas of vulnerability for security breaches.
- Today's attendees expect to see uniformed security. Professional and well-trained security guards or off-duty police officers help to deter crime and increase personal comfort levels.
- Conduct a thorough facility assessment prior to the event. Be alert for possible security breaches.
- Establish a relationship with local law enforcement and fire agencies. They can be valuable resources in your security assessment.
- Recognize the increased risks when high-profile politicians, religious leaders, and celebrities are present. Many VIPs have advance teams that are very proficient in security planning. Protecting high-profile guests requires protocols such as personal security, alias registration, medical coordination, and media planning.
- Establish an access control policy for employees and guests. Studies show that prominent identification deters unwanted guests and reduces security problems.
- Every employee is part of your event security team. Hold employee briefings, conduct frequent training, mandate a security exercise at least once a year to increase awareness, and reinforce responsibilities.

Realistically all conferences, meeting, and events involve some level of risk to your organization. There is no 100 percent guaranteed way to prevent all problems; however, proactive safety and security planning and preparation greatly increase the odds for a successful, crisis-free event.

Conventions and Expositions

Conventions are generally larger meetings with some form of exposition or trade show included. A number of associations have one or more conventions per year. These conventions raise a large part of the association's budget. A typical convention follows a format like this:

1. Welcome/registration
2. Introduction of president
3. President's welcome speech, opening the convention
4. First keynote address by a featured speaker
5. Exposition booths open (equipment manufacturers and trade suppliers)
6. Several workshops or presentations on specific topics
7. Luncheon
8. More workshops and presentations
9. Demonstrations of special topics (e.g., culinary arts for a hospitality convention)
10. Vendors' private receptions
11. Dinner
12. Convention center closes

Figure 12–4 shows a convention event profile for a trade show.

Conventions are not always held in convention centers; in fact, the majority are held in large hotels over a three- to five-day period. The headquarters hotel is usually the one in which most of the activity takes place. Function space is allocated for registration, the convention, expositions, meals, and so on.

Expositions are events that bring together sellers of products and services at a location (usually a convention center) where they can show their products and services to a group of attendees at a convention or trade show. Exhibitors are an essential component of the industry because they pay to exhibit their products to the attendees. Exhibitors interact with attendees with the intention of making sales or establishing contacts and leads for follow-up. Expositions can take up several hundred thousand square feet of space, divided into booths for individual manufacturers or their representatives. In the hospitality industry, the two largest expositions are the American Hotel & Lodging Association's conference held in conjunction with the International Hotel/Motel & Restaurant Show (IHMRS) (held annually in November at the Jacob K. Javits Convention Center in New York) and the National Restaurant Association's annual exposition held every May in Chicago. Both events are well worth attending.

Types of Associations

An association is an organized body that exhibits some variety of volunteer leadership structure, which may employ an activity or purpose that they share in common. The association is generally organized to promote and enhance that

```
16:15:28                                                                    Page: 1
                        Convention Center Corporation                       9506059
                              EVENT PROFILE

                              EVENT STATISTICS

       Event Name:  Apartment Association Trade Show        ID:            9506059
       Sales Person: David Ploskonka              Initial Contact:         8/3/2005
     Event Manager: Kris Roach                    Move In Date:           6/22/2009
       ConVis Contact:                            Move In Day:           Wednesday
       Food Person:                               Move In Time:            6:01 am
        Event Tech.:                              First Event Date:       6/23/2009
      Event Attend.:                              First Event Day:        Thursday
     Nature of Event: LT Local Trade Show         Start Show Time:         6:01 am
    Event Parameter: Convention Center            End Show Time:          11:59 pm
     Business Type 1: 41 Association              # of Event Days:               1
     Business Type 2: 91 LOCAL                    Move Out Date:          6/23/2009
      Booking Status: D Definite                  Move Out Day:           Thursday
      Rate Schedule: III Public Show, Meetings and Location   Out Time:    11:59 pm
      Open to Public: No                          Date Confirmed:         8/3/2005
    Number Sessions: 1                            Attend per Sesn:            3000
      Event Sold By: Facility                     Tot Room Nights:              15
      Abbrev. Name: /6/Apartment Assn            Public Release:              Yes
    Est Bill Amount: Rent - 6,060.00  Equip –          0.00 Food –          0.00
    Last Changed On: 8/20/05 in: Comment Maintenance    By – Alex Gohr
```
This Event has been in the facility before

CLIENT INFORMATION

Company: Apartment Assn, a non-profit Corporation
        Contact Name: Dory Grieve, Sales and Marketing Coord.

ID: SDAA

Alt Contact Name: Ms. Corrina Schultz, Finance & Operations Director

EVENT LOCATIONS

ROOM	MOVE IN	IN USE	ED	MOVE OUT	BS	SEAT	RATE	EST. RENT	ATTEND
A	6/22/09 6:01 am	6/23/09	1	6/23/09 11:59 pm	D	E	III	6,060.00	5000
AS	6/22/09 6:01 am	6/23/09	1	6/23/09 11:59 pm	D	E	III	0.00	10
R01	6/22/09 6:01 am	6/23/09	1	6/23/09 11:59 pm	D	T	III	0.00	450
R02	6/22/09 6:01 am	6/23/09	1	6/23/09 11:59 pm	D	T	III	0.00	350
R03	6/22/09 6:01 am	6/23/09	1	6/23/09 11:59 pm	D	T	III	0.00	280
R04	6/22/09 6:01 am	6/23/09	1	6/23/09 11:59 pm	D	T	III	0.00	280
R05	6/22/09 6:01 am	6/23/09	1	6/23/09 11:59 pm	D	T	III	0.00	460

FOOD SERVICES

ROOM	DATE	TIME	BS ATTEND	EST. COST FOOD SERVICE

There are No Food Services booked for this event

Figure 12–4 • Convention Event Profile for a Trade Show.

INTRODUCING JILL MORAN, CSEP

Principal and Owner, JS Moran, Special Event Planning & Management

In my life, there is no typical day. As the owner of a special event company, I provide a variety of services to corporate, nonprofit, and social clients. I must be able to communicate successfully with a client at one moment, a vendor at the next, and a prospect at another. My job also involves managing the growth of my company, hiring the right staff and vendors for projects, and getting each job done from start to finish in a professional and timely manner.

As a business owner, I am required to keep my eye on many facets of the company almost daily. Some areas are a must to attend to such as billing, scheduling, and marketing. The squeakiest wheel that gets the most grease, though, is the actual ongoing projects. Once a project is secured, the contracting, planning, and execution stages quickly follow after the initial handshake. These components of meeting and event planning can be time and energy consuming as the details are planned out and put into motion. Event details may involve researching, attending meetings, generating event documents, developing creative concepts and themes, securing vendors to satisfy event details, or executing an event. In the planning of any given event or conference, I may be required to attend off-site visits with vendors, venues, or clients as well as use the computer or telephone to facilitate the planning process. Visits to art supply, furniture, fabric stores, or store rooms of linen or décor vendors are also key elements as theme and design elements are worked on. Review of entertainment or speakers, planning of room layouts or trade show and exhibition space, or discussion with graphic artists also fits into the necessary details covered during the planning phase of an event.

A typical day may involve early computer time to work on production schedules, timelines, e-mails to vendors or clients, follow-up on contracts, or focused time spent on a new proposal. I find early morning (before 9 A.M.) or evening (after 8 P.M.) to be the best time for these activities. This is when I get the least telephone interruptions and it is before or after scheduled appointments that would require my time out of the office. During the typical business day, phone calls, planning activities, and appointments occupy most of the day. If I am working on an international project, there is more flexibility with this because of the time differences.

While the execution phase of projects and events keeps me busy moment by moment, the strategic planning and business management of my company also demand attention as well. The challenge for me as the owner of a small business is to carve out time for the marketing and sales arm of the business, taking time to prospect for new business at the same time that I am in the execution phase of events so that when one project comes to an end, another will be waiting in the wings. I do this by developing fresh marketing materials using photos or components of recent meetings and events; creating video or DVD-style materials to post on my web site or to send to clients; making calls to colleagues, prospects, or venues to say "hello" or touch base; and attending luncheons or visits with past clients to keep in touch. I also try to spend time getting a pulse on new markets to explore or niche areas to develop in my business. I typically subscribe to a wide variety of industry and professional magazines and try to end my day flipping through and tearing out articles that may be useful.

One thing I feel strongly about is keeping an eye on the future. I have owned a home-based business since 1988 and have seen the special events industry grow and change in many ways over the years. Passionate about the industry, I made a commitment to share my experience with those starting out, serving as a mentor, speaker, author, and industry leader. I continually examine the direction events and meetings are taking, gaps in the industry that need professional attention, ways to improve the processes or offer new and better services to those who honor the value of events as vehicles for communication, education, or celebration. Whenever possible, I try to attend meetings and conferences, either in my local area or throughout the United States and internationally

continued

to get a pulse on new directions and changes in the industry. These meetings also give me ideas and feed my creative juices to approach new projects with a fresh eye. I have met colleagues who are similar to me and share my challenges or are not at all like me and help me to consider different approaches to events. Many times, these gatherings offer terrific networking opportunities and ways to meet potential vendors or new clients.

Sometimes I feel I eat, sleep, and live special events, and in many ways I do. But work doesn't take up every moment of my life. As a mother and wife, I still try to create a fun, loving home for my family by cooking dinner almost every night and by walking daily with my husband and two dogs. These breaks during the day give me downtime and a chance to regroup. I am also active in the music ministry at my local church as a Youth Choir Director, which offers me spiritual and community involvement. I also belong to a book group, which I often attend without completing the story. There are only so many hours in the day, and I seem to use them up very quickly. But at the end of each day, I am always looking forward to the next!

Source: Courtesy of Jill Moran.

common interest, activity, or purpose. The association industry is significant in many respects—total employees, payroll, and membership—but in one area it is the undisputed leader: It's the big spender when it comes to conventions and meetings. The following are different types of associations that participate in meetings, conventions, and expositions.

Historical Associations

Today's associations find their roots in historical times. Ancient Roman and Asian craftsmen formed associations for the betterment of their trade. Medieval times found associations in the form of guilds, which were created to ensure proper wages were received and to maintain work standards.

Trade Association

A trade association is an industry trade group that is generally a public relations organization founded and funded by corporations that operate in a specific industry. Its purpose is generally to promote that industry through public relations (PR) activities such as advertising, education, political donation, political pressure, publishing, and astroturfing.[1]

Professional Association

A professional association is a professional body or organization, usually nonprofit, that exists to further a particular profession, to protect both the public interest and the interests of professionals.[2]

Medical and Scientific Associations

These associations are professional organizations for medical and scientific professionals. They are often based on their specific specialties and are usually national, often with subnational or regional affiliates. These associations usually offer conferences and continuing education. They often serve in capacities similar to trade unions and often take public policy stances on these issues.

Religious Organizations

Religious organizations include those groups of individuals who are part of churches, mosques, synagogues, and other spiritual or religious congregations. Religion has taken many forms in various cultures and individuals. These groups may come together in meeting places to further develop their faith, to become more aware of others who have the same faith, to organize and plan activities, to recognize their leaders, for fund-raising, and for a number of other reasons.

Government Organizations

There are thousands of government organizations in the United States made up of numerous public bodies and agencies. These types of organizations can range from federal, state, and local organizations. There are five basic types of local governments. Three of these are general-purpose governments; the remaining two include special-purpose local governments that fall into the category of school district governments and special district governments.

Types of Meetings

There are different types of meetings and purposes for having a meeting. Some of the types of meetings are annual meetings that are held by private or public companies, board and committee meetings, fund-raisers, and professional and technical meetings. The following are some of the more popular types of meetings.

Annual Meetings

Annual meetings are meetings that are generally held every year by corporations or associations to inform their members of previous and future activities. In organizations run by volunteers or a paid committee, the annual meeting is generally the forum for the election of officers or representatives for the organization.

Board, Committee Meetings, Seminars and Workshops, Professional and Technical Meetings

Board meetings for corporations must be held annually and most corporations hold meetings monthly or four times a year. Of course, not all are held in hotels, but some are, and that brings in additional revenue at the hotel. Committee meetings are generally held at the place of business and only occasionally are held in hotels. Seminars are frequently held in hotels as are workshops and technical meetings. To meet these needs hotels and convention centers have convention and meeting managers who go over the requirements and prepare proposals and event orders and budgets.

Corporate Meetings, Conventions, and Expositions

Meetings are mostly held by either the corporate or nonprofit industries. Both association and corporate meeting expenditures are in the billions of dollars each year. Corporations in various industries hold lots of meetings mostly for reasons of educating, training, decision making, research, sales, team building, the introduction of a new product, organization or reorganization, problem solving, and strategic planning. Corporate meetings may be held for the employees or for the general public. For employees of a company, a corporate meeting is a command performance. The major objective of corporate meeting planners is to ensure that the meetings are successful.

SMERF

Many participants in meetings are organized by either an association, a corporation, or **social, military, educational, religious, and fraternal groups (SMERF)**. Often these groups are price conscious, because of the fact that the majority of the functions sponsored by these organizations are paid for by the individual, and sometimes the fees are not tax deductible. However, SMERF groups are flexible to ensure that their spending falls within the limits of their budgets; they are a good filler business during off-peak times.

Incentive Meetings

The **incentive market** of MICE continues to experience rapid growth as meeting planners and travel agents organize incentive travel programs for corporate employees to reward them for reaching specific targets. Incentive trips generally vary from three to six days in length and can range from a moderate trip to an extremely lavish vacation for the employee and his or her partner. The most popular destination for incentive trips is Europe, followed closely by the Caribbean, Hawaii, Florida, and California. Because incentive travel serves as the reward for a unique subset of corporate group business, participants must perceive the destination and the hotel as something special. Climate, recreational facilities, and sightseeing opportunities are high on an incentive meeting planner's list of attributes to look for.

A Computer Software Show

▶ Check Your Knowledge

1. What are three different types of meetings described in this chapter and what is their purpose?
2. What is SMERF?

Meeting Planning

Meeting planning includes not only the planning but also the successful holding of the meeting and the post-meeting evaluations. As you shall see, there are a number of topics and lots of details to consider. (See Figure 12–5.)

SAN DIEGO
CONVENTION
CENTER

EVENT MANAGER

DEFINITION

Under moderate direction from the services manager, plans, directs, and supervises assigned events and represents services manager on assigned shifts.

KEY RESPONSIBILITIES

- Plans, coordinates, and supervises all phases of the events to include set ups, move ins and outs, and the activities themselves
- Prepares and disseminates set-up information to the proper departments well in advance of the activity, and ensures complete readiness of the facilities
- Responsible for arranging for all services needed by the tenant
- Coordinates facility staffing needs with appropriate departments
- Acts as a consultant to tenants and the liaison between in-house contractors and tenants
- Preserves facility's physical plant and ensures a safe environment by reviewing tenants plans; requests and makes certain they comply with facility, state, county, and city rules and regulations
- Prepares accounting paperwork of tenant charges, approves final billings, and assists with collection of same
- Resolves complaints, including operational problems and difficulties
- Assists in conducting surveys, gathering statistical information, and working on special projects as assigned by services manager
- Conducts tours of the facilities

MINIMUM REQUIREMENTS

- Bachelor's degree in hospitality management, business, or recreational management from a fully accredited university or college, plus two (2) years of experience in coordinating major conventions and trade shows
- Combination of related education/training and additional experience may substitute for bachelor's degree
- An excellent ability to manage both fiscal and human resources
- Knowledge in public relations; oral and written communications
- Experienced with audiovisual equipment

225 Broadway, Suite 710 • San Diego, CA 92102 • (619) 239-1989
FAX (619) 239-2030
Operated by the San Diego Convention Center Corporation

Figure 12–5 • An Event Manager's Job Description.

Needs Analysis

Before a meeting planner can start planning a meeting a *needs analysis* is done to determine the purpose and desired outcome of a meeting. Once the necessity of the meeting has been established, the meeting planner can then work with the party to maximize the productivity of the meeting. The key to a productive meeting is a meeting agenda. The meeting agenda may not always fall under the responsibility of the meeting planner, but it is essential for the meeting planner to be closely involved with the written agenda and also with the core purpose of the agenda, which may be different from what is stated. For example, a nonprofit organization may hold a function to promote awareness of its objectives through a fun activity, but its hidden agenda is to raise funds for the organization.

The meeting agenda provides the framework for making *meeting objectives*. The meeting planner must know what the organization is trying to accomplish so as to be successful in the management of the meeting or conference. It is helpful for the meeting planner, regardless of what role he or she plays, to plan the meeting with the meeting objectives in mind. The meeting's objectives provide the framework from which the meeting planner will set the budget, select the site and facility, and plan the overall meeting or convention.

Budget

Understanding clients and knowing their needs are both extremely important; however, the budget carries the most weight. Setting the *budget* for the meeting is more successful if the meeting planner is involved in the budget planning throughout and before making a finalized decision on how much to spend in each area. Setting the budget for the meeting is not a simple task. Knowing how much there is available to spend will help the meeting planner to better guide clients with parameters by which the event is designed. Budgets are planned for various activities and the amount of the budget needed fluctuates for different sites. Therefore, a working budget is necessary to be used as a guideline for making decisions for necessary changes. When changes in the budget are made, it is wise to communicate with the meeting planner these decisions so that the planning of activities is within budgetary constraints. Revenue and expenditure estimates must be accurate and be as thorough as possible to make certain that all possible expenditures are included in the budget prior to the event.

Income for a meeting, convention, or exposition comes from grants or contributions, event sponsor contributions, registration fees, exhibitor fees, company or organization sponsoring, advertising, and the sale of educational materials.

Expenses for a meeting, convention, or exposition could include the following but are not limited to rental fees, meeting planner fees, marketing expenses, printing and copying expenses, support supplies, such as office supplies and mailing, on-site and support staff, audiovisual equipment, speakers, signage, entertainment and recreational expenses, mementos for guests and attendees, tours, ground transportation, spousal programs, food and beverage, and on-site personnel.

Request for Proposal and Site Inspection and Selection

No matter how large or small a meeting, it is essential that clear meeting specifications are developed in the form of a written *request for proposal/quote*

(RFQ), rather than contacting hotels by telephone to get a quote. Many larger hotels and convention centers now have online submission forms available.

Several factors are evaluated when selecting a meeting site, including location and level of service, accessibility, hotel room availability, conference room availability, price, city, restaurant service and quality, personal safety, and local attractions. Convention centers and hotels provide meeting space and accommodations as well as food and beverage facilities and service. The convention center and a hotel team from each hotel capable of handling the meeting will attempt to impress the meeting planner. The hotel sales executive will send particulars of the hotel's meeting space and a selection of banquet menus and invite the meeting planner for a site inspection. During the site inspection, the meeting planner is shown all facets of the hotel, including the meeting rooms, guest sleeping rooms, the food and beverage outlets, and any special facility that may interest the planner or the client.

Negotiation with the Convention Center or Hotel

The meeting planner has several critical interactions with hotels, including negotiating the room blocks and rates. Escorting clients on site inspections gives the hotel an opportunity to show its level of facilities and service. The most important interaction is typically with the catering/banquet/conference department associates, especially the services manager, maître d', and captains; these front line associates can make or break a meeting. For example, meeting planners often send boxes of meeting materials to hotels expecting the hotel to automatically know which meeting they are for. On more than one occasion, they have ended up in the hotel's main storeroom, much to the consternation of the meeting planner. Fortunately for most meeting planners, once they have taken care of a meeting one year, subsequent years typically are very similar.

Contracts

Once the meeting planner and the hotel or conference facility have agreed on all the requirements and costs, a contract is prepared and signed by the planner, the organization, and the hotel or convention center. The *contract* is a legal document that binds two or more parties. In the case of meetings, conventions, and expositions, a contract binds an association or organization and the hotel or convention center. The components that make up an enforceable contract include the following:

1. *An offer:* The offer simply states, in as precise a manner as possible, exactly what the offering party is willing to do, and what he or she expects in return. The offer may include specific instructions for how, where, when, and to whom the offer is made.

2. *Consideration:* The payment exchanged for the promise(s) contained in a contract. For a contract to be valid, consideration must flow both ways. For example, the consideration is for a convention center to provide services and use of its facilities in exchange for a consideration of a stated amount to be paid by the organization or host.

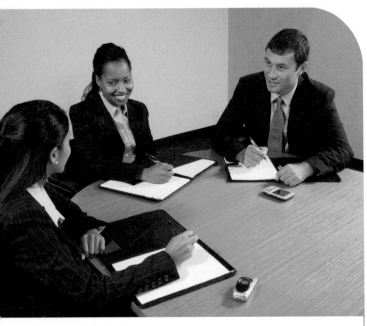

A Preconference Meeting

3. *Acceptance:* The unconditional agreement to the precise terms and conditions of an offer. The acceptance must mirror exactly the terms of the offer for the acceptance to make the contract valid. The best way to indicate acceptance of an offer is by agreeing to the offer in writing.[3]

Most important to be considered legally enforceable, a contract must be made by parties who are legally able to contract, and the activities specified in the contract must not be in violation of the law. Contracts should include clauses on "attrition and performance," meaning that the contract has a clause to protect the hotel or convention facility in the event that the organizer's numbers drop below an acceptable level. Because the space reserved is supposed to produce a certain amount of money, if the numbers drop, so does the money; unless there is a clause that says something like "there will be a guaranteed revenue of $$$ for the use of the room/space." The performance part of the clause means that a certain amount of food and beverage revenue will be charged for regardless of whether it is consumed.

Organizing and Preconference Meetings

The average lead time required for organizing a small meeting is about three to six months; larger meetings and conferences take much longer and are booked years in advance. Some meetings and conventions choose the same location each year and others move from city to city, usually from the East Coast to the Midwest or West Coast.

Conference Event Order

A conference event order has all the information necessary for all department employees to be able to refer to for details of the setup (times and layout) and the conference itself (arrival, meal times and what food and beverages are to be served, and the cost of items so that the billing can be done). An example of a conference event order is given in Figure 12–6.

Postevent Meeting

A postevent meeting is held to evaluate the event—what went well and what should be improved for next time. Larger conferences have staff from the hotel or convention center where the event will be held the following year so that they can better prepare for the event when it is held at their facility.

EVENT DOCUMENT
REVISED COPY
/6/SAN DIEGO INTERNATIONAL BOAT SHOW
Tuesday, January 4, 2005–Tuesday, January 11, 2005

SPACE: Combined Exhibit Halls AB, Hall A - How Manager's Office, Box Office by Hall A, Hall B –
Show Manager's Office, Mezzanine Room 12, Mezzanine Room 13, Mezzanine Rooms 14 A&B, AND
Mezzanine Rooms 15 A&B

CONTACT: Mr. Jeff Hancock
National Marine Manufacturers Association, Inc.
4901 Morena Blvd.
Suite 901
San Diego, CA 92117
Telephone Number: (619) 274-9924
Fax Number: (619) 274-6760
Decorator Co.:   Greyhound Exposition Services
Sales Person: Denise Simenstad
Event Manager: Jane Krause
Event Tech.:   Sylvia A. Harrison

SCHEDULE OF EVENTS:

Monday, January 3, 2005   5:00 am–6:00 pm   Combined Exhibit Halls AB
Service contractor move in GES,
Andy Quintena

Tuesday, January 4, 2005   8:00 am–6:00 pm   Combined Exhibit Halls AB
Service contractor move in GES,
Andy Quintena
12:00 pm–6:00 pm
Combined Exhibit Halls AB
Exhibitor move in

Wednesday, January 5, 2005   8:00 am–6:00 pm   Combined Exhibit Halls AB
Exhibitor move in
Est. attendance: 300

Thursday, January 6, 2005   8:00 am–12:00 pm   Combined Exhibit Halls AB
Exhibitor final move in
11:30 am–8:30 pm   Box Office by Hall A
OPEN: Ticket prices, Adults $6, Children 12 & under $3

Figure 12–6 • Conference Event Document.

Venues for Meetings, Conventions, and Expositions

Most of the time meetings and functions are held in hotels, convention centers, city centers, conference centers, universities, corporate offices, or resorts, but more and more meetings are housed in unique venues such as cruise ships and historical sites.

City Centers

City centers are good venues for some conferences because they are convenient to reach by air and ground transportation. There is plenty of action in a major city center; attractions range from cultural to scenic beauty. Most cities have a convention center and several hotels to accommodate guests.

Convention Centers

Convention centers throughout the world compete to host the largest exhibitions, which can be responsible for adding several million dollars in revenue to the local economy. Convention centers are huge facilities with parking, information services, business centers, and food and beverage facilities included.

Usually convention centers are corporations owned by county, city, or state governments and operated by a board of appointed representatives from the various groups having a vested interest in the successful operation of the center. The board appoints a president or general manager to run the center according to a predetermined mission and goals and objectives.

Convention centers have a variety of expositions and meeting rooms to accommodate both large and small events. The centers generate revenue from the rental of space, which frequently is divided into booths (one booth is about 100 square feet). Large exhibits may take several booths' space. Additional revenue is generated by the sale of food and beverages, concession stand rentals, and vending machines. Many centers also have their own subcontractors to handle staging, construction, lighting, audiovisual, electrical, and communications.

In addition to the megaconvention centers, a number of prominent centers also contribute

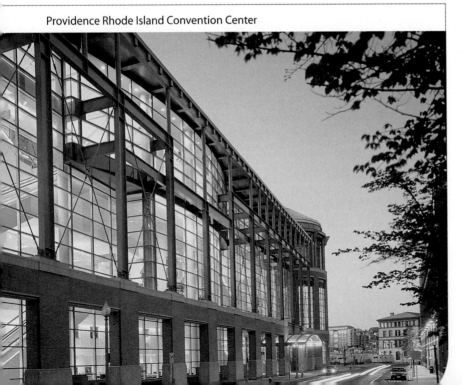

Providence Rhode Island Convention Center

to the local, state, and national economies. One good example is the Rhode Island Convention Center. The $82 million center, representing the second largest public works project in the state's history, is located in the heart of downtown Providence, adjacent to the 14,500-seat Providence Civic Center. The 365,000-square-foot center offers a 100,000-square-foot main exhibit hall, a 20,000-square-foot ballroom, 18 meeting rooms, and a full-service kitchen that can produce 5,000 meals per day. The exhibit hall divides into four separate halls, and the facility features its own telephone system, allowing individualized billing. A special rotunda function room at the front of the building features glass walls that offer a panoramic view of downtown Providence for receptions of up to 365 people. Extensive use of glass on the façade of the center provides ample natural light throughout the entrance and prefunction areas.

Conference Centers

A conference center is a specially designed learning environment dedicated to hosting and supporting small to medium-sized meetings, typically between twenty and fifty people.[4] The nature of a conference meeting is to promote a distraction-free learning environment. Conference centers are designed to encourage sharing of information in an inviting, comfortable atmosphere, and to focus sharply on meetings and what makes them effective. Although the groups that hold meetings in conference centers are typically small in terms of attendees, there are thousands of small meetings held every month. Increasingly, hotels are now going after executive meetings where expense is not a major issue.

Hotels and Resorts

Hotels and resorts offer a variety of locations from city center to destination resorts. Many hotels have ballrooms and other meeting rooms designed to accommodate groups of various sizes. Today, they all have web sites and offer meeting planners to help with the planning and organizing of conferences and meetings. Once the word gets out that a meeting planner is seeking a venue for a conference, there is plenty of competition among the hotels to get the business.

Cruise Ships

Meeting in a nontraditional facility can provide a unique and memorable experience for the meeting attendee. However, many of the challenges faced in traditional venues such as hotels and convention centers are also applicable to these facilities. In some cases, planning must begin much earlier for alternative meeting environments than with traditional facilities. A thorough understanding of goals and objectives, budget, and attendee profile of the meeting is essential to negotiate the best package possible. A cruise ship meeting is a uniquely different meeting setting and offers a number of advantages to the attendees such as discounts, complimentary meals, less outside distraction while at sea, entertainment, and visiting more than one destination while unpacking only once![5]

Colleges and Universities

More and more, alternative venues for meeting places include facilities such as colleges, universities, and their campuses. The paramount consideration in contemplating use of campus-based facilities is to know the nature of the target audience.[6] A certain knowledge and evaluation of the participants are inevitable and invaluable because the relative cost of campus-based meetings is most of the time less expensive than a medium-priced hotel.

Trends in Meetings, Conventions, and Expositions

- More people are going abroad to attend meetings.
- Some international shows do not travel very well (i.e., agricultural machinery). Thus, organizations such as Bleinheim and Reed Exposition Group airlift components and create shows in other countries.
- Competitiveness has increased among all destinations. Convention centers will expand and new centers will come online.
- The industry needs to be more sophisticated. The need for fiber optics is present everywhere.
- Shows are growing at a rate of 5 to 10 percent per year.
- Compared to a few years ago, large conventions are not as well attended, and regional conventions have more attendees.

CASE STUDY

Double-Booked

The convention bureau in a large and popular convention destination has jurisdiction over the convention center. A seasoned convention sales manager, who has worked for the bureau for seven years and produces more sales than any other sales manager, has rebooked a 2,000-person group for a three-day exposition in the convention center. The exposition is to take place two years from the booking date.

The client has a fifteen-year history of holding conventions, meetings, and expositions in this convention center and has always used the bureau to contract all space and services. In fact, the sales manager handling the account has worked with the client for seven of the fifteen years. The bureau considers this client a "preferred customer."

The convention group meeting planner also appears in a magazine ad giving a testimony of praise for the convention bureau, this particular sales manager, and the city as a destination for conventions.

Shortly after the meeting planner rebooks this convention with the bureau, the bureau changes sales administration personnel, not once, but three times. This creates a challenge for the sales manager in terms of producing contracts, client files, and event profiles, and in the recording and distribution of information. The preferred customer who rebooked has a contract, purchase orders for vendor services, a move-in and setup agenda, and an event profile, all supplied by the sales manager. The sales manager has copies of these documents as well. The two hotels where the group will be staying also have contracts for the VIP group.

As is the nature of this particular bureau, other sales managers have been booking and contracting space for the same time period as the group that rebooked. In fact, the exhibit hall has been double-booked, as have the break-out rooms for seminars, workshops, and food and beverage service. The groups that were contracted later are all first-time users of the facility.

This situation remains undetected until ten days prior to the groups' arrival. It is brought to the attention of the bureau and convention center only when the sales manager distributes a memo to schedule a precon-vention meeting with the meeting planner and all convention center staff.

Because of the administrative personnel changes, necessary information was not disseminated to key departments and key personnel. The convention center was never notified that space has been contracted for the preferred customer. The preferred customer has been told about this potentially catastrophic situation. Now there is a major problem to rectify.

Discussion Questions

1. Ultimately, who is responsible for decision making with regard to this situation?
2. What steps should be taken to remedy this situation?
3. Are there fair and ethical procedures to follow to provide space for the preferred customer? If so, what are they?
4. What measures, if any, should be taken in handling the seasoned sales manager?
5. What leverage does the meeting planner have to secure this and future business with the bureau?
6. What might the preferred customer do if it is denied space and usage of the convention center?
7. How can this situation be avoided in the future?

Summary

1. Conventions, meetings, and expositions serve social, political, sporting, or religious purposes. Associations offer benefits such as a political voice, education, marketing avenues, member services, and networking.
2. Meetings are events designed to bring people together for the purpose of exchanging information. Typical forms of meetings are conferences, workshops, seminars, forums, and symposiums.
3. Expositions bring together purveyors of products, equipment, and services in an environment in which they can demonstrate their products. Conventions are meetings that include some form of exposition or trade show.
4. Meeting planners contract out their services to associations and corporations. Their responsibilities include premeeting, on-site, and postmeeting activities.
5. The convention and visitors bureaus are nonprofit organizations that assess the needs of the client and organize transportation, hotel accommodations, restaurants, and attractions.
6. Convention centers are huge facilities, usually owned by the government, where meetings and expositions are held. Events at convention centers require a lot of planning ahead and careful event management. A contract that is based on the event profile and an event document is part of effective management.

Key Words and Concepts

associations
convention
convention and visitors bureaus (CVBs)
convention center
exposition
familiarization (FAM) trip
incentive market

meeting
meeting planner
meetings, incentive travel, conventions, and exhibitions (MICE)
social, military, educational, religious, and fraternal groups (SMERF)

Review Questions

1. From the Companion Website, what is the relationship of the Convention Center and the Convention and Visitors Bureau?
2. On the Companion Website, what career opportunities does John Moors describe?
3. What are associations and what is their purpose?
4. List the number of different people and organizations involved with meetings, conventions, and expositions.
5. List the primary sources of revenue and expenses involved in holding a meeting, a convention, and an exposition.
6. Describe the main types of meeting setups.
7. Explain the difference between an exposition and a convention.
8. List the duties of CVBs.
9. Describe the topics a meeting planner needs to deal with before, during, and after a meeting.

Internet Exercises

1. Organization: **Best of Boston**
   Web site: www.bestboston.com
   Summary: Best of Boston is an event planning company that specializes in putting together packages for different events, such as conventions, corporate events, private parties, and weddings.
   - (a) Explore this web site for events and list the different kinds of events this organization can organize.
   - (b) After simply browsing the web site, discuss the importance of networking in the meetings, conventions, and expositions industry.

2. Organization: **M & C Online**
   Web site: www.meetings-conventions.com
   Summary: This excellent web site offers in-depth information on meetings and conventions from different perspectives, ranging from legal issues to unique themes and concepts.
   Click the Breaking News heading (it's on the left side near the bottom of the page).
   - (a) What is the breaking news?
   - (b) Click "On the Cover" (on the left side near the top) and see what the cover stories are, and then share your findings with your class.

Apply Your Knowledge

Make a master plan with all the steps necessary for holding a meeting or seminar on careers in hospitality management.

Suggested Activity

Contact meeting planners in your area and, with permission of your professor, invite them to speak to the class about their work and how they do it.

Prepare questions in advance so that they may be given to the speaker ahead of time.

Endnotes

1. Wikipedia, "Industry Trade Group," http://en.wikipedia.org/wiki/Trade_association.
2. Wikipedia, "Professional Body," http://en.wikipedia.org/wiki/Professional_association.
3. Steven Barth, *Hospitality Law: Managing Issues in the Hospitality Industry* (Hoboken, NJ: John Wiley and Sons, 2006), 26–29.
4. Professional Convention Management Association, *Professional Meeting Management*, 4th ed. (Dubuque, IA: Kendall/Hunt, 2004), 557–561.
5. Professional Convention Management Association, *Professional Meeting Management*, 564–565.
6. Professional Convention Management Association, *Professional Meeting Management*, 552.

CHAPTER 13

Special Events

OBJECTIVES

After reading and studying this chapter, you should be able to:

- Define a special event.

- Describe what event planners do.

- Classify special events.

- Outline the skills and abilities required for event management.

- Identify the main professional organizations and associations involved with the special event industry.

*The **special events industry** is a dynamic, diverse field that has seen considerable growth and change over the past forty years. Today, the industry employs professionals who work together to provide a broad range of services to create what is termed a special event. But, what is a special event? Dr. Joe J. Goldblatt, a leading academic and author in the special event field distinguishes between a daily event and a special event in the following manner:*

Daily Events	Special Events Examples	
Occur spontaneously	Are always planned	Convention
Do not arouse expectations	Always arouse expectations	Meeting
Usually occur without a reason	Are usually motivated by a Wedding	Festival reason for celebration

*He uses these contributing factors to shape a definition of a special event: "A special event recognizes a unique moment in time with ceremony and ritual to satisfy specific needs."[1] The scope of this definition is very broad and encompasses many "moments." Special events include countless functions, such as **corporate seminars** and **workshops, conventions** and **trade shows, charity balls** and **fund-raisers, fairs and festivals,** and **social functions** such as **weddings and holiday parties.** It is for that reason the industry has seen such growth and presents so much potential for future careers and management opportunities.*

Food, clothing, and shelter are the accepted basic physical needs that humans require. Following those needs is an emotional need to celebrate, which has a direct impact on the human spirit. All societies celebrate—whether it is publicly or privately, as individuals or in groups. The need to celebrate has been recognized by corporations, public and government officials, associations, and individuals. This has contributed to the rapid growth of the special event industry with a wide range of possible employment opportunities. When you consider all of the planners, caterers, producers, event sites, and others that become part of the "special event," you can only imagine the potential for future careers and employment possibilities.

Event management is a newcomer compared to the hotel and restaurant industries. Yet as you will soon learn, special events is a field that doesn't have rigid boundaries. Closely related fields that may overlap include marketing, sales, catering, and entertainment. Future growth trends in special event management provide plenty of career opportunities in all hospitality sectors.

This chapter gives you an overview of the special events industry. You will learn about the various classifications of special events and where to look for future career opportunities. You will find information on the skills and abilities required to be successful in the field. Information on special event organizations, strategic event planning, and the future outlook of the industry will allow you to take a glimpse into this exiting, rewarding, and evolving field. As Frank Supovitz, Vice President of Special Events for the National Hockey League in New York, says, "The stakes have never been higher. Sponsors are savvier. Audiences are more demanding. And, event producers and managers are held accountable by their clients to meet their financial and marketing goals more than ever before. . . . So before the lights go down and the curtain rises, reach out for the experience and expertise in these pages . . . and explore the opportunities in special event management."[2]

Someone has to manage this incredible event, the Super Bowl

What Event Planners Do

Event planning is a general term that refers to a career path in the growing field of special events. Its forecast includes a growing demand for current and future employment opportunities. Like several other professions, event planning came about to fill a gap—someone needed to be in charge of all the gatherings, meetings, conferences, and so on that were increasing in size, number, and spectacle among business and leisure sectors. Corporate managers had to step away from their assignments to take on the additional challenges of planning conventions and conferences. Government officials and employees were displaced from their assignments to arrange recruitment fairs and military events. Consequently, the planner became a person whose job description did not include "planning" whenever a special event was planned.

The title **event planner** was first introduced at hotels and convention centers. Event planners are responsible for planning the event, from start to finish. This includes setting the date and location, advertising the event, providing refreshments or arranging catering services, speakers, or entertainment. Please keep in mind that this is a general list and will vary depending on the type, location, and nature of the event.

> ❝ Associations can be a valuable resource for students interested in a career in event management. Many offer scholarships and provide a great networking opportunity. ❞
>
> Karen Harris

A VGM Career Book, *Opportunities in Event Planning Careers*, has the following to say about a good candidate: "In addition to good organizational skills, someone with a creative spirit, a flair for the dramatic, a sense of adventure, and a love of spectacle could expect to flourish in this field." Highlighted skills and characteristics of a future professional in this field include:

Computer skills	Follow-through skills
Willingness to travel	Ability to work with high-level executives
Willingness to work a flexible schedule	Budgeting skills
Experience in delegating	Ability to initiate and close sales
Willingness to work long hours	Lots of patience
Negotiating skills	Ability to handle multiple tasks simultaneously
Verbal and written communication skills	Being a self-starter
Enthusiasm	Ability to interact with other departments[3]
Project management skills	

Event Management

Event management can be as small as planning an office outing to something larger like organizing a music festival and on up to a Super Bowl or even the Olympics. Events can be on-off, annual or perennial (happening each year), or every four years, as for the Olympics. Things just do not happen by themselves; it takes a great deal of preparation to stage a successful event. To hold a successful event, the organizer should have a vision and leader–manager skills in the key result areas: marketing, financial, operational, and legal. Getting good sponsorship is a big help. Sponsors provide money or in-kind contributions and receive recognition as a sponsor of the event, including use or display of their logo in the event's promotion. Sponsors expect to get something in return for their sponsorship, so give them something tangible that will help their corporation or organization. Each year thousands go to festivals and events of all kinds, and most, if not close to all, events receive some sponsorship because it is too costly to stage an event without sponsorship.

Event management requires special skills in marketing and sales (attracting the business in the first place); planning (to ensure all details are covered and that everything will be ready on time); organization (to make sure all the key staff know what to do, why, when, where, and how); financial (a budget needs to be made and kept to); human resources and motivation (the best people need to be selected and recruited, trained and motivated); and lots of patience and attention to details and endless checking up on them. To gain business, event managers prepare a proposal for the client's approval and contract signature. There are some important how-to's in preparing an event proposal: Find out as much information as possible

> The art of networking will allow you to build a contact base that will help you succeed in the event industry.
>
> Karen Harris

about the event (if it has been previously held) or what the client really has in mind. Ask organizers, attendees, providers, and others what went right and what went wrong or could be improved on next time the event is organized. Write the proposal in business English, no verbal foliage. Get creative—do something different and better and give them something to talk about; finally, do the numbers—nobody wants a surprise—do a pro-forma invoice so that the client will know the costs, and surprise them by being on time and on budget.

An event can be costly to put on; in addition to advertising there is a location charge, security costs, labor costs, and production costs (this may be food, beverage, and service, but also the staging and decor). Usually, the event manager has a good estimate of the number of ticket sales expected. She or he then budgets the costs to include the entertainment and all other costs, leaving a reasonable profit.

Event management also takes place at convention centers and hotels, where event managers handle all the arrangements after the sales manager has completed the contract. The larger convention center events are planned years in advance. As stated earlier, the convention and visitors bureau is usually responsible for the booking of conventions more than eighteen months ahead. Obviously, both the convention and visitors bureau and the convention center marketing and sales teams work closely with each other. Once the booking becomes definite, the senior event manager assigns an event manager to work with the client throughout the sequence of pre-event, event, and postevent, activities.

The booking manager is critical to the success of the event by booking the correct space and working with the organizers to help them save money by allocating only the space really needed and allowing the client to begin setting up on time. A contract is written based on the event profile. The event profile stipulates in writing all the client's requirements and gives all of the relevant information, such as which company will act as decorator/subcontractor to install carpets and set up the booths.

The contract requires careful preparation because it is a legal document and will guarantee certain provisions. For example, the contract may specify that the booths may only be cleaned by center personnel or that food may be prepared for samples only, not for retail. After the contract has been signed and returned by the client, the event manager will from time to time make follow-up calls until about six months before the event when arrangements such as security, business services, and catering will be finalized. The event manager is the key contact between the center and the client. She or he will help the client by introducing approved subcontractors who are able to provide essential services.

Two weeks prior to the event, an event document is distributed to department heads. The event document contains all the detailed information that each department needs to know for the event to run smoothly. About ten days before the event, a WAG meeting (week at a glance) is held. The WAG meeting is one of the most important meetings at the convention center because it provides an opportunity to avoid problems—like two event groups arriving at the same time or additional security for concerts or politicians. About this same time, a preconvention or pre-expo meeting is held with expo managers and their contractors—shuttle bus managers, registration operators, exhibit floor managers, and so on. Once the setup begins, service contractors marshall the eighteen-wheeler trucks to unload the exhibits by using radio phones to call the trucks from a nearby depot. When the exhibits are in place, the exposition opens and the public is admitted.

The following information provides the stages in the event planning process.

Research

The first stage of event planning is to answer these simple questions:

1. Why should a special event be held?
2. Who should hold it?
3. Where should it be held?
4. What should the focus of the event be?
5. What outcomes are expected?

Once answers to these questions are available, you can move to the second stage.

Design

The second stage in the event planning process can be the most exciting and challenging at the same time. It is the area that allows freedom in creativity and the implementation of new ideas that support the objectives of the special event. The design process is a time when an event manager or team can brainstorm new innovative ideas or develop adaptations to previous events to make them better, grander, and more exciting for the attendees. The design process seeks to obtain original and fresh ideas that will create an event worth investing in. The event may be a corporate meeting or it may be a beachside wedding, yet the design of the event will have a lasting impression on those who attend it.

Planning

Planning, the third stage in the event planning process, is often led by the determined budget for the event. The planning process includes contracting out services and arranging all other activities that will become part of the event. The planning process may include the following tasks:

- Determine event budget
- Select the event site
- Select hotel accommodations
- Arrange transportation
- Negotiate contracts
- Arrange catering
- Arrange speaker, entertainment, music
- Organize audiovisual needs

- Create marketing plan for the event
- Prepare invitations or event packets

The type and size of the event will ultimately determine the necessary steps required for the planning process. The information you obtain about planning from your other courses and studies will help you if you choose to pursue a career in event management.

Coordination

The process of **coordination** can be compared to a director leading a band. The band may have rehearsed a piece of music countless times, and yet during a concert the director still has the ability to "direct" or control the performance. Similarly, the event manager engages in the process of coordinating the event as it unfolds. This may be a stressful time because of unforeseen problems occurring, or it may be a truly rewarding time with a flawless execution. Regardless, coordination of the event may involve decision-making skills and abilities as the event progresses.

Coordination also relates to the human resource aspect of the special event. Event managers are leaders who through example motivate others. As an event manager, you will engage in coordinating staff and/or volunteers to carry out the special event's planned objectives and goals. As mentioned earlier, empowering your staff will create a positive environment and will make your job of coordinating their efforts that much easier.

Evaluation

Evaluation should take place during each of the stages of the event planning process and is a final step that can measure the success of the event in meeting the goals and objectives. If you take a look at the event planning process diagram in Figure 13–1,

Figure 13–1 • Event Planning Process Diagram.

you will notice that it is a continuous process. Outcomes are compared to expectations and variances investigated and corrected.

Challenges for Event Planners and Managers

If you are at this point considering a professional career in event management, there are event planning tools that you can use to your advantage as you pursue a career in this field. There are four primary challenges professional event managers face: time, finance, technology, and human resources.

Time management plays an important role in event planning, and it is an element that can be used effectively by budgeting your time the same way that you would your finances. Delegating tasks to the appropriate people, keeping accurate records and lists, preparing agendas before meetings, and focusing on what items deserve top priority are all examples of how to use time management effectively.

Financial management becomes important for an event planner when it becomes necessary for you to evaluate financial data, management fees, vendor fees, and so forth. This does not mean that you have to be a financial wizard; however, knowledge in this area will greatly enhance your opportunity to make profitable and sound decisions. There are resources that can be used in this area such as obtaining help or counsel from a financial professional and using technology that will help with event accounting.

Utilizing technology as a tool in event management can be a great opportunity to assist in the previous two areas. Software programs for word processing, financial management, and database management can help in daily tasks and event planning. Other technology products that are used by event professionals include laptop computers, cell phones, handheld devices, event management software, and the Internet.

The final tool relates to the effective management of your human resources. Empowering your employees is the key to success. As a manager and leader you must train your employees and/or volunteers, and give them the necessary information to perform their jobs. It is critical to select the right people, "empower" them, and develop their skills. This will ultimately help you succeed in accomplishing your goals. Empowering event staff can be used to allow them to make important decisions—successful events require many decisions to be made, and you as a manager will not have the time to

Guests mingle at a Charity Event in Coral Gables, Florida

make all of them. Empowering your team is the greatest tool you can utilize to become an effective leader and improve the performance of your staff.

▶ Check Your Knowledge

1. Give some examples to distinguish the differences between a daily event and a special event.
2. What are event planners responsible for?
3. Name the stages in the event planning process.

Classifications of Special Events

The development of the special events industry has been divided up into the following classifications:

- Corporate events (seminars, workshops, meetings, conferences)
- Association events (conventions, trade shows, meetings)
- Charity balls and fund-raising events
- Social functions (weddings, engagement parties, holiday functions)
- Fairs and festivals
- Concerts and sporting events

In a poll taken from a wide variety of event professionals in the industry, *Event Solutions Black Book* lists the following as the most popular types of event sites used:

Hotel/resort	62.0%
Convention center	32.5%
Tent/structure	32.6%
Banquet hall	29.0%
Outdoors	21.8%
Corporate facility	28.4%
Museum/zoo/gardens	12.4%
Arena/stadium/theater	18.0%
Restaurant	16.1%
Private residence	22.8%
Club	16.7%[4]

With those figures in mind, take a closer look at the various classifications that make up this exciting industry. Each category has its own unique characteristics, rewards, and challenges. As a human resource specialist would say, "It's important to put the right person in the right position." That statement also holds true for this. Any career selection, and especially for a person seeking the management level in it, should look for the correct "fit." With such a vast array of options you may find one that ignites your passion for the field, you may find several that are the wrong size before finding the right one, or you may decide that this is not the right match for your personality and goals. The following may help you to decide whether your future may hold a professional career in the special event industry.

Corporate Events

Corporate events continue to lead the industry in terms of event business. About 80 percent of the event market is corporate events.

Corporate event managers are employed by the company to plan and execute the details of meetings for the corporation's employees, management, and owners. The growing use of special events in the corporate arena created the need for positions dedicated to the planning and management of them. The corporate event planners engage in the following management activities. They are involved in the planning and organizing of the event, and they also play a key leadership role. Additionally, the planner must possess the following skills: effective communication, ability to coordinate various activities, and attention to detail.

Corporate events include the following: annual meetings, sales meetings, new product launches, training meetings and workshops, management meetings, press meetings, incentive meetings, and awards ceremonies.

Corporate events benefit several sectors of the hospitality industry. For example, a client may hold an event at a major attraction like Sea World or a resort like The Breakers. Each corporate client can provide the hotel, restaurants, airlines, and other businesses in the destination's economy with tens of thousands of dollars. Corporate event planners will consider the factors most important to the attendees when using a hotel as part of the event, including corporate account rates for lodging, amenities such as fitness centers and business centers, airport transportation, and quick check-in and checkout at the hotel. Therefore, corporate event planners should have strong negotiating skills to book lodging and convention services as needed.

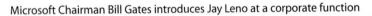
Microsoft Chairman Bill Gates introduces Jay Leno at a corporate function

Association Events

There are more than 6,500 associations in the United States alone. The majority of the large association conventions are planned two to five years ahead of time, and the destination is a determining factor in the planning process. The American

Medical Association and the American Dental Association are two of the most recognized examples. In the hospitality industry, the National Restaurant Association (NRA), American Hotel & Lodging Association (AH&LA), and at a global level the International Association of Convention and Visitors Bureaus are a few of the many associations relating to the field. Associations account for about $60.0 billion in generated revenue. This stems from the millions of people who attend thousands of meetings and conventions. For example, the American Marketing Association holds more than twenty conferences annually, which generates approximately $1,000,000 alone for one hotel.

Events relating to associations can range from a monthly luncheon at a private club or hotel to a yearly convention that may comprise an educational seminar(s) with an opportunity to network with other association members. Associations generally hire full-time paid planners to manage the yearly national membership meeting that is a requirement for most associations as part of their bylaws. Larger associations with greater financial resources often hire full-time meeting and convention management professionals who are involved in the large association events as well as other association events, including board meetings, educational seminars, membership meetings, professional meetings, and regional meetings.

Other opportunities for employment are widespread. They may include a position as a convention manager, special event manager in a hotel, conference manager, or a special event manager at a private club for the events held by local associations.

In the event planning industry, professional associations have a great impact in contributing to the development of their members. Professional associations provide training, certification, networking, and assistance with business plans and other consulting services for their members.

Charity Balls and Fund-Raising Events

Charity balls and fund-raising events provide a unique opportunity for the event manager to work with the particular group or charity, and usually a theme is chosen for the event. The event manager is then responsible for selecting the location and coordinating all of the details that will determine the success of the event, which may include catering, entertainment, décor, lighting, floral arrangements, invitations, rentals, public relations, transportation, security, and technical support.

One of the key skills that a person entering this category must possess is the ability to plan the event on a set and often limited budget. Why is this so critical? The events are used to raise funds toward a set group or charity, and every dollar that is spent on the event is thereby one less dollar that could go toward the cause. Nevertheless, these events are expected to be extravagant—so a little creativity can go a long way in the planning and implementing of the theme. The event manager should also have strong negotiating skills to bargain with vendors on reduced rates or in some cases donated services or products. A smart planner will know how to market and sell the positive public relations that the event could provide to the vendors.

The demand for fund-raising event planners/managers is one that holds solid ground. To prove this point, *Opportunities in Event Planning Careers* quoted an

> " Associations can be a valuable resource for students. Many offer scholarships and provide a great networking opportunity. I received a scholarship from the American Association of University Women and was therefore prompted to join as a student affiliate. Students interested in a career in event management can gain valuable experience by attending the meetings and more importantly—becoming involved. Volunteering is rarely turned down! "
>
> Karen Harris

> " Volunteering is one of the best ways to gain experience in the event industry, and charity/fund-raising events provide a great opportunity. I recently had the opportunity to volunteer as a banquet server for the "Star Night Gala" More importantly, however, I was provided the opportunity to meet various people involved in the planning and ask questions! Check your local paper for "upcoming events" or I found a local Charity Register that provides a calendar of events for the upcoming year.
>
> Volunteers are not paid. Not because they are worthless, but because they are priceless.... "
>
> University of South Florida, Circle K International motto

in-house event planner as stating: "One of the major advantages of working for a nonprofit as an in-house planner for almost six years was that I never had to look for work. There were always new events to take on."[5]

Social Events

Social function planners or managers work on a broad variety of events. This category of special events includes the traditional wedding and party planners that most of us are already familiar with. This category of event planning includes weddings, engagement parties, birthday parties, anniversary parties, holiday parties, graduation parties, military events, and all other social gatherings or events. A social event planner/manager is usually responsible for selecting the venue, determining any themes and/or design schemes, ordering or planning decorations, arranging for catering and entertainment, and having invitations printed and sent out.

SMERF, which stands for social, military, educational, religious, and fraternal organizations, is a category of organizations that also fall into the same category of social events. Individuals of these organizations often pay for the events, meaning they are price sensitive. Needless to say, budgeting skills are important for those working with these groups.

Weddings are the most widely recognized social event. Wedding planners are a key player in the social event category. The title seems glamorous and has a certain perception that most of us will hold; yet the management involved in planning a wedding involves strict attention to detail. Don't forget that the planner is responsible for creating what is considered to be the most important day of a couple's life. "Realize this is a business," says Gerard J. Monaghan, president of the Association of Bridal Consultants. "A fun business to be sure, but a business nonetheless." Effective wedding planners will have contacts formed for a variety of services, such as venues like hotels, wedding locations, decorating, catering, bridal shops, musicians, photographers, florists, and so forth.

Today's weddings are more expensive than those of the past, and they are often longer. Weddings have become true "special events" because of the willingness of family and friends to travel longer distances to celebrate with the bride and groom. Many weddings today have become minivacations for those attending.

▶ Check Your Knowledge

1. What events continue to lead the industry in terms of event business?
2. When are the majority of large association conventions planned?
3. What are the key skills that a person entering the charity ball category must possess?
4. What is SMERF?

Fairs and Festivals

The word *fair* is likely to evoke memories of cotton candy, funnel cakes, Ferris wheels, and other games. These memories are very important to why a fair is considered a special event, but the purpose of most fairs in the United States is usually related to the agriculture industry. A professional staff chosen by the elected committee usually produces them. Fairs are generally held at the local, county, or state level.

Festivals are planned events that are often themed to the celebration's purpose. Cultures, anniversaries, holy days, and special occasions are commonly celebrated as a festival. Mardi Gras, for example, celebrates the beginning of Lent. Food and entertainment are greatly emphasized when planning a festival. Festivals.com is a site that allows you to search for festivals held throughout the globe. The variety of festivals is astounding—art, music, sporting, literary, performing arts, air shows, science, and even children's festivals. The web site describes cultural festivals as: "Magical parades. Fabulous feasts. Dizzying dancing. The spirit of celebration crosses languages, oceans, continents and cultures, as people revel in their heritages and communities."[6]

The following is a small sampling of festivals—some are commonly known, and others are surprising.

Oktoberfest

Mardi Gras

Biketoberfest

Hispanic Heritage Festival

Street Music Festival

American Dance Festival

Polar Bear Jumpoff Festival

Gilroy Garlic Festival

Bagelfest

One of the key strategies in planning special events for fairs and festivals is to determine the purpose of the event early on. It is important to analyze the "available manpower" in the form of both professionals and volunteers who will assist in staging the event. The **International Festival & Events Association (IFEA)** provides an opportunity for event managers from around the world to network and exchange ideas on how other festivals excel in sponsorship, marketing, fund-raising, operations, volunteer coordination, and management. The IFEA is highlighted later in the chapter.

Concerts and Sporting Events

Concert promoters are an alternate career choice relating to special events. For the purpose of this text, smaller concert and music events will be the focus. Woodstock, in 1969, was a large music festival that has been labeled as a transformational event—it transformed the participants and society. Many concerts are planned as fund-raisers such as Live Aid, which raised millions of dollars to benefit starving people of Africa through a concert including major rock performers. On a smaller scale, universities may provide a concert as a special event.

Opening ceremonies, halftime, and postgame shows for sporting events provide another "arena" for an event manager to select as a career path. Shows such as these are highly visible because of the large number of sporting events that are televised. This provides a unique challenge for the event manager—to satisfy the millions of television viewers as well as those watching in the stadium (or whatever the venue may be).

Sporting events have historically been more popular than other forms of entertainment. This is probably because of our competitive nature and a desire to watch those who compete—a kind of flashback to the gladiator days of old. It is important to remember when planning special events in the sport environment that the primary attention should remain on the athletes and the competition. Therefore, the special event should be staged to "add to" and not "subtract from" the sport itself. Special events may be even attracting additional viewers and fans to the sport. The role of special events in the sport category has plenty of room for growth and expansion as professional sports become more and more competitive.

Sports entertainment is a field that will likely see considerable growth in the future. Just think, someone has to plan, organize, and run the halftime shows and events before and after the game. A large audience awaits your Super Bowl–sized imagination, which can ensure that every sporting event is a winning experience for the most important player of all—the fan.

Where Do Event Planners Work?

- Hotels/resorts
- Private corporations
- Associations
- Caterers
- The government
- Private clubs
- Convention centers
- Bridal businesses
- Event production companies
- Nonprofit organizations
- Advertising agencies
- Self-employed

Mega Events

Mega sporting events in the world are some of the biggest moneymakers in the industry. Both large and small communities embrace mega sporting events because of the positive economic impact. Activities in sports have brought forth tremendous economic impacts.

INTRODUCING SUZANNE BAILEY

Event Director

Suzanne graduated from Southern Utah University with a BA in Business Administration, Marketing in 1996. Eager to get her career started, she accepted an entry-level position at Bowl Games of America, a student travel/special event production company that produces several NCAA Bowl Game Halftime Shows including the Orange Bowl (Miami, FL), Sugar Bowl (New Orleans, LA), Liberty Bowl (Memphis, TN), Alamo Bowl (San Antonio, TX), and the Gator Bowl (Jacksonville, FL). BGA recruits high school marching bands and dance groups to perform in the field shows along with guest stars. The students earn an opportunity to perform with BGA by excelling in competition and working fund-raisers to pay for their three- to five-day trip. Within a year, Suzanne settled into the division of the company that interested her most—the tiny but growing dance division of Bowl Games of America, BGA Performance, as an executive assistant.

Suzanne worked with the director of BGA Performance to create an entirely new marketing strategy, which eventually led to great success within the dance division. Rather than working with small high school dance groups exclusively, they set up a commission system with large private dance competition companies, which would market the bowl game performance opportunities to their competition winners. That marketing strategy led to a 300 percent growth in the first year.

Suzanne worked her way up the ladder to associate director and eventually director of BGA Performance. The work changes dramatically with the seasons. During dance competition season, the marketing effort was immense—it was time to make the big sales push. Every day Suzanne created and sent hundreds of invitation packets to private dance competition companies and made as many sales phone calls as possible. She also reviewed audition tapes and selected dancers for the bowl game halftime shows.

Once most of the dancers had signed up for the bowl game that they would perform in, Suzanne's work shifted to roles in customer service and show production. She managed the numerous phone calls from dancers (and their directors and parents) with questions regarding their trip. She also worked with a BGA Performance Operations Director, who books hotel rooms and arranges for transportation and meals for the dancers. Meanwhile, she continued the process of hiring a choreographer for each show and working with the show's producer to create a show concept, including guest stars, props, lighting, music, and costumes.

Suzanne traveled to each city a few months prior to the event with the dance directors and/or chaperones to give them a preview of what would happen during the event with their dancers. These trips were always a lot of fun—"schmoozing" them with elegant dinners and taking them on fun activities. These included day cruises and, of course, a tour of the football stadium. The last few weeks of December (yes, that's right, the holiday season) were always the most hectic of the year for Suzanne. Making sure everything was in place for the bowl games involved confirming choreography, rehearsal sites, costume orders, prop production, and final itinerary packets for the performers.

And finally, the events would take place. Suzanne became an event director during the actual events. Suzanne would travel to the destination city a few days before the dancers would arrive to confirm with hotel group sales managers, caterers, rehearsal site workers, and Bowl Game executives. She would meet and direct her on-site staff (choreography team and event staff). The workdays of the events can be long and exhausting days that are full of excitement and anticipation. Much of the time is devoted to rehearsals, with some fun activities also included. Catered lunches, beach parties, and evening dinner/dance parties for the group at famous spots like Mardi Gras World in New Orleans are a few examples. The dancers enjoy every minute of their week, including the long, hard rehearsals in the sun (or rain, or even snow, depending on the

continued

INTRODUCING SUZANNE BAILEY (continued)

city). Game day (or show day) is always the most exciting of the days. After much hard work and preparation, the dancers go out on the field for their five minutes of fame. They perform, along with famous guest stars and the BGA-recruited marching bands, to a live stadium audience in the tens of thousands and often a national television audience. This is when the position as director of BGA Performance really pays off. The excitement of the show outweighs all the frustrations and the logistics of actually putting it all together. It is extremely rewarding to watch the children have the time of their lives! Then, for Suzanne, the next day is usually spent traveling to the next bowl game city and starting the process all over again. . . .

After working on Bowl Game Halftime Shows for about six years, the 2002 Olympics came to Salt Lake City, Suzanne's hometown. Having worked with the dance choreographer and other directors of the Olympic Opening and Closing Ceremonies team for bowl game shows, she was offered a position as Senior Production Coordinator, Volunteer Cast with the Ceremonies Production Team. She left her position at BGA Performance to work on the Olympic Ceremonies. The Olympic Opening Ceremony is truly the pinnacle of any live production anytime, anywhere. She helped manage a team of fifteen cast coordinators who worked with more than 4,000 volunteer cast members and 200 production staff volunteers. Suzanne facilitated communication between choreographers, stage managers, the producers, and the cast. She managed all aspects of casting for the ceremonies, from recruitment to auditions to performer selection to the actual live performance. This was truly an opportunity of a lifetime for Suzanne. She enjoyed every minute of her work with the Ceremonies Production Team.

After the Olympics, Suzanne started her family and now accepts work as a subcontractor for specific events and shows. She enjoys tackling one project at a time according to her own schedule. The special events world is an exciting, exhausting, and fun place to work.

The *Olympic Games* is the hallmark of all sporting events, attracting more than 6 million people to the host city. That is a lot of people traveling, staying in hotels, eating in restaurants, and possibly looking at the host city's attractions. The Olympics is an international sporting event that takes place every two years and it consists of both summer and winter games. The Olympics attract more people than any other sporting event, making it is easy to see why the Olympics play an important role in the industry.

The *World Cup* features the best soccer teams in the world. It is an international competition that takes place every four years. However, the World Cup is an ongoing competition, as the qualifying rounds take place over the three years before the final rounds in which the championship is awarded. Close to one million people actually attend the World Cup and millions more tune in via television or Internet.

The *Super Bowl* is an annual competition between the two best American football teams. It is a tradition that the game is held on "Super Bowl Sunday." Over the years, this day has become a holiday to many Americans. Super Bowl is one of the most-watched U.S. broadcasts of the year and not just for the game. People also tune in to see the millions of dollars spent on—you guessed it—commercials! People also tune in to watch the halftime show, during which some of the most popular musical artists perform. Another interesting fact is that this day is the second largest food consumption day in the United States (the largest day is of course Thanksgiving). It is estimated that about 44 million people attend 7.5 million Super Bowl parties each year!

The *World Series* is the final fight for the title of best baseball team. It is a championship series of the Major League Baseball (MLB) postseason that leads up to the series every year starting in October. It is played between the American League and National League champions. Today, the series winner is determined through a best-of-seven playoff. The winning team is awarded the World Series Trophy and each player receives a World Series ring.

There are four major men's golf championships known as the *Majors*. The *Masters Tournament* is an annual gathering of the world's best golf players on Augusta Golf Course. Champions of the Masters are automatically invited to play in the other three majors for the following five years, and earn a lifetime invitation to the Masters. The *U.S. Open Championship* is a men's open championship held in June of each year. The U.S. Open Championship is on the official schedule of the PGA Tour and the European Tour. The U.S. Open takes place on a variety of golf courses. The *British Open* is the oldest of the four major championships in men's golf. It is played annually on a links course (located in coastal areas causing frequent wind, on sandy soil, often amid dunes, with few water hazards and few if any trees). *U.S. PGA Championship* is the final championship of the year held in August. Champions of the PGA are also automatically invited to play in the other three majors for the next five years and are exempt from qualifying for the PGA Championship for life.

There are a number of boat races held on an annual basis. *America's Cup* is perhaps the most famous of yachting races. In addition to the yacht races, it is also a test of boat design, sail design, fund-raising, and managing people. The races are held in a series that currently involves a best-of-nine series of match racing (a duel between two boats).

Cruise lines are also creating specialized sports cruises, enabling spectators and participants to enhance their skills, to meet professional athletes, to attend major events, and to simply immerse themselves in their favorite sports.

Required Skills and Abilities for Event Management

Special events management, like any other form of management, requires certain skills and abilities. The act of carrying out a successful event takes more than just an idea—it takes leadership, communication, project management, effective negotiating and delegating skills, working within a budget, the ability to multitask, enthusiasm, social skills, and even the ability to make contacts. The following information will provide an overview of skills critical to effective event management.

Leadership Skills

As a leader, the event manager will wear many hats. The first is to inspire the staff and volunteers by providing valid reasons as to why they should want to assist in achieving the established goals for the event. In this role the event manager will also act as a salesperson. The second hat represents the event manager's responsibility to provide tools for the staff and volunteers to achieve the goals. This includes training and coordination. The third hat the event manager will wear will be that of a coach. The event manager as a leader will act as mentor and provide a support system to build a team. Staff and volunteer motivation is an important factor for effective event management. Leadership ability is the number one skill for successful event managers. The goal of an event manager is to become a leader who can direct a team of employees and/or volunteers who will respect, admire, and follow your direction to accomplish the established goals.

Effective event leadership can transform the people on your team. Empowering your event team to find their own solutions will benefit both the people and the event. It will allow the team members to create new opportunities for themselves and stimulate personal growth. For the event, empowerment will enable goals and objectives to be quickly achieved. Following are suggestions given by Dr. Joe Jeff Goldblatt, CSEP, for event leadership:

- Event leadership enables your team members to find the motivation to continue achieving the event goals and objectives.

- You cannot motivate others; they must motivate themselves by identifying clear personal goals and objectives.

- Volunteers are the lifeblood of most events. Recruiting, training, coordinating, and rewarding are critical to the success of this activity.

- The three styles of event leadership are democratic, autocratic, and laissez-faire. Each style may be used during the course of the event.

- Policies, procedures, and practices serve as the blueprint for event decision making.[7]

Ability to Communicate with Other Departments

The success of an event manager greatly depends on the ability of involved individuals to effectively communicate with one another. Communication can take different forms: oral, written, and electronic. It is very important for event managers to become effective communicators to maintain clear communications with all staff, volunteers, stakeholders, and other departments.

Written communications are an essential tool for record keeping and providing information to be mass distributed. Another tool to communicate with other departments is through a meeting.

Project Management Skills

Event planning and management can be time consuming. Therefore, a good planner should have effective project management skills to be equipped to balance all of the elements of one event (or more if there are other events going on at the same time). Project management is the act of completing the project(s) on time and within budget. Project management is a perfect fit for the special event industry, where the entire event or components of an event can be managed as projects. Following are management tools by George G. Fenich that may be used to assist in event project management:

- Flow charts and graphs used for scheduling certain programs that will happen at the event. Look at any program of a meeting, and you will see start times and end times of a particular seminar, when the coffee break is to occur, when and where the lunch will be held, followed by the resumption of the meeting. A charting of scheduling of the activities helps to guide your attendees and guests.

Meeting Planners Coordinating Events during a Meeting

- Clearly defined work setup and breakdown schedules for the event. This provides the event manager with an opportunity to determine tasks that may have been overlooked in the initial planning process for the event.

- Policy statements will need to be developed to help guide in the decision-making process and the fulfilling of commitments. Some of the commitments would be to human resources, sponsorships, security, ticketing, volunteers, and even to paid personnel for the event.[8]

Negotiating Skills

Negotiation is the process by which a meeting planner and supplier (hotel representative, for example, or other suppliers) reach an agreement on the terms and conditions that will govern their relationship before, during, and after a meeting, convention, exposition, or event. Effective negotiators will enter the negotiation with a good idea of what they want.

A negotiator gives the following tips:

- Do your homework. Develop a "game plan" of the outcomes sought, and prioritize your needs and wants. Learn as much about the other side's position as you can.

- Keep your eyes on the prize. Do not forget the outcome sought.

- Leave something on the table. It may provide an opportunity to come back later and renew the negotiations.

- Do not be the first one to make an offer. Letting the other person make the first move sets the outside parameters for the negotiation.

- Bluff, but do not lie.

- When there is a roadblock, find a more creative path. Thinking "outside the box" often leads to a solution.

- Timing is everything. Remember that time always works against the person who does not have it and that 90 percent of negotiation usually occurs in the last 10 percent of the time allocated.

- Listen, listen, listen . . . and do not get emotional. Letting emotions rule a negotiation will cause one to lose sight of what result is important.[9]

The planning and execution of a special event may involve the negotiation of several contracts. The most important is generally the one with the facility or event site. Contracts with other services may include destination management, entertainment, catering, temporary employees, security, and audiovisual equipment to name a few. Event managers should keep the following two words in mind to strengthen their negotiating skills and position: information and flexibility.

Coordinating and Delegating Skills

The management of staff and volunteers involves coordinating their duties and job performance to enable you to accomplish the goals of the event. As the manager, you are responsible for assigning supervisors or group leaders to oversee the performance of the employees and/or volunteers. It is important to provide coaching and mentoring when working with staff and volunteers to arrive at the event's goals and objectives. When employees can see the purpose and value of their work as well as the outcomes they usually become more excited about achieving the goals and objectives.

Budgeting Skills

Budgeting is an activity that allows managers to plan the use of their financial resources. In the event industry, the event planner may be working with a fixed budget determined by an association, SMERF group, or an individual (a wedding or engagement). In other cases, the budget may be more flexible—a large corporation, for example, that has greater financial resources. Budgeting is a required skill in all hospitality fields, including the special event industry.

The financial history of previous identical or similar events, the general economy and your forecast of the future, and the income expenses you reasonably believe you can expect with the resources available are all factors to be considered in creating an event budget. Even though most event managers will view the budgeting aspect as the least interesting in their job, it is an area that should be carefully managed and is critical for success. The better you become with budgeting skills the more you will be able to use resources for other "more creative" activities.

Ability to Multitask

Because of the nature of the business, an effective event manager should have the ability to multitask. During the planning and staging of the event, your ability to administrate, coordinate, market, and "manage" will be put to the test. Your job is ultimately to conduct and take control of whatever needs to be done to carry out your goals and objectives. You may encounter several problems arising at the same time, and an effective solution would be to delegate tasks accordingly.

Enthusiasm

As you've probably heard time and time again by now, in any hospitality field the risk of burnout is high and the work is demanding. At the same time, however, the rewards are great and so is the satisfaction when the event is a complete success. As perfectly stated by Norman Brinker, chairman of the board of Brinker International, "Find out what you love to do and you'll never work a day in your life. . . . Make work like play and play like hell!" Enthusiasm and passion. Drive and determination. These are all qualities that will contribute to the success of an event manager/planner. As shown in the profile of Suzanne Bailey, the special event industry is an "exciting, exhausting, and fun place to work." For those with the right enthusiasm and passion, it can be a truly rewarding career path.

Effective Social Skills

Social skills are an important trait for any management position, including one in the special event industry. Social skills are critical in making those you do business with feel comfortable, handling situations appropriately, and eliminating barriers that get in the way of accomplishing your goals. Communication is a critical social skill as is the other skill—listening. Social etiquette is another skill that can make or break a career, and it is a practiced skill that can be acquired. Social etiquette is defined as exhibiting good manners established as acceptable to society and showing consideration for others. Professionals in the hospitality industry, including the special event field, must be proficient in proper social etiquette. Service is one of the largest products offered; therefore, social skills and etiquette are required to be successful. Proper social etiquette is required in planning special events, and correct social manners are key to business success.[10] Effective social skills are also critical to leading a motivated group of staff and/or volunteers. How well you communicate, coach, instruct, lead, and listen is a reflection of how well you will succeed as a manager.

Ability to Form Contacts

Many of us have heard the phrase: "It's not what you know . . . but who you know." Does this statement hold any value in the special event industry? It certainly does. An event may require various services, vendors, suppliers, or products. Here's how it works: An event planner prepares a specification of what is required and requests potential suppliers to submit their prices. The event planner then goes over this information with the client and they make a decision as

" We've all heard the term "networking" before. It is a practice worth the time and effort. Networking is one of the benefits of joining an association (explained in the next section). The art of networking will allow you to build a contact base that will help you succeed in the event industry. What would happen if your caterer backed out of a contract at the last minute? First of all, make sure you have a contract. Beyond that, having a strong contact base will allow you to plan for those "unexpected" occurrences that are bound to happen at some point in your career. "

Karen Harris

to who will provide the services. Over time, event planners quickly find out who is the best provider and therefore the one they prefer to work with.

► Check Your Knowledge

1. What does the International Festival & Events Association (IFEA) provide?
2. What is project management?
3. Define the process of negotiation.

Special Event Organizations

Like other hospitality industries, professional associations are a key contributor to the professional development of the special event field. Professional associations provide training and prestigious certification to their members, and membership provides an opportunity to network with other professionals in the field. Furthermore, associations can help members connect with vendors that provide products and services relating to special events.

Professional associations also provide their members with help in creating a business plan and other forms of consultation. Job banks and referral services are even provided by some associations. The following information provides a brief overview of the key associations relating to the special event industry.

International Festivals & Events Association

The International Festivals & Events Association (IFEA) has provided fund-raising and modern developmental ideas to the special events industry for forty-five years. The IFEA began the program to enhance the level of festival management training and performance with a Certified Festival and Event Executive (CFEE) in 1983. Those seeking to achieve this distinguished title are committed to excellence in festival and event management, are using it as a tool for career advancement, and are in the search to further their knowledge. The organization currently has more than 2,700 professional members who are informed through IFEA publications, seminars, an annual convention and trade show, and ongoing networking.[13]

"The CFEE Program is a four-part process based on festival and event management experience, achievements and knowledge. Enrolling in the program and fulfilling the requirements listed above is the first step. Completing the application is next. Successfully completing an oral interview with member(s) of the CFEE Commission is the third. After achieving the CFEE designation, the fourth step is to maintain the designation through continuing education and participation in the profession," according to an IFEA statement.

The benefits of joining this association and meeting the CFEE requirements include being able to negotiate a better income or financial package, recognition by other industry professionals, and the "inside" knowledge that it provides for the festival industry. Visit the IFEA web site at **www.ifea.com** for further information.

CORPORATE PROFILE

International Special Events Society

Members of the ISES organize events like the Macy's Thanksgiving Day Parade.

The **International Special Events Society (ISES)** was founded in 1987 and now has grown to involve nearly 4,000 members who are active in thirty-eight chapters around the world. The organization has professionals representing special event producers (from festivals to trade shows), caterers, decorators, florists, destination management companies, rental companies, special effects experts, audiovisual technicians, party and convention coordinators, hotel sales managers, specialty entertainers, and many others.

The ISES was founded with the objective to "foster enlightened performance through education while promoting ethical conduct. ISES works to join professionals to focus on the 'event as a whole' rather than its individual parts." The organization has formed a solid network of peers that allow its members to produce quality events for their clients while benefiting from positive working relationships with other ISES members.

The ISES awards a designation of Certified Special Events Professional (CSEP), which is considered to be the benchmark of professional achievement in the special events industry. "It is earned through education, performance, experience, service to the industry, portfolio presentation and examination, and reflects a commitment to professional conduct and ethics," as stated by ISES. The program includes a self or group study program, point assessment of experience and service, application form, and exam.[11] Visit the ISES web site at **www.ises.com** for further information.

ISES Mission Statement

The mission of ISES is to educate, advance and promote the special events industry and its network of professionals along with related industries.

To that end, we strive to . . .

- Uphold the integrity of the special events profession to the general public through our "Principles of Professional Conduct and Ethics"
- Acquire and disseminate useful business information
- Foster a spirit of cooperation among members and other special events professionals
- Cultivate high standards of business practices[12]

Meeting Planners International

Meeting Planners International (MPI) is a Dallas-based association with nearly 19,000 members. "As the global authority and resource for the $102.3 billion meeting and event industry, MPI empowers meeting professionals to increase their strategic value through education, clearly defined career pathways, and business growth opportunities," as stated on the MPI web site. MPI offers professional development in two certification programs:

- Certified Meeting Professional (CMP)
- Certification in Meeting Management (CMM)

The CMP Program is based on professional experience and academic examination, which then allows the professional to use the CMP designation after his or her name on business cards, letterheads, and other printed items. Additionally, studies show that CMPs earn up to $10,000 more annually than non-CMPs.[14]

Certification in Meeting Management is directed toward senior-level meeting professionals and provides an opportunity for continuing education, global certification and recognition, potential career advancement, and a networking base.[15] Visit the MPI web site at **www.mpiweb.org** for more information.

Local Convention and Visitors Bureaus

A convention and visitors bureau (CVB) is a not-for-profit organization that is located in almost every city in the United States and Canada. Many other cities throughout the world also have a CVB or convention and visitors association (CVA). Simply stated, the CVB is an organization with the purpose of promoting tourism, meetings, and related business for its city. The CVB has three primary functions:

- Encourage groups to hold meetings, conventions, and trade shows in the city or area it represents
- Assist those groups with meeting preparations and during the event
- Encourage tourists to visit the historic, cultural, and recreational opportunities the destination offers

The CVB does not engage in the actual planning or organizing of meetings, conventions, and other events. However, the CVB assists meeting planners and managers in several ways. First of all, it will provide information about the destination, area attractions, services, and facilities. Second, it provides an unbiased source of information to the planner. Finally, most of the services offered by the CVB are at no charge because they are funded through other sources including hotel occupancy taxes and membership dues. Therefore it can provide an array of services to event planners and managers. A sample of general services provided by a CVB include the following:

- CVBs act as a liaison between the planner and the community.
- CVBs can help meeting attendees maximize their free time through the creation of pre- and postconference activities, spouse tours, and special evening events.

- CVBs can provide hotel room counts and meeting space statistics.

- CVBs can help with meeting facility availability.

- CVBs are a network for transportation—shuttle service, ground transportation, and airline information.

- CVBs can assist with site inspections and familiarization tours.

- CVBs can provide speakers and local educational opportunities.

- CVBs can provide help in securing auxiliary services, production companies, catering, security, and so forth.

The Special Event Job Market

Becoming a special event consultant or an off-premise catering/event specialist requires a delicate balance of many skills. Experience gained from several avenues will propel you to the heights of success. As with any career, an "experience ladder" must be climbed.

First, allow yourself to gain all the experience you can in the food and beverage aspect of the hospitality industry. If time and resources permit, it is highly recommended that you gain knowledge from a culinary arts program. Second, experience gained as a banquet food server in a high-volume convention or resort hotel property is invaluable. Also, paying your dues as a guest service agent at a hotel front desk or as a concierge provides you with the opportunity to hone your customer service skills. Promote yourself to a banquet manager or a CSM (convention service coordinator), which provides the opportunity to learn and perfect organizational skills—to which end is the ability to multitask and deal with hundreds of details simultaneously. After all, the business of special events is the business of managing details.

The next step is obtaining a sales position. An excellent appointment to aspire to is an executive meeting manager, sometimes called a small meeting manager, in a convention or conference hotel. Here, you are responsible for booking small room blocks (usually twenty rooms or less), making meeting room arrangements, meal plans, and audiovisual requirements. On a small scale, hundreds of details are coordinated for several groups at any one time. From this position, you may laterally move to a catering sales position within a hotel.

The catering sales position in a hotel will expose you to many different kinds of events: weddings, reunions, corporate events, holiday events, and social galas and balls. In this position, one either coordinates or has the opportunity to work with various vendors. This is where the florists, prop companies, lighting experts, entertainment agencies, rental companies, and audiovisual wizards come into play. Two to three years in this capacity grooms you for the next rung on the ladder.

Now, you can pursue several different angles: a promotion to a convention service manager within a hotel, moving into off-premise catering as a sales consultant, joining a production company, or perhaps affiliating yourself with a destination management company (DMC). Typically, without sales experience

Figure 13–2 • A Career Path to an Event Manager.

within a DMC, your first experience with them will be as an operations manager. Once proficient in this capacity, you then join the sales team.

After another two years creating and selling your heart out, you will be ready for the big leagues. The palette is now yours to paint your future. How about aspiring to be the next Super Bowl halftime creator and producer? Or perhaps creating the theme and schematics for the Olympics is in your future. Many avenues are available for exploring. Call on your marketing ideas, your business sense, your accounting skills, your aptitude for design, or your discriminating palette for creating unique entertaining and dining concepts. Continually educating yourself and discovering fresh ideas through adventurous experiences are essential to designing and selling special events. Don't forget to embark on as many internships as you can in the name of gaining knowledge and experience. Show your enthusiasm for what is different and unconventional. Know that creativity has no boundaries. Visualize the big picture and go for it! Figure 13–2 shows a career path for an event manager.

Trends in the Special Event Industry

- The special event industry is forecast to grow because clients want ever more spectacular events.

- Events are increasingly more complex involving multimedia presentations, elaborate staging, and frequently upscale food and beverage service.

- Technology presents both an opportunity and a challenge, an opportunity in that it can facilitate event planning and management, and a challenge in that new software programs must be mastered.

CASE STUDY

Not Enough Space

Jessica is the event planner for a large convention center. A client has requested an exhibition that would not only bring excellent revenue but is an annual event that several other convention centers would like to host.

Exhibitions typically take one or two days to set up, three or four days of exhibition, and one day to break down. Professional organizations handle each part of the setup and breakdown.

When Jessica checks the space available on the days requested for the exhibition, she notices that another exhibition is blocking part of the space needed by her client.

Discussion Question

1. What can Jessica do to get this exhibition to use the conventon center without inconveniencing either exhibition too much?

Summary

1. Special events differ from daily events, which occur spontaneously, do not arouse expectations, and usually occur without reason in that they recognize a unique moment in time with ceremony and ritual to satisfy specific needs and are always planned.
2. The special event industry is a growing field that will provide many professional career opportunities in event management and planning.
3. Special event planners and managers have filled a "need" that was first introduced at hotels and convention centers. They are responsible for planning the event, from start to finish.
4. The special event industry can be grouped into several smaller classifications including corporate events, association events, charity balls and fund-raising events, social functions, fairs and festivals, and concert and sporting events.
5. The event planning process includes the following steps: research, design, planning, coordination, and evaluation.
6. Special event planners can work in a variety of settings. They range from hotels/resorts, convention centers, and private clubs to self-employment.
7. Critical skills and abilities that are required for a career in special event management include leadership skills, effective communication, project management skills, negotiating skills, coordinating and delegating skills, budgeting skills, multitasking abilities, enthusiasm, effective social skills, and the ability to form contacts.
8. The special event industry has its own selection of professional associations that offer certification, continuing education, and networking to their members. The International Special Events Society (ISES), International Festivals & Events Association (IFEA), and Meeting Planners International (MPI) are three of the largest and most recognized professional associations in the field. Local convention and visitors bureaus (CVBs) are organizations that can be a valuable resource to the special event industry. A CVB has the purpose of promoting tourism, meetings, and related business for its city.

9. The management of time and finances, along with the utilization of technology and human resources are event planning tools that can be utilized to your advantage as you pursue a career in this field.

10. The special events industry does not have rigid boundaries. Closely related fields that may overlap include catering, marketing, sales, and entertainment.

Key Words and Concepts

charity balls
conventions
coordination
corporate events
corporate seminars
event planner
event planning
fairs and festivals
fund-raisers

International Festival & Events Association (IFEA)
International Special Events Society (ISES)
Meeting Planners International (MPI)
social functions
special events industry
trade shows
weddings and holiday parties
workshops

Review Questions

1. On the Companion Website, how does Judy Gallagher trace the recent evolution of American food?
2. From the Companion Website, what qualities and characteristics does Judy Gallagher describe for success in catering?
3. What do event planners do?
4. What are the challenges for event planners and managers?
5. Describe three of the classifications of special events.
6. Explain the skills and abilities required for event management.

Internet Exercises

1. Go to **www.ises.com** and click "Education." Look for Event World and see what an ISES Event World can do for professional development and who should attend.
2. Go to **www.mpiweb.org/resources/jobs/default.asp**, scroll down to career tools, look under that heading for the job bank, and check out a couple of good jobs.

Apply Your Knowledge

Make a plan for a local event in your area. List all the headings and formulate a budget.

Suggested Activity

Attend a special event and write a brief report on the event and its planning and organization.

Endnotes

1. Joe J. Goldblatt, *Special Events: Best Practices in Modern Event Management*, 2nd ed. (New York: John Wiley and Sons, 1997), 2; Joe J. Goldblatt, *Special Events: The Art and Science of Celebration* (New York: Von Nostrand Reinhold, 1990), 1–2.
2. Frank Supovitz, Foreword, in *Special Events: Best Practices in Modern Event Management*, 2nd ed., by Joe J. Goldblatt (New York: John Wiley and Sons, 1997), iv.
3. Blythe Cameson, *Opportunities in Event Planning Careers*. (VGM Career Books. 2002), 4–7.
4. Event Solutions, *2004 Black Book* (Tempe, AZ: Event Publishing, 2004), 22, www.eventsolutions.com.
5. Blythe Cameson, *Opportunities*, 115.
6. Festivals.com, "Culture," www.festivals.com/culture/.
7. Goldblatt, *Special Events: Best Practices*, 129–139.
8. George G. Fenich, *Meetings, Expositions, Events, and Conventions: An Introduction to the Industry* (Upper Saddle River, NJ: Pearson Education, 2005), 181–182.
9. Fenich, *Meetings, Expositions, Events, and Conventions*, 366.
10. Judy Allen, *Event Planning Ethics and Etiquette: A Principled Approach to the Business of Special Event Management* (Etobicoke, Ontario, Canada: John Wiley and Sons, 2003), 79.
11. International Special Events Society (ISES), "Introduction to Certified Special Events Professional (CSEP)," www.ises.com/csep/intro.cfm.
12. ISES, "Introduction to Certified Special Events Professional (CSEP)," www.ises.com/csep/intro.cfm.
13. International Festivals & Events Association (IFEA), "About the IFEA," www.ifea.com/about_ifea_main.htm.
14. Blythe Cameson, *Opportunities*, 36–41.
15. Meeting Professionals International, "CMM: Global Certification in Meeting Management," www.mpiweb.org/CMS/MPIweb/cmm2007/cmm07.aspx?id=5794.

PART VI

Managerial Areas
of the Hospitality Industry

CHAPTER **14**

Leadership and Management

OBJECTIVES

After reading and studying this chapter, you should be able to:

- Identify the characteristics and practices of leaders and managers.

- Define *leadership* and *management*.

- Differentiate between leadership and management.

- Describe the key management functions.

Leadership

Our fascination with **leadership** goes back many centuries. Lately, however, it has come into prominence in the hospitality, tourism, and other industries as these industries strive for perfection in the delivery of services and products in an increasingly competitive environment. Leaders can and do make a difference when measuring a company's success.

One person working alone can accomplish few tasks or goals. You have probably already experienced being part of a group that had good leadership. It might have been with a school, social, sporting, church, or other group in which the leader made a difference. The reverse might also be true: You may have been in a group with ineffective leadership. Few groups can accomplish much without an individual who acts as an effective leader. The leader can and often does have a significant influence on the group and its direction.

Characteristics and Practices of Leaders

So, what are the ingredients that result in leadership excellence? If you look at the military for examples of leadership excellence, you see that leaders can be identified by certain characteristics. For example, the *U.S. Guidebook for Marines* lists the following leadership traits:

- Courage
- Decisiveness
- Dependability
- Endurance
- Enthusiasm
- Initiative
- Unselfishness
- Integrity
- Judgment
- Justice
- Knowledge
- Loyalty
- Tact

A Marine officer would likely choose integrity as the most important trait. Integrity has been defined as "doing something right even though no one may be aware of it."

In addition to these leadership traits, the following identifiable practices are common to leaders:

1. *Challenge the process* Be active, not passive; search for opportunities; experiment and take risks.
2. *Inspire a shared vision* Create a vision; envision the future; enlist others.
3. *Enable others to act* Do not act alone; foster collaboration; strengthen others.
4. *Model the way* Plan; set examples; strive for small wins.
5. *Encourage the heart* Share the passion; recognize individual contributions; celebrate accomplishments.

Definitions of Leadership

Because of the complexities of leadership, the different types of leadership, and individual perceptions of leaders, leadership has several definitions. Many definitions share commonalities, but there are also differences. In terms of hospitality leadership, the following definition is appropriate: "Leading is the process by which a person with vision is able to influence the activities and outcomes of others in a desired way."

Leaders know what they want and why they want it—and they are able to communicate those desires to others to gain their cooperation and support. Leadership theory and practice has evolved over time to a point where current industry practitioners may be identified as transactional or transformational leaders.[1]

INTRODUCING HERB KELLEHER

Former CEO of Southwest Airlines

Herb Kelleher, who recently gave up his Executive Chairman title, is the living embodiment of the phrase "one of a kind." With his charismatic personality, he is a person who leaves a distinctive mark on whatever he does. Since the birth of Southwest Airlines in 1971 (actually, Rollin W. King, a legal client of Herb's at the time, conceived Southwest Airlines after he had drawn, on a cocktail napkin, a triangle connecting Texas's three major cities: Dallas, Houston, and San Antonio), Herb Kelleher—"Herb" to even his most distant acquaintances—nurtured Southwest Airlines into the seventh largest airline. The company has been profitable every year since 1973. When other carriers lost billions or were struggling with bankruptcy, Southwest was the only company that remained consistently profitable—a record unmatched in the U.S. airline industry—cheerfully pursuing its growth plans by buying more planes, expanding into new cities, and hiring personnel. Southwest is also a model of efficiency: It is a multiple-time winner of the U.S. Department of Transportation's Triple Crown, a monthly citation for the best on-time performance, fewest lost bags, and fewest overall complaints. Kelleher's operation, based on flights covering relatively short distances for prices that are sometimes shockingly low, is likely to experience rapid growth and become even more of a leading power.

One of the keys to this success lies in the company's mission. Southwest Airlines aims at providing cheap, simple, and focused airline service. Kelleher devoted enormous attention to thousands of small decisions, all designed to achieve simplicity. Among these small but tremendously strategic decisions were the removal of closets at the front of the planes to improve passengers' speed in boarding and departing and no onboard food, except snacks, which is justified by the number of short flights (those of about 400 miles). Southwest also refused full participation on computerized reservations systems used by travel agents. More than 80 percent of all Southwest tickets are sold directly to customers, saving the company millions annually. There is no assigned seating and no first-class seating. Planes have been

continued

INTRODUCING HERB KELLEHER *(continued)*

standardized: Southwest operates only one type of aircraft, the 737, which simplifies flight crew training and maintenance personnel training.

These relatively minor privations have their positive counterpart in the fact that Southwest ground crew can turn around a plane at the gate in about twenty minutes! The airline's customers especially appreciate its low fares and on-time schedules.

Who is behind all this? The airline's success is credited to Kelleher's unorthodox personality and entrepreneurial management style. Born and raised in New Jersey, he was the son of the general manager of Campbell Soups, Inc. He began to show leadership qualities as student body president both in high school and in college. From his original idea of becoming a journalist, Kelleher shifted his goal to the practice of law. By the mid-1960s, he was successfully practicing in San Antonio, Texas, his wife's hometown. However, he was always seeking the possibility of starting a venture of his own. The big chance came in 1966 when a legal client, Rollin King, suggested that Texas needed a short-haul commuter airline. That was the trigger: Southwest was born in 1971.

While CEO, Herb directly supervised his business, personally approving expenses over $1,000. His outstanding hands-on efforts also led to unusually good labor–management relations, on the basis of the motto "People are the most important of resources." In fact, he managed to establish a strong bond of loyalty between employees and their company that may have disappeared elsewhere in the American corporate environment.

He still represents some sort of a father figure to SWA, as well as the jester, and the "Lord of Ha-Ha." The effort that he was able to get out of his employees made the real difference. Unlike workers at most other carriers, Southwest employees are willing to pitch in no matter what the task. For example, a reservations sales clerk in Dallas took a call from an anxious customer who was putting his eighty eight-year-old mother aboard a flight to St. Louis. The woman was quite frail, the fellow explained, and he wasn't quite sure she could handle the change of planes in Tulsa. "No sweat!" replied the clerk. "I'll fly with her as far as Tulsa and make sure she gets safely on the St. Louis flight."

Kelleher's outstanding leadership ability is also demonstrated by his long-term thinking. He gathered a top-rank team of successors, which will guarantee the airline's future prosperity. Kelleher is the leader who inspires, the amiable uncle to consult, the cheerleader who motivates, and the clown who spreads cheer. There are many great stories about Herb Kelleher; this is one of the most popular: Southwest was being threatened by an aviation services company over the advertising slogan "Plane Smart." Instead of incurring huge attorneys' fees and dealing with months-long litigation, the two CEOs agreed to settle the matter with an arm-wrestling contest. Herb actually lost the contest, but the other CEO had so much fun that the lawsuit was dropped. Both companies saved a bundle in legal fees.

Transactional Leadership

Transactional leadership is viewed as a process by which a leader is able to bring about desired actions from others by using certain behaviors, rewards, or incentives. In essence, an exchange or transaction takes place between leader and follower. Figure 14–1 shows the transactional leadership model. This concept illustrates the coming together of the leader, the situation, and the followers. A hotel general manager who pressures the food and beverage director to achieve certain goals in exchange for a bonus is an example of someone practicing transactional leadership.

Figure 14–1 • Transactional Leadership Model.

Transformational Leadership

Leadership involves looking for ways to bring about longer-term, higher-order changes in follower behavior. This brings us to transformational leadership. The term **transformational leadership** is used to describe the process of eliciting performance above and beyond normal expectations. A transformational leader is one who inspires others to reach beyond themselves and do more than they originally thought possible; this is accomplished by raising their commitment to a shared vision of the future.

Transformational leaders practice a hands-on philosophy, not in terms of performing the day-to-day tasks of subordinates, but in developing and encouraging their followers individually. Transformational leadership involves three important factors:

1. Charisma
2. Individual consideration
3. Intellectual stimulation

Of course, it is also possible to be a charismatic transformational leader as well as a transactional leader. Although this does involve a measurable amount of effort, these leaders are guaranteed to rake in success throughout their careers.

Examples of Excellence in Leadership

Dr. Martin Luther King Jr. was one of the most charismatic transformational leaders in history. King dedicated his life to achieving rights for all citizens by nonviolent methods. His dream of how society could be was shared by millions of Americans. In 1964, Dr. King won the Nobel Peace Prize.

Another transformational leader is Herb Kelleher, former president, CEO, and current board

Martin Luther King Jr. One of the Most Charismatic Transformational Leaders of the Twentieth Century, Giving His Famous "I Have A Dream" Speech

member of Southwest Airlines, who is profiled in this chapter. He was able to inspire his followers to pursue his corporate vision and reach beyond themselves to give Southwest Airlines that something extra that set it apart from its competitors.

Kelleher recognizes that the company does not exist merely for the gratification of its employees. He knows that Southwest Airlines must perform and must be profitable. However, he believes strongly that valuing individuals for themselves is the best way to attain exceptional performance. Passengers who fly Southwest Airlines may have seen Herb Kelleher because he travels frequently and previously was likely to be found serving drinks, fluffing pillows, or just wandering up and down the aisle, talking to passengers. The success of Southwest and the enthusiasm of its employees indicate that Herb Kelleher achieved his goal of weaving together individual and corporate interests so that all members of the Southwest family benefit. Kelleher is a great transformational leader who is able to lead by visioning, inspiring, empowering, and communicating.[2]

In their fascinating book *Lessons in Leadership: Perspectives for Hospitality Industry Success*, Bill Fisher, former president and CEO of the American Hotel & Lodging Association and currently Darden Eminent Scholar at the University of Central Florida, and Charles Bernstein, editor of *Nation's Restaurant News*, interviewed more than 100 industry leaders and asked each to give advice in an up-close-and-personal manner. Here is an example of the leaders' answers:

"Experience is a hard teacher. It gives the test first, and then you learn the lesson." Richard P. Mayer, former chairman and CEO of Kentucky Fried Chicken and president of General Foods Corporation, says that the key traits and factors that he looks for in assessing talent include the following:

- Established personal goals
- The drive and ambition to attain those goals, tempered and strengthened with integrity
- Proven analytical and communications skills
- Superior interpersonal capabilities
- A sense of humor
- An awareness and appreciation of the world beyond her or his business specialty
- Receptivity to ideas (no matter the source)
- A genuine, deep commitment to the growth and profitability of the business

The essence of success has as many meanings as there are people to ponder it. One concept of success is to couple one's personal and family interests, dreams, and aspirations with a business or professional career such that they complement and fortify each other. Another aspect of leadership is the ability to motivate others in a hospitality working environment; decision making is also essential. These are discussed later in the chapter.

FOCUS ON LEADERSHIP

Leadership—The Basis for Management

William Fisher, Darden Eminent Scholar in Restaurant Management, author and former executive vice president of the National Restaurant Association and the American Hotel & Lodging Association

The concept and practice of leadership as it applies to management carries a fascination and attraction for most people. We all like to think we have some leadership qualities and we strive to develop them. We look at leaders in all walks of life, seeking to identify which qualities, traits, and skills they possess so that we can emulate them. A fundamental question remains: What is the essence of leadership that results in successful management as opposed to failed management? At least part of the answer can be found within the word itself.

1. *Loyalty.* Leadership starts with a loyalty quadrant: loyalty to one's organization and its mission, loyalty to organizational superiors, loyalty to subordinates, and loyalty to oneself. Loyalty is multidirectional, running up and down in the organization. When everyone practices it, loyalty bonds occur, which drives high morale. Loyalty to oneself is based on maintaining a sound body, mind, and spirit so that one is always "riding the top of the wave" in service to others.

2. *Excellence.* Leaders know that excellence is a value, not an object. They strive for both excellence and success. Excellence is the measurement you make of yourself in assessing what you do and how well you do it; success is an external perception that others have of you.

3. *Assertiveness.* Leaders possess a mental and physical intensity that causes them to seek control, take command, assume the mantle of responsibility, and focus on the objective(s). Leaders do not evidence self-doubt as they are comfortable within themselves that what they are doing is right, which, in turn, gives them the courage to take action.

4. *Dedication.* Leaders are dedicated in mind, body, and spirit to their organization and to achievement. They are action oriented, not passive, and prefer purposeful activity to the status quo. They possess an aura or charisma that sets them apart from others with whom they interact, always working in the best interest of their organization.

5. *Enthusiasm.* Leaders are their own best cheerleaders on behalf of their organization and people. They exude enthusiasm and instill it in others to the point of contagion. Their style may be one of poise, stability, clear vision, and articulate speech, but their bristling enthusiasm undergirds their every waking moment.

6. *Risk management.* Leaders realize that risk taking is part of their management perch. They manage risk, rather than letting it manage them, knowing full well that there are no guaranteed outcomes, no foregone conclusions, no preordained results when one is dealing with the future. Nonetheless, they measure risk, adapt to it, control it, and surmount it.

7. *Strength.* Leaders possess an inner fiber of stamina, fortitude, and vibrancy that gives them a mental toughness, causing them to withstand interruption, crises, and unforeseen circumstances that would slow down or immobilize most people. Leaders become all the more energized in the face of surprises.

8. *Honor.* Leaders understand they will leave a legacy, be it good, bad, or indifferent. True leaders recognize that all their relationships and actions are based on the highest standard of honor and integrity. They do the right things correctly, shun short-term, improper expediency, and set the example for others with high-mindedness, professional bearing, and unassailable character.

continued

FOCUS ON LEADERSHIP (continued)

9. *Inspiration.* Leaders don't exist without followers. People will follow leaders who inspire them to reach beyond the normal and ordinary to new levels of accomplishment, new heights of well-being, and new platforms for individual, organizational, and societal good. Inspiration is what distinguishes a leader from a mere position holder, as the leader can touch the heart, mind, and soul of others.

10. *Performance.* At the end of the day, leader–managers rise or fall on the most critical of all measurements: their performance. Results come first, but the ways in which results are achieved are also crucial to sustaining a leader's role. Many dictators don't last despite results, and many charismatics don't last despite personal charm.

Putting the ten elements together spells LEADERSHIP! Always remember, if you want to develop a leadership quality, act as though you already possess it!

Demands Placed on Leaders

Demands on a leader in the hospitality industry include those made by owners, the corporate office, guests, employees, regulatory agencies, and competitors (Figure 14–2). In response to many demands, the leader must balance two additional forces: how much energy to expend on getting results and how much to expend on relationships (Figure 14–3).

Applied social scientists such as Peter Drucker, powerful industry leaders such as Bill Marriott, and public service leaders such as former New York mayor Rudolph Giuliani all seem to have common traits, among which are the following:

1. High ego strength
2. Ability to think strategically
3. Orientation toward the future

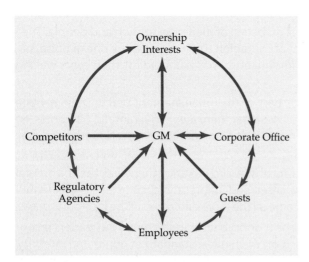

Figure 14–2 • Dynamics of Demands on General Managers in the Hospitality Industry.

Figure 14–3 • Amount of Energy the General Manager Needs to Spend on Getting Results and Maintaining Relationships.

4. A belief in certain fundamental principles of human behavior
5. Strong connections that they do not hesitate to display
6. Political astuteness
7. Ability to use power both for efficiency and for the larger good of the organization

Leaders vary in their values, managerial styles, and priorities. Peter Drucker, the renowned management scholar, author, and consultant of many years, has discussed with hundreds of leaders their roles, goals, and performance. These discussions took place with leaders of large and small organizations, with for-profit and volunteer organizations. Interestingly, Drucker observes:

> All the leaders I have encountered—both those I worked with and those I watched—realized:
>
> 1. The only definition of a leader is someone who has followers. Some people are thinkers. Some are prophets. Both roles are important and badly needed. But without followers, there can be no leaders.
> 2. An effective leader is not someone who is loved or admired. She or he is someone whose followers do the right things. Popularity is not leadership. Results are.
> 3. Leaders are highly visible. They therefore set examples.
> 4. Leadership is not about rank, privileges, titles, or money. It is about responsibility.[3]

Drucker adds that regardless of their enormous diversity with respect to personality, style, abilities, and interests, effective leaders all behave in much the same way:

1. They did not start out with the question "What do I want?" They started out asking, "What needs to be done?"
2. Then they asked, "What can and should I do to make a difference?" This has to be something that both needs to be done and fits the leader's strengths and the way she or he is most effective.
3. They constantly asked, "What are the organization's mission and goals? What constitutes performance and results in this organization?"
4. They were extremely tolerant of diversity in people and did not look for carbon copies of themselves. It rarely even occurred to them to ask, "Do I like or dislike this person?" But they were totally—fiendishly—intolerant when it came to a person's performance, standards, and values.
5. They were not afraid of strength in their associates. They gloried in it. Whether they had heard of it or not, their motto was the one Andrew Carnegie wanted to have put on his tombstone: "Here lies a man who attracted better people into his service than he was himself."
6. One way or another, they submitted themselves to the mirror test—that is, they made sure the person they saw in the mirror in the morning was the kind of person they wanted to be, respect, and believe in. This way they

fortified themselves against the leader's greatest temptations—to do things that are popular rather than right and to do petty, mean, sleazy things.[4]

Finally, these leaders were not preachers; they were doers.

The most effective leaders share a number of skills, and these skills are always related to dealing with employees. The following suggestions outline an approach to becoming a hotel leader rather than just a manager:

- *Be decisive.* Hotel managers are confronted with dozens of decisions every day. Obviously, you should use your best judgment to resolve the decisions that come to roost at your doorstep. As a boss, make the decisions that best meet both your objectives and your ethics and then make your decisions known.

- *Follow through.* Never promise what you can't deliver, and never build false hopes among your employees. Once expectations are dashed, respect for and the reputation of the boss are shot.

CORPORATE PROFILE

The Ritz-Carlton Hotel Company: A Commitment to Excellence and Quality Service Worldwide

The Ritz-Carlton Hotel Company was officially organized in the summer of 1983, although the Ritz-Carlton history and tradition long precede that date. Indeed, this tradition has entered our language: To be "ritzy" or "putting on the ritz" denotes doing something with class. With the purchase of The Ritz-Carlton Boston and the acquisition of the exclusive rights to use the name came a rich heritage.

The legacy of the Ritz-Carlton begins with the celebrated hotelier Cesar Ritz, the "king of hoteliers and hotelier to kings." His philosophy of service and innovations redefined the luxury hotel experience in Europe through his management of the Ritz Paris and the Carlton in London. The Ritz-Carlton Boston revolutionized hospitality in the United States by creating luxury in a hotel setting.

Cesar Ritz died in 1918, but his wife Marie continued the expansion of hotels bearing his name. In the United States, the Ritz-Carlton Investing Company was established by Albert Keller, who bought and franchised the name. In 1927, the Ritz-Carlton Boston was opened by Edward N. Wyner, a Boston real estate developer, with room rates at $15 per night. Because of the reputation of Ritz in Europe and the cosmopolitan society in Boston, Wyner knew the Ritz-Carlton name would secure immediate success.

Fast-forward to 1983 when William B. Johnson acquired the rights to establish the Ritz-Carlton Hotel Company. The company now operates seventy-two hotels world-wide (24 countries). Further expansion plans are included for Europe, Africa, Asia, the Middle East, and the Americas.

The Ritz-Carlton Hotel Company was named the winner of the prestigious Malcolm Baldrige National Quality Award in 1992 and again in 1999. The Ritz-Carlton is the only hospitality organization ever to have won this coveted honor for quality management, given by the U.S. Department of Commerce. Seven categories

- *Select the best.* A boss, good or bad, is carried forward by the work of his or her subordinates. One key to being a good boss is to hire the people who have the best potential to do what you need them to do. Take the time and effort to screen, interview, and assess the people who have not only the skills that you require, but also the needed values.

- *Empower employees.* Give people the authority to interact with the customer. The more important people feel, the better they work.

- *Enhance career development.* Good bosses recognize that most of their people want to improve themselves. However, career development is a two-edged sword: If we take the initative to train and develop our people properly, then the competition is likely to hire them. The only way a boss can prevent the loss of productive workers looking for career development is to provide opportunities for growth within the organization.

In recent years, the role of the hotel general manager has changed from that of being a congenial host, knowledgeable about the niceties of hotelmanship, to

make up the award criteria: leadership, strategic planning, customer and market focus, information and analysis, human resources focus, process management, and business results. At the Ritz-Carlton, a focus on these criteria has resulted in higher employee and customer satisfaction, and increased productivity and market share. Perhaps most significant is increased profitability.

Simon F. Cooper was named president and chief operating officer of the Ritz-Carlton in February 2001. He took over from Horst Schultze, founding president and CEO, whose vision and leadership was the driving force behind the success in obtaining the Malcolm Baldrige Awards. Since joining the company, Cooper has been responsible for the successful opening of twenty three hotels. This expansion continues with more than a dozen hotels and resorts slated for opening over the next decade. The Residences at the Ritz-Carlton Residences and the Ritz-Carlton Club have also been successfully developed and launched under Cooper's tenure.

Committed employees rank as the most essential element. All employees are schooled and carry a pocket-sized card stating the company's Gold Standards, which include a credo, motto, three steps of service, and twenty Ritz-Carlton basics. Each employee is expected to understand and adhere to these standards, which describe processes for solving problems that guests may have as well as detailed grooming, housekeeping, and safety and efficiency standards. "We are Ladies and Gentlemen serving Ladies and Gentlemen" is the motto of the Ritz-Carlton, exemplifying anticipatory service provided by all staff members. "Every employee has the business plan of The Ritz-Carlton—constantly reinforcing that guest satisfaction is our highest mission," says Cooper.

The company has quickly grown a collection of the finest hotels around the world. Several of these hotels are historic landmarks, following a commitment of the company to preserving architecturally important buildings. Some examples are the Ritz-Carlton, Central Park; the Ritz-Carlton, San Francisco; the Ritz-Carlton, Philadelphia; the Ritz-Carlton, New Orleans; and the Ritz-Carlton, Huntington Hotel & Spa. Each property is designed to be a comfortable haven for travelers and a social center for the community. The architecture and artwork are carefully selected to complement the hotel's environment. "We go to great lengths to capture the spirit of a hotel and its locale," says Cooper. "This creates a subtle balance and celebrates a gracious, relaxed lifestyle. The Ritz-Carlton is warm, relaxed yet refined; a most comfortable home away from home." The Ritz-Carlton Hotel Company is now owned and operated by Marriott International.

that of a multigroup pleaser. Guests, employees, owners, and community should all be not only satisfied but delighted with the operation's performance.

Many general managers (GMs) are so bogged down with meetings, reports, and "putting out fires" that they hardly have any time to spend with guests. One GM who makes time is Richard Riley, GM of the fabulous Shangri-La Hotel Makati in Manila, the Philippines. Richard extends an invitation for guests to visit with him in the hotel lobby between 5:00 and 7:00 P.M. every Thursday. As GM of a luxury Caribbean resort in Barbados, West Indies, the author personally greeted every guest to the property. Obviously, there is a difference between a small resort and a large city hotel. Resort guests stay for at least two, sometimes four, weeks in high season, so they need the individual attention.

▶ Check Your Knowledge

1. What three factors does transformational leadership involve?
2. Define *leadership*.
3. Describe some examples of leadership.
4. Explain the demands placed on leaders.

Hospitality Management

Managers plan, organize, make decisions, communicate, motivate, and control the efforts of a group to accomplish predetermined goals. Management also establishes the direction the organization will take. Sometimes this is done with the help of employees or outside consultants, such as marketing research specialists. Managers obtain the necessary resources for the goals to be accomplished, and then they supervise and monitor group and individual progress toward goal accomplishment.

Managers, such as presidents and chief executive officers, who are responsible for the entire company, tend to focus most of their time on strategic planning and the organization's mission. They also spend time organizing and controlling the activities of the corporation. Most top managers do not get involved in the day-to-day aspects of the operation. These duties and responsibilities fall to the middle and supervisory management. In hospitality lingo, one would not expect Bill Marriott to pull a shift behind the bar at the local Marriott hotel. Although capable, his time and expertise are used in shaping the company's future. Thus, although the head bartender and Bill Marriott may both be considered management, they require slightly different skills to be effective and efficient managers.

What Is Management?

Management is simply what managers do: plan, organize, make decisions, communicate, motivate, and control. *Management* is defined as "the process of working with and through others to accomplish organizational goals in an efficient and effective way." In looking at this statement, you can see that the functions of

INTRODUCING STEVE PINETTI

Senior Vice President of Sales and Marketing, Kimpton Hotels & Restaurants

Steve Pinetti grew up in the San Franciso Bay area, worked for Hilton and Hyatt, taught at all the San Francisco Bay area colleges and universities, founded his own marketing company, and was one of Bill Kimpton's first partners in founding Kimpton Hotels & Restaurants. Steve now is the senior vice president of sales and marketing for Kimpton Hotels & Restaurants. Steve oversees branding efforts, Internet presence, public relations, strategic partnerships, and new hotel openings. He has an interesting challenge balancing the competition from both existing large hotel chains and Kimpton's own new hotel openings. Additionally, existing large hotel chains and new hotel companies claim to be the "boutique" hotel leader. In fact, Kimpton invented the concept in 1981: a unique, independent boutique hotel paired with a chef-driven/fine dining restaurant. Says Steve, "The need to stay ahead of the growing competition as well as on top of our own game is never ending. We stay tuned to our customers' behavior, needs, and purchasing process to better understand where consumer thinking influences and spending are headed."

"Because word of mouth is the number one source of our business, we need to stay close to what our guests want, need, say, and do. We have developed a skill set around niche marketing. Since the advent of search on the Net, we have been able to get out from the shadow of the large bully brands and market to consumers who put value on personal preferences and individual style in all they do, especially travel. Since 9-11 we have found that there is a movement toward thinking about what is important to one's life today versus putting things off to be done in the future. People's purchasing decisions are showing that there is a focus on what's important to me today. What is that 'thing' I keep putting off? Now is the time to do it. Wellness, pampering, learning nuggets of information (how to read a painting), discovery skills (cooking classes) are what are becoming important. These are the types of people looking for and staying at Kimpton Hotels." The biggest project on Steve's plate is the recent rollout of new Kimpton brand. "Getting every employee to understand the Kimpton brand, its promise, and the guests' expectations around our promise is proving to be a very large ongoing project. The other half of this proposition is making sure every guest in every hotel each day knows he or she is in the hotel that is part of a larger collection--Kimpton Hotels.

"You need to do the basics in order for your business to survive, but you also need to take calculated risks in order to outdistance and separate yourself from the competition as well as gain notice by the unchained shopper. Taking risks is not in one's human nature, but it is something we value highly at Kimpton. By taking risks we have come up with some of the firsts in our industry. They include social wine hour every night in every Kimpton hotel, tall rooms for tall travelers, complimentary goldfish, first company to offer complimentary high-speed Internet access, and many different specialty suites."

Advice

Anything that requires understanding and implementation by employees needs to be fully communicated well before being instituted operationally. The communication process around understating why and how as well as the benefits to all involved is more important than the actual action. It creates buy-in and buy-off. It ensures that the people who are going to be responsible for implementing it or designing the process buy in versus inheriting some program cooked up from the corporate offices.

Thoughts

Success comes from involving and harnessing all the technical and human resources available. It is vital to keep balance in one's life to keep up with trends and times.

Source: Courtesy of Steve Pinetti

management and working with and through the work of others are ongoing. Additionally, management involves getting efficient and effective results.

Efficiency is getting the most done with the fewest number of inputs. Managers work with scarce resources: money, people, time, and equipment. You can imagine the rush in the kitchen to be ready for a meal service. But it's not enough to just be efficient; management is also about being effective. **Effectiveness** is "doing the right thing." As an example, cooks do the right thing when they cook the food correctly according to the recipe and have it ready when needed.

Who Are Managers?

The changing nature of organizations and work has, in many hospitality organizations, blurred the lines of distinction between managers and nonmanagerial employees. Many traditional jobs now include managerial activities, especially when teams are used. For instance, team members often develop plans, make decisions, and monitor their own performance. This is the case with total quality management.

So, how do we define who managers are? A manager is someone who works with and manages others' activities to accomplish organizational goals in an efficient and effective way. Managers are often classified into three levels: **front-line managers** are the lowest-level managers; they manage the work of line employees. They may also be called supervisors. A front-office supervisor, for example, takes charge of a shift and supervises the guest service agents on the shift.

Middle managers are akin to department heads; they fall between front-line managers and top management. They are responsible for short- to medium-range plans, and they establish goals and objectives to meet these goals. They manage the work of front-line managers.

Top managers are responsible for making medium- to long-range plans and for establishing goals and strategies to meet those goals. Figure 14–4 shows the three levels of management plus nonmanagerial employees.

Key Management Functions

The key management functions are planning, organizing, decision making, communicating, human resources and motivating, and controlling. These management functions are not conducted in isolation; rather they are interdependent and frequently happen simultaneously or at least overlap. Figure 14–5 shows the key management functions leading to goal accomplishment.

Top Managers
Middle Managers
Front-line Managers
Nonmanagerial Associates

Figure 14–4 • Three Levels of Management Plus Nonmanagerial Associates.

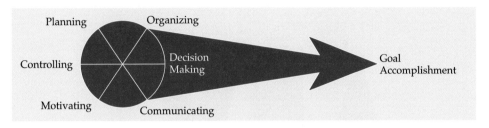

Figure 14–5 • Key Management Functions Leading to Goal Accomplishment.

Hospitality companies exist to serve a particular purpose, and someone has to determine the vision, mission, goals, and strategies to reach or exceed the goals. That someone is management. The **planning** function involves setting the company's goals and developing plans to meet or exceed those goals. Once plans are complete, **organizing** is the process of deciding what needs to be done, who will do it, how the tasks will be grouped, who reports to whom, and who makes decisions.

Decision making is a key management function. The success of all hospitality companies, whether large, multinational corporations or sole proprietorships, depends on the quality of the decision making. Decision making includes determining the vision, mission, goals, and objectives of the company. Decision making also includes scheduling employees, determining what to put on the menu, and responding to guest needs.

Communication with and motivation of individuals and groups are required to get the job done. **Human resources and motivating** involves attracting and retaining the best employees and keeping morale high.

Controlling is the final management function that brings everything full circle. After the goals are set and the plans formulated, management then organizes, communicates, and motivates the resources required to complete the job. Controlling includes the setting of standards and comparing actual results with these standards. If significant deviations are seen, they are investigated and corrective action taken to get performance back on target. This scientific process of monitoring, comparing, and correcting is the controlling function and is necessary to ensure that there are no surprises and that no one is guessing.

Managerial Skills

In addition to the management functions of forecasting, planning, organizing, communicating, motivating, and controlling, managers also need other major skills: conceptual, interpersonal, and technical.

Conceptual skills enable top managers to view the corporation as a complete entity and yet understand how it is split into departments to achieve specific goals. Conceptual skills allow a top manager to view the entire corporation, especially the interdependence of the various departments.

Managers need to lead, influence, communicate, supervise, coach, and evaluate employees' performances. This necessitates a high level of interpersonal human skills. The abilities to build teams and work with others are human skills that successful managers need to cultivate.

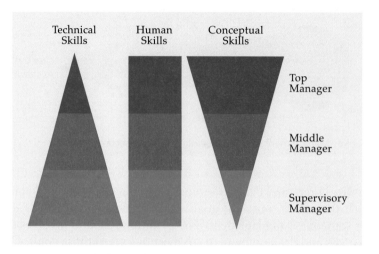

Figure 14–6 • Management Skill Areas.

Managers need to have the technical skills required to understand and use modern techniques, methods, equipment, and procedures. These skills are more important for lower levels of management. As a manager rises through the ranks, the need for technical skills decreases and the need for conceptual skills increases.

You next need to realize the critical importance of the corporate philosophy, culture, and values, and a corporation's mission, goals, and objectives. Figure 14–6 shows the degree of managerial skills required by top managers, middle managers, and supervisory managers.

The Manager's Changing Role

Managers may still have subordinates, but today's successful manager takes more of a team leader/coach approach. There are, of course, other ways to "slice and dice" what managers do. For example, managers don't just plan, organize, make decisions, communicate, motivate, and control. They wear a variety of hats, including the following:

- *Figurehead role.* Every manager spends some time performing ceremonial duties. For example, the president of a corporation might have to greet important business guests or clients or represent the corporation by attending dinners.

- *Leader role.* Every manager should be a leader, coaching, motivating, and encouraging employees.

- *Liaison role.* Managers spend a lot of time in contact with people in other departments both within the organization and externally. An example would be the sales manager liaising with the rooms division director.

- *Spokesperson role.* The manager is often the spokesperson for the organization. For example, a manager may host a college class visit to the property.

- *Negotiator role.* Managers spend a lot of time negotiating. For example, the head of a company along with qualified lawyers may negotiate with a union representative to establish wages and benefits for employees.

These roles, together with the management functions, encompass what managers do. Remember, managers need to be many things—often in quick succession—even to the point of wearing two or more hats at once.

Twenty-first-century managers face not only a more demanding and increasingly complex world, but also a more dynamic and interdependent one. The "global village" is a reality, and sociocultural traditions and values must be understood and diversity respected and encouraged by future managers. The two most important changes going on right now are the technological advances and the internationalization of hospitality and tourism. The extent to which you as a future **leader–manager** can master these events and functions will determine your future.

The manager's role is not only internal but also external. For instance, a manager must be responsive to market needs and income generation. Managers must continually strive to be innovative by realizing efficiencies in their respective areas of responsibility through process improvement—for example, by determining how to reduce long check-in lines at airports and hotels. Some companies use innovative and creative ways to streamline the check-in procedures to make the process a more worthwhile experience for the guests. Disney, for instance, uses the creative approach of sending Mickey and the gang to entertain the guests while they stand in line.

A General Manager's Survival Kit

Ali Kasiki is a top-level manager at the Peninsula Beverly Hills, California. He holds the title of managing director and is involved in creating and implementing broad and comprehensive changes that affect the entire organization. Ali offers his list:

- Know yourself, your own core competencies, and your values.
- Hire a seasoned management team.
- Build barriers of entry; that is, make yourself indispensable.
- Be very flexible.

You, Too, Are a Manager

Your classmates have just voted you to be the leader–manager of the summer study-abroad trip to France. None of you knows much about France or how to get there, what to do when you get there, and so on. Where would you start? (Resist the temptation to delegate the whole trip to a travel agent, please.)

You might start by thinking through what you need to do in terms of planning, organizing, deciding, communicating, motivating, and controlling. What sort of plans will you need? Among other things, you'll need to plan the dates your group is leaving and returning, the cities and towns you'll visit, the airline you'll take there and back, how the group will get around France, and where you'll stay when you're there. As you can imagine, plans like these are very important: You would not want to arrive at Orly Airport with a group of friends who are depending on you and not know what to do next.

Realizing how much work is involved—and that you cannot do it all and still maintain good grades—you get help. You divide up the work and create an organization by asking someone to check airline schedules and prices, another person to check hotel prices, and someone else the sights to see and the transportation needs. However, the job won't get done with the group members simply working by themselves. Each person requires guidance and coordination from you: The person making the airline bookings can't confirm the bookings unless she knows what city and airport the trip will originate in. Similarly, the person making the hotel arrangements can't make any firm bookings until he knows what cities are being visited. To improve communications, you could set up regular meetings with e-mail updates between meetings. Leadership and motivation could be a challenge because two of the group members do not get along well. So, ensuring that everyone stays focused and positive will be a challenge.

Of course, you'll have to make sure the whole project remains "in control." If something can go wrong, it often will, and that's certainly the case when groups of people are traveling together. Everything needs to be double-checked. In other words, managing is something managers do almost every day, often without even knowing it.

Source: Adapted from Gary Dessler, *A Framework for Management* (Upper Saddle River, NJ: Prentice Hall, 2002) 8.

- Get close to your guests and owners to define reality versus perception.
- Show leadership, from both the top and the bottom.
- Delegate. There is no way you can survive without delegation.
- Appeal to trends.
- Trust your instincts.
- Take risks and change the ground rules.
- Don't become overconfident.
- Look successful, or people will think you're not.
- Manage the future—it is the best thing you can do. Bring the future to the present.[5]

Distinction between Leadership and Management

Managing is the formal process in which organizational objectives are achieved through the efforts of subordinates. Leading is the process by which a person with vision is able to influence the behavior of others in some desired way. Although managers have power by virtue of the positions they hold, organizations seek managers who are leaders by virtue of their personalities, their experience, and so on. The differences between management and leadership can be illustrated as follows:

Managers
- Working in the system
- React
- Control risks
- Enforce organizational rules
- Seek and then follow direction
- Control people by pushing them in the right direction
- Coordinate effort

Leaders
- Working on the system
- Create opportunities
- Seek opportunities
- Change organizational rules
- Provide a vision to believe in and strategic alignment
- Motivate people by satisfying basic human needs
- Inspire achievement and energize people[6]

▶ Check Your Knowledge

1. What is management and what are the three management skill areas?

2. Explain levels of management.

3. Describe the key management functions.

4. What is the distinction between leadership and management?

Ethics

Ethics is a set of moral principles and values that people use to answer questions about right and wrong. Because ethics is also about our personal value system, there are people with value systems different from ours. Where did the value system originate? What happens if one value system is different from another? Fortunately, certain universal guiding principles are agreed on by virtually all religions, cultures, and societies. The foundation of all principles is that all people's rights are important and should not be violated. This belief is central to civilized societies; without it, chaos would reign.

Today, people have few moral absolutes; they decide situationally whether it is acceptable to steal, lie, or drink and drive. They seem to think that whatever is right is what works best for the individual. In a country blessed with so many diverse cultures, you might think it is impossible to identify common standards of ethical behavior. However, among sources from many different times and places, such as the Bible, Aristotle's *Ethics*, William Shakespeare's *King Lear*, the Koran, and the *Analects* of Confucius, you'll find the following basic moral values: integrity, respect for human life, self-control, honesty, and courage. Cruelty is wrong. All the world's major religions support a version of the Golden Rule: Do unto others as you would have them do to you.[7]

In the foreword to *Ethics in Hospitality Management*, edited by Stephen S. J. Hall,[8] Dean Emeritus of Cornell University, Robert A. Beck poses this question: "Is overbooking hotel rooms and airline seats ethical? How does one compare the legal responsibilities of the innkeeper and the airline manager to the moral obligation?" He also asks, What is a fair or reasonable wage? A fair or reasonable return on investment? Is it fair or ethical to underpay employees for the benefit of investors?

English Common Law, on which American law is based, left such decisions to the "reasonable man." A judge would ask the jury, "Was this the act of a reasonable man?" Interestingly, what is considered ethical in one country may not be in another. For instance, in some countries it is considered normal to bargain for room rates; in others, bargaining would be considered bad form.

Ethics and morals have become an integral part of hospitality decisions, from employment (equal opportunity and affirmative action) to truth in menus. Many corporations and businesses have developed a code of ethics that all employees use to make decisions. This became necessary because too many managers were making decisions without regard for the impact of such decisions on others.

Stephen Hall is one of the pioneers of ethics in hospitality; he has developed a code of ethics for the hospitality and tourism industry:

1. We acknowledge ethics and morality as inseparable elements of doing business and will test every decision against the highest standards of honesty, legality, fairness, impunity, and conscience.
2. We will conduct ourselves personally and collectively at all times so as to bring credit to the hospitality and tourism industry.
3. We will concentrate our time, energy, and resources on the improvement of our own products and services and we will not denigrate our competition in the pursuit of our success.
4. We will treat all guests equally regardless of race, religion, nationality, creed, or sex.
5. We will deliver all standards of service and product with total consistency to every guest.
6. We will provide a totally safe and sanitary environment at all times for every guest and employee.
7. We will strive constantly, in words, actions, and deeds, to develop and maintain the highest level of trust, honesty, and understanding among guests, clients, employees, employers, and the public at large.
8. We will provide every employee at every level all the knowledge, training, equipment, and motivation required to perform his or her tasks according to our published standards.
9. We will guarantee that every employee at every level will have the same opportunity to perform, advance, and be evaluated against the same standard as all employees engaged in the same or similar tasks.
10. We will actively and consciously work to protect and preserve our natural environment and natural resources in all that we do.
11. We will seek a fair and honest profit, no more, no less.[9]

As you can see, it is vitally important for future hospitality and tourism professionals to abide by this code. Here are some ethical dilemmas in hospitality. What do you think about them?

Ethical Dilemmas in Hospitality

Previously, certain actions may not have been considered ethical, but management often looked the other way. A few scenarios follow that are not seen as ethical today and are against most companies' ethical policies.

1. As catering manager of a large banquet operation, the flowers for the hotel are booked through your office. The account is worth $15,000 per month. The florist offers you a 10 percent kickback. Given that your colleague at a sister hotel in the same company receives a good bonus and you do not,

despite having a better financial result, do you accept the kickback? If so, whom do you share it with?

2. As purchasing agent for a major hospitality organization, you are responsible for purchasing $5 million worth of perishable and nonperishable items. To get your business, a supplier, whose quality and price are similar to others, offers you a new automobile. Do you accept?

3. An order has come from the corporate office that guests from a certain part of the world may only be accepted if the reservation is taken from the embassy of the countries. One Sunday afternoon, you are duty manager and several limos with people from "that part of the world" request rooms for several weeks. You decline, even though there are available rooms. They even offer you a personal envelope, which they say contains $1,000. How do you feel about declining their request?

Trends in Leadership and Management

- Leading a more diverse group of associates.
- Many entry-level employees do not have basic job skills.
- An increasing need for training.
- The need to create leaders out of line managers.
- Managing sales revenue all the way to the bottom line.
- Establishing independent business units to make their own profit, or subcontracting out that department.
- Instead of keeping a person on payroll for a function that is only needed occasionally, outsourcing that service to specialists.
- Cutting down on full-time employees and hiring more part-time employees to avoid paying benefits.
- An increasing challenge to keep up with technological advances and their benefits.
- Social and environmental issues continuing to increase in importance.
- A greater emphasis placed on ethics.

CASE STUDY

Performance Standards

Charles and Nancy both apply for the assistant front office manager position at a 300-room upscale hotel. Charles has worked for a total of eight years in three different hotels and has been with this hotel for three months as a front office associate. Initially, he had a lot of enthusiasm. Lately, however, he has been dressing a bit sloppily and his figures, cash, and reports have been inaccurate. In addition, he is occasionally "rattled" by demanding guests.

Nancy recently graduated from college, with honors, with a degree in hospitality management. While attending college, she worked part-time as a front desk associate at a budget motel. Nancy does not have a lot of experience working in a hotel or in customer service in general, but she is quite knowledgeable as a result of her studies and is eager to begin her career.

It appears that Charles would have been considered a prime candidate for the office manager position because of his extensive experience in other hotels and his knowledge of the hotel's culture. In view of his recent performance, however, the rooms division manager will need to sit down with Charles to review his future career development track.

Discussion Questions

1. What are the qualifications for the job that should be considered for both applicants?
2. How should the discussion between the rooms division manager and Charles be handled? Make specific recommendations for the rooms division manager.
3. Who would be the better person for the job? Why?

CASE STUDY

Reluctant to Change

You have just been appointed assistant manager at an old, established, but busy, New York restaurant. Your employees respond to your suggested changes with, "We have always done it this way." The employees really do not know any other way of doing things.

Discussion Question

1. How should you handle this situation?

Summary

1. Leadership is defined as the process by which a person is able to influence the activities and outcomes of others in a desired way.
2. Contemporary leadership includes transactional and transformational types of leadership.
3. Increased demands placed on hospitality leaders include ownership, corporate, regulatory, employee, environmental, and social interests. Leaders must balance results and relationships.
4. Managing is the process of coordinating work activities so that they are completed efficiently and effectively with and through other people.
5. Leaders, according to Drucker, realize four things and behave in much the same way.
   a. A leader is someone who has followers—some people are thinkers, and some are prophets.
   b. An effective leader is not someone who is loved or admired, but rather someone whose followers do the right things. Popularity is not leadership; results are.
   c. Leaders are highly visible. Leaders set examples.
   d. Leadership is not about rank, privileges, titles, or money. It is about responsibility.
6. There are six key management functions: planning, organizing, decision making, communicating, motivating, and controlling. However, in addition to these functions, managers occasionally have to fill roles such as figurehead, leader, spokesperson, or negotiator.
7. The difference between management and leadership is that the former is the formal process in which organization objectives are achieved through the efforts of subordinates, and the latter is the process by which a person with vision is able to influence the behavior of others in some desired way.

Key Words and Concepts

communication
controlling
decision making
effectiveness
efficiency
ethics
front-line managers
human resources and motivating
leader–manager

leadership
management
managing
middle managers
organizing
planning
top managers
transactional leadership
transformational leadership

Review Questions

1. From the DVD, what is the most fun thing that John Saputo has done in a leadership capacity?
2. What kind of leader–manager will you be?
3. Give examples of the management functions as they apply to the hospitality industry.
4. Discuss the changing role of managers.
5. Define leadership and name the essential qualities of a good leader.
6. Distinguish between transactional and transformational leadership.

Internet Exercises

1. Organization: **WetFeet.com**
   Web site: www.wetfeet.com
   Summary: WetFeet.com is an organization dedicated to helping you make smarter career decisions. WetFeet.com provides inside insight on jobs and careers for both job seekers and recruiters. By all means, take the time to check this one out!
   Click the "Careers" icon and scroll down to "General Management." Answer the following questions.
   (a) What are the requirements for becoming a GM, and what tips does WetFeet.com have to offer?
   (b) The "Career Overview" section illustrates several attributes that managers have in common. In groups, list these attributes and discuss their significance.
2. Organization: **American Management Association**
   Web site: www.amanett.org
   Summary: The American Management Association (AMA), a practitioner-based organization, offers a wide range of management development programs for managers and organizations.
   Find the section titled "AMA Research." Choose two current reports. Read through these and make a bullet list of the key information. Then, write a description of how this information might affect the way a hospitality manager plans, organizes, makes decisions, communicates, motivates, and controls.
3. Organization: **Ritz-Carlton Hotel Company**
   Web site: www.ritzcarlton.com
   Summary: Ritz-Carlton hotels are known for their superior luxury and service in the hospitality industry. This particular Web exercise illustrates how the Ritz-Carlton maintains its culture of service excellence. Take a look at the Ritz-Carlton Leadership Center. Click the "About Us" icon. Then, click "Other Ritz-Carlton Businesses." Now go to the "Ritz-Carlton Leadership Center" and answer the following questions.
   (a) What is Ritz-Carlton's Leadership Orientation?
   (b) What are the seven habits of highly effective people?

Apply Your Knowledge

Your resort has management vacancies for the following positions: executive chef, executive housekeeper, and front office manager. List the traits and characteristics that you consider essential and desirable for these positions.

Suggested Activity

Think of someone you admire as a leader. Make a list of the qualities that make him or her a good leader.

Endnotes

1. For a more detailed review of the many leadership theories, consult one of the many texts on the topic.
2. Jay R. Schrock, presentation to University of South Florida students and faculty, May 2, 2005.
3. This draws on Peter F. Drucker, Foreword, in *The Leader of the Future*, ed. F. Hesselbein et al. (San Francisco: Jossey-Bass, 1996), xii–xiii.
4. Drucker, Foreword, ix.
5. Personal correspondence with Ali Kasiki. August 4, 2005.
6. Vadim Kotelnikov, Ten3 Business e-Coach, version 2005a, www.1000ventures.com.
7. www.religioustolerance.org. nettme.htm
8. Stephen S. Hall, ed., *Ethics in Hospitality Management: A Book of Readings* (East Lansing, MI: Educational Institute, American Hotel & Lodging Association, 1992), 75.
9. Hall, *Ethics in Hospitality Management*, 108.

CHAPTER 15

Planning

OBJECTIVES

After reading and studying this chapter, you should be able to:

- Describe the importance of planning.

- Discuss the merits of the different types of planning.

- Explain how goals are set and strategies are developed and give examples.

- Identify the seven steps in operational planning.

What Is Planning?

Things don't just happen by themselves—well, at least not the way we'd like them to. Remember the time, on a hot day, when you walked into an ice cream store and ordered your favorite flavor, only to be told they were out if it. You were expecting to be delighted but instead were disappointed. A lack of planning was likely the root cause of this negative experience. Someone forgot to order the flavor of ice cream in time for you to enjoy it. This is an example of simple but important planning. There are, as we shall see, more complex forms of planning.

Planning involves selecting the various **goals** that the organization wants to achieve and the **strategies** (actions) to be taken to ensure that those goals are accomplished. In organizations, executives determine where the organization is and where it wants to go. Goals are established for each of the **key operating areas.** In the hospitality industry these would include, but not be limited to, the following key operating areas:

Guest satisfaction: The goal is 100 percent guest satisfaction. The current score may be 89 percent, so the planning element would be to plan strategies as to how to reach 100 percent.

Employee satisfaction: The goal is 100 percent employee satisfaction. Let us assume it is currently 87 percent; a plan is then made to create strategies to bring it up to 100 percent.

Productivity: Productivity is measured in many different ways across departments; for example, the kitchen would look at the number of meals served, and the front desk of a hotel would look at the number of guests checked in and out. Another way is to divide the total revenue by the number of full-time equivalent employees or person-hours worked. A goal might be set to increase the earnings per employee by 10 percent, and the plan would call for strategies to meet or exceed the goal. Similar examples would apply to these key result areas: food and beverage preparation, foodservice, guest services, marketing and sales, rooms division, operating ratios, human resources, physical property, security, and finances. Strategies are then developed to ensure that the goals are met or exceeded.

All managers do some form of planning, whether informal or formal. Informal planning is often done at the last minute, and there is little or no sharing of goals and strategies with others in the organization. The owner has a vision of what he or she wants to accomplish and just goes ahead and does it. This is frequently the situation in small businesses; however, informal planning also occurs even in larger organizations. A weakness of informal planning is that it lacks continuity.

Formal planning occurs when specific goals covering a period of up to several years are identified and shared with all associates, and strategies are developed stating how each goal will be reached. When planning is discussed in this chapter, we are referring to formal planning. Several types of planning exist, but we will examine the main ones used in the hospitality industry.

Think back to the summer trip to France that was introduced in the previous chapter. Your plans might include the following: how you plan to get to the airport, your airline and flight times, the airport of arrival, how you'll get into Paris, your hotel, and the itinerary of what to do each day in each city visited.

Think for a moment: what if you didn't plan? The group would not know what flight to take or, on arrival in France, how to get into central Paris and then how and where to find a place to stay. This would be chaotic and stressful, to say the least. Now think of your career plans. Perhaps your goal is to have a successful career in one of the many areas of hospitality management. Successfully completing your degree along with work experience would facilitate accomplishing your goal. So we can see that planning provides direction and a sense of purpose.[1] Remember the wonderful line in *Alice's Adventures in Wonderland* when Alice is lost and asks the Cheshire Cat which way to go? The Cat asks her where she wants to go. Alice replies, "I don't much care—." The Cat replies, "Then it doesn't matter which way you go."

Planning can also help identify potential opportunities and threats. Planning helps facilitate the other functions of management—organization, decision making, communication, motivation, and especially control—because planning establishes what needs to be done and how it is to be done, and control looks at how well we have done compared to how well we expected to do.[2]

The Purpose of Planning

Planning gives direction not only to top management but to all associates as they focus on goal accomplishment. The purpose of planning is to determine the best goals and strategies to achieve organizational goals. Figure 15–1 shows the hierarchy of planning in organizations. Notice that top executives do most of the strategic planning and first-line managers do most of the operational planning.

Executive Committee Planning the Future Direction and Performance of "Their" Property

Planning provides the road map of where the organization is going. Planning also helps coordinate the efforts of associates toward goal accomplishment. Planning assists in risk reduction by forcing managers to look ahead and anticipate change so they can plan scenarios to react to those potential changes.

Strategic Planning and Strategic Management

The two main categories of plans are strategic (long-term) plans and operational (short-term) plans. Associated with strategic plans are business plans and feasibility studies, which deal with the structure of the plan and provide the details necessary for obtaining finance or other approvals for the operation.

Strategic planning creates the long-range plans that steer an organization toward its goals in the accomplishment of its mission and vision. The strategic planning process involves top management, who, in simple terms, identify where the organization is and where it wants to go. There is a strong link

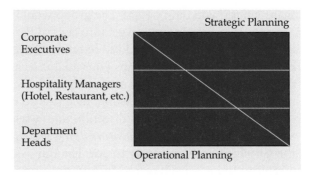

Figure 15–1 • The Hierarchy of Planning in Organizations.

between strategic planning and strategic management. The planners figure out what to do and management implements the plan.

How does a large hospitality company with the mission of being a global entity determine which markets to focus on? Should it focus on expansion in Canada, Europe, Latin America, or Asia? Which market would be more beneficial? And can it enter more than one market at a time? What will the method of entry into these markets be? Will a strategy appropriate for one country work in another? Pick up a copy of the *Wall Street Journal*, *Business Week*, a hospitality trade magazine, or a major newspaper, and you are bound to find articles on or references to business strategy. In the hospitality industry, strategies are devised that become the road map of how to succeed in increasing guest satisfaction, gaining market share, increasing profits, and so on.

Strategic management develops the mission, goals, and strategies by identifying the business of the corporation today and the business it wants for the future, and then identifying the course of action it will pursue, given its strengths, weaknesses, opportunities, and threats (internal and external environments).

Strategic management is a critical part of planning and the management process. There are three main strategic management tasks: (1) developing a vision and mission statement, (2) translating the mission into strategic goals, and (3) crafting a strategy (course of action) to move the organization from where it is today to where it wants to be.

Given the frequency of change in the environment, managers must conduct effective strategic planning in order to respond to the challenges of managing in a highly competitive environment. For example, the terrorist attacks of September 11, 2001, highlighted the need for business to craft effective strategic plans that allow them to respond to such surprises. In other words, a good strategic plan should include detailed prescriptions of how a business wishes to implement its mission in the highly competitive environment, coupled with allowances for responding to extraordinary events.

A direct link exists between the mission of the organization and strategic management—they complement each other. Strategic planning involves creating a long-term strategy for how the organization will meet its mission. The job of strategic management is to translate the mission into strategic goals.

The difference between strategic planning and strategic management is that strategic planning is a systematic process whereby the top management of an organization charts the future course of the enterprise. Strategic management is the process of guiding the organizational strategic plan and acquiring the necessary resources and capabilities to ensure successful implementation of the plan in the context of emergent situations caused by the level of environmental turbulence.[3]

A strategy is the "how to" action necessary to accomplish goals and missions. In the hospitality industry, for instance, there are six steps to strategic planning:[4]

1. Build your vision.
2. Understand your customers.
3. Examine your operating environment.
4. Determine the key issues.
5. Identify strategies for the future.
6. Create your action plan.

Strategic Planning Process

Most of the strategic planning that takes place at the top management level is called *corporate-level strategy*. Figure 15–2 shows the strategic management process. Notice that it begins with identifying the organization's mission, goals, and objectives. It then goes on to analyze the environment and the organization's resources and to identify strengths, weaknesses, opportunities, and

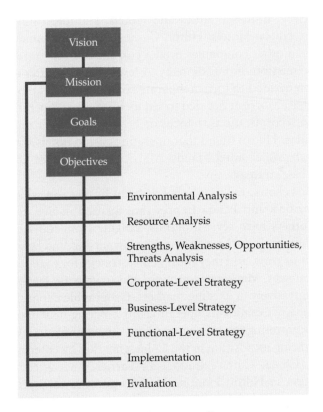

Figure 15–2 • Strategic Management Process.

threats. The organization then formulates strategies, implements them, and evaluates the results.

▶ Check Your Knowledge

1. Name four purposes of planning.
2. What are the two main categories of planning?
3. What are the three main strategic management tasks?

Corporate-Level Strategies

There are three corporate strategies:

1. Growth: (a) Market penetration; (b) geographic expansion; (c) product development; (d) horizontal integration
2. Strategic alliance/joint venture
3. Diversification

At the highest corporate level, many organizations consist of a portfolio of several businesses or divisions. For instance, Disney's portfolio includes movies, theme parks, and the ABC network. Hilton Hotels' portfolio includes Conrad Hotels, Doubletree, Embassy Suites and Hotels, Hampton Inn and Hampton Inns and Suites, Hilton Hotels, Hilton Garden Inn, and Homewood Suites by Hilton. These and other companies need a corporate-level strategy to plan how to best meet the mission of the company. A few years ago, after careful strategic planning, Hilton decided to form a separate company made up of its gaming entertainment hotels; Marriott decided to sell its foodservice operations to Sodexo. This allowed both corporations to focus on best meeting their mission with their lodging operations. Hilton found that operating casino hotels was very different from operating its other hotel brands. Marriott decided that growing its hotel brands was its best strategy.

Corporations choose the number of areas of business in which they want to operate. McDonald's and Panda Express are focused in one area, but Hilton, Marriott, and others have several brands, ranging from full-service hotels and extended-stay hotels all the way to vacation ownership and senior living. Most companies want to grow, and they must plan a strategy for that growth. There are four growth strategies. **Market penetration** aims to increase market share by promoting sales aggressively in existing markets. **Geographic expansion** is a strategy in which a company expands its operations by entering new markets—this is in addition to concentrating on existing markets. An example would be Hilton entering and enhancing its position in the Chinese market by entering into an agreement with Air China, China's leading air carrier. The agreement allows for cross-participation in Hilton Honors, Hilton's guest reward program, and Air China's Companion Club. The aim of the partnership between one of the world's most recognized hotel brands and China's leading airline is to provide enhanced

A DAY IN THE LIFE OF JESSICA LEIBOVICH

Chef/Owner, Entree Nous, San Diego, California; "Best Personal Chef,"
San Diego Magazine

I begin planning my day as a personal chef the night before I cook for a client. Using a program called Mastercook, a recipe database software, I begin menu planning and customize a menu for the clients that I will be cooking for the following day. I usually choose five entrees and side dishes, trying to keep a variety of one seafood, two chickens, one beef or pork, and one vegetarian selection. The side dishes are combinations of fresh vegetables, whole grains, and starches. This combination of meals may change based on the likes and dislikes of each client along with any special diets that they may be on. After the menu planning, I enter the recipes, using Mastercook, into a shopping list and create a shopping list for my cook date. This is all done the night before a cook date.

The day I am going to cook, I start my workday at approximately 8:30 A.M. I begin at my computer by printing out the shopping list for the day along with each of the recipes I will be preparing for my client. I also type up heating instructions for the client. Before I leave the house, I go through the shopping list for the day and place all of the nonperishable items I have already in my rolling cooler. Then I go through the list and identify which stores I will need to shop for each of the items.

Before leaving, I load my car with my cooler and my portable kitchen kit. I make sure to bring my shopping list, recipes, and heating instructions. I am in my car, ready to leave, around 9:15 A.M.

I usually need to go to at least three stores: one store for my dry goods, one store for my meat and produce, and one for seafood. Occasionally, I may need to visit a store if I cannot locate something I need at the others. As I shop, I check off my shopping list as I go.

I am finished shopping around 10:00 A.M. and begin to drive to my client's home. Each day, I go to a different client's house. Some of my clients I cook for every week, and others may only be once a month. Once I arrive, I bring in all of the groceries, my cooler from home, my portable kitchen kit, and the recipes and heating instructions.

Once everything is in from the car, I remove it from the bags and place it on the counters. I put all perishable items such as meat and dairy in the refrigerator. I then set up a cutting board and knife and wash my hands. I quickly go over my recipes and decide which ones need the longest cooking time and need to be started first. I also need to decide on the rotation of the items in the oven so I will not have more than two things in the oven at any given time. Eventually, I get in a rhythm and cook for about four to five hours, preparing each entree and side dish. My day cooking is spent washing, cutting, and trimming vegetables and meat. Then I may sauté, braise, roast, bake, or stew any particular dish, depending on what the menu selections are for that day. Sometimes I am preparing desserts and need to bake as well. Fresh salads are also often requested so the blender may be buzzing with homemade salad dressings. At one time, there may be items on three burners while two different items are in the oven. One thing I always make sure to do is to clean as I go. Otherwise, I would have quite a mess at the end of the day. As I am finished with an item, I clean it up and set it aside to dry.

As I finish preparing items, I place them in ovenproof Pyrex and Corningware containers to store them in the refrigerator or freezer, depending on the client. As each item cools, I place a label identifying each item along with the date and number of servings on a sealable lid. I leave the items to cool briefly and then place them in the refrigerator. If the client will not be eating them within the next two days, they place it in the freezer to enjoy at a later date.

At the end of the day, it all comes together, and the full menu is completed. As I am finished with an item, I place it back in my cooler. That way, when I am done, there will be no more items left on the counters. Once all the cooking is complete, I carefully clean the kitchen and leave it exactly the way it was when I arrived. I then load up my car with my portable kitchen and rolling cooler. This is usually at about 3:00 P.M.

When I arrive back home, about 4:00 P.M., I bring in my things and unload my cooler. I place everything back in its place in the cabinets. That evening I will prepare the menu and shopping list and begin again for the next day.

For more information, including menus and background information, please visit my web site at www.chefjessica.com.

global service for the increasing number of business travelers in China and to address the strong competitive situation with international airlines in the local business travel market after China's entry into the World Trade Organization.[5]

The third form of growth strategy is **product development,** such as Hilton's Garden Inn or a new restaurant menu item. The fourth type of growth strategy is **horizontal integration,** which is the process of acquiring ownership or control of competitors with similar products in the same or similar markets. Hilton's purchase of Promus Corporation (Embassy Suites) was an example of horizontal integration.

Strategic alliances or **joint ventures** are yet other methods for a corporation to fulfill its mission. They work like this: American Airlines has as its mission "to be the world's leading airline by focusing on industry leadership in the areas of safety, service, network, product, technology, and culture." It wanted to expand operations into Asia and Europe—the two main air travel growth areas—but lacked the resources necessary for opening up routes to several additional countries, and it was not allowed to do so by foreign governments because of the competition it would bring to national airlines. So American Airlines formed a "One World" alliance with several other airlines including Aer Lingus, British Airways, Cathay Pacific, Finnair, Iberia Airlines, LAN Chile, and Qantas and more than 20 affiliate carriers to feed each other passengers, code share some flights, and share resources, thus saving money and offering the consumer a better deal with the economy of scale.

Another strategy is **diversification,** in which companies expand into other types of business—related or unrelated. Celebrity chef Emeril "Bam!" Lagasse's expansion into TV dinners is an example of diversification.

Strengths, Weaknesses, Opportunities, and Threats Analysis

A major strategic planning technique that is widely used in the hospitality and tourism industry is a **SWOT analysis:** an analysis of *s*trengths, *w*eaknesses, *o*pportunities, and *t*hreats. A SWOT analysis is used to assess the company's internal and external strengths and weaknesses, to seek out opportunities, and to be aware of and avoid threats. A SWOT analysis is conducted in comparison with a company's main competitors. This makes it easier to see the competitors' strengths, weaknesses, opportunities, and threats. It also makes it easier to plan a successful strategy. Each operator can decide what the key points are for inclusion in the SWOT analysis. The eleven P's of hospitality marketing include the traditional four P's of marketing—place (or location), product, price, promotion—but add three others (people, process, physical evidence) and four new P's (personalization, participation, peer-to-peer, and predictive modeling). All plans need to be implemented; Figure 15–3 shows how plans follow goals and strategy. Notice that strategic plans are implemented through action plans, operating plans, and standing plans.

Environmental Scanning and Forecasting

Environmental scanning is the process of screening large amounts of information to anticipate and interpret changes in the environment. Environmental scanning creates the basis for forecasts. **Forecasting** is the prediction of future outcomes. Information gained through scanning is used to form scenarios. These, in turn,

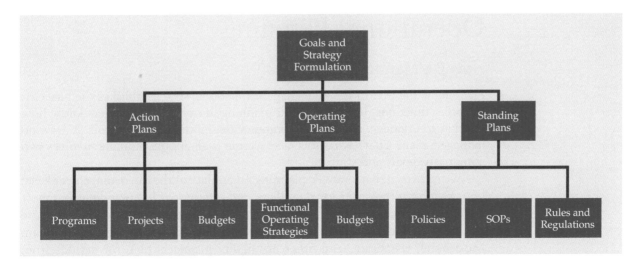

Figure 15–3 • How Plans Follow Goals and Strategies.

establish premises for forecasts, which are predictions of future outcomes. The two main types of outcomes that managers seek to forecast are future revenues and new technology breakthroughs. However, any component in the organization's general or specific environment may receive further attention. Both Marriott International and Magic Mountain's sales levels drive purchasing requirements, production goals, employment needs, inventories, and numerous other decisions. Similarly, your university's income from tuition and state appropriations will determine course offerings, staffing needs, salaries, and the like. These examples illustrate that predicting future revenue is a crucial first step in planning for success.

As you can imagine, the forecasting done by the president of Hilton Hotels is very different from the forecasting done by a restaurant manager or department head. The president of Hilton needs to assess the broad economic, political, social, cultural, technological, and financial implications that may impact any forecast. For instance, should Hilton open a hotel in Providence, Rhode Island, or a different city? The desire of Hilton to have a presence in these markets must be considered along with the economic and other environmental factors in each market location. The president must also consider the probability of success of the new property. Another scenario is that of the president of a major chain restaurant corporation trying to forecast in a changing business environment. What if minimum wage is increased? What if health care is mandated? How would these changes affect the corporation?

▶ Check Your Knowledge

1. Briefly explain the four growth strategies of corporations: (a) market penetration, (b) geographic expansion, (c) product development, and (d) horizontal integration.

2. What does SWOT analysis stand for?

3. What is environmental scanning?

Operational Planning

How Do Managers Plan?

Planning is the first of the management functions, so it establishes the basis for the other functions. In fact, without planning, how would managers know how or what to organize, decide on, communicate, motivate, or control? So how do managers plan? That's what this next section is all about. Planning involves two main parts: goals and strategies.

We have seen that strategic planning takes place at the top management level; now we look at the operational midlevel and supervisory levels and see that most hospitality managers have a shorter planning horizon. **Operational plans** are generally created for periods of up to one year and fit in with the strategic plan. Most hotel, restaurant, and other hospitality managers plan for periods from hourly, daily, weekly, monthly, and up to 90 days.

Operational plans provide managers with a step-by-step approach to accomplish goals. The overall purpose of planning is to have the entire organization moving harmoniously toward the goals. These are the seven steps in operational planning:

1. *Setting goals.* The first step in planning is identifying expected outcomes—that is, the goals. The goals should be specific, measurable, and achievable, and should reflect the vision and mission of the organization.

2. *Analyzing and evaluating the environment.* This involves analyzing political, economic, social, and other trends that may affect the operation. The level of turbulence is evaluated in relation to the organization's present position and the resources available to achieve goals.

3. *Determining alternatives.* This involves developing courses of action that are available to a manager to reach a goal. Input may be requested from all levels of the organization. Group work is normally better than individual input.

4. *Evaluating alternatives.* This calls for making a list of advantages and disadvantages of each alternative. Among the factors to be considered are resources and effects on the organization.

5. *Selecting the best solution.* This analysis of the various alternatives should result in determining one course of action that is better than the others. It may, however, involve combining two or more alternatives.

6. *Implementing the plan.* Once the best solution is chosen, the manager needs to decide the following:
   - Who will do what?
   - By when?

A Management team listens to customers for feedback.

- What resources are required?
- At what benefit?
- At what cost?
- What reporting procedures will there be?
- What authority will be granted to achieve goals?

7. *Controlling and evaluating results.* Once the plan is implemented, it is necessary to monitor progress toward goal accomplishment.

Operational Goal Setting

Goal setting is the process of determining outcomes for each area and associate. In Chapter 1, we looked at organizational vision, mission, goals, and objectives. Once the vision and mission have been determined, organizations set goals in order to meet the mission. The goals are set for each of the key operating areas mentioned earlier. No one can work effectively without specific goals and daily, weekly, monthly, quarterly, semiannual, and annual evaluation reports to assess progress toward goal accomplishment or whether adjustments must be made to change course.[6] Examples of the goals and information a sales department should record and analyze each month follow.

Group Room Nights

- Booked this month and year-to-date by market segment and salesperson
- Actual consumed room nights this month, year-to-date by month, by market segment, and "on the books" for months to come
- Actual average group room rates by month, year-to-date, and on the books for months to come

Individual Room Nights

- Actual room nights booked by month and year-to-date by market segment
- Local corporate clients—actual individual and group room nights booked by month and year-to-date
- Occupancy—actual by month, year-to-date, and same time last year
- REV PAR—actual by month, year-to-date, and same time last year
- Packages—number sold for each type by month, year-to-date, and zip code origin[7]

Another example would be setting productivity goals. Productivity refers to the amount of labor (input) it takes to do a particular task (output). Productivity is measured in labor costs, which are expressed as a percentage of sales, for each department. Because labor costs are the highest of the operational costs, it is critical to keep them in line with budget. Productivity and labor costs can be compared across similar operations to determine which is more efficient. Suppose the goal for a family restaurant's labor costs is 23 percent of sales. If sales go up, then so too can the labor cost—but proportionately. But what if sales go down? Then so will labor costs—again, proportionately. The skill of management is to operate efficiently and effectively. It is easy to operate a hospitality business when it is busy; the skill comes in running a hospitality business that is operating at only 50 to 60 percent capacity, or worse still, even less.

Expressing goals in specific, measurable terms is important because it allows us to measure our progress toward goal accomplishment. Goals are set for each of the key result areas (departments or elements of a business that determine its success; for example, in a restaurant, guest satisfaction scores, sales, food costs, labor costs, and beverage costs are all key result areas).

An example would be a restaurant where guest satisfaction scores are currently 87 percent. The goal is a score of 95 percent. A time by which the goal is to be met is also identified, as is the individual who is to be responsible for its accomplishment.

Planning expert George Morrisey presents a four-point model for use in formulating goals:[8] Here is an example using Morrisey's model:

1. Increase guest satisfaction scores
2. From 87 to 95 percent
3. By December 31, 20XX
4. At a cost of $500 for training

Operational Objectives

Objectives state how the goals will be met. Objectives are operational statements of activities that should be quantifiable and attainable within a stated time. If the goal is to achieve a food cost percentage of 28.5 percent by October 15 and maintain it until further notice at a cost not to exceed $100 or 10 working hours, the food and beverage director and executive chef must do the following:

- Achieve the desired food cost percentage by having the menu items priced and their costs calculated.
- Control portion sizes by establishing an exact portion for each menu item and watching to see that it is maintained.
- Ensure that regular and spot checks are done on inventory and the food cost is calculated correctly. Take a physical count of all food items accurately, including all items in the freezers, the kitchen, the storeroom, the banquet kitchen, and so on, and calculate their costs accurately.
- Ensure that all sales and food costs are included in the calculations. Check that all guest food charges are included in the calculations—especially any functions for the day of the inventory if the food is included—and that the sales are also included.
- Use any leftover food within 48 hours.
- Maintain a vigilant loss prevention program with security. Check bags leaving the property and do not allow any bags in the kitchen.
- Ensure that all food sales are recorded and paid for.

Collectively, these objectives ensure that the goal will be met. Each goal needs to have written step-by-step objectives that state how they will be met.

INTRODUCING TIM MULLIGAN

Area Director of Human Resources, Sheraton Hotels, San Diego

Meet Tim Mulligan, area director of human resources for Sheraton Hotels, San Diego, California. Tim feels that the important elements in planning are knowing what the desired outcome will be, having the instructions followed by the organization, and being a good time manager to help ensure goal attainment.

Goal setting can be divided into two types: annual goals for managers, which have to be in line with career growth, annual bonuses, and so forth, and annual goals for employees, which need to be stated in terms of individual development. According to Tim, the objectives need to be in line with company objectives, individual hotel objectives, and personal growth objectives.

- *Operational plans* are important to meet financial goals (profit), guest satisfaction goals, and employee satisfaction goals.
- *Specific plans* are important to reach day-to-day success with goals and objectives (e.g., check-in, recruiting, hiring process, room cleaning).
- *Single-use plans* are used only for special events, such as holiday parties or HR receptions.
- *Standing plans* are annual plans, such as benefit enrollment and management screening plans. They are also used for company policies, such as tuition reimbursement or training programs.

Tim gave these examples for contingency factors in planning. If the occupancy of the hotel decreases, the HR department has a plan for layoffs. On the other hand, if a need to hire a significant amount of new staff exists, then the HR department has a plan in place for a mass-hiring action.

Forecasting in the HR department differs from forecasting in other departments, according to the HR director. In the HR field, there is a need for more accurate information on a business level, to determine needs on a staffing level, and the need for dollar amounts for advertising, recruiting, background checks, drug tests, training, and so forth.

In response to a question about which benchmarking practices he believes are the most successful, Tim named turnover rates, employee retention, the employee satisfaction index, and the guest satisfaction index.

In the field of technology, a new trend in planning is the optimal business model. This model works with drivers and is based on the business practice. As an example, this model can determine the amount of hours available for scheduling and the maximum amount of money you can spend to stay within a budget. Two more trends are an online employee evaluation model and a goal-setting process called the performance management process.

Management Concepts and Approaches

We can see from the preceding examples that it makes sense if the associates who are going to be responsible for achieving the goals are also the ones involved in setting them. Some years ago this concept lead to **management by objectives (MBO)**, a managerial process that determines the goals of the organization and then plans the objectives, that is, the how-tos of reaching the goals. With MBO, associates usually establish the goals and objectives and review them with management. MBO works because associates have been involved with setting goals and objectives and are likely to be motivated to see them successfully achieved. The MBO process consists of six steps:

1. *Set organizational goals.* Top management sets goals for the company in each key result area.
2. *Set departmental goals.* Department heads and their team members jointly set supporting goals for their departments' key result areas.
3. *Present goals.* Department heads present goals and gain approval from senior management.
4. *Discuss department goals.* Department heads present department goals and ask all team members to develop their own individual goals.
5. *Set individual goals.* Team members set their own goals with their supervisor, and timetables are assigned for accomplishing those goals.
6. *Give feedback.* The supervisor and team members meet periodically to review performance and to assess progress toward goals.

MBO goals need to be specific, measurable, and challenging but attainable, just like any other goals. The main purpose of an MBO program is to integrate the goals of the organization and the goals of the associates so that they are in focus. Over the years MBO has proved very successful and has, in some organizations, been superseded by **total quality management (TQM),** which was introduced in Chapter 1. TQM not only involves planning but also touches on the other functions of management. The idea of improving efficiency and increasing productivity while placing a larger emphasis on quality has caught on fast. Originally designed by Japanese businesses to help reconstruct the economy after World War II, today TQM is widely applied in most industrialized countries. The hospitality industry has embraced quality management with open arms, asking for input from all levels of employees and calling for teamwork. Ultimately the customer rates the team on quality, value, and product—and the customer does not lie. An example of TQM is asking a group of associates to suggest ways to improve the guest experience by addressing specific challenges (actually problems, but industry professionals prefer to be positive and call them *challenges*) that the hospitality operation has in delivering exceptional service.

Take guest check-in as an example. The TQM team would include members from the front office and guest services (bellpersons, etc.) who identify lineups for check-in from 4:00 to 7:00 P.M. The group writes a challenge or problem statement and various ways of improving the situations are presented. They may include the following:

- Using a special desk for airport check-ins
- Handling convention and group guest check-ins in another location (the rooming list is made up in advance and rooms allocated with keys encoded and ready for distribution to guests)
- Cross-training and using associates from other departments to assist with the check-ins

- Adopting an "all hands on deck" approach to have members of management available to assist with check-ins in various ways

- Having additional help available for housekeeping to get the rooms ready more quickly

An example of TQM in the restaurant industry is asking servers in a restaurant for help solving the challenge of reducing the guests' waiting time for a table by turning tables more quickly during rush periods. Once the problem or challenge statement is written, the TQM team can focus on ways to improve the guest experience by suggesting ideas to reduce the guest waiting time. The head chef might automatically take on the role of coach, as opposed to that of supervisor. Implementing TQM will have the natural outcome of teamwork because one employee cannot improve quality on his or her own. The chef uses motivation and inspiration to keep the team in high spirits, and each employee is important in his or her own way. Emphasis is placed on recruiting, training, and keeping quality employees to ensure that the TQM approach will be a success.

Benchmarking is a concept that identifies the best way of doing something and which companies excel in that area (*best-practices companies*). The best practice is noted and emulated or even improved on by other companies. In the spirit of cooperation, companies are expected to share information, so you need to give as well as receive.

The history of benchmarking begins with the 1970s.[9] Japanese companies would take trips to industrialized nations to study their large, successful industrial companies and take that knowledge home to apply to their local companies. By aggressively copying others, they were able to supersede the company being copied by improving on the success strategy. Meanwhile, benchmarking has become a global trait. Some companies are even copying companies outside their own industry. For example, IBM carefully studied Las Vegas casinos to apply their strategy of reducing employee theft at IBM.

How do you benchmark? First of all, a team is formed. The duty of this team is to identify companies to be benchmarked. Next, the team must determine the best possible way of collecting the data, which can be collected internally as well as externally. Once collected, it must be analyzed to determine where the success lies and where the differences lie. The last step is to create an action plan on how to improve on the newly gained data—that is, what steps need to be taken to implement it.

The question to be answered is, "How do these companies obtain internal information on other companies they are benchmarking?" An initial team is formed, the members of which may have contacts among customers, suppliers, or employees of the company they are planning on benchmarking. Companies often are glad to swap success stories and information with others, not only informing them but being informed about others as well. Successful companies can often be identified by the number of quality awards they have won. Also, trade associations typically know who the successful companies are, and analyzing financial data will help determine which companies to benchmark. Having employees who will implement the benchmarked changes helps ensure their commitment to service or product improvement.

Benchmarking is an operational tool that can be used to guide corporate strategy as well as operations strategies.[10] The process in an ideal setting is to

Hank Christen, *Unconventional Concepts, Inc.*
Paul Maniscalco, *George Washington University*

It is unrealistic to expect any level of success in disaster operations without a formal comprehensive emergency management plan (CEMP). A hospitality industry CEMP must meet two important objectives:

- Support emergency response agencies. Hospitality companies have facilities, personnel, and supplies that enhance emergency response efforts.
- Provide support and direction to facility recovery. Returning to normal operations is the goal; the CEMP must address the human, financial, and material resources needed for effective recovery.

An effective hospitality industry CEMP is divided into seven major functions: (1) threat assessment, (2) vulnerability analysis, (3) management, (4) operations, (5) logistics, (6) planning, and (7) administration and finance.

The threat assessment and vulnerability analysis functions are similar to the SWOT analysis (strengths, weaknesses, opportunities, and threats) discussed in this chapter. Threats are categorized into three groups: (1) natural threats: severe weather, wild fires, earthquakes, disease outbreaks; (2) technological threats: chemical spills, utility failures, explosions, urban fires, transportation accidents, cyber failure; and (3) human-made threats: terrorism, cyber attacks, violence, criminal activities, bomb threats, arson.

Vulnerability analysis is the identification of weaknesses or deficiencies relating to a specific threat. For example, a resort in a wilderness area is vulnerable to wildfires.

The management section of the CEMP identifies the incident manager (the person in charge) during disaster operations. The incident manager may or may not be the chief executive of the organization. He or she is responsible for directing team members as well as ensuring a direct liaison between the hospitality facility and the local on-scene incident commander.

Operations are the direct and hands-on activities of hospitality industry personnel that support emergency operations and/or assist the hospitality facility in returning to normalcy. Operations cover a wide spectrum, from evacuation and security procedures to restoration of guest services and rehabilitation of the facility.

Logistics play a vital role; by definition, a disaster exhausts the resources of responders. Logistics includes facilities (buildings), communications, supplies, utilities, fuel/maintenance, food, and water. A climate-controlled room with telephones, computers, and a fax machine serves as an ideal incident command post for fire, law enforcement, and EMS command officers. Food and hot coffee from the facility's restaurants provides rehabilitation to firefighters. Construction materials and equipment are needed during long-term rescue efforts.

A planning section is established to monitor the CEMP and develop action plans during disaster operations to facilitate response to real-time issues and surprises that emerge during disasters. Action plans are usually updated on a 12-hour or full-day cycle as needs dictate and are less formal than the CEMP.

Administration and finance relates to the tracking of all documents and expenditures relating to the disaster event, including employee-related issues such as salary, overtime, and workers' compensation. Documents may include computer records, video, and photographs, as well as paper files.

Sources of low-cost disaster planning expertise include county or city emergency management office, fire departments, law enforcement crime prevention officers, the Internet, the American Red Cross, EMS offices, and the Federal Emergency Management Agency (FEMA). Conduct at least one internal exercise a year to test your plan. Evaluate your plan and make appropriate changes continuously.

compare company operations with those of other companies that exhibit best practices. Note that best practices are often found outside the company's industry grouping. For example, the FAA has contracted with Disney to help reduce the long lines at airports occasioned by more severe security measures due to the threat of terrorism. In many instances, best practices adopted from outside the hospitality industry sometimes must be modified to fit the context.

CORPORATE PROFILE

Choice Hotels International

The awesome story of Choice Hotels began in 1968 when Gerald Petitt, a Dartmouth engineering and business student, was seeking summer employment with IBM[1]. He blew the roof off the company's preemployment test scores. The test scores were brought to the attention of Robert C. Hazard, Jr., who was in charge of the Coors Brewery account. This had an appeal for the ski-bum in Petitt, who was originally from Denver. Robert Hazard says that Jerry Petitt did more in one summer for IBM's efforts to design a production system for the brewery than a team of five engineers did in two years.

Robert Hazard decided then, more than 25 years ago, to keep this talented person. They progressed in their careers with spells at American Express and Best Western; they eventually went on to Silver Spring, Maryland, where they took a sleepy, stagnating lodging company called Quality Inns from 300 properties to more than 5,000 hotels in 48 countries and territories. Because they had been so successful at Best Western, they were enticed to join Quality in 1980 for equity plus $500,000 annual salaries.

Bob and Jerry brought to Quality a combination of engineer-builders and entrepreneur-marketers. They quickly set about changing the mausoleum management style—"where you don't get creative thinking, where you try to pit good minds against each other." Instead, you get "What will the chairman think?" and "We can all go along with it—or look for another job."[2]

To illustrate the change of management style, Bob Hazard draws the upside-down management organization, where the bosses are the millions of guests at 5,000 hotels worldwide. He and Jerry Petitt, of course, were on the bottom.[3]

The strategy of changing the corporate culture, of taking advantage of emerging technological and management trends with emphasis on marketing-driven management over operations, has worked for Choice Hotels. The development of brand segmentation was perhaps its best move. Choice Hotels International is now an international hotel franchisor consisting of the following brands: Comfort Inn, Comfort Suites, Quality, Sleep Inn, Clarion, Cambria Suites, MainStay Suites, Suburban, Econo Lodge, and Rodeway Inn.

More recently, Choice has reorganized, creating market area management teams strategically placed so that licensees can be closer to support staff. Each field staff manager has 45 properties and helps with sales, training, quality assurance reviews, and operations consolidations.

[1] This draws on Philip Hazard, "The Bob and Jerry Show," *Lodging* 19, (December 1993): 37–41.

[2] Ibid., 58.

[3] www.choicehotels.com.

Policies, Procedures, and Rules

Policies, procedures, and rules are examples of standing plans. **Policies** set broad guidelines for associates to use when making decisions. For example, it is the policy of most hotels to pay the room and tax at another hotel and provide a taxi or hotel limo when "walking" a guest.

Procedures specify what to do in given situations. An example would be when a former classmate calls you to request a room for the next weekend. However, the hotel is forecasting 94 percent occupancy, and company procedures, unfortunately for your friend, state that no employees or their friends may stay at complimentary or discounted rates if the hotel is forecast to be more than 90 percent occupied. Policy and procedures often go together.

A **rule** is a specific action guide that associates must follow. Consider this example: Under no circumstances shall an employee serve alcoholic beverages to minors or intoxicated guests.

Budgeting

Most of us are familiar with budgets; we learned about them when we received our first "allowance." Remember how often we had it spent before the week was up? That's why organizations plan the use of their financial resources. A **budget** is a plan allocating money to specific activities. There are budgets for revenues (sales) and costs (expenses) for capital equipment—equipment that has an expected life of several years.

Budgets are popular because they force managers to anticipate expected sales and budget expenses accordingly—that is, not to spend it all before the week is up! Budgets are used extensively in all levels of hospitality organizations, from the corporate level to the smallest departments. Once an estimate of a particular department's revenues is determined, the costs are then budgeted, leaving a portion for profit. This is also called the bottom line. Here's an example of a budget: A restaurant expects 750 guests in a given week; at an average check of $15, this means sales of $39,250 for the week. This allows management to budget labor costs, usually to a predetermined percentage of sales (normally between 18 and 24 percent, depending on the type of restaurant). Food, beverage, and other costs are budgeted in the same way. Figure 15–4 shows a detailed restaurant budget listing all the items of expenditure. Note that the column on the right-hand side is for the percentage of sales to which the dollar amount refers. This percentage is helpful in that it can be easily compared with other similar restaurant operations. In fact, restaurant companies use percentages to check on a manager's performance. If one restaurant manager gets a food cost percentage of 28.5 and another gets 33 percent, then the corporate office will be asking the latter manager questions!

Budgets are popular because they can be used with a variety of applications, all over the world. Budgets are planning techniques that force managers to be fiscally responsible. Notice that the actual and variance columns have no entries in them yet. As soon as the period (usually a month) is over, the results can be totaled and any variances recorded.

Budgets are created by department heads once a year and revised monthly or as necessary. First, the projected revenue is forecasted, and then all fixed and variable

Restaurant Operational Budget

	Budget ($ Thousands)	%	Actual Variance +(−)
Sales			
Food	750.0	75	
Beverage	250.0	25	
Other	0.0		
Total Sales	1,000.0	100	
Cost of Sales			
Food	225.0	30.0	
Beverage	55.0	22.0	
Other	0.0		
Total Cost of Sales	280.0	28.0	
Gross Profit	720.0	72.0	
Controllable Expenses			
Salaries and wages	240.0	24.0	
Employee benefits	40.0	4.0	
Direct operating expenses	60.0	6.0	
Music and entertainment	10.0	1.0	
Marketing	40.0	4.0	
Energy and utility	30.0	3.0	
Administrative and general	40.0	4.0	
Repairs and maintenance	20.0	2.0	
Total Controllable Expenses	480.0	48.0	
Rent and other occupation costs	70.0	7.0	
Income before interest, depreciation, and taxes	170.0	17.0	
Interest	10.0	1.0	
Depreciation	20.0	2.0	
Net Income before Taxes	140.0	14.0	

Figure 15–4 • Restaurant Operational Budget.

costs are allocated to ensure that the required profit is attained. Forecasting revenues is not easy—there are so many variables—but it has to be done. If the business was operating the previous year(s), there is a history. For a new business, the operator's experience, information from similar operations, environmental factors, forecasting models, and calculated guesswork equal a "guesstimate" of sales.

Budgets intertwine with (1) scheduling, because scheduling equals labor costs, the largest controllable budget item; (2) purchasing, because that contributes to food, beverage, and other costs; and (3) controlling, because we want to compare budget to actual revenue and expenditure results.

Check Your Knowledge

1. What is the difference between operational planning and strategic planning?
2. Define benchmarking.
3. Why is it important to have a budget?
4. Give an example of goal setting.
5. Briefly describe the six steps of the MBO process.

Scheduling

Scheduling of associates is a planning activity that involves taking the business forecast and allocating an appropriate number of staff to give the necessary level of service. Because of the increasing cost of wages and benefits, schedules must be planned very carefully to avoid being overstaffed or understaffed. Because the hospitality industry mostly operates 24/7, we need to staff all departments, with appropriate coverage day and night.

In Chapter 1, we briefly introduced the main shifts as early or opening, middle or swing, and late or closing plus the night. Staffing each area or department with an adequate number of associates costs money and is necessary just to open the doors. For example, a restaurant needs a host to greet and seat guests, a server or two, a prep cook or two, a cook or two, a dishwasher, a bartender, and a manager. This is the minimum acceptable staffing level regardless of the number of guests. The same holds true for all areas of the hospitality industry. The problem is that we never know exactly how many guests we will have, and one day can be busy and the next quiet. That's why accurate forecasting, as discussed earlier, is so important.

Obviously the level of service will vary from one lodging operation to another. A full-service hotel may have 24-hour bell service, whereas a limited service hotel will not offer it. An amusement park may be open up to 12 hours a day and may need at least two shifts. A restaurant may be open for up to 12 hours a day and may need two shifts, depending on whether it serves breakfast, lunch, or dinner. The hospitality industry, in order to keep costs down and remain competitive, uses a large number of part-time employees. Many hospitality departments have a skeleton staff of full-time employees augmented by several part-time ones, as the business needs them.

Project Management

Project management means exactly that—managing a project. Project management is the task of completing the project on time and within budget. In the hospitality industry, we have a variety of projects at each level of the corporation. At the corporate level, for instance, there is the construction of a new hotel or restaurant. At the unit level, there is the alteration or renovation of an existing building; at the department level, there is the installation of a new piece of equipment or a new point-of-sale system. But project management is broader than these examples. What about the senior prom? That's a project, too. So are most of the catering functions that take place at convention centers and hotels.

Hospitality companies are increasingly using project management because the approach fits well with the need for flexibility and rapid response to perceived market opportunities. Sometimes an organization has a specific need for a project that does not fit into a regular planning schedule, so it uses project management. Project management works like this: Say the project is to become more environmentally friendly. A hospitality organization will create a team of associates from various departments and challenge them to come up with a plan to accomplish the goal of becoming more environmentally friendly. Figure 15–5 shows the steps in the project-planning process.

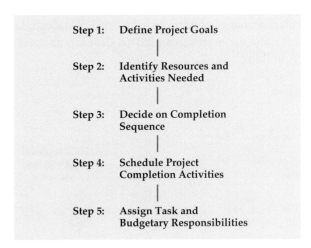

Step 1:	**Define Project Goals**
Step 2:	**Identify Resources and Activities Needed**
Step 3:	**Decide on Completion Sequence**
Step 4:	**Schedule Project Completion Activities**
Step 5:	**Assign Task and Budgetary Responsibilities**

Figure 15–5 • Steps in the Project Planning Process.

Activity	Week						
	1	2	3	4	5	6	7
Consult with beverage staff	✓						
Establish goals and determine wines to be tasted		✓					
Arrange tasting			✓				
Taste wines				✓			
Make selection and determine pricing					✓		
Prepare and print wine list						✓	✓

Figure 15–6 • A Gantt Chart for a Restaurant Owner Planning a New Wine List.

The process begins with clearly defining the project's goals. This step is necessary because the manager and team need to know exactly what's expected. All activities and the resources needed to do them must then be identified. What labor and materials are needed to complete the project? Once the activities have been identified, the sequence of completion needs to be determined. What activities must be completed before others can begin? Which can be done simultaneously? This step is actually done using flowchart-type diagrams such as a Gantt chart or a PERT network (see Figure 15-6 and 15-7). Next, the project activities need to be scheduled. Time estimates for each activity are done, and these estimates are used to develop an overall project schedule and completion date.[11]

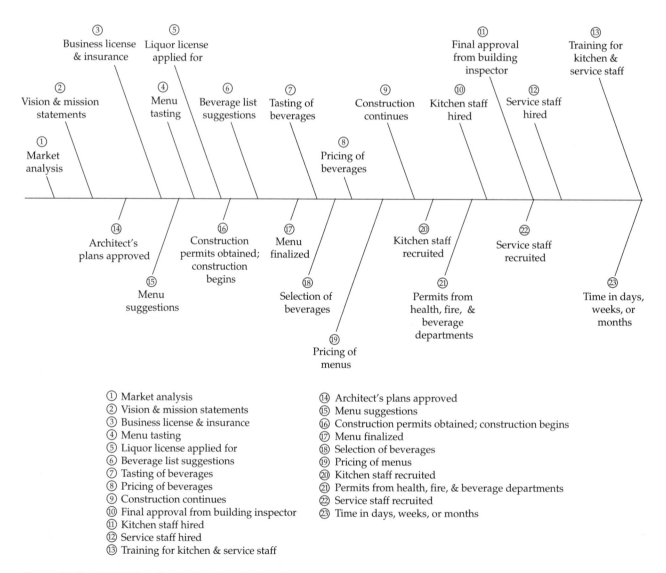

① Market analysis
② Vision & mission statements
③ Business license & insurance
④ Menu tasting
⑤ Liquor license applied for
⑥ Beverage list suggestions
⑦ Tasting of beverages
⑧ Pricing of beverages
⑨ Construction continues
⑩ Final approval from building inspector
⑪ Kitchen staff hired
⑫ Service staff hired
⑬ Training for kitchen & service staff
⑭ Architect's plans approved
⑮ Menu suggestions
⑯ Construction permits obtained; construction begins
⑰ Menu finalized
⑱ Selection of beverages
⑲ Pricing of menus
⑳ Kitchen staff recruited
㉑ Permits from health, fire, & beverage departments
㉒ Service staff recruited
㉓ Time in days, weeks, or months

Figure 15–7 • A PERT Chart for the Opening of a New Restaurant.

▶ **Check Your Knowledge**

1. Describe the minimum acceptable staffing level for a restaurant as it relates to scheduling.

2. What are the steps in project management?

Trends in Planning

Given today's hospitality business environment of rapid change, planning needs to be done on time, yet methodically to keep pace with rapid environmental/global changes. Technology, especially the Internet, can be used to overcome time and distance, allowing for more people to have input into the planning process. Associates can contribute to the planning process online instead of going to meetings.

CASE STUDY

Shell's Seafood Restaurant

Shell's Seafood Restaurant caters weddings and other events in a small New England town. The following is an overview of the planning—or lack of planning—that took place last summer. Jason, the restaurant's general manager, together with the wedding couple, planned a garden wedding and reception in a town park near the restaurant. At first, it seemed as if there were too many choices and decisions to be made, but as they went through the lists they had prepared, they were all pleased with the arrangements.

They chose a wedding ceremony time of 2 P.M. followed by a reception at 2:30 P.M. The wedding couple and their families wanted it to be a special occasion but did not want to spend a fortune, so they decided to use Shell's Seafood Restaurant because they had enjoyed meals there in the past. Jason prepared a menu that the couple liked: cream of asparagus soup, chicken fricassee, potatoes au gratin, cauliflower mornay, and for dessert, crème brûlée. Jason also suggested white and red house wines with an allocation of $^3/_4$ bottle per person. The wedding couple's aunt made the cake and it was delivered to the park, but when Jason's staff assembled it, the weight of the top two tiers caused the cake to sink into the thin layer of icing and fall over.

The wedding ceremony was a success, but as you can imagine, the reception was not.

Discussion Question

1. List the planning errors that were made.

Summary

1. Planning involves selecting the various goals that the organization wants to achieve and the actions (objectives) that will ensure that the organization accomplishes the goals.
2. Goals are set for each of the key operating areas.
3. Planning gives direction, not only to top managers, but to all associates as they focus on goal accomplishment.
4. Strategic (long-term) planning and strategic management involve identifying the business of the corporation and the business it wants for the future, and then identifying the course of action it will pursue, given its strengths, weaknesses, opportunities, and threats.
5. There are three main strategic management tasks: developing a vision and mission statement, translating the mission into strategic goals, and creating a strategy or course of action to move the organization from where it is today to where it wants to be.
6. Strategic planning and management take place at the higher levels of management. This is known as corporate-level strategy.
7. There are four growth strategies: market penetration, geographic expansion, product development, and horizontal integration.
8. A strengths, weaknesses, opportunities, and threats (SWOT) analysis is a key strategic management technique.
9. Environmental scanning is the process of assessing information about the economic, social, political, and technological environment to anticipate and interpret changes in the environment.
10. Operational plans are generally for periods of up to one year and dovetail with the strategic plan.
11. There are seven steps in operational planning: setting goals, analyzing and evaluating the environment, determining alternatives, evaluating alternatives, selecting the best solution, implementing the plan, and controlling and evaluating results.
12. Benchmarking is a concept that identifies the best way of doing something and which companies excel in the area under study.
13. Policies, procedures, and rules are examples of standing plans. Policies set broad guidelines, procedures specify what to do in given situations, and rules are specific action guides that associates must follow.
14. Budgets are plans allocating money for specific activities. They are popular because they force managers to anticipate expected sales and budget expenses accordingly.
15. Goal setting is determining the outcomes for the organization and associates.
16. Objectives state how goals will be met. Management by objectives is a managerial process that determines the goals of the organization, then plans the objectives.
17. Project management is the task of completing a project on time and within budget.

Key Words and Concepts

benchmarking
budget
environmental scanning
forecasting
geographic expansion
goal
goal setting
horizontal integration
joint venture
key operating areas

management by objectives (MBO)
market penetration
objective
operational plans
policy
procedure
product development
project management
rule

scheduling
strategic alliance
strategic management
strategic planning
strategy
SWOT analysis
total quality management (TQM)

Review Questions

1. What does planning involve?
2. How are goals and objectives different?
3. What is strategic planning?
4. What is the distinction between SWOT analysis and environmental screening analysis?
5. Why do companies use policies, procedures, and rules?

Internet Exercise

Organization: Your restaurant chain
Web site: The company's URL
Summary: Fast-food chains need to know what their competitors are doing or going to do. In this exercise, you will select fast-food company web sites and see what you can find out about your competitors.

Apply Your Knowledge

1. Benchmarking can be an important tool and source of information for managers. It can also be useful to students, as you'll see in this team-based exercise. In your small group, discuss study habits that each of you has found to be effective from your years of being in school. As a group, come up with a bulleted list of at least eight effective study habits in the time allowed by your professor. When the professor calls time, each group should combine with one other group and share ideas, again in the time allowed by the professor. In this larger group, be sure to ask questions about suggestions that each small group had. Each small group should make sure it understands the suggestions of the other group with which it is working. When the professor calls time, each small group will then present and explain the study habit suggestions of the other group it was working with. After all groups have presented their suggestions, the class will come up with what it feels are the "best" study habits of all the ideas presented.

2. In groups of four, develop a plan for your formal class graduation dinner with a prominent guest speaker.

Endnotes

1. Draws on Gary Dessler, *A Framework for Management*, 2nd ed. (Upper Saddle River, NJ: Prentice Hall, 2002), 99.
2. Ibid., 100.
3. Personal conversation with Kenneth E. Crocker, Ph.D., professor, Francis Marion University College of Business, May 15, 2008.
4. www.cleggsassociates.com.
5. www.apn.btbtravel.com/s/Editorial-Hotels-And-Resorts.asp?ReportID531401.
6. Personal conversation with Stephen Deuker, director of marketing, Ritz-Carlton, Sarasota, FL, April 18, 2008.
7. Ibid.
8. Dessler, *A Framework for Management*, 108.
9. Stephen P. Robbins and Mary Coulter, *Management*, 8th ed. (Upper Saddle River, NJ: Prentice Hall, 2005), 228–230.
10. Personal conversation with Kenneth E. Crocker, June 15, 2005.
11. Robbins and Coulter, *Management*, 240.

CHAPTER **16**

Organizing

OBJECTIVES

After reading and studying this chapter, you should be able to:

- Describe organizational structure and organizational design.

- Explain why structure and design are important to an organization.

- Identify the key elements of organizational structure.

- Explain team-based structures and why organizations use them.

- Describe matrix structures, project structures, independent business units, and boundaryless organizations.

From Planning to Organizing

Howard Schultz, head of Starbucks Corporation, knows that with more than 16,000 Starbucks stores worldwide, organizing the company is no easy task.[1] Such an organization needs training departments to turn college students into café managers (who know, for example, that every espresso must be pulled within 23 seconds or be thrown away), departments that sell coffee to United Airlines and supermarkets, and a way to manage stores in locations as far away as the Philippines and China. How to organize is, therefore, not an academic issue to Schultz. He has discovered that planning and organizing are inseparable. When his company was small, its strategy focused on high-quality coffee drinks provided by small neighborhood coffeehouses. This strategy in turn suggested the main jobs for which Schultz had to hire lieutenants—for example, store management, purchasing, and finance and accounting. Departments then grew up around these jobs.

As Schultz's strategy evolved to include geographic expansion across the United States and abroad, his organization also had to evolve. Regional store management divisions were established to oversee the stores in each region. Today, with Starbucks coffee also sold to airlines, bookstores, and supermarkets, the company's structure is evolving again, with new departments organized to sell to and serve the needs of these new markets. What Schultz discovered is that the organization is determined by the plan; that is, strategy determines structure.

Schultz has talked about making sure growth doesn't dilute the company's culture. Analysts (who watch companies for investment purposes) believe that Starbucks must determine how to contend with higher materials prices and enhanced competition from lower-priced fast-food chains, including McDonald's and Dunkin' Donuts.[2] Schultz announced his five-point plan on March 19, 2008, to reaffirm the chain's place as the world's coffee authority. "By embracing our heritage, returning to our core—all things coffee—and our relentless commitment to innovation, we will reignite the emotional connection we have with our customers and transform the Starbucks Experience."[3] Chris Muller, writing in *Restaurants and Institutions* magazine, says that Starbucks is a mature product offering in a significantly different marketplace. Upmarket coffee is not as relevant to every portion of the consuming public as it was 10 years ago. Energy drinks, healthy menus, and online music delivery are all factors that were not present when Starbucks caught the growth wave. Muller suggests the following:[4]

1. Starbucks should loosen its "centralized command and control" organization model and move to franchising in a "federalist" model. Franchises should be offered only to current store managers and long-term employees.

2. Starbucks is in the "lifestyle" beverage business and needs to reestablish its product offerings to connect to the core, but unfortunately, the aging baby-boom generation, which made Starbucks so successful, now wants healthy choices (e.g., lower calories, smaller portions).

3. Many members of the millennial generation (born after 1982), do not drink coffee on a regular basis, but do like high-energy drinks and possibly adult chocolate beverages. According to Muller, this demographic group is less focused on an "individual" moment spent in the "Third Place" (the place between home and work), and more on doing team-based activities with a social message for their community. (E-mail is out; Facebook is in.)

4. Starbucks should lower its prices, offer less bitterness and faster service across the system, and realize that coffee aroma is not as meaningful as convenience of purchase. Starbucks needs to offer food—healthy, good-tasting, authentic, and made-for-you menu items with low carbon footprints.

Howard Schultz inviting guests into one of the new Starbucks outlets

Muller also suggests that Starbucks needs to remember that 50 years ago McDonald's had only one protein and five total items. Focus is great for efficiency and rapid growth, but it will not sustain a business model as it reaches maturity and needs billions of dollars in sales.[5] Starbucks announced that it is realigning and reducing its nonretail workforce by 600 and closing 600 stores in an effort to strengthen its focus on customers. Of course, skeptics would ask how such a reduction would actually improve the focus on its customers.

The Purpose of Organizing

The purpose of **organizing** is to get a job done efficiently and effectively by completing these tasks:

- Divide work to be done into specific jobs and departments.

- Assign tasks and responsibilities associated with individual jobs.

- Coordinate diverse organizational tasks.

- Cluster jobs into units.

- Establish relationships among individuals, groups, and departments.

- Establish formal lines of authority.

- Allocate and deploy organizational resources.

This chapter covers these important aspects of organization, but first we need to know what organization is. *Organization* refers to the arrangement of activities so that they systematically contribute to goal accomplishment. No one person can do all the things necessary for a hospitality organization to be successful. Imagine just one person trying to do all the different tasks that make a restaurant meal memorable.

Defining Organizational Structure

In the past few years, organizational structures have changed quite a bit. Traditional approaches were questioned and reevaluated as managers searched for structures that would best support and facilitate employees doing the organization's work. The structure needs to be efficient but also have the flexibility needed in today's dynamic environment. The challenge for managers is to design an organizational structure that allows employees to efficiently and effectively do their work.

An **organizational structure** is like a skeleton in that it supports the various departments in an organization. It provides the total framework by which job tasks are divided, grouped, and coordinated. In today's leaner and meaner hospitality business environment, organizations are flatter, meaning they have fewer levels of managers. They are also structured to better fulfill the needs of the guests. A typical example is the change of mind-set that turned the traditional organizational chart upside down, as shown in Figure 16–1. The general manager used to be at the top of the organizational chart and the front-line associate at

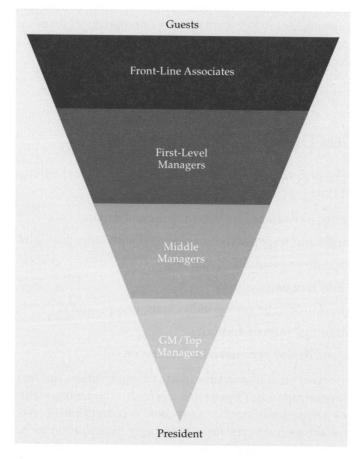

Figure 16–1 • The New "Upside-Down" Organizational Chart.

the bottom—the guest never appeared on the chart! Now we have the guest at the top of the inverted pyramid and the general manager at the bottom. Given higher labor costs, there are also fewer associates to do the same amount of work. Organizations have had to become more flexible in their desire to delight the guest. Some hotels have created rapid-reaction teams of associates who respond to urgent guest needs. These teams are from several different departments but come together in an effort to please the guest. More about this type of team and other teams are discussed later in this chapter.

Work Specialization and Division of Labor

You may recall the humble beginnings of Marriott International as a Hot Shoppe. Mr. and Mrs. Marriott probably decided what was going to be on the menu, then purchased the food, cooked it, and served it. They also collected the money and made sure everything was to their guests' liking. It's fun and stimulating to have your own business and see the results of food well prepared and served and gratified guests returning. Now consider the organizational structure of Marriott International today.

Today, **work specialization** is used to describe the extent to which jobs in an organization are divided into separate tasks. One person does not do the entire job. Instead, it is broken down into steps and a different person completes each step. In the hospitality industry, we use work specialization in various departments but not to the extent that heavy industry does. The reason is that in the hospitality industry we are not producing a commodity, so the line cook is likely to continue to prepare a variety of different dishes. However, the concept does apply to a banquet kitchen when a line is created to plate the food. In such a situation, each person adds a particular part of the meal to the plate, and someone checks it and places it in the heated rolling cart. In other departments, such as housekeeping, work specialization has some application: in making up guest rooms, housekeepers may work in pairs, with each specializing in a particular task. However, because the tasks are very repetitive, housekeepers prefer to do more than one task to avoid boredom.

Work specialization allows professionals to focus on their specialty

Departmentalization

We are all familiar with government departments such as the department of motor vehicles and the department of labor, and your college probably has departments of admissions, financial aid, and student affairs, to name just a few. Once jobs have been divided up by work specialization, they have to

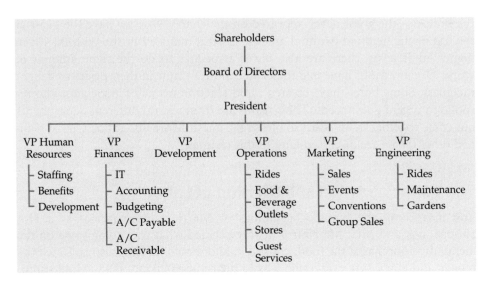

Figure 16–2 • Organization Chart for a Theme Park.

be grouped back together so that the common tasks can be coordinated. This is called **departmentalization**. Every organization has its own form of departmentalization according to its needs. The organization's structure is shown in its **organization chart** (Figure 16–2).

Departments are created to coordinate the work of several associates in a given area. An example is housekeeping in a hotel or marketing and sales for a convention center. The main question facing company presidents is, "What form of organization will best meet the organization's goals?" Should it be organized by function, product, service, guest, or territory, or a combination of these?

The simplest form of departmentalization is by **function**. A large hotel rooms division has a reservations department, uniformed service department, front desk, communications department, concierge, housekeeping, and so on—each with its own specialized function.

Choice Hotels International departmentalizes its lodging properties by **product** in the form of brands: Comfort Inn, Comfort Suites, Quality, Sleep Inn, Clarion, Cambria Suites, MainStay Suites, Suburban, Econo Lodge, and Rodeway Inns. Each brand attracts a slightly different target market, offers slightly different services, and is managed independently.

Sodexo and ARAMARK, both huge multinational corporations with billions of dollars in sales, departmentalize by **guest** needs. They have departments or divisions for education, business and industry, health care, and so on. The sales department of a convention and visitors bureau may departmentalize itself by market served: travel industry, medical, legal, insurance, leisure travel, incentive travel, or military.

Many larger companies departmentalize by **territory** when they have representation in several states, provinces, and countries. For example, Avis Rent A Car has representation in a number of states, provinces, and countries. It recognizes that each geographic market has its own nuances.

Authority and Responsibility

Authority is closely associated with chain of command because it gives managers the right to exercise their power in a given situation. Authority should be commensurate with responsibility. In other words, managers should exercise power only in accordance with their position. In any organization, there is a two-way obligation regarding authority: Managers can expect their associates to do the work required, and, in return, associates need to perform their duties by working efficiently and effectively. In recent years, managers have increasingly empowered associates to make more decisions—particularly in the hospitality industry. We have to ensure that our guests are delighted. Some companies have empowered their employees to do whatever it takes to please the guest, even to the extent of **comping** a room if necessary.

In the hospitality industry it is very important to have not only formal authority but also respect. Associates are quick to gauge the credibility of new supervisors or managers to see how much they know and to determine whether they can help out by getting their hands dirty in an emergency. Someone who has "been there" is likely to gain the associates' respect if he or she can step in and help out during a crisis. Managers are often given authority but lack the in-depth knowledge of the department to really be able to lead by example. Simply put, "You've got to know your onions." When managers lack credibility and therefore respect, it is much more difficult for associates to work with them to get the job done. Thus, many companies require that a newly appointed manager have experience in the area or at least an accelerated apprenticeship in the area he or she will be responsible for, thus building up his or her credibility.

When authority is delegated, so should commensurate **responsibility**. That means that you are responsible for the performance of your operation and the associates who work with you. That can sometimes be a big responsibility. What if an associate serves an alcoholic drink to a guest who is intoxicated, and that guest later drives off and has an accident, injuring not only himself but also another innocent party? Are you responsible? Yes! As manager of the department or restaurant you are not only responsible but liable as well.

▶ Check Your Knowledge

1. Why is organizing important?
2. What are the drawbacks of work specialization?
3. Describe ways managers can departmentalize work activities.

Chain of Command

Organization charts show not only the structure and size of the organization but also the **chain of command** (Figure 16–3). Departments are clearly indicated, and titles may be used to show each associate's position. The chain of command begins at the top of the organization—in the case of a large, publicly traded

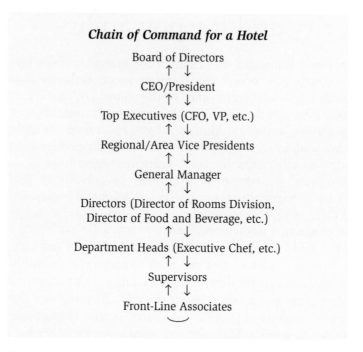

Figure 16–3 • An Example of a Hotel's Chain of Command.

company such as Marriott International, with the board of directors, who are elected by the shareholders. The board of directors select a president or chief executive officer (CEO), and the president selects the top executives such as the chief financial officer (CFO) and vice president of marketing. The president and the executive team develop plans that are presented to the board for approval and then implement those plans. The chain of command is helpful for associates who have questions or need advice because they will know whom to ask. Similarly, they know to whom they are responsible for their work performance. The chain of command should flow from the top to the bottom of the organization and up from bottom to top. This is usually illustrated by lines of authority that indicate who is responsible for what or over whom.

Increasing Span of Control

How many associates can a manager supervise? The answer used to be between 8 and 12. Now, however, the answer is likely to be 12 to 18. The reason for this increase in span of control is that organizations needed to become more competitive with not only other U.S. companies but foreign ones, too. Consider the cost savings realized by eliminating levels of management: if there are two organizations, both with 4,000 employees, and one organization has a span of control of 10 and the other 15, the wider span of control will have fewer

The Guest Is God

An industry consultant was once in Japan giving a seminar with another colleague. The colleague began by saying that in business today the guest is king, and as he was saying that a gentleman rushed down from the back row and grabbed the microphone and told the audience that the guest is not king but God! The gentleman was the company president. Reflecting on this unusual happening, the consultant realized just how much the Japanese revere their guests.

levels of management and lower costs because there will be fewer managers. But how much will that save? Well, if the average manager makes $65,000 a year, then the total savings would be $9.36 million. Having said that many hospitality corporations have increased their span of control, it is also fair to say that they realize that there is a point when the number of people reporting to managers overburdens associates. At that point, managers don't have the time to give advice, nor do they have time to properly supervise their associates, so standards decline. So what factors determine the appropriate span of control? It depends on the type of work being done. Is it straightforward or complex? Are the associates highly skilled and well trained, or is there a training need? Other factors include the degree to which standardized procedures are in place, the information technology available, the leadership style of the manager, and how experienced the manager is in the area of concern.

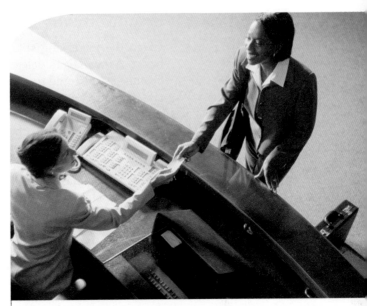

Empowerment allows associates to own the guest request and check to see that it has been fulfilled

A DAY IN THE LIFE OF ANDREA KAZANJIAN

Ritz-Carlton Members Club, Sarasota, Florida

Andrea Kazanjian serves as director of membership for the Ritz-Carlton Members Club in Sarasota, Florida. In her role, Kazanjian is charged with developing and implementing strategies that shape the membership experience for this unique and exclusive luxury tier brand extension.

A day in the life of Andrea Kazanjian consists of conducting membership training workshops, developing professional and successful Membership Sales Executive and Members Services teams, designing all membership collateral and messaging, and managing a number of marketing campaigns. These are just a few of the techniques she will use to help the organization meet the aggressive membership recruitment and sales goals outlined by the ownership.

Kazanjian earned a B.S. in Hotel, Restaurant, and Travel Administration from the University of Massachusetts, Amherst, on a swimming scholarship as a Division I swimmer and team captain. A native of Albany, New York, she is a board member on the Sarasota Chamber of Commerce Young Professionals Group and a volunteer for the community outreach subcommittee, a member of the Junior League of Sarasota, a representative of the Sarasota Chamber of Commerce Leadership Luncheon Series, a member of the United Way of Sarasota, and a leader of the Ritz-Carlton, Sarasota, campaign.

An extension of the Ritz-Carlton Hotel Company, LLC, the Ritz-Carlton Members Club is a luxury-tier, non-equity membership that combines the benefits of a private social club with the tradition of personalized Ritz-Carlton services and world-class amenities designed to complement the Sarasota lifestyle. Members have the opportunity to access the Members Beach Club on Lido Key, the Members Spa Club, and the Tom Fazio–designed Members Golf Club.

Empowerment

Given the increasing span of control, **empowerment** has become an industry norm. As managers delegate more authority and responsibility, associates have become empowered to do whatever it takes to delight the guest. Front-line associates are in a better position to know guests' wants and needs than management, so it makes sense to empower them to take care of delighting guests. In the old days, associates had to check with management before making a decision to ensure guest delight. Let's look at an example. A husband and wife check into a hotel that advertises a room rate that includes a buffet breakfast. Unfortunately, the wife catches a nasty virus and is not well enough to go down to enjoy the buffet breakfast. Her husband says that he will call her to let her know what's offered at the buffet, so she can choose something and he can bring it up for her. He goes down to the restaurant and dutifully calls her to tell her what's available. She tells him what she wants: scrambled eggs and bacon. When the husband explains to a server that his wife is sick and not able to come down for the buffet and requests a tray to carry up her breakfast, the server listens and goes to consult a more senior server, but not the manager. The husband then explains all over again and once more asks for a tray. This time he is told that food cannot be taken upstairs. The husband then says, "My wife is sick and needs something to eat and drink. We've already paid for it. . . . Get the manager here now!" The server later comes over to say that the duty manager says the husband can choose anything from the cold section of the buffet but not the hot part. That does it. The guest demands that the general manager, not the duty manager, be summoned. You get the picture. All of this could have been avoided if only the associates had been empowered to use a little discretion.

Centralization and Decentralization

Some organizations make most of the decisions at the corporate office and inform unit managers of them. This process is called **centralization**. If the top managers make the organization's key decisions with little or no input from subordinates, then the organization is centralized. Other organizations make most of the decisions at the unit level or with input from associates. This is **decentralization**. In reality, organizations are never completely centralized or decentralized because they could not function if all decisions were made by the CEO, nor could they function properly if all decisions were made at the lowest level. Figure 16–4 illustrates the difference between a centralized and a decentralized organization.

Many companies have become more centralized in an effort to save costs and improve service to associates. Because of rapid changes in the hospitality business, organizations are becoming more flexible and responsive. This means the organizations are becoming more decentralized. A good example is Choice Hotels' restructuring of its franchise services. It has centralized franchising services under one umbrella and created one brand management position that oversees the company's eight brands. As a result, the company closed five market offices. In large companies especially, lower-level managers who are "closer to the action" and typically have more detailed knowledge about problems and how best to solve them are empowered to delight the guest.

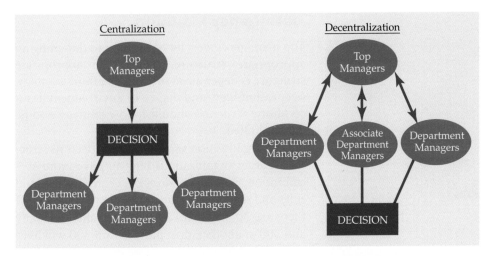

Figure 16–4 • Centralization versus Decentralization in an Organization.

▶ Check Your Knowledge

1. How are the chain of command and span of control used in organizing?
2. Describe the factors that influence greater centralization and the factors that influence greater decentralization.

Organizational Design Decisions

Organizations are structured in different ways, depending on which structure best suits their needs. A company with 20 associates will look very different from one with 10,000 associates. But even organizations of comparable size don't necessarily have similar structures. What works for one organization may not work for another. How do managers decide which is the best structure for them? That decision depends on certain contingency factors that we are about to discuss.

Coordination of Activities

When there are only a few associates in an operation, everyone can catch up quickly, but as the business expands, problems can and do occur unless there is good **coordination of activities**. The hospitality business is fast paced—guests want something now or even sooner! Departments need to communicate quickly and often to keep up with guest requests. You may have experienced an occasion when something did not go as planned—perhaps a checkout delay at your hotel or charges on your bill that were not yours—but now you're in a rush to get to the airport. You get the picture—someone made a mistake!

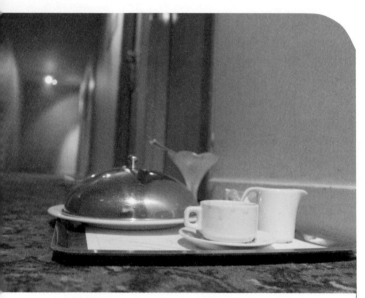

Coordination of various functions and areas is critical in exceeding guest expectations. Room service requires the coordination of a variety of people, including those who take the order from the guest, kitchen personnel who cook the food, and, of course, those who deliver the meal and later retrieve the tray and dishes.

Contingency Planning

Top managers give a lot of thought to designing an appropriate structure. What that appropriate structure is depends on the organization's strategy, size, technology, and degree of environmental uncertainty. Structure should follow strategy and be closely linked.

An organization's size generally affects its structure. Larger organizations tend to have more specialization, departmentalization, centralization, and rules and regulations than do small organizations. If there are 30 associates at one hospitality company and 300 at another, then the one with 300 will have more departments and be more mechanistic.

Every organization has some form of technology that relates to structure. Consider a hotel company that has a central reservations center. It can hold the inventory of all the hotels in the chain and be far more efficient in offering available rates and rooms to callers and also make the inventory available to travel agents and Internet travel organizations. A central reservations center can also do a better job of controlling and maximizing revenue for the available rooms than many decentralized centers.

Technology has enabled restaurant chains to transfer data and store menus and operations and training manuals via the Internet. In some cases this has led to a change in organizational structure. In the hospitality industry, technology has tended to help the existing structure perform better—sometimes with fewer associates. A convention center may have the latest software program for reserving and allocating space, but it will not significantly change the organization's structure; someone must take the guest requests and enter them into the program.

Contingency factors deal with what hospitality organizations refer to as the *what-ifs*. What if such-and-such happens? The company plans and organizes for several possible outcomes. After the terrorist attacks on September 11, 2001, many hospitality companies immediately planned and organized for a drastic drop in business. Departments were greatly reduced, reorganized, or even closed in an effort to reduce the losses.

Contemporary Organizational Designs

Team-Based Structures

In response to competitive market demands for organizations that are lean, flexible, and innovative, managers are finding creative ways to structure and organize work and to make their organizations more responsive to guest needs. The first of the contemporary designs is a **work team structure;** either the complete organization or a part of it is made up of teams that perform the duties necessary to delight

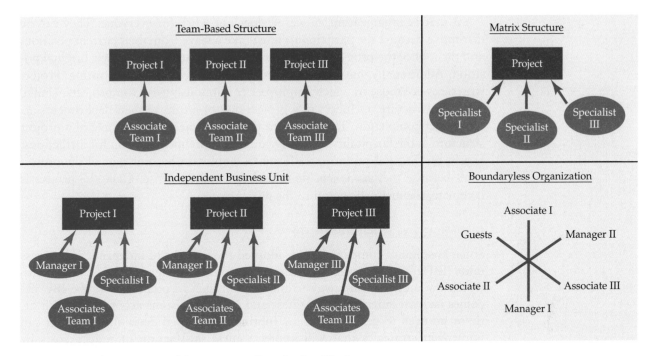

Figure 16–5 • The Four Types of Contemporary Organizational Designs.

the guest (Figure 16–5). This concept is, like many, borrowed from business but has relevance for hospitality managers. Perhaps the best use of this concept for hospitality managers is with TQM, which you may remember we introduced in Chapter 1. Basically, teams of mostly front-line associates take on the challenge of improving guest services and products. At first, these teams are often made up of associates from one department but later can be made up of associates from different departments. This actually improves coordination between departments. Sales departments can work well in teams, as can the banquet kitchen, and for that matter most departments in a hospitality operation. However, the team is more likely to consist of associates from one department as opposed to associates from several departments. In any event, teams tend to be more productive. There are two main types of work teams: integrated and self-managed. *Integrated work teams* are given a number of tasks by the manager, and the team gives specific assignments to members. *Self-managed work teams* are assigned a goal, and the team plans, organizes, leads, and controls to achieve the goal.[6]

Matrix and Project Structures

The **matrix structure** is an organizational structure that assigns specialists from different departments to work on a project—for example, a new attraction, restaurant, or hotel opening. The specialists come together to pool their knowledge and experience to work on the project. During this time they may have two bosses: their department head plus the project manager. To work effectively, project managers and department heads need to communicate on a regular basis. Matrix structures are appealing to organizations that want to speed up the decision-making process or get projects accomplished more quickly.

A matrix organization, however, does not work for everyone. They can be disruptive because the participants must take a leave from their current position, and then, once the project is completed, they need to return to their original position. Additionally, having more than one manager can be frustrating. **Project structures** are those in which employees continuously work on projects. Unlike a matrix structure, members of a project do not return to their departments after project completion. They go on to the next project. An example of a project structure in the hospitality industry would be a preopening team for attractions, hotels, resorts, and restaurants. Teams of employees become part of the project team because they have specific knowledge and expertise. Once the project is complete, the members go on to the next project.

Independent Business Units

Some hospitality companies have adopted the concept of **independent business units (IBUs)** to encourage departments not only to delight the guest but also to watch the money all the way to the bottom line. In other words, the IBU becomes its own independent business and makes decisions accordingly, with little or no need to get approval for routine operational decisions. The unit can implement strategies that will improve guest satisfaction or reduce costs by

INTRODUCING ISADORE SHARP

Chairman, President, and Founder, Four Seasons Regent Hotels

Isadore Sharp, a first-generation Canadian, is the founder, chief executive officer, and chairman of the board of Four Seasons Regent Hotels. From one motel on Toronto's Jarvis Street in the early 1960s has grown the world's largest luxury hotel chain—a multimillion-dollar global hotel empire. Four Seasons Regent's success is largely a reflection of the drive, determination, and personal taste and style of Isadore Sharp.

Four Seasons was built slowly, deal by deal. From the first little motel that Sharp literally helped construct to the complex Asian agreement in which Four Seasons acquired Regent Hotels International Inc., the growth of this company is largely the result of one man's vision. Isadore Sharp (called "Issy" by friends and family) has created a company that friends and foes alike agree is a model for how Canadian companies can compete globally in an increasingly interconnected world economy.

Currently, the Four Seasons Regent manages and owns 65 properties in 29 countries, with 20 more under construction, and continues to move ahead with more hotel plans in different countries. Isadore Sharp's success is all the more remarkable because he did not inherit vast wealth and did not rise through the ranks of a major corporation with ready access to international money markets. He is a self-made man who is consistent and has control of his spirit. He believes in excellent quality for both his hotels and his company. Sharp clearly loves his business and credits the Four Seasons Regent team with the successes of the company. He has been inducted into the Canadian Business Hall of Fame and has received the International Distinguished Entrepreneur Award. Sharp still spends one day in each hotel meeting with employees. Interestingly, none of his three sons is interested in taking over Dad's job.

finding a quicker or better way of doing something. Forming IBUs is an excellent strategy to get associates to realize the total picture of revenue and expenses for a department. It forces associates to engage in all elements of management to make a profit. IBUs also enable management to seriously look at departments not making a sufficient profit contribution, with a view toward making changes and improvements or eliminating the department. Departments that once had a loss are now making a profit as a result of the company installing an IBU system of organizational design.

Boundaryless Organizations

Another contemporary approach to organizational design is the **boundaryless organization,** an organization whose design is not defined by, or limited to, the horizontal, vertical, or external boundaries imposed by a predefined structure.[7] The term was coined by Jack Welch, former chairman of General Electric, who wanted to eliminate vertical and horizontal boundaries within GE and break down external barriers between the company and its customers and suppliers. This idea may sound odd, yet many of today's most successful organizations are finding that they can most effectively operate in today's environment by remaining close to the guest and being flexible and unstructured. The boundaryless organization seeks to eliminate the chain of command, to have appropriate spans of control, and to replace departments with empowered teams. Hospitality organizations are moving in this direction but are not there yet. Some may feel that this is not a concept that will work for hospitality organizations, whereas others may think it's a great idea. Hospitality companies recognize that it is important to stay close to the guest but are challenged to create a boundaryless organization.

Teams and Employee Involvement

Teams are task-oriented work groups; they can either be formally appointed or evolve informally. We all work with others, to a greater or lesser extent, in order to meet or exceed goals. Both formal and informal teams make important contributions to the company and to associates' need satisfaction. For example, an informal team from one hotel saved the company more than $250,000 a year after the team made a proposal about energy savings. Not only did each team member receive a sizable bonus, but their employee satisfaction scores were significantly higher than those of associates who did not participate in the team.

Teams are great for doing work that is complex, interrelated, or more than one person can handle. Harold Geneen, while chairman of ITT, said, "If I had enough arms and legs, I'd do it all myself." We all know that associates cannot do everything themselves because of limitations of arms and legs, time, expertise, knowledge, and other resources. There is a certain "buzz" in a restaurant on a busy Friday night; when the kitchen is getting "slammed," you know what teamwork is or isn't!

The funny thing about teams, as you have probably experienced by now, is that you don't always get to choose who you work with—just as when you do term papers and projects in teams. And even when you do get to choose classmates, it sometimes doesn't work out. They don't do their fair share or something else doesn't work. Yet in the hospitality industry we are constantly working in teams to exceed guest expectations. So how can we make teams more effective?

Group Dynamics

Why are some groups more successful than others? Why does a team of mediocre players sometimes beat a team of superior players? You've probably experienced a situation in which, seemingly against all odds, a team excels. Remember the survival programs on television in the early 2000s? A group of people was dropped off in some remote place, and over a period of time the group members had to survive as teams, *but* they could vote people "off the island." Imagine if we did that in the hospitality industry!

Why and how this happens is called *group dynamics* and includes variables such as the abilities of the group's members, the size of the group, the level of conflict, and the internal pressures on members to conform to the group's norms. Sometimes external influences inhibit the group's performance. Corporate may dictate policies that make it more difficult for the group to succeed, or there may be a shortage of resources. One of the fascinating aspects of group dynamics is the members of the group. You may have experienced a group project at college. Sometimes you had to choose whom you worked with, and sometimes your group members were selected randomly. Which worked best?

How Companies Use Teams at Work

Hospitality companies use teams at work in a variety of ways. One way is to structure the organization into teams from the start. Instead of departments, they are called teams. This implies, of course, that employees must be **team players,** which is vital in the fast-paced hospitality industry. Another way management can use teams is through total quality management (TQM) programs that involve associates working in teams to constantly improve the guest experience. Teams are formed from either individual departments or several different departments. They choose an area of the operation that needs improvement, usually one of guest concern, and proceed to make changes that will benefit the guest. TQM teams have made important contributions to the industry and continue to do so.

Self-managed teams make decisions that were once made by managers. This saves managers time, allowing them to concentrate on more important things. We saw an example in Chapter 4; hotel housekeepers who score highly on room inspections no longer need to have their rooms checked by a floor housekeeper. These teams of housekeepers actually receive a bonus for superior performance, and the hotel saves the salary of the floor housekeepers. Self-managed teams work successfully in several types of hospitality organizations such as theme parks and convention centers.

Principles of Organization for Disaster Operations

Hank Christen, *George Washington University*
Paul Maniscalco, *Unconventional Concepts Inc.*

The development of a comprehensive emergency management plan (CEMP) is based on a functional organization, not a hierarchy. The normal top-down flow of orders, instructions, and information through multiple levels of management (a hierarchy) does not translate effectively to disasters. The function, not the title or level of the player(s), is the key.

Disaster management is organic, loose, and flexible. The first principle of this function-based system is decentralization. It is a "flat system" with only three layers: manager/staff, functional directors (operations, logistics, etc.), and sectors. Sectors are established as needed to support the primary functions (e.g., a food/water sector assigned by the logistics director).

The second key principle is chain of command. Someone is in charge; there are functional directors and there are sector leaders. Information and direction flows from the manager to the functional directors, to the sector leader, and vice versa. Bottom-up information flow is as relevant in a disaster as top-down information flow. Sector leaders who are physically involved often have more knowledge and insight into specific problems than the boss at the top. Senior managers must empower their subordinates and trust them.

The third key principle of organization is span of control. The span of control in disaster operations is much narrower than in normal business management. A span of control of three to four should be maintained. The environment is stressful, with poor communications, inadequate resources, and short decision times.

An effective organizational tool to keep the span of control within limits is branching: dividing a functional level into two or more segments called branches. For example, the logistics director can divide responsibilities into two areas: a service branch, which is responsible for communications and food/water, and a support branch, which is responsible for facilities, supplies, and maintenance.

The incident manager needs a staff (called the management staff) for assistance. The three key positions on the management staff are as follows:

- *Liaison*—serves as a point of contact with emergency responders and other involved agencies, companies, or organizations
- *Public information*—coordinates with the local public information officer; drafts and implements public information strategy
- *Safety officer*—coordinates with incident safety officer; is responsible for safety monitoring of all employee activities; has authority to suspend unsafe procedures or practices

During emergency activities, the planning director must maintain a disaster organizational chart listing positions and names of employee assignments. Organizational restructuring and personnel assignments must be charted during each briefing period to ensure that all team members fully understand their positions: whom they direct and whom they report to. A preprinted chart (legal size, 8½" × 14") showing sector boxes under each functional box needs to be developed. As sectors are established or disbanded, they should be added to or deleted from the chart. A bulletin-board-size chart (4' × 6'; use dry-erase material) should be posted in the internal management center. A disaster demands a very flexible and organic structure; sectors are frequently established and dismantled in response to unpredictable event dynamics.

Job descriptions are another organizational tool that helps ensure effective disaster management. All positions must be defined. The descriptions should be brief and concise. Employees should be assigned to functions and sectors based on their skill sets. For example, a maintenance director is a good choice for the position of logistics director. An individual may shift jobs during emergencies; for example, a marketing manager with previous military planning experience is the logical choice for planning director during an emergency. Everyone must understand his or her role in the crisis setting, especially if roles change from normal assignments.

How to Build Productive Teams

Building productive teams is critical to the success of any organization, especially in the service-oriented hospitality industry. In recent years, the introduction of TQM processes has significantly increased the number of teams in the hospitality industry. At the heart of TQM is process improvement, and associate participation is the heartbeat. **Productive teams** are built by giving associates the authority, responsibility, and encouragement to come together to work on guest-related improvements that will not only enhance the guest experience but also make the associates' jobs easier. Teams need leadership, which is either appointed

CORPORATE PROFILE

Six Flags

Six Flags is a world-renowned theme park company. It owns and operates 38 different parks spread out over North America, Latin America, and Europe. Locations include Mexico City, Belgium, France, Spain, Germany, and most major metropolitan areas in the United States. In fact, having a park in 40 of the 50 major metropolitan areas in the United States has earned Six Flags the title of world's largest regional theme park company. Annually, more than 50 million visitors entertain themselves at Six Flags theme parks worldwide. The company prides itself in claiming that 98 percent of the U.S. population is within an eight-hour drive to a Six Flags theme park.

Who is behind this huge success? The founder of the first theme park was Angus Wynne, a Texas oil baron with a vision. His vision was to create a family entertainment park that was fun as well as affordable and, most important, within a reachable distance from where people lived. Wynne transformed a simple amusement park into a theme park by adding innovative rides with theme presentations. His first park opened in Texas in 1961. The transformation proved to be a huge success with the public; crowds flocked to the newly opened theme park.

The park was named after the six different flags that flew over Texas at one time, representing the six different countries that marked Texas's past history. The theme park was divided into six different regions, each modeled after the country it represented. Visitors could marvel at Spanish haciendas or French bistros, all the while in the company of Southern belles and pirates.

Today, Six Flags has a licensing agreement with DC Comics and Warner Bros. This means that characters such as Batman, Superman, and Bugs Bunny and the gang can be found wandering around the parks and having their pictures taken with park visitors. With fantastic rides and show-stopping entertainment, the parks have become one of the first-choice amusement parks for entertainment-seeking families and individuals.

Funding for expansion of the company was drawn primarily from the profits made from the first successful parks opened, including the first one in Texas. In 1996 Six Flags went public for the first time, meaning it allowed the public to purchase its stock as opposed to hand-picked private investors. The shares were sold at $18 each, and their purchase totaled nearly $70 million. Only one year later the company had raised $200 million with its public offering. With these kinds of funds, Six Flags continued purchasing land or old amusement parks and turning them into Six Flags theme parks, rapidly expanding its reach. Currently Six Flags employs 42,000 people, representing a 10 percent year-on-year growth rate. The parks have become so successful and have such a high income that large corporations, including AOL, Kodak, Perrier, Pringles, and Univision, have signed major sponsorship deals with Six Flags.

by management or chosen by the team. As with any other endeavor, goals and objectives need to be set and the team given the resources it needs to accomplish those goals. It is amazing to see the enthusiasm that teams can generate as they work on improving the guest experience. Associates come up with great ideas that can save money and provide guests with better service. Team building happens when members interact to learn how each member thinks and works. Through close interaction, team members learn to develop increased trust and openness. When a team focuses on setting goals, determining who will plan on accomplishing what by when, and so on, the team should be on its way to becoming a high-achieving team.

Job Rotation

Job rotation is an excellent way to relieve the possible boredom and monotony that can be a disadvantage of work specialization because it gives associates a broader range of experiences. Once associates have mastered the jobs they were hired to do, boredom tends to set in. Job rotation creates interest and helps develop associates to take on additional responsibilities. The management training programs of some of the major hospitality corporations are good examples of job rotation; graduates spend a few months in several departments before selecting an area of specialization. Even then, front-line managers are likely to move through a few departments to build up their knowledge and experience. Job rotation does create some additional costs, mostly in the area of training and reduced productivity, because as associates move into new positions, they need time to become proficient in their new roles. A major benefit of job rotation is that associates become well rounded in the operation of the corporation, and many associates are promoted as a result of gaining the additional knowledge and experience.

Job Enlargement and Job Enrichment

Job enlargement increases the scope of the associates' work. Originally it was intended as a way of maintaining interest in the work; more recently, it has become an economic necessity. Today, hospitality management professionals have more work and responsibilities than ever before—that's why workplace stress has become an issue. However, no one in the hospitality industry can say that his or her job is uneventful. In our business no two days are alike, and for many that's one of the fascinations of the hospitality business, despite the increased workload. **Job enrichment** adds some planning and evaluating responsibilities to a position. It gives associates greater control over their work by allowing them to assume some tasks typically done by their supervisors.

Trends in Organizing

- Computerized scheduling programs save the organizer time and limit the error margin for being overstaffed or understaffed.

- The fact that recipes are just a click away on the Internet helps speed the organizational process tremendously.

- The new dynamic of multitasking has caused a drastic change in the organizational chart. For example, today, front-desk workers are responsible for much more than just checking guests in and out. Through multitasking, they simultaneously act as phone operators, customer service agents, tour guides, and occasionally concierges.

- A new trend following the September 11, 2001, tragedy is to decentralize organizations.

- Reduced occupancies at most hotels have led to a reduction in staff and managerial positions. This in turn has led to more decentralized organizations with fewer levels of management.

CASE STUDY

The Organization of Outback Steakhouse

Chris Sullivan, Bob Basham, Trudy Cooper, and Tim Gannon—cofounders of the Outback Steakhouse concept—began their restaurant careers as a busboy, dishwasher, server, and chef's assistant, respectively. So how did they manage to build one of the all-time most successful restaurant concepts? Their careers may have had humble beginnings, but they had the money to excel. Chris and Bob met at Bennigan's (part of Steak and Ale). They honed their management skills under the mentorship of industry legend Norman Brinker, who later financed Chris and Bob's franchised chain of Chili's restaurants in Georgia and Florida. They later sold the Chili's restaurants back to Brinker for $3 million. This seed money allowed them to develop a restaurant concept they had been toying with.

The concept was for a casual themed steakhouse, and because the partners did not like a western theme (it had already been done by others), they opted for an Australian theme because, at the time, there was a lot of hype about Australia. Australia had just won the America's Cup (a major sailboat race held every four years), and the movie *"Crocodile" Dundee* was popular. As with all new restaurant concepts, they searched for a suitable name. Beth Basham came up with the idea of Outback for the name of the steakhouse—she wrote it on a mirror in lipstick. The Outback themed concept was just what the partners wanted—a casual, fun, family atmosphere and the highest-quality food, which is reflected in Outback's 40 percent food cost (the industry norm for steakhouses is about 36 percent). Chris and Bob asked Tim Gannon, who at the time hardly had enough money to buy the gas to drive to Tampa, to join them. Organizationally, each of the partners "brought something to the table." Chris was the visionary, Bob the operations person, Tim the chef, and Trudy the trainer. Later they realized they needed a numbers guy, and in 1990 Bob Merritt became chief financial officer (CFO).

Instead of fancy marketing research, the partners did lots of talking and observation on what people were eating—remember, this was a time when eating red meat was almost taboo. The partners figured that people were not eating as much red meat at home, but when they dined out they were ready for a good steak.

Initially, the partners thought of setting up one restaurant and then a few more, which would allow them to spend more time on the golf course and with their families. So the success of Outback surprised the partners as well as the Wall Street pundits. The organization grew quickly, and by the mid-1990s more than 200 stores were open; they also signed a joint venture partnership with Carrabba's Italian Grill, giving them access to the high-end Italian restaurant segment.

Same-store sales increased year after year, and the partners looked forward to 500 or even 600 units. Financial analysts were amazed at the rise in Outback's stock. So, to what can we attribute Outback's success? It's a well-defined and popular concept, has a great organizational mantra of "No Rules—Just Right," and serves the best-quality food and service in a casually themed Australian outback–decor restaurant. The typical Outback is a little more than 6,000 square feet, with about 35 tables seating about 160 guests and a bar area that has 8 tables and 32 seats. Outback's target market is "A" demographics and a "B" location, which is often a strip mall. Another aspect of Outback's organization is that servers handle only three tables at a time; this increases their guest contact time and allows for more attention to be paid to each table. They also offer an Australian-themed menu with a higher flavor profile than comparable steakhouses. The design of the kitchen takes up about 45 percent of the restaurant's floor space—12 percent more than other similar restaurants. This extra space represents a potential loss of revenue, but that is the way Outback wanted it done because they realized the kitchen does not run well when it's being "slammed" on a Friday or Saturday night.

There is no organization chart at Outback Steakhouse; everyone at the unpretentious corporate headquarters in Tampa is there to serve the restaurants. There is no corporate human resources department, but applicants are interviewed by two managers and must pass a psychological profile test that gives an indication of the applicant's personality. Outback provides ownership opportunities at three levels in the organization: individual restaurant level, multistore joint venture and franchises, and an employee stock ownership plan. Because there is no middle management, franchisees report directly to the president. Outback's founders had fun setting up the concept and want everyone to have fun too—they sometimes drop in on a store and ask employees if they are having fun. Not only are they doing that—they are laughing all the way to the bank!

Discussion Questions

1. From an organizational perspective, can Outback continue to grow with so little organizational structure?
2. What kind of organizational structure would you suggest for Outback Steakhouse?

Summary

1. The purpose of organizing is to get jobs done efficiently and effectively.
2. Goals are accomplished by organizing the work to be done into specific jobs and departments; assigning tasks and responsibilities associated with individual jobs; coordinating diverse organizational tasks; clustering jobs into units; establishing relationships among individuals, groups, and departments; establishing formal lines of authority; and allocating and deploying organizational resources.
3. Organizational structure is the total framework through which job tasks are divided, grouped, and coordinated.
4. Organizational structure is divided into work specialization, departmentalization, authority and responsibility, chain of command, delegation, increasing span of control and empowerment, and centralization and decentralization.
5. Organizational designs and decisions consist of mechanistic and organic organizations, coordination, contingency factors, common organizational design, contemporary organizational design, IBUs, and the boundaryless organization.
6. Teams are task-oriented work groups; they can either be formally appointed or evolve informally.

Key Words and Concepts

authority	function	productive teams
boundaryless organization	guest	project structure
centralization	independent business unit (IBU)	responsibility
chain of command	job enlargement	self-managed teams
comping	job enrichment	team
contingency factors	job rotation	team player
coordination of activities	organizational structure	territory
decentralization	organization chart	work specialization
departmentalization	organizing	work team structure
empowerment	product	

Review Questions

1. Would you rather work in a mechanistic or an organic organization? Why?
2. Looking to the future, which is the best organization structure for a theme park? A 50-room resort? A midpriced Italian restaurant? An economy 100-room hotel? A 3,000-room casino hotel?
3. Describe a team-based structure.
4. Compare and contrast a matrix structure and a project structure.
5. When might an organization design its structure around independent business units?

Internet Exercise

Organization: Your choice of company
Web site: The company's URL
Summary: Pick a major corporation, such as one mentioned in the text, and go to its web site to look for answers to the following questions.
    (a) What different types of product offerings does the company have?

(b) In how many countries or regions is it represented?
(c) What kind of divisions does it have?
(d) Have different types of guest groups been identified?

Apply Your Knowledge

1. Mini Project: This project is based on a real-life experience of the executive chef at the Sheraton Hotel in San Diego. The project is to organize an off-site event, which is an event that is planned and organized by the Sheraton staff but does not take place at the hotel itself.

2. The Sheraton typically caters the annual San Diego Zoo fund-raiser every year. The attendance for this event is roughly 1,000 people. The caterers organize and cater a reception followed by dinner. Your challenge is to plan this off-site event using the planning techniques and organizational skills you have learned so far.

Endnotes

1. www.starbucks.com/aboutus/company_factsheet.pdf
2. www.rimag.com/blog-starters/2008-03-28.asp.
3. Ibid.
4. "An Alternate Plan for Starbuck's Renewal" at:www. rimeg.com/blog/910000491/post/1500025350.html?
5. Ibid.
6. Robert N. Lussier, *Management Fundamentals*. Cincinnati, OH: South-Western, 2003, p. 198.
7. See, for example, G. G. Dess, A. M. A. Rasheed, K. J. McLaughlin, & R. L. Priem, "The New Corporate Architecture," *Academy of Management Executive*, August 1995, pp. 7-20.

CHAPTER 17

Communication and Decision Making

OBJECTIVES

After reading and studying this chapter, you should be able to:

- Define communication.

- List barriers to effective interpersonal communication and how to overcome them.

- Differentiate between formal and informal communication.

- Explain communication flows and networks.

- Outline the eight steps in the decision-making process.

- Know the difference between rational, bounded rational, and intuitive decisions.

- Identify situations in which a programmed decision is a better solution than a nonprogrammed decision.

- Differentiate the decision conditions of certainty, risk, and uncertainty.

Managerial Communication

Communication is the oil that lubricates all of the other management functions of forecasting, planning, organizing, motivating, and controlling. Additionally, because managers spend a high percentage of their time communicating, the communication function becomes doubly important. Managers interact with others throughout the day by the following means:

- Personal face-to-face meetings
- Telephone
- Mail/fax
- Memos, reports, log books, and other internal/external written communication
- E-mail, web sites

The simplest method of communication involves a sender, a message, and a receiver. However, merely sending a message does not ensure that the message will be received and understood correctly. Several factors can lead to distortion of the message, such as noise interference, poor listening skills, and inappropriate tuning. The middle of a busy lunch service is not the right time to be asking the chef a question about the company's policy on sick-pay benefits. In this chapter we explore these various barriers to effective communication and the importance of good communication to a manager.

What Is Communication?

Communication is the exchange of information and meaning. The essence of communication is the exchange of information. Another important aspect of communication is understanding the meaning. The sole transfer of information is not enough to ensure successful communication; the actual meaning must be understood as well. An employee receiving information from a manager in Spanish will find that information of little use if the employee does not understand Spanish. Perfect communication results when a sender communicates a thought or idea and the receiver perceives it exactly as envisioned by the sender. Just because the receiver does not agree with the message does not mean that the communication process has failed. You can disagree with something even though you fully understand it.

Managerial communication includes two different types: **Interpersonal communication** occurs between two or more individuals, and **organizational communication** includes all the different forms, networks, and systems of communication that occur among individuals, groups, or departments within an organization.

Interpersonal Communication Process

Communication between two or more people is described as interpersonal communication.[1] The **interpersonal communication process** is made up of seven elements: the sender, encoding, the message, the channel, the receiver, decoding, and feedback (Figure 17–1). Before communication can take place, a *message* must exist and be conveyed. This message is sent from the sender and passed to the receiver. The message will travel in converted form because it has to be *encoded* and then passed by way of a medium, a *channel*, from the sender to the receiver. It is then retranslated by means of *decoding*. When successful communication has taken place, the receiver gives *feedback* to the sender indicating that he or she has correctly understood the message being conveyed.

Noise is often a part of the interpersonal communication process. Noise can consist of various activities going on in the background, such as sounds of machinery or coworkers, or it can be as simple as static in the telephone line or illegible print. Therefore, noise is considered a somewhat constant disturbance in the communications process and the cause of distortions of the message. Each element in the process can be influenced and distorted by disturbances. The sender conveys a message by encoding it. During this process, major things could go wrong and distort the message. The sender can have too little or too much knowledge. He or she can't communicate what he or she does not know.

However, if the proper explanations aren't given, the receiver could falsely interpret the message. Too much knowledge may cause the message not to be understood at all. Preexisting attitudes and the cultural system of the sender can influence the encoding of the message as well. Attitudes and beliefs about subject matters will leave their traces in the message and may be picked up by the receiver.

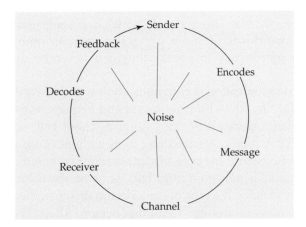

Figure 17–1 • Interpersonal Communication Process. (Derived from Stephen P. Robbins and Mary Coulter, *Management*, 8th ed. Upper Saddle River, NJ: Prentice Hall, 2005, p. 258.)

The message itself, such as a written document, an oral speech, or gestures and facial expressions, can be influenced by disturbances. Noise will influence listening skills during an oral speech. Faulty equipment can lead to disruption of the message if it is conveyed through e-mail or fax. Symbols such as pictures, words, and numbers that are selected by the sender to convey his or her message can be influenced by noise.

The channel used to convey the message is important to the whole communications process. If you choose to use speech to communicate with a person who has a hearing impairment, naturally the message will not be understood as the sender intended it to be. Whether the sender chooses to use an office memorandum, a phone call, e-mail, gestures, or pictures to convey the message will play a large role in how accurately the receiver will understand it. Using two channels can sometimes eliminate distortion—for example, oral speech followed by a written summary.

The receiver is limited by the same factors as the sender. If he or she has too little knowledge of the subject, distortions will take place. Likewise, if he or she has too much knowledge, too much can be read into a simple message. The preexisting attitudes and beliefs of the individual also play a role in how distorted the message will be after the decoding has taken place.

Communicating Interpersonally

Managers can communicate in various ways. Examples include face-to-face, telephone, e-mail, fax, group discussions and meetings, memos, formal presentations, bulletin boards, mail, employee publications, and teleconferencing. Communication experts generally agree that when two people are engaged in a face-to-face conversation, only a small fraction of the total message they share is contained in the words they use. A large portion of the message is contained in vocal elements such as tone of voice, accent, speed, volume, and inflection. The largest part of the message—and arguably the most important—is conveyed by a combination of gestures, postures, facial expressions, and clothing. Although people may listen closely to what is said, nonverbal behavior may constitute two-thirds or more of total communication. And although people have an option not to speak, they can never be uncommunicative nonverbally.[2]

Nonverbal communication is communication without words. Taking examples from everyday life shows how important and frequent nonverbal communication is. Ambulance sirens, a honking horn, a school bell, or the sound of a ringing phone all communicate something to us without using any words. Similarly, gestures, actions, and the type of clothes worn communicate messages to us. A person wearing a police uniform tells us he or she belongs to the police force. In the same manner, the type of car a person drives or the size of his or her house conveys to others a message about that person. All of these forms of communication are nonverbal.

Body language consists of facial expressions, gestures, and any other ways of communicating a message with your body. For example, when you smile or laugh, you convey a message of joy or friendliness. In the same manner, rolling your eyes indicates disbelief or even annoyance. Emotions are typically conveyed purely by body language.

Verbal intonation is using your voice to emphasize certain parts of a phrase or certain words. For example, consider the phrase, "What are you doing?" An abrasive, loud intonation of the voice will indicate that the person is upset, angry, and even defensive. However, if the same sentence is said in a calm, soft voice, it will be perceived as genuine interest or concern or a friendly inquiry. Verbal intonation is almost more important than the words themselves. A common saying is that it is not what you say but *how* you say it. Managers should keep this very important fact in mind.

Facial expressions, a part of body language, convey different meanings

▶ Check Your Knowledge

1. What is the difference between interpersonal and organizational communication?
2. What are three ways of communicating interpersonally?
3. Describe the interpersonal communication process.

Barriers to Effective Interpersonal Communication

Many elements can influence interpersonal communication.[3] The following are some of the major barriers.

Perception

Everybody perceives things differently. This is due to different backgrounds, upbringing, personal experiences, and major influences in their lives. No two people are alike, and neither is their perception. Whereas one person may be optimistic and perceive a message in a positive light, another may be a pessimist and see only negative aspects of the message. Unwanted news is easily screened out and forgotten whereas things we want to hear are remembered for a longer period of time.

Semantics

The actual meaning of words, or **semantics,** is the cause of many failed communication efforts. The literal meaning of words and the actual meaning can be two different things, but they can be expressed in the same way. For instance, if a restaurant manager tells a server to make the guests feel comfortable, she doesn't necessarily mean that the server will bring pillows, blankets, or even beds into the dining area. The manager may have meant to make the customers feel comfortable in a nonphysical way, by attending to them, making sure they are satisfied with their order, and making sure their water glasses are refilled promptly. Using jargon, specialized terminology, or technical language that may be used widely within an organization may be ineffective if used with new employees or people who are not familiar with it.

Nonverbal Communication

Nonverbal communication—communication through body language—is a typical means of communication. However, it can also be considered a barrier to effective communication. The weight of decoding a message lies with the nonverbal communication rather than on the actual encoded message. For example, if a supervisor comes to work in the morning disgruntled about morning traffic, his or her subordinates may misinterpret the angry facial expression as the supervisor being dissatisfied with their work, although he or she never actually said so. The next time you have a conversation with someone, be aware of your own nonverbal communication: what you are expressing with gestures and facial expressions.

Misinterpretations of nonverbal communication are especially dominant in cross-cultural communication. Gestures and expressions mean different things in different cultures. For example, in most Asian and African countries, it is considered impolite to make direct eye contact with the person you are speaking to, whereas it is considered courteous to look the speaker in the eye in most Western cultures.

Ambiguity

Ambiguity, vagueness, or uncertainty can occur in a message being conveyed. A message may be ambiguous, meaning the person receiving the message is uncertain about the actual meaning. If a manager asks an employee to come to her office as soon as possible, it could mean immediately or next week when the employee has some free time. When the words of a message are clear, but the intentions of the sender aren't, ambiguity occurs. The employee may be unclear as to why the manager wants to see him in the office now. Ambiguity may also be described as the receiver's uncertainty about the consequences of the message. The employee may think or ask, "What will happen if I don't go to her office immediately?"

Nonverbal Communication as a Barrier to Effective Communication

Defensiveness

When people feel that they are being verbally attacked or criticized, they tend to react defensively. The reaction could be making sarcastic remarks, being overly judgmental, or simply screening out the unpleasant parts of the conversation. This often happens when employees refuse to realize personal flaws. Using defense mechanisms helps them screen out the negative image of themselves, so they can keep their self-esteem. However, acting defensively is a barrier to effective communication.

Overcoming Barriers to Effective Interpersonal Communication

Because barriers to effective interpersonal communication do exist, there are ways to improve on the communication to largely overcome them. An essential part of a manager's job is to be an effective communicator. The following suggestions should help make interpersonal communication more effective.

Use Feedback

Right off the bat, offering feedback,[4] the last step in the communication process, will eliminate misunderstandings and inaccuracies regarding the message being conveyed. The feedback can be verbal or nonverbal. After the receiver has decoded the message, the sender should make sure the message has been understood. It can be as simple as asking the employee, "Did you understand what I said?" The ideal response to this question will be more than a yes or no answer. The best form of verbal feedback is a quick restatement and summary of the message that has been conveyed: "You said you switched my shift tomorrow to the night shift." This way the sender can be sure that the message has been correctly understood.

The nonverbal form of feedback consists of various reactions to a message. First, the sender can watch for nonverbal cues as to whether the message has been understood. Eye contact, facial expression, scratching the head, or shrugging the shoulders all can indicate how accurately the message has been received and understood. Furthermore, the actions following the message can be used as feedback. A manager who is explaining a new serving procedure to the staff will know how accurately the message has been understood by observing the staff to see whether they follow the new procedure. If some servers do not follow the new procedure, the manager will have to clarify or restate the message.

Active Listening

There is a difference between hearing and actually listening.[5] You may hear what your manager is saying, but did you *really* listen? Hearing is passive, and listening is a deliberate act of understanding and responding to the words being heard. The first step to **active listening** is listening for the total meaning. For example, if a manager tells an employee that the room occupancy is down this quarter, instead of responding, "Don't worry, it'll be fine," the employee can recognize that a problem exists. The second step is to reflect the feelings. This is an important step for the sender of the message because it helps him or her communicate the emotional part of the message. The receiver would reflect it by saying something like, "This situation must be stressful for you." The last step is to note all nonverbal cues and respond to them. These cues might include hand gestures or facial expressions.

Avoid Triggering Defensiveness

Defensiveness is one of the main barriers to effective communication. By avoiding the tendency to criticize, argue, or give advice, senders can avoid triggering defensive behavior. People don't like being criticized because it diminishes their self-image. Phrases that convey blame or finger-pointing are typically useless.

The receiver will respond by arguing or storming off, and the communication has largely failed. A solution to this is to allow a cooling-off period so that both parties can regain their composure. Generally, managers should avoid overly negative statements.

Interpersonal Dynamics

Leaders will get the best results with and through their associates if they adopt these simple suggestions: You must have a great attitude toward your associates, meaning you accept them as colleagues and treat them fairly, with respect; establish a climate of trust; and include your associates in as much decision making as possible. Be sensitive to cultural differences and learn more about the cultures of your associates. Learn the best ways to communicate with your associates. Make sure that your associates know what is expected of them. Actively listen to associates. Involve your associates. Train associates and develop them so they can reach their full potential. Above all, have fun!

▶ Check Your Knowledge

1. Define semantics.
2. Explain ambiguity as it relates to communication barriers.
3. What are three ways of overcoming communication barriers?

Organizational Communication

Organizational communication is necessary in managerial communication. The fundamentals include formal communication versus informal communication, communication flow patterns, and formal and informal communication networks.

Formal and Informal Communication

The two major forms of organizational communication are formal and informal communication. Formal communication is used by managers to communicate job requirements to their employees. It follows the official chain of command. **Formal communication** occurs when, for instance, a manager tells an employee his or her schedule for the following week. The subject matter is always job related and seen as essential to the employment.

Informal communication does not follow a company's chain of command or structural hierarchy. The subject matter may be job related but may not be essential to performing job duties. Examples of informal communication are employees talking at the water fountain, lunchroom, or company gatherings. In every organization employees form relationships with each other, whether as acquaintances or as friends. Employees use informal communication to satisfy their need for social interaction, and it can also improve an organization's performance by fostering better employee relationships and providing a faster, more efficient communication channel.[6] The "grapevine" is a form of informal communication.

Communication Flows and Networks

Communication flows in various directions: upward, downward, laterally, diagonally, and so on, as we will see next.

Upward Communication

Upward communication takes place when managers or superiors rely on their subordinates for receiving information. It flows upward from employees to managers. This type of communication is important to managers because it helps them determine the satisfaction level of their employees and how they feel about their jobs, the organization in general, or problems with coworkers or even with the manager. Some managers even encourage their subordinates to give them ideas about how to make improvements in the organization. Some examples of upward communication include manager performance reports, employee surveys, suggestion boxes, and informal group sessions with other coworkers.

Downward Communication

Communication flowing down from supervisor to employee is considered **downward communication.** Managers use this type of communication for various purposes: to inform employees of company policies, procedures, employee evaluations, or job descriptions and to discuss the future of the employee. Downward communication is often used to inform, direct, coordinate, and evaluate employees.

Lateral Communication

Communication that takes place between the employees of a company who are on the same hierarchical level in the organization is called *lateral communication*. This type of communication is used by employees to discuss their environment and the organization in general. Lateral communication is also used by cross-functional teams to facilitate communication. The important thing to remember is to always let the supervisor know about decisions made through lateral communication.

Diagonal Communication

Communication that takes place between employees who are on different hierarchical levels and in different departments of the organization is called *diagonal communication.* An example of this type of communication is that of a chef communicating with a front-desk receptionist. The two employees are not on the same level, nor are they in the same department of a hotel. Through e-mail, almost every employee is able to communicate efficiently with any other employee

Figure 17–2 • Three Organizational Communication Networks.
(Derived from Stephen P. Robbins and Mary Coulter, *Management*,
7th ed. Upper Saddle River, NJ: Prentice Hall, 2002, p. 295.)

in the same organization. However, as with lateral communication, the employees must make a point to update their managers on decisions made during this type of communication.

Two of the forms of communication flow, vertical and lateral, can be combined in various forms. These new forms are called **communication networks**. The most common are chain, wheel, and all-channel (Figure 17–2), as well as the grapevine.[7]

Chain, Wheel, and All-Channel Communication Networks

Communication in a chain network flows according to the existing chain of command of an organization. This includes downward as well as upward communication flow. This type of network is highly accurate; no information can be lost, and the path the message travels is precise. On the downside, the chain network is only moderately fast and moderately popular with employees.

The wheel network is a network in which communication flows between a strong leader and each individual in a group or team. In this network the coworkers do not need to communicate with each other; they communicate solely with their leader. The advantage to this type of communication is that it is relatively fast in speed and accuracy. However, this type of communication is usually not very popular with employees.

The all-channel communication network is differentiated from others by its freely flowing communication between all members of a group or team. This means that the leader communicates with employees, and employees all communicate with each other. This type of network is very popular with employees, and messages travel very fast. However, the accuracy of the message is not always at 100 percent.

One thing to remember is that every unique situation will require a different communication network. No one network is perfect for every situation.

The Grapevine

The grapevine may be the most popular and important communication network in an organization. One survey reported that 75 percent of employees hear about matters first through rumors on the grapevine.[8] The grapevine is an informal organizational communication network and an important source of communication for the managers of an organization. Through the local informal grapevine, issues that employees consider a reason for stress and anxiety are made known. This network acts as a very effective feedback mechanism and as a filter that sorts out only the issues that employees find important. The negative aspect of this communication network is the occasional rumor that travels through it. This is pretty much unavoidable; however, successful managers can eliminate the negative impact of rumors. This can be done by speaking openly and honestly with employees about any negative feelings or important decisions that are made.

▶ Check Your Knowledge

1. Define informal communication.
2. What is the difference between lateral and diagonal communication?
3. Elaborate on the wheel communication network.

The Decision-Making Process

All individuals in organizations, small or large, are faced with the task of decision making. This can involve decisions as simple as where to have lunch or as complex as the best place to locate a new franchise. A comprehensive, detailed **decision-making process** is used to make a complex decision. However, the same model can also be used for simple decisions.

The decision-making process consists of eight major steps (Figure 17–3):

1. Identification and definition of problem
2. Identification of decision criteria

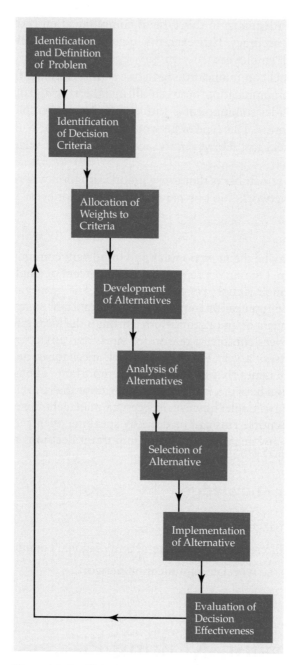

Figure 17–3 • Eight-Step Decision-Making Process.

3. Allocation of weights to criteria
4. Development of alternatives
5. Analysis of alternatives
6. Selection of alternative
7. Implementation of alternative
8. Evaluation of decision effectiveness

This model can be used for most decisions, from simple ones such as what to buy for dinner to complex corporate decisions about new marketing strategies. So let's take a closer look at each step of the decision-making process.

Step 1: Identification and Definition of Problem

Let's say that we are experiencing a discrepancy between current and desired results. In this case, the decision-making process begins with identifying and defining the problem(s). It is not always easy to identify the problem because other issues may muddy the waters. In a hotel setting, problem situations can be identified with respect to, say, guest check-in. In some of the larger city-center, convention-oriented hotels, long lines of guests are frequently waiting to check into the hotel. Defining this problem is best done by writing a problem statement: "The problem is that it takes too long for guests to register." Once the problem has been accurately stated, it becomes easier to move to the next step in the decision-making process.

Another example comes to us from Herb Kelleher, former president of Southwest Airlines, when he decided to remove the closets at the front of Southwest planes. This was in response to a problem: it took too long to turn around the planes. To be competitive and successful, it is necessary to reduce the turnaround time in order to squeeze more flights into each day. The situation that caused or contributed to the turnaround problem was that the first people on the plane typically went to the closets first and then grabbed the nearest seats. On landing, the departing passengers were held up while the people in the front rows rummaged through the closets for their bags. The airline now turns around about 85 percent of its flights in 20 minutes or less and is one of the most profitable airlines.

Step 2: Identification of Decision Criteria

Once the problem has been identified and defined, we need to determine the criteria relevant to the decision. Suppose the problem is that we are hungry; then the decision criteria might be the following:

1. What type of food would we prefer?
2. How much time do we have to eat?
3. How much do we want to spend?
4. How convenient is parking?
5. What is the restaurant's reputation?
6. How is the food quality?
7. How is the service?
8. How is the atmosphere?

These criteria must have been developed by a group that wants to eat out at a restaurant. Criteria that are not identified are usually treated as unimportant.

INTRODUCING PATRICIA TAM

Vice President of Standards and Corporate Relations, Halekulani Corp., Waikiki, Hawaii

Patricia Tam is a role model to everyone who wants to pursue a career in the hospitality industry. It is not hard to see why. Patricia is a woman of great ambition and ability. She has proved herself capable of succeeding at almost anything she attempts to do.[1] Patricia is of Chinese heritage and was brought up in Hawaii. During her childhood years, her ambition was to become an English teacher. Joining the hospitality industry never entered her mind. In fact, she didn't stay in a hotel until she was a young adult: "I was going along with some friends to the mainland for one of the first times I'd been off the island."

When she finished college at age 23, she became proprietor of a bakery. She was then recruited by Amfac Corp. to open a bakeshop at its Royal Lahaina Hotel on Maui in 1975. She says, "When I opened the bakeshop there, I liked the whole aura of resort life, not just because of the guests' experience, but because of the beach and the large infrastructure." She enrolled in the resort's management training program, which would be the start of a long and successful career journey in the lodging industry. Patricia started working at Halekulani in 1983. Halekulani was first constructed in 1907 as a beachfront home accompanied by five bungalows. In 1983, it reopened as a 466-room low-rise complex. It is Waikiki's premier five-diamond resort.

When Patricia became general manager of Halekulani, the situation was less than desirable. She was promoted in the post–Gulf War period, and the once-glorious Pacific destinations had stagnated. Because most of Hawaii's visitors were Asian, Japan's ongoing recession added to the difficult times. In the 1960s, Hawaii experienced its tourist boom years. But during the early 1990s, Hawaii had to fight for every bit of the global destination market it could capture. Patricia says, "We're sitting in an arena right now where the first one to the finish line is the winner. And I think that it's more exciting to be working in this business now than it would have been in the boom years, when all you had to worry about was how many people you couldn't accommodate tonight."

Patricia realizes that the hotel business can make either a profit or a loss. "I think for a lot of us who get into the business, we see the fun part of it: the bartending, the wait help, the restaurant excitement, the chance to meet really fabulous people from around the world. We see one side of the vision of what luxury properties are all about," she explains. "But there's the other side of it, which is that it is a business, and what do businesses do? They've got to make money."

Patricia believes that outstanding guest services make a good hotel and maintain guest loyalty. She pays careful attention to detail and perfection and lets nothing pass her by. Even guest complaints are discussed one by one. She says, "You can get so worked up about the attention to detail that unless you're communicating with staff, it can be pretty challenging for them in terms of how to keep this hotel perfect. Not everybody knows how. But everybody tries to keep it that way." Maintaining her great reputation as a general manager as well as the hotel's reputation as a superior destination is reflected by her drive for perfection. John Sharpe, president of the Toronto-based Four Seasons hotel, nominated Patricia to be hotelier of the year. Halekulani, meaning "house benefiting heaven," was voted best hotel in the world by *Gourmet* magazine. It has held its AAA five-diamond rating for years. It was a finalist for Condé Nast Traveler's Reader's Choice Best Tropical Resorts award and ranked in the top three hotels in the country in Zagat's U.S. hotel, resort, and spa survey. Its well-known restaurant, La Mer, is Hawaii's only AAA-rated five-diamond restaurant, and it has been known as such for years.

Patricia served as a hotel assistant manager, rooms division director, and acting general manager, and also as general manager of Halekulani's adjacent sister property, the four-diamond Waikiki Parc hotel. In 1993, she became the general manager of Halekulani. Through it all, she always wanted more. She says, "I could work the operations in a very good management way, but I never had to be the person responsible for the final decision making on a lot of things. The challenge, the intimidation of that process, coming back over as the general manager, was quite overwhelming to me. But that was also my proudest moment because that's when I realized that I really had to buckle down." The readers of *Hotels* magazine have named Patricia Hotelier of the World.

As for her personality, Patricia is a genuine person who doesn't credit only herself. She doesn't forget that her success depends on an ongoing and mutually beneficial relationship between Halekulani's owner, Halekulani Corp., and herself. She says, " I always look at it as a kind of management proposition where you can always learn every day." She adds, "Every day you can learn something new, not only about how to maintain a luxury property, but how to develop it and take it to the next level, because that's what it's all about."

[1]This profile draws on Tony De la Cruz, "Independent Hotelier of the World, Patricia Tam, Reaching for Resort Perfection," *Hotels* (November 1999): 64; and www.bizjournals.com/pacific/stories2004/08/02/daily56htm.

Courtesy Patricia Tam

Step 3: Allocation of Weights to Criteria

To decision makers, decision criteria all have different levels of importance. For instance, is the expected cost of the meal more important than the atmosphere? If so, a higher weight should be attached to that criterion.

One method used to weigh the criteria is to give the most important criterion a weight of 10 and then score the others according to their relative importance. In the meal example, the cost of the meal may receive a weight of 10, whereas the atmosphere may be awarded a weight of 6. Figure 17–4 lists a sample of criteria and weights for restaurant selection.

Step 4: Development of Alternatives

In developing alternatives, decision makers list the viable alternatives that could resolve the problem. No attempt is made to evaluate these alternatives—only to list them. Using the restaurant scenario, the alternatives are shown in Figure 17–5.

How much do we want to spend?	10
What type of food would we prefer?	8
How much time do we have?	6
How is the food quality?	9
How is the atmosphere?	6
How is the service?	7
How convenient is parking?	6
What is the restaurant's reputation?	6
How far do we want to go to a restaurant?	7

Figure 17–4 • Criteria and Weights in Restaurant Selection.

KFC

Taco Bell

Pizza Hut

McDonald's

Applebee's

The Olive Garden

Wendy's

Figure 17–5 • Restaurant Alternatives.

Step 5: Analysis of Alternatives

The alternatives are analyzed using the criteria and weights established in Steps 2 and 3. Figure 17–6 shows the values placed on each of the alternatives by the group. (It does not show the weighted values.) The weighted values of the group's decision about which restaurant to go to are shown in Figure 17–7.

	KFC	Taco Bell	Pizza Hut	McDonald's	Applebee's	Olive Garden	Wendy's
Price	9	10	10	10	7	7	9
Type of food	7	8	9	8	8	9	9
How much time	9	9	7	10	7	6	10
Quality of food	7	7	8	7	8	8	8
Atmosphere	7	7	8	7	9	9	7
Service	6	6	7	7	8	9	7
Convenient parking	10	10	10	9	10	10	10
Restaurant reputation	8	8	8	7	8	9	8
How far away	8	8	8	10	7	7	8
Total	71	73	75	76	72	74	75

Figure 17–6 • Analysis of Alternatives.

	KFC	Taco Bell	Pizza Hut	McDonald's	Applebee's	Olive Garden	Wendy's
Price	90	100	100	100	70	70	90
Type of food	56	64	72	64	64	72	72
How much time	54	54	42	60	42	36	60
Quality of food	63	63	72	63	72	72	72
Atmosphere	42	42	48	42	54	54	42
Service	42	42	49	49	56	63	49
Convenient parking	60	60	60	56	60	60	60
Restaurant reputation	48	48	48	42	48	54	48
How far away	56	56	56	70	49	49	56
Total	511	529	547	546	515	530	549

Figure 17–7 • Weighted Values Analysis.

Once the weighted values are totaled, we can see that Pizza Hut and Wendy's are the restaurants with the highest scores. Notice how these are not the restaurants with the highest scores before the weighted values were included.

Step 6: Selection of Alternative

The sixth step is to select the best alternative. Once the weighted scores for each alternative have been totaled, it will become obvious which is the best alternative.

Step 7: Implementation of Alternative

We next need to ensure that the alternative is implemented so that the decision is put into action. Sometimes good decisions fail because they are not put into action.

Step 8: Evaluation of Decision Effectiveness

The final step in the decision loop is to evaluate the effectiveness of the decision. As a result of the decision, did we achieve the goals we set? If the decision was not effective, then we must find out why the desired results were not attained. This would mean going back to Step 1. If the decision was effective, then no action, other than recording the outcome, needs to be taken.

How Managers Make Decisions

Managers are the main decision makers in any organization. Although all employees face daily decisions, the choices a manager makes impact the future of the organization. Decision making is an integral part of all four primary managerial functions: planning, organizing, leading, and controlling.

Making Decisions: Rationality, Bounded Rationality, and Intuition

The first criterion for making a decision is that it must be rational. Several assumptions are made to define what a rational decision really is. First, the decision itself would have to maximize value and be consistent within natural constraining limits. This means that the choice made must maximize the organization's profitability. Tying in with this is the natural assumption that the manager making the decision is pursuing the organization's values and profitability, not his or her own interest.

One assumption of **rationality** as it relates to the decision maker is that he or she is fully objective and logical. When making the decision, a clearly stated goal must always be kept in mind. This goes hand in hand with starting with a problem statement.

Bounded rationality means that managers make decisions based on the decision-making process that is bounded, or limited, by an individual's ability to gain information and make decisions. Managers know that their decision-making skills are based on their own competency, intelligence, and, last but not least, their rationality. They are also expected to follow the decision-making process model.

FOCUS ON COMMUNICATING DURING DISASTERS

Hank Christen, *George Washington University*
Paul Maniscalco, *Unconventional Concepts, Inc.*

Communication during a disaster requires complex interactions. If communications are not effective, myriad problems for the organization result, including irreparable harm to the organization's reputation, significant fiscal harm, and drastically reduced organizational business opportunities after the event.

Many hospitality industry managers fail to grasp the importance of preventing significant damage to their organization's reputation and future business prospects that is due to disasters. The situation is further complicated by a lack of familiarity with successful crisis communication techniques. The manager must confront events that are emergent and fluid, make quick and effective decisions, and communicate effectively and expeditiously, especially to the media.

Fundamental components of effective disaster communication are (1) defining the disaster/crisis, (2) assembing a communication team, (3) designating and training a spokesperson, and (4) releasing a statement.

1. *Define the disaster/crisis.* A disaster or crisis is any situation that threatens the health, safety, integrity, or reputation of the organization and its employees or patrons. Usually it originates as an unusual event or emergency, such as an accident, crime, fire, or flood; it can be a natural, technological, or human-made disaster. It also is a situation in which the media or the public feels that the organization did not react to a critical situation in a timely or appropriate manner.

2. *Assemble a communication team.* This team is responsible for writing the organizational communication response delivered during an incident. The team should be comprised of key individuals: the chief executive officer or top manager at the facility, the head of public relations, the operations manager, the director of safety and/or security, legal counsel, and the area manager involved in the crisis (an ad hoc assignment in emergent situations).

3. *Designate and train a spokesperson.* Every hospitality management team should have at least one person solely responsible for speaking to the media to represent the organization during a crisis. The organization must speak with a single voice. The speaker needs to be professional, reassuring, and factual and must have appropriate orientation and education on media relations.

4. *Release a statement.* After researching the events and confirming facts, an event reference sheet should be crafted. It should contain an incident summary, including confirmed particulars, for media release; it should be updated as events or responses change. Collaboration with legal counsel is also necessary to ensure compliance with privacy and organizational security.

Expeditious communication is also critical. Prompt delivery helps control event interpretation and present the organization's version of the incident. The first statement must identify who, what, where, and when (the four W's). Only confirmed facts received from competent authorities should be given, and the legality of a release should be confirmed before it is issued. The speaker should not speculate.

Providing the four W's and showing compassion and concern for those involved (public and employees) during initial media interactions is the basis of successful communication. Demonstration of genuine compassion and concern secures patron and employee confidence and loyalty. The spokesperson should take the initiative to share information and engender an open and inclusive environment; otherwise, alienated patrons or employees will not be supportive during the company's recovery.

However, certain aspects of this model are not realistic with respect to true-life managerial decisions, which are made with respect to bounded reality. This comes into play, for example, when decision makers cannot find all of the necessary information to analyze a problem and all of its possible alternatives. Therefore, they find themselves **satisficing,** a term used by management scholar and author Peter Drucker, or accepting a solution that is just "good enough" rather than maximizing. Consider this example: A chef for a major hotel chain has to prepare a banquet for 50 people. On the menu is half a chicken for every guest, which means that the chef needs 25 whole chickens for this banquet. He purchases the chickens at a market 25 miles away, where he has made the same purchase before for $60. Because he has made purchases from this market before, he knows the quality of the food they sell. What the chef does not know was that there is a free-range chicken farm only 10 miles away that would have sold him the 25 chickens for the same price. Instead of researching his alternatives, the chef satisficed himself with the first option that came to mind and settled on it, assuming it was probably not the best but "good enough." This behavior is rationally bounded because the best solution to be found was bounded by the chef's ability to research all alternatives instead of settling on the first acceptable one that came to mind.

Most decisions that managers make are not based on perfect rationality because of various factors, such as time constraints on researching all possible solutions or lack of resources to do the research. Therefore, decisions are typically based on bounded rationality. In other words, managers make decisions based on alternatives that are just satisfactory. At the same time, though, the decision maker will be strongly influenced by an organization's culture, power considerations, internal politics, and an **escalation of commitment**. An escalation of commitment happens when the commitment to a prior decision is increased despite evidence to the contrary. For example, consider the decline of the Planet Hollywood restaurant chain. At the launch of the chain, the team of marketing professionals deemed it economically sensible to set a high price on burgers and other food items. The restaurant set out to be a novelty establishment, although the target customers were middle-class citizens. Although it was evident that the decision to have high-priced products in a middle-class establishment was doomed for failure from the beginning, the decision makers stuck with it. The inevitable took place, and Planet Hollywood went belly up and was forced to close locations all around the world. The negative consumer reaction was predictable, but the decision makers escalated their commitment to the set prices even though it was a bad decision. Rather than search for new alternatives, they did not want to admit to making a bad decision and simply increased their commitment to the original one.[9]

Using rationality and common sense to influence decision making is very important—we must not forget the role of plain and simple human intuition. Intuition is used in everyday life, such as knowing not to grab a hot baking pan with your bare hands. It ranges all the way to the corporate level, where managers often use their own intuition when making corporate decisions. **Intuitive decision making** is a subconscious process of making decisions on the basis of experience and accumulated judgment. Five different identified aspects of intuition comply with the different types of decisions made. The first is a *values-* or *ethics-based decision*. Managers will recall the ethics system they were raised with and base their

A DAY IN THE LIFE OF DENISE SIMENSTAD

National Sales Manager, San Diego Convention Center, San Diego, California

Denise Simenstad is the national sales manager at the San Diego Convention Center. Her work here starts early and usually ends when the timing is good. What she does in those hours, though, is good customer service and remarkable work.

Denise comes into work at about 8 A.M. When she arrives at her office, she checks her voice mail, e-mail, and inbox messages. From then on, the day is not her own. She's working and attending to customer activity.

Her day-to-day activities keep her busy throughout the day. First, Denise responds to customer inquiries. These inquiries consist of prospective customers calling her to inquire about date and space availability at the convention center, the cost of renting meeting rooms or exhibit halls, and checking whether other, similar shows are booked in the facility.

She then usually leads a tour or, as it is better known, a "site inspection" of the facility to show customers the available physical space, including the lobby, exhibit halls, ballroom, meeting space, and outdoor space. Then she shows them the ancillary services that the convention center provides, such as the audiovisual facilities, food and beverage, telecommunications, security services, business services center, and so on. All of this makes for a complete tour.

Denise then prepares proposals (dates, rates, and space letter) for prospective customers. This ranges from a group of 100 people for one day to a trade show for 15,000 people to 250,000 guests for five days. She includes a package of information concerning the floor plans, rates, regulations, and other pertinent information.

After all of that, Denise answers customers' questions about the facilities available and capabilities. She fields questions on the sizes of rooms, capacities of the facilities, rates, distance between pillars on the exhibit floor, floor loads, dimensions of freight doors, number of committable hotel rooms in the downtown area, number of packages available, and more.

Then comes the duty of issuing and negotiating license agreements (contracts) with outlines, dates, space and rates, insurance requirements, indemnification issues, cancellation classes, guarantees, and so on.

To start wrapping up, Denise attends meetings with other sales managers in the office to discuss business strategy concerning who is considering them for a meeting, how they can close the deal, what other managers are working on, what type of business seems to be prevalent right now, and so on. The sessions continue with yet another meeting with event managers, the people responsible for the operational aspect of an event once it is contracted. In this meeting they all go over any operational concerns and check to ensure that promised sales are delivered. If a client is in-house, they send a gift to his or her hotel room (just prior to arrival) and then go on the floor to check the show and ensure that clients are satisfied with service received.

The day usually ends at about 5:30 P.M. for Denise. The day can go on even longer if a customer is in town. In this case, she makes sure that her customers are wined and dined and attended to well by entertaining them; providing breakfast, lunch, and/or dinner; and basically showing them what San Diego is all about.

Courtesy Denise Simenstad

decisions on personal morals. The second is an *experience-based decision.* Through trial and error, the manager has gained experience and will base a decision on past learning. *Affect-initiated decisions* are those that are based on a manager's emotions and feelings. The fourth type is a *cognitive-based decision.* The manager's previous training, learned skills, and gained knowledge influence the decision-making process. Last, the manager may use his or her subconscious mind to retain data and process it in such a way that it will influence the type of decision he or she will make.

Intuition and rationality are separate but are often used in combination in most decision making. The two complement each other to offer the manager an ideal solution for the decision-making process. As an example, consider a manager who has to make a decision on a situation that is similar to one he has come across in the past. Instead of using careful analytical rationality, he will make a decision based on a "gut feeling" and act quickly with what appears to be limited information. The decision is ultimately made based on his experience and accumulated judgment.

▶ Check Your Knowledge

1. List criteria for making a rational decision.
2. Give an example of satisficing.
3. What are the five aspects of intuition?

Types of Problems and Decisions

Several different types of decisions match different types of problems. They are applied as solutions, depending on the various situations that arise. Managers who are aware of these differences can use them to their advantage.

The two major types of decisions are programmed decisions and nonprogrammed decisions. A **programmed decision** involves situations that recur on a regular basis, allowing the response to be a handled with a "programmed" response. In a programmed decision, the response will occur on a repetitive basis; for example, when the number of New York steaks goes below a specified number, an order for more is automatically placed. Programmed decisions generally become a standard operating procedure. Alternatives are not necessary most of the time because the problem statement is familiar, and therefore the solution is in close reach because of past successful decisions made. The response to a shortage of New York steaks is simply a reorder; the alternatives are truly limited. A programmed decision is made in response to a recurring problem; the approach to dealing with it has become repetitive and therefore does not require a careful analysis.

A **nonprogrammed decision** is nonrecurring and made necessary by unusual circumstances. The type of problem that induces a nonprogrammed decision is a poorly structured problem. These types of problems are usually new or unusual to the decision maker. More often than not, the information on the problem is incomplete or unavailable. This generally increases the difficulty gradient of finding an appropriate solution. Most important, though, the problem is unique and nonrecurring, such as which computer hardware and software a restaurant should install or whether to expand through franchising or company-owned

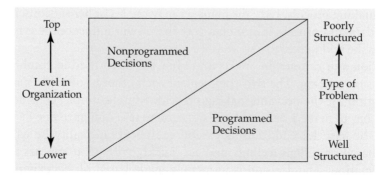

Figure 17–8 • Nonprogrammed and Programmed Decisions. (Derived from Stephen P. Robbins and Mary Coulter, *Management*, 7th ed. Upper Saddle River, NJ: Prentice Hall, 2002, p. 161.)

restaurants. These distinctive decision situations are not likely to recur for several years and require a custom-made decision.

The more sophisticated a company is, the more programmed decisions are made. Many large corporations have policy and procedure manuals to guide managerial and supervisory decision making. Nonprogrammed decisions call for greater analysis, innovation, and problem-solving skills. Figure 17–8 diagrams programmed and nonprogrammed decisions and the level in the organization.

Decision-Making Conditions

In a perfect world, we would have all the information necessary for making decisions. However, in reality, some things are unknowable. This leads us to decision-making conditions. Decision making includes three major conditions: certainty, risk, and uncertainty. These three conditions all have individual characteristics that define each.

The ideal situation for making a decision is one of **certainty**. A decision of certainty includes knowing all of the alternatives and therefore having no risk involved when making a decision, because the outcome is known. A good example for this condition is illustrated by a hotel investment specialist who is allotted a share of the hotel's profit. The investor's options are clear and defined. He knows exactly how much interest is earned on bonds and how much interest is offered by various banks, the security issues, and how many years it will take for them to mature.

Making a decision that involves **risk** is one of the most common situations. Here the decision maker is not certain of the outcome of the situation. However, through personal experience, or a simple "gut feeling," she can estimate the probability of the outcome. Although not all alternatives are properly researched, by using historical data, probabilities can be assigned to various alternatives and the best probable outcome ultimately chosen. This is called a *risk condition* as it relates to decision making and is characterized by having some knowledge of the outcome of the various alternatives, combined with the element of unpredictability.

For example, a popular hotel is thinking about adding on family apartments to its property. So far the largest room they have is a double; the family rooms would

4. Managers use formal communication to communicate job requirements to their employees. It follows the official chain of command. Informal communication does not follow a company's chain of command or structural hierarchy. The subject matter is typically not job related and is not essential to performing job duties.

5. Communication flows are part of the organizational communication process. Upward communication flows from the employees to the manager. Downward communication flows from manager to employees. Lateral communication takes place among employees who are on the same organizational level. Diagonal communication cuts across organizational levels as well as work areas. The four different types of communication networks are the chain, the wheel, the all-channel, and the grapevine.

6. The decision-making process consists of eight steps: (1) identification and definition of problem, (2) identification of decision criteria, (3) allocation of weights to criteria, (4) development of alternatives, (5) analysis of alternatives, (6) selection of alternative, (7) implementation of alternative, and (8) evaluation of decision effectiveness.

7. Although all employees in a company make decisions on a regular basis, in the end it is the manager's decisions that count. His or her decisions usually represent the final word and are valued as "the right decision." Decision making is a large part of all four primary managerial functions: planning, organizing, leading, and controlling. Hence, *managing* is a synonym for *decision making.*

8. A rational decision is based on the following assumptions: The decision is value maximizing and within natural limits, and the manager making the decision is fully objective and logical and has the organization's economic interest in mind. As a result, the rational decision-making problem is simple and has a clearly defined goal, limited alternatives, minimal time pressure, low cost for seeking and evaluating alternatives, an organizational culture that supports risk taking and innovation, and measurable and concrete

outcomes. Bounded rationality suggests that managers make decisions that are bounded by an individual's ability to process information. Managers often cannot possibly analyze all available information and all alternatives, so they satisfice instead of maximize. Finally, intuitive decision making is a subconscious process of making decisions on the basis of experience and accumulated judgment, including ethics learned.

9. Programmed decisions require a problem situation that is a frequent occurrence, allowing the response to be handled with a routine approach. Programmed decisions generally become standard operating procedures. A nonprogrammed decision is nonrecurring and made necessary by unusual circumstances. These types of problems are usually new or unusual to the decision maker. More often than not, the information on the problem is incomplete or unavailable.

10. The decision condition of certainty includes knowing all of the alternatives and therefore having no risk involved when making a decision, because the outcome is pretty much known. Uncertainty situations are characterized by having to make a decision when the outcome is not certain and reasonable outcome estimates can't be made because of lack of adequate information. In risk situations, the decision maker is not certain of the outcome of the situation. However, through personal experience, historical data, or a simple "gut feeling," he or she can estimate the probability of the outcome.

11. Decision-making styles vary depending on a person's way of thinking—rational or intuitive—and a person's tolerance for ambiguity, which can be low or high. Combinations of these differences give us the directive style (low tolerance for ambiguity and rational way of thinking), the analytic style (high tolerance for ambiguity and rational way of thinking), the conceptual style (high tolerance for ambiguity and intuitive way of thinking), and the behavioral style (low tolerance for ambiguity and intuitive way of thinking).

Key Words and Concepts

active listening
allocation of weights to criteria
analytic style
analysis of alternatives
behavioral style
body language
bounded rationality
certainty
communication
communication networks
conceptual style
decision-making process
development of alternatives
directive style

downward communication
escalation of commitment
evaluation of decision
    effectiveness
formal communication
identification and definition of
    problem
identification of decision criteria
implementation of alternative
informal communication
interpersonal communication
interpersonal communication
    process
intuitive decision making

nonprogrammed decision
nonverbal communication
organizational communication
programmed decision
rationality
risk
satisficing
selection of alternative
semantics
tolerance for ambiguity
uncertainty
upward communication
verbal intonation

Review Questions

1. The most important aspect of a manager's job is typically described as decision making. Do you believe this is so? Explain.
2. When reviewing some important decisions you have made, would you describe them as mostly rational or intuitive decisions? What are the characteristics of each? How does intuition affect the decision-making process?
3. During the communications process, if the receiver disagrees with the sender, does this always mean that the message has not been properly understood? Or could it mean something else? Explain.
4. How can the grapevine be used to a company's advantage?
5. When communication is not effective, is it always the fault of the receiver? Discuss all options.

Internet Exercise

Organization: Starbucks
Web site: www.starbucks.com
Summary: Starbucks founder Howard Schultz has resumed his role of chief executive officer and made plans for the reorganization of Starbucks to restore what he calls the "distinctive Starbucks experience" and to focus on the guest. He has made several decisions, including focusing on espresso standards and other important tenets of coffee education, and all Starbucks locations were closed for a three-hour training session one day. Schultz continues to communicate via his messages on the company web site.

(a) Read about Starbucks and see if you agree with Schultz's decisions.
(b) What do you think about his communications? How could communications be improved?

Apply Your Knowledge

1. Select a hospitality-related problem and write a problem statement. Then, using the decision-making steps, show how you would solve the problem.

Endnotes

1. Draws on Stephen P. Robbins and Mary Coulter, *Management,* 8th ed. (Upper Saddle River, NJ: Prentice Hall, 2005), 282.
2. Paul Preston, "Nonverbal Communication: Do You Really Say What You Mean?" *Journal of Healthcare Management,* (March/April 2005): 83.
3. Anne E. Beall, "Body Language Speaks," *Communication World* (March/April 2004): 18.
4. Draws on Gary Dessler, *A Framework for Management,* 3rd ed. (Upper Saddle River, NJ: Prentice Hall, 2004), 282.
5. Draws on Robbins and Coulter, *Management,* 265.
6. Ibid., 293–296.
7. Ibid., 294–295.
8. "Heard It through the Grapevine," cited in *Forbes* (February 10, 1997): 22.
9. Personal conversation with John Horne, president, Anna Maria Oyster Bar restaurants, April 14, 2008.
10. Adapted from Robbins and Coulter, *Mamagement,* 147.

CHAPTER 18

Human Resources

OBJECTIVES

After reading and studying this chapter, you should be able to:

- Explain the importance of job descriptions.

- Give an example of how productivity standards are determined.

- Name and describe the employment-related laws.

- Discuss how to select, recruit, and orient employees.

- Identify methods of employee appraisal and compensation.

- Describe motivation theories and industry practice.

Human Resources Leadership and Management Issues

Human resources are frequently cited as a company's most valuable asset and a competitive advantage, meaning that the employees of one company are better than another. This, as you know, may be true for some companies but not for all. The challenge of finding, retaining, and developing great employees has become greater in recent years. Some issues compounding the employment crunch in the hospitality industry are that employees are now looking for a trusting relationship with their employer; this is even truer because of the recent corporate scandals. Previously, the most important thing was benefits. Benefits are still important, but a stable and trusting relationship is more important.[1]

Changing Demographics

In the United States, the birth rate has slowed, and the American population is aging; millions of baby boomers are about to enter their retirement years. There are now more women and minorities in and entering the hospitality workforce; this brings a fascinating cultural mix to the workplace. The latest figure for the U.S. population is 302,669,480; in 2020 that figure is expected to reach 333,805,000 with more of the increase coming from Hispanic and African Americans.[2] In the age range from 16 to 64, there are 239.7 million White, 44.3 million Hispanic, and 38.3 million African Americans. In California, New Mexico, and Texas, for example, Asian, Hispanic, and African Americans are now the majority. In the United States more than 10 million employees work in the hospitality industry, and most of them are women and minorities.

The hospitality workforce is increasingly diverse, with many cultures adding to the richness of the work environment

Diversity and Inclusion

Given our increasingly diverse and multicultural society, hospitality leaders and associates need to not only understand but embrace diversity and inclusion. Diversity is about the following cultural and physical aspects that distinguish us individually and as groups. This list is not meant to be all inclusive because diversity is much more than what is listed.[3]

Culture

Ethnic group

Race

Religion

Language

Age

Gender

Physical abilities and qualities

Sexual orientation

Culture, ethnic group, and *race* are related terms. Culture is a learned behavior consisting of a unique set of beliefs, values, attitudes, habits, customs, and traditions. Culture influences the way people behave and varies from one group to another. Ethnic groups share a common and distinctive culture, including elements such as religion and language. *Race* refers to a group of people related by common descent.[4]

Equal opportunity laws, discussed later in this chapter, have encouraged diversity, as have a number of hospitality industry leaders and corporations. Marriott International, one of *Fortune* magazine's 100 best companies to work for, says that its commitment to diversity is absolute. Encouraging diversity is the only way to attract, develop, and retain the best talent available.[5] By contrast, failure to understand and respect the diverse cultural backgrounds of employees and the differences among them can result in misunderstandings, tension, poor performance, poor employee morale, and higher rates of absenteeism and turnover. On the other hand, when differences are respected, the working environment is richer, much more fun, and even more interesting.[6] Gerry Fernandez, president of the Multicultural Foodservice Alliance, urges the pursuit of diversity in four areas: workforce, customer, community, and suppliers.[7]

Inclusion means exactly what it says: to include everyone regardless of gender, marital status, race, national origin, religion, age, disability, sexual orientation, weight, and looks.[8] People who are overweight or less beautiful should not be discriminated against—only the ability to do the job should be the employment criteria. Sexual orientation is another example; the fact that a person is gay or lesbian has no bearing on the quality of his or her work.[9]

Turnover

Ask any hospitality leader what the biggest challenge is, and he or she is likely to respond, "Staff—getting them and keeping them!" Not only are there fewer job applicants, but the applicants often lack experience or if they have experience, they do not stay long, adding to a high turnover, which in many companies is more than 100 percent per year. This means that all the employees who are here today will not be here at this time next year. Actually, it doesn't quite work out that way: some people stay, while others come and go two or three times. The complexity of human resources leadership, management, and development in the hospitality industry is increased by the fact that many unskilled workers are employed for entry-level positions, often with little or no training, which contributes to turnover.

Human resources directors say that they need to earn the trust of their employees. Some companies do this by having an "Employee Promise" to guarantee respect, a safe and hospitable workplace, training, mentoring, fair treatment, equal treatment, employee assistance programs, and advancement opportunities.[10] Employee satisfaction means retention, and employee satisfaction is achieved by creating and maintaining a great working environment. A hospitality company should be the employer of choice, the company that employees prefer to work for, not only when compared to other hospitality companies, but also when compared to other industries, such as retail. Supervisors and managers need to be energetic and participative in leading their employees by showing them what to do and how to do it, because if you wait until they ask you, they are already dissatisfied.

Legal Issues

Legislation and the enforcement of laws relating to the workplace have increased in recent years, mostly to protect workers and the workplace; these laws have increased the human resources workload and complexity. As one manager said to the human resources director, "Your job is to keep me out of court."[11] Later in the chapter we will review some of the laws that affect the hospitality industry.

The Importance of Human Resources

Progressive employers seek to become the employer of choice in their respective industry sector. To become an employer of choice, the employer needs to realize that the leadership and management of human resources are important because the hospitality experience is intangible—meaning that one hotel, restaurant, or tourism enterprise is often much the same as another. What makes the difference is service, service, service, and professionalism. (Remember the quote in Chapter 1 from the general manager of the Oriental Hotel in Bangkok, Thailand? He said, "The reason we are rated one of the best hotels in the world is service, service, and service.") As we already know, the hospitality industry is the largest in the world, employing some 70 million people worldwide. No other industry has as much front-line entry-level employee–guest contact as the hospitality industry. Employment ranges from entry-level positions to specialized, supervisory, and managerial–executive positions. Human resources is all about attracting, selecting, orienting, training, coaching, counseling, disciplining and mentoring, developing, evaluating, and supporting and retaining an organization's most important resources: the people.

It is difficult to recruit, hire, train, and retain great employees; the challenge of finding great employees has increased, in part because of the

A Human Resources Director and Assistant in Their Office

changing demographics of the workplace, one element of which is the aging American population (remember the baby boomers?). Baby boomers are now retiring or about to retire, have the disposable income to travel, and are doing so in record numbers. Ironically, this is contributing to the problem of finding enough good employees to serve them and the other guests. Also, there is enormous diversity within the industry. In the next few years, an increasing number of immigrants, minorities, and women will be entering the hospitality workforce. In this chapter we will examine each function of the human resources department. The processes and functions will be explored sequentially from hiring to retirement or termination. Figure 18–1 illustrates the importance of human resources in achieving the corporation's vision and mission.

The importance of human capital, whether it is called *people, labor, intellectual capital, human resources, talent,* or some other term meaning the resource that lies within employees and how they are organized, is increasingly recognized as critical to strategic success and competitive advantage.[12] Progressive companies are moving toward the performance of talent and making decisions about people's talent with the same rigor, logic, and distinctiveness as their decisions about other resources such as money and technology.[13]

In addition to recruiting, hiring, and training, several other functions are a part of human resources: creating job descriptions, developing job specifications, managing payroll and benefits, handling grievances, managing finances,

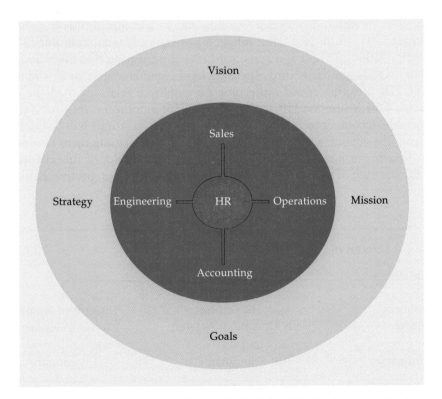

Figure 18–1 • Human resources plays a critical role in achieving the corporation's vision and mission.

promoting community involvement, and ensuring conformance to federal, state, and provincial legislation.

The Human Resources Department

In a large hospitality operation, the human resources department is headed by the director of human resources. The HR director is an executive position and carries with it the enormous responsibilities of running an efficient and effective HR department. The HR director sets the overall tone of how employee relations will be conducted and establishes the vision for the company's human resources. The director is the executive-level advocate for employees. The HR department generally has a co-coordinator, who ensures that all employee and management inquiries are handled with courtesy and given to the appropriate HR manager or director. Most HR departments have an employment manager, who checks applications and does the employment suitability interviews and reference checks. The benefits manager ensures that all employees apply for and receive their appropriate benefits. Figure 18–2 shows the organization chart of a midsized hospitality company's human resources department.

Human Resources Planning

The human resources department is responsible for creating and maintaining an environment in which people can flourish, and to accomplish this it does four main things: (1) recruit and select talented associates; (2) maintain outstanding employee relations; (3) act as a standard-bearer by ensuring that every associate meets or exceeds standards; and (4) ensure legal compliance, training, and development. HR directors spend more time on employee relations than the other functions. This is because HR is the advocate for employees; they need to feel comfortable in coming to HR and knowing that conversations will be confidential. Being the advocate for associates also means representing them to management, department heads, and supervisors. In the remainder of this chapter we will examine each of these areas in detail from an industry perspective. Before we

Figure 18–2 • The Human Resources Division of a Midsize Hospitality Company.

can recruit applicants, we must first determine what these applicants will do. We begin with an examination of the job to be performed, which is called *task analysis*, followed by *job description.*

No hospitality organization can be successful without an outstanding team of dedicated service professionals. Superior human resources are a competitive advantage that companies can benefit from all the way to the bank! Human resources planning is a continuous process by which hospitality companies identify their future needs and how those needs can be met. Imagine opening a theme park and the human resources planning that needs to be done. You would need to consider what rides the park will have, what other attractions there would be, what knowledge and skills successful employees should have, and a strategy for attracting employees and the staffing levels required.

Human resources planning must interface with the company's strategic plan. If, for example, a regional company plans to go national, then human resources will need to have fully trained employees ready to operate the units.

In the United States, the workforce is changing rapidly; a high and increasing percentage of hospitality industry employees consists of minorities and women. Progressive companies are planning for and embracing diversity and inclusion, particularly among supervisory and management levels.

Human resources planning also includes the development of future supervisors and managers. The critical elements of developing employees of excellence, including supervisors, and leader–managers, are leadership development, team building, mentoring, TQM, training, employee empowerment, employee recognition, and praise.

If a new hospitality business is to be set up, then part of the planning involves scrutinizing the tasks that when combined constitute a job. Task analysis may also be done to find the one best way to do a job. Later in the chapter, we look at productivity, which is linked to task analysis. Figure 18–3 illustrates the human resources management and development process.

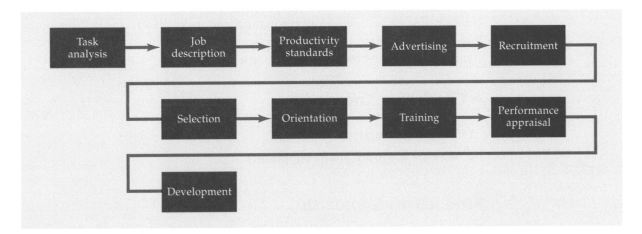

Figure 18–3 • Human Resources Management and Development Process.

Task Analysis, Job Description, and Job Specification

Because human resources or labor costs are the single highest cost of being in business, it has become necessary, through **task analysis,** to examine every task of each employee to determine the best way of doing the particular task and its potential outcome on the guest experience. For example, think of a housekeeper making up a guest's room; several tasks are involved. What should the housekeeper do and in what order? Hotels seek the best way to make up a guest room so that they can maximize efficient use of human resources. From the task analysis, a description of the job can be formulated. It simply lists the various jobs that are required to meet the goals of the position and department.

A **job description** is a detailed description of the activities and outcomes expected of the person performing a specific job. Most hospitality organizations find it very helpful to have job descriptions, not only as a guide for employees and supervisors, but also for quality standards and guest expectations. It is important for each employee to know what the job entails and that they can do the job to the performance standard required. The job description is important because it is a legal document. Some cases have come before the courts and administrative agencies in which employees who were dismissed have sued the former employer, claiming that they did not know or were not properly informed of the duties required. Surprisingly, a few large multinational hospitality companies still do not use job descriptions because they do not want to have employees tied to specific tasks. Job descriptions are not a contract of employment, and management needs to be able to change them with the changing needs of the corporation. Most job descriptions have the section "and all other duties assigned by management." Today, many companies have employees sign their job descriptions to avoid any confusion or misunderstanding about their job and its responsibilities. The job description specifies the knowledge, qualifications, and skills necessary to do the job successfully. Job descriptions can be used as good performance measurement tools.

Job specifications are sometimes a part of the job description and sometimes a separate document. The job specification does exactly what it says: it specifies the qualities and knowledge the person will need to do the job. For example, a prep cook may have to lift 50-pound bags of potatoes. Or a cook may need to scale a recipe up or down from the manual and make up a recipe in 20 minutes. It would be important to see if the applicant has good knife skills and can understand and follow instructions in making a recipe.

▶ Check Your Knowledge

1. What is task analysis?
2. Why are job descriptions important?

Productivity Standards

With today's high labor costs, increasing employee productivity has become a major issue. Productivity standards may be established for each position within the organization. Measuring or timing how long it takes to do a given task determines the **productivity standards**. Departments are staffed according to forecasted demand, whether for restaurant guests, hotel check-ins, or attendance at a theme park. For example, if there are 200 check-ins at a hotel, management would staff the front desk with three employees to give the level of service the hotel guests expect. Of course, the assistant or front-office manager will assist as necessary.

Employee productivity is measured in dollar terms by dividing sales by labor costs. If sales totaled $46,325 and labor costs were $9,265, productivity would be measured as a factor of five. This means that for every dollar in labor costs, $5 in sales was generated. Another way of expressing employee productivity is to divide the sales by the number of employees to arrive at the sales generated per employee. Other measures of productivity might be the number of tables or guests served by a foodservice employee or the number of rooms serviced by a housekeeping associate.

One good way to set productivity standards is to have a group of the best and quickest employees do the tasks and see how long they take; then average the time it takes. For example, if it takes a group of housekeepers 2.5 minutes to properly make a bed, then that time becomes the standard and benchmark. An additional benefit will be to come up with the best way of doing the task, which can then be made into a DVD for training purposes. Some companies have training manuals or web sites where employees can see how something should look—for example, guest rooms or room service setups.

Employment Law

Employment law has become increasingly more important in recent years because of the number of lawsuits brought against employers and the amount of the settlements and jury awards, often into the millions of dollars. Several laws affect the way hospitality and other corporations conduct themselves with regard to human resource leadership and management. Among the most important legislative acts are the following:

- *The Civil Rights Act of 1964*[14] prohibits discrimination on the basis of race, color, religion, sex, or national origin.

- Equal Employment Opportunity Title VII of the Civil Rights Act[15] established the *Equal Employment Opportunity Commission,* which is charged by law to enforce equal employment opportunity for all persons seeking employment. It is critical that all applicants be treated equally and that all employment decisions be job related.

- *The Equal Pay Act of 1963*[16] requires that women and men performing equal jobs receive equal pay. This act was passed because men and women were being paid different amounts for the same work being performed.

- *The Age Discrimination in Employment Act (ADEA) of 1967*[17] prohibits discrimination in employment for people over age 40. With rising productivity expectations and other job-related pressures, older workers

CORPORATE PROFILE

Marriott International, Inc.

Marriott International is a leading worldwide hospitality company. Its heritage is traced back to a root beer stand opened in Washington, D.C., in 1927 by J. Willard and Alice S. Marriott. Today, Marriott International has more than 2,600 lodging properties in the United States and 65 other countries and territories. Marriott International operates and franchises hotels under the following brands:

Marriott Hotels and Resorts: The flagship brand of quality-tier, full-service hotels and resorts with features such as fully equipped fitness centers, gift shops, swimming pools, concierge levels, business centers, meeting facilities, and high-speed Internet.

JW Marriott Hotels and Resorts: The most elegant and luxurious Marriott brand, offering business and leisure travelers a deluxe level of comfort and personal service.

Renaissance Hotels and Resorts: A quality-tier, full-service brand offering guests the ambiance of a boutique. Brand signatures include business library, swimming pool, fitness centers, and conference and banqueting facilities.

Courtyard by Marriott: A moderately priced lodging brand designed by business travelers for business travelers that has recently increased the number of downtown locations often through conversions of historical buildings. Features include 80 to 150 guest rooms, high-speed Internet access, restaurant, lounge, meeting space, central courtyard, exercise room, swimming pool, and 24-hour access to food.

Residence Inn by Marriott: Designed as a home away from home for travelers staying five or more nights and includes a residential atmosphere with spacious accommodations. Features include complimentary hot breakfast, evening hospitality hour, swimming pool, sport court, personalized grocery shopping, guest suites with separate living and sleeping areas, fully equipped kitchen, and work space with data ports and voice mail.

Fairfield Inn by Marriott: A consistent, quality lodging at an affordable price. Features include spacious guest rooms, daily complimentary breakfast, and swimming pool. Future plans call for exercise rooms.

Marriott Convention Centers: A quality-tier brand specializing in small to midsized meetings. Properties provide the latest audiovisual communications technology, experiential learning facilities, gourmet conference dining, golf, and recreational/fitness facilities.

Towne Place Suites by Marriott: A midpriced, extended-stay brand that provides all the comforts of home in a residential atmosphere.

SpringHill Suites by Marriott: A moderately priced, all-suite lodging brand that offers up to 25 percent larger than standard hotel rooms. Features include complimentary continental breakfast, self-serve business center, indoor pool, whirlpool spa, high-speed Internet access, and exercise room.

Marriott Vacation Club International: A leading developer and operator of vacation ownership resorts with an average weekly interval price of $18,700. Features include spacious living and dining area, one-, two-, and three-bedroom villas, master bedroom and bath with whirpool spa, private balcony, kitchen, and laundry area.

Horizons by Marriott Vacation Club: A value-oriented vacation ownership resort community with fun amenities and activities for the entire family, the average price of which is $12,000 for a week a year. Features include roomy and functional two-bedroom, two-bath villas, family-friendly living and dining areas, private balcony, "everything but food" kitchen, and washer and dryer.

The Ritz-Carlton Hotel Company, LLC: The worldwide symbol for the finest in hotel and resort accommodations, dining, and service. Twice recipient of the Malcolm Baldrige National Quality Award, offering signature service amenities, fine dining, 24-hour room service, twice-daily housekeeping, fitness centers, business centers, and concierge services.

The Ritz-Carlton Club: A collection of private residences in highly desirable resort areas that are exclusive to members and their guests. Three- to five-week ownership fractions range from $136,000 to $510,000.

Marriott ExecuStay: Fully furnished corporate housing for executives and travelers who need temporary accommodations for a month or longer. Features include well-maintained properties in convenient locations, flexible lease terms and options, consistently high level of service, competitive pricing, and rooms attractively furnished and customized to satisfy each individual need.

Marriott Executive Apartments: A corporate housing brand designed to meet the needs of business executives on an overseas assignment for 30 days or more by offering residential accommodations with hotel-like amenities.

Marriott Grand Residence Club: Fractional property ownership in premier second home destinations offering the services and amenities of a fine hotel. Three- to 13-week ownership fractions range from $83,900 to $550,000.

Marriott has been ranked the number one most admired company in the lodging industry by *Fortune* for the past five years and also one of the "100 Best Companies to Work For" for the past seven years.

were being displaced in greater numbers than younger workers and then finding it difficult to find alternative employment. The intent of the law is that no employer shall discriminate against an employee over age 40 because of his or her age. The law applies to both employees and applicants.

- *The Immigration Reform and Control Act of 1986* makes it illegal to hire undocumented employees, and it is the employer's responsibility to verify the documents of the prospective employee. Documentation of proof of employment eligibility (an I-9 form) is required for every employee hired after November 6, 1986, and employers cannot discriminate on the basis of national origin or citizenship.

- *The Americans with Disabilities Act (ADA)*[18] is a far-reaching act forbidding discrimination against people with disabilities in employment and the workplace. Employers need to make "reasonable accommodations" to assist people with disabilities and make the workplace accessible to them if they are qualified for the job they applied for. Similarly, guest accommodations must be accessible to people with disabilities. Under the ADA, a person is considered qualified if he or she can perform the "essential functions of the job." In practice, ADA policies are subjective because there is much debate about what constitutes a disability. Currently, a number of cases are going through the courts relating to the ADA and workers' compensation dealing with issues such as carpal tunnel syndrome, which employees regard as a debilitating medical condition. However, the Supreme Court has ruled that carpal tunnel syndrome is not a disability. The ADA does include and protect those who are HIV-positive or have hepatitis B.

- *The Fair Labor Standards Act of 1938,*[19] as amended, established the minimum wage and the maximum number of workweek hours. Managers are exempt from this standard as long as they are spending the majority of their time in managerial activities. Several multimillion-dollar settlements have recently been made to so-called managers who were supposedly exempt, but when they filed suit, the court found them to be doing the work of hourly paid (nonexempt) employees; therefore, they were awarded millions of dollars in back pay and compensation. The Fair Labor Standards Act is a broad federal statute that covers the following:

  Federal minimum wage law

  Employee meals and meal credit

  Equal pay

  Child labor

  Overtime

  Tips, tip credits, and tip-pooling procedures

  Uniforms and uniform maintenance

  Record keeping

  Exempt versus nonexempt employees

- *The Pregnancy Discrimination Act of 1978*[20] provides various protections for pregnant women. It makes it unlawful to discriminate against women because they are or may become pregnant, are giving birth, or have other related medical conditions. It is also unlawful not to hire or promote someone because she is pregnant, and employers cannot set the beginning and end of an employee's maternity leave. If in good faith an employer, for example, offers a pregnant employee server an alternative position as a cashier, she must be paid her server salary, including tips.

- *The Family and Medical Leave Act of 1993* allows associates to take up to 12 weeks of unpaid leave per year for any of the following reasons: (1) birth or adoption of a child, (2) serious health condition of a child, (3) serious health condition of a spouse or parent, or (4) the employee's own health condition.

Another employment-related act is the Drug-Free Workplace Act of 1988, which allows drug testing of all applicants.

Recruitment

Recruitment is finding the most suitable and talented employee for an available position. The process begins with announcing the opportunity; sometimes this is done first within the organization and then outside. Applications are received from a variety of sources: internal promotion, employee referrals, applicant files from people who may have sent in résumés, transfers within the company, advertising, colleges and universities, and government-sponsored employment services.

Application forms and résumés are accepted and screened by the human resources department. Many companies require applicants to come to the property and personally fill out an application form, and some companies use an online application process. Once the application is submitted, the human resources department reviews the application form and résumé for accuracy and checks to ensure that the prospective employee is legally entitled to work in this country. See Figure 18–4 for a description of the recruitment and selection process.

Applicants are invited to attend an interview with the employment manager. This is a general screening interview to determine that the applicant is suitable for employment, which means that he or she meets the minimum standards required to be employed. Some hospitality companies call this a *prescreening interview*, in which the interviewer looks for eye contact, grooming (hair, nails, clean clothes, and, yes, a *smile*. (One HR manager will not hire people who do not smile as many times as she does during the interview, and another will not hire people who do not walk as quickly as she does.) One question that may be asked during a prescreening interview is, "What motivated you to apply for a

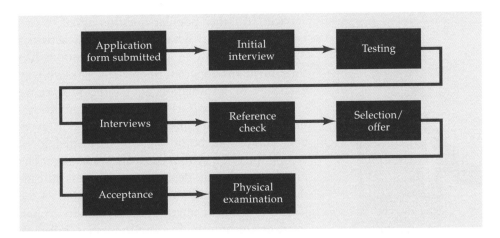

Figure 18–4 • Recruitment and Selection Process.

position here?" The answer should not be, "I need a job," or, "I thought it would fit my schedule at school." Some hospitality companies require applicants to do a talent interview to assess their natural talent (caring, positive, energetic, honest, loyal, and natural need for knowing other people). This type of interview also examines the applicant's relationship extension or aggressive hospitality. Is the person likely to speak to the guest first? Can she confront difficult issues (such as an unhappy guest at the front desk)? Does he have *persuasion*—meaning he can act graciously when a guest is unhappy because she made a reservation six months ago for interconnecting rooms, and when she arrives, there are no connecting rooms available?

There are three kinds of interviews. In the *structured interview,* the questions are prepared in advance, and the interviewer asks only the questions listed on the interview sheet. The advantage of the structured interview is that all candidates are asked the same questions (this is particularly important when an unsuccessful candidate claims that he or she was discriminated against in some way); remember how important it is to treat all applicants the same. Of course, there's a downside to the structured interview: it does not allow for responses to the candidate's answers.

With the *unstructured interview,* general questions are prepared before the interview, and interviewers ask additional questions in response to the candidate's answers to questions. An example might be, "Why are you applying for this position?" This might be followed with, "What qualifications do you have that make you a good candidate for the position?"

The third type of interview is a *semistructured interview.* This is a combination of the structured and unstructured interviews. A prepared list of questions is asked of all candidates, followed by other questions that arise from the prepared questions.

Employment managers look for dress, mannerisms, attentiveness, attitude, and interest. They also ask questions that encourage the applicant to answer in some detail. This necessitates asking open-ended questions, such as, "What did you like most and least about your last job?" or, "Tell me about a time when. . . ," or "Describe your idea of great guest service." Another popular question asked of college graduates is, "What extracurricular activities did you participate in at school?" Questions like these invite the applicant to open up. The two-way exchange of information allows the prospective employee to ask or learn about the job and the corporation. Assuming the applicant makes a favorable impression, he or she will be invited for a second interview with a department manager. The interview within the department will assess the candidate's ability to do the essential functions of the job and his or her interpersonal suitability to join the department team. It is important that skilled interviewers conduct the decision-making interview.

Recruiting qualified applicants and selecting the best candidate include interviewing several people

▶ Check Your Knowledge

1. Describe the employment laws.
2. What are the important topics in recruitment and selection?

Selection

Selection means to select the best-qualified (not necessarily the most qualified) candidate for the available position. Provided that candidates meet the minimum requirements stated in the job specification, the best individual may be selected from the qualified applicants. Part of the selection process may involve tests (personality, intelligence, skill, aptitude, integrity, psychological) to ensure that candidates possess the requisite interpersonal skills or knowledge to do the job. In addition, some companies, as a condition of employment, require new employees to take a drug-screening test. It is advisable to do extensive background checks. For legal reasons, most previous employers will generally give only a neutral reference of the beginning and ending dates of employment and the position held and may state whether the individual is eligible for reemployment. One high-end hospitality company that does extensive background checks even asked an applicant whether he paid a parking ticket he got five years earlier! Assuming that reference and background checks are positive, a formal offer is sometimes made in writing to the prospective employee. (In many companies, written offers are made only for management positions.) The offer outlines the terms and conditions of employment. The offer should include the title of the position offered, the location, hours of work, and job description. It will be signed by the new employee, showing that he or she understands the duties and responsibilities, the benefits and orientation schedule, and the performance evaluation methods. The offer may conclude with a date by which the offer must be accepted. The last step in the recruitment and selection process may be a medical examination. The medical examination acts as a precaution for both the employee and the corporation. Proactive companies have a one-day hiring process as a standard for selection.

Orientation

The **orientation** is a way to introduce new employees to the company and the specifics of the workplace and associates. When planned and presented properly, an employee orientation is a useful tool for retention—a large percentage of new employees leave within the first 90 days, citing among other reasons, lack of training or poor training—and when we add the average cost of thousands of dollars to replace an employee, we realize the importance of orientation all the more. New employees need to have someone help them to get acquainted and settle into the new work environment.

Either prior to beginning or during the first few days of employment, new hires are required to attend a new-hire orientation session. At the orientation, new employees learn details about the corporation's history, policies, procedures, and compensation and benefits. Safety and fire prevention are also introduced,

INTRODUCING PATRICIA ENGFER

General Manager, Hyatt Regency Orlando International Airport, Orlando, Florida

Patricia Engfer began her career 25 years ago as a management trainee in Hilton Head, South Carolina. She then worked as an assistant executive housekeeper in Pittsburgh, followed by jobs at a long list of Hyatt properties, including a stint as rooms executive at the Hyatt Regency Long Beach during that hotel's opening. She first became a general manager at the Hyatt City of Commerce, California, and held similar positions in Los Angeles, Edgewater, and Newport Beach, California. Patricia took her current position of general manager (GM) at the Hyatt Regency Orlando International Airport a few years ago. Here are Pat's answers to our questions:

How have your responsibilities changed at Hyatt?

My responsibilities as a GM have not changed. They include three areas of focus: employees, guests, and owners. What has changed are the tools and sophistication needed to succeed. Our guests, employees, and owners have higher expectations than ever. So we have to be open to innovations that help us meet their expectations.

How did you grow into your position as a GM?

Hyatt does a great job of developing careers one position at a time. That gives each of us the opportunity to develop skills while preparing for the next step. Coming up through the rooms division and working in convention, resort, airport, and city-center hotels prepared me to manage hotels in different markets. The common thread is how you interact with people in each location.

What is the biggest challenge of your job?

We all know that the current business climate is challenging and requires focus and dedication from every member of the team to look at opportunities to drive sales and manage costs.

Do women and minorities have equal opportunities at Hyatt?

Yes. But you must have drive and determination and be willing to give 100 percent. Being a woman has never been a disadvantage. To the contrary, Hyatt has provided an environment that makes it possible to have the best of both worlds—a career and a fabulous family.

Do you have a mentor at Hyatt?

Over the years I have looked to several mentors who have helped me develop in several ways. Steve Trent hired me, and we have kept in close contact through the years. Locally, I have developed friendships with women who are true leaders, including Glenda Hood, former mayor of Orlando and now Florida secretary of state. Another is Linda Chaplin, our past county chairperson, who runs an economic think tank at the University of Central Florida. These women started out raising families, began volunteering time, and today are driving the vision of central Florida. That is truly inspirational.

How do you welcome new employees to your property?

I tell employees the only limits they face are the ones they put on themselves. Hyatt offers training to be successful, but only they can bring the personality and commitment. How many other companies offer a great work environment and the opportunity to live almost anywhere and to grow rapidly, while never having to hop from one company to another? If you put forth the effort, Hyatt provides a platform for success where employees of all races and genders are embraced.

as well as the property's service philosophy. Department heads and the general manager usually introduce themselves to the new employees and wish them well in their new positions. Smart companies ask new associates to evaluate the company. This information provides valuable insights for making improvements. The Ritz-Carlton Company has a two-day orientation followed by a review after 21 days. At the review, the HR department can find out how everything went for the new employee and make any necessary adjustments.

Training and Development

Training in many organizations is an ongoing activity conducted by a training department, a training manager, line management, or specially trained individuals within each department. The first step in establishing a training program is to identify the training needs and then set training objectives. Because the training must be geared toward fulfilling guests' expectations, training often focuses on areas where current service falls short of guest expectations, as noted in guest surveys.

There are five main types of employee training: apprentice, simulation, certification, corporatee-required, and on-the-job training (OJT). *Apprentice training* is given to people who are new to a particular job. The training is specially designed to teach participants the correct way to do a particular task. This often follows the "tell me, show me, do it" routine. Many chefs are involved in an apprenticeship program, which includes a mixture of classroom and OJT with seasoned professionals.

Simulation training simulates the actual workplace. For example, there are specially prepared simulation exercises for travel agents on the Sabre and Apollo airline reservation systems. Once the trainee has reached the required level of proficiency, he or she is allowed to do real ticketing. Hotel front-desk employees use simulation software packages for beginner and advanced training.

Certification training enables individuals to gain corporate or professional certification by attaining passing scores on practical or theoretical tests. These tests are generally job specific and are helpful in motivating employees. For example, T.G.I. Friday's has a certification for each station in the kitchen, and it's a challenge for the line cooks to become certified. Once employees become certified, however, they have a tremendous feeling of accomplishment. ServSafe is a popular certification that is widely used in foodservice operations.

Corporate-required training includes the many workshops and seminars on topics such as safety, workplace values, ethics, harassment, supporting service excellence, service essentials, and valuing differences.

On-the-job training helps maintain standards by having managers, supervisors, trainers, or fellow employees coach individuals in the most effective way to do the required work. OJT allows the trainee to

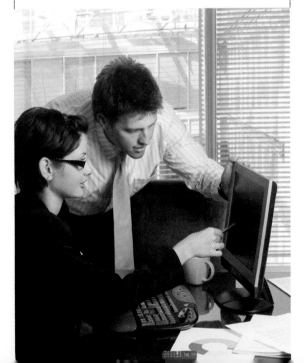

On-the-job training is essential in maintaining standards

quickly learn the best way to do the work based on the experience of trial and error. New hotel housekeepers may work with an experienced employee for a few days to learn the preferred way to do rooms.

Performance Appraisal

The purpose of **performance appraisal** is to compare an employee's performance to preestablished standards as described in the job description. Performance appraisal has been viewed by the industry as positive as well as negative. The positive attributes of performance appraisal include giving feedback to employees, building the appraisal into a personal development plan, establishing a rationale for promotion and wage or salary increases, and helping to establish objectives for training programs.

A major difficulty with most performance appraisal systems is that the judgments involved are frequently subjective, relating primarily to personality traits or observations that cannot be verified. The following are three common distortions in performance appraisals:

1. *Recent behavior influence.* An evaluator's judgment may be overly influenced by the employee's recent behavior (good or bad). Many supervisors wait until the last minute to conduct an appraisal and look at only a short window of employee performance.

2. *The halo effect.* The halo effect occurs when a supervisor is overly concerned with one particular aspect of the overall job, such as punctuality. An employee who is punctual will likely receive a better evaluation than one who is occasionally late, even if his or her productivity is somewhat better. Of course, the opposite is also true and is known as "horns."

3. *Like-me syndrome.* We all tend to like people who are similar to ourselves; naturally, there is a tendency to give a better appraisal to employees who are most like ourselves. This occurs when managers rate employees high because they have similar traits.

There is another inherent weakness in all appraisals. Any system by which a superior rates a subordinate is likely to cause resentment in the person being rated or anxiety in the rater. The basic answer to the anxiety problem is to develop a supportive social system aimed at reducing individual anxiety and thus freeing up energies for constructive purposes. The supportive system includes help from peers and supervisors that will make the employee feel more positive toward the experience and offer a real chance for improvement. One main problem with employee evaluations is a lack of management training in doing employee evaluations. That's why companies such as Hyatt have a "walk a mile in my shoes" program so that managers will have a better understanding of how it is to actually do the job.

Ken Blanchard, the respected author and management speaker, says that there is no such thing as an unmotivated person; an unmotivated employee may be a superstar at the local bowling alley. But imagine that as Fred, the unmotivated employee, rolls the ball down the alley, a supervisor stands there and says, "You only knocked down seven pins; why didn't you knock them all down?" Then, to make matters worse, the manager places a curtain in front of

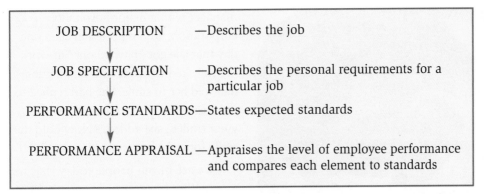

Figure 18–5 • Flow between Job Description, Job Specification, Performance Standards, and Performance Appraisal.

the pins so that Fred cannot see and will not know what to aim for or how well he bowled. Finally, the supervisor removes both the curtain and the pins. When Fred is asked to bowl again, he replies, "I can't, and I don't have anything to aim at!" This is analogous to the many people who work for organizations without knowing job performance expectations and the criteria for appraisal.[21]

Performance appraisals make the link between performance standards and organizational goals. Another critical element is the link among the job description, job specification, performance standards, and performance appraisal. Figure 18–5 shows the importance of the linkage among these factors. Performance appraisals need to be fair, consistent, equal, and nondiscriminatory.

Employee Development

Employee development is a natural progression from appraisal. The employee and his or her supervisor make a development plan. The plan will outline the development activity and indicate when the development will take place. In well-run corporations, employee development is ongoing; it may take the form of in-house training or workshops and seminars on specific topics. Development is a way of enhancing existing skills and is used as motivators for midlevel managers. Development is usually used for nontechnical training, such as effective communications, team building, motivation, and leadership. A popular topic is Stephen Covey's *Seven Habits of Highly Effective People.*[22] Other training and development include English classes, which are handled by outside experts. These training methods help individuals quickly learn the job and improve their performance. Some interesting anonymous industry comments heard in training sessions include the following:

- "People in the organization are a reflection of the leadership."
- "We don't run restaurants, we manage associations."
- "We hire cheerleaders."
- "What! You want my employees to smile? SMILE! I'm lucky if they don't look as if they are in pain!" (This quote is from a restaurateur who shall remain anonymous. It reminds me of a former student, now a food and beverage

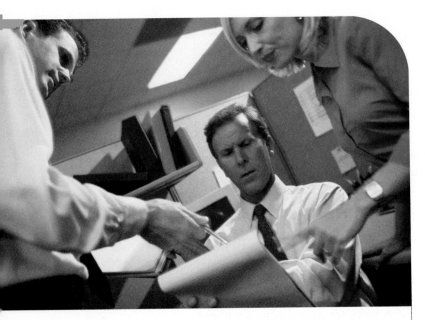

Performance appraisals allow managers and associates to review past performance and establish goals for the future

manager with a major hospitality corporation, who reported in class one day that she got "bawled out" at work. When asked why, she said that a guest had told her to smile. She had replied to the guest, "Sir, *you* smile." When the guest smiled, she added, "Now hold that smile for eight hours – you sucker!")

- "We are hiring people today that we wouldn't have let in as customers a few years ago."
- "You can teach nice people, but you can't teach people to be nice."
- "You achieve what you inspect, not what you expect."

Certification is an excellent form of employee development because it validates a person's ability to do an excellent job and become more professional. Certification can be internal or external. Internal certification occurs when a company has identified certain criteria associated with a position (such as knowing the menu or being able to describe each item). External certification occurs when an employee takes courses toward a professional designation, such as the National Restaurant Association's Foodservice Management Professional (FMP). The American Hotel & Lodging Association also has a number of certification programs. For human resource managers, there is the Professional of Human Resources (PHR) and the Senior Professional of Human Resources (SPHR).

▶ Check Your Knowledge

1. Describe the selection and orientation process.
2. What are a few of the most important legislative acts affecting human resources in the hospitality industry?
3. Describe the key elements of performance appraisal.
4. What is the difference between exempt and nonexempt employees?

Employee Assistance Programs

Employee assistance programs (EAPs) have been instituted at many progressive companies. The purpose of an EAP is to offer confidential and professional counseling and referral services to employees. Employees who have problems may request help in confidence, without losing their jobs. The emphasis of most EAPs

INTRODUCING ROB WESTFALL

Bar Manager, The Speakeasy, Siesta Key, Florida

The Speakeasy has been a staple in Siesta Key's Village for more than five years. Known for its exceptional variety of live music, it is also a place where locals feel right at home. Newly remodeled in November 2004, The Speakeasy now features ice-cold air conditioning in a polished, clean environment. Located at the back of the room is our pool table with plenty of space to allow for professional play. Specialty drinks are another draw for patrons at The Speakeasy. Our menu is loaded with innovative cocktails that are tough to find in another establishment. Along with our extensive list of wines by the glass, we also offer many premium single-malt scotches, cognacs, bourbons, and a host of fine liqueurs. The Speakeasy is owned and operated by Café Gardens, which also owns the Daiquiri Deck located directly next door. For more information on The Speakeasy or the Daiquiri Deck, visit our web site at www.daiquirideck.com.

A typical day for a manager at the Speakeasy goes like this:

9:45 A.M.: Arrive for manager meeting at the Daiquiri Deck. All Daiquiri Deck managers, the owners, and I are present at this meeting. The meeting consists of a variety of issues. Typically, the first order of business is reviewing the numbers from the previous week. Numbers such as net sales, cost of labor, cost of goods, and promotional costs are discussed. Additionally, budgets are a major concern every week. Budgets are set based on sales projections from the previous year and are very important to the success of the business. Next, we discuss any issues from the previous week. In the bar business, an "issue" could be just about anything from fights to vandalism. We find it extremely important to discuss all of these issues so that the management team is all on the same page. The meeting is adjourned after everyone around the table is given a chance to raise any issues they feel necessary. After everything has been discussed, it's time to go to work.

11:00 A.M.: Mondays are very important in the bar business. Inventory must be taken to ensure that costs are in line and that you know what product you need. First, I take an inventory of all beverage products at The Speakeasy. Liquor, beer, wine, cigarettes, cigars, and mixers are all items that must be counted.

12:00 P.M.: Upon completion of the inventory, it is time to put your orders together for the week. Knowing your usage is extremely important when placing an order. Buying in bulk is always superior to simply filling holes from week to week. Simply, it allows you more buying power and, essentially, more free goods. Bar supplies also need to be monitored. Straws, olive picks, stir sticks, bar glass cleaner and sanitizer, and bar napkins all need to be kept in stock. The absence of one item can often make or break a busy night at the bar.

1:00 P.M.: Confirm the band schedule. Booking bands and maintaining an entertainment schedule can sometimes be one of the most frustrating areas of the bar business. However, it can also be the most rewarding. The experience you gain from working with so many different types of entertainment is difficult to replace. Most bands show up on time and treat their job professionally but some do not.

2:00 P.M.: Typically there is always some bar maintenance that needs to be addressed. I always take a walk around and check everything out to make sure that everything is working properly. Bathrooms, lightbulbs, and bar cleanliness are all part of this maintenance.

3:00 P.M.: Work on any upcoming promotions and ensure their success. Spirit tastings, holidays, full moon parties, and private parties are examples of these types of events. Planning is extremely important for the ultimate success of these events.

4:00 P.M.: Send a memo to corporate office regarding what checks need to be written for entertainment that week. Ensure that each band has proper paperwork filled out for tax purposes.

5:00 P.M.: Every day the staff needs to be reminded to step it up. Motivation comes from the top down. The bar business is a stage, and the bartenders are on a stage. The staff will typically need to be reminded of this on a consistent basis. Open lines of communication are very important and allow you to offer constructive criticism or accolades, as they are appropriate.

6:00 P.M.: It's time to have a drink.

That's the management side of the bar. The nighttime is another animal entirely.

is on prevention and on intervening before a crisis stage is reached. Typically, EAP programs assist employees with drug- and alcohol-related problems and personal finance, marital, career and job, and legal issues.

Motivation

Motivation is the art or process of initiating and sustaining behavior toward certain goals. Motivating people is all about inspiring them to do something because they want to do it, not because someone tells them to do it. As the American and Canadian hospitality and tourism industries have "right-sized" the organizational structure by reducing the number of levels of management, the need for motivation has increased. Hotel general managers say that their biggest challenge is how to motivate employees. This section should help you understand your own motivation and influence that of those you will lead in the future. A number of theories about motivation have been developed over the years by experts in motivational psychology. Each has made a contribution to where we are today. What follows is only a brief look at the important topic of motivation. Other hospitality courses will examine this in more detail.

Herzberg's Motivation–Hygiene Theory

A widely accepted and influential theory of motivation is psychologist Frederick Herzberg's *motivation and hygiene factors theory*. While studying managers in the work environment, Herzberg concluded that two separate and distinct sets of factors influenced individual motivation (see Figure 18–6). Herzberg referred to these groups of factors as satisfiers and dissatisfiers, or motivators and hygiene factors. **Motivators** are the intrinsic factors that increase job satisfaction and, hence, lead to increased motivation in employees. Herzberg identified the motivators as

1. Work itself
2. Recognition
3. Responsibility

Motivators	Hygienes
Work itself	Company policies and administration
Recognition	Salary
Responsibility	Working conditions
Achievement	Relationships with supervisors
Growth	Relationships with peers
Advancement	Relationships with subordinates
	Security
	Status

Figure 18–6 • Herzberg's Motivation and Hygiene Factors.

4. Achievement

5. Growth

6. Advancement

The *hygiene factors,* on the other hand, were identified as factors that eliminate job dissatisfaction but by themselves fail to motivate. The hygiene factors are

1. Company policies and administration

2. Salary

3. Working conditions

4. Relationships with supervisors

5. Relationships with peers

6. Relationships with subordinates

7. Security

8. Status

The main premise of Herzberg's theory is that if the hygiene factors are not met, it is unlikely that much motivation will occur, no matter how many of the motivators are met. However, once the hygiene factors have been met, significant motivation will occur once the motivator factors are present.

Maslow's Hierarchy of Needs

Maslow's theory of the *hierarchy of needs* has influenced motivational techniques for many years. The theory suggests that there are five basic needs or motives common to adults:

1. *Physiological needs* are necessities for life, including food, air, and fluids, all of which are essential to our physical existence

2. *Safety needs* provide us with the security and assurance that our physiological needs will be met in the future

3. *Love and belonging needs* are social needs, such as the need for affection and the need for acceptance by others

4. *Esteem needs* are the needs of self-respect and respect from others

5. *Self-actualization needs* are the need for self-fulfillment and the need to reach one's potential

Figure 18–7 shows Maslow's five needs together with examples of how each might be satisfied in an organizational setting. Although Maslow's theory was first proposed years ago, it is still widely and highly regarded as having a significant influence on management and employee motivation.

Now let's relate Maslow's theory to practical hospitality applications. Ask any poor student with unmet physiological and security needs about what motivates him or her. The student will most surely say money and security. So

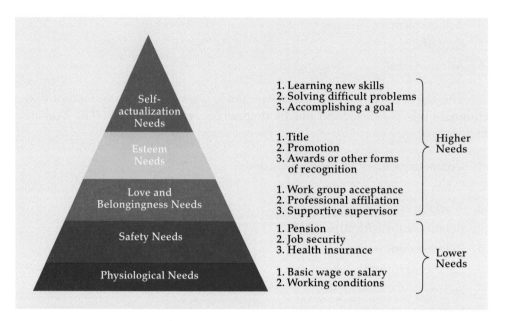

Figure 18–7 • Maslow's Hierarchy of Needs in an Organizational Setting. (From Donald D. White, *Organizational Behavior: Understanding and Managing People at Work*, 2nd ed. Boston: Allyn & Bacon, 1991, p. 149.)

wages, benefits, and job security are important and motivating to the lower-level needs. But once those needs have been met by a certain level of job performance, they cease to be motivators for greater job-related efforts. Moving up the hierarchy, the hospitality industry has no problem in fulfilling social and affiliation needs. Hospitality associates work in departments that have built-in groups or teams, allowing for plenty of social interaction. Now, of course, that can be good or bad, depending on the "climate" or culture in the department—but then it's up to management to make it a positive working experience. A win–win situation exists when associates identify with the department and organization and, better yet, when they feel that they are accepted and that they belong. In such a case, they will be motivated to achieve organization and personal goals.

In the social affiliation context, outstanding managers care for their associates and offer praise in public by having award and recognition ceremonies. Additionally, managers who do something unexpected such as giving baseball tickets to an associate who is a fan increase the associate's feeling of belonging.

Make everyone a winner. As a manager, if you can remove obstacles and make your team winners by providing a good climate, incentives, and rewards, you will have a motivated group. Managers can help motivate associates' natural need for self-esteem by giving them the opportunity to be a winner. Consider this example: One day I was walking through the hotel lobby with a GM of the Westgate Hotel. He bumped into his director of marketing and introduced her as the most professional and best DOM he had ever worked with because she was able to "fill rooms" even in a difficult economy. George went on for a few minutes and was very enthusiastic in his praise; it was a perfect self-esteem builder for the director of marketing.

Self-actualization is the need to achieve for its own sake and is expressed in several ways, including slogans such as "Developing service excellence" or "We are ladies and gentlemen serving ladies and gentlemen" or "We try harder."

Trends in Human Resources

- There is increasing diversity among new employees in the hospitality industry. More women and minorities are not only entering the industry, but are also gaining supervisory and managerial positions.

- Understanding the emotional aspects of motivation will change the way we manage. Emotional intelligence refers to skills in intrapersonal and interpersonal relations. In the future, managers will view employees from a deeper emotional standpoint rather than on the surface level.

- Increased globalization is making the hospitality workplace even more diverse. Individual differences go past traditional demographics to varying deep-level attitudes and beliefs, particularly with nontraditional cultures that are relatively new to the United States. For example, cruise lines are recruiting extensively from Eastern European countries, forcing managers to change the way they interact with employees.

- Advancing employee skills will help satisfy needs, particularly in the "new workforce." The "Generation X" group and the younger "Generation Y" group are very concerned with increasing marketability through learning and developing. Managerial efforts to develop skills and knowledge will help in this regard.

- Economic challenges are forcing hospitality organizations to operate "leaner." Hospitality managers will be forced to develop quick, inexpensive methods of maintaining workplace morale. Rather than greater resources to motivate, creativity will be the key.

- The advent of telecommuting is changing how we motivate employees. Many teams are now "virtual," meaning that face-to-face interaction between supervisors and employees is decreasing. In the future, may need to motivate from afar.

- A critical labor-shortage is becoming a problem.

- An increased focus on employee retention is becoming important.

- An increased use of flextime is becoming popular.

- Food and beverage management positions are increasingly difficult to fill.
- Fewer people in the labor pool have basic reading, writing, and math skills.
- Legal issues in hospitality employment are of increasing concern to hospitality operators as more lawsuits are brought against them.
- Training has become more important as hospitality corporations strive to gain a competitive advantage by offering outstanding guest service.

CASE STUDY

Latasha's Challenge

Latasha Hinkson recently graduated with a bachelor's degree in hospitality management and has been hired as the front-desk manager in a medium-size hotel in New York City. The hotel's clientele is truly international, and so is its staff, which originates from more than 20 different nations. Many of the employees speak more than one language, often at work. Latasha is from the midwestern United States and has had little experience in managing and motivating a multicultural work group. Indeed, she knows little or nothing about many of the cultures that surround her.

One challenge put to Latasha when she was hired was to give a "lift" to the staff and try to create more of a team atmosphere. Currently, the employees at the front desk operate as a bunch of individuals, with little sense of teamwork. It seems as though the differences in culture are preventing the group from getting closer. As a result, the atmosphere at the front desk is cool and functional, rather than warm and friendly.

In addition, Latasha must contend with a number of employee problems if the department is going to function properly. For example, Maria, who originally comes from Spain, is excellent with customers but often comes to work late. Even when confronted by past supervisors about her tardiness, Maria failed to see this as a real problem. Bjorn is a Norwegian hospitality student working part time in the hotel. Although Bjorn is always on time and works very efficiently, his demeanor with the customers is lacking. Often, guests and coworkers perceive him as being aloof or standoffish. Bjorn rarely smiles at guests. Finally, Peng from Asia is very diligent about his work and gives 100 percent to any task he is given. Unfortunately, Peng has some difficulty speaking English and has little confidence in his speaking ability. As a result, he tends to rush through interactions with guests and limits his conversations, saying only what he must to complete the task.

Discussion Questions

If you were in Latasha's place as the new front-desk manager, what methods would you use to answer the following?

1. How will you address each of the work-related problems and motivate Maria, Bjorn, and Peng?
2. How will you facilitate a greater understanding of differences in national culture among the team members at the front desk?
3. Decide on how to build a sense of teamwork within this multicultural group.

Summary

1. The hospitality industry has a large number of entry-level, guest-contact employees, many with little or no training. Human resources management is about attracting, selecting, orienting, training, developing, and evaluating the performance of an organization's most important resource—the human ones.

2. Task analysis examines the tasks that constitute a job to determine whether they are necessary and to gauge their impact on the guest experience. When approved and listed, the tasks are incorporated into the job description.

3. Productivity standards are established for each position. Productivity is measured in how long it takes an associate to do a particular task or job function. Another way to measure productivity is to divide the sales by labor costs and arrive at a factor.

4. Hospitality human resources managers need to know and abide by several employment-related laws.

5. Recruitment is about finding the most suitable candidate for an available position. There are three types of interviews: structured, unstructured, and semistructured.

6. Selection means to select the best candidate, and orientation means to introduce new employees to the company and their job.

7. There are four kinds of training: apprenticeship, simulation, certification, and on-the-job. Employee development is a natural progression from the appraisal; it may consist of training, attending seminars, or obtaining a certification.

8. The performance appraisal compares an employee's actual performance with preestablished standards, and compensation is the complete reward system. Some benefits are mandated by law: Social Security, workers' compensation, and unemployment compensation. Others are made available if the employer decides to offer them and may include pension plans; medical, dental, optical, and life insurance; tuition reimbursement; and employee stock ownership plans.

9. Motivation is the art or process of initiating and sustaining behavior toward certain goals. Motivating people is basically inspiring them to do something because they want to do it, not because someone tells them to do it. The motivational process begins with a need or a demand that is not met. This creates an uncomfortable situation. The person who experiences this need will search for goals that, if obtained, will satisfy that need or demand, therefore eliminating the uncomfortable situation.

10. Herzberg's theory suggests that hygiene factors reduce employee dissatisfaction, while motivators take it a step further and produce job satisfaction. Maslow's hierarchy states the five needs that humans thrive for in a hierarchical pattern: the most basic first, physiological; then safety; social; esteem; and the highest, self-actualization.

Key Words and Concepts

employee assistance program (EAP)
job description
job specification
motivation

motivators
orientation
performance appraisal
productivity standards
recruitment

selection
task analysis
training

Review Questions

1. Why are productivity standards important?
2. What are some good questions to ask at an interview?
3. Describe the elements of a performance appraisal and the things to avoid when doing an appraisal.
4. Why is motivation such an important part of everyday work? Managers are always concerned about new ways to motivate their employees. Explain the importance.
5. Use an example from the hospitality industry to illustrate Herzberg's and Maslow's motivational theories.
6. Depict the main obstacles that exist when motivating low-level employees, such as the housekeeping staff of a hotel. Give specific examples. How does this differ from motivating professionals such as the head chef?
7. How can the early motivational theories be related to motivating a diverse workforce?
8. What motivational technique would work best for your own individual demands? Which technique would be less effective? Explain your answer.

Internet Exercise

Organization: Society for Human Resource Management
Web site: www.shrm.org
Summary: The Society for Human Resource Management is one of the largest human resource associations. Their web site provides in-depth information to both students and professionals around the world.

(a) Briefly discuss two of the latest news articles and how they affect the hospitality industry.
(b) Click on the "Student Program" icon and look at "Getting Started" in HR management. What are some of the current career options being addressed?

Apply Your Knowledge

1. Develop the criteria for and role-play an employee appraisal.
2. Write a job description and the performance evaluation criteria for a position in the hospitality industry.
3. Plan and role-play an interview for a position in the hospitality industry.
4. Interview three hospitality associates—preferably one manager, one supervisor, and one associate—to find out what motives them.
5. Ask your librarian for help in finding interesting hospitality trade magazine articles in an area of human resources that interests you. Share your findings with your classmates.

Endnotes

1. Personal interview with Charlotte Jordan, retired director of human resources, Ritz-Carlton Hotels, April 25, 2008.
2. www.census.gov.
3. Personal conversation with Rita Ingraham, U.S. Census Bureau, July 1, 2006.
4. Personal correspondence with Dr. Chad Gruhl, professor, Metropolitan State College of Denver, February 16, 2008.
5. www.marriott.com/corporateinfo/culture/diversity.
6. John R. Walker, *Supervision: Leading Human Resources in Hospitality*, 6th ed. (Hoboken, NJ: Wiley, 2010): 40.
7. Dina Berta, "MFHA: Industry Gets a Barely Passing Grade on Diversity Issues," *Nation's Restaurant News* (August 21, 2006): 14.
8. Personal correspondence with Dr. Chad Gruhl, February 16, 2008.
9. Walker, *Supervision*, 41; and www.eeoc.gov/abouteeo/overview_laws.html.
10. Personal interview with Charlotte Jordan, April 25, 2008.
11. Personal interview with Angelia Gomez, human resource director, Hyatt Hotels, April 21, 2006.
12. John W. Boudreau and Peter M. Ramstad, *Beyond HR: The New Science of Human Capital* (Boston: Harvard Business School Press, 2007), 4.
13. Ibid.
14. U.S. Equal Employment Opportunity Commission, "Laws Enforced by the EEOC," www.eeoc.gov/policy/laws.html.
15. www.eeoc.gov/abouteeo/overview_laws.html.
16. U.S. Equal Employment Opportunity Commission, "Laws Enforced by the EEOC."
17. Ibid.
18. www.eeoc.gov/ada/.
19. U.S. Department of Labor, "The Fair Labor Standards Act (FLSA)," www.dol.gov/compliance/laws/comflsa.htm.
20. www.eeoc.gov/types/pregnancy.html.
21. Ken Blanchard, address to the National Restaurant Association, Chicago, IL, May 18, 2001.
22. Stephen Covey, *Seven Habits of Highly Effective People: Powerful Lessons in Personal Change* (New York: Simon & Schuster, 1989).

CHAPTER **19**

Control

Did you ever get to the end of the week or the month and discover that you'd run out of money? Well, at one time or another, we all have, and, yes, it's because we did not exercise proper control. But control is not only about keeping our finances in order—it has a much more broad and important role to play in hospitality management. All hospitality managers need to use a variety of control measures to check and see whether the results they achieve are in line with expectations and, if not, to take corrective actions. The control process even sets the parameters for managerial action by setting up control by exception, meaning that managers take action only if the results are outside the acceptable range. Control is often used in conjunction with techniques such as total quality management by allowing associates and management to establish guest service levels.

Control is about keeping score and setting up ways to give us feedback on how we are doing. The feedback leads to corrective action, if necessary. For instance, if a chef and restaurant manager forecast 250 covers and 320 actually come, then they will have to "prep" more food items in a hurry and guide servers to recommend certain dishes in order to avoid running out of too many menu items. These and the many other examples we will read about in this chapter are all control related.

Control has close links to each of the other management functions, especially planning, which, as we know, includes setting goals and making plans on how to reach the goals.

What Is Control?

Control provides a way to check actual results against expected results. Action can then be taken to correct the situation if the results are too far from the expected outcome. If labor costs are 26 percent and they were expected to be 23 percent, the difference is only 3 percent, but that 3 percent could add up to thousands of dollars.

Control is the management function that provides information on the degree to which goals and objectives are being accomplished. Management engages in controlling by monitoring activities and taking corrective actions whenever the goals are not being met. An effective control system ensures that activities are completed that lead to the attainment of the organization's goals.

Control is far broader than you might think. It's not just about checking on outcomes; it is also about providing guidelines and mechanisms to keep things on track by making sure there are no surprises when the results are known. Control is also about keeping your eyes and ears open. Every place seems to have someone who steals, so, as a Swiss hotel manager mentor once said to me in his heavy accent, "John, before you can stop someone else stealing the chicken, you must first know how to steal the chicken." The best way to avoid these losses is to have a tight control system.

Why Is Control Important?

Why is control so important? Control is important because it's the final link in the management functions. It's the only way managers know whether organizational goals are being met and, if not, why not. Controlling is involved with planning, organizing, and leading. Figure 19–1 shows the relationship between controlling and the other management functions.

Goals give specific direction to managers. Effective hospitality managers need to constantly follow up to ensure that what others are supposed to do is being done and goals are being met. Managers need to develop an effective control system—one that can provide information and feedback on employee performance. An effective control system is important because managers need to delegate duties and empower employees to make decisions. But because managers are responsible for performance results, they also need a feedback mechanism, which control provides.

Given that management involves leading, planning, organizing, communicating, motivating, and controlling, one may easily get the impression that maintaining control is just something managers do after they are finished planning, organizing, and leading. For example, controlling always requires that some

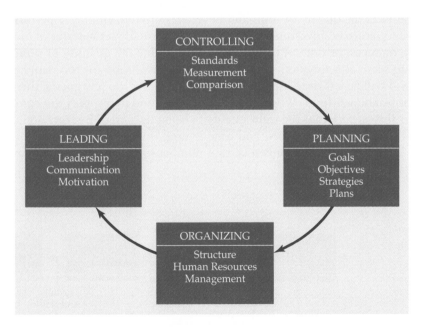

Figure 19–1 • Relationship between Controlling and the Other Management Functions. (Modified from Stephen P. Robbins and Mary Coulter, *Management*, 8th ed. Upper Saddle River, NJ: Prentice Hall, 2005, p. 460.)

desirable outcomes, such as targets, standards, or goals, be set. Similarly, much of what managers do when they have their leadership hats on involves making sure that employees are doing and will do the things they are supposed to do. However, as we learned in the chapter on human resources, the sort of self-motivation that derives from empowering teams and putting them in charge is often the better alternative.

▶ Check Your Knowledge

1. Define control.
2. Why is control important?

The Control Process

The **control process** is a five-step process of determining goals, setting standards, measuring actual performance, comparing actual performance against those standards, and taking managerial action to correct deviations or inadequate performances (Figure 19–2). These standards are the specific goals created during the planning process against which performance progress can be measured.

Setting Standards

In the hospitality industry, setting standards generally means establishing the levels of service, the quality of food and beverages offered, employee performance levels, and return on investment. Standards are normally set in terms of quantity, quality, finances, or time. A caterer has to determine the quantity or number of guests to serve at a function. If the caterer purchases food for too many guests, then food will be left over, but if he or she prepares for too few guests, then there will not be enough food. When a chef purchases food items, they are controlled on arrival to ensure that the right quality is being delivered. Budgets are used to control financial expenditures, and time is used, for example, to control labor costs—a cook should take only a certain number of minutes to prepare a batch of pasta and vegetables.

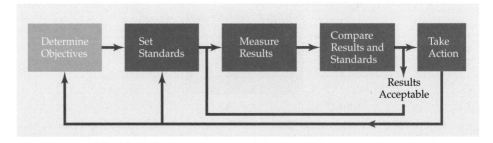

Figure 19–2 • The Control Process.

A word of caution: when developing a method of measurement, one must be absolutely sure first that the goals are indeed measurable. Now, as convoluted as that may sound, let's illustrate the point.

Suppose after careful planning, with input from staff, all agree that labor costs are too high at 28 percent. So the decision is made to reduce labor costs, and that becomes a stated goal—one that is hard to object to. At the end of the month, the kitchen still has a labor cost of 28 percent, so it has not achieved the goal. During your discussion with the personnel responsible, they claim that their plan to reduce labor costs will not be effective until two months hence. You remind them that the goal was to reduce labor costs, they agree that it was, and you point out that last month's labor cost and this month's are the same. Who is correct here? The answer: neither. The goal of reducing labor costs is inadequate and it is not measurable or attainable on your part. The kitchen staff has put a plan into

Information for control purposes can be acquired by a variety of methods, including the telephone

effect that they feel will reduce labor costs by the end of the following month; they feel they are doing all that you asked. The dilemma is that the goal lacks specificity. Had the goal been to decrease labor costs to 24 percent by the end of February, it would be measurable and attainable. Then we could say to the kitchen staff that they hadn't met the stated goal, but because we didn't quantify the goal, they are correct.

Measuring

Managers must first know what they are **measuring** and how they are measuring it before they can measure expected performance. Personal observation, by monitoring subordinates to make sure things are done right, is the simplest and most common way of comparing actual performance to standards. So the chef can see whether the cook is cutting, slicing, and dicing correctly and whether the right amount is being prepared according to the standardized recipe.

Direct Supervision

The purpose of direct supervision is to detect problems of associate-specific actions as they occur and to make corrections immediately in order to keep associate actions in line with management expectations.

How We Measure

Four common sources of information frequently used by managers to measure actual performance are personal observation, statistical reports, oral reports, and written reports.

Management by walking around (MBWA) is the best way to make personal observations. MBWA is a phrase used to describe when a manager is out in the work area, interacting directly with associates and exchanging information about what is happening. MBWA can pick up factual omissions, facial expressions, and tones of voice that may be missed by other sources. Front-office managers will not be aware of how guests are being checked in during the busy early evening check-in period if they are in their offices at that time.

A DAY IN THE LIFE OF CHERRY CERMINARA

Dietitian and General Manager, Sodexo, Gibsonia, Pennsylvania

I am a registered dietitian and general manager operating a K–12 school foodservice program. I work for the management company Sodexo. Sodexo has been contracted to manage the food and nutrition program for the school I serve. It is a five-building, 4,000-student operation. Sodexo School Services leads the nation in providing food and facilities management solutions that support the educational process. From nutrition education to monitoring air quality, our efforts enable students and faculty to consistently perform at a high level. Every day, Sodexo serves the needs of more than 400 school districts. Our expertise allows school administrators to focus on education leadership activities. Best of all, our partnering approach always saves money. Our programs have been tested, and the results are conclusive: Sodexo's food service and facilities management solutions improve the quality of life for students, faculty, and the communities we serve.

As the general manager for this operation, a day in my life includes hiring, training, and managing of employees; ordering foods; taking inventory; managing budgets; financial reporting; menu preparation; production; and nutrition. School meals operations are regulated by the USDA for nutrition according to age-specific needs. Both breakfast and lunch are served. We even provide nutrition education both in the classroom and in the lunchroom.

Other areas of concentration include food safety following HACCP and physical safety for the employees and our customers. We are audited every year by NSF and at least twice per year by the county health department. As a manager, customer service is extremely important in my day-to-day operations. Although the audience is captive, they are still our customers. We look at the students, staff, parents, and administration as our customers. If I cannot train my employees to respect this aspect of their performance, we will lose revenue, and perhaps lose the business to someone perceived to provide a better service. Providing management services to Pine-Richland School District in Gibsonia, Pennsylvania, is really a pleasure. Students are interested in what they eat. They enjoy their meal periods and expect great service. Well-managed, trained, and enthusiastic employees work at Pine-Richland. All of these elements contribute to the company's success.

Statistical reports provide information in the form of data that measure results and can be used for comparative purposes. They also use charts, graphs, and other displays that are easy to visualize. Some managers keep charts on the key result areas and plot the department's progress. Others place safety charts on the associate notice board. These charts visually display the importance of safety and the number of accident-free days, which is another type of goal often sought.

Control information can be acquired through oral reports, conferences, meetings, one-on-one conversations, or telephone calls. The advantage of oral control reports is that they can both be quick and allow instant feedback in the form of a two-way conversation. A manager can inquire about the status of a function and get immediate feedback from the banquet captain. In the often fast-paced hospitality industry, oral control communication is often more effective than other forms of communication. Every time a restaurant service team has an "alley rally" (a quick huddle/meeting), they are, in part, using oral control communications to let servers know what to sell, what the specials are—so guests can be encouraged to order them—instead of "slamming" the kitchen with multiple à la carte orders.

Written reports are also used to measure performance. Like statistical reports, these are slower yet more formal than personal observation or oral reports. Written reports generally have more information than oral ones and are usually easy to file and retrieve. General managers usually expect to see the "daily report," which gives details of the performance results from yesterday, on their desks as they walk into their offices. However, they also want a verbal report from any department they may visit on the way to the office, like "Did we sell out last night?"

Given the varied advantages of each of these measurement approaches, comprehensive control efforts by managers should use all four.

What We Measure

We measure results to see how they compare with expectations. What we measure is more critical than how we measure—what if we are measuring the wrong thing? The results we measure include guest satisfaction, labor costs, food and beverage costs, employee satisfaction, rooms and room rates, bed sheets, energy costs, insurance, and labor turnover.

In simple terms, we measure labor costs because they are the highest of the variable costs. Did we meet our goal of a 24 percent labor cost reduction? Next, did we meet our goal of a 28 percent food cost? To find out if we met our goals, we would need to set up control measuring procedures regarding the daily monitoring of labor costs. Estimates of sales are given to department heads, who then plan and organize their labor costs accordingly. In other words, if you know your sales you can then keep your labor costs at 24 percent. For example, for food and beverage cost control we would scrutinize ordering, purchasing, storing, issuing, preparing, and serving of the various food items. We would take inventory, calculate the actual cost of the food, and express the cost as a percentage of sales. Remember, it's the cost over sales times 100.

Whenever performance results can be measured, it is desirable to consider a results-accountability system. Some control criteria are applicable to any management situation. For instance, because all managers, by definition, coordinate the work of others, criteria such as employee satisfaction or turnover and absenteeism rates can be measured.

Most managers have budgets set in dollar costs for their area of responsibility. Keeping costs within budget is, therefore, a fairly common control measure. However, one of the main purposes of control is to influence behavior. Therefore, a results-accountability control system must be able to detect deviations from desired results quickly enough to allow for timely corrective management action.

> ### Effective Managers
>
> Effective managers first control the "big ticket" items that will be costly if not controlled. Once the more costly items are under control, they can move on to other, less costly items.

Having timely information and acting on that information is crucial in avoiding the following situation: why is it that at some hospitality operations each month's income statement results take almost a month to complete? Because of the delay in producing the results, thousands of dollars are lost before any problems can be fixed.

Comparing Results

Comparing results with expectations shows the amount of variation between actual performance and the standard or expected results. Some variation is generally seen between the expected and the actual results—but how big is the variation? The range of variation is the acceptable difference between the actual and expected results.

Managers are concerned with the size and direction of the variance. Let's look at an example: If guest surveys show that one department is not performing up to expectations, then management would make decisions to have the problem fixed. But what if that didn't work? Then more drastic action would be necessary. Meanwhile the survey scores would continue to drop. Management would quickly find out in which direction and how fast the barometer of guest satisfaction was moving.

Taking Managerial Action

The final step in the control process is taking managerial action. **Correcting actual performance** is used by managers if the source of the performance variation is unsatisfactory. For instance, **corrective action** may include changing the way the job tasks are done, changing strategy (doing different tasks), changing structure (changing supervisors/managers' compensation practices), changing training programs, redesigning jobs, or firing employees.

A manager who decides to correct actual performance then has to make another decision: Does he or she use **immediate corrective action,** which corrects problems at once to get performance back on track, or **basic corrective action,** which looks at how and why performance has deviated and then proceeds to correct the source of deviation? Many managers say they don't have time to take corrective action, yet they are the ones perpetually "putting out fires."

Effective managers analyze deviations and, when the benefits justify it, take the time to pinpoint and correct the causes of variance. This kind of control begins with effective associate selection and training. Hiring the right person for the job and ensuring that associates are properly trained increase the chance that they can be trusted to do the right thing.

Whom Do We Bill?

A funny lack-of-control story happened at a five-star hotel restaurant close to Christmas, when a guest signed the check for his table's extravagant business lunch "S. Claus." The server, thinking that the guest had signing privileges, gave the check to the restaurant cashier, who in turn sent it up to the billing office so that it would go out to the client at the end of the month. Three days later, the check came back to the restaurant with the question "Which company is he with?"

Good communication is critical to associate control for a number of reasons. The most important reason is that good communication helps associates understand what is expected of them. Employee performance reviews take on added significance when viewed from the control perspective. Rather than a method of reviewing past performance, they become a control technique. By rewarding and praising desired behavior, management can use performance reviews to shape future behavior. The opposite will be true of undesirable behavior. Performance reviews are also a good time to consider training, reassignment, raises, and promotion decisions.

▶ **Check Your Knowledge**

1. What are the elements of the control process?
2. Briefly describe the four common sources of information managers use to measure employee performance.
3. Explain the difference between immediate corrective action and basic corrective action.

It is important to note the motivating influences of raises and promotions and how they act as a form of control. Granting raises and awarding promotions based solely on operating results criteria and desired behavior send an important message to all associates. Those actions say that performance and behavior are being monitored and are the basis for personnel decisions. In this way employee actions are controlled.

Types of Control

Managers can use controls *in advance* of an activity (feedforward control), *during* the activity (concurrent control), and *after* the activity (feedback control) has been completed. Figure 19–3 shows the three types of control.

Feedforward control focuses on preventing anticipated problems because it takes place in advance of the work activity. For example, by carefully explaining the policy on billing for catering functions, a catering manager uses feedforward

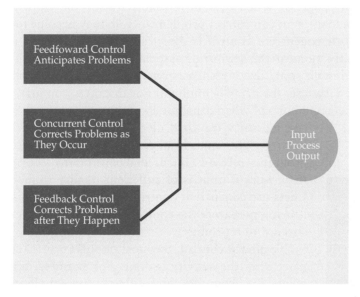

Figure 19–3 • Three Types of Control.

control to explain to the client that an accurate number of people attending the function must be given in order for the correct space to be allocated for the function. A follow-up number is to be given three months, one month, and two weeks before the event, and final guaranteed numbers are required 48 hours before a function. This is the number for which food is purchased, prepared, and charged accordingly. By working closely with the client, the catering manager ensures that there are no surprises.

In the kitchen, recipes are an example of feedforward control; they prescribe the quantity of each ingredient necessary to make a particular dish. Recipes also help with consistency by making each dish look and taste the same. (Now that could be good or bad!) Without recipes, we know the result is going to be a disaster.

Another example of feedforward control occurred when McDonald's opened in Moscow. McDonald's sent quality control experts to help Russian farmers learn techniques for growing high-quality potatoes and bakers to teach processes for baking high-quality breads. Why? Because McDonald's strongly emphasizes product quality no matter the geographic location. They want a McDonald's cheeseburger in Moscow to taste like the one in New York.[1]

Airlines do preventive maintenance on their aircraft; restaurants do the same on their kitchen equipment to prevent any breakdowns during operation. Resorts and hotels also conduct preventive maintenance on the building, the air conditioning system, and so on. These are all examples of feedforward controls.

Feedforward controls are helpful in that they encourage managers to *prevent* problems rather than *react* to them. The challenge is that feedforward controls take more time to organize than the other types of control, yet they save time in the long run.

Concurrent control is a type of control that takes place while a work activity is in progress. When control is enacted while the work is being performed, management can correct problems before they become too costly. The best form of concurrent control is direct supervision, when a manager can concurrently monitor the actions of associates and correct problems as they occur. Although some delay results between the activity and the manager's corrective response, the delay is minimal. For instance, you may have experienced concurrent control when using a computer program such as word-processing software that alerts you to misspelled words or incorrect grammar. In addition, many organizational quality programs rely on concurrent controls to inform workers if their work output is of sufficient quality to meet standards. Chefs use concurrent control when checking on how a recipe is being prepared; the cook can be guided on the correct consistency of a product.

Feedback control, the most popular type of control, takes place after the activity is done. For example, financial statements are examples of feedback control. If, for instance, the income statement shows that sales revenues are declining,

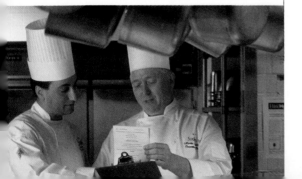

Chefs frequently use concurrent control

the decline has already occurred. The manager's only option is try to determine why sales decreased and to correct the situation.

Feedback control is helpful in hospitality industry situations in which a number of activities repeat themselves: guests make reservations, are welcomed, checked in, roomed, wined and dined, and so on, so resorts and hotels have developed several controls that help measure and report on these activities. These controls include guest surveys, comment cards, and outside checkers who stay at a property and give a detailed report to management on their findings.

Feedback control has two advantages over feedforward and concurrent control. First, feedback provides managers with meaningful information on how effective their planning efforts were. Feedback that indicates little variance between standard and actual performance is evidence that the planning was generally on target. If the deviation is significant, a manager can use the information when formulating new plans to make them more effective. Second, feedback control can enhance employee motivation. Associates generally want information on how well they have performed.

Remember the profile of T.G.I. Friday's earlier in this book, in which the food cost percentage was expected to be 27 percent and the actual was 27.2 percent, meaning the variance was 0.2 of a percentage point? That is feedback control. When a theme park forecasts an attendance of 30,000 on a particular day and the actual comes in at 32,000, that's feedback control.

Other Types of Control

Corporate Control

The catering manager of a large convention and banqueting department received a memo stating that no overtime could be worked unless the F&B director authorized it in advance. Now, for a busy department that did thousands of dollars in business every day and was responsible for most of the F&B division's profit, that memo from the corporate office was not well received—how can we prevent clients from changing their minds at the last minute, and how dare they impose on our operation in this way? In retrospect, the department was caught up in a blanket policy to reduce labor costs by using feedforward control, and it worked because many of the not-so-profitable departments were abusing overtime payments to their associates. The convention and banqueting department services manager planned and scheduled the work more effectively, and the catering managers were able to persuade clients to avoid last-minute room changes by explaining that it would involve additional charges at overtime rates. Incentives were also given to clients to select room setups that would involve fewer complete room changes (from a dinner to a classroom setup when a cabaret might be equally as suitable). Substantial company-wide savings were made, and the conference and banqueting department reacted positively to the change (after a brief period of complaining). They also saved several thousand dollars, which, of course, went straight to the bottom line.

Food and Beverage Controls

Ask any food and beverage operator about controls and you are likely to get a serious look followed by a comment about how important control is to the operation. Lots of money can be made or lost depending on how tight the control is. Most operations take inventory and calculate the food and beverage costs expressed as a percentage of sales at least once, sometimes twice, a month. A glance at this book's index will indicate several pages where food and beverage controls are discussed in detail, so here we will look at control from a management perspective.

When you become a manager and assume responsibility for controlling food and beverage items, the first thing to do is to get the locks changed because you have no idea who has access to what. The second thing is to review all control procedures. If you really want to exercise tight control, then insist that all orders have your signature or approval—that way, you know what should be received. Next, the stores need to be under the authority and responsibility of one person who is held accountable for all items under his or her control.

▶ Check Your Knowledge

1. When is feedforward control used?
2. What is the difference between concurrent control and feedback control?

Operational Financial Controls

At the operational level in the hospitality industry, the financial controls mainly consist of **budgets** and **income statements**. Budgets "guesstimate" the sales figure for the month/year and allow for up to a specific dollar amount to be spent on any cost of goods sold or controllable-costs item. Just preparing the budget has a control-like effect on managers. They are responsible for the financial outcome of their departments and rely heavily on budgets. Instead of just allowing departments to budget the same amount year in and year out, the concept of **zero-based budgeting** has managers begin with a budget of zero dollars and justify all the cost of goods sold, controllable costs, and capital expenditures (such as equipment) they plan on making so that there will be an appropriate amount of profit.

Income statements show the actual sales and expenditures for a month or year. They are used extensively in the hospitality industry as a means of control because they are results driven. Managers use the results for controlling the next period's performance. For example, if the results of the beverage department come in below expectations, then corrective action in the form of increased spot-checks would immediately be instigated along with more frequent inventory checks. Figure 19–4 shows a hotel income statement.

As stated earlier, but worth repeating, good managers first control the "big ticket" items that will be most costly if not controlled. Once the most costly items are under control, managers can move on to controlling other items. Looking at

INCOME STATEMENT
APRIL 2006

	CURRENT MONTH						YEAR TO DATE					
	CURRENT	%	BUDGET	%	LAST YR	%	CURRENT	%	BUDGET	%	LAST YR	%
REVENUE												
ROOMS	291,371	61.5%	310,270	66.3%	312,768	66.5%	1,106,897	63.5%	1,150,835	66.1%	1,167,731	64.3%
FOOD	136,868	28.9%	111,503	23.8%	108,176	23.0%	453,192	26.0%	414,868	23.8%	449,848	24.8%
BEVERAGE	22,830	4.8%	23,717	5.1%	26,470	5.6%	90,041	5.2%	84,787	4.9%	100,355	5.5%
TELEPHONE	5,473	1.2%	4,593	1.0%	6,686	1.4%	18,634	1.1%	17,390	1.0%	28,852	1.6%
SUNDRIES	367	0.1%	651	0.1%	798	0.2%	2,020	0.1%	2,368	0.1%	2,868	0.2%
OTHER INCOME	16,605	3.5%	17,270	3.7%	15,109	3.2%	72,914	4.2%	71,108	4.1%	66,559	3.7%
TOTAL REVENUE	473,514	100.0%	468,004	100.0%	470,007	100.0%	1,743,698	100.0%	1,741,356	100.0%	1,816,213	100.0%
DEPT EXPENSES												
ROOMS	68,874	23.6%	68,671	22.1%	63,403	20.3%	272,356	24.6%	273,771	23.8%	246,979	21.2%
FOOD	138,332	101.1%	115,108	103.2%	96,580	89.3%	468,515	103.4%	427,109	103.0%	398,509	88.6%
BEVERAGE	12,809	56.1%	11,080	46.7%	11,464	43.3%	46,567	51.7%	41,676	49.2%	49,675	49.5%
TELEPHONE	4,636	84.7%	4,867	106.0%	5,628	84.2%	20,543	110.2%	19,793	113.8%	21,234	73.6%
SUNDRIES	213	58.0%	418	64.2%	990	124.1%	1,957	96.9%	1,578	66.6%	2,744	95.7%
OTHER INCOME	10,531	63.4%	12,741	73.8%	12,956	85.8%	43,047	59.0%	56,513	79.5%	44,364	66.7%
TOT DEPT EXPENSES	235,395	49.7%	212,885	45.5%	191,021	40.6%	852,985	48.9%	820,440	47.1%	763,505	42.0%
DEPT PROFIT	238,119	50.3%	255,119	54.5%	278,986	59.4%	890,713	51.1%	920,916	52.9%	1,052,708	58.0%
UNDIST EXPENSES												
ADMIN & GENL	47,054	9.9%	38,531	8.2%	43,762	9.3%	206,582	11.8%	168,784	9.7%	184,744	10.2%
MARKETING	26,619	5.6%	30,139	6.4%	15,458	3.3%	91,079	5.2%	88,953	5.1%	57,023	3.1%
REPAIR & MAINT	26,767	5.7%	39,621	8.5%	37,668	8.0%	142,323	8.2%	165,966	9.5%	130,646	7.2%
GROUNDS	22,662	4.8%	26,650	5.7%	29,897	6.4%	108,114	6.2%	107,024	6.1%	95,284	5.2%
UTILITIES	20,494	4.3%	26,785	5.7%	19,010	4.0%	85,988	4.9%	99,652	5.7%	83,380	4.6%
TOT UNDIST EXP	143,596	30.3%	161,726	34.6%	145,795	31.0%	634,086	36.4%	630,379	36.2%	551,077	30.3%
GROSS OPER PROFIT	94,523	20.0%	93,393	20.0%	133,191	28.3%	256,627	14.7%	290,537	16.7%	501,631	27.6%
FIXED EXPENSES												
PROP TAXES	5,734	1.2%	5,734	1.2%	5,099	1.1%	27,015	1.5%	26,983	1.5%	24,443	1.3%
INSURANCE	2,622	0.6%	2,622	0.6%	1,700	0.4%	10,488	0.6%	10,488	0.6%	6,800	0.4%
INTEREST	1,220	0.3%	1,252	0.3%	1,345	0.3%	4,944	0.3%	5,008	0.3%	5,442	0.3%
INCOME TAXES	0	0.0%	0	0.0%	0	0.0%	0	0.0%	0	0.0%	0	0.0%
DEPREC	26,000	5.5%	26,000	5.6%	26,000	5.5%	104,000	6.0%	104,000	6.0%	100,000	5.5%
TOT FIXED EXP	35,576	7.5%	35,608	7.6%	34,144	7.3%	146,447	8.4%	146,479	8.4%	136,685	7.5%
NET INCOME	58,947	12.4%	57,785	12.3%	99,047	21.1%	110,180	6.3%	144,058	8.3%	364,946	20.1%

	CURRENT	BUDGET	LAST YR		CURRENT	BUDGET	LAST YR
ROOMS AVAIL	2,580	2,580	2,670		10,320	10,320	10,680
ROOMS OCCUPIED	1,495	1,670	1,797		5,747	6,078	6,529
OCCUPANCY %	57.9%	64.7%	67.3%		55.7%	58.9%	61.1%
AVG RATE	$151.63	$147.30	$141.56		$147.84	$147.09	$142.50

Figure 19-4 • Hotel Income Statement. (Courtesy of Hospitality Concepts, San Diego.)

the labor costs in Figure 19–4, we can see that payroll is the largest of the controllable costs. Labor costs, like any other, need to be controlled in line with sales. Each department will have its own desired labor cost expressed as a percentage of sales. If sales go up, it is easier to control labor costs. However, if sales go down, then management must "control" labor costs to avoid losing more than absolutely necessary. Management also needs to be fair with associates. After the September 11, 2001, tragedy, Marriott set an example at many of its hotels and resorts by not laying off any associates—it instead reduced everyone's hours, which did a lot to keep associates loyal.

In managerial accounting, food and beverage costs are the next largest to be controlled after labor costs. Attractions such as Sea World, clubs, resorts, hotels, and restaurants all offer food and beverages to their guests. All food and beverage items need to be costed and priced in advance to yield a certain percentage—let's say 24 percent. We all know that these percentages will vary from one organization to another, the point is that both food and beverage departments need to be controlled to produce the expected results, and income statements provide written feedback control.

Things such as recipes, portion control, proper purchasing, storage, issuing, and preparation of all food and beverage items help ensure that items reach the guest correctly. Next, we need to ensure that all monies reach the bank—no fingers in the cash register! No bags in the kitchen, no internal trades between departments. A proper system must be in place for recording all sales and ensuring that the correct amount is received from guests. Hospitality operators can choose from several point-of-sale systems and front- and back-of-the-house systems to assist the control process in making the job easier.

Qualities of an Effective Control System

Effective control systems tend to have certain characteristics in common.[2] The importance of these qualities varies with the situation; effective control systems have 10 characteristics.

1. *Accuracy.* An effective control system is reliable and produces valid data.
2. *Timeliness.* An effective control system provides timely information.
3. *Economy.* An effective control system is economical to operate.
4. *Flexibility.* An effective control system is flexible enough to adjust to changes and opportunities.
5. *Understandability.* The users can understand an effective control system.
6. *Reasonable criteria.* Control standards must be reasonable and attainable.
7. *Strategic placement.* Because managers can't control everything, they must choose to control factors that are strategic to the organization's performance.

8. *Emphasis on exceptions.* Managers can't control all activities; control devices should call attention only to the exceptions.

9. *Multiple criteria.* Measures decrease tendencies toward a narrow focus.

10. *Corrective action.* The control system not only indicates significant deviations, but also suggests appropriate corrective action.

Experienced managers use effective controls by exception, meaning that if the results are outside the acceptable predetermined limits, then they take action; otherwise they concentrate on something else.

Contingency Plans and Control

The most important contingency plan factor that affects the design of an organization's control system is the size of the organization. The control system should vary according to the organization's size. A small organization relies more on informal and personal control approaches. Here, concurrent control (direct supervision) is probably the most cost effective. However, as organizations increase in size, direct supervision is likely to be supplemented by an expanding formal control system of reports, regulations, and rules. Very large organizations typically have highly formalized and impersonal feedforward and feedback controls. Contingency plans and control cover the *what-ifs*—what if our sales dip 8 percent? What will we do? Reduce associate hours, reduce expenditures, and attempt to boost sales.

As you move up in the organization's hierarchy, there is a greater need for several different types of control; this reflects increased operational complexities. Additionally, the greater the degree of decentralization, the more managers will need feedback on employees' decisions and performance results. Managers who delegate authority for making decisions and performing work are still ultimately responsible for the actions of those to whom it was delegated.

The importance of an activity influences whether and how it will be controlled. However, if an error can be highly damaging to the organization, extensive controls are likely to be implemented. It simply makes sense to control the big-ticket items.

Adjusting Controls for Cultural Differences

Control is used quite differently in other countries.[3] The differences in organizational control systems of global organizations are seen primarily in the measurement and corrective-action steps of the control process. In a global hospitality corporation, managers of foreign operations tend to be controlled less directly by the home office, for no other reason than that distance keeps managers from being able to observe work directly. Because distance creates a tendency to formalize controls, the home office of a global company often relies on extensive formal reports for control. Global companies rely on the power of information technology to provide speedy control reports of results.

FOCUS ON CONTROL AND COMMAND IN TIME OF DISASTER

Hank Christen *George Washington University*
Paul Maniscalco *Unconventional Concepts, Inc.*

Before any emergency or disaster occurs, an organization's responsibility for the control of the situation and for the command of each organizational element need to be clearly specified in the emergency/disaster plan. Individual departments and contractors (who provide goods and services) are integral to ensuring the organization's continued operation, reputation, management, and event survivability. One of the most important tasks is defining control of the organizational response to the event in the planning phase. Once this requirement has been identified, the next step is to implement an interim command and control framework that functions as the highest authority responsible for management of the event.

This command configuration places critical departments and subunits under the control of a single authority—the person on site ultimately in charge of all the organization's resources: the incident commander. This new organizational structure is designed for the sole purpose of resolving the crisis, and it is in effect only in times of emergency. After the crisis has been resolved, the command structure relinquishes its authority to the standard daily managerial configuration. Even though this command structure serves at the direction of the organization and depends on it for logistical support, its characteristics and qualities are unique to itself and to the mission.

The incident command structure requires an effective command and control design—a system providing for critical department interaction and ensuring that all efforts are directed toward achieving a common goal. Without a robust, sustaining support mechanism, the chain of command and communications are fragmented, confusing, and vastly ineffective. By establishing a control mechanism in advance, the organization's command structure is highly adaptable for large- and small-scale emergencies and is flexible enough to integrate resources from different corporate and vendor areas. Several critical issues should be considered when designing a command and control system:

- Every emergency event demands a structured plan. Although more minor emergencies generally do not require a fully scripted response, some guidance is required in all emergency scenarios. Without a response plan, the organization's incident commander is unable to seek the advice and employ the expertise of subordinate commanders.

- The command structure must provide a manageable span of control to be effective. Without a manageable span of control, the incident commander quickly becomes overloaded with data and requests. This phenomenon is frequently referred to in the emergency response field as OBE, "overwhelmed by events." OBE must be avoided. Early recognition of span-of-control issues enables the manager to assign subordinate commanders and avoid OBE.

- Comprehensive resource management, distribution, and accountability are also required. Some required resources may have a limited service time, and replacements must be arranged for. Radio batteries must be exchanged and recharged. Repair parts from distant locations may be needed. Personnel must be fed and relieved. These factors demand that the incident manager assign a current status condition to all resources and provide for efficient operation.

- Communications systems must be reliable, efficient, and secure. Frequently facility communications are disabled because of the incident. The result is an inability to communicate, control, and prioritize subordinate tasking. In the military, communications is called "the voice of command." Commanders who cannot communicate cannot control. The manager should work with the organization's security department and enhance its radio capacity so that internal resources are in place to sustain crisis communications.

Critical Factors

- Control begins with a structured plan.
- A narrow span of control should be maintained to avoid OBE (overwhelmed by events).
- Operational control is not possible without effective communications.

Technology's impact on control also can be seen when comparing technologically advanced nations with less technologically advanced countries. In countries such as the United States, Japan, Canada, the United Kingdom, France, Germany, and Australia, managers of global companies use indirect control devices, particularly computer-related reports and analyses in addition to standardized rules and direct supervision, to ensure that work activities are going as planned.

In less technologically advanced countries, managers tend to rely more on direct supervision and highly centralized decision making for control. Also, constraints on what corrective actions managers can take may affect managers in foreign countries because laws in some countries do not allow managers the option of choosing the facilities, laying off employees, taking money out of the country, or bringing in a new management team from outside the country.

Contemporary Issues in Control

One issue that can arise as managers begin to design efficient and effective control systems includes technological advances in computer hardware and software that have made the process of controlling much easier, but these advances have brought with them difficult questions regarding what managers have the right to know about employee behavior.[4] Another issue is workplace privacy.

Workplace Privacy

If you work, do you think you have a right to privacy at your workplace? What can your employer find out about you and your work? You may be surprised by the answer. Why do managers feel they must monitor what employees are doing? A reason is that employees are hired to work, not to surf the Web checking stock prices, placing bets at online casinos, or shopping for presents for family or friends.

Personal on-the-job Web surfing costs millions of dollars a year in wasted computer resources and billions of dollars in lost work productivity. Another reason why managers monitor employee e-mail and computer usage is that they don't want to risk being sued for creating a hostile workplace environment

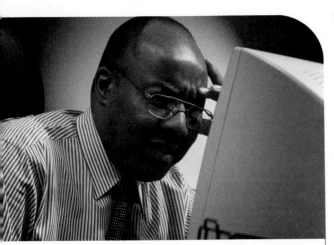

Increased use of computers at the workplace poses risk for privacy issues

A Prepay Restaurant

There is a great hole-in-the-wall restaurant in New York City where arguably the best front-end control system is in place. Servers have to pay the cooks for the guest's food—so you know that they will get the money from the guests.

because of offensive messages or an inappropriate image displayed on a coworker's computer screen. Concern about sexual harassment is one of the reasons why companies may want to monitor or keep backup copies of all e-mail. This can help establish what actually happened if an incident arises and can help managers react instantly. Managers also need to be certain that employees are not inadvertently passing information on to others who could use that information to harm the company.

Employee Theft

Would it surprise you to know that a high percentage of all organizational theft and fraud is committed by employees, not outsiders? Any unauthorized taking of company property by employees for their personal use constitutes employee theft, including fraudulent filing of expense reports and removing equipment, software, and office supplies from the company premises. Hospitality businesses have long faced serious losses from employee theft caused by loose financial controls, especially at the start-up of a business.

Why do employees steal? There are several perspectives. Industrial loss-prevention professionals suggest that people steal because the opportunity presents itself through lax controls and favorable circumstances. Some people have different social financial problems or pressures such as gambling debts. People steal because they can rationalize whatever they're doing as being correct and appropriate behavior. Hospitality associates also steal because they often feel underpaid, so whether it's a phone call here or a knife, fork, and spoon there, if the opportunity arises, they may take advantage of it. Notice how the concepts of feedforward, concurrent, and feedback control to identify measures for deterring or reducing employee theft apply.

Workplace Violence

Factors contributing to workplace violence include employee stress caused by long working hours, information overload, daily interruptions, unrealistic deadlines, and uncaring managers.

This list may not look like the place you work, but some of these factors appear in a good many corporations, especially with the pressure of making a profit in the increasingly competitive 24/7/365 environment.

Control is critical in the hospitality industry because we need to know how we are doing all the time. We need to know whether goals are being met and standards reached or exceeded. According to the situation, well-managed hospitality businesses use a variety of controls to provide the necessary information to management for decision-making purposes.

INTRODUCING MICHAEL R. THORPE

The Leader of the Future Will Be a Holistic One

Michael R. Thorpe, who has earned a bachelor of science degree in hotel and restaurant management, is an outstanding example of the leadership skills that can be acquired throughout the school and college career.

Mike's leadership abilities developed from an early age, with his involvement in the Boy Scouts of America. Looking back at that memorable time, Mike recognizes how important it is for a leader to be a good role model. He emphasizes the fact that it is necessary to make a sharp distinction between "good" leaders and "bad" leaders, thus establishing a learning process that is based on the identification of both "shoulds" (positive examples, experiences, activities, skills) and "should nots" (mistakes, negative attitudes). Mike's experience with the Boy Scouts provided him with fundamental values and skills, which were acknowledged when he achieved the rank of Eagle Scout.

In high school as well as in college, Mike progressively developed and used his leadership skills. He believes that the key to learning is involvement. In fact, he always took part in school activities, also emphasizing the importance of maintaining a broad horizon of interests. In particular, Mike chose to actively participate in a variety of extracurricular activities, including academic, service-oriented, and sports organizations. He stressed the belief that there is a strict correlation among such fields that shapes the overall personality of the leader. "The leader of the future will be a holistic one," Mike says.

Mike's involvement in academic organizations, such as the student body government council; in sports, as captain of the football team and vice president of the football club; and in service-oriented enterprises, such as the Hosteur's Society HRTM Club, to which he was elected president, helped him develop the necessary skills for high-quality interaction with people. He learned that a good leader is someone who can gather a group of individuals and coordinate each single talent, skill, propensity, and personality into a successful team, joining forces in the pursuit of one common goal. Each member of the team must be fulfilled in his or her need for belonging, personal satisfaction, recognition, and so on. To accomplish this task, Mike understood that a leader must also be extremely respectful of each individual's personal life, needs, problems, cultural background, and diversity, setting aside personal likes and dislikes. Diversity also provides an opportunity for the leader to learn from the people he or she guides, an opportunity that every leader must have the humility and willingness to pursue.

In Mike's words, the leader must act as a "glue" that unites people and the organizer who finds the "right place" for each individual, a place in which he or she will be able to excel and perform at his or her full potential.

Work experience throughout his college career also taught Mike that workers will function at their best in a work environment that is appealing and challenging and that provides them with the right tools—in terms of knowledge, motivation, rewards, and climate—to produce the optimal outcome.

To achieve such results, Mike excludes, as much as possible, the carrot-on-a-stick approach. He feels that such a method is a superficial remedy that doesn't get to the root of the problem—and thus doesn't solve it—and doesn't consider that a leader deals with human beings intrinsically characterized by a distinct intelligence and personality. Furthermore, when dealing with subordinates' failures or mistakes, Michael prefers to approach the person(s) in question from his or her point of view, trying to understand the cause of the inefficiency and establish whether that person's poor performance is determined by his own possible leadership mistake.

Mike greatly respects a leader who creates a sense of cooperation, community, and teamwork. Just as in a family, the leader should step down from an ivory tower and be open to each member of the team, listen, and be willing to help with possible personal problems, emphasizing the importance of open communication. And as in a family, the leader must be a caring parent who can also progressively impose discipline and obtain the results expected depending on the members' potential.

Mike understands the role of a father because he has a six-year-old who represents, among other things, the ultimate challenge for leadership. "Workers' livelihoods do depend on the employer/leader."

▶ **Check Your Knowledge**

1. Briefly explain zero-based budgeting.
2. List the qualities of an effective control system.
3. What are some contributors to workplace violence?

Trends in Control

Increasing use of technology for control helps make the job of control not only easier but also much quicker. Quicker results mean decisions to make necessary changes are made sooner, thus avoiding further losses. Handheld devices that take inventory are an example of how technology can assist management with inventory taking.

CASE STUDY

The Ritz-Carlton

The Ritz-Carlton is an outstanding hotel providing luxury service to its guests. In contrast with the standard goals of typical business hotels—to provide a home away from home—the Ritz-Carlton decided to take it a step further and provide luxury accommodation to industry executives, meeting and corporate travel planners, and other affluent travelers. The chain is based in Atlanta and runs 25 luxury hotels that pursue excellence in each market.

Recently the hotel company was awarded the U.S. government's Malcolm Baldrige National Quality Award. The award praised Ritz-Carlton for its participatory leadership, thorough information gathering, coordinated planning and execution, and trained workforce that was ready "to move heaven and earth" to satisfy its customers. Thinking about control, what types of control mechanisms did Ritz-Carlton need to achieve excellence?

The corporate motto is "Ladies and gentlemen serving ladies and gentlemen." All employees are expected to practice the company's "Gold Standards." These standards are made up of a service credo and the basics of premium service, including processes for solving any problem guests may have.

The difference between this luxury chain and other hotel companies is that its employees are "certified" after the common basic orientation followed by an on-the-job training. This certification to work for Ritz-Carlton is reinforced daily by frequent recognition for achievement, performance appraisal, and daily "lineups." Annual surveys are given to make sure the employees know the quality standards the hotel company expects of them as well as to determine their level of satisfaction with the company. One year 96 percent of the employees surveyed ranked excellence in guest services as their primary duty. Workers are empowered by the company to do whatever it takes to solve any sort of problem a customer may encounter. Employees are required to assist their coworkers in dealing with a guest satisfaction issue, leaving no room for any excuse as to why a customer problem was not solved on the spot. In this way, the guest is truly treated as a king; guest satisfaction comes first—always.[5]

Discussion Questions

1. In what ways does Ritz-Carlton use control to ensure high-quality service?
2. How does the company maintain and foster its employees' high level of commitment?

Summary

1. Control is the management function that provides information on the degree to which goals and objectives are being accomplished.

2. Control is important because it's the final link in the management function. An effective control system is important because managers need to delegate duties and empower employees to make decisions.

3. The control process can be described as setting standards, measuring actual performance, comparing actual performance against those standards, and taking managerial action to correct deviations or inadequate performances.

4. Managers can use controls *in advance of* an activity, which is called feedforward control; *during* the activity, which is called concurrent control; and *after* the activity, which is called feedback control.

5. Budgets and income statements are primarily used for financial control. Budgets "guesstimate" the sales figure for the month or year and allow for up to a specific dollar amount to be spent on any cost of goods sold or controllable costs item. Income statements show the actual sales and expenditures for a month or year.

6. Effective control systems have ten characteristics: accuracy, timeliness, economy, flexibility, understandability, reasonable criteria, strategic placement, emphasis on exceptions, multiple criteria, and corrective action.

7. Contemporary issues in control include the increasing use of technological advances, which raise the issue of workplace privacy. Additionally, workplace violence and employee theft are issues in the control process.

Key Words and Concepts

accuracy
basic corrective action
budget
concurrent control
control
control process
correcting actual performance
corrective action
economy

emphasis on exceptions
feedback control
feedforward control
flexibility
immediate corrective action
income statement
management by walking
  around (MBWA)
measurement

multiple criteria
reasonable criteria
strategic placement
timeliness
understandability
zero-based budgeting

Review Questions

1. Imagine a restaurant that is lacking any kind of control. Describe the negative and positive aspects of this environment and then answer the following question: Why is control necessary?

2. If you were a manager of a Hilton resort in the Bahamas, what way of measuring actual employee performance would you use and why? What are the pros and cons of your chosen method?

3. Explain the three different types of control. Think of a situation in which you have been controlled. Which type of control works best for you?
4. Describe how you envision an effective control system. What types of control would you use?

How would you measure employee performance? How would you keep employee theft under control? What about workplace violence? Which operational financial control would you implement?

Internet Exercise

Organization: The ePolicy Institute
Web site: www.epolicyinstitute.com/disasters/stories.html
Summary: This site summarizes e-disaster stories.

a. Do you think that it's fair for employers to monitor their employees' e-mails?
b. What would you do if you caught your boss reading your e-mails?

Apply Your Knowledge

You are a restaurant manager. The month-end food cost percentage has just arrived on your desk, and it shows that the actual food cost percentage is 12 percent above budget. What will you do?

Endnotes

1. Stephen P. Robbins and Mary Coulter, *Management,* 8th ed. (Upper Saddle River, NJ: Prentice Hall, 2005), 486.
2. W. H. Newman, *Constructive Control Design and Use of Control Systems* (Upper Saddle River, NJ: Prentice Hall, 1975), 33.
3. Robbins and Coulter, *Management,* 475.
4. Ibid.
5. Adapted from Gary Dessler, *A Framework for Management* (Upper Saddle River, NJ: Prentice Hall, 2002), 376–377.

Glossary

Accounting director   The person in charge of accounting and money-related topics.

Accounts payable   Balances owed to suppliers that need to be paid; source of funds.

Accuracy   A precise and effective control system—one that is reliable and produces valid data.

Active listening   Listening for full meaning without making premature judgments or interpretations.

Actual market share   The market share that a business actually receives; compare with the fair market share, which is an equal share of the market.

ADA   *See* Americans with Disabilities Act.

ADR   *See* Average daily rate.

Age Discrimination in Employment Act   A law that protects individuals over 40 years of age from age discrimination in matters of hiring, discharge compensation, and other terms of employment.

Agenda 21   A charter produced during the 1992 Earth Summit held in Rio de Janeiro, Brazil, that addresses issues pertaining to the environment and sustainable development; it is intended to prepare the world to successfully meet the challenges of the twenty-first century.

AHMA   American Hotel and Motel Association.

Airport hotel   A hotel located near an airport that caters to travelers; classified as a luxury, midscale, economy, or suite hotel.

À la carte   1. A menu on which food and beverages are listed and priced individually. 2. Foods cooked to order rather than in advance and held for later service.

Alcohol   A naturally occurring and easily synthesized compound that induces intoxication when consumed.

All-suite extended-stay hotel   A type of hotel that is classified as a luxury, midscale suite hotel.

Allocation of weights to criteria   Allocating different levels of importance to decision criteria according to a weighting method.

Ambience   The combined atmosphere created by the décor, lighting, service, possible entertainment (such as background music), and other amenities, which enhances the dining or lodging experience.

Amenities   Features that add material comfort or convenience to a guest's stay; for example, hair shampoo, an iron and ironing board in each room, and an in-room coffee maker.

American service   Food is dished onto individual plates and served to guests.

Americans with Disabilities Act (ADA)   A law that prohibits discrimination against persons with disabilities and stipulates that employers must make "readily achievable" modifications to their premises and to work practices and working conditions for those with disabilities.

Analysis of alternatives   Analyzing alternatives according to the "weights to criteria" method.

Analytic style   A style of decision-making marked by great tolerance for ambiguity and consideration of several alternatives, fostering adaptability to various situations.

Aperitif   A fortified wine flavored with one or more herbs and spices, usually consumed before a meal.

Apollo   The name of a commonly used airline reservation system.

Application service provider (ASP)   Delivers a complete booking system tied to the hotel's inventory in real time via the Internet.

Atmosphere   The combination of mood, lighting, furnishings, and music that has an immediate conscious as well as subconscious effects on guests.

Auditing   The physical, and official, examination of financial records to determine accuracy.

Authority   The rights inherent in a managerial position to tell people what to do and to expect them to do it.

Average daily rate (ADR)   One of the key operating ratios that indicates the level of a hotel's performance. The ADR is calculated by dividing the dollar sales by the number of rooms rented.

Average food service check   A measure of the average bill owed by food service customers.

It is calculated by dividing total food sales by the total number of food covers, or guest counts.

Average guest check   The average amount each group spends; used primarily in a restaurant setting.

Baby boomers   Persons born in the 21-year period from 1946 through 1965. Baby boomers represent the largest segment of the population—about 76 million United States residents in 2004. Baby boomers travel more frequently than their parents and regard travel as a necessity rather than a luxury.

Baccarat   A traditional table game in which the winning hand totals closest to nine.

Back-of-the-house operations   The support areas behind the scenes in a hotel or motel, including housekeeping, laundry, engineering, and foodservice. Also refers to individuals who operate behind the scenes to make a guest's stay pleasant and safe.

Banquet   A formal dinner.

Bar mitzvah   A Jewish religious ritual and family celebration commemorating the entrance into adulthood of a boy on his 13th birthday.

Basic corrective action   An action that examines how and why performance deviated and then proceeds to correct the source of deviation.

Batch cooking   The cooking of food in quantities for consumption throughout a meal period. Used in noncommercial foodservice to avoid putting out all the food at 11:30 and having it spoil. Batches are cooked for readiness at 11:30, 12, 12:30, etc.

Bed and breakfast   A rate that combines a night's accommodation with breakfast the following day. The breakfast may be either a full breakfast or a continental breakfast.

Behavioral style   A decision-making style characterized by a low tolerance for ambiguity and an intuitive way of thinking.

Benchmarking   Searching for the best practices among competitors or noncompetitors that lead to their superior performance.

Bet   An amount wagered or put into play during a gaming activity.

Beverage cost budget   A budget prepared to meet the inventory needs of beverage sales.

Big 6   A casino game involving a wheel spun by a dealer in which players wager on six possible outcomes.

Blackjack   A table game in which the winning hand is determined by whether the dealer or the player gets cards that add up to a number closest to or equal to 21 without going over.

Boardroom-style meeting   A type of meeting setup designed for a small number of participants who sit around a rectangular table.

Body language   Gestures, facial expressions, body postures, and other movements of the body that convey meaning, such as the emotional state and attitude of the person.

Bonding   A recreational process by which people form relationships built on the experiences they have enjoyed together.

Bounded rationality   Decision-making based on or limited by an individual's ability to gain information.

Boundaryless organizations   Organizations not limited to or bound by vertical or horizontal boundaries.

Brigade   A team of kitchen personnel organized into stations.

Budget   An itemized listing, usually prepared annually, of anticipated revenue and projected expenses.

Budgeting   The process of forecasting sales and costs.

Cage   An area under the control of a casino cashier in which cash is exchanged for chips and coins.

California menu   A menu from which guests can order any item at any time of the day.

Call accounting system (CAS)   A system that tracks guest room phone charges.

Call package   In bar operations, the group of spirits that the bar offers to guests who ask for specific name brands.

Capture rate   In hotel food and beverage practice, the number of hotel guests who use the food and beverage outlets.

Cash budget   A budget to plan for the availability of the necessary cash resources for uninterrupted business operations.

Cash flow management   The process by which the business operation's cash flows are monitored, analyzed, and adjusted as needed.

Cash inflow   Accounts for business activity and decisions regarding cash flows into a business.

Cash outflow   Accounts for business activity and decisions regarding cash flows out of a business.

Casino   An area in which gaming activities involving table games and slot machines take place.

Casino hotel   A hotel that combines accommodations with gambling.

Casual dining   Relaxed dining; includes restaurants from several classifications.

Catastrophe plan   A plan to maximize guest and property safety in the event of a disaster.

Catchment area   The geographical area that falls within a specific radius established to determine the size of a restaurant's market (usually one to five miles).

Catering   The part of the food and beverage division of a hotel that is responsible for arranging and planning food and beverage functions for conventions and smaller hotel groups, and local banquets booked by the sales department.

Catering director   Head of all catering operations.

Catering service manager   Head of the catering services department.

CBX   The telecommunications department. Also called PBX.

Celebrity restaurant   A restaurant owned, or partially owned, by a celebrity.

Central reservations office (CRO)   The central office of a lodging company, where reservations are processed.

Central reservations system (CRS)   A reservation system that is commonly used in large franchises to connect their reservation systems with one another; enables guests to call one phone number to reserve a room at any of the chain properties.

Centralization   The degree to which decision-making is concentrated at a single point in the organization.

Certainty   The condition of knowing in advance the outcome of a decision.

CFA   Culinary Federation of America.

Chain network   Within this network, communication flows according to the existing chain of command of an organization; includes upward and downward communication flow.

Chain of command   The continuous line of authority that extends from upper organizational levels to the lowest levels in the organization and clarifies who reports to whom.

Champagne   Sparkling wine made in the Champagne district of France.

Charity ball   A gala dinner-dance event whose purpose is to raise funds toward a group or charity.

Charter of Sustainable Tourism   An outcome of the World Conference on Sustainable Tourism held in Spain in 1995; recognizes the objective of developing a tourism industry that meets economic expectations and environmental requirements, and respects not only the social and physical structure of the location, but also the local population.

Chef de partie (shef de par-tée)   Produces the menu items for a station under the direct supervision of the chef or sous chef. Also known as *station chef*.

Chef tournant   A chef who rotates the various stations in the kitchen to relieve the station chefs.

Chief steward   The individual in a hotel, club, or foodservice operation who is responsible for the cleanliness of the back of the house and dishwashing areas and for storage and control of china, glassware, and silverware.

CHRIE   Council on Hotel, Restaurant, and Institutional Education.

City center hotel   A hotel located in the center of a city.

City ledger   A client whose company has established credit with a particular hotel. Charges are posted to the city ledger and accounts are sent once or twice monthly.

Civil Rights Act of 1964   A law that bans discrimination based on race, religion, color, sex, or national origin.

Class III gaming   A class of gaming created by the Indian Gaming Regulatory Act that includes most casino games. In a state that has class III gaming, casino gaming is legalized for commercial (non-Indian) gaming operators and is conducted in conformance with a contract, or agreement, between the state government and the tribes.

Classroom-style meeting   A type of meeting setup generally used in instructional meetings, such as workshops.

Clinic   A form of meeting whose attendees learn by doing.

Club   An association of persons with some common objective, usually jointly supported, that meets periodically.

Cold calling   A type of prospecting whereby sales representatives call on individuals or organizations with no idea of whether these people will turn out to be true sales prospects.

Commercial foodservice   Operations that compete for customers in the open market.

Commission cap   A limit on the commission earned by travel agents booking airline tickets. The caps were imposed in 1995, changing commissions to $25 each way for domestic flights and reducing commissions for international flights from 11 to 8 percent.

Communication   The exchange of information and the transfer of meaning.

Communication networks   Networks that enable and facilitate the communications process.

Comparison matrix   Used to analyze competitors' strengths and weaknesses to help determine which strategies to use in a marketing action plan.

Competitor analysis   An analysis of competitors' strengths and weaknesses.

Comping   Offering a complimentary service without charge.

Compressed workweek   A workweek in which employees work longer hours per day but fewer days per week.

Computer information system (CIS)   An information system that uses electronic computing technology to create the information system.

Concept   The elements in a foodservice operation that contribute to its function as a complete and organized system serving the needs and expectations of its guests.

Conceptual style   A decision-making style that involves considering numerous alternatives in order to find creative solutions to the problem.

Concierge   A uniformed employee of a hotel who works at a desk in the lobby or on special concierge floors and answers questions, solves problems, and performs the services of a private secretary for the hotel's guests.

Concurrent control   Control that occurs while the work is being done.

Confirmed reservation   A reservation made by a guest that is confirmed by the hotel for the dates they plan to stay.

Contingency factors   Factors contingent upon various circumstances occurring; planning for the *what-ifs*.

Contingency perspective   An approach that says that organizations are different, face different situations (contingencies), and require different methods of managing.

Contractor   A company that operates a foodservice for the client on a contractual basis.

Contribution margin   Key operating figure in menu engineering, determined by subtracting food cost from selling price as a measure of profitability.

Control   The provision of information to management for decision-making purposes. The process of monitoring activities to ensure that they are being accomplished as planned and of correcting any significant deviations.

Control process   A three-step process including measuring actual performance, comparing actual performance against a standard, and taking managerial action to correct deviations or inadequate standards.

Controllable expenses   Expenses that can be controlled by means of cost-effective purchasing systems, a controlled storage and issuing system, and strict control of food production and sales. These expenses are usually watched over by management.

Controller   Head accountant, who manages the accounting department and all financial dealings of a business.

Convention   A generic term referring to any size business or professional meeting held in one specific location, which usually includes some form of trade show or exposition. Also refers to a group of delegates or members who assemble to accomplish a specific goal.

Convention center A large meeting place.

Convention hotel A large hotel that provides accommodation for attendees at conventions; usually located near a convention center.

Convention and visitors bureau 1. An organization responsible for promoting tourism at the regional and local level. 2. A not-for-profit umbrella organization that represents a city or urban area in soliciting and servicing all types of travelers to that city or area, whether for business, pleasure, or both.

Coordination of activities The process of achieving unity of action among interdependent activities.

Corporate culture The overall style or feel of a company. Governs how people relate to each other and their jobs.

Corporate events Annual meetings, sales meetings, new product launches, training meetings, workshops, management meetings, press meetings, incentive meetings, and awards ceremonies.

Corporate philosophy The core beliefs that drive a company's basic organizational structure.

Corporate seminar A corporate meeting whose purpose is to exchange ideas; a conference.

Corporate travel agency An agency that specializes, either partly or wholly, in handling corporate or government accounts. Also known as an *outplant*.

Corporate travel manager An individual employed by a corporation, an association, a government agency, or some other type of organization to coordinate the organization's travel arrangements.

Correcting actual performance An approach used to correct poor performance; may include redefining job tasks, changing work compensation, offering training programs, or laying off staff.

Corrective action An action that is tending or intended to correct.

Covers The guest count of a restaurant.

Creative financing The cross-collateralization of several properties.

Creditor The person or business operation to whom a liability is owed.

Cuisine Food cooked and served in styles from around the world.

Curbside appeal Visual appeal and cleanliness designed to encourage people to dine in a particular restaurant.

Currency fluctuations Changes in the value of one currency compared to another or of one currency compared to itself.

Current assets Operating resources such as cash, accounts receivable, inventories, and prepaid operating expenses that are expected to be used in a year or less. Liquid assets.

Current liabilities Short-term financial obligations.

Customer relationship management (CRM) Businesses attempt to manage the relationship with their customers or guests for long-term mutual benefit.

Cyclical menu A menu that repeats itself over a period of time, usually every 10, 14, or 18 days.

Daily report A report prepared each day to provide essential performance information for a particular property to its management.

Data Raw, unanalyzed facts.

Database A collection of data arranged for ease and speed of retrieval, as by a computer.

Database management system (DBMS) A system for managing databases.

Decentralization The degree to which lower level employees provide input or actually make decisions.

Decision-making process The process of developing and analyzing alternatives and choosing from among them.

Demographics Statistical study of the characteristics of human populations.

Departmentalization Organizing resources into departments.

Desk clerk An employee who works at the front desk to register guests; supplies rates, information, and guest reports.

Destination   A location where travelers choose to visit and spend time.

Destination-management company   Organization in charge of developing and implementing tourism programs.

Development of alternatives   Listing possible alternatives that could resolve a problem.

Dinner house restaurant   A restaurant with a casual, eclectic décor that may promote a particular theme.

Directive style   A decision-making style characterized by a rational way of thinking and low tolerance for ambiguity.

Diversification   A corporate strategy whereby managers try to utilize their organization's resources more effectively by developing new products and new markets.

Diversity   An increase in the heterogeneity of an organization through the inclusion of different ethnic groups.

Division of labor   Dividing labor and tasks.

DOC   Director of catering.

Downward communication   Communication flow within the organization from supervisor or manager to employees.

Dram shop legislation   Laws and procedures that govern the legal operation of establishments that sell measured alcoholic beverages.

Drop   Total amount wagered in a casino during a period of time.

Du jour   French expression used on menus, meaning "of the day."

Economical   Effective work with the smallest amount of resources or input.

Economics   The science relating to the production, distribution, and use of goods and services.

Economy/budget hotel   A hotel that offers rooms at lower rates than do midscale or upscale hotels.

Ecotourism   Responsible travel to natural areas that conserves the environment and sustains the well-being of the local people.

EEO   *See* Equal employment opportunity.

EEOC   *See* Equal Employment Opportunity Commission.

Effectiveness   Completing activities so that organizational goals are attained; also referred to as "doing the right things" or "getting things done."

Efficiency   Getting the most output from the smallest amount of inputs; also referred to as "doing things right" or "getting things done well."

Eighty-sixed (86'ed)   A restaurant expression meaning that an item is canceled and is no longer available.

Elastic   Demand that changes with economic conditions.

Electronic data interchange (EDI)   A way for organizations to exchange standard business transaction documents using direct computer-to-computer networks.

Electronic mail (e-mail)   The instantaneous transmission of written messages by computers.

Emphasis on exceptions   The practice of not questioning a certain routine or way of doing things as long as everything goes well. Only cases of exceptions to routine, such as problems or complaints, have the potential to change the routine.

Employee assistance program (EAP)   A program of various kinds of assistance for employees.

Employee right to know   Per U.S. Senate Bill 198, information about chemicals must be made available to all employees.

Employee training   For many organizations, an ongoing activity that is conducted by a training department, a training manager, or by line management or specially selected individuals within each department.

Empowerment   The act of giving employees the authority, tools, and information they need to do their jobs with greater autonomy.

Encoding   Converting the message into symbolic form.

Engineering director   Head of the engineering and maintenance department and supervisor of its employees; may also maintain the hotel blueprints.

Enterprise information system   *See* Organizational information system.

Entrepreneur   An individual who creates, organizes, manages, and assumes the risk of an enterprise or business.

Environmental analysis   An analysis of the effect of uncontrollable and controllable factors on a hospitality and travel organization's direction and success. It is an element of situation, market, and feasibility analyses; it provides a foundation for long- and short-term marketing plans.

Environmental scanning The screening of large amounts of information to anticipate and interpret changes in the environment.

Equal employment opportunity (EEO) The legal right of all individuals to be considered for employment and promotion on the basis of their ability and merit.

Equal Employment Opportunity Commission (EEOC) The organization that individuals may turn to if they feel that they have been discriminated against by an employer.

Equal Pay Act A law that prohibits discrimination in which employers pay men more than women for jobs requiring substantially equal skills, effort, and responsibility.

Equity theory The theory that an employee compares his or her job's inputs–outcomes ratio with that of relevant others and then corrects any inequity.

Escalation of commitment Increased commitment to a previous decision despite evidence that it may have been wrong.

Ethics The study of standards of conduct and moral judgment; also, the standards of correct conduct.

Ethnic restaurant A restaurant featuring a particular cuisine such as Chinese, Mexican, or Italian.

European plan An accommodation-only rate that includes no meals.

Evaluation of decision effectiveness Determination of whether specified goals have been achieved.

Event planner An individual who is responsible for planning an event from start to finish. Duties include setting the date and location; advertising the event; and providing refreshments or arranging catering services; and arranging speakers and/or entertainment.

Event planning A general term that refers to a career path in the growing field of special events.

Executive chef The head of the kitchen.

Executive committee A committee of hotel executives from each of the major departments within the hotel; generally made up of the general manager, director of rooms division, food and beverage director, marketing and sales director, human resources director, accounting and/or finance director, and engineering director.

Exempt employees Employees who, under Section 13(a)(1) of the Federal Minimum Wage Law, are not required to receive pay for overtime work because they are engaged primarily in managerial or administrative functions.

Expectancy theory The theory that an individual tends to act in a certain way based on the expectation that the act will be followed by a given outcome and on the attractiveness of that outcome to the individual.

Expense account An account used primarily for entertainment purposes.

Exposition An event held mainly to promote informational exchanges among trade people. A large exhibition in which the presentation is the main attraction, as well as being a source of revenue for an exhibitor.

Fair Labor Standards Act of 1938 A law that established a policy for minimum wage and a maximum length for the workweek.

Fair market share A market share based on each business receiving an equal share of the market.

Fairs and festivals Planned events that are often themed to the celebration's purpose.

Familiarization (fam) trip A free or reduced-price trip given to travel agents, travel writers, or other intermediaries to promote destinations.

Feedback control A type of control that takes place after the activity is done and uses the obtained information to remedy the situation.

Feedforward control A type of control that focuses on preventing anticipated problems because it takes place in advance of the actual work activity.

Fermentation The chemical process in which yeast acts on sugar or sugar-containing substances, such as grain or fruit, to produce alcohol and carbon dioxide.

FIFO *See* First-in, first-out.

Financial statement   The end result of the accounting process for a specified period of time (daily, quarterly, yearly).

Financing activities   Activities involving financial resources (cash) obtained from owners and creditors, and the associated repayments of the resulting obligations.

Fine dining   Upscale dining, usually with white tablecloths, à la carte menus, and table service.

Finger foods   Appetizers and bits of foods that can be eaten without the aid of utensils.

Fining   The process by which wine that has matured is filtered to help stabilize it and remove any solid particles still in the wine.

First-in, first-out   The supplies that are ordered first are used first.

First mortgage loan   The most common type of real estate loan taken out by a borrower to buy property over time.

Fixed cost   A cost or expense for a fixed period and range of activity that does not change in total but becomes progressively smaller per unit as volume increases.

Flexibility   The ability to undergo change and modification readily.

Flextime/flexible work hours   A scheduling system in which employees are required to work a certain number of hours per week but are free, within limits, to vary the hours of work.

Floor supervisor   Supervises day-to-day work of room attendants at larger motels. Also called *assistant housekeeper*.

Focus group   A gathering of 8 to 12 people who are interviewed as a group by a facilitator.

FOM   *See* Front office manager.

Food and beverage cost control   Documents and reports used to track food and beverage purchases and usage. Includes food and beverage cost budgets and the analysis of cost activity, including the calculation of two key cost ratios: the food cost percentage and the beverage cost percentage.

Food and beverage director   The individual responsible for the successful operation of all restaurant and kitchen duties, including guest satisfaction and profitability.

Food cost budget   A budget prepared to meet the inventory needs of food costs.

Forecasting   Predicting future outcomes.

Formal communication   Communication that takes place within a prescribed organizational work agreement.

Fortified wine   Wine to which brandy or other spirits have been added to stop further fermentation or to raise its alcoholic content.

Forum   A public assembly or lecture involving audience discussion.

Franchise   1. The authorization given by one company to another to sell its unique products and services. 2. The name of the business format or product that is being franchised.

Franchisee   A person who purchases the right to use or sell the products and services of the franchiser.

Franchiser   An individual or company that licenses others to sell its products or services.

Franchising   A concept that allows a company to expand quickly by allowing qualified people to use the systems, marketing, and purchasing power of the franchiser.

Freeway hotel   A hotel near a freeway.

French service   Restaurant service in which one waiter (a captain) takes the order, does the tableside cooking, and brings the drinks and food, and the secondary or back waiter serves bread and water, clears each course, crumbs the table, and serves the coffee.

Front-of-the-house operations   Comprises all areas with which guests come in contact, including the lobby, corridors, elevators, guest rooms, restaurants and bars, meeting rooms, and restrooms. Also refers to employees who staff these areas.

Front-line manager/supervisor   A low-level manager who manages the work of line employees and has guest contact.

Front office manager (FOM)   The person who manages the front office department.

Full-service hotel   A hotel that has restaurants, lounges, concierges, and many more facilities to cater to guests' needs.

Full-service restaurant   1. A restaurant that has more than a dozen main course items on the menu. 2. A restaurant that cooks food to order.

Function   An assigned duty or activity.

Fund-raiser   An event whose purpose is to raise funds for a group or charity.

Gainsharing plan   A group incentive program that shares the gains of the efforts of group members with those group markets.

Gaming   Wagering of money or other valuables on the outcome of a game or other event.

Gaming entertainment industry   Businesses that offer games of risk as part of a total package of entertainment and leisure time activities, including resort hotel, various foodservice concepts, retail shopping, theme parks, live entertainment, and recreational pursuits.

GDP   *See* Gross domestic product.

General manager   The head manager in an organization, who is ultimately responsible for the operation of the hospitality establishment and the supervision of its employees. Held directly accountable by the corporation or owners for the operation's level of profitability.

Generally Accepted Accounting Principles (GAAP)   Rules set up by the accounting profession that provide guidelines for the financial measurement of operating activity and the preparation of financial statements for external use. GAAP incorporates input from the SEC and FASB.

Geographic expansion   A strategic growth alternative of aggressively expanding into new domestic and/or overseas markets.

Global (international) information system   An information system that allows worldwide companies to remain linked, communicate with each other, and make transactions.

Globalization   The spread of companies beyond their borders to several other countries.

Goal   A specific result to be achieved; the end result of a plan.

Goal setting   Traditionally, goals are set at the top level of an organization and then broken down into subgoals for each level of the organization so that all levels work together toward the achievement of the ultimate goals.

Goal-setting theory   The proposition that specific goals improve performance and that difficult goals, when accepted, result in a higher level of performance than do easily attainable goals.

Government-sponsored recreation   Recreation paid for by government taxes; includes monies sent to cities for museums, libraries, and municipal golf courses.

Grievance   A complaint filed by an employee against the employer or employer's representative.

Gross domestic product (GDP)   The total value of goods and services produced within a country, minus the net payments on foreign investments.

Gross gaming revenue (GGR)   The net spending of customers on gaming. Does not include spending on nongaming operations such as food and beverage, hotel rooms, and other retail expenditures.

Gross operating profit   Revenues minus operating costs before taxes.

Gross operating revenue   Total payments received for goods and services.

Group dynamics   Includes individual abilities of group members, size of the group, level of conflict, and the internal pressures on members to conform to the group's norms; a very important factor for group performance.

Guaranteed reservations   If rooms are available on guest demand, the hotel guarantees the guests rooms on those days.

Guest   A person who is the recipient of hospitality in the form of entertainment—at someone's home, as a visiting participant in a program, or as a customer of an establishment such as a hotel or restaurant.

Guest accounting module   A system that increases the hotel's control over guest accounts and significantly modifies the night audit routine.

Guest counts (covers)   The number of guests dining in a restaurant.

Guest satisfaction   The desired outcome of hospitality services.

Guest service department   The department that takes care of guests and their needs.

Handle   The dollars wagered, or bet; often confused with *win*. Whenever a customer places a bet, the handle increases by the amount of the bet. The handle is not affected by the outcome of the bet.

Harassment   Persistent disturbance of a person verbally, physically, or sexually.

Hard count   The procedure for counting the coins and tokens removed from slot machines.

Haute cuisine   Elaborate or artful cuisine; contemporary cuisine.

Hold   The total amount of win in a casino during a period of time.

Hops   The dried, conical fruit of a special vine that imparts bitterness to beer.

Horizontal integration   The acquisition of ownership or control of competitors that are competing in the same or similar markets with the same or similar products.

Horseshoe-style room setup   A meeting room containing tables arranged in the shape of a U.

Hospice   An old French word meaning to provide care/shelter for travelers. The word *hospitality* is derived from this word.

Hospitality   1. The cordial and generous reception of guests. 2. A wide range of businesses, each of which is dedicated to the service of people away from home.

Hospitality information system (HIS)   A collection of components that work together to provide information to the operations and management of a hospitality organization.

Host/hostess   A greeter and "seater" at the entrance of a restaurant.

Hotel general manager   The manager in a hotel organization who is ultimately responsible for the operation of the hospitality establishment and the supervision of its employees. Held directly accountable by the corporation or owners for the operation's level of profitability.

Hotelier   The keeper, owner, or manager of the property.

Housekeeping   The department responsible for cleaning and servicing guest rooms; considered a back-of-the-house department.

Human resources manager or director   The individual who manages and develops the company's employees and their benefits program and monitors compliance with laws that relate to equal opportunity in hiring and promotion.

Identification of decision criteria   Identifying criteria important for making decisions.

Illegal alien   An individual who moves to another country illegally, without permission to enter as either an immigrant or a refugee. Also called an *undocumented worker*.

Immediate corrective action   Corrective action that corrects problems at once to get performance back on track.

Implementation of alternative   Implementing the selected alternative.

Incentive travel   A marketing and management tool used to motivate people by offering travel rewards for achieving a specific goal.

Income statement   A report that lists the amount of money or its equivalent received during a period of time in exchange for labor or services, from the sale of goods or property, or as profit from financial investments.

Independent business unit (IBU)   A business that makes decisions with little or no need to obtain approval for routine operational decisions from higher up in the organization.

Independent restaurant   A nonfranchise restaurant, privately owned.

Indian Gaming Regulatory Act   A federal act that created a statutory basis for the operation of gaming by Indian tribes in order to promote tribal economic development, self-sufficiency, and strong tribal governments.

Inflation   An increase in the volume of money and credit, resulting in a continuing rise in the general price level.

Informal communication   Does not follow a company's chain of command or structural hierarchy, and the subject matter is typically not job related or essential to performing job duties.

Information   Processed and analyzed data.

Information system (IS)   A set of people, data, and procedures that work together to retrieve, process, store, and disseminate information to support decision making and control.

Information technology (IT)   Any processes, practices, or systems that facilitate the processing and transportation of data or information.

Infusion   The extraction of flavors from foods.

Inseparability   The linkage of hospitality products and services.

Institutional foodservice   An operation that serves people who are members of particular societal institutions, such as a hospital, a college, a school, a nursing home, the military, or industry.

Interest rate   A rate set by the Federal Reserve Bank and banks in general that determines the rate of interest charged for loans.

International Festivals & Events Association   An organization that provides an opportunity for event managers from around the world to network and exchange ideas on how other festivals excel in sponsorship, marketing, fund-raising, operations, volunteer coordination, and management.

International information system   *See* Global (international) information system.

Interpersonal communication   Communication between two or more people.

Interpersonal communication process   Consists of seven elements: the communication source, the message, encoding, the channel, decoding, the receiver, and feedback.

Intuitive decision-making   A subconscious process of making decisions on the basis of experience and accumulated judgment.

Inventory control   A method for keeping track of all resources required to produce a product.

Investing activities   The purchase and sale of operating equipment or other assets intended to produce revenue in the long run. Also includes activities related to non-operating assets intended strictly for investment purposes, such as stock investment in other companies.

Jargon   The specialized or technical language of a trade, profession, or similar group.

Job description   A description of the duties and responsibilities involved in the performance of a particular job.

Job enlargement   A horizontal increase in the number of similar tasks assigned to a job.

Job enrichment   A vertical expansion of a job involving the addition of planning and evaluating responsibilities that act as motivators and make the job more challenging.

Job rotation   The systematic movement of workers from job to job to improve job satisfaction, reduce boredom, and enable employees to gain a broad perspective over the work processes within the entire organization.

Job shadowing   A method enabling a person working in a certain field to train for work in another field.

Job sharing   The practice of having two or more people split a full-time job.

Job specification   The minimum acceptable qualifications that an incumbent must possess to perform a given job successfully.

Joint venture   An approach to going global that involves a specific type of strategic alliance in which the partners agree to form a separate, independent organization for some business purpose.

Keno   A type of bingo game in which players wager on randomly drawn numbers.

Key operating areas   The most important functional areas of an organization that work and interact toward the achievement of the organization's goals.

Kitchen brigade   An element of kitchen organization in which the staff is divided into specialized departments, all contributing collectively to the preparation of a meal.

Kitchen manager   The individual who manages the kitchen department.

Labor cost budget   A budget prepared to meet the salaries, wages, and employee benefits.

Labor cost control   Management of labor costs.

Labor intensive   Relying on a large workforce to meet the needs of guests.

Lager beer   A beverage that is normally referred to simply as beer; it is clear, light bodied, and refreshing.

Lead   In the lingo of convention and visitors bureaus, a prospective client.

Leader-manager   An individual whose duties combine the functions of leadership and management.

Leadership   The influence of one person over another to work willingly toward a predetermined objective.

Leading   Influencing the behavior of others in some desired way.

Lease   A contract granting the use of real estate for a number of years in exchange for rent.

Leasing arrangement   The details of the leasing contract.

Leisure   Freedom from activities, especially time free from work or duties.

Leveraged money   Loans used to finance most of the purchase price.

Liaison personnel   Workers who are responsible for translating corporate philosophy for the contractor and for overseeing the contractor to be sure that he or she abides by the terms of the contract.

Liquid assets   Operating resources such as cash, accounts receivable, inventories, and prepaid operating expenses that are expected to be used in a year or less. *See also* Current assets.

Local-area network (LAN)   A computer network that enables employees of an organization to communicate and work with each other simultaneously through different computers inside a complex or building.

Maître d'hotel   The head waiter.

Malt   Germinated barley.

Managed services   Services that can be leased to professional management companies.

Management   The process of coordinating work activities so that an organization's objectives are achieved efficiently and effectively with and through other people.

Management by objectives (MBO)   A managerial process that determines the goals of the organization and then plans the objectives and the method to be used to reach the goals.

Management by walking around (MBWA)   A management style in which the manager goes into the work area, interacts with associates, and exchanges information about work; enables the manager to pick up information communicated through body language and tone of voice, and shows employees and clients that the manager is available and cares about them.

Management contract   A written agreement between an owner and an operator of a hotel or motor inn by which the owner employs the operator as an agent (employee) to assume full responsibility for operating and managing the property.

Manager   A person who works with and through other people by coordinating their efforts to achieve organizational goals.

Marker   A type of check that documents the amount of credit extended to a casino guest.

Market demand   The demand for a product or service.

Market niche   A specific share or slot of a certain market.

Market penetration   A growth strategy to boost sales of current products by more aggressively permeating the organization's current markets.

Market share   The share of the market that a particular operation owns.

Marketing action plan   A plan based on place, product, price, and promotion; used to set realistic goals and strategies for achieving the desired results.

Marketing consortium or referral organization   An organization made up of independent hotels that refer guests to each of the other members' hotels. Offers similar benefits to franchisees but at a lower cost; properties share a centralized reservations system, image, and logo.

Marketing mix   The term for the pertinent Ps: place, price, promotion, partnership, packaging, programming, and people.

Marketing and sales director   The individual responsible for marketing and sales for a property.

Mash tub   A large stainless steel or copper container used in the making of beer to mix and heat water and grains.

Mashing   In the making of beer, the process of grinding the malt and screening out bits of dirt.

Matrix structure   An organizational structure in which specialists from different functional departments are assigned to work on one or more projects.

Measurement   An evaluation or basis of comparison in order to ascertain the dimensions, quantity, or capacity of something.

Mechanistic organization   An organization that is rigid and tightly controlled.

Meeting   A gathering of people for a common purpose.

Meeting planner   An individual who coordinates every detail of meetings and conventions.

Meeting Planners International (MPI)   A Dallas-based association with nearly 19,000 members, MPI offers professional development in two certification programs: Certified Meeting Professional (CMP) and Certification in Meetings Management (CMM).

Megaresort   An extremely large gaming entertainment complex with thousands of guest rooms; a large gaming area; a number of ballrooms and breakout facilities; numerous food and beverage outlets, including room service and banquet facilities; and numerous retail and recreational offerings.

Mentor   A person who offers advice and counsel to someone who is new to a job or career track.

Menu   A list of the chef's dishes.

Menu development   The process of determining what type of food will be offered in a restaurant.

Menu engineering   Use of the menu as a whole, rather than individual items that make up the menu, as a measure of profitability.

Microbrewery   A small brewery that makes beer.

Middle manager   A manager between the first-line level and the top level of the organization who manages the work of first-line managers.

Minibar   A small refrigerated bar in a guest room.

Mise en place (meez en plás)   A French phrase meaning "everything in its place"; state of overall preparedness; having all the necessary ingredients and cooking utensils at hand and ready to use at the moment work on a dish begins.

Mission statement   A statement of the central purpose, strategies, and values of an organization.

Motivation   The willingness to exert high levels of effort to reach organizational goals, conditioned by the effort's ability to satisfy some individual need.

Motivators   Factors that increase job satisfaction and motivation.

Multiple criteria   An effective control system needs to take into consideration multiple criteria in order to get a more realistic grasp of the situation and narrow down tendencies.

Multiplier effect   A concept that refers to new money that is brought into a community to pay for hotel rooms, restaurant meals, and other aspects of leisure. To some extent, that income then passes into the community when the hotel or restaurant orders supplies and services, pays employees, and so on.

Mundo Maya   A joint ecotourism endeavor comprising the countries in which the Mayan civilization was, and still is, found. These countries are Belize, El Salvador, Guatemala, Honduras, and the five Mexican states of Quitana Roo, Yucatán, Campeche, Tabasco, and Chiapas.

Must   A mixture of grape pulp, skins, seeds, and stems.

National Center for Responsible Gaming (NCRG)   A research and education foundation created by the gaming entertainment industry to fund gambling addiction research.

National Gambling Impact and Policy Commission Act   A law that established a nine-member federal commission to assess the impact of all types of gambling in the United States.

National Restaurant Association (NRA)   The association representing restaurant owners and the restaurant industry.

National School Lunch Program   The program that provides free lunches to students from a certain income level.

National Tourism Organization (NTO)   The organization through which national governments promote their countries.

Net food and beverage revenue   The food and beverage revenue that remains after all expenses have been paid.

Networking   The process of meeting with and gathering information from an ever-expanding channel of acquaintances.

Niche   A specific share or slot of a certain market.

Night auditing   The process of verifying and balancing the guests' accounts.

Night auditor   The individual who verifies and balances guests' accounts.

Nonprogrammed decision   A unique decision that requires a custom-made solution.

Nonverbal communication   Communication transmitted without words through body posture, gestures, and mimics.

Note   A debt of money borrowed and owed to lender(s); a payable.

Nouvelle cuisine   A mid-twentieth-century movement away from classic cuisine principles. Includes shortened cooking times and innovative combinations. A lighter, healthier cuisine based on more natural flavors, including herbs.

NRA   *See* National Restaurant Association.

NTO   *See* National Tourism Organization.

Nutrition education programs   Programs ensuring that food served in school cafeterias follows the nutrition standards set by government programs.

Objective   A specific result toward which effort is directed.

Occupancy forecast   A forecast of a hotel's occupancy for a given period.

Odds   The statistical probabilities of the outcomes of a particular gaming activity.

Online   Access to a computer via a terminal.

Open-book management   A management style in which a company opens its books to the employees, sharing financial data, explaining numbers, and rewarding workers for improvement.

Operating activities   Financial activity associated with running a business on an ongoing basis.

Operational plans   Plans for operation and organization.

Organic organization   An organization that is flexible and highly adaptive.

Organization chart   A chart that illustrates the organization-wide division of work by charting who is accountable to whom and who is in charge of what department.

Organizational communication   All the patterns networks and systems of communication within an organization.

Organizational information system   An information system that is controlled by several remote computers and can be used throughout a company and accessed by a number of associates.

Organizational structure   Formal arrangement of jobs and tasks in an organization.

Orientation   A meeting for new employees in which the operation of the business is explained; usually occurs within the first few days of employment.

Other   Different from that or those implied or specified.

Other operating cost percentage   A financial ratio calculated to assess the effectiveness of operating activities and the target or budgeted percentage. Total Other Operating Costs divided by Total Sales Revenue.

Overbooking   A practice in lodging of booking 5 to 15 percent more rooms than are available in order to combat the loss of revenue resulting from guests who make reservations but who do not arrive.

Overvalued   The condition of a property that is for sale for more than it is worth.

Owner's equity   Total assets minus total liabilities. A financial measure of the owner(s) right or financial interest in a business.

PABS   *See* Profit analysis by segment.

Par stock   The level of stock that must be kept on hand at all times. If the stock on hand falls below this point, a computerized system automatically reorders a predetermined quantity of the stock.

Pathological gambling   An addiction involving a chronic and progressive failure to resist impulses to gamble; includes gambling behavior that compromises, disrupts, or damages personal, family, or vocational pursuits.

Pay for performance   Any compensation method based on merit or performance rather than across-the-board non-output-based pay.

PBX   The telecommunications department. Also called *CBX*.

Performance appraisal A meeting between a manager and one of his or her employees to (1) let the employee know how effectively he or she has met company standards, and (2) let the manager know how well he or she is doing in hiring and training employees.

Perishability The limited lifetime of hospitality products; for example, last night's vacant hotel room cannot be sold today.

Perpetual inventory A running inventory that automatically updates itself.

Personal digital assistant (PDA) A computer system that transmits information or orders and retrieves and posts guest payments; often used in restaurants to improve time management and allow faster service.

Piecework play plan Payment to associates for the amount, or piece, of work produced.

Pilferage Stealing.

Planning The process of defining the organization's goals, establishing an overall strategy for achieving those goals, and developing a comprehensive set of plans to integrate and coordinate organizational work.

PMS *See* Property management system.

Point-of-sale (POS) system A system used in restaurants and outlet stores that records and posts charges; consists of a number of POS terminals that interface with a remote central processing unit.

Poker A card game in which participants play against each other instead of the casino.

Policy A guideline that establishes parameters for making decisions.

Political analysis Analysis of the impact that current and pending legislation may have on the organization.

Pool bar A bar located near or, in some cases, in the pool.

Portfolio financing The grouping of several investments in a portfolio to spread the investment risk.

Positioning The process of establishing a distinctive place in the market (and in the minds of potential guests).

Pour-cost percentage Similar to food cost percentage, except used in beverage control.

Prime cost The cost of food sold plus payroll cost (including employee benefits). This is the largest segment of a restaurant's costs.

Privilege taxes Taxes paid by gaming companies to local, regional, and state governments for the privilege of operating a gaming business; often determined as a percentage of gross gaming revenue.

Procedure A series of interrelated sequential steps that can be used to respond to a well-structured problem.

Product A tangible good or intangible service produced by human or mechanical effort or by a natural process.

Product development The strategy of improving products for current markets to maintain or boost growth.

Product life cycle The stages of market acceptance of products and services.

Product specification The establishment of standards for each product, determined by the purchaser. For example, when ordering meat, the product specification includes the cut, weight, size, percentage of fat content, and so forth.

Production control sheet A checklist/sheet itemizing the production.

Productive teams Workplace teams built by giving associates the authority, responsibility, and encouragement to come together to work on guest-related improvements that will enhance the guest experience and make the associates' jobs easier.

Productivity standards Standards of measurement established to gauge employee productivity.

Profit analysis by segment (PABS) A calculation, using a combination of marketing information and cost analysis, of the average revenues generated by different market segments and the contribution margin for each of the segments considering the cost of making those sales.

Program An organized list of procedures, events, or other pertinent information; a schedule.

Programmed decision A repetitive decision that can be handled by a routine approach.

Project A one-time-only set of activities that have a definite beginning and ending point in time.

Project management The process of completing a project's activities on time, within budget, and according to specifications.

Project structure An organizational structure in which employees work continuously on projects.

Proof A figure representing liquor's alcohol content.

Property management system (PMS) A computerized system that integrates all systems used by a lodging property, such as reservations, front desk, housekeeping, food and beverage control, and accounting.

Purchasing The act of buying all items necessary for the operation of a business.

Purchasing stocks and materials The determination of proper stock levels, accurate ordering points, and approved vendors.

Quick-service restaurant A restaurant that offers quick service.

Rate of return on sales Net income divided by total revenue.

Rationality Consistent with or based on reason; logical. A rational decision needs to be value maximizing and consistent within natural restraining limits.

Real Estate Investment Trust (RIET) A method that enables small investors to combine their funds and protects them from the double taxation levied against an ordinary corporation or trust; designed to facilitate investment in real estate in much the same way a mutual fund facilitates investment in securities.

Reasonable criteria Control standards in an effective control system must be attainable and realistic.

Receiver A device that retranslates the sender's message.

Receiving The back-of-the-house area devoted to receiving goods.

Recession A downturn in the economy.

Recreation Refreshment of strength and spirits after work; a means of diversion.

Recreation for special populations Recreation designed to accommodate persons with disabilities, for example the Special Olympics.

Recruitment The process by which an organization attracts prospective employees.

Referents The persons, systems, or selves against which individuals compare themselves to assess equity.

Reinforcement theory The theory that behavior is a function of its consequences—that is, a reward is a consequence that triggers a desired response or performance.

Reinforcer Any consequence immediately following a response that increases the probability that the behavior will be repeated.

Reorder point The point in time at which an item needs to be reordered so that the company does not run out of it by the time the next delivery is received.

Reservations department The department responsible for taking reservations.

Resort A place that provides recreation and entertainment, especially to vacationers.

Resort hotel A hotel that provides recreation and entertainment, especially to vacationers.

Responsibility The obligation to perform any assigned duties.

Responsible gaming Strategies employed by the gaming entertainment industry to mitigate pathological and underage gambling, including prevention and education and awareness programs for employees, customers, and local communities.

Restaurant accounting The calculation of all costs and preparation of taxes, usually done by the accountant.

Restaurant forecasting The process of estimating the number of future guests, their menu preferences, and the revenue from them.

Restaurant manager The head of operations in a restaurant.

Return on Assets (ROA) An important financial measure that determines how well management uses business assets to produce profit; also used for planning and forecasting. It provides insight into how efficiently a company is being run by management with regard to its ability to generate profits from the assets available to the company. ROA = Net Profit After Taxes divided by Total Assets.

Rev par *See* Revenue per available room.

Revenue per available room (Rev par) Total Rooms Revenue for Period divided by Total Rooms Available During a Period.

Risk The conditions under which the decision maker is able to estimate the likelihood of certain outcomes.

Rollover The transfer of a booking from one occasion to the next.

Room management module A system that tracks the status of rooms; it assists the housekeeping department and the front desk with their duties.

Room occupancy percentage The number of rooms occupied divided by rooms available; a key operating ratio for hotels.

Room rates The various rates charged for hotel rooms.

Room service The cleaning of rooms and resupplying of materials (towels, soap, etc.) by the housekeeping staff.

Roulette A traditional table game in which a dealer spins a wheel and players wager on which number a small ball will fall.

Roux A paste for thickening sauces, made from equal quantities of fat and flour.

Rule A very specific action guide that associates must follow.

Russian service Restaurant service in which the entree, vegetables, and starches are served from a platter onto the diner's plate by a waiter.

SABRE The name of a commonly used airline reservation system.

Sales budget A financial plan detailing expected sales volume and sales revenue for a specified period of time.

Sanitation safety The ability to keep a property in a workable, safe condition.

Satisficing Acceptance of solutions that are good enough.

Scheduling Detailing what activities have to be done, the order in which they are to be completed, who is to do each, and when they are to be completed.

Seat turnover A measure of the number of seats turned over (number of guests) during a meal period. Average Daily Covers (guest counts) divided by Number of Available Seats.

Security/loss prevention A security department that provides guest protection and retrieves lost valuables.

Segmenting Splitting the market into user groups with common characteristics.

Selection The process of determining the eligibility and suitability of a prospective employee.

Selection of alternative Choosing the alternative with the highest weighted score.

Self The essential qualities distinguishing one individual from another; individuality.

Self-managed team A type of work team that operates without a manager and is responsible for a complete work process or a segment of it.

Self-operator A company that manages its own foodservice operations.

Semantics The study of the actual meaning of words.

Seminar A type of meeting that involves a lecture and a dialog; allows participants to share experiences in a particular field.

Service bar A bar, usually behind the scenes of a banquet or other event, from which servers dispense drinks.

Service encounter The period of time during which a customer interacts directly with either personnel or the physical facilities and other visible elements of a hospitality business.

Sexual harassment Unwanted sexually oriented behavior; it changes an employee's working conditions and/or creates a hostile or abusive work environment.

Shift work Normally a shift is six to eight hours of work.

Shoppers People who are paid to use a bar as regular guests would, except that they observe the operation closely.

Site inspection Previewing of a site (usually a convention center or hotel) to determine its suitability for the event, function, or meeting being planned.

Slot machine An electronic gaming device.

Social analysis Analysis of social trends and customs; used in compiling an upscale marketing plan.

Social functions   Events that include weddings, engagement parties, and holiday functions.

Social responsibility   A business firm's obligation, beyond that required by law and economics, to pursue long-term goals that are beneficial to society.

Soft count   A count of the content of each table game's drop box.

Solvency ratio   A measure of the ability to pay all of one's debts or liabilities.

Sommelier (so-mal-ee-yáy)   In a restaurant, the person with considerable wine knowledge who orders and serves wines.

Sous chef (soo shef)   A cook who supervises food production and who reports to the executive chef; he or she is second in command of a kitchen.

Sous-vide (soo-veed)   Air tight pouches of prepared food that can be reheated quickly.

Span of control   The number of people a supervisor/manager can effectively supervise.

Sparkling wine   Wine containing carbon dioxide, which provides effervescence when the wine is poured.

Special events industry   An industry that employs professionals who work together to provide a broad range of services to create what is termed a *special event*.

Specialty restaurant   A restaurant that falls under a specific category; for instance, a seafood or steak restaurant.

Spirits   Distilled drinks.

Spreadsheet   A computerized version of an accountant's ledger book that not only records numeric information but also performs calculations using that information.

Standing plans   Plans that are ongoing and that give guidance for repeated situations or activities.

Statement of cash flow   A financial report that provides information about the operations of a business using cash receipts and cash payments for a period. Used by investors, creditors, and management for information on a business's most liquid asset: cash.

Stewarding   The department in a hotel or food-service operation responsible for back-of-the-house cleanliness in the food and beverage areas; the cleanliness of the china, cutlery, glassware; and the custody of related food and beverage equipment.

Stock option plan   A plan by which employees are offered options to buy stocks in the company.

Strategic alliance   An approach to the expansion of a business's activities (entering new markets) that involves a partnership with another organization(s) in which both share resources, guests, and knowledge in serving existing clients and in the development of new products and services.

Strategic management   The process of identifying and pursuing the organization's strategic plan by aligning internal capabilities with the external demands of its environment, and then ensuring that the plan is being executed properly.

Strategic placement   In an effective control system, the emphasis that managers place on certain factors that are vital to the system's performance.

Strategic planning   Identifying the current business of a firm, the business it wants for the future, and the course of action it will pursue.

Strategy/tactics   Actions taken to achieve goals.

Suggestive selling   Servers in a restaurant increase sales by suggesting appropriate additional items to customers. For example, a server may suggest a Mondavi fumée blanc to complement a fish dish.

Suite   A combined living space with kitchen facilities, or a bedroom section with an attached parlor.

SWOT analysis   A strategic planning tool for analyzing a company's strengths, weaknesses, opportunities, and threats.

Symposium   A formal meeting at which several specialists deliver short addresses on a specific topic or related topics.

Syndicate   A group of investors.

System   A set of interrelated and interdependent parts arranged in a manner that produces a unified whole.

Table d'hôte   French for "table of the host." During medieval times, poorer travelers had to eat with the landlord and his family in the kitchen and they were served the "ordinary" fare at a nominal cost.

Task analysis Analysis of the tasks required to complete a particular job.

Tavern An establishment that serves some food but specializes in alcoholic beverages.

Taxes payable A debt of money owed to the IRS.

Team A task-oriented work group that either evolves informally or is appointed formally.

Team-based structure An organizational structure in which the entire organization is made up of work groups or teams.

Team player An employee who is committed to the team's objectives, members, and goals.

Technological analysis An analysis of the technological changes that may impact the company.

Technology All of the uses derived from discoveries and innovations to satisfy needs; generally refers to industrial technology.

Telecommuting A job approach in which employees work at home and are linked to the workplace by computer and modem.

Territory The area for which a person is responsible as a representative or agent; a sphere of action or interest.

Texture Referring to food and wine, texture is the combination of the qualities in food or wine that correspond to sensations of touch and temperature, such as softness, smoothness, roundness, richness, thickness, creaminess, chewiness, oiliness, harshness, silkiness, and coarseness.

Theater-style meeting setup A meeting setup usually intended for a large audience that is not likely to need to take notes or refer to documents. It generally consists of a raised platform and a lectern from which the presenter addresses the audience.

Theme park A recreational park based on a particular setting or artistic interpretation; may operate with hundreds or thousands of acres of parkland and hundreds or thousands of employees.

Theme restaurant A restaurant distinguished by its combination of decor, atmosphere, and menu.

Timeliness Occurring at a suitable time; well timed; opportune.

TIPS Training for Intervention Procedures by Servers. Sponsored by the NRA, TIPS is a certification program that informs participants about alcohol and the effects of alcohol on people, the common signs of intoxication, and methods for helping customers avoid drinking too much.

TO *See* Tourism office.

Tolerance for ambiguity Individuals with a high tolerance for ambiguity are very time efficient in making decisions because they are able to process many thoughts at the same time. Those with a low tolerance for ambiguity need more time to make a decision because they process information in a consistent and ordered way in order to minimize ambiguity.

Top manager A manager at or near the top level of the organization who is responsible for making organization-wide decisions and establishing the goals and plans that affect the entire organization.

Total quality management (TQM) A managerial approach that integrates all of the functions and related processes of a business such that they are all aimed at maximizing guest satisfaction through ongoing improvement.

Tour operator An agency that sells tour packages to groups of tourists and usually includes an escort or guide with the tour.

Tourism Travel for recreation or the promotion and arrangement of such travel.

Tourism office (TO) An organization in charge of developing and implementing tourism programs for an individual state. Also referred to as a destination marketing organization.

Tourist An individual who takes a trip of 100 miles or more and who stays away from home at least one night.

TQM *See* Total quality management.

Trade show Generally, a large display of products and services available for purchase, promoting information exchange among trade people. Trade shows frequently take place in convention centers where space is rented in blocks of 10 square feet. Also called *exposition*.

Training   An activity conducted by a training department, a training manager, line management, or specially selected individuals within each department to orient and teach new employees how to perform their jobs.

Transactional leadership   A type of leadership that focuses on accomplishing the tasks at hand and on maintaining good working relationships by exchanging promises of rewards for performance.

Transformational leadership   A type of leadership that involves influencing major changes in the attitudes and assumptions of organization members and building commitment for the organization's mission, objectives, and strategies.

Transit occupancy tax   Tax paid by people staying in a city's hotels.

Travel and tour wholesaler   A company or individual who designs and packages tours.

Trend   A prevailing tendency or general movement.

Triple net lease   A lease in which the lessee must pay for all alterations, insurance, utilities, and possible commercial fees (e.g., landscaping or parking upkeep, security).

Truth-in-menu laws   Provisions that prohibit misrepresentation of items being sold. They require that descriptions on menus be accurate.

Turnover rate   Calculated by dividing the number of workers replaced in a given time period by the average number of employees needed to run the business.

Uncertainty   A situation in which a decision maker has neither certainty nor reasonable probability estimates available.

Understandability   To have understanding, knowledge, or comprehension; being easy to understand.

Undocumented worker   An individual who enters from another country illegally, without permission to enter as either an immigrant or a refugee. Also called *illegal alien*.

Uniform system of accounts   A system of accounts used in the hospitality industry whereby all accounts have the same type of coding and all accounting procedures are done the same way.

Upward communication   Upward information flow within the organization from employees to supervisors or managers.

Vacation ownership   Offers consumers the opportunity to purchase fully furnished vacation accommodations in a variety of forms, such as weekly intervals or points in point-based systems, for a percentage of the cost of full ownership.

Variable cost   A cost that varies according to the volume of business.

Variable pay plan   A compensation plan that may reduce or increase some portion of an individual employee's pay, depending on whether the company meets its financial goals.

Verbal intonation   Use of the voice to emphasize certain parts of a phrase or certain words.

Vertical integration   The ownership of or linkage with suppliers of raw materials or airlines owning hotels.

Vintage   The year in which a wine's grapes were harvested.

Voluntary organization   A nongovernmental, nonprofit agency serving the public.

Web reservations system (WRS)   A reservations system that allows guests to seek information such as room availability and to make reservations and payments over the Internet.

Weddings and holiday parties   Of all social gatherings, weddings are the most widely recognized social event.

Weighted average   A method of menu pricing that takes into account the food costs, percentage contribution margin, and sales volume.

Well package   In bar operations, the least expensive pouring brand of drinks that the bar uses when customers do not ask for a specific name brand.

Whisky   A liquor distilled from a fermented mash of grain to which malt, in the form of barley, is added.

White spirits   Gin, rum, vodka, and tequila.

Wide-area network (WAN)   A network that permits high-speed communication among large franchises.

Win   Dollars won by the gaming operation from its customers. The net spending of customers on gaming is called the *win*, also known as *gross gaming revenue (GGR)*.

Wine   Fermented juice of grapes or other fruits.

Work group information system   Data and information shared within a department.

Work specialization   The degree to which tasks in an organization are divided into individual jobs; also called *division of labor*.

Work team structure   Work structured into teams of employees to delight the guest.

Workshop   A usually brief, intensive educational program conducted by a facilitator or a trainer, designed for a relatively small group of people, that focuses especially on techniques and skills in a particular field. Emphasizes interaction and exchange of information among a relatively small number of participants.

Wort   In the making of beer, the liquid obtained after the mashing process.

Yacht club   A private club located near a large body of water whose primary purpose is to provide facilities such as marinas to boat owners.

Yield management   The practice of analyzing past reservation patterns, room rates, cancellations, and no-shows in an attempt to maximize profits and occupancy rates and to set the most competitive room rates.

Zero-based budgeting   Managers begin with a budget of zero dollars and justify all the costs of goods sold, controllable costs, and planned capital expenditures in order to ensure an appropriate profit after the deduction of all expenses.

Index

Photo Credits

p. 183: Jeff Zaruba, Zaruba Photography

p. 189: PureStockX

p. 191: Jochen Tack, Das Fotoarchiv

Part III

(p. 199): Melanie Acevedo, Image Bank/Getty Images

Chapter 6

pp. 200–201: Ryan McVay, Getty Images, Inc. – Riser

p. 203: PureStockX

p. 204, top: MGM Grand

p. 204, bottom: Bettmann Archive

p. 205: Hulton Archive/Getty Images

p. 207: Richard Melman

p. 209: PureStockX

p. 219: AP Wide World Photos

p. 220: William B. Martin

p. 221: Tavern on the Green © Gayle Gleason, 1998

p. 222: Greg Ward © Rough Guides

p. 223: Sarah Stegner

p. 224: © Alan Levenson / CORBIS. All Rights Reserved.

p. 225: James Schnepf Photography, Inc.

p. 226: Demetrio Carrasco © Rough Guides

p. 227: PureStockX

p. 229: Corbis/Bettmann

Chapter 7

pp. 236–237: David Oliver, Getty Images, Inc. – Stone Allstock

p. 239: SuperStock

p. 241: John Self

p. 242: Doug Menuez, Getty Images Inc. – Photodisc

p. 243: Photo by Ron Calamia, 2007, courtesy Emeril's

p. 244: MICROS Systems, Inc.

p. 245: SoftCafe, LLC

p. 246: MICROS Systems, Inc.

p. 248: SuperStock

p. 249: James Lorenz

p. 257: Michael Newman, PhotoEdit Inc.

p. 258: T.G.I. Friday's

Chapter 8

pp. 274–275: Tony Weller, Getty Images – Digital Vision

p. 278: Peter Bennett, Ambient Images

p. 279: Sodexho

p. 282: PureStockX

p. 284: Almay Images Royalty Free

p. 285: Manuel Lorenzo

p. 288: ARAMARK

p. 291: Regynald G. Washington

p. 295, top: ARAMARK

p. 295, bottom: Sodexho

p. 296: ARAMARK

p. 297: Fred J. DeMicco

Chapter 9

pp. 306–307: FoodPix / Stone / Getty Images

p. 309: PureStockX

p. 310: Clive Streeter © Dorling Kindersley

p. 311, top: Linda Whitwam © Dorling Kindersley

p. 311, bottom: PureStockX

p. 312, top: PureStockX

p. 312, bottom: Steve Mason, Getty Images, Inc. – Photodisc

p. 313: Jay R. Schrock

p. 316: PureStockX

p. 317: Robert Mondavi

p. 319: © Dorling Kindersley

p. 320: Rob Westfall

p. 322: Peter Arnold, Inc.

p. 324: PureStockX

p. 325: EyeWire Collection, Getty Images – Photodisc

p. 326: Bernini's

p. 327: Starbucks Coffee Company

p. 329: Amy C. Etra, PhotoEdit Inc.

p. 333: Rob Reichenfeld © Dorling Kindersley

p. 335: PureStockX

p. 337: AP Wide World Photos

Part IV

(p. 345): John Warden, Getty Images Inc. – Stone Allstock

Chapter 10

pp. 346–347: Robert Laberge, Getty Images, Inc.

p. 349: PureStockX

p. 588: Patricia Engfer
p. 589: PureStockX
p. 592: PureStockX
p. 593: Rob Westfall

Chapter 19
pp. 602-603: PureStockX
p. 607: PureStockX

p. 608: Cherry Cerminara
p. 612: Sodexho
p. 616: ARAMARK
p. 621: PureStockX
p. 622: Michael R. Thorpe